Artificial Intelligence

T0184353

Springer

Berlin
Heidelberg
New York
Barcelona
Hong Kong
London
Milan
Paris
Singapore
Tokyo

Alexander Bochman

A Logical Theory of Nonmonotonic Inference and Belief Change

 Springer

Dr. Alexander Bochman

Holon Academic Institute of Technology (HAIT)
Computer Science Department
52 Golomb Street
Holon 58102
Israel

bochmana@barley.cteh.ac.il

Library of Congress Cataloging-in-Publication Data applied for

Die Deutsche Bibliothek - CIP-Einheitsaufnahme
Bochman, Alexander:
A logical theory of nonmonotonic inference and belief change /
Alexander BochmanE. - Berlin ; Heidelberg ; New York ; Barcelona ;
Hong Kong ; London ; Milan ; Paris ; Singapore ; Tokyo : Springer,
2001
  (Artificial intelligence)

ACM Computing Classification (1998): I.2.3

ISBN 978-3-642-07516-2

Springer-Verlag Berlin Heidelberg New York,
a member of BertelsmannSpringer Science + Business Media GmbH

http://www.springer.de

© Springer-Verlag Berlin Heidelberg 2010
Printed in Germany

Cover design: KünkelLopka Werbeagentur, Heidelberg

Preface

The main subject and objective of this book are *logical foundations of nonmonotonic reasoning*. This bears a presumption that there is such a thing as a general theory of nonmonotonic reasoning, as opposed to a bunch of systems for such a reasoning existing in the literature. It also presumes that this kind of reasoning can be analyzed by logical tools (broadly understood), just as any other kind of reasoning.

In order to achieve our goal, we will provide a common logical basis and semantic representation in which different kinds of nonmonotonic reasoning can be interpreted and studied. The suggested framework will subsume basic forms of nonmonotonic inference, including not only the usual skeptical one, but also various forms of credulous (brave) and defeasible reasoning, as well as some new kinds such as contraction inference relations that express relative independence of pieces of data. In addition, the same framework will serve as a basis for a general theory of belief change which, among other things, will allow us to unify the main approaches to belief change existing in the literature, as well as to provide a constructive view of the semantic representation used.

This book is a monograph rather than a textbook, with all its advantages (mainly for the author) and shortcomings (for the reader). It is primarily intended for specialists in Artificial Intelligence and Knowledge Representation who are interested in having versatile tools for describing commonsense reasoning tasks, as well as in knowing representation capabilities of such tools. It also could be of interest to general logicians; our study demonstrates, after all, that nonmonotonic reasoning is just a special kind of logical reasoning that can and should reach the level of sophistication common to established logical formalisms.

Rishon-LeZion, February 2001   *Alexander Bochman*

Contents

1. Introduction

What is nonmonotonic reasoning?

Taken in a broader perspective, a theory of nonmonotonic reasoning gives us (or, more exactly, should give) a more direct and adequate description of the actual ways we think about the world. More often than not we reason and act in situations where we do not or even cannot have complete information. So, deductive reasoning, taken by itself, simply cannot help us in such situations. Still, we usually need to act in such situations in a reasonable way, and it is here that nonmonotonic reasoning finds its place. This means, in particular, that the necessity of nonmonotonic reasoning does not stem from computational considerations, as is sometimes supposed in Artificial Intelligence; it is not the question of speeding or simplifying our reasoning. Rather, it is a matter of vital necessity: we have to act reasonably in situations of partial knowledge in order to achieve our practical and theoretical goals.

Human rational activity is not reducible to collecting facts and deriving their consequences; it embodies an active epistemic attitude that involves making assumptions and wholesale theories about the world and acting in accordance with them. In other words, we do not only perceive the world, we also give it structure in order to make it intelligible and controllable. Nonmonotonic reasoning in this sense is just a special case of a general scientific methodology; its important ingredients are abduction and explanation (see [Poo88]).

The way of thinking in partially known circumstances suggested by nonmonotonic reasoning consists in using justified *beliefs* and reasonable assumptions that can guide us in our decisions. In fact, nonmonotonic reasoning can also be described as a theory of reasonable use of assumptions. It is characterized, however, by a special status it assigns to such assumptions and beliefs; namely, it makes them *default* assumptions. Default assumptions (or simply defaults) are seen as acceptable in all circumstances unless they conflict with other defaults and current evidence[1]. This presumptive reading has a semantic counterpart in the notion of *normality*; default assumptions are considered as holding for normal circumstances, and the theory tells us to

---

[1] Cf. the discussion of the belief-doubt epistemology as opposed to the cartesian doubt-belief epistemology in [Fuh96].

always assume that the world is as normal as is compatible with the known facts. This kind of belief commitment is a novel aspect contributed by nonmonotonic reasoning to a general theory of reasoning. It implies, in particular, that our assumptions and beliefs are not abandoned, in general, in the light of evidence, but only postponed, and hence can still be used when the situation changes. As was rightly noted by David Poole, the default "Birds fly" is not a statement that is true or not of a world; some birds fly, some do not. Rather, it is an assumption used in building our theory of the world. Actually, this kind of reasoning constitutes an essential ingredient of natural sciences as well. Explanations of physical phenomena and experiments are commonly based on such "normality assumptions" that find their expression in *ceteris paribus* (all else being equal) clauses accompanying formulations of practically all physical laws (see [Hem88]).

Clearly, default beliefs and assumptions are *defeasible*; they might give wrong predictions in certain circumstances. This makes nonmonotonic reasoning a risky business. Still, in most cases such beliefs are useful and give desired results, and hence they are worth the risk of making an error. But what is even more important, more often than not we simply have no 'safe' replacement for such a reasoning strategy. That is why it is worth teaching robots and computers to reason in this way.

Nonmonotonic Reasoning and Artificial Intelligence

The above considerations imply a certain position on the question about the relation between Nonmonotonic Reasoning and Artificial Intelligence. A recurrent misconception of nonmonotonic reasoning in the artificial intelligence community consists in viewing it as a kind of "shortcut-logic" in which we simply "jump to conclusions" instead of a careful logical reasoning, especially when the latter exceeds our computational capabilities. In fact, some of the founders of nonmonotonic reasoning in AI could be held responsible for this attitude. This occasional abuse of nonmonotonic reasoning leads to a search for efficient nonmonotonic formalisms while disregarding questions of correctness or adequacy, and to rejection of more adequate accounts solely on the basis that they are not efficient. It is also the main source of disappointment with Nonmonotonic Reasoning, since the latter usually suggests models of high computational complexity.

Part of our intentions in this book consists in dispelling such misconceptions. Nonmonotonic reasoning is not a simplification of classical logic, but its extension providing a way of using logic in situations of incomplete knowledge. Accordingly, it should only be expected that *general nonmonotonic reasoning is bound to be at least as complex as classical logical reasoning.*

We believe that healthy and fruitful relationships between Nonmonotonic Reasoning and AI could be established only on the basis of an acknowledgment that Nonmonotonic Reasoning is not an applied, surrogate logic for

Artificial Intelligence, but a fully fledged logical theory with its own subject and objectives. True, Artificial Intelligence is (so far) the main application area of Nonmonotonic Reasoning, and the main source of the problems it tries to resolve. However, this change in the status would orient us toward resolving *fundamental problems* of nonmonotonic reasoning, instead of trying to produce short-term, though efficient, solutions. Despite a clear success, twenty years of nonmonotonic reasoning research have also shown that we need a deep breath and long term objectives in order to make Nonmonotonic Reasoning a viable tool for the challenges posed by Artificial Intelligence. There is still much to be done in order to meet the actual complexity of reasoning tasks required by the latter. In fact, the present book will demonstrate that the number of unresolved fundamental problems in Nonmonotonic Reasoning still exceeds the number of resolved ones. But we also have a commonsense hope that an adequate, succinct and human-friendly solution to such problems will give us a way to their efficient representation. In other words, we believe that, as in other areas of human research, *proper solutions of fundamental problems will also make for efficiency.*

Remark. The aim of obtaining *proper* solutions for fundamental problems of nonmonotonic reasoning stems from the fact that not all formally adequate solutions are good ones. Actually, this is one of the reasons why we do not use modal formalisms and possible worlds semantics as our primary tool in this study. Though formally adequate and elegant, we believe that this representation has serious shortcomings from the point of view of actual implementation; namely, it does not suggest a human-friendly framework of concepts that can be discerned from available data.

Nonmonotonic reasoning and logic

Nonmonotonic Reasoning-si, *Nonmonotonic Logic*-no!
[MS93]

As the title of the book indicates, we pursue in this study a broadly logical approach to nonmonotonic reasoning. Still, our approach is not 'narrowly' logical. This means, in particular, that we are not going to suggest some new nonmonotonic logic(s) that should replace the classical one. Basically, our logic will remain the good old classical logic. Following the lead of John McCarthy and David Poole , we do not change the logic in order to accommodate it to nonmonotonic reasoning, only the way the logic is used. Moreover, we will provide in the book many grounds for doubting that a proper representation of nonmonotonic reasoning can be given in terms of some nonstandard logical system. The paradise of classical logical reasoning in which the semantic notion of validity is equivalent to syntactic notions of proof and derivation is hardly achievable for nonmonotonic reasoning. Usually, logical systems provide only a more or less tight and convenient framework in which nonmonotonic reasoning can be represented and performed. A non-trivial aspect of this claim is that it pertains not only to monotonic logical systems, but also to so-called nonmonotonic logical formalisms and inference relations suggested in the literature. For example, we will see that nonmonotonic inference relations forming the main content of Part Two of the book, will serve only as a framework for nonmonotonic (defeasible) reasoning, as sets of logical constraints such a reasoning should obey. Specifically, the notion of a nonmonotonic reasoning cannot be reduced to that of nonmonotonic inference defined by these systems. Furthermore, we should not expect that some strengthening of such inference relations with new postulates and rules would capture the intended system of nonmonotonic reasoning.

Classical nonmonotonic reasoning

As we said, a theory of nonmonotonic reasoning can be seen as a theory of a rational (justified) use of assumptions. Accordingly, the main problem nonmonotonic reasoning deals with is that our default assumptions are often incompatible with one another, or with known facts. Consequently, the use of all our assumptions in the form of a single logical theory is out of the question. In such cases of conflict we must have a reasoned choice.

Despite the diversity of systems of nonmonotonic reasoning suggested in the literature, they can be classified as falling into two large camps with respect to the question of how we should choose our assumptions. The approach to this problem, taken in the present book, can be termed *classical (or preferential) nonmonotonic reasoning*. The main idea behind this approach is that the relevant choice should be made by forming an adequate set of options for choice and establishing appropriate preference relations among available alternatives. Actually, this approach to resolving conflicts makes classical nonmonotonic reasoning a special case of a general methodology that is at least as old as the decision theory and theory of social choice. Viewed from within the nonmonotonic reasoning field, our approach can be seen as a continuation of the research program that has begun with John McCarthy's circumscription [McC80] and continued in the works of D. Poole [Poo88], Y. Shoham [Sho88], and many others after them. As we will see, this research program can be sophisticated to the point where it will subsume the majority of other approaches and components of classical nonmonotonic reasoning.

By restricting our subject to classical nonmonotonic reasoning, we leave outside the scope of the book a major alternative approach to nonmonotonic reasoning that includes, in particular, various default and modal nonmonotonic logics, as well as modern approaches to logic programming (see [MT93] for a comprehensive survey of theories and formalisms belonging to this approach, and also [Boc96] for an attempt of a uniform logical representation). This approach can be called *argumentative nonmonotonic reasoning*, since it is based on a different, argumentative strategy of choosing defaults [BDKT97]. In our view, the relation between these two principal paradigms of nonmonotonic reasoning constitutes the main internal problem for a general theory of nonmonotonic reasoning. A prerequisite to a solution of this problem, however, consists in a clear theoretical understanding of both paradigms.

The main advantage of classical nonmonotonic reasoning over its argumentative counterpart (at least in its current form) is that it provides a direct representation for the main nonmonotonic objects, namely default conditionals of the form "If A, then normally B". It also supplies them with a natural semantics that allows us to assess our default claims. This semantics should determine, ultimately, the actual choice of default assumptions made under different circumstances. Default logic and its relatives take a different, less direct route to assessing what can be inferred from a given set of default rules. Namely, they require the user to provide explicit information about when one default can 'block' (or attack) another default. This information is used as a sole factor in determining acceptable combinations of defaults. This strategy can be remarkably successful in resolving some difficult cases of default interaction. Still, the argumentative approach remains largely syntactic in nature, and sometimes puts a heavy burden on the user by requiring him to foresee and control the results of default interaction. Also, it is significantly weaker, in general, than the corresponding formalisms of classical nonmonotonic reasoning in terms of the information that can be inferred from defaults. All this could be clearly seen from the comparison of the two approaches in their treatment of inheritance reasoning (see Chapter 8).

There are also some specific choices made in the book that go beyond the general preferential methodology. The book describes nonmonotonic reasoning and belief change in terms of *epistemic* states. This presupposes, first of all, a separation of contingent facts and evidences from more stable epistemic attitudes that include, in particular, default information. This distinction is widely acknowledged in the literature on nonmonotonic reasoning (see [Poo91, Gef92]). Also, as we already mentioned, and as is implied by the epistemic perspective, we do not use possible worlds as our primary means of representation. Instead, our elementary objects are propositional in character. Epistemic states will be represented, ultimately, in terms of sets of propositions with an imposed preference structure.

Nonmonotonic reasoning and belief change

One of the most interesting developments in the short history of nonmonotonic reasoning consists in discovering its tight connections with the theory of belief change developed by Gärdenfors and his colleagues [AGM85, Gär88]. Following Gärdenfors and Makinson, these two fields are considered now as "two sides of the same coin". This connection will be strengthened further in the book by considering nonmonotonic reasoning and belief change, respectively, as static and dynamic (constructive) aspects of reasoning in epistemic states.

This view will give us a broader perspective on both belief change and nonmonotonic reasoning. Thus, belief change theories enrich nonmonotonic reasoning with an understanding that default conditionals, though important, are by no means the only tool in reasoning about epistemic states. This follows already from the fact that belief revision is seen as a compound process consisting of contraction and expansion. Accordingly, we will study in Part Two contraction inference relations that constitute a static counterpart of belief contractions in the belief change theory. It should be noted, however, that this is only an instance of a more general lesson to be learned by nonmonotonic reasoning, namely that 'pure' knowledge bases of Poole type are unlikely to provide a proper basis for representing nonmonotonic reasoning in its generality.

There is yet another consequence of taking the belief change perspective on nonmonotonic reasoning. The main subject of nonmonotonic reasoning so far has been how we should represent and use a predefined set of defaults supplied by the user. It does not address the issue of how and when we can make or, alternatively, abandon default assumptions. This is a good instance of a fundamental problem of nonmonotonic reasoning, and belief change theory will be taken to be primarily responsible for dealing with this problem of change in our (default) beliefs.

Turning to the other side of the coin, the representation of nonmonotonic reasoning will reveal that belief sets alone are not sufficient for an adequate representation of belief change process. Moreover, by making explicit the structure of epistemic states that determine such processes, we will obtain an opportunity to establish the basic principles behind the main approaches to belief change suggested in the literature, namely the coherentist AGM theory [Gär88] and foundationalist base-generation approach [Han99]. It will turn out, however, that the change in perspective suggested by our approach will also drastically change the scope and objectives of the general theory of belief change.

An overview of the book

The book is divided into three parts. The first part, *The Framework* gives a uniform logical basis and semantic representations for classical nonmonotonic reasoning and belief change.

In Chapter 2, *Scott Consequence Relations*, we describe a logical basis for the whole enterprise. Scott consequence relations that are well known in the logical literature from the works of Scott, Gabbay, Segerberg, Barwise and others, have also proved to be an adequate logical framework for representing various kinds of nonmonotonic inference and belief change. Actually, the choice of Scott consequence relations as a general logical framework for nonmonotonic reasoning was a natural consequence of the author's previous experience in using this formalism (in [Boc92]) as a unifying framework for analyzing the key concepts in the philosophy of science, i.e., laws, counter-factuals, causation and explanation.

We give a 'biased' introduction to the theory of consequence relations providing necessary logical tools for subsequent chapters. Thus, special attention is paid to *supraclassical* consequence relations that subsume classical entailment. The purposes of our study also required a development of the theory of Scott consequence relations in new directions. Actually, the corresponding study revealed amazing representation capabilities of the formalism. Accordingly, the chapter is abundant with new notions such as right compactness and union-closure, or new classes of consequence relations, namely determinate, ground, base-generated, linear, semi-classical etc., that will play an important role in subsequent chapters.

Chapter 3, *Epistemic States*, describes the second, semantic ingredient of our framework, the notion of an epistemic state. Basically, an epistemic state is a set of deductively closed theories (representing admissible belief states of the agent) ordered by a preference relation. In the simplest case of pure epistemic states, the preference relation is just a set inclusion among theories. It turns out that Scott consequence relations provide a syntactic description of such pure states; in this representation the sequents of the consequence relation describe *dependence relations* holding among admissible beliefs.

Epistemic states subsume practically all representations of nonmonotonic inference and belief change suggested in the literature. We give in this chapter a first classification of epistemic states, and introduce the notions of belief and knowledge sets determined by them. In addition, we show how the preference relation among admissible belief sets can be generated from priorities among defaults. Finally, we describe the main kinds of inference relations that are definable in the framework of epistemic states. These include ordinary skeptical inference relations, as well as credulous ones. Also, we describe contraction inference relations that can be seen as representing independence relations among potential beliefs and constitute a static counterpart of contraction operations in belief change theory.

In Chapter 4, *Equivalence and Decomposition of Epistemic States*, we present some general results concerning equivalence of epistemic states with respect to their functional role in nonmonotonic reasoning and belief change. It will be shown, in particular, that any epistemic state can be decomposed in some well-defined sense into a set of epistemic states that are linearly ordered by preference. Some further results of this kind will be given in subsequent chapters.

Finally, we describe in Chapter 5, *Epistemic Entrenchment and Its Relatives*, a number of expectation relations on propositions that are shown to provide a useful tool in studying nonmonotonic inference.

The second part of the book, *Nonmonotonic Inference*, gives a detailed description of different kinds of inference relations definable on epistemic states.

Chapter 6, *Basic Inference Relations*, determines a common core for systems of skeptical and brave nonmonotonic reasoning described in subsequent chapters.

Chapter 7, *Skeptical Inference*, gives a description of 'ordinary' skeptical inference relations, namely preferential and rational inference from [KLM90], as well as some intermediate systems. It is shown, in particular, that these inference relations can be represented in terms of pure epistemic states and their associated consequence relations. This new representation will allow us to give a much more realistic interpretation of such inference relations than that given by traditional models based on possible worlds. It will also allow us to include skeptical inference relations into a broader context of nonmonotonic reasoning tasks. In addition, it will clarify the role of further constraints imposed on traditional models, such as injectivity. We also show how representations of different kinds can be transformed one into the other.

Chapter 8, *Defeasible Entailment*, discusses what can be seen as the main problem of classical nonmonotonic reasoning, namely the problem of constructing a system of defeasible entailment. To begin with, we describe desiderata for such a reasoning and show ways of their fulfillment using special kinds of epistemic states generated by conditional bases. In the second part of this chapter, as a special case of the preceding construction, we give a semantic representation of inheritance reasoning, an old stumbling block for many theories of nonmonotonic reasoning. Despite the initial pessimistic opinion, we show that it is possible to see inheritance reasoning as a special kind of a logical reasoning in our sense.

Chapter 9, *Credulous Nonmonotonic Inference*, gives an axiomatic description and semantic representation for several systems of credulous, or brave, nonmonotonic reasoning. It is shown, in particular, that pure epistemic states turn out to be sufficient for representing most of these inference relations. In addition, we demonstrate that credulous inference can also be modeled in the expectation-based framework of [GM94]. We also show how brave conditionals can be used in skeptical reasoning to secure strengthening the antecedent and other important reasoning patterns that cannot be obtained by skeptical reasoning alone.

Chapter 10, *Contraction Inference*, gives a description of contraction relations, an inference counterpart of belief contraction studying in Part Three. We provide here a complete characterization of contraction relations determined by epistemic states. It turns out that such inference relations, unlike preferential ones, cannot be represented by pure epistemic states. We also give several representation results covering practically all contraction operations found in the literature. Finally, we describe a 'canonical decomposition' of skeptical (preferential) inference relations in terms of contraction relations.

This decomposition can be seen as an inferential counterpart of the well-known Levi identity in the belief change theory studied in the last part of the book.

The third part of the book, *Belief Change*, deals with the question of how our beliefs and epistemic states are changed.

Chapter 11, *Belief Change and Its Problems*, sets up the stage and describes the problem of belief change. We argue first that the set of beliefs alone cannot serve as a basis of a reasonable belief change process; some more structure and information about our internal states should be taken into account in order to guide the choice of the resulting set of beliefs. Our suggestion here amounts to taking epistemic states as a general framework for describing the belief change process. This representation will allow us to subsume in a single framework the two main (and rival) accounts of belief change, the AGM theory and the theory of base change. In addition, this representation will satisfy the *principle of categorial matching* suggested in [GR95]): the representation of the epistemic state after a change should be of the same kind as that before the change. Apart from aesthetic considerations, compliance with this principle turns out to be essential for an adequate representation of iterated belief change.

Chapter 12, *Contractions of Epistemic States*, describes one of the basic belief change operations, namely removal of beliefs from epistemic states. We give here a detailed description and a formal characterization for several belief contraction functions, both ones existing in the literature and new ones.

Chapter 13, *Merge and Expansion*, describes the ways of composition of epistemic states. As is shown, traditional expansion operations can be seen as a special kind of such a composition. It turns out that such operations (which are trivial in the AGM approach) emerge as a main varying parameter in a belief change process. Basically, they allow us to reflect the degree of certainty or credibility with which we can accept a new proposition, and possible dependence of its acceptance on other beliefs we have. This gives rise to several different expansion operations, all producing the same new belief set, but having different implications for subsequent changes.

Chapter 14, *Compound and Derived Changes*, describes some compound and derived changes on epistemic states, such as the traditional revision operation. We also discuss in this chapter the problem of change in inference and entrenchment relations that are generated by corresponding changes in underlying epistemic states. Finally, we consider some global questions concerning the emerging general theory of change in epistemic states, and explore the expressive capabilities of the main belief change operations in constructing epistemic states.

* * *

Bits and pieces of this book have appeared already in the author's previous publications. A short description of some of the themes from Chapter 9 is contained in [Boc99a]. An abridged version of Chapter 10 has been published as [Boc00a]. Finally, the main topics of Part Three have been discussed in [Boc99b, Boc00c, Boc00b], though the theory of belief change suggested in this book is essentially different in many respects from that described in the latter papers.

Part I

The Framework

2. Consequence Relations

In this chapter we will describe the formalism of consequence relations that will serve as a logical basis for our approach to nonmonotonic reasoning and belief change. We are not intending, however, to give a comprehensive theory of consequence relations. Rather, the following exposition can be seen as a compendium of notions and results that will be used in what follows. In fact, due to this biased description, a lot of the notions described below, such as semi-classicality, groundedness and base-generation, will be quite new and unusual in a general theory of consequence relations. We will show, in particular, that Scott consequence relations is a powerful formalism that allows a concise logical description of many interesting concepts outside their traditional range of applications. Actually, the results of this chapter will also show that common descriptions of consequence relations still only scratch the surface of this notion. And subsequent applications will demonstrate that it is worth being studied in depth.

2.1 Scott consequence relations

Scott consequence relations [Sco74, Gab76, Gab81], known also as multiple-conclusion consequence relations (cf. [Seg82, SS78]), have as their origin Gentzen's sequent calculus, and are based on the idea of taking consequence relation to be a binary relation between sets of propositions. In contrast to ordinary (single-conclusion) Tarski consequence relations, Scott sequents involve sets of formulas as their conclusions. Such conclusions are interpreted as sets of alternatives, implied (or required) by the premises. As we will see, this 'multiple-conclusion' character of Scott consequence relations will be essential for an adequate representation of many interesting concepts.

2.1.1 Basic definitions

Throughout the book, we will denote propositions by $A, B, C, \ldots$, finite sets of propositions by $a, b, c, \ldots$, and arbitrary sets of propositions by $u, v, \ldots$. Also, for any set of propositions u, we will denote by $\overline{u}$ the complement of u, that is the set of all propositions that do not belong to u (with respect to a given language).

Scott consequence relations can be seen as a symmetric generalization of ordinary Tarski consequence relations. They involve rules or sequents of the form $a \Vdash b$, where a and b are finite sets of propositions. An informal reading of such sequents will be:

If all propositions from a are accepted, then one of the propositions from b should also be accepted.

A set of sequents is called a *Scott consequence relation* if it satisfies the following conditions:

Reflexivity $A \Vdash A$;

Monotonicity   If $a \Vdash b$ and $a \subseteq a'$, $b \subseteq b'$, then $a' \Vdash b'$;

Cut   If $a \Vdash b, A$ and $a, A \Vdash b$, then $a \Vdash b$.

In what follows we use ordinary terminological conventions and write, e.g., $a, A \Vdash b, B$ instead of $a \cup \{A\} \Vdash b \cup \{B\}$ and $\Vdash a$, $a \Vdash$ instead of $\emptyset \Vdash a$ and $a \Vdash \emptyset$, respectively.

The notion of a sequent can be extended to include infinite sets of premises and conclusions by requiring that, for any sets of propositions u and v,

(**Compactness**) $u \Vdash v$ if and only if $a \Vdash b$, for some finite $a \subseteq u, b \subseteq v$.

This extension retains all the rules of a Scott consequence relation. Moreover, it can be shown that the resulting extended consequence relations could be characterized alternatively as Scott consequence relations on arbitrary sets of formulas satisfying the Compactness requirement.

Symmetry and duality. The conditions characterizing a Scott consequence relation are completely symmetric with respect to premises and conclusions of sequents. This implies, in particular, that for any Scott consequence relation we can define a *dual consequence relation* as follows:

$$a \Vdash^d b \quad \equiv \quad b \Vdash a$$

As can be seen, this is also a Scott consequence relation. Speaking more generally, any notion definable in this framework has a dual counterpart that in many cases turns out to be no less interesting and useful than the source one. Moreover, the properties of this dual notion can be easily discerned from that of the source one by obvious duality considerations.

Due to the 'Horn' form of the rules characterizing a Scott consequence relation, intersection of a set of Scott consequence relations is again a Scott consequence relation. This implies, in particular, the following

Lemma 2.1.1. *For any set of sequents there exists a least Scott consequence relation containing it.*

Now we introduce the basic notion of a theory of a Scott consequence relation.

Definition 2.1.1. *A set of propositions u will be called a* theory *of a Scott consequence relation* $\Vdash$ *if* $u \not\Vdash \bar{u}$.

Thus, theories are defined as sets of propositions that do not imply propositions outside them. The following lemma shows that theories can be seen as sets of propositions that are closed with respect to the sequents of a consequence relation.

Lemma 2.1.2. *u is a theory of a Scott consequence relation* $\Vdash$ *iff, for any sets of propositions* a, b *such that* $a \Vdash b$, *if* $a \subseteq u$, *then* $u \cap b \neq \emptyset$.

Proof. If $a \Vdash b$, $a \subseteq u$, but $b \subseteq \bar{u}$, then $u \Vdash \bar{u}$ by Monotonicity, and hence u is not a theory of $\Vdash$. In the other direction, if $u \Vdash \bar{u}$, then by compactness there must exist a, b such that $a \Vdash b$, $a \subseteq u$ and $b \subseteq \bar{u}$, so the above condition is violated. $\qquad\Box$

Theories of a Scott consequence relation can be considered as 'multiple-conclusion' analogs of theories of a Tarski consequence relation. Note, however, that theories of a Scott consequence relation do not have all the usual properties of Tarski theories. Most importantly, intersections of Scott theories are not in general theories. Nevertheless, they still have a property of *completeness with respect to directed sets*, stated below.

A set of theories $\mathcal{T}$ will be called *upward (downward) directed*, if for any $u_1, u_2 \in \mathcal{T}$ there is $u \in \mathcal{T}$ that includes (or is included in) both u_1 and u_2.

Lemma 2.1.3. *If* $\mathcal{T}$ *is an upward (downward) directed set of theories of a Scott consequence relation* $\Vdash$, *then* $\bigcup \mathcal{T}$ *(or* $\bigcap \mathcal{T}$*) is also a theory of* $\Vdash$.

Proof. Let $\mathcal{T}$ be an upward directed set of theories and suppose that their union is not a theory, that is, $\bigcup \mathcal{T} \Vdash \overline{\bigcup \mathcal{T}}$. Then for some finite $a \subseteq \bigcup \mathcal{T}$, $b \subseteq \overline{\bigcup \mathcal{T}}$, $a \Vdash b$. Since a is finite, and $\mathcal{T}$ is upward directed, we have that for some $u \in \mathcal{T}$, $a \subseteq u$. But $b \subseteq \bar{u}$ and therefore we have $u \Vdash \bar{u}$—a contradiction with the assumption that u is a theory.

The proof for the intersection is similar, and can be obtained by duality considerations. $\qquad\Box$

The above property implies, as a special case, the existence of inclusion minimal theories containing some set of propositions, and inclusion maximal theories disjoint from a set of propositions:

Theorem 2.1.1.   *1. If* u *is a theory and* v *a set of propositions such that* $v \subseteq u$, *then* u *contains a minimal theory* u' *including* v.

   2. If u *is a theory and* $u \subseteq v$, *then* u *is contained in a maximal theory* u' *included in* v.

Proof. We will prove only the first claim – the second one will follow by duality.

Let u be a theory including v. Consider an arbitrary maximal chain of theories $\mathcal{T}$ such that $u \in \mathcal{T}$, and $v \subseteq w$, for each $w \in \mathcal{T}$ (the existence of such a chain follows from the axiom of choice, as in all such proofs). By the previous lemma, $u' = \bigcap \mathcal{T}$ is also a theory of the consequence relation. Clearly, u' includes v and is included in u. Moreover, u' is a minimal such theory, since otherwise $\mathcal{T}$ would not be a maximal chain.   □

As a special case, we obtain a useful property that any theory is included in some maximal theory of a consequence relation and includes a minimal such theory:

Corollary 2.1.1. *Any theory of* $\Vdash$ *is included in a maximal theory and contains a minimal theory of* $\Vdash$.

2.1.2 Representation theorem

Any set of sets of propositions $\mathcal{T}$ determines a Scott consequence relation $\Vdash_{\mathcal{T}}$ defined as follows:

(GS) $a \Vdash_{\mathcal{T}} b \;\;\equiv\;\;$ For any $u \in \mathcal{T}$, if $a \subseteq u$, then $b \cap u \neq \emptyset$.

If a consequence relation $\Vdash$ coincides with $\Vdash_{\mathcal{T}}$, for some set $\mathcal{T}$, we will say that $\Vdash$ is *generated by* $\mathcal{T}$. The following lemma shows that any set from $\mathcal{T}$ will be a theory of the generated consequence relation.

Lemma 2.1.4. *Any* $u \in \mathcal{T}$ *is a theory of* $\Vdash_{\mathcal{T}}$.

Proof. Assume that some $u \in \mathcal{T}$ is not a theory of $\Vdash_{\mathcal{T}}$, that is, $u \Vdash_{\mathcal{T}} \bar{u}$. By compactness, there must exist $a \subseteq u$ and $b \subseteq \bar{u}$ such that $a \Vdash_{\mathcal{T}} b$ - a contradiction with the definition of $\Vdash_{\mathcal{T}}$.   □

Actually, the above construction of consequence relations is quite general, since any Scott consequence relation can be generated in this way by the set of its theories – this is precisely the basic result about Scott consequence relations, called the Scott Completeness Theorem in [Gab81].

Let $\mathcal{T}_{\Vdash}$ be a set of all theories of a Scott consequence relation $\Vdash$. Then we have

Lemma 2.1.5 (Extension Lemma, [Gab76]). *For any sets of propositions* u, v, *if* $u \nVdash v$, *then there exists a theory* w *of* $\Vdash$ *such that* $u \subseteq w$ *and* $v \cap w = \emptyset$.

Proof. Let $A_1, A_2, \ldots$ be an enumeration of all propositions of the language. Define by induction a sequence of pairs of sets (u_i, v_i) such that $u_i \nVdash v_i$ as follows. First, let $u_0 = u$, $v_0 = v$. Now, given (u_n, v_n) such that $u_n \nVdash v_n$ and

A_n, define (u_{n+1}, v_{n+1}) as equal to $(u_n \cup \{A_n\}, v_n)$, if $u_n, A_n \nVdash v_n$, and as $(u_n, v_n \cup \{A_n\})$ otherwise. Notice that we cannot have both $u_n, A_n \Vdash v_n$ and $u_n \Vdash v_n, A_n$, since by the Cut rule we would obtain $u_n \Vdash v_n$, contrary to our inductive assumption. Consequently, $u_{n+1} \nVdash v_{n+1}$ in either case. Moreover, it is easy to see that $u_n \subseteq u_{n+1}$ and $v_n \subseteq v_{n+1}$.

Now let u' be the union of all u_n, and v' be the union of all v_n. Then $u' \nVdash v'$, since otherwise we would have by compactness $u_i \Vdash v_i$, for some i. This implies, in particular, that u' and v' are disjoint. Moreover, by the construction, each proposition of the language is included either in u' or in v'. Consequently, $v' = \overline{u'}$, and therefore u' is a required theory. $\square$

An immediate consequence of the Extension Lemma is that any Scott consequence relation is generated by its theories:

Theorem 2.1.2 (Representation Theorem). *If $\Vdash$ is a Scott consequence relation, then $\Vdash = \Vdash_{\mathcal{T}_\Vdash}$.*

Proof. By the Extension Lemma and Monotonicity, $a \nVdash b$ holds if and only if there exists a theory w of $\Vdash$ such that $a \subseteq w$ and $b \cap w = \emptyset$. By the definition of $\Vdash_{\mathcal{T}_\Vdash}$, the latter is equivalent to $a \nVdash_{\mathcal{T}_\Vdash} b$. Thus $\Vdash$ and $\Vdash_{\mathcal{T}_\Vdash}$ contain the same sequents. $\square$

An important consequence of the above representation theorem is that Scott consequence relations are uniquely determined by their theories. This will make such consequence relations an adequate tool for describing epistemic states (see Chapter 3). Moreover, for more expressive languages the above Representation Theorem can serve as a basis for constructing full-fledged semantics. In this case the set of theories of a consequence relation will serve, eventually, as its canonical model.

The following simple lemma shows that inclusion among consequence relations is equivalent to inverse inclusion for their sets of theories. So, extending a consequence relation amounts to reducing the set of its theories.

Lemma 2.1.6. $\Vdash \subseteq \Vdash_1$ *iff any theory of $\Vdash_1$ is a theory of $\Vdash$.*

Proof. The direction from left to right is immediate. Let $a \Vdash b$ but $a \nVdash_1 b$, for some a, b. Then there is a theory u of $\Vdash_1$ that includes a and disjoint from b. But $u \Vdash \overline{u}$ by Monotonicity, and hence u is not a theory of $\Vdash$. $\square$

A Scott consequence relation will be called *trivial*, if the empty sequent $\emptyset \Vdash \emptyset$ belongs to it. As can be seen, a consequence relation is trivial if and only if it contains all possible sequents as its rules. It is also easy to see that a Scott consequence relation is non-trivial if and only if it has at least one theory.

2.1.3 Compact sets of theories

As we have seen, if a family of sets of propositions $\mathcal{T}$ generates a Scott consequence relation $\Vdash$, any set from $\mathcal{T}$ will be a theory of $\Vdash$. However, $\Vdash$ will have in general other theories as well. This means, in particular, that the correspondence between consequence relations and sets of theories is not in general one-to-one.

A set $\mathcal{T}$ will be called *compact*, if it coincides with the set of all theories of $\Vdash_{\mathcal{T}}$. The following lemma shows that compactness of $\mathcal{T}$ amounts to the validity of the corresponding 'generating' definition of $\Vdash_{\mathcal{T}}$ for all sequents, not only for finite ones.

Lemma 2.1.7. $\mathcal{T}$ *is compact iff for any sets* u, v

$$u \Vdash_{\mathcal{T}} v \ \text{iff} \ (w)(u \subseteq w \ \& \ w \in \mathcal{T} \Rightarrow v \cap w \neq \emptyset)$$

Proof. By the Extension Lemma, $u \nVdash_{\mathcal{T}} v$ iff some theory w of $\Vdash_{\mathcal{T}}$ includes u and is disjoint from v. But if $\mathcal{T}$ is compact, w belongs to $\mathcal{T}$ and hence the implication from left to right holds. Now if the right-hand side is true for all u, v, then $u \nVdash_{\mathcal{T}} \overline{u}$ iff some $w \in \mathcal{T}$ includes u and is disjoint from $\overline{u}$ iff $w = u$. Thus the set of theories of $\Vdash_{\mathcal{T}}$ coincides with $\mathcal{T}$ and hence $\mathcal{T}$ is compact. $\square$

The above lemma also shows that there is a one-to-one correspondence between Scott consequence relations and compact sets of theories. Still, the following important result shows that we have a perfect match between *finite* sets of theories and their associated Scott consequence relations.

Lemma 2.1.8. *Any finite set of theories is compact.*

Proof. Let $\mathcal{T} = \{u_1, \ldots, u_n\}$ be a finite set of theories and assume that $u \notin \mathcal{T}$ is a theory of $\Vdash_{\mathcal{T}}$. Then, for any $1 \leq i \leq n$, if $u \nsubseteq u_i$, we choose some $A_i \in u \setminus u_i$, while if $u \subset u_i$, we chose some $B_i \in u_i \setminus u$. Let a be a set of all chosen A_i and b a set of all such B_i. Since u is a theory, we have $a \nVdash b$. However, $\Vdash$ is generated by $\mathcal{T}$, and hence it must contain a theory u_j such that $a \subseteq u_j$ and $b \subseteq \overline{u}_j$. But this is impossible, since, if A_j is chosen, a is not included in u_j, while if B_j is chosen, b is not included in $\overline{u}_j$. $\square$

The above lemma can actually be seen as one of the main incentives behind choosing Scott consequence relations as a representation formalism for our study; it indicates that, at least in the finite case, Scott consequence relations provide a faithful syntactic representation for collections of theories. This property will not hold for ordinary Tarski consequence relations (see below), since their sets of theories will always be closed with respect to intersections, a property that turns out to be undesirable in representing epistemic states.

2.1.4 Right compactness

The following weakening of the notion of a compact set of theories will play an important role in the sequel.

Definition 2.1.2. *A subset $\mathcal{T}$ of theories of a consequence relation $\Vdash$ will be called* right-compact *in $\Vdash$ if, for any proposition A and set v,*

$$A \Vdash v \text{ iff } (w)(A \in w \text{ \& } w \in \mathcal{T} \Rightarrow v \cap w \neq \emptyset)$$

Thus, a right-compact set of theories is sufficient for determining all single-premised sequents $A \Vdash v$ of a consequence relation. Notice that right-compact sets of theories may still be insufficient, in general, for generating a given consequence relation. They will be generating, however, for supraclassical consequence relations (see below) that will form the main logical tool in our study.

We will now give two useful characterizations of right compactness. To begin with, we will prove the following

Theorem 2.1.3. *A set $\mathcal{T}$ of theories is right-compact in $\Vdash$ if and only if any theory of $\Vdash$ is a set-theoretic union of theories from $\mathcal{T}$.*

Proof. Assume first that $\mathcal{T}$ is right-compact in $\Vdash$, but some theory u of $\Vdash$ is not a union of theories from $\mathcal{T}$. Then there must exist a proposition $A \in u$ that does not belong to any theory $v \in \mathcal{T}$ that is included in u. This means that, for any theory $v \in \mathcal{T}$ that contains A, $v \cap \bar{u} \neq \emptyset$. By the definition of right compactness, the latter implies $A \Vdash \bar{u}$, and hence $u \Vdash \bar{u}$ (since $A \in u$), contrary to the assumption that u is a theory of $\Vdash$.

In the other direction, if $A \Vdash v$ and $A \in u$, for some $u \in \mathcal{T}$, then $u \cap v \neq \emptyset$, since u is a theory of $\vDash$. Assume now that the condition of the theorem holds and $A \nVdash v$, for some A and v. We need to show that in this case $\mathcal{T}$ contains a theory w such that $A \in w$ and $w \cap v = \emptyset$. By the Extension Lemma, there must exist a theory u of $\Vdash$ that contains A and is disjoint from v. Since u is a union of theories from $\mathcal{T}$, there must exist a theory $w \in \mathcal{T}$ such that $A \in w \subseteq u$. Accordingly w contains A and is disjoint from v, as required. This concludes the proof. $\square$

A second characterization of right compactness makes use of the following notion of a *small theory*:

Definition 2.1.3. *A theory u of a consequence relation $\Vdash$ will be called* small *if, for some proposition A, u is a minimal theory of $\Vdash$ containing A.*

The following lemma provides an alternative description of such theories.

Lemma 2.1.9. *A set u is a minimal theory containing A if and only if $A \nVdash$ and, for any B,*

$$B \in u \quad \text{iff} \quad A \Vdash B, \bar{u}.$$

Proof. Let u be a minimal theory containing A. If $B \notin u$, then $u \nVdash \overline{u}$ implies $A \nVdash B, \overline{u}$ by Monotonicity. Conversely, if $A \nVdash B, \overline{u}$, there must exist a theory v included in u such that $A \in v$ and $B \notin v$. But u is a minimal theory containing A, and hence $u = v$ and $B \notin u$.

Let us denote by Fm the set of all propositions of the language. Assume now that $A \nVdash$ and a set u satisfies the above condition. By Reflexivity, we immediately conclude that $A \in u$. If there exists a proposition B not belonging to u (that is, $u \neq Fm$), then $A \nVdash B, \overline{u}$, and hence u contains some theory that also contains A. Let v be a minimal theory containing A and included in u, and assume that $v \neq u$, that is, there is $C \in u \setminus v$. $C \in u$ implies $A \Vdash C, \overline{u}$, while $C \notin v$ implies $A \nVdash C, \overline{v}$, and hence $A \nVdash C, \overline{u}$ by Monotonicity – a contradiction. Hence $u = v$, and hence u is a minimal theory containing A. Finally, if $u = Fm$, then $A \Vdash B$, for any proposition B, and hence Fm is the only theory containing A.   □

The following result gives a characterization of right compactness in terms of small theories.

Theorem 2.1.4. *A set of theories $\mathcal{T}$ is right-compact in $\Vdash$ if and only if $\mathcal{T}$ contains all small theories of $\Vdash$.*

Proof. If $\mathcal{T}$ is right-compact and u is a small theory containing A, then u must be a union of theories from $\mathcal{T}$, and hence at least one such theory v will contain A. But u is a minimal theory containing A, and therefore $u = v$. Thus, $u \in \mathcal{T}$.

In the other direction, let u be a theory of $\Vdash$ and $A \in u$. Then u must contain some minimal theory v that includes A. Therefore, any theory of $\Vdash$ is a union of small theories. Now, if all small theories belong to $\mathcal{T}$, we immediately obtain that any theory is a union of theories from $\mathcal{T}$.   □

2.1.5 Determinate and linear consequence relations

Keeping in mind our intended use of Scott consequence relations for representing epistemic states, we will describe below three classes of consequence relations that will correspond to important kinds of epistemic states.

Determination. Determinate consequence relations, defined below, will correspond to determinate epistemic states described in Chapter 3.

Definition 2.1.4. *A consequence relation $\Vdash$ will be called* determinate *if, for any set a, $a \Vdash$ implies $A \Vdash$, for some $A \in a$.*

The following lemma characterizes determinate consequence relations as consequence relations having a unique greatest theory.

Lemma 2.1.10. *A consequence relation is determinate iff it has a greatest theory.*

Proof. Assume that a consequence relation $\Vdash$ has a greatest theory u. Then $A \nVdash$ holds if and only if $A \in u$. Consequently, if $A_i \nVdash$, for any $A_i \in a$, then $a \subseteq u$, and therefore $a \nVdash$. Thus, $\Vdash$ is determinate.

For the other direction, we will show that the set $u = \{A \mid A \nVdash\}$ is a greatest theory of a determinate consequence relation. To begin with, u is consistent. Indeed, otherwise $u \Vdash$, and hence $a \Vdash$, for some finite set $a \subseteq u$. By determination, we would have $A \Vdash$, for some $A \in u$, contrary to the definition of u.

Since u is consistent, it is included in some theory of $\Vdash$. Note, however, that any theory v of $\Vdash$ contains only consistent propositions, and hence is included in u. Thus, u is a greatest theory of $\Vdash$. $\qquad\square$

Let $\Vdash$ be an arbitrary consequence relation, and u a theory of $\Vdash$. Then we can define a determinate consequence relation $\Vdash^u$ generated by all theories of $\Vdash$ that are included in u. The following result gives a syntactic description of this consequence relation.

Lemma 2.1.11. *If u is a theory of $\Vdash$, then $a \Vdash^u b$ iff $a \Vdash b, \overline{u}$.*

Proof. Due to the Extension Lemma and Monotonicity, $a \nVdash b, \overline{u}$ holds if and only if there exists a theory w of $\Vdash$ such that $a \subseteq w$, $b \subseteq \overline{w}$ and $\overline{u} \subseteq \overline{w}$, that is, $w \subseteq u$. Thus w is a theory of $\Vdash^u$, and hence the above condition amounts to $a \nVdash^u b$. $\qquad\square$

Primeness. A Scott consequence relation will be called *prime* if it has a unique least theory. Such consequence relations form an exact dual of determinate consequence relations.

The following lemma gives a syntactic description of primeness.

Lemma 2.1.12. *A Scott consequence relation is prime iff, for any set a, $\Vdash a$ holds only if $\Vdash A$, for some $A \in a$.*

Proof. Assume that $\Vdash$ has a least theory u_0. Then, for any proposition A, if $\nVdash A$, then A does not belong to some theory of $\Vdash$, and consequently it does not belong to u_0. Therefore, if $\nVdash A_i$, for all $A_i \in a$, then a is disjoint from u_0, and hence $\nVdash a$ holds.

In the other direction, if a consequence relation satisfies the above condition, we will show first that the set $u = \{A \mid \Vdash A\}$ is a theory. Indeed, otherwise we would have $a \Vdash b$, for some finite $a \subseteq u$ and $b \subseteq \overline{u}$. Since all elements of a are provable, we would obtain by Cut $\Vdash b$ and hence $\Vdash B$, for some $B \in b$. But B belongs to $\overline{u}$ and hence is not provable in $\Vdash$ – a contradiction.

Clearly, u is included in any theory of $\Vdash$, and therefore $\Vdash$ has a least theory. $\qquad\square$

Linearity. A Scott consequence relation will be called *linear* if its theories are linearly ordered with respect to inclusion. The following lemma gives a syntactic characterization of such consequence relations.

Lemma 2.1.13. *A Scott consequence relation is linear iff, for any propositions A and B, either $A \Vdash B$, or $B \Vdash A$.*

Proof. Assume that $\Vdash$ is a linear consequence relation and $A \nVdash B$. Then there must exist a theory u containing A but not B. In this case any theory v of $\Vdash$ that includes B cannot be included in u. And since the set of theories is linearly ordered with respect to inclusion, any such theory v will include u. Therefore A will belong to any theory of $\Vdash$ that contains B, and hence $B \Vdash A$ will hold.

Assume now that $\Vdash$ is not linear, and u and v are two of its incomparable theories. Then there must exist propositions A and B such that $A \in u \setminus v$ and $B \in v \setminus u$. Consequently we have that $A \nVdash B$ and $B \nVdash A$.   □

As is well-known, any partial order is an intersection of the set of linear (total) orders that extend it. Similarly, the following result shows that any Scott consequence relation is an intersection of its linear extensions.

Lemma 2.1.14. *Any Scott consequence relation is an intersection of the set of linear consequence relations that extend it.*

Proof. The inclusion of left into right is immediate. Let $\Vdash$ be a Scott consequence relation and $a \nVdash b$, for some a and b. Then there exists a theory u of $\Vdash$ that includes a and is disjoint from b. Now, since the union of any chain of theories from $\Vdash$ is also a theory of $\Vdash$, u is included in some maximal chain of theories $\mathcal{T}_l$ (by Zorn's lemma). Let $\Vdash^l$ be a Scott consequence relation determined by $\mathcal{T}_l$. Clearly, $\Vdash^l$ is a linear consequence relation that extends $\Vdash$. In addition, u is a theory of $\Vdash^l$, and hence $a \nVdash^l b$. Thus, $\Vdash$ coincides with the intersection of linear consequence relations that extend it.   □

As will be shown in what follows, a similar 'linear decomposition' will also hold for quite rich partially ordered structures of epistemic states.

2.2 Tarski consequence relations

Definition and properties. Scott consequence relation is a generalization of the usual *Tarski consequence relation*. The latter can be characterized as a set of rules of the form $a \vdash A$ (where A is a single proposition) satisfying the following conditions:

(Reflexivity) $A \vdash A$;
(Monotonicity)   If $a \vdash A$ and $a \subseteq a'$, then $a' \vdash A$;
(Cut)   If $a \vdash A$ and $a, A \vdash B$, then $a \vdash B$.

As before, the rules of a Tarski consequence relation can be extended to include infinite sets of premises by stipulating that $u \vdash A$ holds only if u has a finite subset a such that $a \vdash A$. Then the resulting consequence relation will satisfy the compactness property.

A Tarski consequence relation can also be described using the associated *provability operator* Cn defined as follows: $\mathrm{Cn}(u) = \{A \mid u \vdash A\}$. A *theory* of a Tarski consequence relation is a set of propositions u such that $u = \mathrm{Cn}(u)$. As is well-known, the set of theories of any Tarski consequence relation is closed with respect to arbitrary intersections as well as with respect to unions of upward directed sets (with respect to inclusion).

Tarski subrelation of a Scott relation

If $\Vdash$ is a Scott consequence relation, then the set of all rules of the form $a \Vdash A$ constitutes an ordinary Tarski consequence relation. We will call the latter a *Tarski subrelation of* $\Vdash$ and will denote it by $\vdash_{\Vdash}$. We will also denote by $\mathrm{Cn}_{\Vdash}$ the provability operator corresponding to $\vdash_{\Vdash}$.

As we mentioned, the set of theories of a Tarski consequence relation is closed with respect to arbitrary intersections. It turns out that intersections of theories of a Scott consequence relation give us the set of theories of its Tarski subrelation.

Lemma 2.2.1. *Theories of $\vdash_{\Vdash}$ are precisely intersections of theories of $\Vdash$, plus the set of all propositions.*

Proof. It is easy to check that any theory of $\Vdash$ is also a theory of $\vdash_{\Vdash}$. Since theories of $\vdash_{\Vdash}$ are closed with respect to intersections, all intersections of theories from $\Vdash$ are theories of $\vdash_{\Vdash}$. Finally, it is easy to check that the set of all propositions of the language is always a theory of a Tarski consequence relation.

In the other direction, assume that u is a theory of $\vdash_{\Vdash}$ which is distinct from the set of all propositions, that is $A \notin u$, for some A. Then $u \nVdash A$, and hence there is a theory v of $\Vdash$ such that $u \subseteq v$ and $A \notin v$. Consequently, any theory of $\vdash_{\Vdash}$ coincides with an intersection of all theories of $\Vdash$ that include u. □

The following lemma will be used in the sequel.

Lemma 2.2.2. *A theory u of a Scott consequence relation $\Vdash$ is a least theory containing a set of propositions v if and only if $u = \mathrm{Cn}_{\Vdash}(v)$.*

Proof. Clearly, $\mathrm{Cn}_{\Vdash}(v)$ is an intersection of all theories of $\Vdash$ containing v. Therefore, if it is a theory by itself, it must be a least theory containing v. Assume now that u is a least theory containing v, but $\mathrm{Cn}_{\Vdash}(v)$ is not a theory. Then there exists c such that $v \Vdash c$, though no $C \in c$ is a consequence of v. The latter condition implies that, for any $C \in c$ there exists a theory u_C that contains v but does not contain C. Since u should be included in all these theories, we have that u is disjoint from c, contrary to the fact that $v \Vdash c$. □

Tarski relations as singular Scott relations

Generally speaking, a Tarski consequence relation can also be seen as a special case of a Scott consequence relation. More exactly, there is a one-to-one correspondence between Tarski consequence relations and *singular* Scott consequence relations satisfying the following condition:

(**Singularity**) If $a \Vdash b$, then $a \Vdash B$, for some $B \in b$.

A characteristic 'semantic' feature of a singular Scott consequence relation is that intersection of any set of its theories is also a theory of a consequence relation.

Lemma 2.2.3. *A Scott consequence relation $\Vdash$ is singular if and only if*

1. *The set of all propositions of the language is a theory of $\Vdash$;*
2. *If $\mathcal{T}$ is a set of theories of $\Vdash$, then $\bigcap \mathcal{T}$ is also a theory of $\Vdash$.*

Proof. Note first that if $\Vdash$ is singular, all its sequents must have nonempty sets of conclusions. Therefore any set of propositions is consistent in $\Vdash$. In particular, the set of all propositions of the language is consistent and hence it is a maximal theory of $\Vdash$.

Assume that $\mathcal{T}$ is a set of theories of a singular consequence relation $\Vdash$, though $\bigcap \mathcal{T}$ is not a theory. Then there must exist finite sets a and b such that $a \Vdash b$, $a \subseteq \bigcap \mathcal{T}$, and $b \cap \bigcap \mathcal{T} = \emptyset$ (see Lemma 2.1.2). Since $\Vdash$ is singular, $a \Vdash B$, for some $B \in b$. Note, however, that any $u \in \mathcal{T}$ is a theory and $a \subseteq u$. Consequently, $B \in \bigcap \mathcal{T}$, which contradicts the assumption that b is disjoint from $\bigcap \mathcal{T}$.

Assume now that $\Vdash$ is not singular, that is there exist sets a and b such that $a \Vdash b$, though $a \nVdash B$, for any $B \in b$. Two cases should be considered.

(a) $b = \emptyset$. Then $a \Vdash$, and hence the set of all propositions is not a theory of $\Vdash$.

(b) $b \neq \emptyset$. Then, for any $B \in b$, there must exist a theory u_B that includes a but not B. Let v be an intersection of such theories, one for each $B \in b$. Clearly, v includes a and is disjoint from b. Therefore it cannot be a theory of $\Vdash$. This concludes the proof. $\square$

As can be shown, the second condition above can be replaced by a weaker claim that intersection of any two theories is also a theory.

It can be verified that any singular Scott consequence relation is uniquely determined by its Tarski subrelation. Also, if $\vdash$ is a Tarski consequence relation, we can define the corresponding singular Scott consequence relation as follows (cf. [Gab81], Theorem 11):

$$a \Vdash_\vdash b \text{ iff } a \vdash A, \text{ for some } A \in b.$$

It is easy to check that $\vdash$ and $\Vdash_\vdash$ have actually the same theories. So, we have an exact correspondence between Tarski consequence relations and singular Scott consequence relations. In what follows we will often implicitly use this correspondence. It will allow us, in particular, to extend all the notions definable for Scott consequence relations to Tarski consequence relations.

Linear Scott versus linear Tarski consequence relations. The set of theories of a linear Scott consequence relation is always closed with respect to intersections. So, such consequence relations are 'almost singular' in that they satisfy the following condition: for any a and any *nonempty b*,

$$a \Vdash b \text{ iff } a \Vdash B, \text{ for some } B \in b.$$

Linear Scott consequence relations do not satisfy, however, the first characteristic property of singular consequence relations, since the set of all propositions does not always form a theory. Still, such consequence relations can be studied in the framework of Tarski consequence relations, with the only reservation that Scott consequence relations are capable of distinguishing between cases where the set of all propositions is a theory and those where it is not.

2.3 Supraclassicality

Now we will consider consequence relations in languages containing the usual classical connectives $\{\vee, \wedge, \neg, \rightarrow\}$. As usual, $\vDash$ will denote the classical entailment relation with respect to these connectives, and Cl its associated classical derivability operator. Also, for a finite set of propositions a, we will denote by $\bigwedge a$ the conjunction of all propositions from a. As a special case, $\bigwedge \emptyset$ will denote an arbitrary tautology $\mathbf{t}$.

2.3.1 Supraclassical Tarski consequence relations

A Tarski consequence relation $\vdash$ is called *supraclassical* if $\vDash \subseteq \vdash$. In other words, a Tarski consequence relation is supraclassical if it subsumes classical inference.

Supraclassicality is equivalent to the requirement that all theories of a consequence relation are deductively closed sets.

Lemma 2.3.1. *A Tarski consequence relation is supraclassical iff all its theories are deductively closed sets.*

Proof. Theories of a Tarski consequence relation are sets of propositions that are closed with respect to its rules. Consequently, if $\vdash$ is supraclassical, all its theories will also be closed with respect to the classical entailment. In the other direction, if $a \vDash B$, but $a \nvdash B$, then there exists a theory of $\vdash$ that contains a but not B. Clearly, such a theory will not be deductively closed. $\qquad\square$

Supraclassicality allows for replacement of classically equivalent formulas in premises and conclusions of the rules. In addition, it allows to replace sets of premises by their classical conjunctions: $a \vdash A$ will be equivalent to $\bigwedge a \vdash A$. Accordingly, supraclassical Tarski consequence relations can be reduced to certain binary relations among classical propositions. This fact will play an important role in Chapter 5.

It should be noted, however, that provable equivalence with respect to a supraclassical consequence relation does not imply that the corresponding formulas are interchangeable in all contexts. For example, even if $A \vdash B$ and $B \vdash A$ hold, this does not imply, in general, $\neg A \vdash \neg B$ or $A \vee C \vdash B \vee C$. This property will hold, however, for 'fully' classical Tarski consequence relations described below.

2.3.2 Classical consequence relations

A Tarski consequence relation will be called *classical* if it is supraclassical and satisfies the deduction theorem:

Deduction   If $a, A \vdash B$, then $a \vdash A \to B$.

Classical consequence relations satisfy already all the familiar rules of classical inference, such as Contraposition, Disjunction in the Antecedent, etc. Moreover, the following result shows that adding each of these rules to a supraclassical consequence relation is sufficient for classicality. We leave the proof to the reader as an exercise.

Lemma 2.3.2. *A supraclassical consequence relation is classical iff it satisfies one of the following rules:*

Deduction   *If $a, A \vdash B$, then $a \vdash A \to B$;*
Contraposition   *If $a, A \vdash B$, then $a, \neg B \vdash \neg A$;*
Disjunction   *If $a, A \vdash C$ and $a, B \vdash C$, then $a, A \vee B \vdash C$.*

Notice that even classical consequence relations still do not coincide, in general, with the classical entailment $\vDash$; the latter can be described as the least classical (or, equivalently, least supraclassical) consequence relation. There is, however, an intimate connection between classical entailment and classical consequence relations. Notice that any rule $A \vdash B$ of a classical consequence relation is equivalent to $\vdash A \to B$. Consequently, any classical consequence relation can be seen as a classical entailment with some set of propositions added as additional, nonlogical axioms. And in this respect arbitrary supraclassical consequence relations allow additional freedom in that they permit the use of auxiliary nonlogical *inference rules* of the form $A \vdash B$ that are not reducible to the corresponding material implications.

In what follows, we will always use Th to denote the provability operator of some classical Tarski consequence relation.

Classical subrelation of a supraclassical Tarski relation. Any supraclassical Tarski consequence relation ⊢ contains a classical consequence relation defined as follows:

$$A \in \text{Th}_\vdash(a) \quad \equiv \quad \vdash \bigwedge a \to A$$

The following result shows that this consequence relation is a greatest classical consequence relation included in ⊢.

Lemma 2.3.3. *For any supraclassical Tarski consequence relation* ⊢, $\text{Th}_\vdash$ *is a greatest classical consequence relation included in* ⊢.

Proof. Assume that Th is some classical consequence relation included in ⊢. Then $A \in \text{Th}(a)$ implies $\bigwedge a \to A \in \text{Th}(\emptyset)$, and hence ⊢ $\bigwedge a \to A$, that is, $A \in \text{Th}_\vdash(a)$. Thus, Th is included in $\text{Th}_\vdash$.   □

The classical subrelation of a supraclassical consequence relation will play the role of an 'internal logic' of the latter.

2.3.3 Semi-classical consequence relations

We will describe below a very special kind of Tarski consequence relation that will play a central role in our analysis of nonmonotonic inference.

A supraclassical Tarski consequence relation will be called *semi-classical* if it is closed with respect to the following weak rule of reasoning by cases:

Weak Factoring   If $a, A \vee B \vdash A$ and $a, A \vee \neg B \vdash A$, then $a \vdash A$.

Clearly, any classical consequence relation is semi-classical, though not vice versa. A semantic characterization of such consequence relations can be given in terms of so-called saturatable theories introduced in [Lev91].

Definition 2.3.1. *A deductively closed set u will be called* saturatable *with respect to a proposition A, if* $\text{Cl}(u \cup \{A\})$ *is a world (maximal deductively closed set).*

It is easy to see that a theory u is saturatable with respect to A if and only if, for any proposition B, either $A \to B$ or $A \to \neg B$ belongs to u.

Lemma 2.3.4. *A consequence relation* ⊢ *is semi-classical iff any maximal theory of* ⊢ *that is consistent with some proposition A is saturatable with respect to A.*

Proof. If $a \nvdash A$, there must exist a maximal theory u that is consistent with $\neg A$ and includes a. If u is saturatable with respect to $\neg A$, either $A \vee B$ or $A \vee \neg B$ belongs to u, and therefore either $a, A \vee B \nvdash A$ or $a, A \vee \neg B \nvdash A$. Hence Weak Factoring holds. It is easy to check also that if ⊢ is semi-classical and u is a maximal theory such that $u \nvdash \neg A$, then either $\neg A \vee B$ or $\neg A \vee \neg B$ should belong to u by Weak Factoring, and hence $\text{Cl}(u \cup \{A\})$ is a world.   □

The next result shows that Weak Factoring is equivalent to a certain weak form of Disjunction in the Antecedent.

Lemma 2.3.5. *A supraclassical consequence relation is semi-classical iff it satisfies the following rule:*

Weak Disjunction *If* $a, A \vee B \vdash A$ *and* $a, A \vee C \vdash A$, *then* $a, A \vee B \vee C \vdash A$.

Proof. Replacing C by $\neg B$ in the above rule, we immediately obtain Weak Factoring. In the other direction, if $a, A \vee B \vdash A$ and $a, A \vee C \vdash A$, then the former implies

$$a, A \vee B \vee C, A \vee B \vdash A,$$

while the latter implies $a, A \vee B \vee C, A \vee C, A \vee \neg B \vdash A$. Now notice that

$$A \vee B \vee C, A \vee \neg B, A \vee \neg C \vdash A$$

belongs to any supraclassical consequence relation, and hence also

$$a, A \vee B \vee C, A \vee \neg B, A \vee \neg C \vdash A.$$

Applying Weak Factoring to this and the previous rule, we conclude $a, A \vee B \vee C, A \vee \neg B \vdash A$. Applying Weak Factoring to the latter and (1), we finally obtain $a, A \vee B \vee C \vdash A$. □

It is interesting to note that Weak Disjunction can be reduced to the following 'premise-free' special case:

Weak Disjunction$_0$ If $A \vee B \vdash A$ and $A \vee C \vdash A$, then $A \vee B \vee C \vdash A$.

We will use the latter characterization in Chapter 5.

Substituting **f** for A in the Weak Factoring rule, we obtain the following rule:

(W) $$\frac{a, B \vdash \qquad a, \neg B \vdash}{a \vdash}$$

This rule can be shown to correspond to the requirement that maximal theories of a consequence relation are worlds (that is, maximal deductively closed sets).

Lemma 2.3.6. *Any maximal consistent theory of a semi-classical consequence relation is a world.*

In what follows, we will also use the following feature of semi-classical consequence relations:

Lemma 2.3.7. *If* $\vdash$ *is a semi-classical consequence relation, then* $B \to A \vdash B$ *holds if and only if, for any* a, *if* $a, B \vdash A$, *then* $a \vdash B$.

Proof. Since $B \to A, B \vdash A$ by Supraclassicality, we can substitute $B \to A$ for a in the above condition and obtain $B \to A \vdash B$.

Assume that $B \to A \vdash B$ and $a, B \vdash A$. The first condition implies $a, B \to A \vdash A \wedge B$, which is equivalent to $a, (B \to A) \vee (A \wedge B) \vdash A \wedge B$. It can be easily seen that the second condition is equivalent to $a, B \vee (A \wedge B) \vdash A \wedge B$. Applying Weak Disjunction to the two latter conditions we obtain

$$a, B \vee (B \to A) \vee (A \wedge B) \vdash A \wedge B.$$

It can be checked that the last premise in the above rule is a tautology, and hence it can be removed. Thus, $a \vdash A \wedge B$ and consequently $a \vdash B$, as required. $\square$

2.3.4 Supraclassical Scott relations

So far, we have defined supraclassicality only for Tarski consequence relations. The following definition provides a straightforward extension of this notion to Scott consequence relations.

Definition 2.3.2. *A Scott consequence relation will be called* supraclassical, *if it satisfies:*

Supraclassicality   *If $a \vDash A$, then $a \Vdash A$.*

As can be seen, a Scott consequence relation is supraclassical if and only if its Tarski subrelation is supraclassical. And just as for the latter, it requires all theories of a Scott consequence relation to be deductively closed.

Lemma 2.3.8. *A Scott consequence relation is supraclassical if and only if all its theories are deductively closed sets.*

Moreover, the Representation Theorem for Scott consequence relations immediately implies that such a consequence relation is supraclassical if and only if it is generated by a set of deductively closed theories.

Just as for Tarski consequence relations, supraclassicality allows for replacement of classically equivalent formulas in premises and conclusions of sequents, as well as replacement of sets of premises by their classical conjunctions: $a \Vdash b$ will be equivalent to $\bigwedge a \Vdash b$. Multiple conclusions, however, cannot be replaced in this way by their classical disjunctions. Taking a simplest case, a sequent $\Vdash B, C$ is not reducible to $\Vdash B \vee C$; the latter says that any theory should contain $B \vee C$, while the former asserts a stronger constraint that any theory should contain either B or C.

Since finite premise sets in sequents can always be replaced by their conjunctions, supraclassical Scott consequence relations are determined, in effect, by sequents of the form $A \Vdash b$ that contain a single premise. As a result, we will show now that in the supraclassical case the Representation Theorem for Scott consequence relations can be modified to a claim that any such consequence relation is uniquely determined by its small theories.

Theorem 2.3.1. *Any supraclassical Scott consequence relation is generated by the set of its small theories.*

Proof. To begin with, any theory containing some finite set a includes a minimal such theory – see Theorem 2.1.1. Consequently, by the Representation Theorem, $a \Vdash b$ holds iff $b \cap u \neq \emptyset$, for any minimal theory u containing a. In addition, for supraclassical consequence relations, any finite set of premises a can be replaced by its conjunction $\bigwedge a$. Therefore, the set of small theories is sufficient for determining $\Vdash$. $\qquad\qquad\square$

As a consequence of the above result, we obtain that any right-compact set of theories of a supraclassical consequence relation will also be a generating set of theories.

Corollary 2.3.1. *If a set of theories $\mathcal{T}$ is right-compact in a supraclassical consequence relation, then the latter is generated by $\mathcal{T}$.*

Proof. Follows from the fact that $\mathcal{T}$ is right-compact if and only if it includes the set of small theories. $\qquad\qquad\square$

A supraclassical Scott consequence relation will be called *classically consistent* if the set of all propositions is not its theory. It is easy to show that this condition can be replaced by the requirement $\mathbf{f} \Vdash$, where $\mathbf{f}$ is an arbitrary classical contradiction.

Classical subrelation of a Scott consequence relation. As we established earlier, any supraclassical Tarski consequence relation contains a greatest classical subrelation. Similarly, any supraclassical Scott consequence relation contains a greatest classical consequence relation defined as follows:

$$A \in \mathrm{Th}_{\Vdash}(a) \quad \equiv \quad \Vdash \bigwedge a \to A$$

We will call such a consequence relation the *classical subrelation* of $\Vdash$. As can be easily seen, $\mathrm{Th}_{\Vdash}$ is also a classical subrelation of the Tarski subrelation of $\Vdash$.

The following lemma has the same proof as the corresponding claim for Tarski consequence relations.

Lemma 2.3.9. *For any supraclassical Scott consequence relation $\Vdash$, $\mathrm{Th}_{\Vdash}$ is a greatest classical consequence relation included in $\Vdash$.*

As for Tarski consequence relations, the classical subrelation of a Scott consequence relation will play the role of an internal logic of the latter.

Linear supraclassical consequence relations. In the supraclassical case linearity admits the following quite useful characterization that will be extensively used in the book:

Lemma 2.3.10. *A supraclassical Scott consequence relation is linear if and only if it satisfies the following condition:*

If $a \Vdash c$, then $A \Vdash c$, for some $A \in a$.

Proof. If $\Vdash$ satisfies the above condition, then, in particular, $A, B \Vdash A \wedge B$ implies that either $A \Vdash A \wedge B$, or $B \Vdash A \wedge B$, that is, either $A \Vdash B$ or $B \Vdash A$. As was shown earlier, this is sufficient to guarantee that the relevant consequence relation is linear. In the other direction, it is easy to check that the above condition is valid if a set of theories is linearly ordered.   □

2.4 Grounded Scott consequence relations

In this section we will consider supraclassical Scott consequence relations that are generated, in a certain sense, by sets of propositions. The construction below describes one of the important ways of building Scott consequence relations. Though it could be given in a more general setting, the level of generality chosen will be sufficient for our purposes.

Let Th be an arbitrary classical consequence relation, and Δ a set propositions. A Scott consequence relation will be called *classically generated by a pair* (Δ, Th) if it is generated by a set of theories $\{\mathrm{Th}(D) \mid D \in \Delta\}$. In this case we will also say that a consequence relation is *classically generated by a set of propositions* Δ (relative to Th).

It turns out that there exists a purely internal characterization of classically generated consequence relations. To begin with, the following result shows that the classical consequence relation Th in the generating pair (Δ, Th) can always be replaced by the classical subrelation $\mathrm{Th}_{\Vdash}$ of $\Vdash$.

Lemma 2.4.1. *If $\Vdash$ is generated by (Δ, Th), then it is generated by $(\Delta, \mathrm{Th}_{\Vdash})$.*

Proof. It is sufficient to show that (Δ, Th) and $(\Delta, \mathrm{Th}_{\Vdash})$ produce the same generating theories, that is, $\mathrm{Th}(B) = \mathrm{Th}_{\Vdash}(B)$, for any $B \in \Delta$. Indeed, if $A \in \mathrm{Th}(B)$, then $B \to A \in \mathrm{Th}(D)$, for any $D \in \Delta$, and hence $\Vdash B \to A$, that is, $A \in \mathrm{Th}_{\Vdash}(B)$. In the other direction, if $\Vdash B \to A$, then $B \Vdash A$. But $\mathrm{Th}(B)$ is a theory of $\Vdash$ and $B \in \mathrm{Th}(B)$. Consequently, we obtain $A \in \mathrm{Th}(B)$.   □

So, in what follows we will simply talk about consequence relations generated by sets of propositions.

Let us introduce the following notions.

Definition 2.4.1. *Let $\Vdash$ be a supraclassical Scott consequence relation.*

- *A theory of $\Vdash$ will be called* prime, *if $u = \mathrm{Th}_{\Vdash}(A)$, for some proposition A.*

- *A proposition A will be called* prime in $\Vdash$, *if* $\mathrm{Th}_{\Vdash}(A)$ *is a theory of* $\Vdash$.

It is easy to show that if A is a prime proposition, then $\mathrm{Th}_{\Vdash}(A)$ is a least theory of $\Vdash$ containing A. Consequently, any prime theory will be small. Note also that all prime propositions 'generating' a given prime theory are equivalent modulo $\mathrm{Th}_{\Vdash}$.

The next lemma gives an alternative description of prime propositions.

Lemma 2.4.2. *A proposition A is prime iff, for any set c, $A \Vdash c$ implies $\Vdash A \rightarrow C$, for some $C \in c$.*

Proof. Any prime proposition A is contained in some theory, and hence $A \not\Vdash$. Assume that $A \Vdash c$. Since $\mathrm{Th}_{\Vdash}(A)$ is a theory of $\Vdash$, there must exist $C \in c \cap \mathrm{Th}_{\Vdash}(A)$, and hence $\Vdash A \rightarrow C$.

If A is not prime, $\mathrm{Th}_{\Vdash}(A)$ is not a theory of $\Vdash$, that is, there exists c such that $\mathrm{Th}_{\Vdash}(A) \Vdash c$, though c is disjoint from $\mathrm{Th}_{\Vdash}(A)$. By compactness, there exists a proposition $B \in \mathrm{Th}_{\Vdash}(A)$ such that $B \Vdash c$. But then $A \Vdash c$, though $\not\Vdash A \rightarrow C$, for all $C \in c$. This concludes the proof. $\square$

Now we are ready to introduce the following notion of a grounded consequence relation.

Definition 2.4.2. *A Scott consequence relation will be called* grounded *if it is generated by a set of its prime theories.*

The result below shows that grounded consequence relations are precisely consequence relations that are classically generated by some sets of propositions.

Theorem 2.4.1. *A supraclassical Scott consequence relation $\Vdash$ is grounded if and only if it is classically generated by some pair (Δ, Th).*

Proof. If $\Vdash$ is grounded, let us take Δ to be the set of prime propositions of $\Vdash$ and $\mathrm{Th}_{\Vdash}$ to be an appropriate classical consequence relation. Then the set $\{\mathrm{Th}_{\Vdash}(B) \mid B \in \Delta\}$ is clearly a set of theories generating $\Vdash$.

In the other direction, if $\Vdash$ is generated by (Δ, Th), then as was shown earlier, it is generated by $(\Delta, \mathrm{Th}_{\Vdash})$. But any theory of the form $\mathrm{Th}_{\Vdash}(B)$, for $B \in \Delta$, is a prime theory of $\Vdash$, so $\Vdash$ is generated by its prime theories. $\square$

Strong groundedness

Groundedness of a consequence relation does not guarantee that any theory of the generated consequence relation is obtainable as a logical closure of some generating propositions. In many applications, however, we will need such a stronger notion of groundedness.

Definition 2.4.3. *A supraclassical Scott consequence relation $\Vdash$ will be called* strongly generated *by a pair (Δ, Th) if any small theory of $\Vdash$ coincides with $\mathrm{Th}(D)$, for some $D \in \Delta$.*

Since any supraclassical Scott consequence relation is generated by its small theories, if a consequence relation is strongly generated by a set of propositions Δ, it will be classically generated by Δ. Again, it turns out that there exists a purely internal characterization of strongly generated consequence relations.

Definition 2.4.4. *A supraclassical Scott consequence relation will be called* strongly grounded *if all its small theories are prime.*

Then we immediately obtain

Theorem 2.4.2. *A supraclassical consequence relation is strongly grounded iff it is strongly generated by some set of propositions.*

The following result connects the notion of strong groundedness with the general notion of right compactness.

Theorem 2.4.3. *A supraclassical consequence relation is strongly grounded if and only if the set of its prime theories is right-compact.*

Proof. Follows from the fact that a set of theories is right-compact iff it includes the set of small theories.   □

As a result, we immediately obtain the following

Corollary 2.4.1. *A consequence relation is strongly grounded if and only if all its theories are unions of prime theories.*

Let us denote by $\mathbf{P}_{\Vdash}$ the set of prime propositions of a consequence relation $\Vdash$. Then the following consequence of the above result shows that any theory of a strongly grounded consequence relation is a deductive closure of the prime propositions included in it.

Corollary 2.4.2. *If a consequence relation $\Vdash$ is strongly grounded, then any theory u of $\Vdash$ is equal to* $\mathrm{Th}_{\Vdash}(u \cap \mathbf{P}_{\Vdash})$.

Proof. If $\Vdash$ is strongly grounded, then each its theory u is a union of all $\mathrm{Th}(A)$, where $A \in \mathbf{P}_{\Vdash} \cap u$, and hence u coincides with $\mathrm{Th}_{\Vdash}(u \cap \mathbf{P}_{\Vdash})$.   □

Clearly, any strongly grounded consequence relation will be grounded, though not vice versa. The following example illustrates this.

Example 2.4.1. Let Δ be a set of all propositions $B_n = p \wedge p_1 \wedge \cdots \wedge p_n \wedge q_n$, for all natural n. We consider a consequence relation generated by Δ with respect to the classical entailment Cl.

Let u be a logical closure of the set of all p's. Clearly, this theory cannot be prime. We will show, however, that u is a minimal theory containing p. Assume first that there exists a finite set c such that $u \Vdash c$, though c is disjoint from u. Then the conjunctive normal form of any $C \in c$ must contain a disjunction C_d of literals without positive occurrences of p's. Let c_d be a set of such disjunctions, for all $C \in c$. Then we still have that c_d is disjoint from u and $u \Vdash c_d$. Moreover, by compactness, $p, p_1, \ldots, p_n \Vdash c_d$, for some natural n. Consequently, for any $k \geq n$, at least one C_d from c_d must be a logical consequence of B_k. Since C_d does not have positive occurrences of p's, it must contain q_k. Therefore, for any $k \geq n$, at least one disjunction from c_d must contain a positive atom q_k. But this is impossible due to the finiteness of c_d. Thus, u is a theory of this consequence relation. Moreover, assume that there is another theory u_0 such that $p \in u_0 \subset u$, and let p_i be an atomic proposition that does not belong to u_0. Then $i > 1$, since $\Vdash p_1$ belongs to the consequence relation. In addition, it is easy to check that the following sequents belong to the consequence relation, for any $j > 1$:

$$\Vdash p_j, q_j, q_{j-1}, \ldots, q_1$$

Consequently, u_0 must contain q_l, for some $l \leq i$, which is impossible, since u_0 is included in u. Therefore, u is a minimal theory containing p.

Despite the above counterexample, there are many natural classes of consequence relations that are strongly grounded. In particular, imposing some finiteness restrictions will enforce strong generation.

Definition 2.4.5. *A supraclassical Scott consequence relation will be called*

- finite *if it is a least consequence relation containing some finite set of sequents.*
- finitary *if it is generated by a finite set of prime theories.*

Since any finite set of theories is compact, we immediately obtain

Lemma 2.4.3. *Any finitary consequence relation is strongly grounded.*

However, a finite consequence relation has, in general, an infinite number of theories. Nevertheless, we have

Theorem 2.4.4. *Any finite consequence relation is strongly grounded.*

Proof. Assume that $\Vdash$ is generated by a finite set of sequents $\{a_i \Vdash c_i\}$, and let h denote a (finite) set of all propositions occurring in their conclusions, that is, $h = \bigcup_i (c_i)$.

Let u be a minimal theory containing a proposition A. We will show that $u = \mathrm{Cl}(A \wedge H_u)$, where H_u denotes a conjunction of all propositions from h belonging to u. To this end, it is sufficient to show that $\mathrm{Cl}(A \wedge H_u)$ is a theory of $\Vdash$ (since it is included in u). In other words, we need to show that $\mathrm{Cl}(A \wedge H_u)$ is closed with respect to the generating sequents.

For any generating sequent $a_i \Vdash c_i$, if $a_i \subseteq \mathrm{Cl}(A \wedge H_u)$, then $a_i \subseteq u$, and hence there is $C \in c_i$ that belongs to u. Therefore $C \in u \cap h$, and consequently $C \in \mathrm{Cl}(A \wedge H_u)$. Hence, $\mathrm{Cl}(A \wedge H_u)$ is a theory of $\Vdash$.   □

To end this section we will give a direct description of a consequence relation that is strongly generated by a set of propositions Δ.

Let $\Vdash$ be a supraclassical consequence relation and Δ a set of propositions. For any proposition A of the language, we will denote by Δ^A the set of all $D \in \Delta$ such that $A \in \mathrm{Th}_{\Vdash}(D)$. This set can be seen as a set of all possible explanations of A on the basis of Δ. Then we have

Theorem 2.4.5. *A supraclassical consequence relation $\Vdash$ is strongly generated by a set of propositions Δ iff it satisfies the following conditions:*

1. *Any proposition from Δ is prime;*
2. *$A \Vdash \Delta^A$, for any proposition A.*

Proof. If $\Vdash$ is strongly generated by Δ, then any proposition from Δ will be prime in $\Vdash$. Also, if $A \in \mathrm{Th}_{\Vdash}(D)$, for some $D \in \Delta$, then $D \in \Delta^A$, and hence $\mathrm{Th}_{\Vdash}(D)$ will not be disjoint from Δ^A. Therefore $A \Vdash \Delta^A$ by right compactness.

Assume that $\Vdash$ satisfies the above two conditions, and let u be a minimal theory of $\Vdash$ containing some proposition A. Since u should be closed with respect to the sequent $A \Vdash \Delta^A$, we have $D \in u$, for some $D \in \Delta^A$. But D is a prime proposition, and hence $\mathrm{Th}_{\Vdash}(D)$ will be a theory of $\Vdash$ that contains A and is included in u. Due to minimality of u, we have $u = \mathrm{Th}_{\Vdash}(D)$. Thus, $\Vdash$ is strongly generated by Δ. $\qquad\square$

2.5 Base-generated consequence relations

In this section we will give a characterization of Scott consequence relations that are generated by subsets of a certain set of propositions called its *base*. As we will see later, such consequence relations will correspond to epistemic states generated by default bases. As for grounded consequence relations, the following constructions will provide a purely logical way of describing base-generation. It will be shown, in particular, that propositions from the base can be characterized as propositions that behave classically in the context of supraclassical consequence relations.

Base-generated consequence relations will be defined as consequence relations that are classically generated by all *nonempty* subsets of a certain set of propositions[1].

Definition 2.5.1. *Let* Th *be a classical consequence relation and Δ a set of propositions. A Scott consequence relation will be called* base-generated *by a pair (Δ, Th) if it is generated by a set of theories $\{\mathrm{Th}(\Delta_0) \mid \Delta_0 \neq \emptyset \ \& \ \Delta_0 \subseteq \Delta\}$. In this case Δ will be called a* base *of $\Vdash$ (relative to* Th*)*.

---

[1] We modify here the definition of base-generation as compared with [Boc99b] in that we exclude the empty subset from consideration. A slight complication created by this decision at the present stage will be compensated in subsequent chapters by more transparent representation results.

If Δ is a base, we will denote by $\Delta^\wedge$ the set of propositions $\{\bigwedge a \mid a \subseteq \Delta\}$.

The following result shows that base-generation is a special case of classical generation.

Theorem 2.5.1. *Any base-generated consequence relation is grounded.*

Proof. Let Δ be a base generating $\Vdash$ with respect to Th. Due to compactness of Th, finite subsets of Δ are sufficient for determining the generating consequence relation. Moreover, such finite sets can always be replaced by their conjunctions. Consequently, $\Vdash$ will be generated, in effect, by $\Delta^\wedge$ relative to the same classical consequence relation. □

The construction in the proof of the above theorem shows, in particular, that base-generation by Δ amounts to a generation by a set of propositions $\Delta^\wedge$.

A set of propositions Δ will be called $\wedge$-*closed*, if, for any $A, B \in \Delta$, $A \wedge B$ also belongs to Δ. Then we immediately obtain

Corollary 2.5.1. $\Vdash$ *is base generated iff it is generated by a $\wedge$-closed set of propositions.*

Propositions from a base of a consequence relation can be freely combined in order to produce new theories. In particular, it is easy to show that $\mathrm{Th}(\Delta)$ is the greatest theory of such a consequence relation. Thus, base-generation implies determination:

Lemma 2.5.1. *Any base-generated consequence relation is determinate.*

Proof. If $A \nVdash$, there must exist a subset b of the base such that $A \in \mathrm{Th}(b)$. Now if $A_i \nVdash$, for all $A_i \in a$, and $\{b_i\}$ the corresponding subsets of the base, then $b_a = \bigcup(b_i)$ is a subset of the base such that $a \subseteq \mathrm{Th}(b_a)$. Consequently, $a \nVdash$. □

For any set of propositions w, we will denote by $A \to w$ the set $\{A \to B \mid B \in w\}$.

Definition 2.5.2. *Let $\Vdash$ be a supraclassical Scott consequence relation.*

- *A proposition B will be called* basic *in $\Vdash$ if $a, B \Vdash b$ always implies $a \Vdash B \to b$.*
- *B will be called a* base proposition *of $\Vdash$ if it is basic and prime.*

The above condition for basic propositions is a generalized form of a deduction theorem for Scott consequence relations. Consequently, basic propositions are, in a sense, propositions that behave classically in our supraclassical context. The following result provides a semantic characterization of such propositions.

Theorem 2.5.2. *A is a basic proposition of* $\Vdash$ *iff, for any theory u of* $\Vdash$, $\mathrm{Cl}(\{A\} \cup u)$ *is also a theory of* $\Vdash$.

Proof. Let u be a theory of $\Vdash$. If $\mathrm{Cl}(\{A\} \cup u)$ is not a theory of $\Vdash$, there must exist finite sets $a \subseteq u$, $c \subseteq \overline{\mathrm{Cl}(\{A\} \cup u)}$ such that $a, A \Vdash c$. If A is a basic proposition, we have $a \Vdash A \to c$, and since u is a theory, there is $C \in c$ such that $A \to C \in u$. Consequently, $C \in \mathrm{Cl}(\{A\} \cup u)$, contrary to the assumption that c is disjoint from $\mathrm{Cl}(\{A\} \cup u)$.

In the other direction, if $a \nVdash A \to c$, then there is a theory u such that $a \subseteq u$ and $A \to c \subseteq \overline{u}$. But then $\mathrm{Cl}(\{A\} \cup u)$ is a theory of $\Vdash$ that includes A and a and is disjoint from c. Therefore, $A, a \nVdash c$, and hence A is a basic proposition. $\square$

Base propositions are even more 'classical' in this respect than basic propositions, since their closures are theories of a consequence relation. Note that if $\Vdash$ is a prime consequence relation, then any basic proposition in $\Vdash$ will be a base proposition[2].

We are going to show now that the set of all base propositions forms a base of a base-generated consequence relation. We begin with demonstrating that any proposition belonging to some base of a base-generated consequence relation is a base proposition.

Lemma 2.5.2. *If Δ is a base of* $\Vdash$, *then any proposition from $\Delta^{\wedge}$ is a base proposition of* $\Vdash$.

Proof. Let $\Vdash$ be a consequence relation generated by a base Δ with respect to Th, and $B \in \Delta^{\wedge}$. Note that B is a prime proposition of $\Vdash$ (cf. the proof of Theorem 2.4.1).

Now, if $a \nVdash B \to c$, there must exist $B_1 \in \Delta^{\wedge}$ such that $a \subseteq \mathrm{Th}(B_1)$ and $B \to c \subseteq \overline{\mathrm{Th}(B_1)}$. The later condition implies that c is disjoint from $\mathrm{Th}(B \wedge B_1)$. In addition, $\mathrm{Th}(B \wedge B_1)$ includes both B and a. But $B \wedge B_1$ belongs to $\Delta^{\wedge}$, and hence $a, B \nVdash c$. Therefore, B is a base proposition of $\Vdash$. $\square$

Theorem 2.5.3. *A is a base proposition of a base-generated consequence relation* $\Vdash$ *if and only if it is prime in* $\Vdash$.

Proof. Let $\Vdash$ be a consequence relation generated by a base Δ with respect to Th, and assume that A is prime, that is, $\mathrm{Th}_{\Vdash}(A)$ is a theory of $\Vdash$. If $a \nVdash A \to c$, there must exist $B \in \Delta^{\wedge}$ such that $a \subseteq \mathrm{Th}(B)$ and $A \to c \subseteq \overline{\mathrm{Th}(B)}$. But B is a finite proposition of $\Vdash$, and hence $\mathrm{Th}(B) = \mathrm{Th}_{\Vdash}(B)$ (cf. the proof of Theorem 2.4.1). Consequently, we have $B \to c \subseteq \overline{\mathrm{Th}_{\Vdash}(A)}$, and hence $A \nVdash B \to c$ (since $\mathrm{Th}_{\Vdash}(A)$ is a theory). Therefore there must exist $B_1 \in \Delta^{\wedge}$ such that $A \in \mathrm{Th}(B_1)$ and $B \to c \subseteq \overline{\mathrm{Th}(B_1)}$. The later condition implies that c is disjoint from $\mathrm{Th}(B \wedge B_1)$. In addition, $\mathrm{Th}(B \wedge B_1)$ includes

---

[2] This was the case considered, in effect, in [Boc99b].

both A and a. But $B \wedge B_1$ belongs to $\Delta^\wedge$, and hence $a, A \not\Vdash c$. Therefore, A is a base proposition of $\Vdash$. $\square$

As was shown earlier, any base-generated consequence relation is grounded, that is, generated by its prime theories. Moreover, the set of base propositions can be easily shown to be $\wedge$-closed. Consequently, we immediately obtain the following

Corollary 2.5.2. *A consequence relation $\Vdash$ is base-generated if and only if the set of its base propositions forms a base of $\Vdash$ (relative to $\mathrm{Th}_{\Vdash}$).*

In other words, the set of all base propositions of a base-generated consequence relation can be seen as its *canonical base*.

2.5.1 Union-closure and strong base-generation

In this section we will give an important alternative characterization of base-generated consequence relations.

A set $\mathcal{T}$ of deductively closed theories will be called *union-closed* if, for any theories u_1, u_2 from $\mathcal{T}$, $\mathrm{Cl}(u_1 \cup u_2)$ also belongs to $\mathcal{T}$. A Scott consequence relation will be called *union-closed* if its set of theories is union closed.

The following lemma will be used later in this section.

Lemma 2.5.3. *A supraclassical Scott consequence relation $\Vdash$ is union-closed if and only if some right-compact set of its theories is union-closed.*

Proof. The direction from left to right is immediate. Let $\mathcal{T}$ be a union-closed right-compact set of theories of $\Vdash$, and u and v are two arbitrary theories of $\Vdash$. Since $\mathcal{T}$ is right-compact, $u = \bigcup \mathcal{U}$ and $v = \bigcup \mathcal{V}$, for some subsets $\mathcal{U}$ and $\mathcal{V}$ of $\mathcal{T}$. Now consider the set $\mathcal{W}$ of theories $\mathrm{Cl}(u_i \cup v_j)$, for all $u_i \in \mathcal{U}$ and $v_j \in \mathcal{V}$. Since $\mathcal{T}$ is union-closed, $\mathcal{W}$ is included in $\mathcal{T}$, and hence all theories are theories of $\Vdash$. Moreover, the set $\mathcal{W}$ is directed. Indeed, any two theories $\mathrm{Cl}(u_1, v_1)$ and $\mathrm{Cl}(u_2, v_2)$ from $\mathcal{W}$ are included into the theory $\mathrm{Cl}(\mathrm{Cl}(u_1, u_2), \mathrm{Cl}(v_1, v_2))$, which also belongs to $\mathcal{W}$. Consequently, the union $\bigcup \mathcal{W}$ is also a theory of $\Vdash$. But it can be easily checked that this theory coincides with $\mathrm{Cl}(u, v)$. So, $\mathrm{Cl}(u, v)$ is also a theory of $\Vdash$, and hence $\Vdash$ is union-closed. $\square$

The next result connects the notion of union-closure with that of base-generation.

Lemma 2.5.4. *If a set of theories of a grounded consequence relation $\Vdash$ is union-closed, then $\Vdash$ is base-generated.*

Proof. Let Δ be a set of all prime propositions of $\Vdash$, and $A, B \in \Delta$. Then $\mathrm{Th}_{\Vdash}(A)$ and $\mathrm{Th}_{\Vdash}(B)$ are theories of $\Vdash$, and hence $\mathrm{Cl}(\mathrm{Th}_{\Vdash}(A) \cup \mathrm{Th}_{\Vdash}(B))$ is also a theory. We will show that the latter is equal to $\mathrm{Th}_{\Vdash}(A \wedge B)$. Indeed, $\mathrm{Cl}(\mathrm{Th}_{\Vdash}(A) \cup \mathrm{Th}_{\Vdash}(B))$ is clearly included in $\mathrm{Th}_{\Vdash}(A \wedge B)$. In addition, if

$\Vdash (A \wedge B) \to C$, then $B \to C \in \mathrm{Th}_{\Vdash}(A)$, $B \in \mathrm{Th}_{\Vdash}(B)$, and hence $C \in \mathrm{Cl}(\mathrm{Th}_{\Vdash}(A) \cup \mathrm{Th}_{\Vdash}(B))$.

Since $\mathrm{Th}_{\Vdash}(A \wedge B)$ is a theory of $\Vdash$, $A \wedge B$ is a prime proposition of $\Vdash$. Thus, the set Δ that generates $\Vdash$ is $\wedge$-closed, and consequently $\Vdash$ is base-generated. □

The reverse implication will hold for strongly grounded consequence relations. To begin with, the following result clarifies the meaning of strong groundedness for base-generated consequence relations.

Let $\Delta_{\Vdash}$ be the set of all base (= prime) propositions of a base-generated consequence relation $\Vdash$. Let us denote by $\mathcal{T}_{\Vdash}^{\Delta}$ the set of generating theories:

$$\mathcal{T}_{\Vdash}^{\Delta} = \{\mathrm{Th}_{\Vdash}(\Delta_0) \mid \Delta_0 \subseteq \Delta \ \& \ \Delta_0 \neq \emptyset\}$$

Then we obtain

Theorem 2.5.4. *A base-generated consequence relation $\Vdash$ is strongly grounded iff the set of theories of $\Vdash$ coincides with $\mathcal{T}_{\Vdash}^{\Delta}$.*

Proof. A base-generated consequence relation is strongly grounded iff any of its theories is a union of prime theories. Consequently any theory u will coincide with $\mathrm{Th}(u \cap \Delta_{\Vdash})$, and hence all theories of $\Vdash$ will be deductive closures of base propositions. □

Since $\mathcal{T}_{\Vdash}^{\Delta}$ generates $\Vdash$, the above result immediately implies

Corollary 2.5.3. *A consequence relation is base-generated and strongly grounded iff the set of theories $\mathcal{T}_{\Vdash}^{\Delta}$ is compact.*

The next result shows that, for strongly grounded consequence relations, base-generation is equivalent to union closure.

Theorem 2.5.5. *A strongly grounded consequence relation is base-generated if and only if it is union-closed.*

Proof. The direction from right to left follows from Lemma 2.5.4. Also, if a consequence relation is strongly grounded and base-generated, then the set its prime theories is union-closed and right-compact. Hence the reverse implication follows from Lemma 2.5.3. □

The following example shows that the restriction to strongly grounded consequence relations is essential for the above result.

Example 2.5.1. Let Δ be a set of all propositions of the form $p_0 \wedge p_1 \wedge \cdots \wedge p_n \wedge q_n$ or $q_0 \wedge (q_1 \to r) \wedge \cdots \wedge (q_n \to r) \wedge (p_n \to r)$, for all natural n. We consider a consequence relation generated by the base Δ with respect to the classical entailment.

It is easy to check that $p_0, q_0 \Vdash r$ holds in this consequence relation. Let u be a logical closure of the set of all p's, and v a logical closure of q_0 and the set of formulas $q_i \to r$, for all natural i. It can be shown that u and v are theories of this consequence relation (cf. Example 2.4.1). However, r is not a logical consequence of $u \cup v$, and hence $\mathrm{Cl}(u \cup v)$ is not a theory of this consequence relation. Thus, the set of theories of this base-generated consequence relation is not union-closed.

The above example shows, in particular, that even if a consequence relation is generated by a union-closed set of theories, it will not always be union-closed.

2.5.2 Base-generated Tarski consequence relations

Since Tarski consequence relations can be seen as a special kind of Scott consequence relations, the notion of base-generation can be easily transferred to the latter. In particular, any base-generated Tarski consequence relation will be generated by its *basic propositions* defined as propositions B validating the deduction theorem: if $a, B \vdash A$, then $a \vdash B \to A$, for any a and A. Moreover, for Tarski consequence relations, any proposition is prime, so basic propositions will also be base propositions of a consequence relation. Note, however, that the set of basic propositions of a Tarski consequence relation will be closed not only with respect to conjunctions, but also with respect to disjunctions:

Lemma 2.5.5. *If A and B are basic propositions of a Tarski consequence relation $\vdash$, then $A \vee B$ is also a basic proposition of $\vdash$.*

As for general consequence relations, any union-closed Tarski consequence relation will be base-generated, and the reverse implication will hold only for strongly grounded consequence relations. The following lemma gives an important alternative characterization of union-closure for Tarski consequence relations:

Lemma 2.5.6. *A supraclassical Tarski consequence relation is union-closed if and only if it satisfies*

$$\mathrm{Cn}(A \wedge B) = \mathrm{Cl}(\mathrm{Cn}(A), \mathrm{Cn}(B))$$

Proof. The direction from left to right is immediate. Let u and v be two theories of $\vdash$ and $u, v \vdash A$. then there must exist $B \in u$ and $C \in v$ such that $B, C \vdash A$. By the above condition, this implies $A \in \mathrm{Cl}(\mathrm{Cn}(B), \mathrm{Cn}(C))$, and hence there must exist $B_1 \in \mathrm{Cn}(B)$ and $C_1 \in \mathrm{Cn}(C)$ such that $C_1, B_1 \vdash A$. But B_1 belongs to u, while C_1 belongs to v, and therefore $u, v \vdash A$. Consequently, $\vdash$ is union-closed. $\square$

The above condition will be used in Chapter 7 in characterizing injective preferential inference relations.

Exercises

1. Show that Scott consequence relations can be alternatively characterized as binary relations on arbitrary sets of propositions satisfying Reflexivity, Monotonicity, Cut and Compactness.
2. Show that if $\Vdash$ is a supraclassical Scott consequence relation, then $a \Vdash b$ is equivalent to $\bigwedge a \Vdash b$.
3. Show that if an intersection of any two theories of a consequence relation is also a theory, then the set of its theories is closed with respect to arbitrary intersections.
4. Show that a Tarski consequence relation $\vdash$ is classical if and only if its theories are deductively closed and satisfy the following condition: any world containing a theory of $\vdash$ is also a theory of $\vdash$.
5. Show that, for supraclassical Tarski consequence relations, Weak Disjunction is equivalent to the rule

   If $A \vee B \vdash A$ and $A \vee C \vdash A$, then $A \vee B \vee C \vdash A$.

   Hint. Notice that $C, A \vee B \vdash A$ is equivalent to $(C \wedge A) \vee (C \wedge B) \vdash C \wedge A$.
6. Let $\vdash$ be a semi-classical consequence relation. Show that if u is a maximal theory of $\vdash$ that does not contain a proposition A, then $\mathrm{Cl}(u, A)$ is also a theory of $\vdash$.
7. Let $\vdash$ be a supraclassical Tarski consequence relation generated by a finite set of propositions Δ. For any proposition A, A^Δ will denote a disjunction of all $D \in \Delta$ such that $A \in \mathrm{Th}_\vdash(D)$.

   (i) Show that $A \vdash B$ iff $A^\Delta \vdash B^\Delta$;

   (ii) Show that $\vdash$ is generated by a finite set Δ if and only if (a) any proposition from Δ is prime and (b) $A \vdash A^\Delta$, for any A.

3. Epistemic States

Introduction

Semantic interpretation constitutes one of the main components of a viable reasoning system, monotonic or not. A formal inference engine, though important in its own right, can be effectively used for representing and solving commonsense reasoning tasks only if its basic inference steps possess a clear meaning allowing us to discern them from a description of a situation at hand. This also means that not all formally adequate semantic representations will do on the final score, but only those which provide a human-friendly framework of concepts that can be easily and systematically discerned from (or imposed upon) the informal description.

In this chapter we are going to describe a general representation framework for nonmonotonic reasoning and belief change that will be used throughout this book. This general framework admits a lot of qualifications, so we will make efforts to single out representations that will be both necessary and sufficient for particular reasoning tasks. In this way we will try to avoid both over-simplification and excessive abstraction of our models. Throughout this chapter we will also establish links and relations between our semantic representation and other models of nonmonotonic reasoning and belief change suggested in the literature.

3.1 General epistemic states

As we said in the introduction, humans do not just collect data and make logical conclusions, they try to explain what they see and predict consequences of their potential actions, even if not all aspects and facts about the situation are known. Accordingly, the main task of nonmonotonic reasoning consists in a reasonable use of assumptions and beliefs we adopt to describe partly unknown situations.

At first sight, it might seem that what we need in order to give a logical representation of this behavior is simply to add a set of current beliefs or hypotheses to known facts. Unfortunately, this will not do. In most cases of interest, our beliefs are only an output of a more complex structure of epistemic states. The latter guide our decisions as to what to believe and what not to believe when, for example, the situation changes.

Studies in nonmonotonic reasoning have suggested a new general approach to such 'belief support' systems according to which our beliefs are formed with the help of defaults, or expectations, that we are willing to accept in the absence of evidence to the contrary. In many situations, however, different defaults may conflict both with one another and with known facts, and this gives us several admissible subsets of defaults forming a basis for different plausible sets of beliefs we can hold in such situations. Practically all systems of nonmonotonic reasoning, such as Reiter's default logic [Rei80], or an abductive system of Poole [Poo88] (see below), reflect this feature of default-based systems. Consequently, the intended notion of an epistemic state should also reflect this structure.

Taking a more holistic view on this understanding of the role of epistemic states, we will focus our attention on potential (admissible) *belief states* that are generated by all allowable combinations of defaults. They will be taken to be the only options for choice; borrowing (and taking literally) Isaac Levi's terminology [Lev91], admissible belief states will represent what is considered by the agent as serious possibilities. Propositions supported by such admissible belief states will represent admissible *belief sets* that are actually envisaged by the agent. Notice, however, that different combinations of defaults may sometimes produce the same logical conclusions. Accordingly, we may have different admissible belief states that generate identical belief sets.

The set of all admissible belief states in the above sense will be considered as the principal component of our epistemic states. It is important to note that this structure implicitly reflects dependence relations among potential beliefs. The latter, even if logically consistent, can be based on incompatible defaults and expectations, and hence cannot always be held simultaneously. Accordingly, admissible belief sets are not homogeneous; not all deletions or additions to them constitute justifiable belief sets, but only those that are supported by some admissible sets of defaults. In other words, potential beliefs are correlated, and some of them serve as reasons, or justification, for others. This dependence structure will be described below using consequence relations associated with epistemic states. Accordingly, epistemic states will be shown to embody some important features of a foundational approach to belief acceptance.

The second component of our notion of an epistemic state is a *preference relation* on admissible belief states. This relation reflects the fact that not all admissible combinations of defaults constitute equally preferred options for choice. For example, defaults are presumed to hold, so an admissible belief state generated by a larger set of defaults is normally preferred to an admissible state generated by a smaller set of defaults. In addition, not all defaults are born equal, so they may have some priority structure that imposes, in turn, a certain additional preference structure on admissible belief states (later in this chapter we will give a more detailed description of such structures). Alternatively, we may have some global measures allowing the comparison of admissible belief states in terms of their informational content, reliability, etc. All these constructions lead to imposing a preference order on the set of admissible belief states.

We are ready now to introduce our definition of a general epistemic state. But first we need to fix the underlying language.

Let $\mathcal{L}$ be a propositional language containing the usual classical connectives $\{\neg, \lor, \land, \rightarrow, \leftrightarrow\}$. As in the preceding chapter, $\vDash$ will denote the associated classical entailment relation, and Cl the corresponding classical derivability operator. As usual, a set of propositions u will be called a *deductively closed theory* if $u = \mathrm{Cl}(u)$.

Definition 3.1.1. *A* general epistemic state $\mathbb{E}$ *in a language* $\mathcal{L}$ *is a triple* $(\mathcal{S}, l, \prec)$, *where* $\mathcal{S}$ *is a set of objects called* admissible belief states, $\prec$ *is a preference relation on* $\mathcal{S}$, *while* l *is a labelling function assigning a deductively closed theory in* $\mathcal{L}$ *(called* an admissible belief set*) to every belief state from* $\mathcal{S}$.

If $s \prec t$ holds, we will say that the admissible belief state t is *preferred* to s[1]. We will assume "by default" that the preference relation is a *strict partial order*. We can safely make such an assumption, since practically all constructions in this book will be hospitable to this understanding, and hence we will have no incentive to consider more abstract relations. It should be mentioned, however, that in many cases such an assumption will not actually be needed, and $\prec$ can be taken to be an arbitrary irreflexive relation. In what follows we will occasionally use also a reflexive variant of $\prec$ defined as

$$s \preceq t \equiv s \prec t \text{ or } s = t$$

Clearly, if $\prec$ is a strict partial order, it is definable, in turn, as a strict counterpart of the above weak partial order. Actually, in many applications the preference relation of an epistemic state will be obtained in the same way as a strict counterpart of some weak preference relation $\preccurlyeq$; namely it will defined as

$$s \prec t \equiv s \preccurlyeq t \text{ and } t \npreccurlyeq s$$

The qualification 'epistemic' in the name of our epistemic states is not accidental. Epistemic states say nothing directly about what is actually true, but only what is believed (or presumed) to hold. They are intended to reflect, in particular, the requirement of separating background and contingent knowledge suggested by several authors (see [Poo91, Gef92]). This will make epistemic states relatively stable entities; change in facts and situations will not necessary lead to change in epistemic states. The actual conclusions and

---

[1] Notice that we reverse the direction of preference as compared with common representations of nonmonotonic inference.

assumptions made by the agent in particular situations will be obtained by combining her epistemic state with available facts. More exactly, such conclusions will be obtained by choosing preferred admissible belief states *that are consistent with the facts.*

An admissible belief state $s \in S$ will be said to *support* a proposition A, if A belongs to its associated belief set, that is, $A \in l(s)$. The set of all admissible states that does *not* support A will be denoted by $]A[$. Clearly, the set of admissible belief states consistent with some proposition A will coincide with $]\neg A[$. Similarly, for a set of propositions w, we will denote by $]w[$ the set of admissible states that support no proposition from w.

Finally, notice that the very distinction between admissible belief states and belief sets allows for the possibility that different admissible states may have identical belief sets. A most natural understanding of such general epistemic states emerges if we adopt a broader view of epistemic states advocated, for example, by Isaac Levi in a number of works (see, e.g., [Lev91]). According to this view, epistemic states are essentially non-linguistic entities, and they can be described, in general, only partially by available language means. In other words, a description of an epistemic state in a particular language is only an 'approximation' to the full information contained in it. And as any approximation, it can sometimes be made more precise by extending our linguistic capabilities. It may well happen, however, that on the present level of precision, two essentially different belief states are indistinguishable in terms of propositions formulated in the current language. And though language is the only tool we posses for describing our epistemic states, taking into account such a possibility may sometimes influence the conclusions we make.

Infinite states and smoothness. It should be kept in mind that epistemic states are intended to serve as idealized representations of real (e.g., human) epistemic states. Accordingly, they are generated through a reasoning process that results in forming admissible combinations of defaults. In many cases such epistemic states will be finite. The following definition describes two important understandings of finiteness of epistemic states that will be used in what follows.

Definition 3.1.2. *An epistemic state will be called* finite *if it has a finite number of admissible states, and* finitary *if it is finite, and any admissible belief set is a logical closure of a single proposition.*

A finitary epistemic state is representable, in effect, as a finite set of propositions ordered by preference. Indeed, for any admissible belief state s of a finitary epistemic state, we can choose a proposition A_s in such a way that different admissible states will correspond to syntactically different propositions. Due to this correspondence between admissible states and their associated propositions, the latter can be identified with their corresponding admissible states. Then the epistemic state will consist of a set of propositions ordered by preference, while the label of each such proposition will be supposed to coincide with its logical closure.

Still, it is unreasonable to restrict our attention to finite epistemic states, or to epistemic states containing only finitely generated admissible belief sets. The above considerations imply, however, that such admissible belief states should always satisfy certain 'accessibility' constraints; namely, we can suppose that any such admissible belief set is obtainable via a potentially infinite set of finite approximations.

There are several ways of reflecting the above informal requirement on epistemic states. For applications concerning nonmonotonic inference, the condition of *smoothness* (cf. [Mak89, KLM90]) will be sufficient for all purposes.

Let $\prec$ be an irreflexive preference relation on an arbitrary set of objects X. An object $s \in X$ will be said to be *preferred in* X (with respect to $\prec$) if there is no $t \in X$ such that $s \prec t$. The set X will be called *smooth* with respect to $\prec$ if, for any $s \in X$, there exists $t \in X$ such that $s \preceq t$, and t is preferred in X.

Definition 3.1.3. *An epistemic state* $\mathbb{E}$ *will be said to be* smooth *if any set of admissible belief states of the form* $]A[$ *is smooth with respect to the preference order.*

Though adequate for nonmonotonic reasoning, the above smoothness requirement will not be sufficient, however, for representing belief change. The reason is that smoothness is not preserved by the main belief change operations (studied in Part Three), so, for example, a contraction of a smooth epistemic state may produce an epistemic state that is not smooth. Accordingly, in dealing with belief change, we will need a stronger, 'hereditary' notion of smoothness that will already be invariant under the main belief change operations. This notion is captured in the following definition.

Definition 3.1.4. *1. An epistemic state will be called* m-smooth *if every set of admissible states of the form* $]w[$ *is smooth.*

2. An epistemic state will be called finitely m-smooth *if, for any finite set* w, $]w[$ *is smooth.*

The above notions of m-smoothness will also play an essential role in Chapter 4, where we will consider the notions of equivalence and similarity among epistemic states. It should be clear, however, that all the variant properties of smoothness trivially hold for finite epistemic states.

Belief and knowledge sets of an epistemic state

Epistemic states are purported to represent beliefs and other mental dispositions of the agent. In this respect, the above notion of an epistemic state clearly allows us to represent a richer repertoire of epistemic attitudes than plain belief sets[2]. As we will see, the basic concepts and notions associated with nonmonotonic reasoning can be viewed as reflecting some of these epistemic attitudes.

As its first and most important function, an epistemic state gives rise to the notion of belief that we are going to describe below. In fact, this understanding of belief can be discerned from the above informal description of epistemic states as generated by defaults or expectations. Under this understanding, we should believe in propositions that are supported by all preferred admissible states of an epistemic state.

Definition 3.1.5. *A proposition will be said to be* believed *in an epistemic state* $\mathbb{E}$ *if it is supported by all preferred admissible belief states from* $\mathbb{E}$. *The set of all propositions believed in* $\mathbb{E}$ *will be called a* belief set *of* $\mathbb{E}$ *and denoted by* $\mathbf{B}_{\mathbb{E}}$.

Thus, even if an epistemic state involves multiple preferred admissible belief sets, we can still believe in propositions that belong to all of them. As we shall see in due course, such a notion of belief is implicitly presupposed in practically all formalisms of nonmonotonic reasoning and belief change. It is also explicitly adopted, for example, in [FH99].

It should be noted that the above definition of belief only makes sense if an epistemic state always has maximally preferred admissible belief states. This requirement is satisfied, however, for smooth epistemic states.

Though the notion of a belief set is defined for all epistemic states, there is an obvious uneasiness in applying this notion to cases when an epistemic state contains inconsistent preferred admissible states. In particular, if all preferred admissible states are inconsistent, the resulting belief set will also be inconsistent. It turns out, however, that in such cases a more natural notion of belief is provided by restricting the universe of discourse to consistent admissible states.

By a *consolidation* of an epistemic state $\mathbb{E}$ we mean an epistemic state obtained from $\mathbb{E}$ by removing all admissible states labelled with an inconsistent theory. As we will see in due course, this notion corresponds to Hansson's consolidation operation in the theory of belief change that amounts to contracting falsity from an epistemic state. Accordingly, the consolidated epistemic state will be denoted by $\mathbb{E} - \mathbf{f}$.

Definition 3.1.6. *A proposition A will be said to be a* refined belief *in an epistemic state* $\mathbb{E}$ *if it is believed in* $\mathbb{E} - \mathbf{f}$. *The set of all refined beliefs will be called a* refined belief set *of* $\mathbb{E}$.

It should be noted already at this stage that the refined belief set may be distinct from the 'canonical' belief set of an epistemic state even if the latter is

---

[2] See [Gär88] for discussing epistemic attitudes expressible in different representations of epistemic states.

consistent. This could happen if only some of the preferred admissible states are inconsistent; eliminating the latter could then result in making some new admissible states preferred ones, which could change the resulting belief set.

Despite the naturalness of taking the refined belief set as representing beliefs associated with an epistemic state, there are certain technical advantages in keeping both notions of belief in use.

A proposition that is not believed may still constitute an *admissible belief* with respect to an epistemic state if it belongs to at least one admissible belief set. A proposition A will be said to be *disbelieved* in an epistemic state $\mathbb{E}$ if there is no admissible belief set in $\mathbb{E}$ that includes A. This notion of disbelief highlights still another 'foundational' feature of our epistemic states: a proposition A is disbelieved if it is not supported by any admissible belief state, even though it may be logically consistent with all of them. Clearly, disbelief is a stronger notion than simple absence of belief. The contraction operation on epistemic states, described in Part Three, will be based on this notion.

Our epistemic framework also allows us to define a distinction between believed and known propositions.

Definition 3.1.7. *A proposition will be said to be* known *in an epistemic state* $\mathbb{E}$ *if it belongs to all admissible belief sets. Otherwise it will be called* contingent. *The set of all known propositions of* $\mathbb{E}$ *will be called the* knowledge set *of* $\mathbb{E}$ *and denoted by* $\mathbf{K_E}$.

The notion of a knowledge set of an epistemic state will play an important role in the present study, since it will determine the monotonic internal logic of an epistemic state. More exactly by an *internal logic* of an epistemic state $\mathbb{E}$ (notation $\mathrm{Th}_\mathbb{E}$) we will mean a least classical Tarski consequence relation containing the knowledge set of $\mathcal{E}$ as the set of auxiliary axioms. Accordingly, $B \in \mathrm{Th}_\mathbb{E}(A)$ will hold if and only if B is classically derivable from A and the knowledge set of $\mathbb{E}^3$.

As we will see in Part Two, all nonmonotonic inference relations will have a monotonic component coinciding, ultimately, with the internal logic of the associated epistemic state.

Remark. In order to prevent some philosophical misunderstandings concerning the above notion of knowledge, we recall that our epistemic states are thoroughly epistemic, and hence they explicitly describe only what is believed to hold rather than what is actually true. Accordingly, known propositions of an epistemic state can be best seen as propositions that are *believed to be known* (or, if you prefer, firmly believed). Nevertheless, viewed from within epistemic states, such propositions behave precisely as propositions that are known to the reasoning agent, and this will be sufficient for our purposes.

---

[3] As can be verified, this holds iff $A \to B$ is known.

3.2 Main kinds of epistemic states

Our study will reveal a number of special kinds of epistemic states that
will play an important role in representing particular forms of nonmonotonic
inference and belief change. In this section we will give a first, rather rough
classification of epistemic states that will be refined in the course of our
exposition.

To begin with, the definition of general epistemic states does not impose
any correlations between the preference relation among admissible states and
the informational (propositional) content of the latter. Our first classification,
given in the definition below, singles out the main constraints on the correspondence between these two factors.

Definition 3.2.1. *A general epistemic state will be called*

- standard *if it satisfies*
  Injectivity   *If $l(s) = l(t)$, then $s = t$.*
- persistent *if it satisfies*
  Persistence   *If $s \prec t$, then $l(s) \subseteq l(t)$.*
- monotonic *if it satisfies*
  Monotonicity   *If $l(s) \subset l(t)$, then $s \prec t$.*
- pure *if it satisfies*
  Pure Monotonicity   *$s \preceq t$ if and only if $l(s) \subseteq l(t)$.*

Below we will give a brief description of these classes of epistemic states.

3.2.1 Standard epistemic states

An epistemic state is standard if its labelling function is injective, that is,
different admissible states are labelled with different theories. Such epistemic
states can be represented simply as pairs $\langle \mathcal{E}, \prec \rangle$, where $\mathcal{E}$ is a set of deductively closed theories, while $\prec$ is a preference relation on $\mathcal{E}$. As we will
see, all current models of belief change, as well as early models suggested
for nonmonotonic inference, correspond to standard epistemic states. Still,
experience with nonmonotonic formalisms has shown the importance of generalizing earlier semantic representations to models in which different states
may correspond to the same set of supported propositions. Moreover, we will
show that a similar generalization will also be required for representing belief
change, since standard epistemic states still cannot give us an adequate representation of some important concepts. We will suggest, however, at least
two natural ways of understanding general epistemic states that will recon-
cile them with the 'standard' notion. For this and many other reasons, the
relation between standard and general epistemic states will occupy an important place in our study. We will obtain, in particular, somewhat surprising
results that stand in opposition to the current picture. First, we will show,
that standard (and even pure) epistemic states are sufficient for representing

the main kinds of nonmonotonic inference. Second, we will demonstrate that the basic belief change operations, namely contraction and expansions, are most naturally representable in terms of non-standard epistemic states.

As we already mentioned, there are plausible understandings of general epistemic states that allow us to see them as derived from standard epistemic states. The first one consists in the assumption that admissible belief states determining the same set of beliefs may arise due to *language indeterminacy* of such states with respect to available linguistic means: potential belief states may be determined by information that simply has not found its way to the set of associated beliefs. A second possible interpretation of nonstandard epistemic states consists in seeing them as arising due to an inherent *indeterminacy of the preference relation*: if we have several possibilities of ordering admissible belief states with respect to preference, we can express this indeterminacy by including all such possibilities into our epistemic state using multiple 'copies' of admissible belief sets with varying preferences among them.

In Chapter 4, both the above interpretations will receive a formal justification. Namely, we will demonstrate that any general epistemic state can always be decomposed into a set of standard epistemic states, all having the same admissible belief sets, though with varying preference order. Also, it will be shown that any general epistemic state can be seen as a language restriction of some standard epistemic state.

3.2.2 Monotonicity and its kinds

The monotonicity condition above can be seen as a realization of a strong version of the *principle of informational economy* according to which all potential beliefs are valuable, and hence any extension of an admissible belief set makes the corresponding admissible state better than the source one. Monotonic epistemic states implement this principle in the form of the requirement that the preference relation should subsume the relation of set inclusion among admissible belief sets. As with standardness, monotonicity is also a common feature of the major paradigms of belief change representation, as well as models for nonmonotonic inference suggested in the literature.

Standardness and monotonicity jointly amount to the strengthening of the monotonicity condition to the corresponding reflexive relations:

Strict Monotonicity   If $l(s) \subseteq l(t)$, then $s \preceq t$.

Thus, epistemic states satisfying Strict Monotonicity are precisely epistemic states that are standard and monotonic.

It is easy to verify that monotonic epistemic states satisfy the following *maximizing property*:

Maximizing If s is a preferred admissible belief state in $]A[$, then $l(s)$ is a maximal admissible belief set that does not contain A.

In many cases, maximizing will be the only property of monotonic epistemic states that will be actually used in derivations. The following example shows, however, that, even for finite epistemic states, maximizing does not imply monotonicity.

Example 3.2.1. Consider a standard epistemic state consisting of theories

$$\{\mathrm{Cl}(p), \mathrm{Cl}(p \wedge q), \mathrm{Cl}(p \wedge r), \mathrm{Cl}(p \wedge (q \vee r)), \mathrm{Cl}(p \wedge q \wedge r)\}$$

with a preference order that coincides with set inclusion on all theories except $\mathrm{Cl}(p)$; for the latter we will assume only that $\mathrm{Cl}(p) \prec \mathrm{Cl}(p \wedge q)$ and $\mathrm{Cl}(p) \prec \mathrm{Cl}(p \wedge r)$. Since $\mathrm{Cl}(p \wedge (q \vee r))$ is incomparable with $\mathrm{Cl}(p))$, this epistemic state is not monotonic. Nevertheless, its preference order is maximizing. Checking this for $\mathrm{Cl}(p)$ is the only non-trivial case. Assume that $\mathrm{Cl}(p)$ is a preferred theory in $]A[$, for some proposition A. Then A must belong both to $\mathrm{Cl}(p \wedge q)$ and to $\mathrm{Cl}(p \wedge q)$. Consequently, it also belongs to $\mathrm{Cl}(p \wedge (q \vee r))$, and hence $\mathrm{Cl}(p)$ is a maximal theory of the epistemic state that does not contain A. Note also that any theory of our epistemic state is a preferred theory for some proposition; for example, $\mathrm{Cl}(p)$ is a preferred theory in $]q \vee r[$. Using the terminology of Chapter 4, this means that the epistemic state is normal.

Though important, the monotonicity condition is by no means a universally applicable requirement. Thus, Isaac Levi has argued in [Lev91] that the above mentioned strict version of the principle of informational economy should be replaced by a weaker principle stating that only *valuable* information is relevant for establishing preferences between admissible alternatives. Furthermore, we will see below that some natural constructions of epistemic states from sets of defaults produce epistemic states that are not monotonic. They will satisfy, however, some weaker monotonicity conditions that are described in the next definition.

Definition 3.2.2. *An epistemic state will be called*

- semi-monotonic *if $l(s) \subset l(t)$ implies $s \prec t'$, for some t' such that $l(t) = l(t')$;*
- weakly monotonic *if $s \prec t$ implies $l(t) \not\subseteq l(s)$.*

In many respects, semi-monotonicity can be considered as a most plausible replacement of 'full' monotonicity in the context of general epistemic states. Notice, for example, that semi-monotonicity coincides with monotonicity for standard epistemic states. Also, semi-monotonic epistemic states will satisfy the above mentioned maximizing property, so in most cases they will have the same properties as monotonic epistemic states.

Weak monotonicity amounts to the requirement that the preference order should not conflict with set inclusion in the sense that smaller belief sets should not be preferred to larger ones. As we will show in the next chapter, weak monotonicity can be safely imposed on epistemic states without restricting their expressivity.

3.2.3 Persistent epistemic states

For persistent epistemic states, the informational content of admissible states is always preserved (persists) in transitions to more preferred states. In other words, any admissible state preferred to a given one should support all propositions sanctioned by the latter. This property reflects the idea that the informational content of an admissible state is an essential (though presumably not the only) factor in determining the place of this state in the preference structure.

Persistent epistemic states are formally similar to a number of *information models* suggested in the logical literature, such as Kripke's semantics for intuitionistic logic, Veltman's data semantics, etc. (see [Ben88] for an overview). All such models consist of a partially ordered set of informational states. The relevant partial order represents possible ways of information growth, so it is assumed to satisfy the persistence requirement by its very meaning. Actually, our description of nonmonotonic inference given in Part Two will have much in common with the interpretation of counterfactual conditionals suggested in this framework.

If a persistent epistemic state is also standard, it satisfies the following stronger version of the persistence condition:

Strong Persistence   If $s \prec t$, then $l(s) \subset l(t)$.

Compared with the original persistence condition, strong persistence excludes, in addition, preferentially comparable admissible states that support the same belief set. Actually, we will see later that any persistent epistemic state can always be transformed into an equivalent epistemic state that satisfies Strong Persistence.

The importance of persistent epistemic states for our study stems from the fact that they will be shown to constitute a smallest natural class of epistemic states that is closed under belief change operations that do not involve prioritization among defaults. Such epistemic states also emerge as a nearest counterpart in our framework of a foundational approach to belief change. In addition, they will admit a natural finitary representation in terms of flocks of bases suggested in [FUKV86] (see below).

3.2.4 Pure epistemic states

For pure epistemic states, the preference relation among admissible belief states is determined solely by their informational content. Such epistemic states can also be seen as standard epistemic states in which the preference order on theories coincides with the relation of (proper) set inclusion. Accordingly, a pure epistemic state can be defined simply as a set of theories, with the intended understanding that the relation of set inclusion among such theories plays the role of a preference relation. For example, a belief set of a pure epistemic state can be defined as an intersection of its maximal theories.

Similar reformulation can also be given for other notions defined earlier for general epistemic states.

Note that pure epistemic states are not only standard, but also both persistent and monotonic. In fact, pure epistemic states can be concisely described as general epistemic states that are standard, monotonic and persistent. Consequently, they own all the properties of the latter.

As we will show in Part Two, pure epistemic states will be adequate for representing the main kinds of nonmonotonic inference. An additional advantage of such epistemic states is that they admit a natural syntactic representation in terms of Scott consequence relations, described in Chapter 2.

Since a pure epistemic state $\mathcal{E}$ can be seen simply as a set of deductively closed theories, it generates a supraclassical Scott consequence relation $\Vdash_{\mathcal{E}}$ such that all admissible belief sets from $\mathcal{E}$ are theories of $\Vdash_{\mathcal{E}}$. Moreover, our earlier results show that if $\mathcal{E}$ is finite, the set of theories of $\Vdash_{\mathcal{E}}$ is precisely $\mathcal{E}$ (see Lemma 2.1.8). These facts allow us to see supraclassical Scott consequence relations as a faithful syntactic representation of pure epistemic states. The virtues and advantages of such a syntactic translation should be obvious; instead of descriptions in terms of sets of theories, we will be able to express our objects of interest in terms of consequence relations among propositions. In many cases, this will give us rather compact and computationally feasible representations.

Due to the correspondence between consequence relations and pure epistemic states, all the notions defined earlier for epistemic states can be immediately extended to Scott consequence relations. Thus, we obtain the following definition of propositions believed with respect to a consequence relation:

Definition 3.2.3. *A proposition A will be said to be* believed *with respect to a consequence relation* $\Vdash$*, if it belongs to all maximal theories of* $\Vdash$*. The set of all believed propositions will be called a* belief set *of* $\Vdash$*.*

The following simple result shows that a proposition is believed in a consequence relation $\Vdash$ if and only if it can be added to any set of propositions that is consistent in $\Vdash$ (we leave the proof to the reader).

Lemma 3.2.1. *A is believed in* $\Vdash$ *iff, for any a, $a \nVdash$ implies $A, a \nVdash$.*

A proposition has been said to be known in an epistemic state if it belongs to all admissible belief sets. Translating this into the terminology of consequence relations, we obtain

Definition 3.2.4. *A proposition A will be said to be* known *with respect to a consequence relation* $\Vdash$ *if* $\Vdash A$ *holds.*

As we already said, the internal logic of an epistemic state is determined by its knowledge set. Accordingly, the *internal logic* of a supraclassical Scott consequence relation will be identified with its classical subrelation (as defined in Chapter 2).

Notice that, for classical consequence relations, the definition of belief collapses to provability of A in $\Vdash$, that is, to $\Vdash A$. Thus, only in the supraclassical case our definitions of belief and knowledge provide us with distinct concepts.

The correspondence between pure epistemic states and consequence relations will be used in what follows also in the other direction, namely for extending the notions defined earlier for consequence relations to their associated epistemic states. Thus, a pure epistemic state will be called base-generated if it is generated by all subsets of some set of propositions, as described in Chapter 2 (see below).

Dependencies and expectations

Not only pure epistemic states, but actually any epistemic state $\mathbb{E}$ generates a Scott consequence relation $\Vdash_{\mathbb{E}}$ determined by all admissible belief sets of $\mathbb{E}$. This consequence relation reflects, in effect, the justificational structure of the source epistemic state. A rule $A \Vdash B$ says on this interpretation that any admissible belief set of the epistemic state that contains A should contain also B. We will take this as meaning that the agent cannot believe A without believing B or, in other words, that her belief in A *depends* on belief in B. Similarly, if b is a set of propositions, $A \Vdash b$ will mean that the agent cannot believe A without accepting at least one proposition from b. In this way, the consequence relation will be considered as reflecting *dependence relations* that hold among admissible beliefs of the underlying epistemic state. Consequently, if A and B are believed propositions, and $A \Vdash B$ holds, we can say that A is believed *just because* B is believed. This understanding will exactly correspond to a definition of "just because" given by Rott in [Rot95] (see condition (DJB) in the paper).

It should be stressed that Scott consequence relations generated by epistemic states should not be identified with the *logic* of the agent in a strong sense of the word, something belonging to her intellectual capabilities independently of the world and current assumptions. This could be seen already from the fact that the direction of dependence can often be opposite to that of logical inference:

Example 3.2.2. Suppose that a pure epistemic state $\mathcal{E}$ contains an admissible belief set u of the form $\mathrm{Cl}(A)$, for some proposition A. Assume now that u is the only admissible belief set of $\mathcal{E}$ that includes $A \vee B$. Then $A \vee B$ depends on A in this epistemic state, and hence $A \vee B \Vdash A$ will belong to the associated consequence relation. Notice that if u is also the only admissible belief set containing $A \vee C$, then we will have that $A \vee B$ and $A \vee C$ are mutually depended propositions, since they both depend on the same 'justification', namely A. Accordingly, we will have that both $A \vee B \Vdash A \vee C$ and $A \vee C \Vdash A \vee B$ will hold.

The above example shows also that it would be unwise to put much weight on the claim that our dependence relations always correspond to the intuitive understanding of dependence. This would be unreasonable, however, already because there is no single or uniform concept of dependence that could be applicable to all its uses. Still, we will claim that the suggested notion reflects a reasonable and natural notion of dependence that plays an important role in structuring and correlating our beliefs.

An alternative view of epistemic states suggested by the above interpretation in terms of dependence relations indicates that our notion of an epistemic state is broader than its initial motivation, and it can have its own life, independent of the original informal understanding as formed by admissible combinations of default assumptions. Speaking more generally, this interpretation shows that, at least in some cases, epistemic states can also be described by imposing certain non-logical relations on all propositions of the language. This 'change of gestalt' has actually been suggested by Gärdenfors and Makinson in their expectation-based approach to nonmonotonic reasoning and belief change (see [GM94]). According to their theory, nonmonotonic inferences can be formed not only by using auxiliary sets of default assumptions, or expectations, but also by establishing *expectation relations* on the set of all propositions of the language according to which some propositions are more expected (or less surprising) than others. Then "A nonmonotonically entails B" can be interpreted as saying that B follows from A together with all propositions that are "sufficiently well expected" in the light of A. Gärdenfors and Makinson have also established a close correspondence between this expectation-based representation and their previous work on belief revision.

Expectation relations and their generalizations will be described in Chapter 5. For now, it is sufficient to note that the original expectation relations of Gärdenfors and Makinson are exactly equivalent to linear consequence relations. As a result, the expectation-based theory of nonmonotonic inference and belief change will correspond to a special case of our general representation.

3.2.5 Homogeneous and worlds-based states

Pure epistemic states trivialize the preferential component of epistemic states by reducing it to set inclusion among admissible theories. This means that such epistemic states embody no non-trivial preference relations among potential beliefs, and its structure is wholly determined by dependence relations holding among them. This makes such states 'purely foundational' in the sense that acceptance or rejection of admissible beliefs is made in them only on the basis of their position in the dependence structure that provides justifications for some beliefs in terms of other beliefs.

At the other extreme, we may have epistemic states that are wholly determined by the preference relation among (sets of) potential beliefs. Such epistemic states have only a trivial dependence structure, namely the logical entailment. Accordingly, they provide no distinction between basic and derived beliefs, and hence all logically consistent combinations of potential beliefs would constitute admissible belief sets. This is embodied in the following definition of homogeneous epistemic states.

Definition 3.2.5. *An epistemic state* $\mathbb{E}$ *will be called* homogeneous *if its set of admissible belief sets coincides with the set of all deductively closed theories that include the knowledge set of* $\mathbb{E}$.

Homogeneous epistemic states presuppose, in effect, that no dependence relations hold among potential beliefs, except for logical ones, and hence any deductively closed set is admissible. Consequently, the structure of such a state is determined solely by a preference relation on all theories of the language that agree with the internal logic of the epistemic state.

As will be shown in Chapter 4, homogeneous epistemic states are adequate for representing all (skeptical) inference relations. In addition, they are closely related to well-known possible worlds models.

By a *possible worlds-based epistemic state* we will mean an epistemic state in which every admissible belief state is labelled with a world (maximal deductively closed set). Actually, such epistemic states coincide with preferential models from [KLM90]. These models constitute, in turn, a most common instance of the *possible worlds semantics*, that is, of relational structures on possible worlds. It will be shown in Chapter 4 that such models are exactly equivalent to monotonic homogeneous epistemic states.

Possible worlds semantics constitutes a very expressive representation framework. In fact, the only problem it has in certain applications is a burden of responsibility it imposes on the users of such models. As was aptly remarked in [LM92], possible worlds models require from the user to have, "in his mind", a picture of possible worlds together with a preference relation among them. However, possible worlds are world-size entities that are not so easy to keep in mind and, moreover, order with respect to preference. What makes things worse still is the very distinction between states and worlds, which is unavoidable if we want to have an adequate representation in terms of such models. Apparently, it is this excessively idealized character of such representations that could be seen as the source of a rather skeptical attitude toward these models, expressed in [KLM90]. The authors of the latter paper considered the associated formal systems of nonmonotonic inference as the main object of interest, while the relevant semantics were relegated merely to a technical tool that does not provide an 'ontological justification' for nonmonotonic inference. It will be one of our objectives in Part Two, however, to show that such systems of nonmonotonic inference can be given user-friendly semantic representations.

Homogeneous epistemic states will also be used as a formal representation of a coherentist approach to belief change. Actually, we will use for this purpose a restricted version of the homogeneity principle in which only subsets of the belief set are considered as admissible options for choice. This is reflected in the following definition.

Definition 3.2.6. *A general epistemic state* $\mathbb{E}$ *will be called* **B***-homogeneous if its set of admissible belief sets* $\mathcal{E}$ *coincides with the set of all deductively closed theories that include the knowledge set and are included in the belief set of* $\mathbb{E}$.

As we will see in due course, however, **B**-homogeneous epistemic states have much the same properties as their unrestricted counterparts.

3.2.6 Kinds of preference order

A detailed analysis of nonmonotonic inference and belief change will give prominence to epistemic states with certain special kinds of the preference order.

The belief set associated with an epistemic state is actually an intersection of maximal admissible belief sets. Still, it does not always constitute an admissible belief set by itself. The latter will hold, however, in an ideal situation when an epistemic state contains a unique preferred admissible belief state.

Definition 3.2.7. *An epistemic state will be called* determinate *if it has a unique preferred admissible belief state.*

Clearly, if an epistemic state is determinate, its belief set will coincide with the label of its unique preferred admissible state. Such epistemic states do not cause any deliberations about what to believe. As we will see, many important systems of nonmonotonic reasoning, and practically all representations of belief change existing in the literature, will correspond to determinate epistemic states. Nevertheless, non-determinate epistemic states will be shown to be essential for an adequate representation of both nonmonotonic reasoning and belief change.

A further, 'hereditary' strengthening of determination leads us to the notion of a linear epistemic state. For such epistemic states, the set of admissible belief states that are consistent with any proposition A will always have a unique preferred element.

Definition 3.2.8. *A general epistemic state will be called* linear *if its preference order is connected, that is, for any two distinct admissible belief states* s *and* t, *either* $s \prec t$ *or* $t \prec s$.

Linear epistemic states constitute a simplest and most regular kind of epistemic states. This could be seen as a reason of the fact that such epistemic states correspond to most popular and well-studied models suggested for nonmonotonic reasoning and belief change. Note, for example, that if we represent a deductively closed theory via a set of worlds that include it, then a pure linear epistemic state will correspond to a *nested system of spheres* or, in other words, to Grove's model of belief change [Gro88]. This correspondence will provide us with links between linear epistemic states and other well-known models that will be extensively discussed in the book.

Finally, there are also two generalizations of the linear order that will play an important role in our study.

Definition 3.2.9. • *An epistemic state will be called* modular *if its preference order is modular:*

Modularity   *If $s \prec t$, then either $s \prec r$, or $r \prec t$.*

• *An epistemic state will be called* tree-ordered *if its preference order satisfies:*

Tree order   *If $s, r \preceq t$, then either $s \preceq r$, or $r \preceq s$.*

As we will see in Part Two, modular orders have much the same properties as linear orders from the point of view of their associated inference relations. As to the tree-orders, it will be shown in the next chapter that any epistemic state is equivalent to some tree-ordered epistemic state.

3.3 Base-generated epistemic states

In this and the next section we will give a formal description of epistemic states that are generated by default bases. As we will see, such epistemic states have some special properties that do not hold for epistemic states in general. These descriptions will also provide us with further clues about characteristic properties of epistemic states arising in particular reasoning contexts.

To begin with, we will describe epistemic states that are generated by pure (non-prioritized) bases.

Given a set of defaults Δ, we will define the corresponding epistemic state $\mathbb{E}_\Delta = \langle \mathcal{P}(\Delta), l, \prec \rangle$, where

• the set of admissible belief states $\mathcal{P}(\Delta)$ is the set of all non-empty subsets of Δ;
• l is a function assigning each $\Gamma \subseteq \Delta$ its deductive closure, that is, $l(\Gamma) = \mathrm{Cl}(\Gamma)$;
• the preference order is defined as: $\Gamma \prec \Phi$ iff $\Gamma \subset \Phi$.

As can be seen from the above description, the epistemic state associated with a pure base Δ is uniquely determined by the latter. Such epistemic states will be called *purely base-generated* in what follows. As we will see in what follows, such epistemic states will faithfully represent sets of defaults in their role of supporting nonmonotonic inference, as well as the role of bases in belief change.

The above defined epistemic state will in general be neither standard, nor monotonic; this is because two incomparable sets of defaults Γ and Φ may be such that $\mathrm{Cl}(\Gamma) \subset \mathrm{Cl}(\Phi)$, or even $\mathrm{Cl}(\Gamma) = \mathrm{Cl}(\Phi)$. Still, it is easy to check that $\mathbb{E}_\Delta$ is a persistent epistemic state: if $\Gamma \prec \Phi$, then clearly $\text{Cl}(\Gamma) \subseteq \text{Cl}(\Phi)$. In addition, this epistemic state satisfies the following important property:

Union-closure For any two admissible states s, t there exists an admissible state r such that $s \preceq r$, $t \preceq r$ and $l(r) = \text{Cl}(l(s) \cup l(t))$.

Indeed, the union $\Gamma \cup \Phi$ of any two sets of defaults constitutes an admissible state in $\mathbb{E}_\Delta$ that satisfies the above condition. Consequently, we have

Theorem 3.3.1. $\mathbb{E}_\Delta$ *is a persistent and union-closed epistemic state.*

The set of admissible belief sets of $\mathbb{E}_\Delta$ coincides with the set of deductive closures of all subsets of Δ. This set of theories can be considered as a pure epistemic state that we will denote by $\mathcal{E}_\Delta$. The latter epistemic state will also be union-closed. In fact, under the correspondence between pure epistemic states and Scott consequence relations, $\mathcal{E}_\Delta$ will correspond to the consequence relation that is base-generated by Δ. Moreover, it will be shown in Chapter 4 that $\mathbb{E}_\Delta$ and $\mathcal{E}_\Delta$ are equivalent in some well-defined sense; this will mean that they will generate the same nonmonotonic inference relations and will produce the same beliefs under all belief change operations.

3.3.1 General and normal base-generation

Pure base-generated epistemic states constitute an important special case of a broad class of epistemic states that are generated by bases. This class includes, in particular, epistemic states in which the preference relation is not reduced to set inclusion, but is determined, for example, by some priority order on the elements of the base (see below). In addition, the underlying monotonic logic of such epistemic states need not be restricted to classical entailment; instead, we can use an arbitrary classical consequence relation that will accommodate what is considered as known in the epistemic state. All such kinds of base-generation will be subsumed by the following generic definition of base-generation.

Definition 3.3.1. *An epistemic state will be called* base-generated *by a set of propositions Δ with respect to a classical consequence relation* Th *if*

- *the set of its admissible belief states is the set $\mathcal{P}(\Delta)$ of all non-empty subsets of Δ;*
- *l is a function assigning each $\Gamma \subseteq \Delta$ a theory $\text{Th}(\Gamma)$;*
- *the preference order is monotonic on $\mathcal{P}(\Delta)$: if $\Gamma \subset \Phi$, then $\Gamma \prec \Phi$.*

Base-generated epistemic states in the above sense will not in general be persistent. Still, as for pure base-generation, monotonicity will imply that all such epistemic states will be union-closed.

Lemma 3.3.1. *Any base-generated epistemic state is union-closed.*

The above observation indicates that union-closure will play an important role in what follows. In fact, it will be shown in the next chapter that, in the finite case, any union-closed epistemic state will be equivalent to a base-generated epistemic state. Actually, the very distinction between union-closed and more general epistemic states will allow us to account in a systematic way for some subtle differences among the main representations suggested for nonmonotonic inference and belief change.

Union-closure immediately implies that $\mathbb{E}$ is a determinate epistemic state, that is, it has a unique preferred admissible state. Another important consequence of union-closure is semi-monotonicity:

Lemma 3.3.2. *Any union-closed epistemic state is semi-monotonic.*

Proof. If s and t are two admissible states such that $l(s) \subset l(t)$, then by union-closure there must exist an admissible state t' such that $s, t \preceq t'$ and $l(t') = \mathrm{Cl}(l(s) \cup l(t)) = \mathrm{Cl}(l(t))$. Hence the result. $\square$

The above construction of base-generated epistemic states also suggests a natural generalization of the notion of a basic proposition that has been defined in the preceding chapter with respect to consequence relations.

Definition 3.3.2. *A proposition A will be called* basic *in an epistemic state $\mathbb{E}$ if, for any admissible state s such that $A \notin l(s)$, there exists an admissible state t such that $s \prec t$ and $l(t) = \mathrm{Cl}(A, l(s))$.*

It is easy to check that the above definition reduces to our earlier definition of basic propositions in pure epistemic states, given in Chapter 2. Note that, in addition to requiring that A should be a basic proposition of the associated pure epistemic state $\mathcal{E}_\Delta$, this definition requires also that adding A should always produce a better admissible state in the preference order. Still, it is easily verified that any proposition from a base of a base-generated epistemic state will be a basic proposition in the above sense. Note, however, that the base-generated state will have, in general, basic proposition that do not belong to its initial base. This follows from the following simple observation showing that basic propositions are closed with respect to conjunctions:

Lemma 3.3.3. *If A and B are basic propositions of $\mathbb{E}$, then $A \wedge B$ is also a basic proposition of $\mathbb{E}$.*

Note also that the set of basic propositions is not closed, in general, with respect to disjunctions: the disjunction $A \vee B$ of two basic propositions will not always be basic. This fact will have important implications for representing belief change in the framework of epistemic states.

Normal base-generation

The above definition of base-generation deliberately excludes the empty subset of the base from consideration. This is done because the resulting notion of base-generation will be shown to be more suitable for representing some natural classes of epistemic states (see the next chapter). However, epistemic states generated by *all* subsets of a base (including the empty set) turn out provide a more adequate representation for default bases. Notice, for example, that an epistemic state $\mathbb{E}_{\{A\}}$ generated by a singular base $\{A\}$ in accordance with the above definition involves a single admissible belief state, namely $\{A\}$, and hence A is not only believed, but is actually known in this epistemic state. Clearly, such a representation will be inadequate if we want to consider A as only a (default) belief. The relevant modification consists in adding to $\mathbb{E}_{\{A\}}$ a new admissible state corresponding to the empty subset of $\{A\}$; then A will not be known, but only believed, in the resulting epistemic state. Notice now that this latter epistemic state is also base-generated; namely, it is generated by the base $\{A, \mathbf{t}\}$, where $\mathbf{t}$ is an arbitrary tautology. This observation is quite general, and it suggests the following definition:

Definition 3.3.3. *An epistemic state will be called* normally base-generated *by a set of propositions* Δ *with respect to a classical consequence relation* Th *if it is base-generated by the set* $\Delta \cup \{\mathbf{t}\}$ *with respect to* Th.

Thus, normal base-generation is just a special case of base-generation that amounts to adding $\mathbf{t}$ to the base. Notice, in particular, that any normally base-generated epistemic state will have a unique least preferred admissible state $\{\mathbf{t}\}$, and this is its only distinction from the corresponding 'ordinary' base-generated epistemic state. In most cases of interest, this modification does not influence the behavior of such epistemic states in inference and belief change. Consequently, we will return to normal base-generation only in the last two chapters of the book, where we will study merge and expansions of epistemic states with new basic propositions.

3.4 Prioritized base-generation

A most natural understanding of the preference order among admissible belief states consists in seeing it as derived in some way or other from basic priorities among individual defaults. In this section we will describe the main construction of a preference order on sets of defaults from priority relations on defaults. To this end, we briefly describe first some general results about combining preference relations given in [ARS95]. Actually, the results of this fundamental work will be intensively used throughout our study.

3.4.1 Combining preference relations

As we will see, the task of constructing a preference order based on priorities among individual defaults is actually a special case of a general problem of combining a set of preference relations into a single 'consensus' preference order. This problem plays an important role in the theory of social choice. Below we will describe a general way of solving this problem suggested in [ARS95].

To simplify the exposition, we will restrict our attention to the case when all the relevant preference relations are weak partial orders. Then the above problem amounts to defining a general operator o that maps a set of preference relations $\{\preccurlyeq_x \mid x \in V\}$ on the same set of objects M to a single preference relation $\preccurlyeq = o(\{\preccurlyeq_x \mid x \in V\})$. Not any such operator will do, however; it will be required that this operator should satisfy at least the following *Arrow's conditions*:

- The resulting preference $\preccurlyeq$ on elements of M depends only on argument preferences on the same elements;
- The operator o is invariant with respect to isomorphic mappings of M that preserve the argument preferences;
- The operator is unanimous with abstentions: if all $\preccurlyeq_x$ determine the same relationship (vote) between s and t, apart from those which abstain (that is, not $s \preccurlyeq_x t \wedge t \preccurlyeq_x s$), then $\preccurlyeq$ also determines the same vote between s and t;
- $\preccurlyeq$ should be a weak partial order[4].

The main result of [ARS95] consists in showing that any finitary operator on preference relations satisfying the above conditions is definable using the following construction.

A *priority graph* is a triple $(N, \lhd, v)$, where N is a set of nodes, $\lhd$ is a strict partial order on N (representing the priority relation), and v is a labelling function assigning each node a variable (corresponding to an index of some preference relation). Thus, the priority graph defines, in effect, a prioritization on a set of preference relations, though it allows different nodes in the hierarchy to be labelled with the same preference relation. Just us for epistemic states, this generalization turns out to be essential for an adequate representation of all operators satisfying Arrow's conditions.

Let $\{\preccurlyeq_x \mid x \in V\}$ be a set of preference relations, and $(N, \lhd, v)$ a priority graph such that $v(N) = V$. Then the priority graph determines a single resulting preference relation obtained by combining the source preferences using the following *lexicographic rule*:

$$s \preccurlyeq t \ \equiv \ \forall i \in N(s \preccurlyeq_{v(i)} t \vee \exists j \in N(j \lhd i \wedge s \prec_{v(j)} t))$$

---

[4] The original, more general formulation in [ARS95] requires only that the operator o should preserve transitivity of preference relations.

The above lexicographic rule says roughly that t is weakly preferred to s overall if it is weakly preferred for each argument preference, except possibly those for which there is a prior preference that strictly prefers t to s. As we will see later, this rule is a generalization of some well-known constructions suggested in the literature. As has been shown in [ARS95], the corresponding strict preference can be defined as follows:

$$s \prec t \equiv s \preccurlyeq t \wedge \exists i \in N(s \prec_{v(i)} t)$$

The operator on preference relations generated by some priority graph will be called a *priority operator*. Then the following basic result shows that such operators are precisely operators satisfying Arrow's conditions.

Theorem 3.4.1 ([ARS95]). *A finitary operator satisfies Arrow's conditions iff it is a priority operator.*

The above result shows that the lexicographic rule constitutes in a sense a canonical way of combining preference relations. It is interesting to observe that, due to the fact that relevant preference relations are not required to be total, the above construction successfully avoids the famous Arrow's impossibility theorem saying that no such operator could be constructed for total preference orders. More generally, priority operators do not satisfy the property of *decidedness*, according to which the global preference is decided when at least one the individual preferences is decided. Consequently, they are immune also to the impediments for combining preferences discussed in [DW91]. It should be noted, however, that the above Arrow's conditions, though very natural, are nevertheless not universally acceptable. Notice, for example, that the last requirement, according to which the resulting preference should be a weak partial order, effectively excludes combining preference relations based on the majority principle.

In the next section we will apply the above construction to prioritized default bases.

3.4.2 Default priorities

Let us suppose now that the set of defaults Δ is ordered by some *priority relation* $\lhd$ which will be assumed to be a strict partial order. For two defaults $\alpha, \beta \in \Delta$, $\alpha \lhd \beta$ will mean that α *is prior to* β[5]. Prior defaults will be considered more important, or better, than posterior ones. We will occasionally use also $\unlhd$ to denote the reflexive counterpart of $\lhd$.

Notice that no logical constraints were imposed on the priority relation, so we may have, in general, that $\alpha \lhd \beta$, though β logically implies (or even equivalent to) α.

Recall that defaults are considered as beliefs we are willing to hold insofar as it is consistent to do so. This can be interpreted as a claim that any default

---

[5] Notice that, in contrast to preference, priority growths downwards.

determines a primary preference relation according to which admissible belief sets containing the default are preferred to belief sets that do not contain it. In particular, for any default δ, we can define the following weak preference relation $\preccurlyeq_\delta$ on the set $\mathcal{P}(\Delta)$ of all subsets of Δ:

$$\Gamma \preccurlyeq_\delta \Phi \;\equiv\; \text{if } \delta \in \Gamma \text{ then } \delta \in \Phi$$

The above preference relations are very simple: each $\preccurlyeq_\delta$ forms a weak total order having just two equivalence classes, namely sets of defaults that contain δ, and sets that do not contain δ. As can be seen, the corresponding strict preference relation $\Gamma \prec_\delta \Phi$ is definable as $\delta \in \Phi \backslash \Gamma$.

The above construction assigns each default a preference relation on $\mathcal{P}(\Delta)$. Moreover, the prioritized base $(\Delta, \lhd)$ can be viewed in this respect as a priority graph in which every node δ is assigned a preference relation $\preccurlyeq_\delta$. Consequently, we can apply the lexicographic rule for constructing a consensus preference order on sets of defaults.

Unfolding the lexicographic rule for our case using the above description of the primary preference relations $\preccurlyeq_\delta$, we arrive at the following condition:

$$\Gamma \preccurlyeq \Phi \;\equiv\; (\forall \alpha \in \Gamma \backslash \Phi)(\exists \beta \in \Phi \backslash \Gamma)(\beta \lhd \alpha)$$

The above condition says that $\Gamma \preccurlyeq \Phi$ holds when, for each default in $\Gamma \backslash \Phi$, there exists a prior default in $\Phi \backslash \Gamma$. Similarly, the corresponding strict preference is definable as follows:

$$\Gamma \prec \Phi \;\equiv\; \Gamma \preccurlyeq \Phi \land \Gamma \neq \Phi$$

Note 3.4.1. Though the above construction has been used for a long time outside nonmonotonic reasoning and belief change, Lifschitz was apparently the first to use it in the framework of prioritized circumscription. [Gef92] employed it for defining preference relations among sets of defaults. Grosof was the first to recognize the general character of the lexicographic rule (see [Gro91]). Finally, Hans Rott has studied it in application to prioritized bases in [Rot92a].

If the priority relation is *modular*, then the above definition reduces to a more familiar notion (see, e.g., [Neb92]). In this case the priority relation can be alternatively described by splitting the set of defaults Δ into a set of layers $\{\Delta_i\}$, for $1 \leq i \leq n$, that collect equally preferred defaults, with an understanding that the larger the index of the layer, the higher is the priority of defaults it contains. In other words, if $\alpha \in \Delta_k$ and $\beta \in \Delta_m$, then $\alpha \lhd \beta$ if and only if $m < k$. Then, for two sets of defaults Γ and Φ, we will have that $\Gamma \prec \Phi$ in accordance with the above definition if and only if there exists an index i such that $\Gamma \cap \Delta_i \subset \Phi \cap \Delta_i$ and $\Gamma \cap \Delta_j = \Phi \cap \Delta_j$, for any $j > i$.

If $\lhd$ is a total order (that is, all layers Δ_i are singletons), then the corresponding preference relation will also be a total order on sets of defaults: for any two distinct sets of defaults Γ and Φ, we will have that either $\Gamma \prec \Phi$, or $\Phi \prec \Gamma$. Note, however, that this property is not extendable to modular orders; preference relations produced by modular priority orders will not in general be modular.

The above construction of a preference relation in terms of priorities determines quite a special kind of partial orders on sets of defaults. Thus, an important feature of such preference orders is that they are monotonic relative to inclusion between default sets:

If $\Gamma \subset \Phi$, then $\Gamma \prec \Phi$

Still, even monotonicity does not characterize the relevant priority-based preference orders completely. Nevertheless, we will show now that priority-based preference relations are quite versatile in the sense that additional preferences can be always added to a given preference relation by refining the underlying priority relation. We will make use of this feature in Chapter 4, where we will show that associated prioritized epistemic states can be decomposed in some well defined sense into a set of linear prioritized states.

To begin with, we have that refining a priority relation among defaults produces a refinement of the generated preference relation. The proof is immediate from the definition of a generated preference relation.

Lemma 3.4.1. *If $\lhd$ and $\lhd_1$ are priority relations on Δ generating, respectively, preference relations $\prec$ and $\prec_1$ on $\mathcal{P}(\Delta)$, then $\lhd \subseteq \lhd_1$ implies $\prec \subseteq \prec_1$.*

Our next result shows that a priority-based preference relation can be always refined to include a given new preference through refining the underlying priority relation.

Theorem 3.4.2. *Let $\prec$ be a preference relation generated by a priority relation $\lhd$ on Δ. Then if $\Phi \not\prec \Gamma$, for two different subsets of Δ, then there exists a refinement $\lhd_1$ of $\lhd$ such that $\Gamma \prec_1 \Phi$ holds for the generated preference relation.*

Proof. Since $\Phi \not\prec \Gamma$, there must exist a default $\alpha \in \Phi \setminus \Gamma$, such that no default in $\Gamma \setminus \Phi$ is prior to α. Let us denote by Γ_0 the set of all defaults in $\Gamma \setminus \Phi$, for which there are no prior defaults in $\Phi \setminus \Gamma$. Now we will refine the underlying priority relation $\lhd$ by making α prior to all defaults in Γ_0. Actually, this can be done by defining the following new priority relation on Δ:

$$\beta \lhd_1 \gamma \equiv \beta \lhd \gamma \text{ or } (\exists \gamma_0 \in \Gamma_0)(\beta \trianglelefteq \alpha \ \& \ \gamma_0 \trianglelefteq \gamma)$$

Due to our choice of α and Γ_0, it can be easily verified that $\lhd_1$ is a strict partial order. Moreover, we clearly have that $\lhd$ is included in $\lhd_1$ and, for any $\gamma_0 \in \Gamma_0$, $\alpha \lhd_1 \gamma_0$. Due to this fact and the preceding lemma, we have that the preference relation $\prec_1$ generated by $\lhd_1$ is a refinement of $\lhd$ and, moreover, $\Gamma \prec_1 \Phi$, since for any default in $\Gamma \setminus \Phi$, there is now a prior default in $\Phi \setminus \Gamma$. This completes the proof. $\square$

Despite all its virtues, the above definition of a preference relation in terms of priorities among defaults still does not give us the generality needed for some of our intended applications. The reason is that it is based on absolute, unconditional priorities. As we will see in the next part, inheritance hierarchies are representable in terms of priorities that are conditional upon presence of other defaults. It turns out, however, that the essence of the above definition, as well as the main features of the generated preference relation, can be preserved in this more general setting. The corresponding construction will be described in Chapter 8.

Prioritized base-generated epistemic states. Since a prioritized base determines a non-trivial preference relation among sets of defaults, we can incorporate this preference relation into a definition of the associated epistemic state

$$\mathbb{E} = \langle \mathcal{P}(\Delta), l, \prec_\lhd \rangle,$$

where, as before, $\mathcal{P}(\Delta)$ is a set of all subsets of Δ, and l is a function assigning each $\Gamma \subseteq \Delta$ its deductive closure with respect to some classical consequence relation Th. Thus, the only difference between this definition and earlier ones is that the preference order $\prec_\lhd$ is now determined by the underlying priority relation $\lhd$ among defaults. Moreover, since $\prec_\lhd$ is monotonic on $\mathcal{P}(\Delta)$, the above epistemic state will be base-generated by Δ in accordance with our earlier definition. Note that, since no logical constraints were imposed on the priority relation, we may have now that $\Gamma \prec_\lhd \Phi$, even though $\mathrm{Th}(\Gamma)$ is actually included into $\mathrm{Th}(\Phi)$. This means that the generated epistemic state $\mathbb{E}$ will not, on general, be persistent. Nevertheless, it will still be union-closed. In addition, any proposition from Δ will be a basic proposition of $\mathbb{E}$ in accordance with our earlier definition.

As will be shown in Chapter 4, any prioritized base-generated epistemic state is reducible to an equivalent epistemic state which will be both standard and monotonic.

Prioritized homogeneous states. The above construction of prioritized epistemic states can also be used for defining a preference order for homogeneous epistemic states. The idea behind this definition is that the comparison between arbitrary admissible states can be based on the comparison between sets of defaults that are supported by these states, irrespective of what else is accepted in such admissible states. In other words, given a prioritized set of defaults Δ, we can define the preference relation among arbitrary admissible states as follows:

$$s \prec_\Delta t \equiv l(s) \cap \Delta \prec l(t) \cap \Delta$$

This construction has been actually used by Nebel in [Neb92] in defining preference relation between arbitrary sets of propositions. It will be employed also in Chapter 7 in constructing models of nonmonotonic inference. Clearly, if admissible belief states are generated by sets of defaults, we return back to prioritized base-generated epistemic states.

3.5 Flocks

Base-generated epistemic states constitute a quite special kind of epistemic states. Note, for example, that any base-generated epistemic state will be determinate, since the set of all propositions of the base will always produce a unique most preferred (and greatest) admissible belief state. As we will see in Part Two, determinate epistemic states produce only a restricted class of inference relations, so many natural inference relations are not representable using such epistemic states. In addition, we will show in Part Three that one of the main operations on epistemic states, namely contraction, does not preserve the properties of base-generation and union-closure, so the process of belief change is not representable in the framework of base-generated states.

There exists, however, a generalization of the base representation that will already be free from these shortcomings. This representation has been suggested in [FUKV86] and consists in using sets (or 'flocks') of bases.

By a *flock* we will mean an arbitrary set of sets of propositions $\mathcal{F} = \{\Delta_i\}$, for $i \in I$. Such a flock can be considered as a collection of bases Δ_i, and the following construction of the epistemic state generated by a flock can be seen as a natural generalization of pure base-generated epistemic states.

Any flock generates an epistemic state $\mathbb{E}_{\mathcal{F}} = \langle \mathcal{F}_{\downarrow}, l, \prec \rangle$ defined as follows:

- the set of admissible belief states $\mathcal{F}_{\downarrow}$ is a set of all nonempty sets Γ such that $\Gamma \subseteq \Delta$, for some $\Delta \in \mathcal{F}$;
- l is a function assigning each $\Gamma \in \mathcal{F}_{\downarrow}$ its deductive closure, that is, $l(\Gamma) = \mathrm{Cl}(\Gamma)$;
- the preference order is defined as: $\Gamma \prec \Phi$ iff $\Gamma \subset \Phi$.

As can be seen, flocks constitute a generalization of pure bases. Namely, any default base Δ can be identified with a singular flock $\{\Delta\}$.

As in our study, the flock representation was used in [FUKV86] as a framework for describing belief change operations. Our subsequent results will be somewhat different, however, from that of [FUKV86]. The main difference can be described as follows.

Let us say that two flocks are *identical* if they generate the same epistemic state. Now, let $\mathcal{F}$ be a flock and Δ_0 a set of propositions such that $\Delta_0 \subseteq \Delta$, for some $\Delta \in \mathcal{F}$. Then it is easy to see that flocks $\mathcal{F}$ and $\mathcal{F} \cup \{\Delta_0\}$ produce the same epistemic state, and consequently they are identical in the above sense. This shows that a flock is determined, in effect, by its inclusion-maximal elements. According to the approach of [FUKV86], however, the above two flocks are distinct, and hence the validity of propositions with respect to a flock is determined, in effect, by *minimal* sets belonging to the flock. As we will see in due course, this understanding produces inadequate results for the theory of belief change based on flocks. In particular, the contraction operation defined in [FUKV86] turns out to be non-commutative, which makes the resulting theory less plausible and more complex than it could be. In fact, our definitions of the basic belief change operations on flocks will be practically the same as in [FUKV86]. So, the only essential difference between the two understandings of flocks will amount to the above mentioned feature that non-maximal bases can be eliminated from a flock without changing its informational content.

It should be said already now that the above feature, though plausible in many respects that will be explained later, gives rise to a high sensitivity of flocks to the syntactic form of the propositions occurring in it.

Example 3.5.1. Let us consider the flock $\mathcal{F} = \{\{A'\}, \{A, B\}\}$, where A' is logically equivalent to A. Replacing A' with A, we obtain a different flock $\mathcal{F}' = \{\{A\}, \{A, B\}\}$, which is identical to $\{\{A, B\}\}$. Note that $A \wedge B$ is believed in the epistemic state generated by the latter flock, though only A is believed in the epistemic state generated by the source flock $\mathcal{F}$.

The above example shows that flocks do not admit replacements of logically equivalent propositions, at least in cases when such a replacement leads to identification of propositions with other propositions appearing elsewhere in the flock. This makes flocks more syntax-dependent objects that pure bases (that admit such replacements). Note, however, that the epistemic state generated by a flock is a syntax-independent object. Nevertheless, purely syntactic differences in flocks may lead to significant differences in epistemic states generated by them.

Note 3.5.1. Unfortunately, the above interpretation is significantly different also from the (inadequate) interpretation of flocks in terms of pure epistemic states suggested in [Boc99b]. As we will see in what follows, flocks are not representable, in general, even in terms of standard epistemic states. Actually, the interpretation given in [Boc99b] produced adequate behavior for contractions, but has turned out to be inadequate for representing expansions and revisions; in this respect, the original theory of [FUKV86] suggested, in effect, the right solution.

It is easy to check that flock-generated epistemic states do not satisfy union-closure. Moreover, they are not in general even semi-monotonic. Still they are always persistent; this follows immediately from the fact that $\Gamma \prec \Phi$ holds in such a state if and only if $\Gamma \subset \Phi$, and hence $\mathrm{Cl}(\Gamma) \subseteq \mathrm{Cl}(\Phi)$. Thus, we have

Proposition 3.5.1. *Any epistemic state generated by a flock is persistent.*

Moreover, we will see in Chapter 4 that any finitary persistent epistemic state is representable by some flock. This will make flocks an adequate syntactic formalism for representing persistent epistemic states and belief changes on them.

Normal flock-generation Just as for base-generation, we will also need in what follows the notion of a normal flock-generation that will take into account the empty set of propositions. Namely, we will say that an an epistemic state $\mathbb{E}$ is *normally generated* by a flock $\mathcal{F}$ if all subsets of its component bases (including the empty set) are admissible states of $\mathbb{E}$. As can be easily verified, however, normal flock-generation amounts to ordinary flock-generation with respect to a modified flock $\mathcal{F}^+ = \{\Delta_i \cup \{\mathbf{t}\}\}$ obtained by adding $\mathbf{t}$ to each base of the flock $\mathcal{F}$. We will meet such epistemic states in Chapter 13 where we will consider merge and expansions of flocks.

3.6 Nonmonotonic inference and its kinds

In this section we will describe the main forms of nonmonotonic inference in epistemic states that will be studied in Part Two. As a preparation, we will briefly describe Poole's approach to formalizing nonmonotonic reasoning; this will give us a good starting point for determining the essential properties of the relevant notions.

3.6.1 Poole's abductive framework

Poole's abductive system [Poo88] can serve as a primary example of our approach to representing nonmonotonic formalisms in terms of epistemic states[6].

An *abductive framework* is a pair $\langle \mathcal{F}, \Delta \rangle$, where $\mathcal{F}$ and Δ are sets of propositions denoting, respectively, *facts* and *possible hypotheses*. A *scenario* of an abductive framework is a consistent set of the form $\mathcal{F} \cup \Delta^0$, where $\Delta^0 \subseteq \Delta$. A proposition A is said to be *explainable* in an abductive framework if it is a logical consequence of some scenario. *Extensions* of an abductive framework are defined by Poole as deductive closures of maximal scenaria. Clearly, a proposition is explainable if and only if it belongs to some extension. Finally, a proposition will be said to be *predictable* in an abductive framework if it belongs to all its extensions.

There are actually two principal ways of representing the above abductive framework in terms of epistemic states. The first way consists in forming a pure epistemic state, say $\mathcal{E}_f$, consisting simply of deductive closures of scenaria. Then extensions of an abductive framework will correspond to maximal admissible belief sets. Accordingly, a proposition will be predictable (respectively, explainable) in an abductive framework if and only if its is believed (respectively, admissible) in the associated pure epistemic state. In this way the latter will capture the basic notions defined in the source abductive framework.

Though formally adequate, the above representation has, however, a certain deficiency from the point of view of our informal understanding of epistemic states, since it does not provide a clear separation of objective facts and

---

[6] We will deviate a bit from the original Poole's representation in order to confine the description to propositional language.

epistemic (default) information. Actually, this inconvenience can be traced back to Poole's notion of a scenario itself, since the latter combines objective facts and epistemic hypotheses, as opposed to recommendations about separation of evidences from background knowledge made in his other writings (e.g., in [Poo91]). As a result, the set of facts $\mathcal{F}$ turns out to be included into the knowledge set of the above defined epistemic state. Consequently, such an epistemic state will be always rigidly tailored to the current factual situation.

The way to circumvent this shortcoming in representation consists in representing Poole's framework using another epistemic state, namely the epistemic state $\mathbb{E}_\Delta$ that is base-generated by the set of hypotheses Δ (see above). This epistemic state will already be 'purely epistemic', since it does not involve factual information given by $\mathcal{F}$. This will require, however, a corresponding change in the definitions of explainable and predictable propositions, since the latter are determined by combining facts and hypotheses. Accordingly, instead of absolute notions of belief and admissibility, we will need their *conditional* counterparts.

To simplify the exposition, we will assume that the set of facts $\mathcal{F}$ is finite, and that F corresponds to the conjunction of all propositions from $\mathcal{F}$. Then in order to determine propositions that are explainable or predictable in an abductive framework, we should consider admissible belief states from $\mathbb{E}_\Delta$ that are *consistent* with the facts F. Specifically, a proposition A is predictable in an abductive framework $\langle F, \Delta \rangle$ if and only if each preferred admissible state in $\mathbb{E}_\Delta$ that is consistent with F, taken together with F itself, implies A. Or, in other words, when

> $F \rightarrow A$ is supported by all preferred admissible states that are consistent with F.

Similarly, a proposition A is explainable in an abductive framework if and only if at least one preferred admissible belief state in $\mathbb{E}_\Delta$ that is consistent with F, taken together with F itself, implies A. In other words,

> $F \rightarrow A$ is supported by some preferred admissible belief state consistent with F.

The above two descriptions will be generalized below to two basic forms of nonmonotonic inference definable in epistemic states, namely to skeptical and credulous inference.

3.6.2 Skeptical inference

Epistemic states represent beliefs, defaults or expectations that the agent has about the world. These epistemic attitudes are relatively stable and normally do not change with changes in the current situation. Instead, in each situation we restrict our attention to admissible combinations of beliefs that are consistent with the current facts, and choose preferred (best) among them. The latter are used to support the conclusions and assumptions we make about the situation at hand. Accordingly, all kinds of nonmonotonic inference relations, described below, presuppose a two-step selection procedure: given a proposition F representing current evidence, we consider admissible belief states that are consistent with F and choose preferred elements in this set. Differences among various kinds of nonmonotonic inference will arise only at this point, due to different use we will make of these preferred belief states.

A *skeptical inference* with respect to an epistemic state is obtained if we decide that, given the set of preferred belief states consistent with the facts, we can reasonably infer only what is supported by each of these states. In other words, A will be a skeptical conclusion from the evidence F in a given epistemic state $\mathbb{E}$ if each preferred admissible belief set in $\mathbb{E}$ that is consistent with F, taken together with F itself, implies A. Or, in still other words,

Definition 3.6.1. *A is a* skeptical consequence *of F (notation $F \hspace{-0.5mm}\mid\hspace{-1.5mm}\sim A$) in an epistemic state if $F \to A$ is supported by all preferred belief states in $]\neg F[$.*

A set of conditionals $A \hspace{-0.5mm}\mid\hspace{-1.5mm}\sim B$ that are valid in an epistemic state $\mathbb{E}$ in accordance with the above definition will be called a *skeptical inference relation determined by $\mathbb{E}$*. Accordingly, we will say that a set of conditionals forms a skeptical inference relation if it is determined by some epistemic state.

The above definition constitutes a straightforward generalization of the corresponding definition of prediction in Poole's system. More exactly, the latter can be identified with the skeptical inference with respect to base-generated epistemic states. The definition will also be shown to provide a generalization of the notion of an expectation-based inference, given in [GM94].

Historical note. The above epistemic definition of conditionals is actually very old. In fact, the 'standard' definition of nonmonotonic inference, given in [KLM90], derives from the relatively modern possible worlds theory of conditionals developed by Stalnaker and Lewis. The above definition, however, can be traced back to the era before the discovery of possible worlds, namely to Frank Ramsey and John S. Mill. This alternative understanding of conditionals is succinctly described in the following quotation taken from [Ram78, page 144]:

> "In general we can say with Mill that 'If p then q' means that q is inferrable from p, that is, of course, from p together with certain facts and laws not stated but in some way indicated by the context."

In fact, our semantic definition can be seen as a particular variant of the *Ramsey test for conditionals* (see [Gär88]). Though less familiar, it has also been used in the so-called 'premise-based' semantics for counterfactuals proposed by Veltman and Kratzer[Vel76, Kra81]. The relation between the two approaches to analyzing conditionals has been studied already by David Lewis in [Lew81].

In many respects, skeptical inference constitutes the most important form of nonmonotonic inference. It will be studied in Chapter 7. As we will see then, the above definition will turn out to be sufficiently general to capture the main systems of such inference discussed in the literature.

Remark. General epistemic states correspond actually to cumulative models of nonmonotonic inference studied in [Mak89, KLM90]. Such models were used in these papers for defining a general notion of a *cumulative inference*. Translated into our terminology, it says that A nonmonotonically implies B if all preferred admissible states among the states *supporting* A support also B. This kind of inference is significantly weaker, however, than skeptical inference, and hence does not fully capture, on our view, the notion of nonmonotonic inference. It also falls out of the general approach to nonmonotonic inference described in Chapter 6. As a result, it falls also out of the scope of this book.

3.6.3 Contraction inference

The above epistemic definition of skeptical inference displays the latter as a composite notion. Namely, the definition says that $A \mathrel{|\!\sim} B$ holds if and only if the implication $A \to B$ is supported by all preferred belief states that do not contain $\neg A$. This construction resembles quite closely the two-step construction of revision in the belief change theory. According to the latter, in order to revise a belief set with a new, possibly incompatible belief A, we should first contract $\neg A$ from the belief set, and then expand the result by adding A. As we will see later, this resemblance between nonmonotonic inference and belief revision is not accidental. But already now it suggests that skeptical inference can be expressed using a more fundamental, or primitive, concept corresponding to the contraction operation in belief revision. This concept can be described as follows:

Definition 3.6.2. *B is a contraction consequence of A (notation $A \mathrel{\rightthreetimes} B$) in an epistemic state if B is supported by all preferred belief states in $]A[$.*

Thus, $A \mathrel{\rightthreetimes} B$ holds if B *is a plausible belief in the absence of A*. This defines a (slightly unusual) inference relation that will play an important role in our study. We will call an expression of the form $A \mathrel{\rightthreetimes} B$ a *contraction conditional* or, in short, a *contractional*. An informal reading of such contractionals will be *"In the absence of A, normally B"*.

Remark. Rules of the form "In the absence of A, accept B" are actually a simplest kind of *default rules* that constitute the subject matter of Reiter's default logic [Rei80]. The relationship between contractionals and Reiter's default rules remains yet to be explored; presumably, it would be an important step on still a long way towards a future general theory of nonmonotonic reasoning. The similarity suggests, however, that a contractional $A \multimap B$ could be read as "*Unless A, B*", with the only reservation that we do not accept the usual presupposition associated with the latter expression, namely that A is by itself an unexpected (abnormal) condition.

Similarly to conditionals, a set of contractionals that are valid in an epistemic state $\mathbb{E}$ in accordance with the above definition will be called a *contraction inference relation* determined by $\mathbb{E}$. Contraction inference relations will be studied in Chapter 10, while in Part Three we will show that they correspond precisely to the contraction operation in the theory of belief change.

Given the above definition of contraction inference, we can re-define now skeptical inference as follows:

$$A \mathrel{\vcenter{\hbox{$\scriptstyle\sim$}}} B \equiv \neg A \multimap A \to B$$

As can be seen, the above definition, coupled with the semantic definition of contraction inference, gives us exactly the skeptical inference defined earlier. Accordingly, many properties of the latter can be analyzed already on the level of contraction inference relations.

3.6.4 Credulous inference

A *credulous inference* with respect to an epistemic state is defined by assuming that we can reasonably infer (or explain) conclusions that are supported by at least one preferred belief state consistent with the facts. In other words, A will be a credulous conclusion from the evidence F in a given epistemic state $\mathbb{E}$ if at least one preferred admissible belief set in $\mathbb{E}$ that is consistent with F, taken together with F itself, implies A. In still other words,

Definition 3.6.3. *A is a* credulous consequence *of F (notation $F \mathrel{\vcenter{\hbox{$\approx$}}} A$) in an epistemic state if $F \to A$ is supported by at least one preferred belief state in $]\neg F[$.*

As before, a set of conditionals $A \mathrel{\vcenter{\hbox{$\approx$}}} B$ that are valid in an epistemic state $\mathbb{E}$ will be called a *credulous inference relation determined by* $\mathbb{E}$. As for skeptical inference, the above definition constitutes a generalization of the corresponding definition of explanation in Poole's system. More exactly, the latter can be identified with the credulous inference with respect to pure epistemic states.

Credulous inference is only one, though important, instance of a broad range of non-skeptical inference relations. Different systems of non-skeptical inference will be discussed in Chapter 9.

Remark. Just as for skeptical inference, the above definition of credulous inference can be decomposed into a contraction step and an expansion step. Accordingly, we could define the notion of a *credulous contraction inference* saying that B should hold in at least one preferred belief state that does not support A. It remains to be seen, however, whether this notion could be of any use in nonmonotonic reasoning.

3.6.5 A digression: careful and adventurous inference

In addition to skeptical and credulous inference, the reader may find in the literature two special kinds of nonmonotonic inference that have played an important role in the history of nonmonotonic reasoning. Both these kinds of inference are based on selecting a *unique* admissible state for each factual assumption. Consequently, both make good sense only for a special class of epistemic states, namely for union-closed (base-generated) monotonic states; for the latter, any set of admissible belief states has a greatest lower bound and least upper bound in the preference order.

The first kind, that could be called an *adventurous inference*, asserts that A implies B if $A{\rightarrow}B$ belongs to a least admissible state containing all preferred states consistent with A. This kind of inference can be seen as a generalization of the *Closed World Assumption* (CWA); just as the latter, it boldly presumes that any default consistent with the facts can be used for making conclusions. Clearly, this kind of inference is stronger even than credulous inference in the sense that any credulous conclusion will also be an adventurous conclusion from the same premises. As can be expected, however, this principle does not give good results in cases when there is a number of defaults that are individually consistent, but jointly incompatible with the facts. Accordingly, it does not work in presence of multiple preferred alternatives, since it refers in this case to admissible belief sets that are already incompatible with the facts, and hence produces inconsistent results.

The second kind of inference, that could be called a *careful inference*, can be viewed as a mirrored image of an adventurous inference. It says that A implies B if $A{\rightarrow}B$ is supported by the (unique) belief state corresponding to the common part of all preferred states compatible with A. This kind of inference corresponds to the direct inference approach in the inheritance theory [HTT90] and to the well-founded semantics in logic programming. In the theory of belief change it is represented by base revision operations suggested by Hansson [Han93b]. As can be seen, careful inference is more cautious than skeptical one. In addition, it is in general less complex computationally than the latter. The only, though essential, reservation about such kind of inference is that it is too careful, since it does not allow to infer some otherwise reasonable conclusions that do not have the same justification in all cases (they were called *floating conclusions* in [MS91]). Consequently, it is essentially weaker than skeptical inference (see [Sch93]).

Apart from occasional remarks, the above two kinds of inference will not be dealt with in the present study, since its main concern is what ought to be inferred, rather than what could be inferred fast. Still, it should be noted that both these kinds of inference, though inadequate in general, can be very useful in providing computationally feasible approximations to skeptical and credulous inference. It is interesting to note in this respect that both of them are completely adequate for linear epistemic states (which are already union-closed). Actually, linear epistemic states obliterate the distinctions between all these kinds of inference; both adventurous and careful inference, on the one hand, and credulous and skeptical inference, on the other, collapse in such an epistemic state to a single inference relation.

4. Similarity, Equivalence and Decomposition of Epistemic States

Since epistemic states will be used in this book for representing nonmonotonic inference and belief change, we will be primarily interested in the properties of epistemic states that could influence the behavior of generated inference relations and belief change operations. In order to single out the properties of epistemic states that are relevant, we will introduce in this chapter a number of notions of equivalence for epistemic states that will preserve the generated inference relations and belief sets. We will start with the strongest notion of similarity for epistemic states that will be invariant under the basic belief change operations. In other words, similar epistemic states will produce the same response under any future change made to these states; borrowing the terminology of [FUKV86], they will be *equivalent forever*. We will also show that any epistemic state is decomposable in this sense into a set of linear epistemic states. In addition, we will introduce the notion of a selection function which will determine the 'inference profile' of an epistemic state. Epistemic states generating the same selection function will be called equivalent. The notions of equivalence and similarity will supply us with powerful tools for investigating properties of epistemic states that are essential in determining their behavior in nonmonotonic inference and belief change.

4.1 Similarity

We will start with a strong notion of similarity that will establish a kind of bisimulation for epistemic states, a notion familiar from studies in possible worlds semantics. We introduce first some notation.

Two admissible belief states s_1 and s_2 (possibly from different epistemic states) will be called *equal* (notation $s_1 \overset{\circ}{=} s_2$) if they are labelled with the same theory.

Let $\mathcal{T}_1$ and $\mathcal{T}_2$ be two sets of sets of theories. We will say that $\mathcal{T}_1$ *dominates* $\mathcal{T}_2$ (notation $\mathcal{T}_1 \ll \mathcal{T}_2$) if, for any $u \in \mathcal{T}_2$ there exists $v \in \mathcal{T}_1$ such that $v \subseteq u$.

Finally, for any admissible state s from $\mathbb{E}$, we will denote by $\Uparrow s$ the set of all admissible belief sets 'above s', that is, $\Uparrow s = \{l(t) \mid s \prec t\}$.

Definition 4.1.1. *Two epistemic states $\mathbb{E}_1$ and $\mathbb{E}_2$ will be called* similar, *if they satisfy the following two conditions:*

- $(\forall s_1 \in \mathbb{E}_1)(\exists s_2 \in \mathbb{E}_2)(s_1 \stackrel{\circ}{=} s_2 \wedge \Uparrow s_1 \ll \Uparrow s_2);$
- $(\forall s_2 \in \mathbb{E}_2)(\exists s_1 \in \mathbb{E}_1)(s_1 \stackrel{\circ}{=} s_2 \wedge \Uparrow s_2 \ll \Uparrow s_1).$

It can be easily verified that the above definition determines an equivalence relation on epistemic states. Moreover, we will see in due course that similarity will be preserved by all belief change operations on epistemic states. The following example gives a first illustration of this notion.

Example 4.1.1. Let us consider the following two epistemic states. $\mathbb{E}_1$ consists of three admissible states s_1, s_2, s_3 that are labelled, respectively, with $Cl(p)$, $Cl(r)$ and $Cl(q \wedge r)$, and ordered as follows: $s_1 \prec s_2$. The second epistemic state $\mathbb{E}_2$ also has three admissible states t_1, t_2, t_3 that are labelled, respectively, with the same theories as in $\mathbb{E}_1$, but the preference order is $t_1 \prec t_2$ and $t_1 \prec t_3$. In other words, $\mathbb{E}_1$ and $\mathbb{E}_2$ are almost identical, except that $\mathbb{E}_2$ contains an additional preference (namely, $t_1 \prec t_3$).

It can be easily verified that these epistemic states are similar. Notice that we do not have that $\Uparrow t_1$ (which amounts to $\{Cl(r), Cl(q \wedge r)\}$) is included in $\Uparrow s_1$ (which is $\{Cl(r)\}$). Still, it is easy to see that the latter set dominates the former, which is sufficient for similarity.

As a first application of the above notion of similarity, we will characterize a broad class of epistemic states that are similar to pure epistemic states.

To begin with, note that any general epistemic state $\mathbb{E}$ determines a pure epistemic state $\mathcal{E}_\mathbb{E}$ consisting of all admissible belief sets of $\mathbb{E}$. Then the following result is based on the observation that if $\mathbb{E}$ is persistent and semi-monotonic, it will be similar to its associated pure epistemic state.

Theorem 4.1.1. *Any persistent and semi-monotonic epistemic state is similar to a pure epistemic state.*

Proof. Let $\mathbb{E}$ be a persistent and semi-monotonic epistemic state, and $\mathcal{E}_\mathbb{E}$ its associated pure epistemic state.

Given an admissible state s in $\mathbb{E}$, we will take $u = l(s)$ as its equal counterpart in $\mathcal{E}_\mathbb{E}$. Assume that $u \subset v$, for some $v \in \mathcal{E}_\mathbb{E}$. Since v is an admissible belief set of $\mathbb{E}$, there exists an admissible state t in $\mathbb{E}$ such that $l(t) = v$. But then by semi-monotonicity there must exist an admissible state t' equal to t such that $s \prec t'$. This shows that $\Uparrow s$ dominates $\Uparrow u$.

Assume now that u is an admissible belief set in $\mathcal{E}_\mathbb{E}$. Then there exists an admissible state s_0 in $\mathbb{E}$ such that $l(s_0) = u$. Consequently, $s_0 \in]\overline{u}[$, where $\overline{u}$ is a complement of u. By m-smoothness, there must exist an admissible state s such that $s_0 \preceq s$ and s is preferred in $]\overline{u}[$. By persistence, we have, however, that $l(s_0) \subseteq l(s) \subseteq u$, and hence $l(s) = l(s_0) = u$. Let us take s as a counterpart of u in $\mathbb{E}$. If $s \prec t$, then $l(s) \subseteq l(t)$ by persistence, and hence $l(s) \subset l(t)$, since s is preferred in $]\overline{u}[$. Thus, $u \subset l(t)$ in $\mathcal{E}_\mathbb{E}$, which shows that $\Uparrow u$ dominates $\Uparrow s$. This completes the proof. $\square$

As we have seen in Chapter 3, any epistemic state $\mathbb{E}_\Delta$ that is generated by a pure (non-prioritized) base Δ is both persistent and semi-monotonic. Moreover, the corresponding pure epistemic state consisting of admissible belief sets of $\mathbb{E}_\Delta$ will also be union-closed. Consequently, we obtain the following important

Corollary 4.1.1. *Any purely base-generated epistemic state is similar to a pure union-closed epistemic state.*

The above result shows, in effect, that simple bases can be modeled in our framework using pure union-closed epistemic states. In the next section we will show that in the finite case any persistent and union-closed epistemic state is representable by some pure base.

4.1.1 Similarity of pure bases

In this section we will consider epistemic states that are generated by pure bases. To begin with, the notion of similarity is helpful in establishing that pure bases are in a certain sense syntax-independent objects in their role of producing epistemic states.

Definition 4.1.2. 1. *([FUKV86]) A set of propositions Δ_1 will be said to cover another set Δ_2 if each proposition from Δ_2 is logically equivalent to a conjunction of some propositions from Δ_1.*
2. *Two sets of propositions Δ_1 and Δ_2 will be called* basically equivalent, *if each is covered by another.*

Given a base Δ, we will denote by $\mathcal{E}_\Delta$ the pure epistemic state consisting of all admissible belief sets of $\mathbb{E}_\Delta$, namely, all theories of the form $\mathrm{Cl}(\Gamma)$, where $\Gamma \subseteq \Delta$. As has been shown above, these two epistemic states are similar. Now, it can be easily verified that Δ_1 and Δ_2 are basically equivalent if and only if $\mathcal{E}_{\Delta_1}$ coincides with $\mathcal{E}_{\Delta_2}$. Consequently, we immediately obtain

Lemma 4.1.1. *If Δ_1 and Δ_2 are basically equivalent, then their associated base-generated epistemic states are similar.*

Basic equivalence allows for replacement of propositions from the base by their logical equivalents. Also, it allows to add (or, respectively, remove) propositions that are conjunctions of other basic propositions. As we will see later, basic equivalence is a weakest relation among bases that is preserved under belief change operations. Consequently, these transformations practically exhaust possible changes of bases that would preserve their roles in nonmonotonic reasoning and belief change.

We will show now that epistemic states that are persistent and union-closed are representable by pure bases.

Lemma 4.1.2. *Any finitary, persistent and union-closed epistemic state is similar to a purely base-generated epistemic state.*

Proof. Let $\mathbb{E}$ be a finitary, persistent and union-closed epistemic state. As we have mentioned already in the preceding chapter, any finitary epistemic state is representable, in effect, as a finite partially ordered set of propositions $(\Delta, \prec)$, where any proposition A from Δ represents an admissible belief state of $\mathbb{E}$ (that is labelled with $\mathrm{Cl}(A)$). As we will show, in our present case Δ will be a base of an epistemic state $\mathbb{E}_\Delta$ that is similar to $\mathbb{E}$.

Since $\mathbb{E}$ is union-closed, for any nonempty $\Gamma \subseteq \Delta$ there exists $A \in \Delta$ that is logically equivalent to $\bigwedge \Gamma$ and such that $B \preceq A$, for any $B \in \Gamma$. We will take some such A as a counterpart of Γ in $\mathbb{E}$. Assume that $A \prec B$ in $\mathbb{E}$. Then $l(A) \subseteq l(B)$ by persistence, and hence $\mathrm{Cl}(\Gamma \cup \{B\}) = l(B)$ and $\Gamma \prec \Gamma \cup \{B\}$ in $\mathbb{E}_\Delta$. Consequently, $\Uparrow\Gamma$ in $\mathbb{E}_\Delta$ dominates $\Uparrow A$ in $\mathbb{E}$.

In the other direction, for any A from Δ, we will take as its counterpart in $\mathbb{E}_\Delta$ the set Γ of all $B \in \Delta$ that are logically implied by A. Assume that $\Gamma \subset \Phi$ in $\mathbb{E}_\Delta$. Then there exists an admissible state C in Δ such that $l(C) = \mathrm{Cl}(\Phi)$ and $A \preceq C$. Moreover, A is distinct from C, since otherwise we would have that A implies all propositions from Φ, and hence $\Phi \subseteq \Gamma$. Therefore, $A \prec C$, which shows that $\Uparrow A$ dominates $\Uparrow\Gamma$. This completes the proof. $\square$

The above result can be viewed as a concise description of the place of pure base representation in the general representation formalism suggested in this study.

4.1.2 Union-closure and base-generation

Now we will generalize the above result for pure base-generation to arbitrary base-generated epistemic states.

Recall that any base-generated epistemic state is union-closed. The following result shows that, in the finite case, the reverse claim also holds, namely any union-closed epistemic state is similar to a base-generated epistemic state.

Theorem 4.1.2. *Any finitary union-closed epistemic state is similar to a base-generated epistemic state.*

Proof. Let $\mathbb{E}$ be a finitary union-closed epistemic state. As before, we will represent $\mathbb{E}$ as a finite partially ordered set of propositions $(\Delta, \prec)$, and show that Δ will be a base of some epistemic state similar to $\mathbb{E}$.

Since $\mathbb{E}$ is union-closed, for any nonempty $\Gamma \subseteq \Delta$ there exists $A \in \Delta$ that is logically equivalent to $\bigwedge \Gamma$ and such that $B \preceq A$, for any $B \in \Gamma$. We will call such A a *cover* of Γ. Moreover, though $\mathbb{E}$ may contain a number of different (though equal) covers for Γ, the union-closure implies also that there exists a unique most preferred cover among them; we will denote it by $\hat{\Gamma}$.

Now let us consider a base-generated epistemic state $\mathbb{E}_b = (\Delta, \prec_b)$, where $\prec_b$ is defined as follows:

$$\Gamma \prec_b \Phi \text{ iff } \Gamma \subset \Phi \text{ or } \hat{\Gamma} \prec \hat{\Phi}$$

Clearly, this preference relation is monotonic on $\mathcal{P}(\Delta)$. Note also that $\Gamma \subset \Phi$ implies $\hat{\Gamma} \preceq \hat{\Phi}$; this is sufficient for showing that $\prec_b$ will be a strict partial order. Moreover, we will show that $\mathbb{E}_b$ is similar to $\mathbb{E}$.

For any admissible state Γ from $\mathbb{E}_b$, we will take $\hat{\Gamma}$ as its counterpart in $\mathbb{E}$. Assume that $\hat{\Gamma} \prec B$ in $\mathbb{E}$. Then $\hat{\Gamma} \prec \{\hat{B}\}$, and therefore $\Gamma \prec_b \{B\}$ in $\mathbb{E}_b$. This shows that $\Uparrow\Gamma$ in $\mathbb{E}_b$ dominates $\Uparrow\hat{\Gamma}$ in $\mathbb{E}$.

In the other direction, for any A from Δ, we will take as its counterpart in $\mathbb{E}_b$ the set Γ of all $B \in \Delta$ that are logically implied by A. Clearly, $A \in \Gamma$. Assume that $\Gamma \prec_b \Phi$ in $\mathbb{E}_b$, and suppose first that $\Gamma \subset \Phi$. Then $A \preceq \widehat{\Phi \cup \{A\}}$. Moreover, A is not a cover of $\Phi \cup \{A\}$, since Φ contains propositions that are not implied by A. Consequently, $A \prec \widehat{\Phi \cup \{A\}}$. In addition, $\widehat{\Phi \cup \{A\}}$ covers Γ, and hence it implies A. Consequently, $\mathrm{Cl}(\widehat{\Phi \cup \{A\}}) = \mathrm{Cl}(\Phi)$, as required by similarity.

Finally, suppose that $\hat{\Gamma} \prec \hat{\Phi}$. But $\hat{\Gamma}$ covers also A, so $A \prec \hat{\Phi}$, and consequently $\Uparrow A$ dominates $\Uparrow\Gamma$ in $\mathbb{E}_b$. This completes the proof. $\square$

The above result shows that union-closure can be seen as a characteristic property of base-generated epistemic states. Note that base-generated epistemic states are not persistent, so they will not be reducible, in general, to pure epistemic states. We will see later, however, that all such states are reducible to standard monotonic epistemic states.

Remark. Recall that the general notion of base-generation, defined in the preceding chapter, has involved an arbitrary classical consequence relation Th instead of the classical entailment. The above result shows, however, that the use of such an auxiliary consequence relation is not essential in the finite case. Namely, the known propositions can be adjoined to all propositions from the base, and then the corresponding classical consequence relation could be safely replaced with classical entailment. The generalized setting will be useful, however, for some of our subsequent constructions.

4.1.3 Similarity of prioritized bases

We will give in this section an important sufficient criterion for similarity of epistemic states generated by prioritized bases. To simplify the exposition, we will assume that the underlying monotonic logic of such epistemic states coincides with the classical entailment. Note, however, that this assumption will not be essential for subsequent results.

We have established earlier that two basically equivalent pure bases generate similar epistemic states. Clearly, this condition will not be sufficient for equivalence of prioritized bases. Thus, even replacement of logical equivalents in a prioritized base could sometimes change the generated epistemic state. The following example illustrates this.

Example 4.1.2. Let us consider a base $\Delta = \{A, A_1, B, C\}$, where A is equivalent to A_1, B is prior to A, and C is prior to A_1. Due to our subsequent results, the corresponding epistemic state $\mathbb{E}_\Delta$ can be compactly described as an epistemic state that is base-generated by a pure base $\{A, B, C\}$, plus an additional preference $\{A\} \prec \{B, C\}$.

Now let us replace A_1 with A in Δ. As a result, we obtain a prioritized base $\{A, B, C\}$ in which both B and C are prior to A. The corresponding epistemic state $\mathbb{E}_1$ will actually be a refinement of $\mathbb{E}_\Delta$ with additional preferences $\{A\} \prec \{B\}$, $\{A\} \prec \{C\}$, $\{A, B\} \prec \{B, C\}$, and $\{A, C\} \prec \{B, C\}$. We will have, in particular, that $\neg(A \wedge B)$ will skeptically imply $B \wedge C$ in $\mathbb{E}_1$, though not in $\mathbb{E}_\Delta$. Using our later terminology, this means that $\mathbb{E}_\Delta$ will not be even inference equivalent to $\mathbb{E}_1$.

Still, some non-trivial notion of similarity between prioritized bases will be shown now to be sufficient for similarity of their associated epistemic states. As a matter of fact, this notion of similarity is a modification of the notion of equivalence for priority graphs from [ARS95], though adapted to our context where the preference relations are generated by defaults.

Given a prioritized base $(\Delta, \lhd)$ and $\alpha \in \Delta$, we will denote by $\nabla\alpha$ the set of all elements of Δ that are prior to α. In addition, given another prioritized base $(\Delta_1, \lhd_1)$ and some $\beta \in \Delta_1$, we will say that $\nabla\alpha$ *covers* $\nabla\beta$ if, for each default prior to β there exists a logically equivalent default prior to α.

Definition 4.1.3. *Two prioritized bases $(\Delta, \lhd)$ and $(\Delta_1, \lhd_1)$ will be called similar if the following two conditions are satisfied:*

- $(\forall \alpha \in \Delta)(\exists \alpha_1 \in \Delta_1)(\alpha \equiv \alpha_1 \wedge \nabla\alpha$ *covers* $\nabla\alpha_1)$;
- $(\forall \alpha_1 \in \Delta_1)(\exists \alpha \in \Delta)(\alpha_1 \equiv \alpha \wedge \nabla\alpha_1$ *covers* $\nabla\alpha)$.

As can be seen, similarity of prioritized bases presupposes that, for each default β in one of them, there exists a logically equivalent default β' in another base. It requires, in addition, that some such β' should be such that each default prior to it is logically equivalent to some default prior to β.

The following result shows that the above notion of similarity is sufficient for similarity of epistemic states generated by two prioritized bases.

Theorem 4.1.3. *Epistemic states generated by similar prioritized bases are similar.*

Proof. Let $(\Delta, \lhd)$ and $(\Delta_1, \lhd_1)$ be two similar prioritized bases, and $\mathbb{E}$ and $\mathbb{E}_1$ their generated epistemic states.

For an admissible state Γ in $\mathbb{E}$, we will consider the set $\Gamma_1 \subseteq \Delta_1$ consisting of all defaults that are logically equivalent to some default in Γ. Clearly, $\mathrm{Cl}(\Gamma) = \mathrm{Cl}(\Gamma_1)$. Moreover, we will show that $\Uparrow\Gamma \ll \Uparrow\Gamma_1$.

Assume that $\Gamma_1 \prec \Phi_1$ in $\mathbb{E}_1$, and let Φ be the set of all defaults in Δ that are logically equivalent to defaults from Φ_1. Since $\mathrm{Cl}(\Phi) = \mathrm{Cl}(\Phi_1)$, it is sufficient to show that $\Gamma \prec \Phi$ in $\mathbb{E}$.

If $\alpha \in \Gamma \backslash \Phi$, then there must exist an equivalent default $\alpha_1 \in \Delta_1$ such that $\nabla\alpha$ covers $\nabla\alpha_1$. Since $\alpha \in \Gamma$, we have $\alpha_1 \in \Gamma_1$. In addition, $\alpha_1 \notin \Phi_1$, since otherwise we would have that $\alpha \in \Phi$. Thus, $\alpha_1 \in \Gamma_1 \backslash \Phi_1$. Consequently, there exists $\beta_1 \in \Phi_1 \backslash \Gamma_1$ such that $\beta_1 \lhd_1 \alpha_1$ (due to the assumption that $\Gamma_1 \prec \Phi_1$). But $\bigtriangledown \alpha$ covers $\bigtriangledown \alpha_1$, so β_1 has a logically equivalent default $\beta \lhd \alpha$. Clearly, $\beta \in \Phi$. Moreover, $\beta \notin \Gamma$, since otherwise we would have that $\beta_1 \in \Gamma_1$. Thus, $\beta \in \Phi \backslash \Gamma$, which shows that $\Gamma \prec \Phi$. This completes the proof. $\qquad \square$

Though we have shown only that similarity of prioritized bases is sufficient for similarity of associated epistemic states, the defining conditions of similarity give actually a good indication of the (rather restricted) possibilities of varying prioritized bases that would preserve equivalence of corresponding epistemic states. Nevertheless, the similarity condition allows to prove an important result (cf. [ARS95]) that any prioritized base can be transformed into a similar base where the priority relation forms a *tree order*, namely, if $\alpha \trianglelefteq \beta, \gamma$, then either $\gamma \trianglelefteq \beta$, or $\beta \trianglelefteq \gamma$.

Lemma 4.1.3. *For any prioritized base there exists a similar tree-ordered prioritized base.*

Proof. Given a prioritized base $(\Delta, \lhd)$, we will construct the corresponding tree-ordered base $(\Delta_0, \lhd_0)$ as follows. For any finite $\lhd$-chain of defaults $s = (\alpha_0, \ldots, \alpha_n)$ from Δ such that $\alpha_0 \lhd \cdots \lhd \alpha_n$, we will include in Δ_0 a new proposition α_s that is logically equivalent to its first element α_0. Then we order these propositions by priority as follows:

$$\alpha_s \lhd_0 \alpha_t \text{ iff } t \text{ is a tail of } s.$$

Clearly, the above defined priority relation forms a tree order on Δ_0. We will show now that $(\Delta, \lhd)$ is similar to $(\Delta_0, \lhd_0)$.

For any $\beta \in \Delta$, let us take the default $\alpha_{(\beta)} \in \Delta_0$ corresponding to a rudimentary chain (β). Assume that $\alpha_s \lhd_0 \alpha_{(\beta)}$ and γ is an end of s. Then γ is logically equivalent to α_s and $\gamma \lhd \beta$. Consequently, $\bigtriangledown \beta$ covers $\bigtriangledown \alpha_{(\beta)}$. In the other direction, for any $\alpha_s \in \Delta_0$, we will take the first element of s, say α, as its counterpart in Δ. Then, for any $\beta \lhd \alpha$, we will take α_t, where t is a chain obtained from s by adding β as its first element. Clearly, s is a tail of t, so $\alpha_t \lhd_0 \alpha_s$; moreover, α_t is equivalent to β, which shows that $\bigtriangledown \alpha_s$ covers $\bigtriangledown \alpha$. Therefore, $(\Delta, \lhd)$ is similar to $(\Delta_0, \lhd_0)$. $\qquad \square$

The above result will be used in Chapter 13 for showing that any epistemic state generated by a prioritized base is constructible using two basic merge operations on epistemic states.

4.1.4 Persistence and flock-generation

Flocks of bases have been introduced in the preceding chapter as a generalization of simple bases that is already invariant with respect to the main belief change operations. Now we will show that flocks provide, in effect, a syntactic representation for the class of persistent epistemic states. As a general preparation, we will show that any persistent epistemic state is similar to a persistent epistemic state that is tree-ordered with respect to preference. Note that, though it will be shown later that any epistemic state is equivalent to a disjoint sum of its linear refinements (which is tree-ordered), this result cannot help us in the present case, since linear refinements do not preserve persistence. Still, there is a relatively simple direct proof of this fact, which is based on a similar proof for Kripke models of intuitionistic logic (see, e.g., [Gab81]).

Lemma 4.1.4. *Any persistent epistemic state is similar to a persistent tree-ordered epistemic state.*

Proof. Let $\mathbb{E}$ be a persistent epistemic state. We will construct a new epistemic state $\mathbb{E}_t$ as follows: admissible states of $\mathbb{E}_t$ will be taken to be finite sequences $\hat{s} = (s_1, \ldots, s_n)$ of admissible states from $\mathbb{E}$ that are ordered with respect to preference: $s_1 \prec \cdots \prec s_n$. The label of each such sequence will coincide with the label of its last element: $l_t(\hat{s}) = l(s_n)$. Finally we put $\hat{s} \prec \hat{t}$ if $\hat{s}$ is an initial segment of $\hat{t}$.

As can be easily seen, $\mathbb{E}_t$ is a persistent and tree-ordered epistemic state. We will show now that it is similar to $\mathbb{E}$.

For any s from $\mathbb{E}$ we will take a one-element sequence (s) as its counterpart in $\mathbb{E}_t$. Assume that $(s) \prec \hat{t}$ in $\mathbb{E}_t$, and t is the last element of $\hat{t}$. Then s is an initial element of $\hat{t}$, and hence $s \prec t$ in $\mathbb{E}$. In addition, we have $l_t(\hat{t}) = l(t)$, and therefore $\Uparrow s$ dominates $\Uparrow(s)$. In the other direction, if $\hat{s}$ is an admissible state of $\mathbb{E}_t$, we will take its last element, say s, as its counterpart in $\mathbb{E}$. Assume that $s \prec t$, and let $\hat{t}$ be a sequence obtained from $\hat{s}$ by adding t as a last element. Then clearly $\hat{s} \prec \hat{t}$ and $l_t(t) = l(t)$. Therefore $\Uparrow\hat{s}$ dominates $\Uparrow s$. This completes the proof. $\qquad\square$

Now let $\mathcal{F}$ be a flock, and $\mathbb{E}_{\mathcal{F}}$ the corresponding epistemic state generated by $\mathcal{F}$. Then we can show the following

Theorem 4.1.4. *Any finitary persistent epistemic state is similar to $\mathbb{E}_{\mathcal{F}}$, for some flock $\mathcal{F}$.*

Proof. Let $\mathbb{E}$ be a finitary persistent epistemic state. As in preceding proofs, we will represent it as a pair $(\Delta, \prec)$, where Δ is a set of propositions representing admissible states of $\mathbb{E}$. Moreover, due to our preceding result, we can assume that $\mathbb{E}$ is tree-ordered. Then, for any admissible state $A \in \Delta$, we will denote by $\Downarrow A$ the set $\{B \in \Delta \mid B \preceq A\}$. Notice that, since $\mathbb{E}$ is tree-ordered and persistent, propositions from $\Downarrow s$ will be totally ordered with respect to logical entailment, and all of them will be consequences of A. Finally, we define a flock $\mathcal{F}$ as a set of all bases of the form $\Downarrow A$, where $A \in \Delta$. We are going to show that $\mathbb{E}$ is similar to $\mathbb{E}_{\mathcal{F}}$.

Let Γ be an admissible state of $\mathbb{E}_{\mathcal{F}}$. Then $\Gamma \subseteq \Downarrow A$, for some $A \in \Delta$, and hence propositions from Γ are linearly ordered by preference. Let B be a most preferred among them. Then, due to persistence, we have $l(B) = \text{Cl}(\Gamma)$, and hence we can choose B as a counterpart of Γ in $\mathbb{E}$. If $B \prec C$, then $\Downarrow C$ is an admissible state in $\mathbb{E}_\mathcal{F}$, $\Gamma \subset \Downarrow C$ and $\text{Cl}(\Downarrow C) = l(C)$. This gives us one direction of similarity.

Now, for any $A \in \Delta$, we will take $\Downarrow A$ as a counterpart in $\mathbb{E}_\mathcal{F}$. Assume that $\Downarrow A \subset \Gamma$, for some admissible state Γ from $\mathbb{E}_\mathcal{F}$. As before, $\Gamma \subseteq \Downarrow B$, for some $B \in \Delta$, and hence propositions from Γ are linearly ordered by preference. Let A_1 be a preferred proposition in this set. Then clearly $A \prec A_1$, and $l(A_1) = \text{Cl}(\Gamma)$ by persistence. This gives us the second condition of similarity and thereby completes the proof. $\square$

Due to the above result, flocks can be seen as an adequate syntactic representation of (finite) persistent epistemic states. We will return to this representation in Part Three where flocks will be used as a syntactic framework for representing belief changes in persistent epistemic states.

As we have seen, flocks do not admit replacement of logical equivalents. As a result, our interpretation of flocks invalidates a sufficient condition of equivalence for flocks stated in [FUKV86, Theorem 8], according to which two flocks are equivalent if every base from the first flock is basically equivalent to some base from the second flock and vice versa. An exact description of possible transformations of flocks that preserve equivalence of associated epistemic states remains an open problem.

4.2 Decomposition of epistemic states

In this section we describe an important notion of decomposition of epistemic states into a set of epistemic states. This decomposition will serve as a basis of some representation results that will be proved later.

The notion of a sum of a set of structures constitutes one of the powerful tools in many areas of mathematics. As we will see, it turns out to be useful also in analyzing epistemic states. Actually, this operation will be adopted in Part Three as one of the main belief change operations on epistemic states.

Definition 4.2.1. A disjoint sum *of a set of epistemic states* $\mathfrak{E} = \{\mathbb{E}_i \mid i \in I\}$ *is an epistemic state, denoted by* $\sum \mathfrak{E}$, *that is defined as follows:*

- *Admissible states of* $\sum \mathfrak{E}$ *are pairs* (s, i) *such that s is an admissible state in* $\mathbb{E}_i$;
- $l((s, i)) = l_i(s)$, *where l_i is a labelling function of* $\mathbb{E}_i$;
- $(s, i) \prec (t, j)$ *iff $i = j$ and $s \prec t$ in* $\mathbb{E}_i$.

As can be seen from the above description, a disjoint sum of epistemic states is obtained, in effect, by combining all their admissible states, together with the associated preferences. The new description of such admissible states as pairs (s, i) is purported to keep admissible states from distinct epistemic states separate, even if they are equal (hence the name disjoint sum). In this way all constellations of admissible states occurring in the component epistemic states are preserved in the resulting epistemic state.

A set of epistemic states $\mathfrak{E}$ will be called a *decomposition* of an epistemic state $\mathbb{E}$ if $\mathbb{E}$ is similar to $\sum \mathfrak{E}$. In this case we will also say that $\mathbb{E}$ is *similar to the set* $\mathfrak{E}$. As we will see in what follows, such a decomposition will generate a corresponding decomposition of the inference relations associated with an epistemic state.

Notice that even if all epistemic states in $\mathfrak{E}$ are standard, their disjoint sum will not in general be standard, since different epistemic states in $\mathfrak{E}$ may contain equal admissible belief states. In this way, for example, a set of standard epistemic states that represents potential variants of preference ordering on the same set of theories generates a non-standard epistemic state that could directly reflect the indetermination.

The adequacy of this understanding of non-standard epistemic states will be confirmed later by showing that any epistemic state can be decomposed into a set of standard epistemic states. To begin with, we are going to show now that any general epistemic state is decomposable into a set of linear epistemic states. To this end, we will have to make some preparations.

Definition 4.2.2. *An epistemic state $\langle S, \prec, l \rangle$ will be said to be a* refinement *of an epistemic state $\langle S, \prec_0, l \rangle$ if $\prec_0 \subseteq \prec$.*

A refinement of an epistemic state is obtained by extending its preference relation without changing admissible belief states and the labelling function. As a first auxiliary result, we will show that any finitely smooth epistemic state has a linear refinement that is also finitely smooth.

Lemma 4.2.1. *Any finitely smooth epistemic state can be refined to a linear finitely smooth epistemic state.*

Proof. As is well known, any partial order can be extended to a linear (connected) order. Our construction will use this fact, but will also take into account the necessity of preserving smoothness.

Let us assume that $a_1, a_2, \ldots, a_n, \ldots$ is some fixed ordering of all finite sets of propositions (since this set is countable, such an ordering can always be construed). Starting with the source epistemic state $\mathbb{E}$, we will construct a sequence of epistemic states $\{\mathbb{E}_n\}$ as follows. If $\mathbb{E}_{n-1}$ is already given, and $]a_n[$ is empty in $\mathbb{E}$, then we take $\mathbb{E}_n$ to be equal to $\mathbb{E}_{n-1}$. Otherwise we choose an arbitrary preferred state s in $]a_n[$ (which should exist by smoothness) and subordinate to s all admissible states that are not preferred to s; it can be easily checked that the resulting preference relation $\prec^s$ can be defined as follows:

$$r \prec^s t \equiv r \prec t \text{ or } (s \not\preceq r \text{ and } s \preceq t).$$

Notice that, on each step, we refine the preference order without changing the set of admissible belief states. It can also be easily verified that the above refinement preserves finite smoothness. In addition, for any a_k, the epistemic state $\mathbb{E}_k$ will already have a unique preferred state in $]a_k[$. Consequently, this admissible state will also be preferred to all other admissible states in $]A_k[$ in any possible refinement of $\mathbb{E}_k$. This means also that any subsequent refinement of the preference order will preserve the smoothness of $]a_k[$.

Consider now an epistemic state $\mathbb{E}_+$ with the preference order equal to the union of all preference orders from $\{\mathbb{E}_n\}$. In view of what has been said earlier, the new preference order will be finitely smooth; moreover, $\mathbb{E}_+$ will be a refinement of $\mathbb{E}$.

As a final step, we will extend the preference order of $\mathbb{E}_+$ to an arbitrary linear order. Let us denote the resulting linear epistemic state by $\mathbb{E}^l$. Our previous considerations imply that this linear order will also be finitely smooth. Consequently, $\mathbb{E}^l$ will be a linear finitely smooth refinement of $\mathbb{E}$. This completes the proof. $\square$

The above result has the following corollary that will be actually used in the proof of the main theorem.

Corollary 4.2.1. *If s is an admissible state of a finitely smooth epistemic state $\mathbb{E}$, then there exists a linear finitely smooth refinement $\mathbb{E}_l$ of $\mathbb{E}$ such that the set of admissible states preferred to s in $\mathbb{E}$ coincides with the set of admissible states preferred to s in $\mathbb{E}_l$.*

Proof. As a first step, we will refine $\mathbb{E}$ to an epistemic state $\mathbb{E}_s$ by subordinating to s all admissible states that are not preferred to s in $\mathbb{E}$. As we already mentioned in the preceding proof, this transformation preserves smoothness. Clearly, for any admissible state t, $s \prec t$ in $\mathbb{E}_s$ if and only if $s \prec t$ in $\mathbb{E}$. Furthermore, the relations of s to other admissible states in $\mathbb{E}_s$ are completely determined: for any admissible state t, we have that either $s \prec t$, or $t \prec s$. Consequently, any refinement of $\mathbb{E}_s$ cannot change the set of admissible states that are preferred to s in $\mathbb{E}_s$. Therefore, if we refine $\mathbb{E}_s$ to some finitely smooth linear epistemic state $\mathbb{E}_l$, we will obtain that the set of admissible states preferred to s in $\mathbb{E}$ coincides with the set of admissible states preferred to s in $\mathbb{E}_l$. $\square$

Now we are ready to prove our main result in this section.

Theorem 4.2.1. *Any finitely smooth epistemic state is similar to the set of its finitely smooth linear refinements.*

Proof. Let $\mathbb{E} = \langle \mathcal{S}, \prec, l \rangle$ be a finitely smooth epistemic state, and $\mathfrak{E}$ the set of all finitely smooth linear epistemic states that are refinements of $\mathbb{E}$. We have to show that $\mathbb{E}$ is similar to the disjoint union $\sum \mathfrak{E}$.

If s is an admissible state in $\mathbb{E}$, then the preceding corollary implies that there exists a linear refinement $\mathbb{E}_i$ in $\mathfrak{E}$ such that the set of admissible states preferred to s in $\mathbb{E}$ coincides with the set of admissible states preferred to s in $\mathbb{E}_i$. As a result, $\Uparrow s$ coincides with $\Uparrow(s, i)$ in $\sum \mathfrak{E}$.

In the other direction, since each $\mathbb{E}_i$ in $\mathfrak{E}$ is a refinement of $\mathbb{E}$, we always have that $\Uparrow s$ in $\mathbb{E}$ is included in $\Uparrow s$ in $\mathbb{E}_i$. By the construction of the disjoint union we have then that each (s, i) is equal to s and $\Uparrow(s, i)$ includes $\Uparrow s$. This completes the proof. $\square$

The above result will imply, in effect, that any general epistemic state can be replaced in all its functions by a certain set of linear epistemic states. Furthermore, in what follows we will refine this result to the claim that any epistemic state can be modeled in this sense by a set of linear epistemic states that are standard and monotonic.

As a first application of the above decomposition result, we will show that any prioritized Δ-based epistemic state is similar to a set of prioritized Δ-based epistemic states generated by all linear refinements of the underlying priority relation. To avoid complications, we will show this result only for finite Δ.

Theorem 4.2.2. *The epistemic state generated by a finite prioritized base $(\Delta, \lhd)$ is similar to the set of linear epistemic states generated by prioritized bases $(\Delta, \lhd_i)$, where $\lhd_i$ is a linear refinement of $\lhd$.*

Proof. (A sketch) We can adapt the proof given for Theorem 4.2.1, provided that we modify the proofs of Lemma 4.2.1 and its corollary by showing that the refinement obtained by subordinating to s all admissible states that are not preferred to s can be obtained by refining the underlying priority relation. Since Δ was assumed to be finite, this can be easily achieved by a number of application of Theorem 3.4.2 from Chapter 3. Moreover, due to the finiteness of Δ, we do not have to worry about smoothness, so we can refine any given priority order right away to an arbitrary linear priority order. Clearly, the epistemic state generated by the latter will be a linear refinement of the source Δ-based epistemic state. $\square$

The above result shows that the properties of prioritized base-generated epistemic states can be analyzed by using linear refinements of the source priority relation. For example, we have a very natural procedure of finding preferred sets of defaults suggested in a number of works (see, e.g., [Bre91b])

Notice first that in a finite case a linear refinement of a priority relation is simply an *enumeration* of defaults that respects the priority order. Accordingly, the above result shows that all preferred sets of defaults that are consistent with A can be obtained as follows:

Let $\delta_1, \delta_2, \ldots, \delta_n$ be an enumeration of Δ that respects the priority relation. Define the following sequence of default sets: $\Gamma_0 = \emptyset$, and for $0 \le i < n$,

$$\Gamma_{i+1} = \begin{cases} \Gamma_i \cup \{\delta_i\} & \text{if } \Gamma_i \cup \{\delta_i\} \text{ is consistent with } A, \\ \Gamma_i & \text{otherwise.} \end{cases}$$

Then Γ_n is a preferred set of defaults consistent with A.

The justification of the above procedure is based on the fact that, for any preferred set of defaults consistent with A there exists a linear refinement of the priority relation that makes it a unique preferred set consistent with A.

4.3 Normal similarity

An epistemic state may contain 'idle' admissible states that cannot become preferred states for any set of propositions. Such admissible states can be safely eliminated from an epistemic state without changing the behavior of the latter in nonmonotonic inference and belief change. This motivates the constructions described below.

Definition 4.3.1. *An admissible state s will be said to be* normal *in $\mathbb{E}$, if there is no admissible state t in $\mathbb{E}$ such that $s \prec t$ and $l(t) \subseteq l(s)$.*

As we will see in due course, in order to account for dynamic features of epistemic states, we can restrict our attention to admissible states that are preferred in at least one set $]w[$. The following lemma shows that such states are precisely normal admissible states.

Lemma 4.3.1. *1. An admissible state is normal if and only if it is a preferred state in some set $]w[$.*
2. An epistemic state is weakly monotonic if and only if all its admissible states are normal.

Proof. If s is a preferred state in $]w[$, then $l(s)$ is disjoint from w, though any admissible state preferred to s will support at least one proposition from w. Consequently, if $s \prec t$, then $l(t) \not\subseteq l(s)$, and therefore s is a normal admissible state. Conversely, if s is a normal admissible state, then it will be a preferred state in $]\overline{l(s)}[$, where $\overline{l(s)}$ is a complement of $l(s)$. Indeed, $]\overline{l(s)}[$ contains precisely all admissible states r such that $l(r) \subseteq l(s)$. Consequently, $s \in]\overline{l(s)}[$, though for any t such that $s \prec t$ we have $t \notin]\overline{l(s)}[$, since $l(t) \not\subseteq l(s)$.

The second claim above is immediate from the definition of weak monotonicity. $\qquad\square$

It is instructive for what follows to describe the above notion of normality when applied to base-generated epistemic states.

Definition 4.3.2. *A subset Γ of the set of defaults Δ will be said to be* closed *in Δ if $\Gamma = \text{Cl}(\Gamma) \cap \Delta$.*

It turns out that closed subsets of Δ exactly correspond to normal admissible states of the associated epistemic state $\mathbb{E}_\Delta$.

Lemma 4.3.2. *A set Γ is closed in a finite set of defaults Δ if and only if it is a normal admissible state in $\mathbb{E}_\Delta$.*

Proof. It can be verified that Γ is a normal admissible state in $\mathbb{E}_\Delta$ if and only if it does not imply any default from $\Delta \setminus \Gamma$, which is clearly equivalent to the closedness of Γ in Δ. $\square$

If we consider arbitrary base-generated epistemic states, then not all closed sets of defaults will correspond to normal admissible states. Still, due to monotonicity, any set of defaults that is preferred in some set $]w[$ will be closed.

For any set of defaults Γ there exists a least closed set containing Γ, namely, the set $\Gamma^c = \mathrm{Cl}(\Gamma) \cap \Delta$. Notice that $\mathrm{Cl}(\Gamma) = \mathrm{Cl}(\Gamma^c)$, so the two sets of defaults correspond to equal admissible states in $\mathbb{E}_\Delta$. This observation is generalized to the following result.

Lemma 4.3.3. *For any admissible state s of an m-smooth epistemic state there exists a normal admissible state t such that $s \preceq t$ and $l(t) \subseteq l(s)$.*

Proof. If s is an admissible state of $\mathbb{E}$, then it belongs to the set $]\overline{l(s)}[$. By m-smoothness, there must exist a preferred state t in $]\overline{l(s)}[$ such that $s \preceq t$. Clearly, $l(t) \subseteq l(s)$. Moreover, t is normal by Lemma 4.3.1. $\square$

As we said, non-normal admissible states do not influence the generated inference relations or a dynamic behavior of an epistemic state. Therefore, they can be safely eliminated. This motivates the construction below.

Definition 4.3.3. *A normal reduction of an epistemic state $\mathbb{E}$ (denoted by $\mathbb{E}^n$) is an epistemic state obtained by a restriction of $\mathbb{E}$ to its normal admissible states.*

As can be easily checked, a normal reduction of an epistemic state will contain only normal admissible states. In other words, $\mathbb{E}^n$ will always be a weakly monotonic epistemic state.

The above observations suggest that in checking whether two epistemic states are 'the same' we can restrict our attention only to their normal admissible states. In other words, we can check the similarity among normal reductions of these epistemic states. This is reflected in the following definition.

Definition 4.3.4. *Two epistemic states $\mathbb{E}_1$ and $\mathbb{E}_2$ will be called normally similar, if $\mathbb{E}_1^n$ is similar to $\mathbb{E}_2^n$.*

The following lemma gives a more direct (and eventually more convenient) description of normal similarity.

Lemma 4.3.4. $\mathbb{E}_1$ *and* $\mathbb{E}_2$ *are normally similar iff they satisfy the following two conditions:*

- $(\forall$ *normal* $s_1 \in \mathbb{E}_1)(\exists s_2 \in \mathbb{E}_2)(s_1 \overset{\circ}{=} s_2 \wedge \Uparrow s_1 \ll \Uparrow s_2);$
- $(\forall$ *normal* $s_2 \in \mathbb{E}_2)(\exists s_1 \in \mathbb{E}_1)(s_1 \overset{\circ}{=} s_2 \wedge \Uparrow s_2 \ll \Uparrow s_1).$

Proof. Assume first that the above conditions hold, and let s_1 be a normal admissible state in $\mathbb{E}_1$. Then there exists an equal admissible state s_2 in $\mathbb{E}_2$ such that $\Uparrow s_1 \ll \Uparrow s_2$. To begin with, we will show that s_2 is normal in $\mathbb{E}_2$. Indeed, assume that there exists t_2 in $\mathbb{E}_2$ such that $s_2 \prec t_2$ and $l(t_2) \subseteq l(s_2)$. Since $\Uparrow s_1$ dominates $\Uparrow s_2$, we have that there must exist t_1 in $\mathbb{E}_1$ such that $s_1 \prec t_1$ and $l(t_1) \subseteq l(t_2)$. But then $l(t_1) \subseteq l(s_2) = l(s_1)$, contrary to the normality of s_1. Hence s_2 is normal in $\mathbb{E}_2$.

Let us denote by $\Uparrow^n s$ the restriction of $\Uparrow s$ to normal admissible states. Then we need to show that $\Uparrow^n s_1 \ll \Uparrow^n s_2$.

Assume that t_2 is a normal state in $\mathbb{E}_2$ such that $s_2 \prec t_2$. Then there must exist an admissible state t_1 in $\mathbb{E}_1$ such that $s_1 \prec t_1$ and $l(t_1) \subseteq l(t_2)$. By Lemma 4.3.3, there is a normal admissible state r_1 such that $t_1 \preceq r_1$ and $l(r_1) \subseteq l(t_1)$. But then we have $s_1 \prec r_1$ and $l(r_1) \subseteq l(t_2)$, which show that $\Uparrow^n s_1 \ll \Uparrow^n s_2$. Similar proof can be given for the second condition of normal similarity. Consequently, $\mathbb{E}_1$ and $\mathbb{E}_2$ are normally similar.

Assume now that $\mathbb{E}_1$ and $\mathbb{E}_2$ are normally similar, and let s_1 be a normal state in $\mathbb{E}_1$. Then there exists an equal admissible state s_2 in $\mathbb{E}_2$ such that $\Uparrow^n s_1 \ll \Uparrow^n s_2$. To prove the claim, it is sufficient to show that $\Uparrow s_1 \ll \Uparrow s_2$.

Let t_2 be an admissible state in $\mathbb{E}_2$ such that $s_2 \prec t_2$. If t_2 is normal, then we are done. So, assume that t_2 is not normal. Then, by Lemma 4.3.3, there is a normal admissible state r_2 such that $t_2 \preceq r_2$ and $l(r_2) \subseteq l(t_2)$. But then $s_2 \prec r_2$, so there exists r_1 in $\mathbb{E}_1$ such that $s_1 \prec r_1$ and $l(r_1) \subseteq l(r_2)$. Consequently, $l(r_1) \subseteq l(t_2)$, which shows that $\Uparrow s_1 \ll \Uparrow s_2$. This completes the proof. $\qquad\square$

The above result shows that normal similarity amounts to restricting the similarity check to normal admissible states. An immediate consequence of this result is that similarity implies normal similarity.

Corollary 4.3.1. *Similar epistemic states are also normally similar.*

As a direct consequence of the definition of normal similarity, we obtain also the following important result.

Lemma 4.3.5. *Any epistemic state is normally similar to its normal reduction.*

The above observation has a number of useful consequences. To begin with, since the normal reduction is weakly monotonic, we immediately obtain

Corollary 4.3.2. *Any epistemic state is normally similar to a weakly monotonic epistemic state.*

Note that if an epistemic state is standard and monotonic, then it will also be weakly monotonic. Moreover, our next result shows that any linear epistemic state is normally similar to a linear epistemic state which is both standard and monotonic.

Theorem 4.3.1. *Any linear epistemic state is normally similar to some linear epistemic state, which is monotonic and standard.*

Proof. In order to prove the above claim, it is sufficient to show that the normal reduction $\mathbb{E}^n$ of a linear epistemic state $\mathbb{E}$ is both standard and monotonic.

Assume that $l(s) \subset l(t)$, for two admissible states from $\mathbb{E}^n$. Since $\mathbb{E}$ is linear, we have that either $s \prec t$, or $t \prec s$. But in the second case we would obtain that $\mathbb{E}^n$ is not normal. Therefore, $s \prec t$, and hence $\mathbb{E}^n$ is monotonic.

Assume now that $l(s) = l(t)$, for two admissible states from $\mathbb{E}^n$. By the normality condition, s and t should be incomparable with respect to preference, so we conclude $s = t$ by linearity. Thus, $\mathbb{E}^n$ is standard. $\qquad\square$

The above result shows that in the linear case we can safely restrict our attention to epistemic states that are both standard and monotonic.

Replacing normal similarity for similarity in the definition of the decomposition of epistemic states, we obtain the notion of a *normal decomposition*. In this case will say also that an epistemic state in *normally similar to a set* of epistemic states. Then the preceding result will imply the following important

Corollary 4.3.3. *Any finitely smooth epistemic state is normally similar to a set of linear standard and monotonic epistemic states.*

Proof. As can be easily verified, disjoint sums preserve normal similarity in the sense that if we replace one of the component epistemic states by another epistemic state that is normally similar to it, then the new disjoint sum will also be normally similar to the source one. $\qquad\square$

The above result justifies our earlier claim that any general epistemic state is reducible, in effect, to a set of standard and monotonic epistemic states. Note that only a few quite regular kinds of epistemic states are normally similar to monotonic states. Thus, the following example describes a simple epistemic state with a modular preference relation that is not reducible to any monotonic epistemic state.

Example 4.3.1. Let us consider a standard epistemic state $\mathbb{E}$ consisting of two theories $\{u, v\}$ such that $u \subset v$, and an empty preference relation. This epistemic state is (trivially) modular. Notice also that if both u and v belong to $]A[$, then they both are preferred in $]A[$. Clearly, no maximizing epistemic state can produce this result. Consequently, no monotonic epistemic state can even be equivalent to $\mathbb{E}$ (see below). Moreover, no monotonic linear refinement of $\mathbb{E}$ can contain u as a preferred state in $]A[$. Consequently, the above decomposition cannot be achieved without removing u in some refinements.

Standard reduction of base-generated epistemic states. In addition to linear epistemic states, there is yet another broad class of general epistemic states that are reducible to standard states, namely, the class of base-generated epistemic states. As we have seen, all such epistemic states are union-closed. The following theorem shows that any union-closed epistemic state is reducible to a standard monotonic epistemic state.

Theorem 4.3.2. *Any union-closed epistemic state is normally similar to a standard monotonic epistemic state.*

Proof. Let $\mathbb{E}$ be a union-closed general epistemic state, and $\mathbb{E}^n$ its normal reduction. We are going to show that $\mathbb{E}^n$ is both standard and monotonic.

Suppose that $\mathbb{E}^n$ is not standard, and hence we have two distinct normal admissible states s, t in $\mathbb{E}^n$ such that $l(s) = l(t)$. By union-closure there must exist an admissible state r in $\mathbb{E}$ such that $l(r) = l(s) = l(t)$ and $s, t \preceq r$. Since r is distinct from either s or t, we have that either $s \prec r$, or $t \prec r$. But if $s \prec r$, then s is not normal in $\mathbb{E}$; similarly, if $t \prec r$, then t is not normal. This contradiction shows that $\mathbb{E}^n$ is a standard epistemic state. Furthermore, suppose this time that $l(s) \subset l(t)$ for two admissible states in $\mathbb{E}^n$. Then, by union-closure, there must exist an admissible state r in $\mathbb{E}$ such that $l(r) = l(t)$ and $s, t \preceq r$. Clearly, $s \prec r$. Also, if it were the case that $t \prec r$, then t would not be normal. Consequently, $r = t$, and therefore $s \prec t$. Thus, $\mathbb{E}^n$ is also a monotonic epistemic state. This completes the proof. $\square$

It should be mentioned that, though the reduction of a union-closed epistemic state is standard and monotonic, it need not be union-closed. In fact, we will see in Chapter 7 that the restriction to epistemic states that are standard, monotonic and union-closed reduces also the class of generated inference relations.

As can be seen from the above proof, the standard and monotonic reduction of an epistemic state can be obtained for any epistemic state that satisfies the following slight strengthening of semi-monotonicity:

Strict semi-monotonicity If $l(s) \subseteq l(t)$, then there exists an admissible state r equal to t such that $s, t \preceq r$.

The above condition is a consequence of union-closure that was actually used in the proof.

4.4 Language-restricted epistemic states

As has been said in Chapter 3, yet another natural way of understanding non-standard epistemic states consists in the assumption that such states involve information that is not expressible in the current language. We consider now this possibility in more details.

Recall that epistemic states are language-relative objects. Assume now that a language $\mathcal{L}$ is a sub-language of another propositional language $\mathcal{L}_0$, and let $\mathbb{E}$ be some standard epistemic state in $\mathcal{L}_0$. This epistemic state naturally generates a certain epistemic state in the restricted language $\mathcal{L}$. This 'reduced' epistemic state may already be non-standard, since different theories in $\mathcal{L}_0$ might correspond to the same theory in $\mathcal{L}$. Notice that the language-restricted epistemic state will produce nonmonotonic inference relations that are exactly language restrictions of the corresponding 'standard' inference relations in the language $\mathcal{L}_0$. Moreover, it might well happen that these latter, language-restricted inference relations are not representable by any standard epistemic state *in* $\mathcal{L}$.

It seems completely unreasonable to exclude the above 'partial' inference relations from consideration: they can be seen as giving a language-restricted description of some perfectly legitimate inference relations on standard epistemic states. Hence we have to live with the possibility that some quite natural inference relations are not representable by standard epistemic states *in the same language*, and hence we must admit non-standard epistemic states.

It turns out that the above construction of general epistemic states from standard ones is quite general. Namely, we are going to show now that any general epistemic state can be considered as a language-restriction of some standard and monotonic epistemic state.

In what follows, we will use some facts about *eliminants* of classical propositional formulas (see [Bro90]).

Let $\mathcal{L}$ be a classical propositional language and $\mathcal{L}_0$ its restriction obtained by eliminating some propositional atoms from $\mathcal{L}$. Then, for any propositional formula A in $\mathcal{L}$ there exists a formula A_e in $\mathcal{L}_0$, called an *eliminant* of A, that satisfies the following property with respect to $\mathcal{L}$:

For any formula B_0 in $\mathcal{L}_0$, $A \vDash B_0$ iff $A_e \vDash B_0$.

In fact, an eliminant of a propositional formula A can be obtained by iterating the following procedure of eliminating propositional atoms: for any propositional atom p, we replace A with the formula $A_\mathbf{t}^p \vee A_\mathbf{f}^p$, where $A_\mathbf{t}^p$ ($A_\mathbf{f}^p$) is obtained from A by substituting all occurrences of p with $\mathbf{t}$ (respectively, $\mathbf{f}$).

In the proof of the theorem below we will use the notion dual to eliminant. Namely, for any formula A from $\mathcal{L}$, we will consider its $\mathcal{L}_0$-*closure* A_c defined as $\neg(\neg A)_e$. In other words, the closure of A is defined as a negation of the eliminant of $\neg A$. As can be easily shown on the basis of the above property of eliminants, closure satisfies the following property with respect to $\mathcal{L}$:

For any formula B_0 in $\mathcal{L}_0$, $B_0 \vDash A$ iff $B_0 \vDash A_c$.

Now we are ready to prove the following

Theorem 4.4.1. *For any finitely smooth general epistemic state $\mathbb{E}$ in a language $\mathcal{L}$ there exists a finitely smooth standard monotonic epistemic state $\mathbb{E}_0$*

in some language $\mathcal{L}_0$ extending $\mathcal{L}$ such that its restriction to $\mathcal{L}$ is normally similar to $\mathbb{E}$.

Proof. Let $\{\mathbb{E}_i\}$ be a normal decomposition of an epistemic state $\mathbb{E}$ into a set of finitely smooth standard monotonic and linear states. For each such component state $\mathbb{E}_i$, we will introduce a new propositional atom p_i into the language. Then we consider a standard epistemic state in this new language $\mathcal{L}^+$ consisting of all theories of the form $\mathrm{Cl}(u, p_i)$, where u belongs to $\mathbb{E}_i$. These theories will be ordered as follows:

$$\mathrm{Cl}(u, p_i) \prec^+ \mathrm{Cl}(v, p_j) \text{ if and only if } i = j \text{ and } u \prec v \text{ in } \mathbb{E}_i.$$

Let us denote the resulting epistemic state by $\mathbb{E}^+$. It is easy to check that $\prec^+$ is a strict partial order. Moreover, it is monotonic. Indeed, if $\mathrm{Cl}(u, p_i) \subset \mathrm{Cl}(v, p_j)$, then clearly p_i coincides with p_j (since these are the only 'new' atoms in such theories) and $u \subset v$. Due to monotonicity of $\mathbb{E}_i$, we have $u \prec v$ in $\mathbb{E}_i$, and hence $\mathrm{Cl}(u, p_i) \prec^+ \mathrm{Cl}(v, p_j)$ by the definition of $\prec^+$. So, $\prec^+$ is a monotonic preference order.

Now we will show that $\prec^+$ is a finitely smooth order. Assume first that $A \notin \mathrm{Cl}(u, p_i)$, where A is a propositional formula in $\mathcal{L}^+$ and u is a theory from $\mathbb{E}_i$. The later condition is equivalent to $u \nvDash p_i \rightarrow A$. Let A^c denote the closure of $p_i \rightarrow A$ in $\mathcal{L}$. Then by the above mentioned characteristic property of closures we have that, for any theory v from $\mathbb{E}_i$, $A \notin \mathrm{Cl}(v, p_i)$ if and only if $A^c \notin v$.

Now assume that $\mathrm{Cl}(u, p_i)$ belongs to $]w[$, for some finite set w from $\mathcal{L}^+$. Let us denote by w^c the set of all A^c, for $A \in w$. Since $\mathbb{E}_i$ is a finitely smooth epistemic state, it follows that $u \preceq v$, for some theory v from $\mathbb{E}_i$ that is preferred in $]w^c[$. The above observation implies then that $\mathrm{Cl}(v, p_i)$ is a preferred theory in $]w[$ with respect to $\mathbb{E}^+$. Moreover, if $u \neq v$, then we have $\mathrm{Cl}(u, p_i) \prec^+ \mathrm{Cl}(v, p_i)$. This shows that $\mathbb{E}^+$ is a smooth epistemic state.

Finally, let us assume that $A_0 \notin \mathrm{Cl}(u, p_i)$, where A_0 is a proposition of the source language $\mathcal{L}$. It can be easily shown that the closure of $p_i \rightarrow A_0$ with respect to $\mathcal{L}$ coincides with A_0 (the reader can obtain this fact from the construction of eliminants given above). It follows immediately that $A_0 \notin \mathrm{Cl}(u, p_i)$ if and only if $A_0 \notin u$. Combined with the assumption that the set of epistemic states $\{\mathbb{E}_j\}$ provides a decomposition of $\mathbb{E}$, this immediately gives us that the restriction of $\mathbb{E}^+$ to $\mathcal{L}$ is normally similar to $\mathbb{E}$. $\qquad\square$

Thus, any general epistemic state can be seen as a standard and monotonic epistemic state "in disguise". Similarly, the next result shows that persistent epistemic states can be seen as language-restricted pure epistemic states. The corresponding assertion will be proved, however, only for finite epistemic states; this will be sufficient for our present purposes.

Theorem 4.4.2. *For any finite persistent epistemic state $\mathbb{E}$ in a language $\mathcal{L}$ there exists a pure epistemic state $\mathcal{E}$ in some language $\mathcal{L}_0$ extending $\mathcal{L}$ such that the restriction of $\mathcal{E}$ to $\mathcal{L}$ coincides with $\mathbb{E}$.*

Proof. Note first that the construction in the proof of the preceding theorem cannot be directly applied to the present case, since refinements of epistemic states do not preserve persistence. Still, a relatively simple direct proof can be given in the finite case (mainly to avoid questions of smoothness).

Given a finite persistent epistemic state $\mathbb{E}$, we will extend the language $\mathcal{L}$ to a language $\mathcal{L}_0$ by adding new propositional atom s, for every admissible state s in $\mathbb{E}$. $\overleftarrow{s}$ will denote the set of such propositional atoms corresponding to all admissible states t such that $t \preceq s$. Then we consider a pure epistemic state $\mathcal{E}$ in $\mathcal{L}_0$ consisting of theories of the form $\mathrm{Cl}(\overleftarrow{s} \cup l(s))$, for each admissible state s.

To begin with, note that the restriction of a theory $\mathrm{Cl}(\overleftarrow{s} \cup l(s))$ to the language $\mathcal{L}$ coincides with $l(s)$. In addition, we will show that $\mathrm{Cl}(\overleftarrow{s} \cup l(s)) \subset \mathrm{Cl}(\overleftarrow{t} \cup l(t))$ holds if and only if $s \prec t$. Indeed, if $s \prec t$, then $l(s) \subseteq l(t)$ by persistence, and $\overleftarrow{s} \subset \overleftarrow{t}$ by transitivity of the preference relation. Consequently, $\mathrm{Cl}(\overleftarrow{s} \cup l(s)) \subset \mathrm{Cl}(\overleftarrow{t} \cup l(t))$. In the other direction, assume that the latter inclusion holds. Then, in particular, the propositional atom s is a logical consequence of $\overleftarrow{t} \cup l(t)$ in $\mathcal{L}_0$, which is possible only if it belongs to $\overleftarrow{t}$. Therefore $s \preceq t$ in $\mathbb{E}$. But since the above inclusion is proper, we have that s is distinct from t, and hence $s \prec t$.

Due to the above observations, it is easy to see that the restriction of $\mathcal{E}$ to $\mathcal{L}$ gives an epistemic state that is isomorphic to $\mathbb{E}$. $\square$

The above results will be exploited below in showing that standardness and monotonicity are somewhat elusive properties that do not admit a simple characterization by syntactic means. As we will see, none of the nonmonotonic inference relations definable on epistemic states allows a characterization of these properties of epistemic states by means of ordinary inference rules.

4.5 Equivalence

In this section we will introduce an entirely different way of describing epistemic states, which is based on using selection functions.

As we said in the preceding chapter, the use of epistemic states for supporting beliefs and conditional conclusions amounts to a two-step procedure. First, in any given factual situation, we consider the set of all admissible belief states that are consistent with the facts. Second, we choose preferred elements in this set. Though at this point there are several different options how to proceed, in all cases the set of theories corresponding to chosen admissible belief states provides all the necessary information for making plausible conclusions.

As can be seen from the above description, the functional role of an epistemic state in supporting nonmonotonic inference is wholly determined by the function that takes as an input some proposition A and outputs the set of admissible belief sets corresponding to preferred belief states in $]A[$ (in the case of skeptical and credulous inference, we consider sets of the form $]\neg F[$).

It should be kept in mind that the above function provides only a static 'snapshot' of an epistemic state that does not characterize the dynamic behavior of the latter. It turns out, however, that the dynamic behavior of an epistemic state is captured by considering an extension of this function to a function that takes *sets* of propositions as arguments and returns preferred admissible belief sets that are disjoint from such sets. This extended function will determine both the inference relations associated with the epistemic state, and its dynamic behavior in belief change.

Definition 4.5.1. *A selection function associated with an epistemic state* $\mathbb{E}$ *is a function* $f_{\mathbb{E}}$ *assigning every set of propositions* w *a set of theories corresponding to preferred admissible states in* $]w[$:

$$f_{\mathbb{E}}(w) = \{l(s) \mid s \text{ is a preferred admissible state in }]w[\}$$

Note 4.5.1. In fact, the above defined selection function can be reformulated as a special case of a *choice function* on the set of admissible belief sets. More exactly, it can be identified with a function assigning to each set of admissible belief sets its subset corresponding to preferred belief states. Choice functions have proved their usefulness in studying both nonmonotonic reasoning and belief change – see, e.g., [Rot93, Sch97, Leh98]. Moreover, despite the fact that our selection functions are defined on theories instead of possible worlds, they have much the same properties as that investigated in the literature. The study of such functions, however, is beyond the objectives of the present study.

Note that the selection function determines not only corresponding inference relations (see below), but also both the belief and knowledge sets of an epistemic state: the former is definable as $\bigcap f_{\mathbb{E}}(\emptyset)$, while the latter as $\{A \mid f_{\mathbb{E}}(A) = \emptyset\}$.

Since the selection function will determine the essential properties of epistemic states, it is only natural to introduce the following

Definition 4.5.2. *Two epistemic states will be called* equivalent *(notation* $\mathbb{E}_1 \approx \mathbb{E}_2$ *) if they determine the same selection function.*

As will be shown in Part Three, equivalent epistemic state will remain equivalent under practically all 'legitimate' changes of epistemic states. Consequently, they will be indistinguishable for the purposes of this book.

It turns out that there exists an intimate connection between the above notion of equivalence and the notion of (normal) similarity introduced earlier. The results that follow clarify this connection.

To begin with, we will show that normally similar epistemic states are equivalent in the above sense.

Theorem 4.5.1. *Normally similar epistemic states are equivalent.*

Proof. Assume that $u \in f_{\mathbb{E}_1}(w)$. Then there exists an admissible state s_1 in $\mathbb{E}_1$ which is preferred in $]w[$ and such that $u = l(s_1)$. Since s_1 is normal in $\mathbb{E}_1$, there must exist an equal state s_2 in $\mathbb{E}_2$ such that $\Uparrow s_1$ in $\mathbb{E}_1$ dominates $\Uparrow s_2$ in $\mathbb{E}_2$. We will show that s_2 is a preferred state in $]w[$ with respect to $\mathbb{E}_2$. Indeed, assume that there exists $t_2 \in]w[$ such that $s_2 \prec t_2$. Consequently, there must exist t_1 in $\mathbb{E}_1$ such that $s_1 \prec t_1$ and $l(t_1) \subseteq l(t_2)$. But then $t_1 \in]w[$, contrary to our assumption that s_1 is preferred in $]w[$. Thus, s_2 is a preferred state in $]w[$, and consequently $u = l(s_2) \in f_{\mathbb{E}_2}(w)$. This shows that $f_{\mathbb{E}_1}(w) \subseteq f_{\mathbb{E}_2}(w)$. A similar proof can be given for the reverse inclusion. Therefore, $\mathbb{E}_1 \approx \mathbb{E}_2$. $\square$

Combined with the fact that similar epistemic states are normally similar, we immediately obtain that similar epistemic states are also equivalent. In addition, the following result shows that, under some mild constraints, normal similarity is reducible to equivalence.

To begin with, let us say that an admissible belief set of an epistemic state $\mathbb{E}$ is *normal* if it is a label of some normal admissible state in $\mathbb{E}$. Clearly, the set of normal admissible belief sets is precisely the set of theories appearing in the range of the selection function associated with an epistemic state. Actually, it can be easily shown that u is an admissible belief set in $\mathbb{E}$ if and only if $u \in f_{\mathbb{E}}(\bar{u})$. This shows clearly that equivalent epistemic states must have the same normal admissible belief sets. In other words, if $\mathbb{E}_1 \approx \mathbb{E}_2$, then any normal admissible state in $\mathbb{E}_1$ has an equal admissible state in $\mathbb{E}_2$ and vice versa. We will use this observation in the proof below.

A general epistemic state $\mathbb{E}$ will be called *quasi-standard*, if each admissible state of its normal reduction $\mathbb{E}^n$ has no more than a finite number of equal admissible states. Note that the class of quasi-standard epistemic states is quite broad: it includes, for example, all standard epistemic states, as well as all finite epistemic states. In addition, it includes also all linear and union-closed epistemic states.

Theorem 4.5.2. *Two quasi-standard epistemic states are normally similar if and only if they are equivalent.*

Proof. The direction from left to right has been proved earlier. So, let us assume that $\mathbb{E}_1$ and $\mathbb{E}_2$ are equivalent epistemic states that are not normally similar. By symmetry considerations, we can take this as meaning that there is an admissible state s_1 in $\mathbb{E}_1^n$ such that, for any equal admissible state s_2 in $\mathbb{E}_2^n$, $\Uparrow s_1$ does not dominate $\Uparrow s_2$, that is, $\mathbb{E}_2^n$ contains an admissible state t_2 such that $s_2 \prec t_2$, and $l(t_2)$ does not include any admissible set from $\Uparrow s_1$.

Let $\{s_2^1, \ldots, s_2^n\}$ by the set of all admissible states in $\mathbb{E}_2^n$ that are equal to s_1; by quasi-standardness, this set will be finite. In addition, for any s_2^i, we will denote by t_2^i an arbitrarily chosen admissible state satisfying the conditions for t_2 above.

Let us denote by $\mathcal{T}$ the set of sets of propositions of the form $l(t_1)\backslash l(s_1)$, for all t_1 in $\mathbb{E}_1^n$ such that $s_1 \prec t_1$. Assume now that w is an arbitrary *incision set* for $\mathcal{T}$, that is, $w \subseteq \bigcup \mathcal{T}$, and w has a non-empty intersection with every set from $\mathcal{T}$. Clearly, $]w[$ in $\mathbb{E}_1$ will contain s_1, but no admissible state preferred to s_1. Consequently, s_1 will be a preferred admissible state in $]w[$, and hence $l(s_1) \in f_{\mathbb{E}_1}(w)$. Since $\mathbb{E}_1$ and $\mathbb{E}_2$ are equivalent, it follows that one of the admissible states s_2^i in $\mathbb{E}_2^n$ that are equal to s_1 should be a preferred admissible state in $]w[$, which is possible only if one of the admissible states t_2^i does not belong to $]w[$. In other words, w cannot be disjoint from $\bigcup l(t_2^i)$. Now, w has been taken to be an arbitrary incision set in $\mathcal{T}$. Consequently, $\bigcup l(t_2^i)$ must include at least one set $l(t_1)\backslash l(s_1)$ from $\mathcal{T}$ (since otherwise we can construct an incision set that would be disjoint from $\bigcup l(t_2^i)$). Thus, we obtain that, for some t_1 such that $s \prec t_1$, $l(t_1)$ is included in the union of $l(s_1)$ and $\bigcup l(t_2^i)$. Now we can use a known fact from the folklore of classical logic, namely that a deductively closed theory u is included into a union $v_1 \cup \cdots \cup v_n$ of a finite number of theories only if it is included in at least one of them[1]. But $l(t_1) \not\subseteq l(s_1)$, since s_1 is a normal admissible state. Consequently there must exist t_2^i such that $l(t_1) \subseteq l(t_2^i)$, contrary to our assumption that $l(t_2^i)$ does not include any admissible set from $\Uparrow s_1$. The obtained contradiction shows that $\mathbb{E}_1$ and $\mathbb{E}_2$ should be normally similar.   □

Unfortunately, the restriction to quasi-standard epistemic states in the formulation of the above theorem is essential, as is shown by the following example.

Example 4.5.1. Let us consider the following two epistemic states. The state $\mathbb{E}_1$ contains

- admissible states s_i, for all natural $i > 0$, such that $l(s_i) = \mathrm{Cl}(p_i)$;
- admissible states t_i, for all natural $i > 0$, such that $l(t_i) = \mathrm{Cl}(p_0)$;
- a state r such that $l(r)$ is a closure of the set of all propositional atoms p_i, for $i > 0$.

The preference order on these admissible states is defined by: $t_i \prec s_i$, for all $i > 0$.

The state $\mathbb{E}_2$ contains

- admissible states s_i, for all natural $i > 0$, such that $l(s_i) = \mathrm{Cl}(p_i)$;
- an admissible state t such that $l(t) = \mathrm{Cl}(p_0)$;
- a state r such that $l(r)$ is a closure of the set of all propositional atoms p_i, for $i > 0$.

The preference order on these admissible states is defined as $t \prec r$.

It can be easily verified that $\mathbb{E}_1$ and $\mathbb{E}_2$ determine the same selection function, so they are equivalent. Note, however, that $\mathbb{E}_1$ is not quasi-standard,

---

[1] A short proof: if $A_i \in u \setminus v_i$, then the conjunction of all such A_i belongs to u and does not belong to any v_i.

since it contains an infinite number of admissible states labelled with $Cl(p_0)$. Furthermore, $\mathbb{E}_1$ and $\mathbb{E}_2$ are not normally similar, since the state t in $\mathbb{E}_2$ has no counterpart admissible state in $\mathbb{E}_1$ that would satisfy the relevant condition of dominance.

The above example shows that equivalence is a weaker notion, in general, than normal similarity. We will continue our study of these relations in Part Three where we will consider their behavior in belief change.

4.5.1 Static equivalence

As we have said, the nonmonotonic inference relations generated by an epistemic state are wholly determined by the selection function restricted to single propositions as inputs. Such a restricted function will be called a *singular selection function* associated with an epistemic state. It is definable directly as follows:

$$f_{\mathbb{E}}(A) = \{l(s) \mid s \text{ is a preferred admissible state in }]A[\}$$

The definitions for the three main forms of nonmonotonic inference, given in Chapter 3, can be rewritten now as follows:

- $A \vdash B$ holds in $\mathbb{E}$ if and only if $A \to B \in \bigcap f_{\mathbb{E}}(\neg A)$;
- $A \dashv B$ holds in $\mathbb{E}$ if and only if $B \in \bigcap f_{\mathbb{E}}(A)$;
- $A \approx B$ holds in $\mathbb{E}$ if and only if $A \to B \in \bigcup f_{\mathbb{E}}(\neg A)$.

Thus, all three basic kinds of nonmonotonic inference are definable in terms of the singular selection function. It is interesting to note, however, that a singular selection function cannot determine the belief set of an epistemic state; this follows already from the fact that all theories in the range of such a selection function should be consistent. Still, it determines a *refined* belief set, which is definable as $\bigcap f_{\mathbb{E}}(\mathbf{f})$. This subtle discrepancy will reappear in a number of places later in the book.

If epistemic states determine the same selection function, they will be indistinguishable from the point of their role in nonmonotonic inference. We will call such epistemic states statically equivalent.

Definition 4.5.3. *Two epistemic states $\mathbb{E}_1$ and $\mathbb{E}_2$ will be said to be statically equivalent if they determine the same singular selection function.*

As an illustration of the above notion, let us consider pure epistemic states that are generated by consequence relations.

The formalism of Scott consequence relations has been chosen in the book due to its tight correspondence with pure epistemic states. Still, the following result shows that any Scott consequence relation is statically equivalent to its Tarski subrelation.

Lemma 4.5.1. *If* ⊢ *is a Tarski subrelation of a Scott consequence relation* ⊩, *then the pure epistemic state generated by* ⊢ *is statically equivalent to the epistemic state generated by* ⊩.

Proof. It is sufficient to show that, for any A, ⊩ and ⊢ have the same maximal theories that do not include A. Clearly, if u is a maximal theory of ⊩ that does not include A, then it is also a maximal such theory in ⊢. Assume now that u is a maximal theory of ⊢ that does not include A. Since $u \nvdash A$, we have also $u \nVdash A$, and hence there is a maximal theory u_0 of ⊩ that does not include A and such that $u \subseteq u_0$. Since u_0 is also a theory of ⊢, we have that u coincides with u_0. □

Note, however, that, though Scott consequence relations are statically equivalent to Tarski consequence relations, the former will produce different (and more adequate) results after performing contraction operations (see Chapter 12). For example, if ⊩ is generated by two theories $\{\mathrm{Cl}(p), \mathrm{Cl}(q)\}$, then contracting both p and q will give an empty epistemic state (and a trivial consequence relation). But if we will apply the same contractions to ⊢, we will obtain that $p \vee q$ belongs to the resulting belief set; this is due to the fact that theories of a Tarski consequence relation are closed with respect to intersections, and hence $\mathrm{Cl}(p \vee q)$ will also be a theory of ⊢ which will not be eliminated by the two contractions. Notice that this result goes against our intuitions, since $p \vee q$ is a purely derivative belief that was present in the initial belief set solely due to the presence of p and q.

4.5.2 Skeptical equivalence

A common feature of skeptical and contraction inference is that both are based on taking intersections of preferred admissible states. This common feature can be captured by considering the following weakening of the notion of a static equivalence for epistemic states:

Definition 4.5.4. *Two epistemic states* $\mathbb{E}_1$ *and* $\mathbb{E}_2$ *will be called* skeptically equivalent *if, for any proposition* A, $\bigcap f_{\mathbb{E}_1}(A) = \bigcap f_{\mathbb{E}_2}(A)$.

Clearly, statically equivalent epistemic states will also be skeptically equivalent, though not vice versa. It can be easily verified, however, that two epistemic states are skeptically equivalent if and only if they determine the same contraction inference relation. Moreover, since skeptical inference is definable in terms of contraction inference, we obtain that skeptically equivalent epistemic states determine the same skeptical and contraction inference relations; both are definable in terms of intersections of theories in the range of the associated selection function.

Homogeneous epistemic states and possible worlds semantics. We will show now that homogeneous epistemic states are adequate for representing both skeptical and contraction inference. More exactly, we will show that any general epistemic state is skeptically equivalent to a homogeneous epistemic state.

Theorem 4.5.3. *Any general epistemic state is skeptically equivalent to a homogeneous and weakly monotonic epistemic state.*

Proof. Let $\mathbb{E}$ be an arbitrary epistemic state. Due to our previous results, we can assume that it is weakly monotonic. Let $\mathcal{U}$ denote the set of all deductively closed theories that are not admissible belief sets of $\mathbb{E}$, but include its knowledge set $\mathbf{K_E}$. We will consider all such theories as new admissible belief states with identical labels, that is, $l(u) = u$, for any $u \in \mathcal{U}$. The resulting epistemic state will already be homogeneous, so we need only to extend the preference relation in an appropriate way to achieve equivalence and weak monotony. We will do this as follows: for any $u \in \mathcal{U}$ and any proposition A such that $A \notin u$, we will subordinate u to any preferred admissible state s in $]A[$ (with respect to $\mathbb{E}$) such that $l(s) \not\subseteq u$. Finally, we will close the extended preference relation by transitivity in order to obtain a strict partial order. Let us denote the resulting epistemic state by $\mathbb{E}_h$.

To begin with, let us check that the new preference relation is weakly monotonic. Since $\mathbb{E}$ was assumed to be weakly monotonic, we need only to check the new preferences of the form $u \prec t$, where $u \in \mathcal{U}$ and t is an admissible state in $\mathbb{E}$. As can be verified, $u \prec t$ holds in accordance with our construction if and only if there exists an admissible state s in $\mathbb{E}$ such that $s \preceq t$, and u has been subordinated to s because, for some proposition $A \notin u$, s is a preferred state in $]A[$ and $l(s) \not\subseteq u$. Let us suppose now that $l(t) \subseteq u$. Then clearly $s \neq t$, and hence $s \prec t$. But s is a preferred state in $]A[$, and therefore $A \in l(t)$, contrary to our assumption that $l(t)$ is included in u. Thus, $l(t) \not\subseteq u$, which shows that the new preference relation is weakly monotonic.

We will show now that $\mathbb{E}$ and $\mathbb{E}_h$ are skeptically equivalent. If $s \in \mathbb{E}_h$ is an 'old' admissible state, then it is easy to see that it has the same more preferred states in $\mathbb{E}_h$ as it had in $\mathbb{E}$. Consequently, for any A, such a state will be preferred in $]A[$ with respect to $\mathbb{E}_h$ iff it was preferred in $\mathbb{E}$. Let us consider now a new admissible state u from $\mathcal{U}$ such that $A \notin u$. By our construction, u will be a preferred admissible state in $]A[$ with respect to $\mathbb{E}_h$ if and only if $l(s) \subseteq u$, for any preferred 'old' admissible state s in $]A[$. Accordingly, for any A, the intersection of all preferred admissible belief sets in $\mathbb{E}_h$ with respect to A will coincide with the intersection of all such sets in $\mathbb{E}$. This shows that $\mathbb{E}$ and $\mathbb{E}_h$ are skeptically equivalent. $\square$

The above result implies that homogeneous weakly monotonic epistemic states are sufficient for representing all skeptical and contraction inference relations. Actually, if the source epistemic state is standard, the construction given in the proof produces an equivalent standard homogeneous epistemic state. However, the demonstrated representation capabilities of homogeneous epistemic states depend essentially on the fact that they are not supposed, in general, to be standard or monotonic. As we will see in due course, imposing any of these constraints will reduce the class of generated inference relations.

Finally, we will show now that homogeneous epistemic states that are also monotonic are equivalent to semantic models based on possible worlds.

Theorem 4.5.4. *Any monotonic homogeneous epistemic state is statically equivalent to some possible worlds-based epistemic state, and vice versa.*

Proof. Given a monotonic homogeneous epistemic state $\mathbb{E}$, we can construct the corresponding possible worlds-based epistemic state $\mathbb{W}$ by restricting the set of admissible belief states from $\mathbb{E}$ to states labelled with worlds. Notice that, due to homogeneity and monotonicity, all strictly normal admissible states in $\mathbb{E}$ will belong to $\mathbb{W}$. Consequently, $\mathbb{E}$ and $\mathbb{W}$ will determine the same selection function.

In the other direction, any possible worlds-based epistemic state $\mathbb{W}$ can be extended to a monotonic homogeneous epistemic state as follows. First, we add a new admissible belief state for each deductively closed theory of the language that is not among admissible belief sets of $\mathbb{W}$ and includes the knowledge set of $\mathbb{W}$. Second, we order all resulting admissible states by monotonicity (set inclusion). Third, we subordinate each new admissible state that is labelled with a world to all 'old' admissible belief states from $\mathbb{W}$. As can be verified, the resulting homogeneous epistemic state will be equivalent to $\mathbb{W}$. □

The above result provides a natural link between epistemic states and possible worlds models for nonmonotonic inference that prevail in the current literature. More about the relation between these two representations will be said in Part Two.

4.5.3 Belief equivalence

If we exclude credulous inference from consideration and restrict our attention only to skeptical inference relations and belief change operations, then we can use a weaker notion of equivalence for epistemic states described in the following definition.

Definition 4.5.5. *Two epistemic states $\mathbb{E}_1$ and $\mathbb{E}_2$ will be called* belief equivalent *if, for any w,* $\bigcap f_{\mathbb{E}_1}(w) = \bigcap f_{\mathbb{E}_2}(w)$.

Belief equivalence can be seen as a dynamic generalization of the notion of skeptical equivalence defined earlier. Clearly, equivalent epistemic states will also be belief equivalent. The following simple example shows that the reverse implication does not hold in general.

Example 4.5.2. Let us consider the following two standard epistemic states. The state $\mathbb{E}_1$ consists of two theories $\mathrm{Cl}(p)$ and $\mathrm{Cl}(p \wedge q)$ with an empty preference relation, while $\mathbb{E}_2$ consists of a single theory $\mathrm{Cl}(p)$. These epistemic states are not equivalent, since, for example, $f_{\mathbb{E}_1}(\mathbf{f}) = \{\mathrm{Cl}(p \wedge q), \mathrm{Cl}(p)\}$, while $f_{\mathbb{E}_2}(\mathbf{f}) = \{\mathrm{Cl}(p)\}$. Actually, this shows that the two epistemic states determine different credulous inference relations; we have, for example, that $\mathbf{t} \mathrel{\vert\!\approx} p \wedge q$ is valid in $\mathbb{E}_1$, but not in $\mathbb{E}_2$. Still, it is easily verified that these two epistemic states are belief equivalent: any set $]w[$ in $\mathbb{E}_1$ that includes $\mathrm{Cl}(p \wedge q)$, will include also $\mathrm{Cl}(p)$, and hence $\bigcap f_{\mathbb{E}_1}(w)$ will always coincide with $\bigcap f_{\mathbb{E}_2}(w)$.

The following result shows, however, that belief equivalence is sufficient for coincidence of pure epistemic states. This result generalizes the corresponding result obtained in [FUKV86].

Theorem 4.5.5. *Two pure epistemic states are belief equivalent if and only if they coincide.*

Proof. Let $\mathcal{E}_1$ and $\mathcal{E}_2$ be two belief equivalent pure epistemic states, and suppose that $u \in \mathcal{E}_1$. Then u is the only maximal theory in $]\overline{u}[$, where $\overline{u}$ denotes the complement of u. Consequently, $f_{\mathcal{E}_1}(\overline{u}) = \{u\}$, and hence $u = \bigcup f_{\mathcal{E}_1}(\overline{u})$. Since $\mathcal{E}_1$ and $\mathcal{E}_2$ are belief equivalent, we have also $u = \bigcup f_{\mathcal{E}_2}(\overline{u})$, which is possible only if $u \in \mathcal{E}_2$. Therefore, $\mathcal{E}_1 \subseteq \mathcal{E}_2$. A similar argument can be given for the reverse inclusion. Thus, $\mathcal{E}_1$ coincides with $\mathcal{E}_2$. $\qquad\square$

As we have seen earlier, any persistent and semi-monotonic epistemic state is similar to a pure epistemic state. Consequently, the above result implies that belief equivalence is sufficient for similarity of such epistemic states:

Corollary 4.5.1. *Two persistent and semi-monotonic epistemic states are belief equivalent if and only if they are similar.*

Another consequence of the above result is that basic equivalence of two bases is, in effect, a weakest equivalence relation that makes the associated base-generated epistemic states essentially identical.

Corollary 4.5.2. *The sets Δ_1 and Δ_2 are basically equivalent iff their associated base-generated epistemic states are belief equivalent.*

Proof. If $\mathbb{E}_{\Delta_1}$ is belief equivalent to $\mathbb{E}_{\Delta_2}$, then their corresponding pure epistemic states $\mathcal{E}_{\Delta_1}$ and $\mathcal{E}_{\Delta_2}$ will also be belief equivalent, and hence they will coincide. As we have said earlier, this can hold only if Δ_1 and Δ_2 are basically equivalent. $\qquad\square$

The above result implies that if Δ_1 and Δ_2 are not basically equivalent, then their associated epistemic states will not be belief equivalent. As we will see in Chapter 12, the latter means that a certain sequence of contractions performed on these epistemic states will produce epistemic states with different belief sets. Consequently, basic equivalence can be seen as a necessary and sufficient condition for essential equivalence of two pure bases.

4.6 Decomposition of inference relations

As before, we will say that an epistemic state is *equivalent to a set* of epistemic states if it is equivalent to their disjoint union. Then the following lemma shows that decomposition of epistemic states produces a decomposition of their associated selection functions.

Lemma 4.6.1. *If* $\mathbb{E}$ *is equivalent to a set of epistemic states* $\mathfrak{E} = \{\mathbb{E}_i\}$*, then, for any set of propositions* w*,*

$$f_{\mathbb{E}}(w) = \bigcup_i f_{\mathbb{E}_i}(w)$$

Proof. Immediate from the fact that, for any w, (s, i) is a preferred state in $]w[$ with respect to $\sum \mathfrak{E}$ if and only if s is a preferred state in $]w[$ with respect to $\mathbb{E}_i$.   □

As an immediate consequence of the above decomposition, the following result shows that the inference relations determined by epistemic states are also decomposable into inference relations determined by their components. The proof is straightforward.

Theorem 4.6.1. *If* $\mathbb{E}$ *is equivalent to* $\mathfrak{E}$*, then*

1. $A \mathrel{|\!\sim} B$ *holds in* $\mathbb{E}$ *iff it holds in all epistemic states from* $\mathfrak{E}$*.*
2. $A \mathrel{\rightarrowtail} B$ *holds in* $\mathbb{E}$ *iff it holds in all* $\mathfrak{E}$*.*
3. $A \mathrel{|\!\approx}$ *holds in* $\mathbb{E}$ *iff it holds in at least one epistemic state from* $\mathfrak{E}$*.*

Semantics and completeness results for nonmonotonic inference, given in the literature, are usually based on single models. In contrast, semantic notions studied in mainstream logical studies are ordinarily defined with respect to sets of models. The above result allows us to show, however, that the notion of decomposition provides a smooth transition between 'single-model' and 'multiple-model' representations of inference relations. Moreover, this could be done even before a syntactic description of the corresponding inference relations is given.

The following definition describes appropriate notions of validity for different kinds of conditionals with respect to *sets* of epistemic states.

Definition 4.6.1. *Let* $\mathfrak{E}$ *be a set of epistemic states.*

1. B *will be said to be a* skeptical (respectively, contraction) consequence *of* A *with respect to* $\mathfrak{E}$*, if* B *is a skeptical (resp., contraction) consequence of* A *with respect to each epistemic state from* $\mathfrak{E}$*.*
2. B *will be said to be a* credulous consequence *of* A *with respect to* $\mathfrak{E}$*, if* B *is a credulous consequence of* A *with respect to at least one epistemic state from* $\mathfrak{E}$*.*

Recall that skeptical, contraction and credulous inference relations were defined earlier as sets of respective conditionals determined by some epistemic state. Now, a set of epistemic states $\mathfrak{E}$ can be combined into a single epistemic state $\sum \mathfrak{E}$, and the above definitions will give us exactly the conditions of validity for conditionals with respect to $\sum \mathfrak{E}$. Consequently, we immediately obtain

Lemma 4.6.2. *The set of skeptical [contraction, credulous] conditionals determined by a set of epistemic states forms a skeptical [contraction, credulous] inference relation.*

Our second result makes use of Corollary 4.3.3 above according to which any epistemic state is decomposable into a set of linear standard epistemic states.

Theorem 4.6.2. *Any skeptical [contraction, credulous] inference relation is determined by a set of standard linear monotonic epistemic states.*

The above result shows that the main forms of nonmonotonic inference can be analyzed, in effect, in terms of quite regular epistemic states that are standard, linear and monotonic. This fact will be extensively used in what follows.

4.7 Syntactic characterization of inference relations

As an application of the above general results on equivalence and decomposition, we will show that restriction to certain classes of epistemic states does not change some general rules valid for inference relations.

By a *general rule* for (skeptical, contraction or credulous) conditionals we will mean a rule $\mathcal{R}$ of the form

$$\text{If } C_1, \ C_2, \ldots, C_m, \text{ then either } C_{m+1}, \text{ or } \ldots, \text{ or } C_n,$$

where each C_i is an appropriate (skeptical, contraction or credulous) conditional. $C_1, C_2, \ldots, C_m$ will be called the premises of the rule, while $C_{m+1}, \ldots, C_n$ - its conclusions. Note that the set of premises or even conclusions of a rule can be empty.

Syntactic characterizations of inference relations, including the characterizations given later in Part Two, are almost always formulated in terms of the above general rules. A class of inference relations $\mathcal{I}$ will be said to *satisfy* a rule $\mathcal{R}$ (and the rule will be said to be *valid* for the class), if each inference relation from $\mathcal{I}$ is closed with respect to the rule, that is, if all the conditionals in the premises of $\mathcal{R}$ belong to the inference relation, then it contains also at least one of the conclusions of $\mathcal{R}$.

In what follows we will classify general rules for inference relations in accordance with the number of premises and/or conclusions they have. A rule will be called *simple* if it contains at most one premise and a single conclusion; in other words, simple rules are rules of the form *"If C_1, then C_2"*, or *"C_1 holds"*. The basic inference relation described in Chapter 6 will be characterized by simple rules only. A rule will be called *singular* (or *Horn*) one if it contains a single conclusion; otherwise it will be called *disjunctive*. Finally, by a *co-singular* rule we will mean a rule having at most one premise (cf. [Fla98]).

Our first result makes use of the decomposition of epistemic states into linear ones. It says that a restriction to epistemic states that are linear standard and monotonic does not extend the set of singular rules valid for associated skeptical and contraction inference relations.

Theorem 4.7.1. *A singular rule is valid for skeptical or contraction inference relations generated by standard linear and monotonic epistemic states if and only if it is valid for all skeptical (respectively, contraction) inference relations.*

Proof. We will consider only the case of skeptical inference, since the proof for contraction inference is the same.

The direction from right to left is immediate. Assume that a singular rule "If C_1, C_2, ..., C_m, then C" is not valid for all skeptical inference relations. Then there must exist an epistemic state $\mathbb{E}$ that validates all the premises of the rule, and falsifies C. Let $\{\mathbb{E}_i\}$ be a decomposition of $\mathbb{E}$ into a set of standard linear and monotonic epistemic states. Then at least one such epistemic state, say $\mathbb{E}_i$, does not validate C, though it still validates all the premises of the rule. Therefore, the rule will not be valid also for the class of all standard linear and monotonic epistemic states. This completes the proof.   □

As we will see in due course, linear epistemic states generate restricted classes of inference relations for all three basic kinds of inference; in other words, in all three cases there are rules that are valid only for inference relations generated by linear epistemic states. Still, the above result implies that such additional rules for skeptical and contraction inference should be non-singular. For example, skeptical inference relations determined by linear epistemic states will be characterized by adding the well-known rule of Rational Monotony, which is disjunctive (see Chapter 7).

For credulous inference, the restriction to the linear case preserves co-singular rules:

Theorem 4.7.2. *A co-singular rule is valid for credulous inference relations generated by standard linear and monotonic epistemic states if and only if it is valid for all credulous inference relations.*

The proof follows immediately from the decomposition of credulous inference relations, and we leave it to the reader. We will see in Chapter 9 that credulous inference invalidates, in general, familiar Horn rules for skeptical non-monotonic inference such as And, Cut and Cautious Monotony, though these rules will be valid for the linear case. It validates, however, the above mentioned rule of Rational Monotony, which is co-singular, though the latter is valid only for linear skeptical inference relations.

Our next result is based on the fact, established earlier, that any general epistemic state is representable as a language-restricted reduction of an epistemic state that is standard and monotonic. This result says, in effect, that standardness and monotonicity cannot be captured using general rules characterizing associated inference relations.

Theorem 4.7.3. *A general rule is valid for the class of all skeptical, contraction or credulous inference relations determined by standard monotonic epistemic states if and only if it is valid with respect to all such inference relations.*

Proof. To simplify the exposition, we will restrict ourselves to skeptical inference relations, though the same proof will be valid also for contraction and credulous inference.

Assume that a general rule $\mathcal{R}$ is not valid for skeptical inference relations in some language $\mathcal{L}$. This means that there is an inference relation $\vdash$ that includes all premises from $\mathcal{R}$, but does not include any of its conclusions. Let $\mathbb{E}$ be a general epistemic state (in $\mathcal{L}$) that generates $\vdash$. By Theorem 4.4.1 above, this epistemic state can be transformed into an equivalent standard monotonic epistemic state in some extended language. Clearly, $\mathcal{R}$ will not be valid also for the latter epistemic state. Consequently, the rule $\mathcal{R}$ will not hold also for the class of skeptical inference relations generated by standard and monotonic epistemic states.   □

Thus, imposing standardness and monotonicity on epistemic states do not introduce new valid general rules. This makes the characterization of the associated inference relations a difficult task in some cases. We will see, however, that all skeptical and credulous inference relations are representable by pure epistemic states, and hence the reduction to standard and monotonic states does not change the class of generated inference relations in these cases. Still, this result does not hold for contraction inference relations; the restriction to pure epistemic states makes valid new general rules for them. The problem reappears also for skeptical inference relations as a problem of characterizing inference relations generated by standard possible worlds-based (KLM) models. It turns out that the corresponding characterization can be achieved, however, using some conditions that are more complex than general rules.

Finally, Theorem 4.4.2 can be used to show that pure and persistent epistemic states cannot be distinguished by means of general rules characterizing the associated inference relations. In order to apply this theorem, however, we need to prove first that nonmonotonic inference relations satisfy a *finite model property*.

Lemma 4.7.1. *If a general rule $\mathcal{R}$ for skeptical, contraction or credulous inference is invalid with respect to some epistemic state $\mathbb{E}$, then the latter can be restricted to a finite epistemic state $\mathbb{E}_f$ that will also invalidate $\mathcal{R}$.*

Proof. We will prove the claim only for contraction inference, but practically the same proof can be given for the other two kinds of inference relations.

If a rule $\mathcal{R}$ for contractionals is invalid in $\mathbb{E}$, then all the contractionals $A_i \mathrel{\dashv} B_i$ $(1 \leq i \leq k)$ from the premises of $\mathcal{R}$ are valid in $\mathbb{E}$, while all contractionals $C_j \mathrel{\dashv} D_j$ $(1 \leq j \leq n)$ from the conclusions of $\mathcal{R}$ are invalid in $\mathbb{E}$. The latter means that, for any j, there exists an admissible state s_j that is preferred in $]C_j[$ and such that $D_j \notin l(s_j)$. To begin with, let us chose one such 'refuting' admissible state for each contractional $C_j \mathrel{\dashv} D_j$ and denote the resulting finite set of admissible states by S_0.

Now, starting from S_0, we iteratively construct a sequence of finite sets of admissible states S_m as follows. If $s \in S_{m-1}$ is such that $s \in]A_i[$, for some contractional $A_i \mathrel{\dashv} B_i$ from the premises of $\mathcal{R}$, but s is not a preferred admissible state in $]A_i[$, then we choose some preferred admissible state t in $]A_i[$ such that $s \prec t$ and put it into S_m. Notice that the same procedure with respect to A_i will not be applicable neither to t (since it is already preferred in $]A_i[$), nor to any descendants of t obtained on subsequent stages (since they will not already belong to $]A_i[$). Thus, while S_1 contains no more than k descendants for each admissible state in S_0 (where k is the number of premises in $\mathcal{R}$), S_2 will contain no more than $k-1$ descendants for each admissible state in S_1. A little reflection on this behavior will show that the whole procedure will terminate after no more than k steps.

Now let us denote by S_f the union of all S_i obtained by applying the above procedure. Clearly, S_f is a finite set of admissible states. Moreover, any admissible state s in S_f that belongs to some $]A_i[$ will be subordinated to some admissible state t in S_f which is also a preferred state in $]A_i[$ with respect to $\mathbb{E}$.

Finally, we will take $\mathbb{E}_f$ to be a restriction of $\mathbb{E}$ to the set of admissible states S_f. Then the above observation shows that each $A_i \mathrel{\dashv} B_i$ from the premises of the rule $\mathcal{R}$ will be valid in $\mathbb{E}_f$. Moreover, all conclusions of $\mathcal{R}$ will be invalid in $\mathbb{E}_f$, since the latter contains the set of refuting admissible states S_0. Therefore, $\mathbb{E}_f$ will also invalidate $\mathcal{R}$, and we are done. $\square$

Now we are ready to prove the following

Theorem 4.7.4. *A general rule is valid for the class of all skeptical, contraction or credulous inference relations determined by pure epistemic states if and only if it is valid for all persistent epistemic states.*

Proof. We will consider again only contraction inference, though the same proof will be valid also for skeptical and credulous inference.

Assume that a general rule $\mathcal{R}$ for contractionals in a given language $\mathcal{L}$ is invalidated by some persistent epistemic state $\mathbb{E}$. By the preceding lemma, $\mathbb{E}$ can be chosen to be finite. Then by Theorem 4.4.2, this epistemic state can be transformed into a pure epistemic state in some extended language. Clearly, $\mathcal{R}$ will not be valid also for the latter epistemic state. Consequently, the rule $\mathcal{R}$ will not hold also for pure epistemic states.   □

As the preceding result, the above theorem shows that pure and persistent epistemic states validate the same general rules of nonmonotonic inference. Consequently, the study of such rules for persistent epistemic states in general can be made in the framework of pure epistemic states and associated consequence relations.

5. Epistemic Entrenchment and Its Relatives

5.1 Expectation relations

In this chapter we will lay down general foundations for an approach to non-monotonic reasoning and belief change based on establishing certain expectation relations on the set of propositions. As we mentioned in Chapter 3, such an approach arises naturally when we adopt a coherentist position according to which dependencies and justification relations are disregarded. However, we have also seen that the dependence structure is also describable in terms of certain dependence relations on propositions. This creates a rather involved picture in which these relations are actually interdefinable. A first sketch of the emerging picture will be drawn in this chapter. Further details will be added in subsequent chapters when we will consider the role being played by these relations in describing nonmonotonic reasoning and belief change.

Epistemic entrenchment relations have been introduced in studies of belief revision. Peter Gärdenfors (see [Gär88, GM88]) has suggested such relations as a natural mechanism for determining what to retract and what to retain in the process of revision. Gärdenfors and Makinson have employed these relations in [GM94] for describing nonmonotonic inference. A generalization of epistemic entrenchment relations to partial orders has been suggested in [LR91]. An essentially different generalization, called generalized entrenchment relations, has been developed by Hans Rott in [Rot92b]. He showed that a broad range of contraction and revision operations can be grounded on such generalized entrenchment orders.

The use of orderings on propositions for studying conditionals can be traced back to David Lewis [Lew73] who introduced comparative possibility relations and showed that they are interdefinable with counterfactual conditionals. Dubois and Prade have studied the notions of relative possibility and necessity and showed their connection with epistemic entrenchment (see [DP91]). A generalization of this approach to partial plausibility orders has been given in [FH98]. In addition, Freund introduced a related notion of a preferential order in [Fre92] as a convenient tool for analyzing nonmonotonic inference relations.

Epistemic entrenchment and related concepts have proved their usefulness and importance in analyzing nonmonotonic inference and belief change. We will provide below a systematic description of such relations, as well as interfaces connecting them to other basic notions used in the book. Thus, we will give a systematic comparison between the notion of epistemic entrenchment and its generalizations, on the one hand, and consequence relations, on the other. As we will see, both generalized entrenchment relations and dependence consequence relations can be considered as diverging generalizations of the original concept of epistemic entrenchment. Still, we will see also that these notions are intimately connected, and consequently can perform much the same roles in nonmonotonic reasoning and belief change. This will allow us to switch smoothly from one representation to another in order to obtain a richer picture of our constructions.

General expectation relations. By a *general expectation relation* we will mean an arbitrary relation $<$ on the set of classical propositions satisfying the following two conditions of *quasi-monotonicity*:

Right Weakening   If $A < B$ and $B \vDash C$, then $A < C$;
Left Strengthening   If $A \vDash B$ and $B < C$, then $A < C$.

$A < B$ will be interpreted informally as saying "B *is sufficiently well expected (expected enough) as compared with* A". This (presumably vague) description nevertheless conforms with the above postulates without committing us to either reflexive or strict interpretation of these relations– an issue that will play an important role in what follows.

Our reasons for choosing the above conditions as defining a plausible general concept of expectation are two-fold. First, these are the only natural conditions that belong to the common part of all relations that will be described below. Second, these conditions alone are almost sufficient for determining the basic inference relation discussed in the next chapter; the only additions needed deal with special cases of logical contradictions or tautologies.

An expectation relation will be called *non-trivial* if it is non-empty. Due to quasi-monotonicity, this will hold if and only if $\mathbf{f} < \mathbf{t}$.

General expectation relations do not form a homogeneous area; rather, they should be seen as a useful common 'umbrella' for a number of quite diverse concepts. As a first indication of this situation, note that the following two simple operations transform expectation relations into expectation relations. They will be used extensively in what follows.

(Contraposition)	$A <^{\neg} B$	$\equiv$ $\neg B < \neg A$
(Converse Complement)	$A <^{c} B$	$\equiv$ $B \not< A$

The following lemma can be obtained by a straightforward check of quasi-monotonicity for transformed relations.

Lemma 5.1.1. *If $<$ is an expectation relation, then both $<^{\neg}$ and $<^{c}$ are expectation relations.*

As can be seen, double application of either Contraposition or Converse Complement returns us to the source expectation relation. Accordingly, these transformations will be used in what follows in establishing one-to-one correspondences between particular classes of expectation relations.

5.2 Entrenchment, plausibility and dependence

We will introduce below three basic kinds of expectation relations that will be our main subject in this chapter, namely plausibility, entrenchment and dependence relations. These relations will correspond to three major alternative formalisms for representing nonmonotonic inference and belief change, studied in the literature. The usefulness of the general notion of an expectation relation will show itself, however, in the fact that all these rather different kinds of expectation relations will turn out to be interdefinable.

5.2.1 Entrenchment relations

The notion of epistemic entrenchment was intended to reflect relative importance, or 'vulnerability', of believed propositions that can determine what is abandoned, and what is retained, when a belief change is carried out. A 'mature' version of the theory of epistemic entrenchment relations was given in [GM88]. The basic idea behind epistemic entrenchment can be expressed as follows: if we have to reject or remove $A \wedge B$ from our beliefs, we can accomplish this, in general, by removing either A or B. In other words, we have a choice. Then B is more entrenched than A when the best way to accomplish the task consists in retaining B and removing A. We will formulae this as the following maxim:

> B is more entrenched than A if B can be retained whenever we are required to remove $A \wedge B$.

The above principle will receive a formal representation in due course. For the time being, it can assist us in justifying the following definition.

Definition 5.2.1.   *1. An expectation relation will be called an* entrenchment *relation if it satisfies the following condition:*
   Reduction   *If $A \wedge B < B$, then $A < B$.*
   2. An entrenchment relation will be called simple *if it satisfies*
   t-reflexivity $t < t$.
   Otherwise, it will be called strict.

The above definition makes Reduction the basic property of the notion of entrenchment. As can be seen, Reduction agrees with the informal description of entrenchment given earlier.

Strict entrenchment relations is a very abstract generalization of Rott's *generalized epistemic entrenchment* (see [Rot92b]). An exact correspondence between them will be discussed below.

The following lemma gives some useful properties of entrenchment relations. The proof presents no difficulty and is left to the reader.

Lemma 5.2.1. *1. $A < B$ implies $B \rightarrow A < B$;*
2. If $A \wedge C < B \wedge C$, then $A < B$;
3. $A < A$ if and only if $t < A$;
4. $\neg A < A$ if and only if $f < A$;
5. (Simple entrenchment) $A < t$, for any A.

An interesting property of entrenchment relations, revealed by the above lemma, is that such relations are 'almost irreflexive': (3) above shows that the only propositions for which reflexivity holds are propositions that are $<$-equivalent to the tautology t. Accordingly, we immediately obtain

Corollary 5.2.1. *An entrenchment relation is strict iff it is irreflexive.*

Proof. Assume that $A < A$, for some proposition A. Then $t < A$, and hence $t < t$ by Right Weakening. Consequently, the expectation relation will not be strict.   □

Practically all formalizations of entrenchment and plausibility relations, given in the literature, consider them to be either weak (reflexive) or strict (irreflexive) orders. It turns out, however, that this simplicity of familiar orderings does not fit exactly with the behavior of corresponding inference relations or belief change operations they are purported to represent; some qualifications are always required for such orderings in order to give an adequate description for the limit cases of logical tautologies and/or contradictions. Such qualifications become unnecessary, however, if we will choose simple entrenchment relations as our basic formalism; as we have seen, the latter are irreflexive in all cases except for propositions that are equivalent to tautologies. In fact, there is a natural interpretation of possible reflexivity of epistemic entrenchment on logical truths. According to our informal interpretation of entrenchment relations as determining the choice among propositions in deletions, $t < t$ expresses an idea that the logical truth, t, should be retained *even if we are required to remove* t! This means that the potential conflict arising when we attempt to remove t cannot be resolved. As we will see later, this 'deviant' behavior of epistemic entrenchment exactly corresponds to the behavior of belief contractions with respect to logically valid propositions. Consequently, simple entrenchment relations turns out to be more in accord with the internal logic governing the behavior of contractions and related constructs.

5.2.2 Plausibility relations

Plausibility relations can be seen as a generalization of *relative plausibility orders* from [FH98]. The latter are, in turn, a generalization of a vast number of related concepts that have their origin in the notion of comparative probability (see below) and its qualitative generalizations such as comparative possibility (see [BDP97]).

Definition 5.2.2. *1. An expectation relation will be called a* plausibility relation *if it satisfies the following condition:*
Right Strengthening   *If $A < A \vee B$, then $A < B$.*
2. A plausibility relation will be called simple *if it satisfies*
f-reflexivity $f < f$.
and strict *otherwise.*

Plausibility relations will receive considerably less attention in this book than entrenchment or dependence relations. There are two reasons for this. First, we will see below that plausibility relations are perfect duals of entrenchment relations, so we can safely avoid detailed descriptions and proofs for plausibility relations and refer instead to duality considerations. In addition, plausibility relations appear to be more suitable for formalisms and representations based on possible worlds. Furthermore, entrenchment relations look much less natural in such contexts than plausibility relations. Our approach, however, is not based on possible worlds. Moreover, our main representation framework of epistemic states creates an opposite situation in which plausibility relations are much less convenient and natural than entrenchment relations.

5.2.3 Dependence relations

Definition 5.2.3. *An expectation relation will be called a* simple dependence relation *if it is reflexive and satisfies the following condition:*

Antecedence   *If $A < B$, then $A < A \wedge B$.*

Simple dependence relations are 'rudimentary' consequence relations; they are generalizations of dependence relations described in Chapter 3. Such relations will play an important role in this book both by themselves, and as a useful tool for connecting other kinds of expectation relations with the main constructions of our study. These connections will be grounded in the fact that dependence relations constitute actually an alternative generalization of the original epistemic entrenchment relations of Gärdenfors and Makinson. As we will see below, since these epistemic entrenchment relations are highly regular relations (i.e., linear orders) they conflate, in effect, two essentially different notions, namely dependence and entrenchment. These two notions will be clearly distinguishable, both formally and conceptually, in more general contexts.

5.2.4 Correspondences

Now we are going to show that the above three kinds of expectation relations are interdefinable. To begin with, we will show that entrenchment relations are equivalent to plausibility relations. The following lemma shows that Contraposition establishes a natural correspondence between plausibility and entrenchment relations.

Lemma 5.2.2.   *1. $<$ is a plausibility relation if and only if $<^{\neg}$ is an entrenchment relation.*

  2. $<$ is a simple (respectively, strict) plausibility relation if and only if $<^{\neg}$ is a simple (resp., strict) entrenchment relation.

Due to the above duality between entrenchment and plausibility relations, all the results proved below for entrenchment relations can be immediately translated into the corresponding results for plausibility relations.

Our second result shows that simple dependence relations are exactly converse complements of strict entrenchment relations. In other words, the Converse Complement transformation establishes an inter-definability of simple dependence and strict entrenchment relations.

Lemma 5.2.3. *$<$ is a simple dependence relation if and only if $<^c$ is a strict entrenchment relation.*

Finally, we will complete the circle and show that simple dependence relations are equivalent to simple entrenchment relations.

Given a dependence relation $<$, we can define the corresponding entrenchment relation as follows:

(ED) $A <_e B \quad \equiv \quad B \to A < B$

Notice that, due to Antecedence, $B \to A < B$ is equivalent to $B \to A < A \wedge B$. Accordingly, the above condition means, in effect, that $B \to A$ is a purely derivative belief, acceptance of which depends on accepting both A and B. Consequently, B is not involved in acceptance of A, and hence it can be safely retained when we remove $A \wedge B$. As we will see later, this gives a natural support to the claim that B is more entrenched than A.

In the other direction, if $<$ is an entrenchment relation, the corresponding dependence relation is defined by requiring that A depends on B if the implication $A \to B$ is more entrenched than A:

(DE) $A <_d B \quad \equiv \quad A < A \to B$

In what follows, the pair of transformations determined by (ED) and (DE) will be called the *de-mapping*. Then the result below shows that the de-mapping determines a bijection between simple entrenchment and dependence relations.

$<_{ed}$ below denotes a consecutive application of (ED) and then (DE) to $<$; similarly for $<_{de}$.

Theorem 5.2.1. *1. If $<$ is a simple dependence relation, then $<_e$ defined by (ED) is a simple entrenchment relation. Moreover, $<_{ed}$ coincides with $<$.*

2. If $<$ is a simple entrenchment relation, then $<_d$ defined by (ED) is a simple dependence relation. Also, $<_{de}$ coincides with $<$.

Proof. It is immediate to show that both (ED) and (DE) transform expectation relations into expectation relations. So, we will check only specific properties involved.

(1) Assume that $<$ is a simple dependence relation. Then t-reflexivity of $<_e$ follows from reflexivity of $<$, while Reduction follows directly from the definition of $<_e$. Finally, $A <_{ed} B$ is reducible to $(A \to B) \to A < A \to B$, and hence to $A < A \to B$. The latter is equivalent to $A < B$ by Antecedence and Right Weakening for $<$.

(2) Assume now that $<$ is a simple entrenchment relation. Then reflexivity of $<_d$ follows from t-reflexivity of $<$, while Antecedence follows directly from the definition of $<_d$. Finally, $A <_{de} B$ is reducible to $B \to A < B$. The latter implies $A < B$ by Left Strengthening, while $A < B$ implies $A \wedge B < B$ by Left Strengthening, and hence $B \to A < B$ by Reduction. $\square$

As a general consequence of the above correspondences, all basic kinds of expectation relations introduced above (in both strict and simple versions) turn out to be interdefinable. Actually, combining the above mappings, we can obtain direct translations between each two kinds of expectation relations.

For example, the following pair of transformations establishes a direct correspondence between dependence and simple plausibility. These transformations can be obtained by combining Contraposition with the de-mapping.

(PD) $\qquad\qquad A <_p B \quad \equiv \quad B \to A < \neg A$

(DP) $\qquad\qquad A <_{d1} B \quad \equiv \quad A \wedge \neg B < \neg A$

Similarly, the transformation given below determines a one-to-one correspondence between strict and simple entrenchment relations (in both ways). We will call this transformation the rs*-*mapping*. It is obtainable as a combination of the de-mapping and Converse Complement.

(RS*) $\qquad\qquad A <^* B \quad \equiv \quad B \not< B \to A$

Lemma 5.2.4. *1. If $<$ is an entrenchment relation, then $<^*$ is also an entrenchment relation and $<^{**}$ coincides with $<$.*

2. $<$ is a simple entrenchment relation if and only if $<^*$ is a strict entrenchment relation.

Though adequate, the above (derived) rs*-mapping between strict and simple entrenchment relations has a certain deficiency compared with our intuitive understanding of their relationship, since it does not preserve the ordering on 'regular' propositions that are not equivalent to **t**. A more natural mapping between the two will be described in the next section.

5.2.5 Comparative probability

By way of comparison, we will briefly consider below yet another expectation relation that is based on relative probability.

Definition 5.2.4. *An expectation relation will be called a* (comparative) *probability relation if it is reflexive and satisfies the following condition:*

Contraposition   *If $A \wedge B < A \wedge C$, then $A \wedge \neg C < A \wedge \neg B$.*

The above relation can be interpreted as a rudimentary comparative probability relation saying "*B is at least as probable as A*". As can be easily verified, if we interpret $A < B$ as $probability(A) \leq probability(B)$, then the resulting relation will be a comparative probability relation in the above sense. Clearly, the 'full' relative probability will also be a connected and transitive order, and will satisfy some further, less intuitive properties (see [Ben84]). But already Contraposition neatly distinguishes comparative probability relations from the three kinds of expectation relations introduced earlier. As can be shown, for expectation relations Contraposition is equivalent to the following condition:

(Symmetric Difference) $A < B$ if and only if $A \wedge \neg B < \neg A \wedge B$.

The above condition says that probabilistic comparison between propositions is determined, in effect, by their 'logical differences'.

Despite the distinction, it turns out that probability relations are also interdefinable with the above three kinds of expectation relations. Thus, the following definitions give a one-to-one correspondence between probability and dependence relations.

(PRD) $A <_{pd} B \quad \equiv \quad B \rightarrow A < A \rightarrow B$

(DPR) $A <_{dp} B \quad \equiv \quad A < A \rightarrow B$

We will leave the proof of the following theorem as an exercise to the reader.

Theorem 5.2.2. *1. If $<$ is a dependence relation, then $<_{pd}$ defined by (PRD) is a probability relation, and the corresponding dependence relation generated, in turn, by (DPR) coincides with $<$.*

2. If $<$ is a probability relation, then $<_{dp}$ defined by (DPR) is a dependence relation, and the corresponding probability relation generated, in turn, by (PRD) coincides with $<$.

Due to the above correspondence, the inference relations generated by probability relations will have much in common with inference relations produced by other kinds of expectation relations (see the next chapter).

5.3 Regular expectation relations

As we have seen, even simple entrenchment relations are almost irreflexive, that is, they are irreflexive on all propositions that are not $<$-equivalent to the truth $\mathbf{t}$. This suggests another, more natural, way of relating simple and strict versions of epistemic entrenchment. Namely, in order to transform a simple entrenchment relation into a strict one (or vice versa), we should change only its behavior on propositions that are $<$-equivalent to $\mathbf{t}$. These transformations give right results, however, only under certain additional regularity conditions on entrenchment relations.

Definition 5.3.1.   *1. A simple entrenchment relation will be called* regular *if it satisfies*
    t-regularity   *If* $\mathbf{t} < A$ *and* $A < B$, *then* $\mathbf{t} < A \wedge B$.
  2. A strict entrenchment relation will be called regular *if it satisfies*
    t-primeness   *If* $A < \mathbf{t}$ *and* $B \not< \mathbf{t}$, *then* $A < B$.

The condition of t-primeness above has been introduced by Rott in [Rot92b][1] as a supplementary postulate having a certain harmonizing effect on the notion of entrenchment. More exactly, it makes valid the AGM postulate (K–7) for belief contractions. However, Rott has excluded it from the set of his 'basic' postulates due to the fact that it was non-Horn and lacked an independent motivation. We will see later, however, that this condition can be seen as a by-product of the particular definition of epistemic entrenchment in terms of contractions, presupposed by Rott.

The following lemma gives an alternative description of t-regularity in terms of a couple of simpler conditions.

Lemma 5.3.1. *t-regularity is equivalent to the following two conditions:*

- *If* $\mathbf{t} < A$ *and* $A < B$, *then* $\mathbf{t} < B$;
- *If* $\mathbf{t} < A$ *and* $\mathbf{t} < B$, *then* $\mathbf{t} < A \wedge B$.

Proof. If t-regularity holds, then (1) is immediate, while (2) can be obtained when we notice that $\mathbf{t} < B$ implies $A < B$. In the other direction, if $\mathbf{t} < A$ and $A < B$, then $\mathbf{t} < B$ by (1), and hence $\mathbf{t} < A \wedge B$ by (2).   □

Similarly to entrenchment, we will define regularity conditions also for plausibility and dependence relations.

Definition 5.3.2.   *1. A simple plausibility relation will be called* regular *if it satisfies*
    f-regularity   *If* $\mathbf{f} < B$ *and* $B < A$, *then* $\mathbf{f} < A$.
  2. A strict plausibility relation will be called regular *if it satisfies*
    f-primeness   *If* $\mathbf{f} < B$ *and* $\mathbf{f} \not< A$, *then* $A < B$.

---

[1] This condition is called (GEE6') in [GR95].

Definition 5.3.3. *A dependence relation will be called* regular *if it satisfies t-regularity.*

It can be easily shown that all translations defined earlier are extendable to regular expectation relations. Thus, Contraposition will determine the correspondences between regular entrenchment and regular plausibility, Converse Complement will determine the correspondence between regular dependence and strict regular entrenchment, while the de-mapping determines a bijection between regular dependence and regular simple entrenchment. These useful facts are summarized in the following lemma.

Lemma 5.3.2.   *1. If $<$ and $<'$ are, respectively, a simple entrenchment and dependence relations that are related by the de-mapping, then $<$ is regular if and only if $<'$ is regular.*
   2. If $<$ and $<'$ are, respectively, a strict entrenchment and dependence relations that are related by Converse Complement, then $<$ is regular if and only if $<'$ is regular.
   3. If $<$ and $<'$ are, respectively, a simple entrenchment and simple plausibility relations that are related by Contraposition, then $<$ is regular if and only if $<'$ is regular.

As we said, however, regular entrenchment and plausibility relations determine a more natural correspondence between simple and strict variants. Given a regular simple entrenchment relation, we can construct its strict counterpart using the following definition:

(SRE) $A <_s B \quad \equiv \quad A < B \text{ and } \mathbf{t} \not< A$

As can be easily seen, $<_s$ is a subrelation of $<$ that coincides with the latter on all pairs (A, B) such that A is not $<$-equivalent to $\mathbf{t}$.

In the other direction, given a strict entrenchment relation, its simple counterpart is definable as follows:

(RSE) $A <_r B \quad \equiv \quad A < B \text{ or } B \not< \mathbf{t}$

In this case $<_r$ is an extension of $<$ obtained by making all propositions that are not strictly below $\mathbf{t}$ maximal propositions in the order. As before, the two relations coincide on 'regular' propositions.

The pair of transformations determined by (SRE) and (RSE) above will be called the *rs-mapping*. The following result shows that the rs-mapping determines a bijection between regular simple and strict entrenchment relations.

Theorem 5.3.1.   *1. If $<$ is a regular simple entrenchment relation, then $<_s$ defined by (SRE) is a strict entrenchment relation. Moreover, $<_{sr}$ coincides with $<$.*

2. If $<$ is a strict entrenchment relation, then $<_r$ defined by (RSE) is a regular simple entrenchment relation. Also, $<_{bs}$ coincides with $<$.

Proof. It is immediate to check that (SRE) and (RSE) produce expectation relations, so we will prove only specific properties involved.

(1) Assume that $<$ is a regular simple entrenchment relation.

Irreflexivity. $A < A$ implies $\mathbf{t} < A$ (see Lemma 5.2.1). Consequently $A \not<_s A$ by (SRE).

Reduction. Assume $A \wedge B <_s B$, that is, $A \wedge B < B$ and $\mathbf{t} \not< A \wedge B$. Then $A < B$ by Reduction for $<$ and $\mathbf{t} \not< A$ by weak t-regularity. Consequently, $A <_s B$.

t-primeness. Assume $A <_s \mathbf{t}$ and $B \not<_s \mathbf{t}$. Then $\mathbf{t} \not< A$ and $\mathbf{t} < B$. Consequently, $A < B$ (by Left Strengthening) and therefore $A <_s B$.

Finally, assume that $A <_{sr} B$, that is, either $\mathbf{t} < B$ or $A < B$ and $\mathbf{t} \not< A$. Clearly, in both these cases $A < B$. In the other direction, $A < B$ implies that either $\mathbf{t} < B$ or $\mathbf{t} \not< A$ (by weak t-regularity), and hence $A <_{sr} B$. Thus, $<_{sr}$ coincides with $<$.

(2) Assume now that $<$ is a regular strict entrenchment relation.

t-reflexivity of $<_r$ follows directly from (RSE).

Reduction for $<_r$ follows from Reduction for $<$.

t-regularity. Assume that $\mathbf{t} <_r A$ and $A <_r B$. Since $<$ is irreflexive, $\mathbf{t} <_r A$ amounts to $A \not< \mathbf{t}$. Consequently, $A \not< B$, and therefore $A <_r B$ implies $B \not< \mathbf{t}$. But then $A \wedge B \not< \mathbf{t}$. Indeed, if $A \wedge B < \mathbf{t}$ and $B \not< \mathbf{t}$, then $A \wedge B < B$ by t-primeness, and hence $A < B$ by Reduction - a contradiction. Therefore $A \wedge B \not< \mathbf{t}$, and consequently $\mathbf{t} <_r A \wedge B$ by (RSE).

Finally, assume that $A <_{bs} B$, that is, $A < \mathbf{t}$ and either $A < B$ or $B \not< \mathbf{t}$. Clearly, $A < B$ implies both these conditions. In the other direction, $A < B$ follows from $A < \mathbf{t}$ and $B \not< \mathbf{t}$ by t-primeness. Therefore, $<_{bs}$ coincides with $<$.   □

Given the duality between entrenchment and plausibility, we can immediately obtain from the above theorem an alternative correspondence between regular simple and strict plausibility:

(SRP) $A <_s B \quad \equiv \quad A < B$ and $B \not< \mathbf{f}$

(RSP) $A <_r B \quad \equiv \quad A < B$ or $\mathbf{f} \not< A$

Non-commuting. Together with its advantages (that will become clear in what follows), the rs-mapping introduces, however, a complication into our picture that needs to be addressed.

By defining an alternative mapping between strict and simple entrenchment relations, we have created a peculiar situation in which we have a triangle of *non-commuting* mappings consisting of the de-mapping (between simple entrenchment and dependence), Converse Complement (between dependence and strict entrenchment), and rs-mapping (between strict and simple entrenchment). Non-commuting means that no mapping from the three can be obtained as a composition of the other two. In still other words, this means that for each two kinds of expectation relations involved we have now *two* different bijections, one direct and another one obtained by composing the other two mappings. This certainly complicates the picture. But there is a positive side in this story; the above triple of mappings also doubles our possibilities of representing inference relations and related objects, and it turns out that the new possibilities correspond actually to some established ways of defining such inference relations, given in the literature.

In addition to the direct rs-mapping, we have already defined earlier a derived rs*-mapping as a composition of the de-mapping and converse complement. Similarly, the following *de*-mapping determines an alternative correspondence between simple entrenchment and dependence relations (in both ways); it is obtainable by composing the rs-mapping and converse complement.

(DE*) $$A <_{de}^* B \quad \equiv \quad B \not< A \text{ or } \mathbf{t} < B$$

Finally, the following c^*-*mapping* determines an alternative correspondence between strict entrenchment and dependence relations; it is obtainable by composition of the de- and rs-mappings.

(SD*) $$A <_s^* B \quad \equiv \quad B \to A < B \text{ and } \mathbf{t} \not< A$$
(DS*) $$A <_d^* B \quad \equiv \quad A < A \to B \text{ or } A \to B \not< \mathbf{t}$$

As we said earlier, the de-mapping and Converse Complement are bijections on regular expectation relations. So, all three our mappings transform regular expectation relations into regular expectation relations. However, the non-commuting of the mappings shows itself in the fact that if we take, say, a regular dependence relation, transform it into a simple entrenchment via the de-mapping, then transform the result into a strict entrenchment by the rs-mapping, and finally transform the latter back to dependence relations by Converse Complement, we will obtain, in general, a *different* regular dependence relation. This phenomenon will reappear in the next chapter in the form of a duality relation that can be established among regular inference relations.

5.4 Dependence orders, consequence relations and partial epistemic entrenchment

By a *dependence order* we will mean a simple dependence relation that is already transitive. Such dependence relations constitute a 'partial' generalization of the original (reflexive) notions of epistemic entrenchment and expectation relations suggested by Gärdenfors and Makinson: they have all the essential properties of the latter, except connectivity. We will see also that dependence orders constitute a (slight) generalization of the notion of partial epistemic entrenchment from [LR91].

To begin with, notice that dependence orders can be described completely by means of the following three rules:

Dominance   If $A \models B$, then $A < B$.
Transitivity   If $A < B$ and $B < C$, then $A < C$.
Antecedence   If $A < B$, then $A < A \wedge B$.

Indeed, the quasi-monotonicity rules for an expectation relation are obtainable by combining Transitivity and Dominance. Note also that any dependence order satisfies the following important rule:

And   If $A < B$ and $A < C$, then $A < B \wedge C$.

Lemma 5.4.1. *Any dependence order satisfies And.*

Proof. If $A < B$ and $A < C$, then $A < A \wedge B$ by Antecedence from the first condition, and $A \wedge B < C$ by Left Strengthening from the second one. The latter implies $A \wedge B < A \wedge B \wedge C$ by Antecedence, and hence $A \wedge B < B \wedge C$ by Right Weakening. Therefore $A < B \wedge C$ by Transitivity.   □

As we are going to show now, dependence orders are exactly equivalent to supraclassical Tarski consequence relations.

To begin with, recall that sets of premises in rules of a supraclassical consequence relation can be always replaced by their conjunctions. This means that any supraclassical Tarski consequence relation is determined, in effect, by pairs of propositions standing in this relation. Such a binary relation will always be a partial order on the set of classical propositions. And as we will show now, these partial orders are precisely dependence orders.

It is easy to check that the set of rules of the form $A \vdash B$ belonging to a supraclassical consequence relation forms a dependence order. Moreover, for any dependence order $<$, we can define the following consequence relation:

$$a \vdash_< A \quad \text{iff} \quad \bigwedge a < A$$

Then the following lemma says, in effect, that consequence relation and dependence order are equivalent notions.

Lemma 5.4.2. $<$ *is a dependence order if and only if* $\vdash_<$ *is a supraclassical consequence relation.*

Proof. Supraclassicality (and hence reflexivity) follows from Dominance. In addition, $C \wedge B < B$ by Dominance. Consequently, $\bigwedge a < A$ implies $B \wedge \bigwedge a < A$ by Transitivity. Thus, Monotonicity holds. Finally, if $\bigwedge a < A$ and $A \wedge \bigwedge a < B$, then Dominance and Antecedence imply $\bigwedge a < A \wedge \bigwedge a$, and hence by Transitivity $\bigwedge a < B$. Thus Cut is also satisfied.   □

Remark. Partial epistemic entrenchment relations introduced by Lindström and Rabinowicz in [LR91] satisfy all the postulates of dependence orders. Moreover, the notion of a filter, or *fallback*, used in [LR91], exactly corresponds to theories of the associated consequence relation $\vdash_<$. Accordingly, most of the properties of these objects, proved in [LR91], can be immediately obtained on the basis of this identification. Still, partial entrenchment relations are less general than dependence orders; as we will see later, they correspond to determinate consequence relations.

As a final observation in this section, we note that converse complement of dependence orders correspond to a rather special class of strict entrenchment relations, namely to relations that satisfy

Modularity   If $A < B$, then either $C < B$ or $A < C$.

The lemma below follows from the well-known fact that modular relations are exactly converse complements of transitive relations.

Lemma 5.4.3. *Converse complements of dependence orders are exactly modular strict entrenchment relations.*

Notice that modular strict entrenchment relations are not necessary transitive. They will be such, however, when we will add the condition of asymmetry (see below).

5.5 Qualitative expectation relations

In this section we will describe the three kinds of expectation relations that determine skeptical inference relations, namely qualitative entrenchment, qualitative plausibility and qualitative dependence. As before, all these kinds of expectation relations will turn out to be interdefinable.

Definition 5.5.1. • *An entrenchment relation will be called* qualitative *if it satisfies And:*
And   *If $A < B$ and $A < C$, then $A < B \wedge C$.*
• *A plausibility relation will be called* qualitative *if it satisfies*
Or   *If $A < C$ and $B < C$, then $A \vee B < C$.*
• *A dependence relation will be called* qualitative *if it satisfies*
Weak Or   *If $A \vee B < A$ and $A \vee C < A$, then $A \vee B \vee C < A$.*

Qualitative expectation relations are quite rich structures. All of them will already be transitive.

We will begin with qualitative entrenchment. All conditions for qualitative entrenchment relations correspond to Rott's conditions for generalized epistemic entrenchment in [Rot92b] (see also [GR95]), except that the latter are formulated with respect to some fixed underlying classical consequence relation (see below). Actually, Rott's generalized epistemic entrenchment corresponds exactly to strict qualitative entrenchment relations.

The following lemma describes basic properties of qualitative entrenchment (see [Rot92b]).

Lemma 5.5.1. *1. If $A < B$ and $C < D$, then $A \wedge C < B \wedge D$;*
2. If $A < B$ and $B < C$, then $A < C$.
3. If $A \wedge B < C$ and $A \wedge C < B$, then $A < B \wedge C$.

Proof. (i) If $A < B$ and $C < D$, then $A \wedge C < B$ and $A \wedge C < D$ by Right Weakening, and hence $A \wedge C < B \wedge D$ by And.

(ii) $A < B$ and $B < C$, then $A \wedge B < B \wedge C$ by (1) and hence $A \wedge B \wedge C < B \wedge C$ by Left Strengthening. Consequently, $A < B \wedge C$ by Reduction, and therefore $A < C$ by Right Weakening.

(iii) If $A \wedge B < C$ and $A \wedge C < B$, then $A \wedge B \wedge C < B \wedge C$ by (1), and hence $A < B \wedge C$ by Reduction. $\square$

Property (3) above can be shown to be equivalent to a combination of Reduction and And. It has been considered in [Rot94] as expressing the essence of the notion of epistemic entrenchment. Its 'contrapositive' counterpart has been taken as a characteristic postulate of qualitative plausibility in [FH98].

Qualitative dependence relations have been used in [Geo99] under the name weakly disjunctive partial entrenchment orders.

As we are going to show now, qualitative dependence relations are equivalent to semi-classical consequence relations. To begin with, we will show that any qualitative dependence relation is already transitive.

Lemma 5.5.2. *Any qualitative dependence relation is a dependence order.*

Proof. Assume that $A < B$ and $B < C$ hold. The first condition implies $A \wedge (B \to C) < B$ by Left Strengthening, and hence $A \wedge (B \to C) < A \wedge B \wedge C$ by Antecedence. Again, by Left Strengthening, $A \wedge \neg B < A \wedge B \wedge C$. Now, $B < C$ implies $A \wedge B < C$, and hence $A \wedge B < A \wedge B \wedge C$ by Antecedence. Now we can apply Weak Or and obtain $A < A \wedge B \wedge C$. Consequently, $A < C$ by Right Weakening. Thus, transitivity holds. $\square$

Since dependence orders are equivalent to supraclassical consequence relations, qualitative dependence relations will correspond to a special class of consequence relations. The following result shows that these are precisely semi-classical consequence relations described in Chapter 2.

Lemma 5.5.3. *$<$ is a qualitative dependence relation if and only if $\vdash_<$ is a semi-classical consequence relation.*

The following result shows that our earlier definitions of dependence in terms of simple entrenchment and vice versa are extendable to qualitative relations.

Theorem 5.5.1. *The de-mapping determines a bijection between qualitative dependence relations and simple qualitative entrenchment relations.*

Proof. We need only to show that the de-mapping determines a correspondence between the rule And (for entrenchment) and Weak Or (for dependence).

(i) $<_e$ satisfies And if and only if the dependence relation $<$ satisfies

If $B \to A < B$ and $C \to A < C$, then $(B \wedge C) \to A < B \wedge C$.

Now, $B \to A < B$ implies $(A \wedge B \wedge C) \vee (\neg B \vee (A \wedge C)) < B$ by Left Strengthening, and hence

$$(A \wedge B \wedge C) \vee (\neg B \vee (A \wedge C)) < A \wedge B \wedge C$$

by Antecedence. Similarly, $C \to A < C$ implies

$$(A \wedge B \wedge C) \vee (\neg C \vee (A \wedge B)) < A \wedge B \wedge C.$$

Now we can apply Weak Or and obtain

$$\neg B \vee \neg C \vee (A \wedge B) \vee (A \wedge C) < A \wedge B \wedge C$$

which is equivalent to $(B \wedge C) \to A < A \wedge B \wedge C$. The latter implies $(B \wedge C) \to A < B \wedge C$ by Right Weakening. Consequently, And holds for $<_e$, and hence the latter is a qualitative entrenchment relation.

(ii) We have to show validity of Weak Or for $<_d$. Assume $A \vee B <_d A$ and $A \vee C <_d A$. The first condition is reduced to $A \vee B < B \to A$, and hence implies $A < B \to A$ by Left Strengthening. Similarly, the second condition implies $A < C \to A$. Therefore $A < (B \vee C) \to A$ by And. But the latter implies $A \vee B \vee C < (B \vee C) \to A$ by Reduction, which is equivalent to $A \vee B \vee C <_d A$. Thus, Weak Or is valid for $<_d$. This completes the proof. $\square$

Finally, note that transitivity and And imply t-regularity. Accordingly, any simple qualitative entrenchment relation, and any qualitative dependence relation will already be regular. This means, in particular, that we can use the rs-mapping for establishing the correspondence between simple and strict qualitative entrenchment relations. It is interesting to note that, since such relations are already transitive, strict qualitative entrenchment can be equivalently defined as a strict version of simple qualitative entrenchment:

(SBE1) $A <^s B \quad \equiv \quad A < B \ \& \ B \not< A$

Theorem 5.5.2. *The rs-mapping determines a bijection between strict and simple qualitative entrenchment relations.*

Proof. We only need to show the validity of And on both sides.

(i) Assume $A <_s B$ and $A <_s C$. The first condition implies $A < B$ and $\mathbf{t} \not< A$, while the second one $A < C$ and $\mathbf{t} \not< A$. Consequently, $A < (B \wedge C)$ by And for $<$, and hence $A <_s (B \wedge C)$. Thus, And holds for $<_s$.

(ii) Assume $A <_r B$ and $A <_r C$. The first condition holds if either $A < B$, or $B \not< \mathbf{t}$. The second one implies that either $A < C$ or $C \not< \mathbf{t}$. A number of cases should be considered. To begin with, if $B \wedge C \not< \mathbf{t}$, then we immediately obtain $A <_r (B \wedge C)$ by the definition of $<_r$. So, we will assume below that $B \wedge C < \mathbf{t}$.

(a) If $A < B$ and $A < C$, then $A < B \wedge C$ by And for $<$, and hence $A <_r B \wedge C$ holds.

(b) If $A < B$ and $C \not< \mathbf{t}$, then $B \wedge C < \mathbf{t}$ implies $B \wedge C < C$ by t-primeness, and hence $B < C$ by Reduction. Consequently, $A < C$ by transitivity, and hence $A < (B \wedge C)$ by And for $<$. Therefore, $A <_s (B \wedge C)$ holds.

(c) If $B \not< \mathbf{t}$ and $A < C$, then $B \wedge C < B$ by t-primeness, and hence $C < B$ by Reduction. Then $A < B$ by transitivity, and the proof proceeds as in (b).

(d) Finally, assume that $B \not< \mathbf{t}$ and $C \not< \mathbf{t}$. Given $B \wedge C < \mathbf{t}$ and the first condition, we obtain $B \wedge C < B$ by t-primeness, and hence $C < B$. But the latter implies $C < \mathbf{t}$, contrary to our assumptions. This completes the proof. □

As before, a general consequence from the above results is that all the variant notions of a qualitative expectation relation turn out to be interdefinable.

As a last observation in this section, we will show that any dependence order determines a natural qualitative entrenchment relation associated with it.

Recall our informal description of entrenchment relations given at the beginning of the chapter: B is more entrenched than A if B can be retained whenever we are required to reject $A \wedge B$. Now, we can interpret this description in the framework of consequence relations (= dependence orders) as follows:

> B is more entrenched than A if B belongs to all maximal theories of
> a consequence relation that do not contain $A \wedge B$.

The above description justifies the following definition. For any dependence order $<$, we will define the corresponding entrenchment relation as follows:

$$A <_q B \equiv C \wedge B < A \text{ only if } C < B, \text{ for any } C.$$

It can be easily shown that if $<$ is a dependence order, then $A <_q B$ holds if and only if B belongs to all maximal theories of the associated consequence relation $\vdash_<$ that do not contain $A \wedge B$. The following result shows that this definition determines a qualitative entrenchment relation.

Lemma 5.5.4. *If $<$ is a dependence order, then $<_q$ is a simple qualitative entrenchment relation.*

Proof. We will check the validity of the postulates for simple qualitative entrenchment.

t-reflexivity follows immediately from the definition of $<_q$.

Reduction. Assume that $A \wedge B <_q B$ and $C \wedge B < A$. Then $C \wedge B < A \wedge B$ by Antecedence and Right Weakening, and hence $A \wedge B <_q B$ implies $C < B$. Thus, $A <_q B$ holds.

And. Assume that $A <_q B$, $A <_q D$ and $C \wedge B \wedge D < A$, for some C. Then $A <_q B$ implies $C \wedge D < B$, while $A <_q D$ implies $C \wedge B < D$. Consequently, $C < B \wedge D$ by (3) from Lemma 5.5.1. Therefore, $A <_q B \wedge D$ holds. $\square$

It turns out that the above construction of qualitative entrenchment relations is quite general in the sense that any simple qualitative entrenchment is generated by some dependence order.

Lemma 5.5.5. *Any simple qualitative entrenchment relation is generated by some dependence order.*

Proof. Let $<$ be a simple qualitative entrenchment relation, and $<'$ its corresponding qualitative dependence relation (via the de-mapping). Then we will show that $<'$ generates $<$.

Assume first that $A <'_q B$ holds, and take C equal to $B \to A$. Then we will have that $C \wedge B <' A$ holds. Indeed, the latter is equivalent to $C \wedge B < ((C \wedge B) \to A)$, that is, to $A \wedge B < ((A \wedge B) \to A)$, where the right side is equivalent to t. Consequently, $A <'_q B$ gives us $C <' B$, which amounts to $B \to A < B$. But the latter implies $A < B$ by Left Strengthening.

Assume now that $A < B$ and $C \wedge B <' A$, for some C. The second condition is reducible to $C \wedge B < ((C \wedge B) \to A)$. By (1) from Lemma 5.5.1 we infer $A \wedge B \wedge C < B \wedge (C \to A)$. But $A \wedge B \wedge C$ is equivalent to $C \wedge B \wedge (C \to A)$, so we can apply Reduction and infer $C < B \wedge (C \to A)$. But the latter implies $C < C \to B$, which is equivalent to $C <' B$. Consequently, $A <'_q B$ holds, and therefore $<$ coincides with $<'_q$. This completes the proof. $\square$

It should be noted that the above construction does not establish a bijection between dependence orders and qualitative entrenchment relations, since different dependence orders can generate the same entrenchment relation. Still, the construction provides an important way of representing qualitative entrenchment relations.

5.6 Modular and linear expectation relations

A dependence order will be called *linear* if it satisfies

Linearity $A < B$ or $B < A$.

Due to the correspondence between dependence orders and consequence relations, linear dependence orders correspond exactly to linear consequence relations.

Theorem 5.6.1. $<$ *is a linear dependence order iff* $\vdash_<$ *is a linear supraclassical consequence relation.*

Linear dependence orders satisfy already the main property of original epistemic entrenchment relations from [GM88], namely

Conjunctiveness $A < A \wedge B$ or $B < A \wedge B$.

As can be easily seen, Linearity and Conjunctiveness are equivalent (given Antecedence). Actually, linear dependence orders are exactly equivalent to *expectation orderings* from [GM94]. The latter are characterized by the following three postulates:

Dominance If $A \vDash B$, then $A < B$.
Transitivity If $A < B$ and $B < C$, then $A < C$.
Conjunctiveness $A < A \wedge B$ or $B < A \wedge B$.

Lemma 5.6.1. *Linear dependence orders coincide with expectation orderings.*

Proof. Conjunctiveness follows from Linearity and Antecedence. So, we need only to show that expectation orderings satisfy Linearity and Antecedence.

Linearity follows from Conjunctiveness by Right Weakening, while the latter is an immediate consequence of Dominance and Transitivity.

Assume that $A < B$, but $A \not< A \wedge B$. Then $B < A \wedge B$ by Conjunctiveness, and hence $A < A \wedge B$ by Transitivity - a contradiction. Thus, Antecedence holds.   □

As we will see in the next section, there is a strong connection between expectation orderings (and linear consequence relations) and 'full' epistemic entrenchment relations from [GM88].

Turning to other relatives of linear dependence orders, we can notice that the converse complement (or, equivalently, the strict counterpart) of a linear dependence order is exactly a strict modular qualitative entrenchment relation. This result has been obtained, in effect, by Rott in [Rot92b]; he has shown that imposing modularity is the only condition needed in order to transform a strict qualitative entrenchment order into a strict version of the standard epistemic entrenchment of Gärdenfors and Makinson.

Lemma 5.6.2. $<$ *is a linear dependence order if and only if* $<^c$ *is a strict entrenchment relation that is modular and qualitative.*

Proof. As has been shown earlier, converse complements of general dependence orders are strict modular entrenchment relations. Consequently, linear dependence orders correspond in this sense to strict modular relations that are *asymmetric*. Hence, it is sufficient to show that they are qualitative, that is, satisfy And.

Assume that $A < B$, $A < C$, but $A \not< B \wedge C$. By modularity, we have then $B \wedge C < B$ and $B \wedge C < C$. The latter imply, respectively, $C < B$ and $B < C$ by Reduction, contrary to asymmetry. Thus, And holds.

In the other direction, we need only to notice that, since strict qualitative entrenchment relations are transitive, they are asymmetric, and hence their converse complements are linear. $\quad\square$

Finally, the rs-mapping can be used to show that the correspondence between strict and simple entrenchment relations is extendable to qualitative modular relations.

Lemma 5.6.3. *The rs-mapping determines a bijection between simple and strict qualitative modular entrenchment relations.*

Proof. We need only to check Modularity on both sides.

(i) Assume that $<$ is a modular entrenchment relation, and $A <_s B$. Then $A < B$ and $\mathbf{t} \not< A$. If $A < C$, then $A <_s C$, and we are done. So, let us assume that $A \not< C$. Then $C < B$ by modularity. Assume that $\mathbf{t} < C$. Then $A < C$ by modularity (since $\mathbf{t} \not< A$), contrary to our assumption. Therefore $\mathbf{t} \not< C$, and hence $C <_s B$.

(ii) Assume this time that $A <_r B$, for some modular entrenchment relation $<$. Then either $A < B$ or $B \not< \mathbf{t}$. In the first case we have either $A < C$ or $C < B$ by modularity, and hence either $A <_r C$ or $C <_r B$ by the definition of $<_r$. In the second case we have $C <_r B$, again, by the definition of $<_r$. Thus, Modularity holds for $<_r$. $\quad\square$

Thus, in this case also all the notions studied earlier, namely dependence relations, epistemic entrenchment and plausibility will be interdefinable. Notice, however, that the actual mappings that have been chosen for this case are different from the mappings that were chosen earlier for establishing the correspondences on the level of qualitative expectation relations. This change was deliberate, since the de-mapping does *not* relate linear dependence relations and simple modular qualitative entrenchment: though de-counterparts of linear dependence relations will be modular, not all simple modular qualitative entrenchment relations will correspond to linear dependence relations via the de-mapping. Linear dependence and simple modular entrenchment are related, however, via a combination of the Converse Complement and the rs-mapping (that is, via the de*-mapping, described earlier). This is where the non-commuting of our three basic mappings has turned out to be fruitful.

5.7 Belief sets and underlying logics of expectation relations

An *epistemic entrenchment relation* from [GM88] was defined in a predetermined context consisting of a given deductively closed belief set **K** and a classical consequence relation Th; it was required to satisfy the following conditions:

(EE1) $A \leq B$ and $B \leq C$ imply $A \leq C$. (Transitivity)
(EE2)   If $A \in \text{Th}(B)$, then $A \leq B$. (Dominance)
(EE3)   Either $A \leq A \wedge B$ or $B \leq A \wedge B$ (Conjunctiveness)
(EE4)   When $\mathbf{f} \notin \mathbf{K}$, $A \notin \mathbf{K}$ iff $A \leq B$, for all B. (Minimality)
(EE5)   If $B \leq A$, for all B, then $A \in \text{Th}(\emptyset)$. (Maximality)

It turns out, however, that the notions of a belief set and underlying logic can be recovered from any sufficiently rich expectation relation. As a result, the above 'relative' notion of epistemic entrenchment will be shown to be essentially equivalent to the notion of an expectation relation from [GM94] (or, in other words, to that of a linear dependence order).

5.7.1 The internal logic of dependence orders

As we said in Chapter 2, any supraclassical consequence relation $\vdash$ contains a greatest *classical* consequence relation $\text{Th}_\vdash$, which is defined as follows:

$$A \in \text{Th}(a) \quad \equiv \quad \vdash \bigwedge a \rightarrow A$$

This classical subrelation can be seen as determining the 'internal logic' of a supraclassical consequence relation and its associated pure epistemic state. Below we will translate this construction into the framework of dependence orders.

A dependence order will be said to *respect* a classical consequence relation Th if it satisfies the following two conditions:

(Th-**dominance**)   If $B \in \text{Th}(A)$, then $A < B$.
(Th-**preservation**)   If $B < A$, for all B, then $A \in \text{Th}(\emptyset)$.

The above conditions exactly correspond to postulates (EE2) and (EE5) of epistemic entrenchment, given above. In fact, these are the only postulates in the list that describe the connection between epistemic entrenchment and the underlying logic. As can be seen, Th-dominance is a strengthening of the Dominance condition for dependence orders. Th-preservation can by simplified to the following condition:

(TP)   If $\mathbf{t} < A$, then $A \in \text{Th}(\emptyset)$.

As the following result shows, the above two conditions are sufficient for identifying Th with the classical subrelation of the associated supraclassical consequence relation.

Lemma 5.7.1. *A dependence order $<$ respects* Th *if and only if* Th *coincides with the classical subrelation of* $\vdash_<$.

Proof. Assume first that $<$ respects Th. Since Th is classical, $B \in \text{Th}(A)$ if and only if $A \to B \in \text{Th}(\emptyset)$. By Th-dominance and (TP) this is equivalent to $\mathbf{t} < A \to B$. But the later amounts to $B \in \text{Th}_<(A)$, where Th $<$ is a classical subrelation of $\vdash_<$. Consequently, Th coincides with the classical subrelation of $\vdash_<$. In the other direction, it is easy to check that the classical subrelation of $\vdash_<$ is respected by $<$. $\square$

The above result shows, in effect, that the underlying logic of a dependence order is uniquely determined by the order itself.

As we will see now, an almost similar situation occurs with the belief set associated with a dependence order.

5.7.2 Belief sets of dependence orders

The characterization of standard epistemic entrenchment in [GM88] includes only postulate (EE4) that involves the associated belief set **K**. For consistent belief sets, it amounts to the following equivalence

(Bottom) $A \notin \mathbf{K}$ iff $A \leq \mathbf{f}$.

Though Bottom looks like a definition of **K** in our context, it turns out that it implicitly restricts the set of allowable dependence orders due to the fact that **K** is supposed to be a deductively closed set. As we will show now, this restriction amounts to restricting the associated consequence relations to determinate ones.

A dependence order will be called *determinate* if it satisfies the following condition:

(Determination) $A \wedge B < \mathbf{f}$ only if $A < \mathbf{f}$ or $B < \mathbf{f}$.

As can be easily checked, the above condition is equivalent to the characterization of determinate consequence relations given in Chapter 2. Consequently, we have

Lemma 5.7.2. *A dependence order is determinate iff* $\vdash_<$ *is a determinate consequence relation.*

Now the following result shows that the postulate Bottom above amounts, in fact, to restricting the set of dependence orders to determinate ones.

Theorem 5.7.1. *A dependence order $<$ satisfies the postulate Bottom with respect to a consistent belief set* **K** *if and only if $<$ is determinate and* **K** *coincides with the belief set of* $\vdash_<$.

Proof. If $A \wedge B < \mathbf{f}$, then $A \wedge B \notin \mathbf{K}$ by Bottom. Since $\mathbf{K}$ is deductively closed, we have that either $A \notin \mathbf{K}$ or $B \notin \mathbf{K}$, and hence either $A < \mathbf{f}$ or $B < \mathbf{f}$. Thus, $<$ is a determinate dependence order. Moreover, the set of all consistent propositions with respect to a determinate consequence relation forms its greatest consistent theory, and hence $\mathbf{K}$ coincides in this case with the belief set of $\vdash_<$. $\square$

The above theorem shows clearly that the net effect of the postulate Bottom consists in imposing determination on dependence orders. More exactly, accepting Bottom or (EE4) amounts to imposing determination and identifying the belief set $\mathbf{K}$ with the set of all propositions A such that $A \nless \mathbf{f}$.

Partial epistemic entrenchment ordering. A 'partial' generalization of the notion of epistemic entrenchment suggested in [LR91] was also defined in the context of a fixed belief set and an underlying classical consequence relation, and was required to satisfy all the postulates for epistemic entrenchment, except Conjunctiveness (EE3), which was replaced by the And rule. To make this precise, we will introduce the following definition.

Definition 5.7.1. *A dependence order will be said to be a* partial epistemic entrenchment ordering *for a belief set* $\mathbf{K}$ *with respect to a classical consequence relation* Th *if it satisfies* Th-*dominance and* Th-*preservation with respect to* Th, *and Bottom with respect to* $\mathbf{K}$.

It can be easily shown that the above definition is equivalent to the definition of *epistemic entrenchment ordering for* $\mathbf{K}$, given in [LR91]. Now our previous results can be used to 'purify' this notion.

To begin with, Th-dominance and Th-preservation jointly amount to requiring that the dependence order $<$ respects Th. Consequently, Th should coincide with the internal logic $\mathrm{Th}_<$ of the dependence order. In addition, we have seen that Bottom is reducible to the requirement that the dependence order should be determinate, in which case $\mathbf{K}$ should coincide with the belief set of $\vdash_<$. Summing up these facts, we arrive at the following conclusion:

Lemma 5.7.3. *Partial epistemic entrenchment orderings are equivalent to determinate dependence orders.*

5.7.3 Belief set and logic of qualitative entrenchment

Just as for dependence orders, any qualitative entrenchment order determines its own belief set and underlying classical consequence relation. Thus, the *belief set* of a qualitative entrenchment order can be defined as the set of all propositions that are more entrenched than logical falsity:

$$\mathbf{K}_< = \{A \mid \mathbf{f} < A\}$$

The following lemma gives an indirect justification for the above notion of a belief set.

Lemma 5.7.4. *If $<$ is a qualitative entrenchment relation and $<^d$ its corresponding qualitative dependence relation, then $\mathbf{K}_<$ coincides with the belief set of $<^d$.*

Proof. Notice first that, according to our translations, $\mathbf{f} < A$ holds if and only if $\neg A <^d \mathbf{f}$. Also, $<^d$ corresponds to a semi-classical consequence relation, say $\vdash$, and hence all maximal theories of $\vdash$ are worlds. Consequently, A belongs to the belief set of $\vdash$ if and only if $\neg A \vdash \mathbf{f}$. Consequently, the belief set of $<^d$ consists precisely of propositions such that $\neg A <^d \mathbf{f}$. This completes the proof.   □

Further arguments in favor of the above definition of the belief set will be given in due course when we will discuss belief change.

Similarly, the underlying classical consequence relation of a simple qualitative entrenchment order can be defined as follows:

$$A \in \mathrm{Th}_<(B) \quad \equiv \quad \mathbf{t} < (B \to A)$$

As can be seen, the above classical consequence relation is determined by propositions that are as entrenched as the logical truth $\mathbf{t}$.

As before, we will say that a simple qualitative entrenchment order *respects* a classical consequence relation Th, if it satisfies the following conditions:

(QE1)   If $A < B$ and $C \in \mathrm{Th}(B)$, then $A < C$.
(QE2)   If $A < B$ and $A \in \mathrm{Th}(C)$, then $C < B$.
(QE3)   If $\mathbf{t} < A$, then $A \in \mathrm{Th}(\emptyset)$.

The first two conditions exactly correspond to conditions on generalized epistemic entrenchment given in [Rot92b]. The following result describes the impact of these conditions. It shows that $\mathrm{Th}_<$ provides a correct description of the internal logic of $<$.

Lemma 5.7.5. *A simple qualitative entrenchment relation $<$ respects a classical consequence relation Th if and only if Th coincides with $\mathrm{Th}_<$.*

Proof. Let us check first that $<$ respects $\mathrm{Th}_<$. Note that (QE3) follows directly from the definition of $\mathrm{Th}_<$.

(QE1). If $A < B$ and $\mathbf{t} < B \to C$, then the latter implies $A < B \to C$, and hence $A < B \wedge (B \to C)$ by And. But the latter implies $A < C$ by Right Weakening.

(QE2). If $A < B$ and $\mathbf{t} < C \to A$, then the latter implies $C < C \to A$, and hence $A \wedge C < B \wedge (C \to A)$ by Lemma 5.5.1. But the latter is equivalent $C \wedge (C \to A) < B \wedge (C \to A)$, and therefore we obtain $C < B$ by Lemma 5.5.1.

So, $<$ respects $\mathrm{Th}_<$. In the other direction, in order to show that Th coincides with $\mathrm{Th}_<$, it is sufficient to demonstrate that they have the same provable propositions. Now, if $\mathbf{t} < A$, then $A \in \mathrm{Th}(\emptyset)$ by (QE3), while the other direction follows from (QE1).   □

Part II

Nonmonotonic Inference

6. The Basic Inference Relation

6.1 Introduction

The approach to nonmonotonic reasoning based on describing associated inference relations forms one of the most natural and powerful tools in its study. Gabbay's paper [Gab85], a starting point of the approach, has been followed by a number of fundamental works (notably [Mak89, Sho88]) that have reached saturation in the so-called KLM theory [KLM90, LM92] (see also [Mak94] for an overview). In these works a semantic representation of nonmonotonic inference relations was developed based on sets of world-states ordered by a preference relation: a nonmonotonic inference rule $A \vdash B$ was characterized as saying that B should be true in all preferred states satisfying A. Shoham [Sho88] has shown that such a preference-based representation allows us to unify many approaches to nonmonotonic reasoning developed in Artificial Intelligence.

The above notion of a nonmonotonic inference was designed to capture a *skeptical approach* to nonmonotonic reasoning, according to which if there is a number of equally preferred alternatives, we infer only what is common to all of them. However, we have seen earlier (recall Poole's abductive system described in Chapter 3) that for some reasoning tasks, such as explanation and diagnosis, each of the preferred alternatives is considered as an admissible solution. This leads to an alternative understanding of nonmonotonic reasoning, usually called *credulous* or *brave* one, which is based on choosing a particular preferred set of defaults.

Despite obvious differences, it turns out that skeptical and credulous inference systems also have much in common. Moreover, viewing both as species of one general concept of nonmonotonic inference will give us a broader perspective on the latter that will subsume, in addition, many other interesting reasoning patterns.

We describe below a basic system of nonmonotonic inference that will serve as a natural common core both for skeptical and credulous inference systems. To this end, we will make use of the approach to inference relations suggested by van Benthem in [Ben84, Ben86]. The latter will give us a rather rich and neat picture that avoids complications and fancy elaborations created by common approaches in terms of selection functions.

There have been a number of studies in the literature attempting to give a systematic description for a broader spectrum of nonmonotonic inferences than just skeptical ones – see, e.g., [PL92, Bra93, CLS95]. The problem has turned out to be difficult, however. Indeed, on the face of it, skeptical and credulous inference have little in common. For example, credulous inference invalidates the basic postulates of skeptical inference, such as Cut, Cautious Monotony or And. This means, in particular, that in order to obtain a broader picture of nonmonotonic inference that would encompass both credulous and skeptical kinds, we need to find an alternative ground for classifying inference relations. It turns out that van Benthem's approach to inference relations gives us exactly what we need.

The main idea behind van Benthem's approach was that a conditional can be seen as a special kind of a *generalized quantifier* representing a relation between the respective sets of instances or situations supporting and refuting it. In this setting, the nature of a conditional can be described in terms of possible changes made to these sets of situations that still preserve its validity. Such changes can involve adding new confirming instances, deleting refuting ones, etc. In order to make these notions precise, we will introduce some notation.

An implicit presupposition of van Benthem's study was that situations correspond to possible worlds. We will not accept this presupposition, and adopt instead a broader informal understanding of situations according to which the latter can support propositions, though they need not be complete in this respect: situations may be neutral with respect to some propositions and neither support nor refute them.

A situation s will be said to *confirm* a conditional $A \mathrel{|\!\sim} B$ if it supports the classical implication $A \to B$. A situation s will be said to *refute* a conditional $A \mathrel{|\!\sim} B$ if it supports $A \to \neg B$. The validity of a conditional with respect to a set of situations can be seen then as determined by appropriate, 'favorable' combinations of confirming and refuting instances. Whatever the appropriate combinations are, we will assume (together with van Benthem) that adding new confirming instances to a valid conditional, or removing refuting ones, cannot change its validity. Accordingly, we can accept the following principle:

> If all situations confirming $A \mathrel{|\!\sim} B$ confirm also $C \mathrel{|\!\sim} D$, and all situations refuting $C \mathrel{|\!\sim} D$ refute also $A \mathrel{|\!\sim} B$, then validity of $A \mathrel{|\!\sim} B$ implies validity of $C \mathrel{|\!\sim} D$.

The above principle will be practically sufficient for justifying the rules of the basic inference relation, given below. It will support also a representation of conditionals in terms of expectation relations. More exactly, we can assume that a conditional is valid if the set of its confirming situations *is sufficiently good as compared with* the set of its refuting situations. According to this understanding, $A \mathrel{|\!\sim} B$ could be defined as $A \to \neg B < A \to B$ for an appropriate expectation relation, while the above principle secures that this is indeed an expectation relation as defined in Chapter 5. This representation corresponds to the expectation-based theory of nonmonotonic inference suggested in [GM94].

An equally expressive representation of conditionals will be obtained if we would require that $A \mathrel{|\!\sim} B$ holds when the set of situations supporting both A and B is 'sufficiently good' as compared with the set of situations supporting A and $\neg B$. According to this understanding, $A \mathrel{|\!\sim} B$ could be defined as $A \wedge \neg B < A \wedge B$ for an appropriate expectation relation. Actually, this representation will be more in accord with the original 'possible-worlds' understanding of situations presupposed by van Benthem. We will see also that this interpretation is actually a generalization of the representation of conditionals in terms of plausibility relations developed in [FH98], though our conditions on the plausibility relation will be much weaker than the corresponding conditions on the plausibility orders given in that paper.

Remark. It is interesting to note that the latter understanding of conditionals can also be given a purely logical interpretation, namely an interpretation in terms of some three-valued logic. Let us say that a conditional is *true* (respectively, *false*) in an interpretation if the latter supports $A \wedge B$ (resp., $A \wedge \neg B$). Otherwise, a conditional will be said to be *undefined* with respect to an interpretation. This assigns a conditional a three-valued interpretation even with respect to classical models. Moreover, the above derivability principle for conditionals can be reformulated now as a natural and familiar principle of three-valued semantic derivability, according to which derivability should *preserve both truth and non-falsity*. This semantics for conditionals has been suggested by Dubois and Prade (see [BDP97] for an overview).

Whatever the representation we choose, it will lead to the set of postulates, given in the next section.

In what follows, we will systematically overburden our notation and use the expression $A \mathrel{|\!\sim} B$ in two senses. First, $A \mathrel{|\!\sim} B$ will denote an individual conditional of the form '*If A, then (normally) B*'. Second, $\mathrel{|\!\sim}$ will often be used to denote a nonmonotonic inference *relation* among propositions; $A \mathrel{|\!\sim} B$ will mean then that A and B stand in the relation. Furthermore, we will even take a liberty to say in this case that the conditional $A \mathrel{|\!\sim} B$ belongs to the inference relation $\mathrel{|\!\sim}$.

6.2 Postulates

Throughout this book we will follow David Makinson in distinguishing monotonic *consequence* relations from nonmonotonic *inference* relations. This terminological distinction will be especially suitable in contexts where we will study the relations between the two.

By a *basic inference relation* $\mathcal{B}$ we will mean a relation $\mathrel{|\!\sim}$ on propositions satisfying the following postulates:

Reflexivity $A \mathrel{|\!\sim} A$

Left Equivalence   If $\models A \leftrightarrow B$ and $A \mathrel{|\!\sim} C$, then $B \mathrel{|\!\sim} C$

Right Weakening   If $A \mathrel{|\!\sim} B$ and $B \models C$, then $A \mathrel{|\!\sim} C$

Antecedence   If $A \mathrel{|\!\sim} B$, then $A \mathrel{|\!\sim} A \wedge B$

Deduction   If $A \wedge B \mathrel{|\!\sim} C$, then $A \mathrel{|\!\sim} B \to C$

Conjunctive Cautious Monotony   If $A \mathrel{|\!\sim} B \wedge C$, then $A \wedge B \mathrel{|\!\sim} C$

The most salient feature of the above list is that all the above postulates involve no more than one conditional premise. In other words, they all are *simple rules* in the sense defined in Chapter 4. Accordingly, the famous postulates of nonmonotonic inference, such as Cut, And and Or are absent from the list. In addition, the well-known Cautious Monotony rule is expressed in a slightly different, still more cautious, form that has only one premise.

Reflexivity is the only postulate in the above list that unconditionally asserts the validity of some conditional. Actually, given the rest of the postulates, it is equivalent to a quite weak requirement saying that the conditional $\mathbf{f} \mathrel{|\!\sim} \mathbf{t}$ should always belongs to the inference relation.

Reflexivity and Right Weakening immediately imply 'supraclassicality' of basic inference relations:

(**Dominance**)   If $A \models B$, then $A \mathrel{|\!\sim} B$.

Our axiomatization almost coincides with the minimal conditional logic M suggested by van Benthem in [Ben84], with the only exception that, instead of the Deduction rule, van Benthem used the following postulate:

(**Confirmation**)   If $A \mathrel{|\!\sim} B$, then $A \vee C \mathrel{|\!\sim} B \vee C$.

Actually, the above Confirmation rule can be seen as a direct reflection of the principle that adding new confirming interpretations does not change the validity of a conditional. Still, the following simple result shows that, under some weak conditions, Deduction is equivalent to Confirmation.

Lemma 6.2.1. *Given Left Logical Equivalence and Right Weakening, Confirmation is equivalent to Deduction.*

Proof. If Confirmation holds and $A \wedge B \mathrel{|\!\sim} C$, then $(A \wedge B) \vee (A \wedge \neg B) \mathrel{|\!\sim} C \vee (A \wedge \neg B)$, and hence $A \mathrel{|\!\sim} C \vee (A \wedge \neg B)$ by Left Logical Equivalence and $A \mathrel{|\!\sim} B \to C$ by Right Weakening. In the other direction, if Deduction is valid and $A \mathrel{|\!\sim} B$, then $(A \vee C) \wedge (A \vee \neg C) \mathrel{|\!\sim} B$ by Left Logical Equivalence, and hence $A \vee C \mathrel{|\!\sim} (A \vee \neg C) \to B$ by Deduction. Therefore $A \vee C \mathrel{|\!\sim} B \vee C$ by Right Weakening. Thus, Confirmation holds. $\square$

Notice that Deduction (and hence Confirmation) is valid for preferential entailment from [KLM90], but is not valid for more general systems of cumulative inference described in the same paper. Already this fact indicates that our classification of inference relations will not correspond to standard classifications of nonmonotonic inference given in the literature.

The next lemma summarizes the properties of the basic inference relation that we will use in what follows.

Lemma 6.2.2. 1. $A \hspace{1pt}\vdash\hspace{-6pt}\sim \neg A$ *if and only if* $A \hspace{1pt}\vdash\hspace{-6pt}\sim \mathbf{f}$;
  2. *If* $A \vee B \hspace{1pt}\vdash\hspace{-6pt}\sim \mathbf{f}$, *then* $A \hspace{1pt}\vdash\hspace{-6pt}\sim \mathbf{f}$;
  3. *If* $\neg(A \wedge B) \hspace{1pt}\vdash\hspace{-6pt}\sim A$, *then* $\neg(A \wedge B \wedge C) \hspace{1pt}\vdash\hspace{-6pt}\sim A$;
  4. *If* $\neg A \hspace{1pt}\vdash\hspace{-6pt}\sim \mathbf{f}$, *then* $\neg(A \wedge B) \hspace{1pt}\vdash\hspace{-6pt}\sim A$;
  5. *If* $\neg(A \wedge B \wedge C) \hspace{1pt}\vdash\hspace{-6pt}\sim A \wedge B$, *then* $\neg(B \wedge C) \hspace{1pt}\vdash\hspace{-6pt}\sim B$.

Proof. (1) follows immediately by Antecedence and Right Weakening. For (2), if $A \vee B \hspace{1pt}\vdash\hspace{-6pt}\sim \mathbf{f}$, then $A \vee B \hspace{1pt}\vdash\hspace{-6pt}\sim \mathbf{f} \wedge (A \vee \neg B)$ by Right Weakening, and hence $(A \vee B) \wedge (A \vee \neg B) \hspace{1pt}\vdash\hspace{-6pt}\sim \mathbf{f}$ by Cautious Monotony. Therefore $A \hspace{1pt}\vdash\hspace{-6pt}\sim \mathbf{f}$ by Left Logical Equivalence.

For (3). If $\neg(A \wedge B) \hspace{1pt}\vdash\hspace{-6pt}\sim A$, then $\neg(A \wedge B) \vee (A \wedge B \wedge \neg C) \hspace{1pt}\vdash\hspace{-6pt}\sim A \vee (A \wedge B \wedge \neg C)$ by Confirmation, and hence $\neg(A \wedge B \wedge C) \hspace{1pt}\vdash\hspace{-6pt}\sim A$ by Left Logical Equivalence and Right Weakening.

(4) is a direct consequence of (3) and (1).

Finally, if $\neg(A \wedge B \wedge C) \hspace{1pt}\vdash\hspace{-6pt}\sim A \wedge B$, then $\neg(A \wedge B \wedge C) \hspace{1pt}\vdash\hspace{-6pt}\sim A \wedge B \wedge (A \vee \neg B \vee \neg C)$ by Right Weakening, and consequently $\neg(A \wedge B \wedge C) \wedge (A \vee \neg B \vee \neg C) \hspace{1pt}\vdash\hspace{-6pt}\sim A \wedge B$ by Cautious Monotony. The latter is equivalent to $\neg(B \wedge C) \hspace{1pt}\vdash\hspace{-6pt}\sim A \wedge B$ by Left Logical Equivalence, and therefore $\neg(B \wedge C) \hspace{1pt}\vdash\hspace{-6pt}\sim B$ by Right Weakening. Thus, (5) holds.   □

Due to the fact that all rules for $\mathcal{B}$ involve at most one conditional assertion as a premise, this system does not say anything about how to combine different conditionals. As a result, a conditional is derivable in $\mathcal{B}$ from a set of conditionals Γ only if it is derivable from at most one of the conditionals in Γ. Accordingly, derivability in $\mathcal{B}$ is fully described by claims of the form '$C \hspace{1pt}\vdash\hspace{-6pt}\sim D$ is derivable from $A \hspace{1pt}\vdash\hspace{-6pt}\sim B$' (written $A \hspace{1pt}\vdash\hspace{-6pt}\sim B \Vdash_{\mathcal{B}} C \hspace{1pt}\vdash\hspace{-6pt}\sim D$).

The following important result gives a direct description of the derivability relation generated by $\mathcal{B}$ in terms of the classical entailment.

Theorem 6.2.1. $A \hspace{1pt}\vdash\hspace{-6pt}\sim B \Vdash_{\mathcal{B}} C \hspace{1pt}\vdash\hspace{-6pt}\sim D$ *if and only if either* $C \vDash D$, *or* $A \wedge B \vDash C \wedge D$ *and* $A \to B \vDash C \to D$.

Proof. To begin with, let us denote by $\mathbf{R}$ a relation on conditionals determined by the above conditions, namely, let us say that $A \hspace{1pt}\vdash\hspace{-6pt}\sim B \mathbf{R} C \hspace{1pt}\vdash\hspace{-6pt}\sim D$ holds if and only if either $C \vDash D$, or $A \wedge B \vDash C \wedge D$ and $A \to B \vDash C \to D$. As can be easily checked, $\mathbf{R}$ is a reflexive and transitive relation on the set of conditional assertions. Consequently, in order to prove the implication from left to right, it is sufficient to check that each of the rules of $\mathcal{B}$, viewed as a relation on conditionals, is subsumed by $\mathbf{R}$. The relevant check is straightforward. For instance, the check for Confirmation amounts to showing that $A \wedge B \vdash (A \vee C) \wedge (B \vee C)$ and $A \to B \vDash (A \vee C) \to (B \vee C)$ are classically valid inferences.

In the other direction, let us consider first the limit case when $C \vDash D$. Then $C \vdash D$ holds by Dominance, and hence is derived in $\mathcal{B}$ from any conditional.

Assume now that $A \mathrel{\vert\!\sim} B$, $A \wedge B \vDash C \wedge D$ and $A \to B \vDash C \to D$. We need to show that $C \mathrel{\vert\!\sim} D$ is derivable in $\mathcal{B}$. To begin with, we have $A \vee (C \wedge \neg A) \mathrel{\vert\!\sim} B \vee (C \wedge \neg A)$ by Confirmation, and therefore $A \vee C \mathrel{\vert\!\sim} (B \vee C) \wedge (\neg A \vee B)$ by replacing logical equivalents. The latter implies $(A \vee C) \wedge (B \vee C) \mathrel{\vert\!\sim} A \to B$ by Conjunctive Cautious Monotony. But C is a logical consequence of $A \wedge B$, and hence $C \mathrel{\vert\!\sim} A \to B$ by Left Logical Equivalence. Now the second entailment above gives us $C \mathrel{\vert\!\sim} C \to D$ by Right Weakening, and consequently $C \mathrel{\vert\!\sim} D$ holds by Antecedence and Right Weakening. This completes the proof. $\square$

Theorem 6.2.1 makes checking basic derivability among individual conditionals a relatively straightforward matter. Accordingly, we will omit sometimes explicit derivations of this kind and refer the reader to the above theorem for a justification.

The above theorem justifies also the informal description of the meaning of conditionals, given earlier. Notice that $A \wedge B \vDash C \wedge D$ holds if and only if $C \to \neg D \vDash A \to \neg B$. Accordingly, the above result says that $A \mathrel{\vert\!\sim} B$ implies $C \mathrel{\vert\!\sim} D$ if and only if either all situations confirm $C \mathrel{\vert\!\sim} D$ (and hence it is a logically valid conditional), or if all confirming instances of the former are confirming instances of the latter and all refuting instances of the latter are refuting instances of the former.

Note 6.2.1. The limit case $C \vDash D$ in the formulation of the above theorem could be eliminated if we would notice that $C \vDash D$ holds precisely when $C \mathrel{\vert\!\sim} D$ follows from $\mathbf{f} \mathrel{\vert\!\sim} \mathbf{t}$ in accordance with the main condition above. Accordingly, we could eliminate $C \vDash D$ from the right side, but redefine $A \mathrel{\vert\!\sim} B \Vdash_{\mathcal{B}} C \mathrel{\vert\!\sim} D$ as saying that $C \mathrel{\vert\!\sim} D$ is derivable either from $A \mathrel{\vert\!\sim} B$ or from $\mathbf{f} \mathrel{\vert\!\sim} \mathbf{t}$.

Basic inference relation is obviously a very weak inference system, first of all because it does not allow to combine different conditionals. Nevertheless, we will show later that basic inference is in a sense complete so far as we are interested in derivability among individual conditionals. More exactly, it will be shown that basic derivability captures exactly the one-premise derivability of both skeptical and credulous inference relations.

6.3 Basic inference via expectations

Now we are going to give representations of basic inference in terms of the three basic kinds expectation relations studied in the preceding chapter. Each of these kinds gives raise to a particular definition of an inference relation.

As we have said earlier, a conditional can be interpreted as asserting that situations validating $A \to B$ are sufficiently well expectable, as compared with situations supporting $A \rightarrow \neg B$. Accordingly, the following definition provides a description of conditionals in terms of expectation relations:

(IE) $$A \mathrel{\vdash_<} B \;\equiv\; A \rightarrow \neg B < A \rightarrow B$$

The following result demonstrates that any expectation relation that is t-reflexive generates a basic inference relation by the above definition.

Theorem 6.3.1. *If $<$ is a t-reflexive expectation relation, then $\mathrel{\vdash_<}$ as defined by (IE) is a basic inference relation.*

Proof. Let us check validity of the postulates for basic inference. To begin with, Left Logical Equivalence and Antecedence follow immediately from the fact that expectation relations admit replacement of logical equivalents.

Reflexivity amounts to the condition $A < t$, for any proposition A. As has been shown in Chapter 5, this condition is equivalent to **t**-reflexivity.

Right Weakening amounts to the condition that if $A \rightarrow \neg B < A \rightarrow B$ and $B \vDash C$, then $A \rightarrow \neg C < A \rightarrow C$. But $B \vDash C$ implies $A \rightarrow \neg C \vDash A \rightarrow \neg B$ and $A \rightarrow B \vDash A \rightarrow C$. Consequently, $A \rightarrow \neg C < A \rightarrow C$ follows by quasi-monotonicity.

Deduction. Assume that $(A \wedge B) \rightarrow \neg C < (A \wedge B) \rightarrow C$. Notice that $A \rightarrow (B \wedge \neg C) \vDash (A \wedge B) \rightarrow \neg C$ and hence $A \rightarrow (B \wedge \neg C < A \rightarrow (B \rightarrow C)$. But the latter is equivalent to $A \mathrel{\vdash} B \rightarrow C$. Thus, Deduction holds.

Conjunctive Cautious Monotony. Assume $A \rightarrow \neg(B \wedge C) < A \rightarrow (B \wedge C)$. We have $A \rightarrow (B \wedge C) \vDash (A \wedge B) \rightarrow C$ and hence $(A \wedge B) \rightarrow \neg C < (A \wedge B) \rightarrow C$, that is, $A \wedge B \mathrel{\vdash} C$. This completes the proof. $\square$

Thus, a broad class of expectation relations generate basic inference relations. Actually, the proof of the above theorem shows that general expectation relations validate all the postulates for basic inference, except Reflexivity. So, t-reflexivity of $<$ is needed only to secure the latter.

Now we are going to show that the above representation of basic inference in terms of expectation relations is complete in the sense that any such inference relation is produced by some expectation relation.

Given a basic inference relation $\mathrel{\vdash}$, we can define the following expectation relation:

(EI) $$A <_{\mathrel{\vdash}} B \;\equiv\; \neg(A \wedge B) \mathrel{\vdash} B$$

This relation turns out to be a simple entrenchment. Moreover, the following result shows that basic inference relations are actually interdefinable with simple entrenchment relations.

Theorem 6.3.2. *1. If $\mathrel{\vdash}$ is a basic inference relation, then $<_{\mathrel{\vdash}}$, as defined by (EI), is a simple entrenchment relation that generates, in turn, $\mathrel{\vdash}$ via (IE).*

2. *If $<$ is a simple entrenchment relation, and $\vdash_<$ the basic inference relation obtained from $<$ by (IE), then $<$ coincides with the entrenchment relation produced by $\vdash_<$ via (EI).*

Proof. The proof that (EI) defines a simple entrenchment relation is straightforward: it amounts to checking derivability for corresponding conditionals, which can be made easily using Theorem 6.2.1. So, we will check only that $<_\vdash$ generates $\vdash$ via (IE). Assume that $A \to \neg B <_\vdash A \to B$. The latter is unfolded to $(A \wedge \neg B) \vee (A \wedge B) \vdash A \to B$, which is equivalent to $A \vdash A \to B$. Now, $A \vdash B$ implies $A \vdash A \to B$ by Right Weakening, while $A \vdash A \to B$ implies $A \vdash A \wedge (A \to B)$ by Antecedence, and hence $A \vdash B$ follows by Right Weakening.

Assume now that $<$ is a simple entrenchment relation, and $\neg(A \wedge B) \vdash_< B$. The latter condition amounts to $\neg(A \wedge B) \to \neg B < \neg(A \wedge B) \to B$. Replacing logical equivalents, we obtain $B \to A < B$. The latter implies $A < B$ by Left Strengthening, while the reverse implication follows by Reduction. Consequently, $<$ coincides with the entrenchment relation produced by $\vdash_<$ via (EI). This concludes the proof. □

The above theorem establishes, in fact, a one-to-one correspondence between basic inference relations and simple entrenchment relations. Since any t-reflexive expectation relation generates a basic inference relation, for any such expectation relation there exists an 'inference-equivalent' entrenchment relation producing the same basic inference (As we will see below, this will hold also for any expectation relation that is f-reflexive.) Note also that, for entrenchment relations, the definition of the associated inference relation can be simplified to the following condition:

(IE') $$A \vdash B \equiv \neg A < A \to B$$

Due to Reduction, the above definition is equivalent to (IE).

We will say that the pair of translations given by (EI) and (IE) determines the *ie-mapping* between inference and entrenchment relations. Then the above theorem could be reformulated as saying that the ie-mapping establishes a bijection between basic inference relations and simple entrenchment relations. This extends our list of correspondences among different expectation relations, established in the preceding chapter, with a link to basic inference. Accordingly, we can use these correspondences in order to obtain representations of basic inference in terms of simple plausibility and dependence. The proofs of the results below are straightforward and will be omitted.

The following two definitions establish a correspondence between basic inference and simple plausibility. They can be obtained from the above definitions for inference and entrenchment by Contraposition.

(IP) $$A \vdash B \equiv A \wedge \neg B < A \wedge B$$
(PI) $$A < B \equiv A \vee B \vdash \neg A$$

This pair of translations will be called the *ip-mapping* in what follows. Just as before, it can be easily shown that any f-reflexive expectation relation generates a basic inference relation by (IP). The following theorem shows that the ip-mapping determines a bijection between basic inference relations and simple plausibility relations.

Theorem 6.3.3. *1. If $\mathrel{|\!\sim}$ is a basic inference relation, then (PI) defines a simple plausibility relation that generates, in turn, $\mathrel{|\!\sim}$ via (IP).*
2. If $<$ is a simple plausibility relation, and $\mathrel{|\!\sim}_<$ the basic inference relation obtained from $<$ by (IP), then $<$ coincides with the plausibility relation produced by $\mathrel{|\!\sim}_<$ via (PI).

Next, the following two uniform translations establish mutual definability of basic inference and dependence relations; they are obtainable by combining the above ie-mapping with the de-mapping between simple entrenchment and dependence.

(ID) $$A \mathrel{|\!\sim} B \;\equiv\; \neg(A \wedge B) < \neg A$$
(DI) $$A < B \;\equiv\; \neg(A \wedge B) \mathrel{|\!\sim} \neg A$$

The above pair of definitions will be said to determine the *id-mapping*. The following theorem states that the id-mapping is a bijection between basic inference relations and dependence relations.

Theorem 6.3.4. *1. If $\mathrel{|\!\sim}$ is a basic inference relation, then (DI) defines a dependence relation that generates, in turn, $\mathrel{|\!\sim}$ via (ID).*
2. If $<$ is a dependence relation, and $\mathrel{|\!\sim}_<$ the basic inference relation obtained from $<$ by (ID), then $<$ coincides with the dependence relation produced by $\mathrel{|\!\sim}_<$ via (DI).

It is interesting to observe that the de-mapping, ie-mapping and id-mapping actually commute, that is, each pair of them determine the third. Accordingly, we could as well start our description with the id-mapping, and then define the ie-mapping as a composition of the id-mapping and the de-mapping.

Finally, combining the id-mapping with Converse Complement, we can obtain a correspondence between basic inference and strict entrenchment.

(IS*) $$A \mathrel{|\!\sim} B \;\equiv\; \neg A \not< \neg(A \wedge B)$$
(SI*) $$A < B \;\equiv\; \neg(A \wedge B) \mathrel{|\!\!\not\sim} \neg A$$

Theorem 6.3.5. *1. If $\mathrel{|\!\sim}$ is a basic inference relation, then (SI*) defines a strict entrenchment relation that generates, in turn, $\mathrel{|\!\sim}$ via (IS*).*
2. If $<$ is a strict entrenchment relation then (IS) defines a basic inference relation that generates, in turn, $<$ via (SI*).*

Though adequate, the above 'negative' correspondence between basic inference and strict entrenchment is not especially plausible. A more natural, positive correspondence will be described in the next section.

To conclude this section, it is worth mentioning that comparative probability relations are also interdefinable with our three basic kinds of expectation relations, so they will be interdefinable also with basic inference relations. Actually, the corresponding definitions were given in [Ben84]:

(IPR) $A \mathbin{|\!\sim} B \;\equiv\; A \wedge \neg B < A \wedge B$

(PRI) $A < B \;\equiv\; (A \wedge \neg B) \vee (\neg A \wedge B) \mathbin{|\!\sim} B$

As can be seen, the definition (IPR) of an inference relation in terms of comparative probability coincides with the corresponding definition (IP) in terms of plausibility; this should not be surprising due to the probabilistic origins of the latter. Note, however, that probability relations satisfy Contraposition, so the definition (IE) of inference in terms of entrenchment would also be adequate for this purpose.

6.4 Regular inference relations

In this section we will extend the basic inference relation with rules dealing with the limit case of known propositions.

Definition 6.4.1. *A basic inference relation will be called*

1. regular *if it satisfies the following rule:*
   Regularity *If $A \mathbin{|\!\sim} B$ and $B \mathbin{|\!\sim} \mathbf{f}$, then $A \mathbin{|\!\sim} \mathbf{f}$.*
2. strongly regular *if it satisfies:*
   Strong Regularity *If $B \mathbin{|\!\sim} \mathbf{f}$ and $A \mathbin{|\!\sim} C$, then $A \mathbin{|\!\sim} \neg B \wedge C$.*

Though the above rules, unlike the rules of $\mathcal{B}$, involve two conditional premises, they deal with a rather special class of 'contradictory' propositions that imply falsity. The conditional $B \mathbin{|\!\sim} \mathbf{f}$ says, in effect, that B is seen as impossible with respect to the inference relation, that is, no imaginable situation assumed by $\mathbin{|\!\sim}$ is compatible with B. Regularity asserts then a kind of 'backward propagation' for contradictions: if some proposition A implies such a contradictory proposition, it is contradictory by itself. Strong Regularity embodies a stronger assumption that if B is contradictory in this sense, then $\neg B$ should be considered as a known proposition, and consequently it can be conjoined to consequences of any proposition. Strong Regularity will hold for practically all inference relations considered later. An important feature of such inference relations is that they fix their underlying monotonic logic (see below).

The following lemma gives two valid rules of regular inference that we will use later.

Lemma 6.4.1. *1. If $A \hspace{1pt}\vert\!\!\sim \mathbf{f}$ and $B \hspace{1pt}\vert\!\!\sim \mathbf{f}$, then $A \lor B \hspace{1pt}\vert\!\!\sim \mathbf{f}$;*
  2. If $B \hspace{1pt}\vert\!\!\sim \mathbf{f}$ and $A \lor B \hspace{1pt}\vert\!\!\sim \neg A$, then $A \hspace{1pt}\vert\!\!\sim \mathbf{f}$.

Proof. (1) If $A \hspace{1pt}\vert\!\!\sim \mathbf{f}$ and $B \hspace{1pt}\vert\!\!\sim \mathbf{f}$, then $A \lor B \hspace{1pt}\vert\!\!\sim B$ by Deduction and Right Weakening from the first conditional, and hence $A \lor B \hspace{1pt}\vert\!\!\sim \mathbf{f}$ by Regularity.

(2) If $A \lor B \hspace{1pt}\vert\!\!\sim \neg A$, then $A \lor B \hspace{1pt}\vert\!\!\sim B$ by Antecedence and Right Weakening, and hence, given $B \hspace{1pt}\vert\!\!\sim \mathbf{f}$, we infer $A \lor B \hspace{1pt}\vert\!\!\sim \mathbf{f}$ by Regularity. The latter implies $A \hspace{1pt}\vert\!\!\sim \mathbf{f}$ by (2) from Lemma 6.2.2. $\qquad\square$

6.4.1 Regularity and strict expectation relations

To begin with, the following result shows that the ie-mapping, described earlier, determines also a correspondence between regular inference relations and simple regular entrenchment relations.

Theorem 6.4.1. *1. If $\hspace{1pt}\vert\!\!\sim$ is a regular inference relation, then the simple entrenchment relation defined by (EI) is regular.*
  2. If $<$ is a simple regular entrenchment relation, the basic inference relation defined by (IE) is regular.

Proof. (1) Assume that $\hspace{1pt}\vert\!\!\sim$ is a regular inference relation, and $\mathbf{t} < A$ and $A < B$ hold for the corresponding simple entrenchment relation. The first condition amounts to $\neg A \hspace{1pt}\vert\!\!\sim A$, which is equivalent to $\neg A \hspace{1pt}\vert\!\!\sim \mathbf{f}$. The second condition gives $\neg (A \land B) \hspace{1pt}\vert\!\!\sim B$, which implies $\neg (A \land B) \hspace{1pt}\vert\!\!\sim \neg A$ by Antecedence and Right Weakening. Consequently, $\neg (A \land B) \hspace{1pt}\vert\!\!\sim \mathbf{f}$ by Regularity. But the latter is equivalent to $\mathbf{t} < A \land B$. Consequently, t-regularity holds for $<$.

(2) Assume now that $<$ is a simple regular entrenchment relation, and we have $B \hspace{1pt}\vert\!\!\sim \mathbf{f}$ and $A \hspace{1pt}\vert\!\!\sim B$ for the corresponding inference relation. The first condition amounts to $\mathbf{t} < \neg B$, while the second one – to $A \to \neg B < A \to B$, which implies $\neg B < A \to B$. By t-regularity, we infer $\mathbf{t} < \neg B \land (A \to B)$, which implies $\mathbf{t} < \neg A$ by Right Weakening. But the latter condition is equivalent to $A \hspace{1pt}\vert\!\!\sim \mathbf{f}$, so Regularity holds for $\hspace{1pt}\vert\!\!\sim$. $\qquad\square$

As we have mentioned in the preceding chapter, expectation relations used in the literature for representing nonmonotonic inference and belief change are commonly assumed to be strict partial orders. For such expectation relations our earlier definitions of nonmonotonic inference in terms of plausibility (IP) and entrenchment (IE) (see above) will already be inadequate, since they will not validate Reflexivity. In order to circumvent this shortcoming, these definitions should be modified by adding a special condition dealing with the trivial case of false propositions. Fortunately, the 'right' definition for strict entrenchment can be obtained by combining the ie-mapping with the rs-mapping between simple and strict entrenchment, defined in the preceding chapter. This immediately gives us the following conditions determining a new, more natural, correspondence between inference relations and strict entrenchment:

(ISE) $A \mathrel{\mid\!\sim} B \;\equiv\; A \to \neg B < A \to B$ or $\neg A \not< \mathbf{t}$

(SEI) $A < B \;\equiv\; \neg(A \wedge B) \mathrel{\mid\!\sim} B$ and $\neg A \mathrel{\mid\!\!\not\sim} \mathbf{f}$

We have seen in the preceding chapter, however, that the rs-mapping produces the right behavior only for regular entrenchment relations. Moreover, it turns out that the definition (ISE) generates only regular inference relations. The following lemma gives an exact description of this situation.

Lemma 6.4.2. *A strict expectation relation $<$ determines a basic inference relation by (ISE) if and only if it is regular. Moreover, in this case the defined inference relation will also be regular.*

Proof. (1) It is easy to check that if $<$ is an expectation relation, then the inference relation defined by (ISE) unconditionally satisfies all postulates of basic inference, except Deduction. Moreover, it satisfies the latter if and only if $<$ satisfies the following condition (dealing with the limit case):

(*)   If $\neg A < \mathbf{t}$ and $\neg(A \wedge B) \not< \mathbf{t}$, then $A \to (B \wedge \neg C) < (A \wedge B) \to C$.

Substituting $\mathbf{f}$ for C in (*), we obtain

(**)   If $\neg A < \mathbf{t}$ and $\neg(A \wedge B) \not< \mathbf{t}$, then $A \to B < A \to \neg B$.

Clearly, (**) implies, in turn, (*) by quasi-monotonicity, so they are equivalent.

Assume now that $A < \mathbf{t}$ and $B \not< \mathbf{t}$. Then $A \wedge B < \mathbf{t}$ by quasi-monotonicity and $(A \wedge B) \vee B \not< \mathbf{t}$. Consequently, (**) gives $B \to A < B$. Therefore $A < B$, and hence t-primeness holds. In the other direction, if $\neg A < \mathbf{t}$ and $\neg(A \wedge B) \not< \mathbf{t}$, then t-primeness implies $\neg A < \neg(A \wedge B)$, and consequently $A \to B < A \to \neg B$ by Reduction. Thus, (**) is satisfied. Therefore, an expectation relation determines a basic inference relation by (ISE) if and only if it is regular.

(2) Assume that $<$ is a strict expectation relation. By (ISE), $A \mathrel{\mid\!\sim} \mathbf{f}$ belongs to the associated inference relation if either $\mathbf{t} < \neg A$ or $\neg A \not< \mathbf{t}$. However, implies $\neg A < \neg A$, contrary to irreflexivity of $<$. Accordingly, $A \mathrel{\mid\!\sim} \mathbf{f}$ holds if and only if $\neg A \not< \mathbf{t}$.

Assume now that $A \mathrel{\mid\!\sim} B$ and $B \mathrel{\mid\!\sim} \mathbf{f}$ hold for the generated inference relation. Then $\neg B \not< \mathbf{t}$ and either $A \to \neg B < A \to B$ or $\neg A \not< \mathbf{t}$. But $A \to \neg B < A \to B$ implies $A \to \neg B < \mathbf{t}$ by Right Weakening, which is incompatible with $\neg B \not< \mathbf{t}$. So, $\neg A \not< \mathbf{t}$, and consequently $A \mathrel{\mid\!\sim} \mathbf{f}$. Thus, Regularity holds for $\mathrel{\mid\!\sim}$. $\square$

The pair of definitions (ISE) and (SEI) will be said to determine the *is-mapping* between inference relations and strict entrenchment. The following theorem shows that this mapping determines a bijection between regular inference relations and strict regular entrenchment relations. The proof follows immediately from the fact that the is-mapping is a composition of the ie-mapping and rs-mapping, and Theorem 6.4.1.

Theorem 6.4.2. *1. If $\vdash$ is a regular inference relation, then (SEI) defines a strict regular entrenchment relation that generates, in turn, $\vdash$ via (ISE).*

2. If $<$ is a strict regular entrenchment relation, then (ISE) determines a regular inference relation that generates, in turn $<$ via (SEI).

The above result can be used, in turn, for establishing a correspondence between regular inference relations and strict regular plausibility relations. The following pair of translations is obtainable from the is-mapping by Contraposition:

(ISP) $A \vdash B \equiv A \wedge \neg B < A \wedge B$ or $\mathbf{f} \not< A$

(SPI) $A < B \equiv A \vee B \vdash \neg A$ and $B \not\vdash \mathbf{f}$

These definitions correspond, in effect, to that given in [FH98]. The following theorem shows that they establish a one-to-one correspondence between regular inference relations and strict plausibility relations.

Theorem 6.4.3. *1. If $\vdash$ is a regular inference relation, then $<$, as defined by (SPI), is a strict plausibility relation that generates, in turn, $\vdash$ via (ISP).*

2. If $<$ is a strict plausibility relation, and $\vdash$ the basic inference relation obtained from $<$ by (ISP), then $<$ coincides with the plausibility relation produced by $\vdash$ via (SPI).

Finally, combining the is-mapping and Converse Complement, we obtain an alternative correspondence between regular inference relations and regular dependence relations; this correspondence will be called the *id*-mapping*:

(ID*) $A \vdash B \equiv A \rightarrow B \not< A \rightarrow \neg B$ or $\mathbf{t} < \neg A$

(DI*) $A < B \equiv \neg(A \wedge B) \not\vdash A$ or $\neg B \vdash \mathbf{f}$

Theorem 6.4.4. *1. If $\vdash$ is a regular inference relation, then (DI*) defines a regular dependence relation that generates, in turn, $\vdash$ via (ID*).*

2. If $<$ is a regular dependence relation, then (ID*) defines a regular inference relation that produces, in turn, $<$ via (DI*).

The id*-mapping will play an important role in the following chapters, since it will give us a representation both for rational inference relations and for credulous inference.

6.4.2 Duality

It turns out that, for any regular inference relation $\vdash$, we can define a *dual* inference relation as follows:

(Dual) $A \vdash^{\circ} B \equiv A \not\vdash \neg B$ or $A \vdash \mathbf{f}$

Theorem 6.4.5. *If $\mathrel{\vbar\joinrel\sim}$ is a regular inference relation, then $\mathrel{\vbar\joinrel\sim}^\circ$ is also a regular inference relation. Moreover, $\mathrel{\vbar\joinrel\sim}^{\circ\circ}$ coincides with $\mathrel{\vbar\joinrel\sim}$.*

Proof. Reflexivity for $\mathrel{\vbar\joinrel\sim}^\circ$ follows from the fact that $A \mathrel{\vbar\joinrel\sim} \neg A$ always implies $A \mathrel{\vbar\joinrel\sim} \mathbf{f}$. Left Logical Equivalence is immediate, while Right Weakening for $\mathrel{\vbar\joinrel\sim}^\circ$ follows directly from Right Weakening for $\mathrel{\vbar\joinrel\sim}$. Also, Antecedence for $\mathrel{\vbar\joinrel\sim}^\circ$ follows from the fact that $A \mathrel{\vbar\joinrel\sim} A \to B$ implies $A \mathrel{\vbar\joinrel\sim} B$.

Deduction for $\mathrel{\vbar\joinrel\sim}^\circ$ amounts to the following two conditions for $\mathrel{\vbar\joinrel\sim}$:

1. If $A \wedge B \mathrel{\vbar\joinrel\sim} \mathbf{f}$ and $A \mathrel{\vbar\joinrel\sim} B \wedge \neg C$, then $A \mathrel{\vbar\joinrel\sim} \mathbf{f}$;
2. If $A \mathrel{\vbar\joinrel\sim} B \wedge \neg C$, then either $A \wedge B \mathrel{\vbar\joinrel\sim} \neg C$ or $A \mathrel{\vbar\joinrel\sim} \mathbf{f}$.

For the first condition, $A \mathrel{\vbar\joinrel\sim} B \wedge \neg C$ implies $A \mathrel{\vbar\joinrel\sim} A \wedge B$ by Antecedence and Right Weakening, and hence $A \vee C \mathrel{\vbar\joinrel\sim} \mathbf{f}$ by Regularity. For the second condition, $A \mathrel{\vbar\joinrel\sim} B \wedge \neg C$ implies $A \wedge B \mathrel{\vbar\joinrel\sim} \neg C$ by Conjunctive Cautious Monotony.

Conjunctive Cautious Monotony amounts to the following two conditions for $\mathrel{\vbar\joinrel\sim}$:

1. If $A \mathrel{\vbar\joinrel\sim} \mathbf{f}$, then $A \wedge B \mathrel{\vbar\joinrel\sim} \mathbf{f}$;
2. If $A \wedge B \mathrel{\vbar\joinrel\sim} \neg C$, then $A \mathrel{\vbar\joinrel\sim} \neg B \vee \neg C$.

The first condition follows from Lemma 6.2.2, while the second one is a direct consequence of the Deduction rule.

Finally, *Regularity* for $\mathrel{\vbar\joinrel\sim}^\circ$ follows immediately from the fact that $B \mathrel{\vbar\joinrel\sim} \mathbf{f}$ implies $A \mathrel{\vbar\joinrel\sim} \neg B$ with respect to basic inference. $\qquad\square$

Thus, the class of regular inference relations is invariant with respect to the 'duality operation' $^\circ$. This indicates, in fact, that this class of inference relations is not homogeneous and contains quite diverse inference systems.

Our last result in this section shows that Strong Regularity is also preserved by the duality operation.

Lemma 6.4.3. *If $\mathrel{\vbar\joinrel\sim}$ is a strongly regular inference relation, then $\mathrel{\vbar\joinrel\sim}^\circ$ is also a strongly regular inference relation.*

Proof. It sufficient to check that if $\mathrel{\vbar\joinrel\sim}$ satisfies Strong Regularity, then $\mathrel{\vbar\joinrel\sim}^\circ$ also satisfies Strong Regularity. Assume $A \mathrel{\vbar\joinrel\sim}^\circ B$ and $C \mathrel{\vbar\joinrel\sim}^\circ \mathbf{f}$. Then $C \mathrel{\vbar\joinrel\sim} \mathbf{f}$ and either $A \mathrel{\not\vbar\joinrel\sim} \neg B$ or $A \mathrel{\vbar\joinrel\sim} \mathbf{f}$. In the second case $A \mathrel{\vbar\joinrel\sim}^\circ B \wedge \neg C$ will (trivially) hold. So assume $C \mathrel{\vbar\joinrel\sim} \mathbf{f}$ and $A \mathrel{\not\vbar\joinrel\sim} \neg B$. We will show that in this case $A \mathrel{\not\vbar\joinrel\sim} B \to C$. Indeed, otherwise we would have $A \mathrel{\vbar\joinrel\sim} (B \to C) \wedge \neg C$ by Strong Regularity, and hence $A \mathrel{\vbar\joinrel\sim} \neg B$, contrary to our assumptions. Thus, $A \mathrel{\not\vbar\joinrel\sim} B \to C$. But the latter implies $A \mathrel{\vbar\joinrel\sim}^\circ B \wedge \neg C$, as required. Therefore, Strong Regularity holds for $\mathrel{\vbar\joinrel\sim}^\circ$. $\qquad\square$

6.5 The internal logic of an inference relation

It turns out that practically all inference relations discussed in this Part of the book determine their own *internal logic*, namely a greatest classical Tarski consequence relation that is subsumed by the inference relation and allows replacement of equivalent propositions in antecedents and consequents of conditionals. Such an internal logic can be seen as the monotonic component of a nonmonotonic inference relation, and it can be used instead of the classical entailment in all its functions, such as replacement of logical equivalents or right weakening. Moreover, singling out this monotonic ingredient in an inference relation allows to clarify and simplify a number of important issues concerning the behavior of inference relations.

Our first definition specifies in what sense an inference relation complies with some classical consequence relation.

Definition 6.5.1. *An inference relation will be said to* respect *a classical consequence relation* Th *if it allows for replacement of* Th*-equivalent propositions in conclusions of its conditionals:*

Right Th-***Equivalence***   *If* $B \leftrightarrow C \in \mathrm{Th}(\emptyset)$ *and* $A \mathrel{|\!\sim} B$, *then* $A \mathrel{|\!\sim} C$.

Combined with Right Weakening, the above condition immediately implies Right Weakening with respect to Th-entailment:

(**Right** Th-**Weakening**) If $C \in \mathrm{Th}(B)$ and $A \mathrel{|\!\sim} B$, then $A \mathrel{|\!\sim} C$.

Consequently, an inference relation that respects Th also subsumes the latter:

(Th-**Dominance**) If $B \in \mathrm{Th}(A)$, then $A \mathrel{|\!\sim} B$.

Furthermore, the following lemma shows that if an inference relation respects Th, then it allows for substitutions of Th-equivalent propositions also in premises of inference rules:

(**Left** Th-**Equivalence**) If $A \leftrightarrow B \in \mathrm{Th}(\emptyset)$ and $A \mathrel{|\!\sim} C$, then $B \mathrel{|\!\sim} C$.

Lemma 6.5.1. *If an inference relation* $\mathrel{|\!\sim}$ *respects* Th, *then it satisfies Left* Th-*Equivalence.*

Proof. Assume that $A \leftrightarrow B \in \mathrm{Th}(\emptyset)$ and $A \mathrel{|\!\sim} C$. Then $A \mathrel{|\!\sim} C \wedge (A \leftrightarrow B)$ by Right Th-Equivalence, and hence $A \mathrel{|\!\sim} A \wedge C \wedge (A \leftrightarrow B)$ by Antecedence. The latter implies $A \mathrel{|\!\sim} B \wedge C$ by Right Weakening, and hence $A \wedge B \mathrel{|\!\sim} C$ by Conjunctive Cautious Monotony. Therefore $B \mathrel{|\!\sim} A \rightarrow C$ by Deduction. But $A \rightarrow C$ is Th-equivalent to $B \rightarrow C$ (since A and B are Th-equivalent). Consequently, $B \mathrel{|\!\sim} B \rightarrow C$, which is equivalent to $B \mathrel{|\!\sim} C$. $\square$

Notice that Left Equivalence and Right Weakening are the only rules of a basic inference relation that involve references to the underlying logic (namely, to the classical entailment). Accordingly, if a basic inference relation $\vdash$ respects a classical consequence relation Th, the latter can be safely considered as an internal logic of $\vdash$ instead of the classical entailment; all our results and conclusions will persist under such a replacement. This naturally leads us to the following

Definition 6.5.2. *A conditional $A \vdash B$ will be said to be Th-derivable from a set of conditionals Γ (notation $\Gamma \Vdash_B^{Th} A \vdash B$) if $A \vdash B$ is derivable from Γ using the rules of B and Right Th-Equivalence.*

The above definition is equivalent to the claim that $A \vdash B$ belongs to the least basic inference relation that contains Γ and respects Th. Now, since Right Th-equivalence is also a rule containing only one conditional premise, a conditional is Th-derivable from a set of conditionals Γ only if it is derivable from at most one conditional from Γ. Furthermore, the following characterization of one-premise Th-derivability can be obtained as a straightforward generalization of Theorem 6.2.1.

Corollary 6.5.1. $A \vdash B \Vdash_B^{Th} C \vdash D$ *if and only if either $C \to D \in \text{Th}(\emptyset)$, or $C \wedge D \in \text{Th}(A \wedge B)$ and $C \to D \in \text{Th}(A \to B)$.*

The above results show that respect for a classical consequence relation gives us the right behavior when this consequence relation is viewed as a logic underlying an inference relation. Still, the notion of respect does not determine a unique classical consequence relation; this follows already from the fact that if an inference relation respect some classical consequence relation Th, then it also respects any classical consequence relation weaker than Th. Consequently, in order to fix the underlying logic of an inference relation, we need a stronger notion of *consistency preservation* employed in [GM94].

Definition 6.5.3. *An inference relation will be said to* preserve *a classical consequence relation* Th *if it respects* Th *and satisfies:*

Consistency Preservation   *If $A \vdash \mathbf{f}$, then $\neg A \in \text{Th}(\emptyset)$*

We are going to show now that the above definition determines a unique classical consequence relation that can be seen as *the* internal logic of the source inference relation.

For any inference relation $\vdash$, the set of propositions

$$\mathbf{K}_{\vdash} = \{A \mid \neg A \vdash \mathbf{f}\}$$

will be called the *knowledge set* of $\vdash$, and each proposition from $\mathbf{K}_{\vdash}$ will be said to be *known* with respect to $\vdash$. In addition, $\text{Th}_{\vdash}$ will denote the least classical consequence relation containing $\mathbf{K}_{\vdash}$ as its axioms.

The following auxiliary lemma gives two useful properties of knowledge sets for regular inference relations.

Lemma 6.5.2. *If $\mathrel{|\!\sim}$ is a regular inference relation, then*

1. $\mathbf{K}_{\mathrel{|\!\sim}}$ *is a deductively closed set;*
2. $B \in \mathrm{Th}_{\mathrel{|\!\sim}}(A)$ *if and only if $A \to B \in \mathbf{K}_{\mathrel{|\!\sim}}$.*

Proof. (1) It is sufficient to show that $\mathbf{K}_{\mathrel{|\!\sim}}$ is closed with respect to modus ponens. Assume that both A and $A \to B$ belong $\mathbf{K}_{\mathrel{|\!\sim}}$, that is, $\neg A \mathrel{|\!\sim} \mathbf{f}$ and $A \wedge \neg B \mathrel{|\!\sim} \mathbf{f}$. Then $\neg A \vee \neg B \mathrel{|\!\sim} \mathbf{f}$ (see Lemma 6.4.1), and hence $\neg B \mathrel{|\!\sim} \mathbf{f}$ by basic inference. Thus, $B \in \mathbf{K}_{\mathrel{|\!\sim}}$.

(2) Since $\mathbf{K}_{\mathrel{|\!\sim}}$ is deductively closed, it coincides with the least theory of $\mathrm{Th}_{\mathrel{|\!\sim}}$, that is, with $\mathrm{Th}_{\mathrel{|\!\sim}}(\emptyset)$. Now the result follows from the fact that $B \in \mathrm{Th}_{\mathrel{|\!\sim}}(A)$ holds if and only if $A \to B \in \mathrm{Th}_{\mathrel{|\!\sim}}(\emptyset)$. $\qquad\square$

The following result provides a natural alternative characterization of the classical subrelation. This characterization was given in [Leh98].

Lemma 6.5.3. *If $\mathrm{Th}_{\mathrel{|\!\sim}}$ is a classical subrelation of a regular inference relation $\mathrel{|\!\sim}$, then $B \in \mathrm{Th}_{\mathrel{|\!\sim}}(A)$ holds if and only if $A \wedge C \mathrel{|\!\sim} B$, for any C.*

Proof. By the previous lemma, $B \in \mathrm{Th}_{\mathrel{|\!\sim}}(A)$ if and only if $A \wedge \neg B \mathrel{|\!\sim} \mathbf{f}$. The latter implies $C \wedge A \wedge \neg B \mathrel{|\!\sim} \mathbf{f}$ by basic inference, for any proposition C, and hence $C \wedge A \mathrel{|\!\sim} B$ by Deduction. In the other direction, if $A \wedge C \mathrel{|\!\sim} B$ holds for any C, then, in particular, $A \wedge \neg B \mathrel{|\!\sim} B$, and hence $A \wedge \neg B \mathrel{|\!\sim} \mathbf{f}$, which is equivalent to $B \in \mathrm{Th}_{\mathrel{|\!\sim}}(A)$. $\qquad\square$

The above result says that monotonic inferences sanctioned by a non-monotonic inference relation are precisely inferences that 'survive' addition of auxiliary premises, that is, inferences that permit Strengthening of the Antecedent.

The following theorem shows that any strongly regular inference relation uniquely determines its underlying monotonic logic.

Theorem 6.5.1. *1. If an inference relation $\mathrel{|\!\sim}$ respects Th, then Th is included in $\mathrm{Th}_{\mathrel{|\!\sim}}$.*

2. An inference relation is strongly regular if and only if it respects $\mathrm{Th}_{\mathrel{|\!\sim}}$.

Proof. (1) Assume that an inference relation $\mathrel{|\!\sim}$ respects Th, and $B \in \mathrm{Th}(A)$. Then $A \wedge \neg B$ is Th-inconsistent, and hence $A \wedge \neg B \mathrel{|\!\sim} \mathbf{f}$, since $\mathrel{|\!\sim}$ respects Th. The latter implies that $A \to B \in \mathbf{K}_{\mathrel{|\!\sim}}$, and therefore $B \in \mathrm{Th}_{\mathrel{|\!\sim}}(A)$. Thus, Th is included in $\mathrm{Th}_{\mathrel{|\!\sim}}$.

(2) Let $\mathrel{|\!\sim}$ be a strongly regular inference relation. Assume that $C \mathrel{|\!\sim} A$, and A is equivalent to B with respect to $\mathrm{Th}_{\mathrel{|\!\sim}}$. By the preceding lemma, the latter amounts to $A \leftrightarrow B \in \mathbf{K}_{\mathrel{|\!\sim}}$. By Strong Regularity, $C \mathrel{|\!\sim} A \wedge (A \leftrightarrow B)$, and hence $C \mathrel{|\!\sim} B$ by Right Weakening. Therefore $\mathrel{|\!\sim}$ respects $\mathrm{Th}_{\mathrel{|\!\sim}}$. In the other direction, assume that $\mathrel{|\!\sim}$ respects $\mathrm{Th}_{\mathrel{|\!\sim}}$, $B \mathrel{|\!\sim} C$ and $A \mathrel{|\!\sim} \mathbf{f}$. Then $\neg A \in \mathbf{K}_{\mathrel{|\!\sim}}$, and hence C is equivalent to $\neg A \wedge C$ with respect to $\mathrm{Th}_{\mathrel{|\!\sim}}$. Consequently $B \mathrel{|\!\sim} \neg A \wedge C$, and therefore Strong Regularity holds. $\qquad\square$

As an immediate consequence of the above theorem, we obtain

Corollary 6.5.2. *An inference relation $\vdash\!\sim$ preserves a classical consequence relation* Th *if and only if $\vdash\!\sim$ is strongly regular, and* Th *coincides with* $\text{Th}_{\vdash\!\sim}$.

Proof. Notice first that Consistency Preservation says, in effect, that Th must include $\mathbf{K}_{\vdash\!\sim}$. Consequently it is equivalent to the requirement that Th should include $\text{Th}_{\vdash\!\sim}$. AS a result, the above theorem implies that $\vdash\!\sim$ preserves Th only if the latter coincides with $\text{Th}_{\vdash\!\sim}$, in which case it is clearly strongly regular. The reverse implication is immediate.   □

The above result shows that Strong Regularity implies, in effect, that the underlying logic of an inference relation can be identified with $\text{Th}_{\vdash\!\sim}$. Our next result will demonstrate that this shift from classical entailment to $\text{Th}_{\vdash\!\sim}$ exhausts, in a sense, the contribution of the Strong Regularity rule.

By a *regular closure* of a set of conditionals Γ, denoted by $\vdash\!\sim_\Gamma$, we will mean a least strongly regular inference relation including Γ. This inference relation can be alternatively described as the set of all conditionals that can be obtained from Γ by applying the rules of basic inference and Regularity. If $A \vdash\!\sim B$ belongs to $\vdash\!\sim_\Gamma$, we will say that Γ *regularly entails* $A \vdash\!\sim B$. Finally, to simplify the notation, in what follows we will denote by Th_Γ the internal logic of $\vdash\!\sim_\Gamma$, that is, $\text{Th}_{\vdash\!\sim_\Gamma}$.

The following theorem shows that regular derivability is reducible, in effect, to basic derivability that respects the internal logic.

Theorem 6.5.2. Γ *regularly entails* $C \vdash\!\sim D$ *iff* Γ Th_Γ*-entails* $C \vdash\!\sim D$.

Proof. The implication from left to right will be shown by induction on regular derivations. If $C \vdash\!\sim D$ belongs to Γ, then the claim is immediate. Assume that $C \vdash\!\sim D$ was obtained from $A \vdash\!\sim B$ using some basic rule from $\mathcal{B}$. Then $C \vdash\!\sim D$ is clearly Th_Γ-derivable from $A \vdash\!\sim B$. Finally, assume that the conditional $A \vdash\!\sim B \wedge \neg C$ was obtained using Regularity from two derived conditionals, $A \vdash\!\sim B$ and $C \vdash\!\sim \mathbf{f}$. Since the latter conditional is regularly derivable from Γ, $\neg C$ belongs to $\mathbf{K}_{\vdash\!\sim_\Gamma}$, where $\vdash\!\sim_\Gamma$ is a regular closure of Γ. Consequently, $\neg C \in \text{Th}_\Gamma(\emptyset)$, and hence we can apply Right Th-Equivalence to $A \vdash\!\sim B$ to derive $A \vdash\!\sim B \wedge \neg C$. Now, by the inductive assumption $A \vdash\!\sim B$ is Th_Γ-derivable from Γ. Hence $A \vdash\!\sim B \wedge \neg C$ is also Th_Γ-derivable from Γ.

In order to show the reverse implication, it is sufficient to demonstrate that the regular closure of Γ is a basic inference relation that respects Th_Γ. To this end, we need only to show the validity of Right Th_Γ-Equivalence. So, let us assume that $A \vdash\!\sim B$ is regularly derivable from Γ and $B \leftrightarrow C \in \text{Th}_\Gamma(\emptyset)$. The latter condition is equivalent to derivability of the conditional $\neg(B \leftrightarrow C) \vdash\!\sim \mathbf{f}$. Now we apply Regularity to the two derivable conditionals and obtain $A \vdash\!\sim B \wedge (B \leftrightarrow C)$. Finally, using Right Weakening, we conclude $A \vdash\!\sim C$. Thus, the regular closure of Γ respects Th_Γ. Consequently it includes all conditionals that are derivable from Γ using the basic rules and Right Th_Γ-Equivalence.   □

Given a local character of Th-derivability, we immediately obtain the following

Corollary 6.5.3. Γ *regularly entails* $C \mathbin{|\!\sim} D$ *if and only if* $C \mathbin{|\!\sim} D$ *is* Th_{Γ}-*derivable from some conditional from* Γ.

Thus, regular derivability is reducible to basic derivability with respect to the underlying classical consequence relation. Still, this result is not completely satisfying, since Th_{Γ} was defined on the basis of the relevant strongly regular inference relation. Thus, we still do not have a clear separation between monotonic and nonmonotonic components of a regular inference relation.

The following construction gives a more constructive description of the knowledge set $\mathbf{K}_{\Gamma}$ generated by a set of conditionals Γ.

The knowledge set of a regular inference relation is determined by the set of conditionals of the form $A \mathbin{|\!\sim} \mathbf{f}$ belonging to it. If we want to compute all such conditionals that are derivable from a given set of conditionals Γ, we should take into account that each conditional of the form $A \mathbin{|\!\sim} B$, where A is logically inconsistent with B, implies $A \mathbin{|\!\sim} \mathbf{f}$ (by Antecedence and Right Weakening). Also, if we have $A \mathbin{|\!\sim} \mathbf{f}$ and $C \mathbin{|\!\sim} D$ such that B is inconsistent with C, *given* $\neg A$, then we can derive $C \mathbin{|\!\sim} \mathbf{f}$ by Regularity. So, the computation of the knowledge set requires an iterative construction.

A *monotonic core* of a set of conditionals Γ (denoted by $\mathbf{K}_{\Gamma}^{+}$) will be defined as a union of sets of propositions $\mathbf{K}_i$ defined inductively as follows:

$$\mathbf{K}_0 = \emptyset; \qquad \mathbf{K}_{i+1} = \{\neg A \mid A \mathbin{|\!\sim} B \in \Gamma \text{ and } \mathbf{K}_i, A \vDash \neg B\}$$

As can be seen, $\mathbf{K}_{\Gamma}^{+}$ includes negations of antecedents of certain conditionals belonging to Γ. An important property of this set is given in the following lemma.

Lemma 6.5.4. *If* $A \mathbin{|\!\sim} B \in \Gamma$ *and* $\mathbf{K}_{\Gamma}^{+}, B \vDash \neg A$, *then* $\neg A \in \mathbf{K}_{\Gamma}^{+}$.

Proof. If $\mathbf{K}_{\Gamma}^{+}, B \vDash \neg A$, then, for some i, we have $\mathbf{K}_i, B \vDash \neg A$. Consequently, given $A \mathbin{|\!\sim} B \in \Gamma$, we conclude $\neg A \in \mathbf{K}_{i+1}$, and therefore $\neg A \in \mathbf{K}_{\Gamma}^{+}$. $\qquad\square$

The following theorem shows that the monotonic core determines the knowledge set of Γ.

Theorem 6.5.3. *The knowledge set* $\mathbf{K}_{\Gamma}$ *of a set of conditionals* Γ *is a deductive closure of its monotonic core* $\mathbf{K}_{\Gamma}^{+}$.

Proof. In order to demonstrate that the monotonic core is included in the knowledge set, we will show by induction that each set $\mathbf{K}_i$ is contained in the knowledge set. The claim is obvious for $\mathbf{K}_0$, so let us assume that it holds for $\mathbf{K}_i$ and show that it holds also for $\mathbf{K}_{i+1}$.

Assume that $\neg A \in \mathbf{K}_{i+1}$. Then $B, \mathbf{K}_i \vDash \neg A$, for some conditional $A \mathbin{|\!\sim} B$ from Γ. By compactness of $\vDash$, $\mathbf{K}_i$ contains a finite set $\{\neg A_1, \ldots, \neg A_n\}$ such that, taken together with B, implies $\neg A$. Consequently, $A \wedge B \vDash \bigvee A_j$. But $A \vDash B$ implies $A \vDash A \wedge B$ by Antecedence, and hence we can derive $A \vDash \bigvee A_j$ by Right Weakening. Now, by our inductive assumption, each $\neg A_j$, $1 \leq j \leq n$, belongs to the knowledge set of Γ, and hence, for any such j, the conditional $A_j \vDash \mathbf{f}$ is regularly derivable from Γ. Applying Regularity to the latter conditionals and $A \vDash \bigvee A_j$, we obtain $A \vDash (\bigvee A_j) \wedge (\bigwedge \neg A_j)$, and consequently $A \vDash \mathbf{f}$ by Right Weakening. Thus, $\neg A$ belongs to the knowledge set. This shows that the nonmonotonic core is included in the knowledge set.

In order to show the reverse inclusion, let us denote by Th_Γ^+ the least classical consequence relation containing the core $\mathbf{K}_\Gamma^+$, and consider the set of all conditionals that are Th_Γ^+-derivable from Γ. We will denote this set by Γ^+. We are going to show that Γ^+ is a strongly regular inference relation. Clearly, Γ^+ is a basic inference relation. So, it is sufficient to demonstrate that it is closed also with respect to the Regularity rule.

To begin with, according Corollary 6.5.1, a conditional of the form $A \vDash \mathbf{f}$ belongs to Γ^+ if and only if either $A \to \mathbf{f} \in \mathrm{Th}_\Gamma^+(\emptyset)$ or Γ contains a conditional $C \vDash D$ such that $\mathbf{f} \in \mathrm{Th}_\Gamma^+(C \wedge D)$ and $A \to \mathbf{f} \in \mathrm{Th}_\Gamma^+(C \to D)$. In the first case we have $\mathbf{K}_\Gamma^+ \vDash \neg A$. In the second case, the corresponding conditions can be rewritten as follows:

$$\mathbf{K}_\Gamma^+ \vDash \neg(C \wedge D) \qquad \text{and} \qquad C \to D, \mathbf{K}_\Gamma^+ \vDash \neg A$$

Applying the previous lemma to the first condition above, we conclude that $\neg C \in \mathbf{K}_\Gamma^+$. Consequently, the second condition gives us again $\mathbf{K}_\Gamma^+ \vDash \neg A$. So, $A \vDash \mathbf{f} \in \Gamma^+$ only if $\mathbf{K}_\Gamma^+ \vDash \neg A$. We will use this fact below.

Assume now that $A \vDash B$ and $E \vDash \mathbf{f}$ belong to Γ^+. By our previous result, we have $\mathbf{K}_\Gamma^+ \vDash \neg E$, that is, $\neg E \in \mathrm{Th}_\Gamma^+(\emptyset)$. Consequently, we can use Right Th_Γ^+-Equivalence to conclude that $A \vDash B \wedge \neg E$ also belongs to Γ^+. Thus, Γ^+ satisfies Regularity, and consequently it is a strongly regular inference relation.

The regular closure of Γ was defined as a least strongly regular inference relation that includes Γ. Consequently, it should be included in Γ^+. In particular, if A belongs to the knowledge set of Γ, then $\neg A \vDash \mathbf{f} \in \Gamma^+$, and consequently $\mathbf{K}_\Gamma^+ \vDash A$. This concludes the proof.   □

The above results can be summarized as follows. Any strongly regular inference relation has a monotonic, logical component determined by conditionals of the form $A \vDash \mathbf{f}$ belonging to it. Once this component is known, regular derivability can be reduced to basic derivability that respects the associated classical consequence relation.

6.6 Safe inference

Some kinds of nonmonotonic inference (e.g., credulous inference) permit situations in which the same assumption may lead to contradictory conclusions without disproving the assumption. This possibility is excluded in a modified notion of a basic inference relation that is described in the next definition.

Definition 6.6.1. *An inference relation will be called* safe *if it satisfies the following rule:*

Consistency   *If $A \mathrel{|\!\sim} B$ and $A \mathrel{|\!\sim} \neg B$, then $A \mathrel{|\!\sim} \mathbf{f}$.*

To begin with, we will show that any safe inference relation is already regular.

Lemma 6.6.1. *Any safe inference relation is regular.*

Proof. Assume that $A \mathrel{|\!\sim} B$ and $B \mathrel{|\!\sim} \mathbf{f}$. The first conditional implies $A \vee B \mathrel{|\!\sim} (A \vee \neg B) \to B$ by Deduction, and hence $A \vee B \mathrel{|\!\sim} B$ by Right Weakening. The second conditional implies $A \vee B \mathrel{|\!\sim} A \wedge \neg B$ by Deduction, and hence $A \vee B \mathrel{|\!\sim} \neg B$ by Right Weakening. Hence we can apply Consistency to conclude $A \vee B \mathrel{|\!\sim} \mathbf{f}$. But the latter implies $A \mathrel{|\!\sim} \mathbf{f}$ by basic inference.   □

Clearly, if an inference relation is skeptical, that is, satisfies And (see below), it will be safe. In fact, we will show in the next section that Regularity and standard Cautious Monotony are already sufficient for safety:

Lemma 6.6.2. *Any regular inference relation satisfying Cautious Monotony is safe.*

But even for inference relations that do not satisfy Cautious Monotony, safety appears as a desirable requirement in many applications. Fortunately, there is a fairly general way of constructing a 'safe counterpart' for any regular inference relation.

To begin with, it is easy to check the following:

Lemma 6.6.3. *A regular inference relation $\mathrel{|\!\sim}$ is safe iff $\mathrel{|\!\sim} \; \subseteq \; \mathrel{|\!\sim}^{\circ}$.*

Proof. Note that the above condition says that, for any A and B, if $A \mathrel{|\!\sim} B$, then either $A \mathrel{|\!\sim} \mathbf{f}$ or $A \mathrel{|\!\not\sim} \neg B$. Clearly, the latter condition is equivalent to Consistency.   □

So, an inference relation is safe if and only if it is included in its dual counterpart. This suggests the following construction. For any regular inference relation $\mathrel{|\!\sim}$ we can define the following new inference relation $\mathrel{|\!\sim}^{s}$:

$$A \mathrel{|\!\sim}^{s} B \quad \equiv \quad A \mathrel{|\!\sim} B \; \& \; A \mathrel{|\!\sim}^{\circ} B$$

As can be seen, $\mathrel{|\!\sim}^{s}$ is actually an intersection of $\mathrel{|\!\sim}$ and its dual $\mathrel{|\!\sim}^{\circ}$. It is easy to check also that this is indeed a regular inference relation in our sense. Moreover, the following result shows that this inference relation will always be safe.

Theorem 6.6.1.   *1. If $\mathrel{|\!\sim}$ is a regular inference relation, then $\mathrel{|\!\sim}^{s}$ is safe.*

2. A regular inference relation $\mid\hspace{-0.3em}\sim$ is safe if and only if it coincides with $\mid\hspace{-0.3em}\sim^s$.

Proof. (1) Since $\mid\hspace{-0.3em}\sim^s$ is an intersection of two regular inference relations, it should be regular (due to the fact that all rules of a regular inference relation are Horn ones). Now, unfolding the definition of $\mid\hspace{-0.3em}\sim^s$, we immediately obtain that $A \mid\hspace{-0.3em}\sim^s B$ and $A \mid\hspace{-0.3em}\sim^s \neg B$ jointly imply $A \mid\hspace{-0.3em}\sim \mathbf{f}$. As can be checked, the later is equivalent to $A \mid\hspace{-0.3em}\sim^s \mathbf{f}$, so Consistency holds for $\mid\hspace{-0.3em}\sim^s$.

(2) $\mid\hspace{-0.3em}\sim$ coincides with $\mid\hspace{-0.3em}\sim^s$ if and only if $\mid\hspace{-0.3em}\sim \ \subseteq \ \mid\hspace{-0.3em}\sim^\circ$. So the result follows directly from the preceding lemma. $\square$

The second claim in the above theorem says, in effect, that any safe inference relation can be construed as $\mid\hspace{-0.3em}\sim^s$, for some inference relation $\mid\hspace{-0.3em}\sim$. Some special cases of this construction will be considered in what follows.

To conclude this section, we will show that safe inference relations admit a natural interpretation in terms of asymmetric expectation relations.

As has been shown earlier, regular inference relations are representable by irreflexive expectation relations using the translations that we reproduce below for convenience.

(ISP) $A \mid\hspace{-0.3em}\sim B \ \equiv \ A \wedge \neg B < A \wedge B$ or $\mathbf{t} \not< A$

(SPI) $A < B \ \equiv \ A \vee B \mid\hspace{-0.3em}\sim \neg A$ and $B \mid\hspace{-0.3em}\not\sim \mathbf{f}$

It turns out that the same definitions create a one-to-one correspondence between safe inference and asymmetric plausibility relations.

Theorem 6.6.2. *1. If $\mid\hspace{-0.3em}\sim$ is a safe inference relation, then (SPI) defines an asymmetric plausibility relation.*

2. If $<$ is an asymmetric plausibility relation, then (ISP) determines a safe inference relation.

Proof. (1) We need only to check that the corresponding plausibility relation is asymmetric. Let $\mid\hspace{-0.3em}\sim$ be a safe inference relation, and assume that, for some A, B, both $A < B$ and $B < A$ hold for the associated plausibility relation. Then we would have, $B \mid\hspace{-0.3em}\not\sim \mathbf{f}$, $A \vee B \mid\hspace{-0.3em}\sim \neg B$ and $A \mid\hspace{-0.3em}\not\sim \mathbf{f}$. But $A \vee B \mid\hspace{-0.3em}\sim \neg A$ implies $A \vee B \mid\hspace{-0.3em}\sim B$ (by Antecedence and Right Weakening) and hence $A \vee B \mid\hspace{-0.3em}\sim \mathbf{f}$ by Consistency. The latter implies, however, both $A \mid\hspace{-0.3em}\sim \mathbf{f}$ and $B \mid\hspace{-0.3em}\sim \mathbf{f}$ - contradiction. Thus, $<$ is asymmetric.

(2) Now we have to show only that the generated inference relation will satisfy Consistency. Assume that $A \mid\hspace{-0.3em}\sim B$ and $A \mid\hspace{-0.3em}\sim \neg B$. The first conditional is unfolded into $A \wedge \neg B < A \wedge B$ or $\mathbf{f} \not< A$, while the second one – into $A \wedge B < A \wedge \neg B$ or $\mathbf{f} \not< A$. If $\mathbf{f} \not< A$, then $A \mid\hspace{-0.3em}\sim \mathbf{f}$, and we are done. Otherwise we would have both $A \wedge \neg B < A \wedge B$ and $A \wedge B < A \wedge \neg B$, which is impossible due to asymmetry of $<$. Therefore, the generated inference relation satisfies Consistency. $\square$

6.7 Extending the basic relation

In this last section we will introduce the main additional postulates of non-monotonic inference that will be used in subsequent chapters. Practically all these postulates are well known from the literature.

And	If $A \mathrel{|\!\sim} B$ and $A \mathrel{|\!\sim} C$, then $A \mathrel{|\!\sim} B \wedge C$
Cautious Monotony	If $A \mathrel{|\!\sim} B$ and $A \mathrel{|\!\sim} C$, then $A \wedge B \mathrel{|\!\sim} C$
Cut	If $A \mathrel{|\!\sim} B$ and $A \wedge B \mathrel{|\!\sim} C$ then $A \mathrel{|\!\sim} C$.
Consistency	If $A \mathrel{|\!\sim} B$ and $A \mathrel{|\!\sim} \neg B$ then $A \mathrel{|\!\sim} \mathbf{f}$.
Or	If $A \mathrel{|\!\sim} C$ and $B \mathrel{|\!\sim} C$, then $A \vee B \mathrel{|\!\sim} C$.
Rational Monotony	If $A \mathrel{|\!\sim} B$ and $A \mathrel{|\!\not\sim} \neg C$, then $A \wedge C \mathrel{|\!\sim} B$.

It turns out that the framework of basic inference supports some strong and non-trivial connections among the above postulates. The following theorem summarizes the main dependencies.

Theorem 6.7.1. *1. Cut and Cautious Monotony are jointly equivalent to And;*

2. Cut implies Or;

3. Regularity and Cautious Monotony imply Consistency;

4. Cautious Monotony and Or imply Cut;

5. Rational Monotony and Consistency imply And.

Proof. (1) ([KLM90]) If $A \mathrel{|\!\sim} B$ and $A \wedge B \mathrel{|\!\sim} C$, then $A \mathrel{|\!\sim} B \to C$ by Deduction, and hence $A \mathrel{|\!\sim} C$ by And and Right Weakening. So, And implies Cut. In addition, And and Conjunctive Cautious Monotony immediately imply 'standard' Cautious Monotony. In the other direction, assume that $A \mathrel{|\!\sim} B$ and $A \mathrel{|\!\sim} C$. By Cautious Monotony, $A \wedge B \mathrel{|\!\sim} C$. In addition, Dominance gives $A \wedge B \wedge C \mathrel{|\!\sim} B \wedge C$. Hence $A \wedge B \mathrel{|\!\sim} B \wedge C$ by Cut. Combined with $A \mathrel{|\!\sim} B$, this gives us $A \mathrel{|\!\sim} B \wedge C$ by Cut again. So, And holds.

(2) Assume that $A \mathrel{|\!\sim} C$ and $B \mathrel{|\!\sim} C$. Then Confirmation implies $A \vee B \mathrel{|\!\sim} C \vee B$ (from the first conditional) and $B \vee (A \wedge C) \mathrel{|\!\sim} C$ (from the second one). Applying Cut to the two latter conditionals, we conclude $A \vee B \mathrel{|\!\sim} C$. Thus, Cut implies Or.

(3) Assume that $A \mathrel{|\!\sim} B$ and $A \mathrel{|\!\sim} \neg B$. Applying Cautious Monotony, we obtain $A \wedge B \mathrel{|\!\sim} \neg B$, and consequently $A \wedge B \mathrel{|\!\sim} \mathbf{f}$ by Antecedence and Right Weakening. Also, the first conditional implies $A \mathrel{|\!\sim} A \wedge B$ by Antecedence. Now we can use Regularity to infer $A \mathrel{|\!\sim} \mathbf{f}$. So, Cautious Monotony and Regularity imply Consistency.

(4) Assume that $A \mathrel{|\!\sim} B$ and $A \wedge B \mathrel{|\!\sim} C$. The latter implies $A \mathrel{|\!\sim} B \to C$ by Deduction, and hence we infer $A \wedge (B \to C) \mathrel{|\!\sim} B$ by Cautious Monotony. Applying Antecedence and Right Weakening to the latter, we obtain $A \wedge (B \to$

$C) \hspace{0.5mm} \mid\!\sim C$. Finally we use the last conditional and $A \wedge B \mid\!\sim C$ to conclude $A \mid\!\sim C$ by Or and Left Logical Equivalence.

(5) Assume that And does not hold: $A \mid\!\sim B$, $A \mid\!\sim C$, but $A \mid\!\not\sim B \wedge C$. Applying Rational Monotony, we obtain $A \wedge \neg(B \wedge C) \mid\!\sim B$ (using the first conditional) and $A \wedge \neg(B \wedge C) \mid\!\sim C$ (using the second one). Then Deduction gives us, respectively, $A \mid\!\sim B \wedge \neg C$ and $A \mid\!\sim C \wedge \neg B$, and hence $A \mid\!\sim B$ and $A \mid\!\sim \neg B$ by Right Weakening. Now we can use Consistency to conclude $A \mid\!\sim \mathbf{f}$. But the latter implies $A \mid\!\sim B \wedge C$ by Right Weakening, contrary to our assumption.   □

A most interesting consequence of the above results is that And is a very strong postulate in the framework of basic inference, since it implies Cut, Cautious Monotony, Consistency and Or. In addition, And implies Strong Regularity. Indeed, $\neg C \mid\!\sim \mathbf{f}$ implies $A \mid\!\sim C$ by the basic inference, so $A \mid\!\sim B$ and $\neg C \mid\!\sim \mathbf{f}$ imply $A \mid\!\sim B \wedge C$ by And.

Actually, acceptance of And will give us exactly the skeptical inference relation (alias preferential inference relation from [KLM90]) that will be studied in the next chapter. The above dependencies show also that, if we do not accept And (e.g., for credulous inference), we should also reject either Cautious Monotony or Or (and hence Cut). In addition, if we want also to preserve Consistency, we cannot accept Rational Monotony.

The above list of entailments practically exhausts non-trivial relations between the postulates; this will be gradually made clear in subsequent chapters. Below we will describe only a couple of interesting inference relations that separate particular sets of postulates.

As a first example, an inference relation defined below shows that Consistency cannot be obtained without Cautious Monotony.

Example 6.7.1. Let us define the following inference relation:

$A \mid\!\sim B$ iff either $\models \neg A$, or $A \wedge B$ is classically consistent.

It can be verified that this is a regular inference relation that satisfies Cut, Or and Rational Monotony, but not Consistency (and hence neither Cautious Monotony, nor And).

Our second example describes, in effect, an adventurous inference relation that falls out of our framework of basic inference.

Example 6.7.2. (Closed World Assumption) Given an arbitrary base Δ, let us define the following inference relation:

$$A \mid\!\sim C \quad \text{iff} \quad A, \{B \in \Delta \mid A \wedge B \not\models\} \models C$$

Notice that if Δ is a set of negated atoms of the language, then the above inference relation represents the Closed World Assumption principle.

As can be verified, the above inference relation satisfies all basic postulates except Conjunctive Cautious Monotony. (Hint. Notice that $A \mid\!\sim \mathbf{f}$ does not necessarily imply $A \wedge B \mid\!\sim \mathbf{f}$.) Still, it satisfies the rest of the two-premise postulates for non-monotonic inference, namely And, Cut, Or and Rational Monotony.

Classical and quasi-classical inference. Ordinary classical consequence relations can be obtained by adding Transitivity to basic inference. This follows from the fact that consequence orders are characterized by Reflexivity, Antecedence and Transitivity; the rest of the postulates for basic inference will already be derivable. Note also that supraclassical consequence relations are not, in general, basic inference relations, since they do not satisfy Deduction. Consequently, a supraclassical consequence relation will also be a basic inference relation only if it is already classical.

Transitivity implies that the inference relation is already monotonic in the sense that it satisfies:

(Left Monotony)   If $A \mathrel{|\!\sim} B$, then $A \wedge C \mathrel{|\!\sim} B$.

Note, however, that Left Monotony alone still does not give full classicality. This can be immediately seen from the observation that Left Monotony is a simple rule that contain a single premise, so it cannot be used to combine different conditionals. In particular, it does not derive any of the two-premise postulates from the above list. Accordingly, basic inference relations satisfying Left Monotony could be called *quasi-classical*. Though quasi-classical inference relations are weaker than classical consequence relations, they justify the same *simple* rules as the latter. This follows from an easily proved observation that a set of conditionals Γ quasi-classically entails $A \mathrel{|\!\sim} B$ if and only if $C \rightarrow D \vDash A \rightarrow B$, for some conditional $C \mathrel{|\!\sim} D$ from Γ. For example, such inference relations will satisfy contraposition. In addition, they will satisfy disjunctive rules of Rational Monotony and Disjunctive Rationality. Finally, any regular quasi-classical inference relation will already by fully classical.

7. Skeptical Inference Relations

Introduction

In this chapter we are going to consider the notion of a skeptical inference, which constitutes a most important and studied kind of nonmonotonic inference. As we said in Chapter 3, our semantic interpretation of such an inference is derived from the traditional understanding of conditionals suggested by Ramsey and Mill. From a purely technical point of view, the representation of such an inference in terms of epistemic states could also be seen as a 'fusion' of the two main approaches to describing such inference suggested in the literature, namely possible worlds-based preferential models of [KLM90], and expectation-based models of [GM94]. We have already seen that possible worlds models constitute a very special case of epistemic states. On the other hand, our representation provides a generalization of the approach suggested in [GM94] that extends the latter to a broader class of nonmonotonic logics. Moreover, it shares with the latter the change of gestalt consisting in viewing preferences between worlds as merely a by-product of more basic relations holding between our beliefs. As a special case of this representation, we will establish a direct correspondence between preferential inference relations and supraclassical Tarski consequence relations.

We also consider in this chapter a representation for some important extensions of preferential entailment. We show that such extensions can be characterized by imposing some very natural conditions on generating epistemic states. It will be shown, in particular, that the suggested representation for rational inference relations is intimately connected with the expectation-based representation of Gärdenfors and Makinson.

7.1 Preferential inference relations

A basic inference relation will be called *preferential* if it satisfies the rule And:

And   If $A \mathrel{|\!\sim} B$ and $A \mathrel{|\!\sim} C$, then $A \mathrel{|\!\sim} B \wedge C$.

Preferential inference relations have been introduced in [KLM90]. As we will show, such inference relations provide a formalization of skeptical inference with respect to epistemic states (as defined in Chapter 3). We will begin, however, with describing some syntactic features of preferential inference.

The rule And contains two conditional premises. Consequently, it makes it possible to combine different conditionals. As has been established in the preceding chapter, in the framework of basic inference, And is already sufficient for deriving the main 'standard' postulates of nonmonotonic inference, namely Cut, Cautious Monotony and Or. It also turns out that the latter postulates allow us to derive, in turn, the main postulates of basic inference (as well as And). Thus, the following postulates provide a convenient alternative axiomatization of preferential inference relations (see, e.g., [Gef92]).

Dominance   If $A \models B$, then $A \mathrel{|\!\sim} B$.

Cautious Monotony   If $A \mathrel{|\!\sim} B$ and $A \mathrel{|\!\sim} C$, then $A \wedge B \mathrel{|\!\sim} C$

Cut   If $A \mathrel{|\!\sim} B$ and $A \wedge B \mathrel{|\!\sim} C$ then $A \mathrel{|\!\sim} C$.

Or   If $A \mathrel{|\!\sim} C$ and $B \mathrel{|\!\sim} C$, then $A \vee B \mathrel{|\!\sim} C$.

Lemma 7.1.1. *An inference relation is preferential if and only if it satisfies Dominance, Cautious Monotony, Cut and Or.*

Proof. To begin with, we need to show that the postulates of $\mathcal{B}$ are derivable.

Reflexivity follows directly from Dominance.

Right Weakening. If $A \mathrel{|\!\sim} B$ and $B \models C$, then $A \wedge B \mathrel{|\!\sim} C$ by Dominance, and hence $A \mathrel{|\!\sim} C$ by Cut.

Left Logical Equivalence. If $\models A \leftrightarrow C$ and $A \mathrel{|\!\sim} B$, then $A \mathrel{|\!\sim} C$ and $C \mathrel{|\!\sim} A$ by Dominance, hence $A \wedge C \mathrel{|\!\sim} B$ by Cautious Monotony, and therefore $C \mathrel{|\!\sim} B$ by Cut.

Deduction. If $A \wedge B \mathrel{|\!\sim} C$, then $A \wedge B \mathrel{|\!\sim} B \to C$ by Right Weakening, $A \wedge \neg B \mathrel{|\!\sim} B \to C$ by Dominance, and therefore $A \mathrel{|\!\sim} B \to C$ by Or.

Conjunctive Cautious Monotony. If $A \mathrel{|\!\sim} B \wedge C$, then $A \mathrel{|\!\sim} B$ and $A \mathrel{|\!\sim} C$ by Right Weakening, and hence $A \wedge B \mathrel{|\!\sim} C$ by Cautious Monotony.

And. See Theorem 6.7.1 in the preceding chapter.   □

Preferential inference relations make valid the following general rule of combining conditionals; this rule has been introduced in [Ada75].

(**Quasi-conjunction**) If $A \mathrel{|\!\sim} B$ and $C \mathrel{|\!\sim} D$, then $A \vee C \mathrel{|\!\sim} (A \to B) \wedge (C \to D)$.

As will be shown later, preferential inference can be seen as a basic inference augmented with Quasi-conjunction. In other words, derivability with respect to preferential inference is precisely basic derivability plus the above rule of combining conditionals. In particular, preferential derivability from single conditionals will coincide with basic derivability. Actually, preferential inference relations turn out to be syntactically complete with respect to Horn rules, much in the same sense in which basic inference relations are complete with respect to simple rules. In other words, no reasonable extension of preferential inference will validate new Horn rules for nonmonotonic inference.

7.2 Preferential inference via expectations

In this section we will extend the correspondence between basic nonmonotonic inference and expectation relations to preferential inference. The results that follow will demonstrate that the latter corresponds precisely to qualitative expectation relations.

Recall that entrenchment, plausibility and dependence relations are mutually definable. For reasons that will become clear later, we will start this time with the correspondence between preferential inference and dependence relations.

As has been established in the preceding chapter, the following two definitions, called the id-mapping, determine a bijection between basic inference and dependence relations.

(ID) $\qquad\qquad A \mid\!\sim B \ \equiv\ \neg(A \wedge B) < \neg A$

(DI) $\qquad\qquad A < B \ \equiv\ \neg(A \wedge B) \mid\!\sim \neg A$

The result below demonstrates that the above correspondence determines also the correspondence between preferential inference and qualitative dependence relations.

Theorem 7.2.1.   *1. If $\mid\!\sim$ is a preferential inference relation, then (DI) defines a qualitative dependence relation.*

2. If $<$ is a qualitative dependence relation, then (ID) defines a preferential inference relation.

Proof. Due to our previous results, we need to check only that the rule And for inference relations corresponds to the rule Weak Or for dependence relations.

(1) Assume that $A \vee B < A$ and $A \vee C < A$ hold for the associated dependence relation. Then $\neg A \mid\!\sim \neg A \wedge \neg B$ and $\neg A \mid\!\sim \neg A \wedge \neg C$ belong to the inference relation. Applying And, we obtain $\neg A \mid\!\sim \neg A \wedge \neg B \wedge \neg C$, which is equivalent to $A \vee B \vee C < A$. Thus, Weak Or is valid.

(2) Assume that $A \mid\!\sim B$ and $A \mid\!\sim C$ belong to the inference relation generated by the qualitative dependence relation $<$. Then $\neg A \vee \neg B < \neg A$ and

$\neg A \vee \neg C < \neg A$, and hence $\neg A \vee \neg B \vee \neg C < \neg A$ by Weak Or. But the latter is equivalent to $A \mathrel{\vert\!\sim} B \wedge C$, so And holds. $\square$

Qualitative dependence relations are interdefinable with semi-classical consequence relations, and hence the above theorem establishes also a correspondence between the latter and preferential inference relations. This correspondence will play an important role in what follows.

Since qualitative dependence relations are interdefinable with qualitative entrenchment relations, we immediately obtain that the ie-mapping and is-mapping defined in the preceding chapter determine correspondences between preferential inference and, respectively, simple and strict qualitative entrenchment.

Corollary 7.2.1. *1. The ie-mapping determines a bijection between preferential inference relations and simple qualitative entrenchment relations.*
   2. The is-mapping determines a bijection between preferential inference relations and strict qualitative entrenchment relations.

Finally, combining the ie-mapping and contraposition, we obtain the ip-mapping defined in the preceding chapter; it will establish a bijection between preferential inference and simple qualitative plausibility relations.

7.3 Preferential inference as skeptical inference

Now we turn to representation of preferential inference in the framework of epistemic states. To begin with, the following theorem shows that preferential inference relations are sound with respect to skeptical inference in epistemic states.

Theorem 7.3.1. *The set of conditionals that are skeptically valid in an epistemic state forms a preferential inference relation.*

Proof. Dominance follows immediately from the definition of skeptical validity.

   Cut. Assume that $A \mathrel{\vert\!\sim} B$ and $A \wedge B \mathrel{\vert\!\sim} C$ are skeptically valid with respect to an epistemic state $\mathbb{E}$. Then each preferred admissible state s consistent with A supports $A \to B$, and hence it is consistent with $A \wedge B$. This implies, in particular, that s is also a preferred state consistent with $A \wedge B$ (since all 'better' states support already $\neg A$). Consequently, $A \wedge B \mathrel{\vert\!\sim} C$ implies that $(A \wedge B) \to C$ is supported by s, and therefore s supports $A \to C$. Thus, $A \mathrel{\vert\!\sim} C$ is skeptically valid in $\mathbb{E}$.

   Cautious Monotony. Assume that $A \mathrel{\vert\!\sim} B$ and $A \mathrel{\vert\!\sim} C$ hold in an epistemic state $\mathbb{E}$. Then all preferred states consistent with A satisfy both $A \to B$ and $A \to C$. Let s be a preferred state consistent with $A \wedge B$. Then it should also be preferred in $]\neg A[$. Indeed, otherwise there would exist a state t such that

$s \prec t$ and t is preferred in $]\neg A[$. But t should support $A \to B$, and hence it is consistent with $A \wedge B$ contrary to the assumption that s is a preferred such state. But if s is preferred in $]\neg A[$, it supports $A \to C$ and hence it should support $(A \wedge B) \to C$. Therefore $A \wedge B \mid\!\sim C$ holds in $\mathbb{E}$.

Or. Assume that $A \mid\!\sim C$ and $B \mid\!\sim C$ hold in $\mathbb{E}$, and let s be a preferred state consistent with $A \vee B$. This implies that s is preferred either in $]\neg A[$ or in $\langle B \rangle$ (or in both). To show that Or is satisfied, it is sufficient to demonstrate that in either case s satisfies $(A \vee B) \to C$.

Assume that s is preferred in $]\neg A[$ but not in $]\neg B[$, that is, s supports $\neg B$. Then s supports $A \to C$ and hence also $(A \vee B) \to C$. The case of s being preferred in $]\neg B[$ but not in $]\neg A[$ is similar. Finally, assume that s is preferred both in $]\neg A[$ and in $]\neg B[$. Then it should support both $A \to C$ and $B \to C$, and hence also $(A \vee B) \to C$. Therefore, Or is satisfied.   □

As can be seen from the above proof, the smoothness condition on the preference relation of epistemic states is needed only for Cautious Monotony.

Now we will show that preferential inference relations are also complete for skeptical inference. The idea of the following proof is as follows. Any preferential inference relation is equivalent to a qualitative dependence order, which is equivalent, in turn, to some (semi-classical) consequence relation. It turns out that the theories of the latter form a pure epistemic state that generate precisely the original inference relation.

Theorem 7.3.2. *Any preferential inference relation coincides with the skeptical inference relation determined by some epistemic state.*

Proof. Let $\mid\!\sim$ be a preferential inference relation, and $\vdash$ a semi-classical consequence relation corresponding to $\mid\!\sim$. Let us consider a pure epistemic state consisting of the set $\mathcal{T}$ of all theories of $\vdash$. We claim that $\mid\!\sim$ is precisely the set of conditionals that are skeptically valid in $\mathcal{T}$.

Assume first that $A \mid\!\sim B$, though it is not skeptically valid in $\mathcal{T}$. Then there must exist a maximal theory u of $\vdash$ consistent with A such that $A \to B \notin u$. Clearly, $u \nvdash \neg A$ and $u, A \to B \vdash \neg A$ (due to maximality of u). By compactness of $\vdash$, there must exist a proposition $C \in u$ such that $C \nvdash \neg A$ and $C, (A \to B) \vdash \neg A$. The latter condition corresponds to the following condition for $\mid\!\sim$:

$$\neg C \vee A \mid\!\sim \neg C \vee \neg B$$

On the other hand, $A \mid\!\sim B$ implies $\neg C \vee A \mid\!\sim \neg C \vee B$ (by Deduction and Right Weakening). Hence we can apply And and obtain $\neg C \vee A \mid\!\sim \neg C$. But the latter is equivalent to $C \vdash \neg A$, which contradicts our assumptions.

Assume now that $A \not\mid\!\sim B$. Then $\neg A \vee \neg B \nvdash \neg A$ for the associated consequence relation. The latter implies that there exists a maximal theory u of $\vdash$ that is consistent with A and contains $\neg A \vee \neg B$. As can be seen, u cannot contain $A \to B$ (since otherwise it would contain A). Therefore $A \mid\!\sim B$ is not skeptically valid with respect to $\mathcal{T}$. This completes the proof.   □

The above proof is relatively short, but it hides many interesting connections that we will explore in the next section.

Clearly, many quite different epistemic states can generate the same inference relation. Still, it is important to observe that the latter uniquely determines two basic features of the host epistemic state, namely its refined belief set and its knowledge set. Thus, it is easy to see that the refined belief set of any epistemic state $\mathbb{E}$ is precisely the set of propositions that are preferentially provable in the associated inference relation:

$$\mathbf{B_E} \;=\; \{A \mid \mathbf{t} \hspace{0.1em}\vdash_{\mathbb{E}} A\}$$

Similarly, a proposition A is known in $\mathbb{E}$ if and only if $\neg A \hspace{0.1em}\vdash \mathbf{f}$. Thus,

$$\mathbf{K_E} \;=\; \{A \mid \neg A \hspace{0.1em}\vdash_{\mathbb{E}} \mathbf{f}\}$$

As a result, we have that *the internal logic of an epistemic state coincides with the internal logic of the generated inference relation* (see Chapter 6). We will use this fact without further mentioning in what follows.

Expectation relations in epistemic states

Due to inter-definability of preferential inference relations and qualitative expectation relations, we can immediately use the above representation of preferential inference relations in order to give a semantic representation of qualitative expectation relations in terms of epistemic states. Thus, the following definition provides an appropriate description of simple entrenchment relations generated by epistemic states.

Definition 7.3.1. *B will be said to be* more entrenched *than A in an epistemic state $\mathbb{E}$ (notation $A <_{\mathbb{E}} B$), if B is supported by all preferred admissible states in $]A \wedge B[$.*

The above definition determines a relation on the set of propositions that we will call an *entrenchment relation generated by an epistemic state*. As can be seen, the definition conforms with the informal description of entrenchment relations given in Chapter 5: B is more entrenched than A if all preferred ways of removing $A \wedge B$ retain B. The following result shows that this definition determines exactly simple qualitative entrenchment relations.

Theorem 7.3.3. *Simple qualitative entrenchment relations coincide with entrenchment relations generated by epistemic states.*

Proof. Any simple qualitative entrenchment relation is definable as $\neg(A \wedge B) \hspace{0.1em}\vdash B$, for an appropriate preferential inference relation, and the semantic conditions for this conditional with respect to an epistemic state coincide with the definition of an entrenchment relation generated by an epistemic state. Hence the result.   □

A similar semantic description could be given for other kinds of qualitative expectation relations. They will not be needed for the following, however, so we will leave it as an exercise to the reader.

7.4 Consequence-based inference relations

The proof of the completeness theorem, given in the preceding section, was based on the correspondence between inference relations and consequence relations (= dependence orders). In this section we will consider this correspondence in more details.

Recall that a supraclassical consequence relation can be seen as a syntactic description of a pure epistemic state consisting of theories of this consequence relation. Accordingly, any Tarski consequence relation determines the corresponding notion of a skeptical validity defined as follows:

Definition 7.4.1. *A conditional $A \mathrel{\vert\!\sim} B$ will be said to be* skeptically valid *with respect to a supraclassical consequence relation $\vdash$ if $A \to B$ belongs to all maximal theories of $\vdash$ that are consistent with A. The set of conditionals that are skeptically valid with respect to $\vdash$ will be denoted by $\mathrel{\vert\!\sim}_{\vdash}$.*

The above definition describes, in effect, skeptical validity with respect to the pure epistemic state determined by all theories of a consequence relation. Consequently, Theorem 7.3.1 is sufficient to justify the following

Corollary 7.4.1. *If $\vdash$ is a supraclassical Tarski consequence relation, then $\mathrel{\vert\!\sim}_{\vdash}$ is a preferential inference relation.*

It turns out that the validity of a conditional with respect to a consequence relation is equivalent to a closure of this consequence relation with respect to some rule:

Lemma 7.4.1. *$A \mathrel{\vert\!\sim} B$ is skeptically valid with respect to $\vdash$ if and only if $\vdash$ is closed with respect to the following rule, for any a:*

$$\frac{a, A \to B \vdash \neg A}{a \vdash \neg A}$$

Proof. If $A \mathrel{\vert\!\sim}_{\vdash} B$ holds and $a \nvdash \neg A$, then there is a theory u of $\vdash$ that includes a, but is consistent with A. This theory is included in some maximal theory v consistent with A. The latter includes both a and $A \to B$, and hence $a, A \to B \nvdash \neg A$.

In the other direction, assume that $\vdash$ is closed with respect to the above rule, and u is a maximal theory consistent with A and such that $A \to B \notin u$. Due to maximality of u, we have $u, A \to B \vdash \neg A$, and hence by compactness there is a finite set a such that $a, A \to B \vdash \neg A$. Consequently, we have $a \vdash \neg A$, and therefore $u \vdash \neg A$ that contradicts the assumption that u is consistent with A. Therefore, any maximal theory consistent with A should contain $A \to B$, and hence $A \mathrel{\vert\!\sim}_{\vdash} B$ holds. $\qquad\square$

The above result implies, in particular, that a consequence relation can be forced to validate a given conditional by imposing an associated 'monotonic' rule.

Note also that, since an inference relation determines the belief set and internal logic of its generating epistemic state, it will determine the belief set of a generating consequence relation and its classical subrelation. Thus, we have

Lemma 7.4.2. *If $\mathrel{|\!\sim}$ is a preferential inference relation generated by $\vdash$ and* $\mathrm{Th}_{\vdash}$ *its classical subrelation, then* $\mathrm{Th}_{\mathrel{|\!\sim}} = \mathrm{Th}_{\vdash}$.

7.4.1 Semi-classical translation

As has been shown earlier, semi-classical consequence relations (alias qualitative dependence orders) are interdefinable with preferential inference relations. Moreover, the proof of the completeness theorem was actually based on showing that the associated semi-classical consequence relation generates the original inference relation. Accordingly, the essence of this proof amounts to the following result showing that, for semi-classical consequence relations, the characterization of the generated skeptical inference can be drastically simplified[1].

Theorem 7.4.1. *If $\vdash$ is a semi-classical Tarski consequence relation, then* $A \mathrel{|\!\sim_{\vdash}} B$ *if and only if* $\neg(A \wedge B) \vdash \neg A$.

Proof. Note first that, for any supraclassical consequence relation $\neg(A \wedge B) \vdash \neg A$ is equivalent to $\neg(A \wedge B) \vdash A \to B$, while the latter can be rewritten as $(A \to B) \to \neg A \vdash A \to B$. Now, by Lemma 2.3.7 from Chapter 2, if $\vdash$ is a semi-classical consequence relation, then the last condition holds if and only if, for any a, if $a, A \to B \vdash \neg A$, then $a \vdash A \to B$. By the Cut rule, the latter is equivalent to the condition that, for any a, if $a, A \to B \vdash \neg A$, then $a \vdash \neg A$. Now the result follows from Lemma 7.4.1. $\qquad\square$

In addition to the general completeness result with respect to epistemic states, the above theorem gives us also the following

Corollary 7.4.2. *An inference relation is preferential if and only if it is generated by some supraclassical consequence relation.*

The following result shows that the semi-classical consequence relation $\vdash_{\mathrel{|\!\sim}}$ corresponding to a preferential inference relation $\mathrel{|\!\sim}$ occupies a special place among Tarski consequence relations validating the rules from $\mathrel{|\!\sim}$.

Lemma 7.4.3. *For any preferential inference relation $\mathrel{|\!\sim}$, $\vdash_{\mathrel{|\!\sim}}$ is a least Tarski consequence relation making valid all conditionals from $\mathrel{|\!\sim}$.*

---

[1] This result has been independently proved in [Geo99], though in a quite different terminology.

Proof. Let $\vdash$ be a Tarski consequence relation such that its generated preferential inference relation includes $\mathrel{|\!\sim}$. Now, if $A \vdash_{\mathrel{|\!\sim}} B$, then $\neg(A \land B) \mathrel{|\!\sim} \neg A$, and consequently $\vdash$ should be closed with respect to the rule

$$\frac{a, \neg(A \land B) \to \neg A \vdash A \land B}{a \vdash A \land B}$$

By supraclassicality, $A, \neg(A \land B) \to \neg A \vdash A \land B$, and hence by substituting $\{A\}$ for a in the above rule, we immediately obtain $A \vdash A \land B$, which is equivalent to $A \vdash B$. Therefore, $\vdash_{\mathrel{|\!\sim}}$ is included in $\vdash$. $\square$

A constructive characterization of semi-classical consequence relations generating a given set of nonmonotonic inference rules will be given in the next section. It will allow us to reduce preferential derivability to derivability with respect to consequence relations, and eventually to classical entailment.

7.4.2 Basic propositions in nonmonotonic inference

The correspondence between preferential inference relations and consequence relations allows us to single out some important classes of propositions that behave in a monotonic way in the framework of nonmonotonic preferential inference relations.

Engelfriet has described in [Eng98] two interesting classes of propositions that are characterized by their 'almost monotonic' behavior with respect to a preferential inference relation. These classes are described in the following definition.

Definition 7.4.2. *1. A proposition B will be said to be* conservative *with respect to a preferential inference relation $\mathrel{|\!\sim}$ if, for any A, if $A \mathrel{|\!\sim} B$, then $A \land C \mathrel{|\!\sim} B$, for any proposition C.*
   2. A proposition B will be said to be a default *with respect to a preferential inference relation $\mathrel{|\!\sim}$ if, for any propositions A and C, if $A \mathrel{|\!\sim} C$, then $A \land B \mathrel{|\!\sim} C$.*

Conservative propositions are propositions that, once inferred (nonmonotonically) from some premises, remain such even if we add new premises. Default propositions are precisely propositions that can be safely added to any premises without destroying previous nonmonotonic conclusions. As was rightly argued by Engelfriet, the ability to single out such propositions can greatly improve the efficiency of computing preferential entailment. [Eng98] contains a detailed description of such propositions in different nonmonotonic formalisms, as well as some results about their semantic behavior in preferential possible worlds models.

As we are going to show now, conservative and default propositions have a natural characterization in terms of associated consequence relations. Namely, we will show that conservative propositions correspond in this sense to prime propositions of consequence relations, while default propositions correspond precisely to basic propositions.

We begin with conservative propositions. The following lemma gives a simpler characterization of such propositions. It says that a conservative proposition is nonmonotonically inferred from some proposition A only if it is inferred from A with respect to the classical subrelation $\text{Th}_{\vdash}$ of the inference relation (that is, when $A \wedge \neg B \mathrel{\vert\!\sim} \mathbf{f}$). This fact follows immediately from Lemma 6.5.3 in the preceding chapter.

Lemma 7.4.4. *A proposition B is conservative with respect to $\mathrel{\vert\!\sim}$ if and only if, for any A, $A \mathrel{\vert\!\sim} B$ only if $B \in \text{Th}_{\vdash}(A)$.*

The next result shows that prime propositions of a consequence relation (see Definition 2.4.1 in Chapter 2) generate conservative propositions of the associated inference relation.

Lemma 7.4.5. *If $\neg B$ is a prime proposition of a supraclassical consequence relation, then B is a conservative proposition of the generated preferential inference relation.*

Proof. Assume that $\neg B$ is a prime proposition of $\vdash$ and $A \mathrel{\vert\!\sim} B$ belongs to the associated inference relation. Then, for any a, $a, A \to B \vdash \neg A$ implies $a \vdash \neg A$. Substituting $\{A \to \neg B\}$ for a, we obtain $A \to \neg B \vdash \neg A$, which implies $\neg B \vdash \neg A$. Since $\neg B$ is prime, we conclude that $\vdash \neg B \to \neg A$, and hence $B \in \text{Th}_{\vdash}(A)$ (see Lemma 7.4.2 above). Thus, B is a conservative proposition of the generated preferential inference relation. $\qquad\square$

Finally, the following result shows, in effect, that a proposition B is conservative with respect to an inference relation $\mathrel{\vert\!\sim}$ if and only if $\neg B$ is a prime proposition of some consequence relation that generates $\mathrel{\vert\!\sim}$.

Theorem 7.4.2. *B is a conservative proposition in $\mathrel{\vert\!\sim}$ if and only if $\neg B$ is a prime proposition of the corresponding semi-classical consequence relation.*

Proof. The implication from right to left follows from the preceding lemma. Assume that B is a conservative proposition of $\mathrel{\vert\!\sim}$, and $\vdash$ the corresponding semi-classical consequence relation. Then conservativity implies the following condition on $\vdash$: for any A, if $\neg(A \wedge B) \vdash \neg A$, then $\vdash A \to B$. Substituting $C \to B$ for A, we obtain that if $\neg B \vdash C$, then $\vdash \neg B \to C$. Since C is arbitrary, the latter condition is an exact characterization of primeness of $\neg B$ in $\vdash$. Consequently, B is a conservative proposition of $\mathrel{\vert\!\sim}$ only if $\neg B$ is a prime proposition of $\vdash$. $\qquad\square$

Now we will consider default propositions. Notice that if B is a default proposition, then $\neg B$ is conservative. The following lemma shows that basic propositions of a consequence relation will be default propositions of the associated inference relation.

Lemma 7.4.6. *If B is a basic proposition of a supraclassical consequence relation, then it is a default proposition of the generated preferential inference relation.*

Proof. Assume that B is a basic proposition of $\vdash$ and $A \mathrel{|\!\sim} C$ belongs to the associated inference relation. Assume also that $a, (A \wedge B) \rightarrow C \vdash \neg(A \wedge B)$ holds, for some set a. Then $B, a, A \rightarrow C \vdash \neg A$, and hence $A \mathrel{|\!\sim} C$ implies $B, a \vdash \neg A$. Since B is a basic proposition, the latter implies, in turn, $a \vdash \neg(A \wedge B)$. Therefore, $A \wedge B \mathrel{|\!\sim} C$ holds for the associated inference relation, and consequently B is a default proposition of $\mathrel{|\!\sim}$. $\qquad\square$

And finally the next result shows that a proposition is default with respect to an inference relation $\mathrel{|\!\sim}$ if and only if it is a basic proposition of some consequence relation that generates $\mathrel{|\!\sim}$.

Theorem 7.4.3. *B is a default proposition in $\mathrel{|\!\sim}$ if and only if it is a basic proposition of the corresponding semi-classical consequence relation.*

Proof. The implication from right to left follows from the preceding lemma. Assume that B is a default proposition of $\mathrel{|\!\sim}$, and $\vdash$ the corresponding semi-classical consequence relation. Monotonicity of B amounts to the following condition on $\vdash$: for any A, C, if $\neg A \vee \neg C \vdash \neg A$, then $\neg A \vee \neg C \vee \neg B \vdash \neg(A \wedge B)$. Assume now that $B \wedge D \vdash E$ holds, for some D, E. Then $(B \wedge D \wedge E) \vee (B \wedge D \wedge \neg E) \vdash B \wedge D \wedge E$. Consequently, monotonicity of B gives us

$$(B \wedge D \wedge E) \vee (B \wedge D \wedge \neg E) \vee \neg B \vdash (B \wedge D \wedge E) \vee \neg B$$

which is reducible to $\neg B \vee D \vdash (D \wedge E) \vee \neg B$. But the latter implies $D \vdash B \rightarrow E$, and therefore B is a basic proposition of $\vdash$. This completes the proof. $\quad\square$

The results of this section confirm our conviction that many important properties relevant to nonmonotonic inference can be described in terms of consequence relations that generate such an inference.

7.5 Syntactic characterizations

In this section we will obtain two important syntactic characterizations of preferential derivability, first with respect to consequence relations, and then with respect to classical entailment.

7.5.1 Consequence relations generating a set of conditionals

We will describe now a method of constructing a Tarski consequence relation validating a given set of conditionals Δ.

As has been shown above, the validity of a conditional $A \mathrel{|\!\sim} B$ with respect to a Tarski consequence relation $\vdash$ amounts to a closure of $\vdash$ with respect to the rule saying that if $a, A \to B \vdash \neg A$, then $a \vdash \neg A$. Due to the 'Horn' form of this rule, intersections of consequence relations satisfying the rule also satisfy the rule. Consequently, we immediately obtain

Lemma 7.5.1. *For any set of conditionals Δ there exists a least consequence relation validating all the rules from Δ.*

The least consequence relation validating Δ will be denoted by $\vdash_\Delta$. Note that a set of conditionals may be inconsistent, and in this case $\vdash_\Delta$ will be an inconsistent consequence relation.

Example 7.5.1. Consider the set of conditionals $\Delta = \{A \mathrel{|\!\sim} \neg A, \neg A \mathrel{|\!\sim} A\}$. This set is preferentially inconsistent (that is, it implies any conditional of the language). The consequence relation validating Δ should contain the rules $a \vdash A$ and $a \vdash \neg A$, for any set a. Clearly, such a consequence relation is bound to be inconsistent.

By a *preferential closure* of Δ (denoted by $\hat{\Delta}$) we will mean the least preferential inference relation containing Δ. The following result connects the newly introduced consequence relation with our earlier constructions.

Theorem 7.5.1. *For any set of conditionals Δ, $\vdash_\Delta$ coincides with the semi-classical consequence relation corresponding to $\hat{\Delta}$.*

Proof. Let $\vdash^s_{\hat{\Delta}}$ be the semi-classical consequence relation corresponding to $\hat{\Delta}$. Clearly, $\vdash_\Delta$ is included in $\vdash^s_{\hat{\Delta}}$. Moreover, $\vdash^s_{\hat{\Delta}}$ is a least consequence relation validating $\hat{\Delta}$. But the set of conditionals validated by $\vdash_\Delta$ forms a preferential inference relation, and consequently $\hat{\Delta}$ is included in this set. Therefore $\vdash_\Delta$ coincides with $\vdash^s_{\hat{\Delta}}$. $\square$

Since $\vdash^s_{\hat{\Delta}}$ validates precisely $\hat{\Delta}$, we immediately conclude

Corollary 7.5.1. *If Δ is a set of conditionals, then the preferential closure of Δ coincides with the set of conditionals valid in $\vdash_\Delta$.*

The following consequence of the above theorem gives an equivalent description of $\vdash_\Delta$. It follows immediately from Theorem 7.4.1.

Corollary 7.5.2. $\vdash_\Delta$ *is a least semi-classical consequence relation containing a rule $\neg(A \wedge B) \vdash \neg A$ for each conditional $A \mathrel{|\!\sim} B$ from Δ.*

The above facts will help us in giving a constructive description of preferential derivability.

For a finite set of conditionals Δ, we will denote by $\overrightarrow{\Delta}$ the conjunction of their corresponding classical implications, that is, $\bigwedge\{A \to B \mid A \mathrel{|\!\sim} B \in \Delta\}$, and by $\Delta^\vee$ the disjunction of antecedents of Δ, that is, $\bigvee\{A \mid A \mathrel{|\!\sim} B \in \Delta\}$. We will admit also a special case of Δ being an empty set. In this case we will define $\overrightarrow{\Delta}$ to be equal to $\mathbf{t}$, while $\Delta^\vee$ will be equal to $\mathbf{f}$. As can be seen,

$\overrightarrow{\Delta}$ is always a logical consequence of $\neg \Delta^\vee$. Also, we will denote by $I(\Delta)$ the formula $\overrightarrow{\Delta} \to \neg \Delta^\vee$. The formula can be seen as saying that the relevant set of conditionals constitutes a *clash* (see below). In the case when Δ is empty, $I(\Delta)$ will be equivalent to **t**.

By a *quasi-conjunction* of a finite set of conditionals Δ, denoted by $\&(\Delta)$, we will mean a conditional $\Delta^\vee \hspace{0.3em}\vrule\hspace{-0.5em}\sim \overrightarrow{\Delta}$.

Lemma 7.5.2. *([Ada75]) Any finite set of conditionals Δ preferentially entails $\&(\Delta)$.*

Proof. Note first that $A \hspace{0.3em}\vrule\hspace{-0.5em}\sim B$ entails $A \vee C \hspace{0.3em}\vrule\hspace{-0.5em}\sim A \to B$, for any proposition C. Consequently, Δ entails $\Delta^\vee \hspace{0.3em}\vrule\hspace{-0.5em}\sim (A_i \to B_i)$, for any conditional $A_i \hspace{0.3em}\vrule\hspace{-0.5em}\sim B_i$ from Δ. Conjoining these conditionals using And, we obtain the quasi-conjunction of Δ. $\qquad\square$

As a first consequence of the above lemma, we obtain

Lemma 7.5.3. *A consequence relation $\vdash$ validates a finite set of conditionals Δ only if $I(\Delta) \vdash \neg \Delta^\vee$.*

Proof. Let $\hspace{0.3em}\vrule\hspace{-0.5em}\sim_\vdash$ be a preferential inference relation generated by $\vdash$ and $\vdash^s$ the semi-classical consequence relation corresponding to $\hspace{0.3em}\vrule\hspace{-0.5em}\sim_\vdash$. Since $\vdash^s$ is a least consequence relation validating $\hspace{0.3em}\vrule\hspace{-0.5em}\sim_\vdash$, it is included in $\vdash$.

Since $\&(\Delta)$ belongs to $\hspace{0.3em}\vrule\hspace{-0.5em}\sim_\vdash$ by the previous lemma, we have $\neg \Delta^\vee \vee \neg \overrightarrow{\Delta} \vdash^s \neg \Delta^\vee$, which is equivalent to $I(\Delta) \vdash^s \neg \Delta^\vee$. But $\vdash^s$ is included in $\vdash$, and hence $I(\Delta) \vdash \neg \Delta^\vee$. $\qquad\square$

The following theorem gives a direct characterization of the rules of $\vdash_\Delta$.

Theorem 7.5.2. *$a \vdash_\Delta A$ if and only if there exists a finite set $\Delta_0 \subseteq \Delta$ such that*

$$a \vDash I(\Delta_0) \text{ and } a \vdash \overrightarrow{\Delta}_0 \to A.$$

Proof. Let $\vdash^0_\Delta$ be a consequence relation determined by the above condition. We will show first that it is a supraclassical consequence relation.

Monotonicity is obviously satisfied. Taking $\Delta_0 = \emptyset$, we also immediately obtain that $\vdash^0_\Delta$ is supraclassical. Hence it remains only to check Cut.

If $a \vDash I(\Delta_0) \wedge (\overrightarrow{\Delta}_0 \to A)$ and $a, A \vDash I(\Delta_1) \wedge (\overrightarrow{\Delta}_1 \to B)$, then it is easy to check that $a \vDash I(\Delta_2) \wedge (\overrightarrow{\Delta}_2 \to B)$, where Δ_2 denotes $\Delta_0 \cup \Delta_1$. Hence, Cut is satisfied.

Now we will show that $\vdash^0_\Delta$ makes valid all conditionals from Δ. Indeed, if $A \hspace{0.3em}\vrule\hspace{-0.5em}\sim B \in \Delta$ and

$$a, A \to B \vDash I(\Delta_0) \wedge (\overrightarrow{\Delta}_0 \to \neg A),$$

for some set Δ_0, then we immediately obtain

$$a \vDash I(\Delta_1) \wedge (\vec{\Delta}_1 \to \neg A),$$

where Δ_1 denotes $\Delta_0 \cup \{A \vdash\!\!\!\sim B\}$. Consequently $a \vdash^0_\Delta \neg A$.

Finally, we will show that $\vdash^0_\Delta$ is a minimal consequence relation validating Δ (and hence it will coincide with $\vdash_\Delta$).

Let $\vdash$ be an arbitrary consequence relation validating all conditionals from Δ. If $a \vDash I(\Delta_0) \wedge (\vec{\Delta}_0 \to A)$, then by Supraclassicality $a \vdash I(\Delta_0)$ and $a \vdash \vec{\Delta}_0 \to A$. By the preceding lemma we obtain $a \vdash \neg \Delta_0^\vee$ from the first rule, while the second rule implies $a \vdash \neg \Delta_0^\vee \to A$. Consequently we can conclude $a \vdash A$, and therefore $\vdash^0_\Delta$ is included in $\vdash$. This completes the proof of the theorem. □

The last part of the proof of this theorem shows, in effect, that $\vdash_\Delta$ is included in any consequence relation containing the rules $I(\Delta_0) \vdash \Delta_0^\vee$, for all finite subsets Δ_0 of Δ. Consequently we have

Corollary 7.5.3. *For any set of conditionals Δ, $\vdash_\Delta$ is a least consequence relation containing all rules of the form $I(\Delta_0) \vdash \neg \Delta_0^\vee$, where Δ_0 ranges over finite subsets of Δ.*

Below we will use the above results for characterizing preferential derivability in terms of classical entailment.

7.5.2 Classical reduction

As an immediate consequence of the above results, we obtain a direct logical method of checking when a conditional $A \vdash\!\!\!\sim B$ belongs to the preferential closure of a set of conditionals Δ.

Theorem 7.5.3. *([Ada75]) A set of conditionals Δ preferentially entails $A \vdash\!\!\!\sim B$ if and only if there exists a finite $\Delta_0 \subseteq \Delta$ such that*

1. $\vec{\Delta}_0 \vDash A \to B$;
2. $\neg A \vDash I(\Delta_0)$.

Proof. $A \vdash\!\!\!\sim B$ belongs to the preferential closure of Δ iff $\neg(A \wedge B) \vdash_\Delta \neg A$ iff there exists $\Delta_0 \subseteq \Delta$ such that $\neg(A \wedge B) \vDash I(\Delta_0) \wedge (\vec{\Delta}_0 \to \neg A)$. It is easy to check that the latter condition is equivalent to the above two. □

The above theorem provides a very convenient method of proving derivability results for preferential inference relations. Thus, the following result can be obtained as an immediate consequence of the theorem.

Corollary 7.5.4. *A set of conditionals Δ preferentially entails $A \vdash\!\!\!\sim B$ if and only if $\Delta \cup \{A \vdash\!\!\!\sim \neg B\}$ preferentially entails $A \vdash\!\!\!\sim \mathbf{f}$.*

As another application of the above theorem, we will show that preferential derivability can be reduced, in effect, to derivability with respect to the basic inference relation $\mathcal{B}$.

For a set of conditionals Δ, we will denote by $\Delta^{\&}$ the set of all quasi-conjunctions of conditionals from Δ. Then we have

Corollary 7.5.5. $A \mathrel{|\!\!\sim} B$ *is preferentially derivable from Δ if and only if it is basically derivable from $\Delta^{\&}$.*

Proof. To begin with, $A \mathrel{|\!\!\sim} B$ belongs to the preferential closure of Δ if and only if there exists a finite subset Δ_0 of Δ such that (i) $\overrightarrow{\Delta}_0 \vDash A \to B$, and (ii) $\neg A \vDash I(\Delta_0)$. Since $\neg \Delta_0^{\vee}$ logically implies $\overrightarrow{\Delta}_0$, (i) is equivalent to

(i')
$$\Delta_0^{\vee} \to \overrightarrow{\Delta}_0 \vDash A \to B$$

Also, (ii) can be reformulated as $\Delta_0^{\vee} \wedge \overrightarrow{\Delta}_0 \vDash A$. Moreover, given (i), the latter is equivalent to

(ii')
$$\Delta_0^{\vee} \wedge \overrightarrow{\Delta}_0 \vDash A \wedge B$$

But (i') and (ii') are precisely the conditions for derivability of $A \mathrel{|\!\!\sim} B$ from $\&(\Delta_0)$ with respect to the basic inference. This completes the proof. $\square$

The above result shows that the contribution of skeptical derivability to derivability with respect to the basic inference is reducible to forming quasi-conjunctions of the conditionals assumed as premises; after adding such conjunctions, the derivation can proceed by using only the basic derivation rules from $\mathcal{B}$. An especially interesting consequence of this result (proved, in fact, by van Benthem) is that preferential derivability among pairs of conditionals coincides with the basic derivability:

Corollary 7.5.6. *[Ben84] A conditional $C \mathrel{|\!\!\sim} D$ is preferentially derivable from another conditional $A \mathrel{|\!\!\sim} B$ if and only if it is derivable from the latter with respect to the basic inference.*

The above result provides a first justification to our earlier remarks that the basic inference constitutes, in effect, a *conservative* core of nonmonotonic inference; reasonable full-fledged systems of nonmonotonic inference do not change the derivability relations among pairs of conditionals that are sanctioned already by the basic inference. In the next chapter we will see that this holds for non-skeptical inference systems as well.

7.5.3 Belief and knowledge core of conditional bases

The semantic definition of skeptical inference assigns a special role to conditionals of the form $A \mathrel{|\!\!\sim} \mathbf{f}$. Namely, they describe our knowledge rather than beliefs. As we have seen in Chapter 6, any regular inference relation $\mid\!\sim$ determines its own monotonic internal logic $\text{Th}_{\mid\!\sim}$ that is preserved by $\mid\!\sim$. For preferential inference relations, this internal logic corresponds to the set of propositions that are known in an associated epistemic state. A separation of this monotonic component from the rest of the conditionals belonging to an inference relation will turn out to be important for describing defeasible entailment in Chapter 8.

Let us consider the structure of the above monotonic component in more details.

As before, by a *knowledge set* of a set of conditionals Δ we will mean the set

$$\mathbf{K}_\Delta = \{A \mid \neg A \mid\!\sim \mathbf{f} \in \hat{\Delta}\}$$

As has been established earlier, this set determines the internal logic of $\hat{\Delta}$; accordingly, we will denote the latter logic by Th_Δ.

It turns out that any set of conditionals contains a separate subset that is solely responsible for determining its internal monotonic logic.

Definition 7.5.1. *A* knowledge core *of a set of conditionals Δ (denoted by Δ_k) is the set of all conditionals $A \mid\!\sim B$ from Δ such that $\neg A \in \mathbf{K}_\Delta$.*

The knowledge core can be considered as describing what is known in the framework of the conditional base. Actually, conditionals belonging to the knowledge core could hardly be called *nonmonotonic* conditionals at all, since they will determine the monotonic, immutable part of the information embodied in the base.

Following [Gef92], let us say that a finite set of conditionals Γ constitutes a *clash*, if $\models I(\Gamma)$. In other words, Γ is a clash if $\overrightarrow{\Gamma}$ logically implies negations of antecedents of all conditionals from Γ. For example, the set $\{A \mid\!\sim B, A \mid\!\sim \neg B\}$ constitutes a simplest clash. This notion turns out to be useful in describing the knowledge core of a set of conditionals.

To begin with, we have the following characterization of the knowledge set associated with a set of conditionals.

Lemma 7.5.4. $A \in \mathbf{K}_\Delta$ *iff $\neg\Gamma^\vee \models A$, for some clash $\Gamma \subseteq \Delta$.*

Proof. By Theorem 7.5.3, Δ preferentially entails $A \mid\!\sim \mathbf{f}$ if and only if, for some finite subset Γ, we have $\overrightarrow{\Gamma} \models \neg A$ and $\neg A \models I(\Gamma)$. Unfolding these conditions for our case, we obtain that Γ constitutes a clash, and therefore $\overrightarrow{\Gamma}$ is logically equivalent to $\neg\Gamma^\vee$. Hence the result. $\square$

As can be easily verified, the union of two clashes is again a clash. Consequently, any set of conditionals Δ will always contain a unique greatest clash. Moreover, the following result shows that this greatest clash is precisely the knowledge core of Δ.

Corollary 7.5.7. Δ_k *coincides with a greatest clash included in* Δ.

Proof. If a conditional $A \mathbin{\vert\!\sim} B$ belongs to some clash $\Gamma \subseteq \Delta$, then $\neg A \in \mathbf{K}_\Delta$ by the preceding lemma, and hence $A \mathbin{\vert\!\sim} B$ belongs to Δ_k. In the other direction, if $A \mathbin{\vert\!\sim} B$ belongs to Δ_k, then $\neg A \in \mathbf{K}_\Delta$, and hence $\neg \Gamma^\vee \vDash \neg A$, for some clash $\Gamma \subseteq \Delta$. But then it is easy to see that $\Gamma \cup \{A \mathbin{\vert\!\sim} B\}$ is also a clash that contains $A \mathbin{\vert\!\sim} B$. Consequently, any conditional from Δ_k belongs to some clash, and hence Δ_k is included in a greatest clash. $\square$

Example 7.5.2. Let us consider the following set of conditionals:

$$\Delta = \{p \mathbin{\vert\!\sim} \neg q, t \mathbin{\vert\!\sim} p, t \mathbin{\vert\!\sim} q\}$$

Since $\overrightarrow{\Delta}$ is classically inconsistent, Δ itself constitutes a clash. Consequently, the knowledge core of Δ coincides with Δ. Note that the associated knowledge set for this case will also be inconsistent.

Now we will show that the knowledge core of a set of conditionals is solely responsible for determining the knowledge set.

Definition 7.5.2. *A* knowledge base *of a set of conditionals* Δ *is the set*

$$\mathbf{K}_\Delta^+ = \{\neg A \mid A \mathbin{\vert\!\sim} B \in \Delta_k\}$$

As can be seen from the above definition, the knowledge base is a subset of the knowledge set formed by negations of antecedents of all conditionals belonging to the knowledge core. Our terminology is justified by the following observation showing that the knowledge set coincides with the deductive closure of the knowledge base.

Lemma 7.5.5. $\mathbf{K}_\Delta = \mathrm{Cl}(\mathbf{K}_\Delta^+)$.

Proof. If $A \in \mathbf{K}_\Delta$, then $\neg \Gamma^\vee \vDash A$, for some clash $\Gamma \subseteq \Delta$. But negations of antecedents of all conditionals from Γ belong to $\mathbf{K}_\Delta^+$, and consequently $\mathbf{K}_\Delta^+ \vDash A$. This completes the proof. $\square$

As a consequence of the above result, we immediately obtain that the internal monotonic logic associated with Δ is determined by the knowledge base.

Corollary 7.5.8. Th_Δ *is a least consequence relation containing the knowledge base of* Δ.

The notion of a clash, defined earlier, can be generalized to that of a clash with respect to some classical consequence relation Th. Namely, we will say that a set Γ constitutes a *clash with respect to* Th if $I(\Gamma) \in \mathrm{Th}(\emptyset)$. Then, given a set of conditionals Δ, it is natural to ask whether clashes with respect to Th_Δ could include some conditionals beyond the knowledge core of Δ. Fortunately, the following result shows that this is not the case. This fact will be used in Chapter 8.

Lemma 7.5.6. *A subset Γ of Δ is a clash with respect to* Th_Δ *only if* $\Gamma \subseteq \Delta_k$.

Proof. If $\Gamma \subseteq \Delta$ is a clash with respect to Th_Δ, then $\overrightarrow{\Gamma}$ together with $\mathbf{K}_\Delta^+$ logically imply negations of antecedents of all conditionals from Γ. As can be seen, this is sufficient for establishing that $\Gamma \cup \Delta_k$ constitutes a(n ordinary) clash. Consequently, $\Gamma \subseteq \Delta_k$, since Δ_k is a greatest clash in Δ. $\square$

Let us introduce now the following notion.

Definition 7.5.3. *A* belief core *of a set of conditionals Δ is the set* $\Delta_b = \Delta \setminus \Delta_k$.

The belief core of Δ is defined above as the complement of its knowledge core. As can be easily verified, if $\mathbb{E}$ is an epistemic state that generates precisely the preferential closure of Δ, then Δ_b consists of all conditionals $A \mathrel{\vert\!\sim} B$ from Δ that are non-trivially valid in $\mathbb{E}$, that is, $\neg A$ is contingent in $\mathbb{E}$. This means, in particular, that the belief core is *p-consistent* (cf. [Ada75, Gef92]) in the sense that it can be realized as a set of non-trivially skeptically valid conditionals. Actually, many studies in defeasible entailment are based on the assumption that the relevant sets of conditionals are p-consistent in this sense (see Chapter 8). A characteristic property of such sets is that they do not contain a clash. Accordingly, such sets of conditionals have only trivial knowledge sets, namely the set of tautologies.

Thus, any set of conditionals Δ can be split into a belief part Δ_b and a knowledge part Δ_k that determines the underlying monotonic logic. Moreover, we will show now that, once this monotonic logic is known, preferential derivability from Δ is wholly determined by its belief core.

Generalizing corresponding notions from Chapter 6, we will introduce the following notion of preferential derivability with respect to a classical consequence relation Th.

Definition 7.5.4. *A* preferential Th-closure *of a set of conditionals Δ is a least preferential inference relation that contains Δ and respects* Th. *Any conditional belonging to the preferential* Th-*closure will be said to be* preferentially Th-derivable *from Δ.*

Preferential Th-derivability amounts to preferential derivability that allows, in addition, replacement of Th-equivalent propositions. As follows from the results stated in Chapter 6, any regular inference relation respects its internal logic, so 'pure' preferential derivability from Δ coincides with preferential Th_Δ-derivability, where Th_Δ is the internal logic of $\hat{\Delta}$.

Now the following result shows that preferential derivability from Δ is reducible to preferential derivability from its belief core Δ_b with respect to Th_Δ.

Theorem 7.5.4. *The preferential closure of Δ coincides with the preferential* Th_Δ-*closure of Δ_b.*

Proof. If $A \mathrel{|\!\sim} B$ belongs to the preferential Th_Δ-closure of Δ_b, then it belongs also to the preferential Th_Δ-closure of Δ. Moreover, the preferential closure of Δ respects Th_Δ, and hence $A \mathrel{|\!\sim} B$ is preferentially derivable from Δ.

In the other direction, if $A \mathrel{|\!\sim} B$ is preferentially derivable from Δ, then we take a particular derivation of $A \mathrel{|\!\sim} B$ from Δ and modify it as follows: if $C \mathrel{|\!\sim} D$ is a conditional from Δ_k appearing in the derivation, we replace it with a conditional $C \mathrel{|\!\sim} \mathbf{f}$. Note that, since C belongs to $\mathbf{K}_\Delta$, the latter conditional is always Th_Δ-derivable. In addition, it implies $C \mathrel{|\!\sim} D$ by Right Weakening. As a result, the described modification, transforms the source derivation into a Th_Δ-derivation from Δ_b. This completes the proof.   □

The above theorem says that a conditional is preferentially derivable from Δ if and only if it is preferentially derivable from its belief core with respect to Th_Δ. Recall now that the latter consequence relation is uniquely determined by the knowledge core of Δ. Thus, any conditional base Δ can be seen as composed of two mutually independent components, namely the knowledge part and the belief part.

7.6 Inferential equivalence

The representation of preferential inference in terms of general epistemic states will allow us to clarify now the relationship between different kinds of models for preferential entailment existing in the literature. We start with introducing the following weak notion of equivalence among epistemic states.

Definition 7.6.1. *Two epistemic states are* inference-equivalent, *if they generate the same skeptical inference relation.*

As can be verified, skeptically equivalent epistemic states (see Chapter 4) will also be inference-equivalent, though not vice versa. This makes inference equivalence a weakest equivalence relation on epistemic states introduced so far. Accordingly, it can be expected that the equivalence classes with respect to this relation will be quite large. Note, however, that inference relations are interdefinable with expectation relations, and hence inference-equivalence of two epistemic states implies coincidence of their associated entrenchment, dependence and other expectation relations.

For inference-equivalence, the notion of a normal admissible state, given in Chapter 4, can be strengthened to the following notion.

Definition 7.6.2. *An admissible state s will be said to be* strictly normal *in an epistemic state $\mathbb{E}$, if $\bigcap \Uparrow s \not\subseteq l(s)$;*

Unfolding the definition of strict normality, we obtain that an admissible state s is strictly normal if and only if there exists some proposition A such that $A \notin l(s)$ and $A \in l(t)$ for any admissible state t that is preferred to s. In other words, an admissible state is strictly normal if and only if it is a preferred state in some set $]A[$. Consequently, strictly normal admissible states are the only admissible states that participate in determining the main kinds of inference relations associated with an epistemic state. Hence, in considering inference relations associated with an epistemic state, we can restrict our attention to admissible states that are strictly normal. Clearly, any strictly normal admissible state will also be normal, though not vice versa. It should be kept in mind, however, that the inference relations generated by an epistemic state are insufficient, in general, for determining its dynamic behavior in belief change; two epistemic states may generate the same inference relations, though will produce different inference relations after some change, say contraction.

By an *inferential reduction* of an epistemic state $\mathbb{E}$ we will mean a restriction of $\mathbb{E}$ to strictly normal admissible states. Then the following result follows immediately from our earlier observation that only strictly normal admissible states participate in determining the associated inference relations.

Theorem 7.6.1. *Any epistemic state is inference-equivalent to its inferential reduction.*

Let us consider now the role of strictly normality in base-generated epistemic states. Below we will denote by $\neg\Gamma$ the set of negations of all propositions from Γ.

Definition 7.6.3. *A subset $\Gamma \subseteq \Delta$ will be said to be* independent in Δ *if $\Gamma \cup \neg(\Delta \setminus \Gamma)$ is a consistent set of propositions.*

It turns out that independent subsets of Δ exactly correspond to strictly normal admissible states of the associated epistemic state $\mathbb{E}_\Delta$.

Lemma 7.6.1. *Γ is independent in a finite set Δ iff it is a strictly normal admissible state in $\mathbb{E}_\Delta$.*

Proof. Assume that Γ is not independent in Δ. Then there must exist a finite set of defaults $\Gamma_c \subseteq \Delta \setminus \Gamma$ such that $\Gamma \vDash \bigvee \Gamma_c$. Now, if Γ belongs to $]A[$, for some A, then $\Gamma, A \nvDash$. But then there must exist at least one default $\delta \in \Gamma_c$ for which $\Gamma, \delta, A \nvDash$. Consequently, we have that $\Gamma \cup \{\delta\}$ also belongs to $]A[$, and hence Γ cannot be a preferred admissible state in $]A[$.

Assume now that Γ is independent in Δ. Then Γ is a preferred state in $]\bigvee(\Delta \setminus \Gamma)[$ (we use at this point finiteness of Δ), and hence it is strictly normal. Indeed, due to independence, $\bigvee(\Delta \setminus \Gamma)$ is not a consequence of Γ, though each extension of Γ will contain some default from $\Delta \setminus \Gamma$. $\qquad\square$

In the case of arbitrary base-generated epistemic states, any preferred subset of defaults will be independent, though not vice versa. Consequently, the inferential reduction of such an epistemic state will contain only independent sets of defaults. This fact will be used in what follows.

7.7 Model transformations and representative classes of epistemic states

We will describe below a direct transformation of general epistemic states into equivalent preferential models from [KLM90], as well as a similar transformation of general epistemic states into pure epistemic states. These transformations will allow us to single out a number of important classes of epistemic states that will be still sufficient for representing all preferential inference relations.

7.7.1 Epistemic states and possible worlds models

This is the right moment to remind the reader that preferential models from [KLM90] constitute a special case of epistemic states when the admissible belief states are labelled with worlds (maximal deductively closed sets). Moreover, it is easy to see that our definition of skeptical inference, when applied to such epistemic states, is reducible to the claim that $A \mathrel{|\!\sim} B$ holds if and only if B is supported by all preferred admissible belief states that support A. In other words, it coincides with the definition of nonmonotonic inference given in [KLM90]. Accordingly, the completeness result established in [KLM90] constitutes a certain strengthening of our general completeness result, since it shows that epistemic states based on possible worlds are already sufficient for representing all preferential inference relations. We will say in what follows that such epistemic states constitute a *representative class* with respect to preferential inference. It turns out, however, that this representative class of epistemic states is not unique. In fact, our completeness theorem can now be interpreted as saying that pure epistemic states also form a representative class with respect to preferential inference, since any preferential inference relation is representable by some pure epistemic state.

In order to clarify this situation, we will describe below a direct transformation of general epistemic states into inference-equivalent possible worlds models.

Let $\langle S, l, \prec \rangle$ be an epistemic state. We define the corresponding preferential possible worlds model as follows. Let S_0 be a set of all world-state pairs (α, s) such that $l(s) \subseteq \alpha$. Define a preference relation on S_0 as follows:

$$(\alpha, s) \prec_0 (\beta, t) \text{ iff } s \prec t.$$

Finally, we define the corresponding labelling function l_0 in an obvious way: $l_0(\alpha, s) = \alpha$.

Theorem 7.7.1. *If $\mathbb{E} = \langle S, l, \prec \rangle$ is a general epistemic state, then $\mathbb{W} = \langle S_0, l_0, \prec_0 \rangle$ is a preferential possible worlds model that is inference-equivalent to $\mathbb{E}$.*

Proof. The smoothness of $\prec_0$ immediately follows from the smoothness of $\prec$. Hence $\mathbb{W}$ is a preferential model.

If $A \hspace{-0.5mm}\mid\hspace{-2.5mm}\sim\hspace{-0.5mm} B$ is valid in $\mathbb{E}$, and (α, s) is a state in $\mathbb{W}$ that satisfies A but not B, then $A \to B \notin \alpha$ and hence s does not satisfy $A \to B$ and is consistent with A. Therefore s is not a preferred state of $\mathbb{E}$ consistent with A, and consequently there exists a state t consistent with A such that $s \prec t$. Let β be a world including $l(t)$ such that $A \in \beta$. Clearly, (β, t) is a state in $\mathbb{W}$. Moreover, we have that (β, t) satisfies A and $(\alpha, s) \prec_0 (\beta, t)$. Therefore (α, s) is not a preferred state of $\mathbb{W}$ satisfying A, and hence any A-preferred state in $\mathbb{W}$ should satisfy B.

Assume now that $A \hspace{-0.5mm}\mid\hspace{-2.5mm}\sim\hspace{-0.5mm} B$ does not hold in $\mathbb{E}$. Then there exists a preferred state s consistent with A that does not support $A \to B$. Let α be a world containing $l(s)$ such that $A \wedge \neg B \in \alpha$. Then (α, s) is a preferred state in $\mathbb{W}$ satisfying A (since s is a preferred state consistent with A) and it does not satisfy B. Thus, $A \hspace{-0.5mm}\mid\hspace{-2.5mm}\sim\hspace{-0.5mm} B$ holds in $\mathbb{W}$ if and only if it holds in $\mathbb{E}$. $\square$

Since any preferential inference relation is determined by some epistemic state, the above theorem gives an alternative proof of the completeness result from [KLM90]:

Theorem 7.7.2. *An inference relation is preferential if and only if it is determined by some preferential KLM model.*

This fact will allow us now to give yet another important characterization of preferential inference relations.

Let $\mathbb{W} = \langle S, l, \prec \rangle$ be an epistemic state based on possible worlds. We will extend this epistemic state by adding a new admissible state i such that $l(i) = \mathrm{Cl}(\mathbf{f})$, and extend the preference order of $\mathbb{W}$ by requiring that $s \prec i$, for any $s \in S$. Let us denote the resulting epistemic state by $\mathbb{E}_W$. Since the added admissible state is inconsistent, the transformation does not change preferred states for any proposition. Consequently, $\mathbb{E}_W$ will be inference-equivalent to $\mathbb{W}$. Notice now that $\mathbb{E}_W$ is already a (trivially) union-closed and monotonic epistemic state. Therefore, we obtain

Corollary 7.7.1. *Any preferential inference relation is generated by some monotonic union-closed epistemic state.*

As we have established in Chapter 4, any finitary union-closed epistemic state is similar to some base-generated epistemic state. Consequently, the above result shows that, in the finite case, any preferential inference relation can be modeled using some default base with a monotonic preference order on its subsets. Notice, however, that the result refers to general epistemic states, and it cannot be strengthened to standard epistemic states, despite the fact that any union-closed epistemic state is reducible to a standard and monotonic epistemic state (see Chapter 4). The reason is that the normal reduction of a union-closed epistemic state need not be union-closed. Furthermore, we will see below that the epistemic states that are monotonic, union-closed and standard do not form a representative class for preferential inference.

7.7.2 Purification of general epistemic states

Our general completeness result indicates that, for any epistemic state, there must exist an inference-equivalent pure epistemic state. Below we will give an explicit transformation of a general epistemic state into a corresponding pure epistemic state.

Let $\mathbb{E} = \langle S, l, \prec \rangle$ be a general epistemic state. For any admissible state s, $L(s)$ will denote the set of worlds $\bigcup\{l(t) \mid s \prec t\}$. Then $\mathcal{T}_{\mathbb{E}}$ will denote the set of theories such that $u \in \mathcal{T}_{\mathbb{E}}$ if and only if there exist a state s and a world $\alpha \in l(s)$ such that u is an intersection of the set of worlds $\{\alpha\} \cup L(s)$.

Theorem 7.7.3. *If $\mathbb{E}$ is a general epistemic state, then the consequence relation $\vdash_{\mathbb{E}}$ determined by the set of theories $\mathcal{T}_{\mathbb{E}}$ is semi-classical and generates the same preferential inference relation as $\mathbb{E}$.*

Proof. We show first that $\vdash_{\mathbb{E}}$ is semi-classical. If $a \nvdash_{\mathbb{E}} A$, there must exist a theory $u \in \mathcal{T}_{\mathbb{E}}$ that includes a but not A. Let (α, s) (where $\alpha \in l(s)$) be a pair generating u. We consider first the case when s itself is a preferred state consistent with $\neg A$. In this case α is the only world in $\{\alpha\} \cup L(s)$ that includes $\neg A$. Hence, if α includes some proposition B, we have that $A \vee B$ belongs to u, and consequently $a, A \vee B \nvdash_{\mathbb{E}} A$. Otherwise α contains $\neg B$, and then $A \vee \neg B \in u$ and therefore $a, A \vee \neg B \nvdash_{\mathbb{E}} A$.

If s is not a preferred state consistent with $\neg A$, there is a preferred such state t that is better than s. Let β be a world in $l(t)$ containing $\neg A$ and v a theory corresponding to the set of worlds $\{\beta\} \cup L(t)$. Notice that the latter set is included in $\{\alpha\} \cup L(s)$, and hence $u \subseteq v$. Applying to v the same considerations as before, we can obtain that, for any proposition B, either $A \vee B$ or $A \vee \neg B$ belongs to v, and therefore either $a, A \vee B \nvdash_{\mathbb{E}} A$ or $a, A \vee \neg B \nvdash_{\mathbb{E}} A$. Thus, $\vdash_{\mathbb{E}}$ is semi-classical.

Now we will show that $\neg(A \wedge B) \vdash_{\mathbb{E}} \neg A$ holds iff $A \mathrel{\vert\!\sim} B$ is valid in $\mathbb{E}$.

If $A \mathrel{\vert\!\sim} B$ is not valid in $\mathbb{E}$, there exists a preferred state s consistent with A that does not support $A \to B$. Let $\alpha \in l(s)$ be a world including $A \wedge \neg B$. and u a theory corresponding to $\{\alpha\} \cup L(s)$. Then it is easy to see that $\neg(A \wedge B) \in u$ and $\neg A \notin u$. Therefore, $\neg(A \wedge B) \nvdash_{\mathbb{E}} \neg A$. In the other direction, if $A \mathrel{\vert\!\sim} B$ is valid in $\mathbb{E}$, but $\neg(A \wedge B) \nvdash_{\mathbb{E}} \neg A$, there must exist a theory $u \in \mathcal{T}_{\mathbb{E}}$ that includes $\neg(A \wedge B)$ and does not include $\neg A$. Let u be generated by a set of worlds $\{\alpha\} \cup L(s)$. If s were preferred consistent with A, then it would satisfy $A \to B$, contrary to the assumption that $\neg(A \wedge B) \in u$. Otherwise there must exist a preferred A-consistent state t such that $s \prec t$ (since u is consistent with A). Again, t should satisfy both $A \to B$ and $\neg(A \wedge B)$, contrary to the fact it is consistent with A. Therefore $\neg(A \wedge B) \vdash_{\mathbb{E}} \neg A$. $\qquad\square$

The above transformation allows us to see how the use of states in preferential KLM models can be eliminated and replaced by ordinary classical theories[2].

Example 7.7.1. Let us consider a preferential model determined by four world-states $s_0 \prec s_2$ and $s_1 \prec s_3$ such that s_0 satisfies p and $\neg q$, s_1 satisfies $\neg p$ and $\neg q$ and both s_2 and s_3 satisfy p and q. This model was used in [KLM90] as an example of a model that has no equivalent model based on worlds instead of states. The set of theories $\mathcal{T}$ corresponding to this model is $\{\mathrm{Cl}(p \wedge \neg q), \mathrm{Cl}(\neg p \wedge \neg q), \mathrm{Cl}(p), \mathrm{Cl}(p \leftrightarrow q)\}$. Notice that if we were identify, for example, the states s_2 and s_3 (labelled with identical worlds), we would obtain a different set of theories – $\{\mathrm{Cl}(p \wedge \neg q), \mathrm{Cl}(\neg p \wedge \neg q), \mathrm{Cl}(q \to p)\}$. In this way the distinction between states and worlds is captured, in effect, using different sets of theories associated with the same set of worlds.

Our next result shows that any preferential inference relation is generated by some *standard* union-closed epistemic state, provided that the monotonicity requirement is weakened to weak monotonicity.

Theorem 7.7.4. *Any preferential inference relation is generated by some standard epistemic state that is union-closed and weakly monotonic.*

Proof. Let $\mathrel{\vdash\mkern-6mu\sim}$ be a preferential inference relation, $\vdash$ a consequence relation that generates $\mathrel{\vdash\mkern-6mu\sim}$, and $\mathcal{T}$ a set of theories of $\vdash$. We will transform $\mathcal{T}$ into a standard union-closed epistemic state as follows. First, we extend $\mathcal{T}$ with new theories obtained as deductive closures of all unions of theories from $\mathcal{T}$. Clearly, the resulting set of theories, that we will denote by $\mathcal{T}_0$, will already be union-closed. Next, we will define a preference order on $\mathcal{T}_0$ by extending the inclusion order on $\mathcal{T}$ with all pairs (u, v) from $\mathcal{T}_0$ such that $u \in \mathcal{T}_0 \setminus \mathcal{T}$, $v \in \mathcal{T}$ and $v \not\subseteq u$. As a result, any 'new' theory in $\mathcal{T}_0$ will be subordinated to all 'old' theories from $\mathcal{T}$ that are not included in it. As can be checked, the resulting preference order will be transitive and weakly monotonic. Finally, we will show that the new epistemic state, that we will denote by $\mathbb{E}$, will determine the same inference relation as $\mathcal{T}$.

Note first that any preferred (that is, maximal) theory of $\mathcal{T}$ with respect to some proposition A will also be a preferred such theory in $\mathbb{E}$. Consequently, if $A \mathrel{\vdash\mkern-6mu\sim} B$ is valid in $\mathbb{E}$, it will also be valid in $\mathcal{T}$. In the other direction, assume that $A \mathrel{\vdash\mkern-6mu\sim} B$ is valid in $\mathcal{T}$, but not in $\mathbb{E}$. The latter implies that there exists a 'new' theory u that is a preferred theory in $\mathbb{E}$ consistent with A and such that $A \to B \notin u$. By the definition of the preference order, any 'old' theory $v \in \mathcal{T}$ that is not included in u will already contain $\neg A$. Consequently, all maximal theories from $\mathcal{T}$ that are consistent with A will be included in u. But any such maximal theory should contain $A \to B$, contrary to our assumption that $A \to B$ does not belong to u. Thus, $\mathbb{E}$ determines the same inference relation as $\mathcal{T}$, and hence it generates $\mathrel{\vdash\mkern-6mu\sim}$. $\qquad\square$

---

[2] A similar, though a more complex, procedure of eliminating states was suggested in [ACS92].

Thus, standard union-closed epistemic states also form a representative class with respect to preferential inference. The restriction to standard epistemic states was made possible, however, only by relaxing the monotonicity condition to weak monotonicity. As we will see, weak monotonicity cannot be strengthened to monotonicity here without restricting the class of generated inference relations.

Example 7.7.2. (Continued) The preferential model from [KLM90], considered earlier, was shown to be equivalent to a pure epistemic state determined by four theories $Cl(p \land \neg q)$, $Cl(\neg p \land \neg q)$, $Cl(p)$, $Cl(p \leftrightarrow q)$. This epistemic state is not union-closed. We can, however, transform this epistemic state into an inference-equivalent standard union-closed state by adding a new theory $Cl(p \land q)$ and defining a preference order by subordinating the latter theory to both $Cl(p \land \neg q)$ and $Cl(\neg p \land \neg q)$. It can be easily checked that the resulting epistemic state will determine the same inference relation.

The above results show that there is a number of natural classes of epistemic states that are sufficient for representing any preferential inference relation. The following theorem gives a summary of these results. It shows that any two properties chosen from standardness, monotonicity and union-closure are sufficient for determining a representative class of epistemic states.

Theorem 7.7.5. *Any epistemic state is inference-equivalent to an epistemic state that is*

- *standard and monotonic;*
- *standard and union-closed;*
- *union-closed and monotonic.*

There is a natural question that arises at this point, namely whether the class of epistemic states that are monotonic, union-closed and standard is also a representative class with respect to preferential inference. As we will see in the next section, however, the latter class determines a proper subset of inference relations consisting of what will be called injective inference relations.

General union-closed epistemic states have some interesting additional properties that we will use later. To begin with, if such a state is maximizing, that is, its preferred admissible states are also maximal ones, then the construction of an equivalent pure epistemic state, given in Theorem 7.7.3 above can be drastically simplified as follows.

Let $\mathbb{E} = \langle S, l, \prec \rangle$ be a union-closed and maximizing epistemic state. For any admissible state s, $F(s)$ will denote a theory $\bigcup \{l(t) \mid s \preceq t\}$ and $\mathcal{E}$ will denote the pure epistemic state determined by the set of all such theories.

Theorem 7.7.6. *If $\mathbb{E}$ is a union-closed and maximizing epistemic state, then $\mathcal{E}$ is a pure epistemic state that generates the same preferential inference relation as $\mathbb{E}$.*

Proof. To begin with, we will show that for any general epistemic state $\mathbb{E}$, if $A \mathrel{\vdash_{\mathbb{E}}} B$, then $A \mathrel{\vdash_{\mathcal{E}}} B$.

Assume that $A \mathrel{\vdash} B$ is valid in $\mathbb{E}$, and let $F(s)$ be a theory from $\mathcal{E}$ that is consistent with A. Then there must exist a state s_1 in $\mathbb{E}$ such that $s \preceq s_1$ and $\neg A \notin l(s_1)$. Therefore $s_1 \preceq t$, for some preferred state t that is consistent with A. Consequently $F(t)$ is consistent with A. Moreover, since $A \mathrel{\vdash} B$ is valid in $\mathbb{E}$, $A \to B \in l(t)$ and hence $A \to B \in F(t)$ (because $\neg A \in l(t_1)$, for any t_1 that is more preferred than t). Thus, any theory from $\mathcal{E}$ that is consistent with A is included in a theory that is also consistent with A and contains $A \to B$. Therefore $A \mathrel{\vdash} B$ is valid in $\mathcal{E}$.

Assume now that $A \mathrel{\vdash} B$ is valid in $\mathcal{E}$, though it is not valid in $\mathbb{E}$. The latter condition implies that there exists an A-preferred state s in $\mathbb{E}$ that does not support $A \to B$. Consequently, $A \to B$ does not belong to $F(s)$. Clearly, $F(s)$ is consistent with A, and hence there must exists a theory $F(s_1)$ in $\mathcal{E}$ that properly includes $F(s)$ and already contains $A \to B$. Therefore, there exists a state t in $\mathbb{E}$ consistent with A and such that $s_1 \preceq t$, $A \to B \in l(t)$. Notice that this implies that $l(t) \not\subseteq l(s)$ and $F(s) \subset F(t)$. Therefore $\mathrm{Cl}(A, F(s))$ is included in $\mathrm{Cl}(A, l(t))$, and the inclusion is proper, since B belongs to the latter set, but not to the former one. Notice now that $l(s)$ is included in $\mathrm{Cl}(A, F(s))$. Indeed, since $\neg A \in l(s')$, for any s' that is more preferred than s, $A \to C \in F(s)$, for any C belonging to $l(s)$. As a result, we obtain $l(s) \subset \mathrm{Cl}(A, l(t))$. Let us consider now the theory $u = \mathrm{Cl}(l(s), l(t))$. Due to the union-closure of $\mathbb{E}$, u constitutes an admissible belief set in $\mathbb{E}$. In addition, we have that it properly includes $l(s)$ (since $l(t) \not\subseteq l(s)$). Finally, u is consistent with A. Indeed, if it were the case that $\neg A \in u$, then $l(s), l(t) \vDash \neg A$, and hence the set $l(s) \cup l(t) \cup \{A\}$ would be inconsistent. But $l(s) \subset \mathrm{Cl}(A, l(t))$, and hence we would obtain that $l(t)$ is also inconsistent with A, which contradicts our assumptions. Hence A is consistent with u. Therefore, $l(s)$ is not a maximal admissible theory in $\mathbb{E}$ that is consistent with A - a contradiction with the assumption that $\mathbb{E}$ is maximizing. This completes the proof. $\qquad\square$

It should be noted that the derived pure epistemic state $\mathcal{E}$ need not be union-closed; as we will show later, the set of pure union-closed epistemic states also generates a restricted class of injective inference relations.

The following example shows that the assumption of maximizing is essential for the above result.

Example 7.7.3. Consider a standard epistemic state $\mathbb{E}$ consisting of three theories $\mathrm{Cl}(\emptyset)$, $\mathrm{Cl}(p \to q)$, $\mathrm{Cl}(\neg p)$ such that $\mathrm{Cl}(\emptyset) \prec \mathrm{Cl}(\neg p)$. This epistemic state is union-closed and even weakly monotonic, but it is not maximizing since, for example, $\mathrm{Cl}(\emptyset)$ is a preferred theory consistent with p, though it is included in $\mathrm{Cl}(p \to q)$ which is also consistent with p. Now, the corresponding pure epistemic state $\mathcal{E}$ will consists precisely of the above three theories. Consequently, it validates $p \mathrel{\vdash} q$, though the later conditional does not hold in $\mathbb{E}$, since $\mathrm{Cl}(\emptyset)$ is a p-preferred theory that does not contain $p \to q$.

An important consequence of the above result is that preferences imposed on theories of a (pure) union-closed epistemic state amount, in effect, to extending the Tarski consequence relation corresponding to admissible belief sets of this state.

Corollary 7.7.2. *If* $\mathbb{E}$ *is a union-closed maximizing epistemic state, and* $\vdash^{\mathbb{E}}$ *the Tarski consequence relation determined by all admissible belief sets of* $\mathbb{E}$, *then there exists a consequence relation extending* $\vdash^{\mathbb{E}}$ *that generates the same preferential inference relation as* $\mathbb{E}$.

Proof. Follows from the fact that theories of $\mathcal{E}$ are intersections of admissible belief sets from $\mathbb{E}$, and hence all theories from $\mathcal{E}$ are theories of $\vdash_{\mathbb{E}}$. $\square$

7.8 Base-generated inference relations

In this section we will give a syntactic description of inference relations produced by a given base of default propositions Δ. This will serve as a theoretical preparation for our study of defeasible entailment in Chapter 8.

Δ-grounded inference

Given a finite set of propositions Δ and a classical consequence relation Th, we will say that an epistemic state $\mathbb{E}$ is *Δ-grounded* (with respect to Th) if, for each admissible state s, $l(s) = \mathrm{Th}(A)$, for some $A \in \Delta$. As a first step in our exposition, we will give a syntactic description of inference relations generated by Δ-grounded epistemic states.

Below we will use the following auxiliary notions.

Definition 7.8.1.   *1. A Δ-interior of a proposition A, denoted by A_Δ, is a proposition $\bigvee\{\delta \mid \delta \in \Delta \ \& \ A \in \mathrm{Th}(\delta)\}$.*
   2. A Δ-closure of a proposition A, denoted by A^Δ, is a proposition $\bigwedge\{\neg\delta \mid \delta \in \Delta \ \& \ \neg A \in \mathrm{Th}(\delta)\}$.

As can be checked, A^Δ is equivalent to $\neg(\neg A)_\Delta$. The following simple lemmas collect the properties of Δ-interior and Δ-closure that we will need in what follows. The proofs are straightforward.

Lemma 7.8.1.   *1. $A \in \mathrm{Th}(A_\Delta)$;*
   2. $(A_\Delta)_\Delta$ is equivalent to A_Δ;
   3. For any A and any $\delta \in \Delta$, $A \in \mathrm{Th}(\delta)$ if and only if $A_\Delta \in \mathrm{Th}(\delta)$.

Lemma 7.8.2.   *1. $A^\Delta \in \mathrm{Th}(A)$;*
   2. $(A^\Delta)^\Delta$ is equivalent to A^Δ;
   3. For any A and any $\delta \in \Delta$, $\neg A \in \mathrm{Th}(\delta)$ if and only if $\neg(A^\Delta) \in \mathrm{Th}(\delta)$.

Inference relations generated by Δ-grounded epistemic states will satisfy a characteristic property described in the next definition.

Definition 7.8.2. *An inference relation $\mathrel{\vdash\mkern-7mu\sim}$ will be called Δ-reductive if it satisfies the following condition (with respect to its internal logic $\mathrm{Th}_{\mathrel{\vdash\mkern-7mu\sim}}$):*

Δ-**reduction** $A \mathrel{\vdash\mkern-7mu\sim} B$ *if and only if* $A^{\Delta} \mathrel{\vdash\mkern-7mu\sim} (A \to B)_{\Delta}$

As can be seen, Δ-reduction allows to reduce any conditional of an inference relation to a conditional involving only defaults from Δ. More exactly, any conditional is reducible to a conditional of the form

$$\neg\delta_1 \wedge \cdots \wedge \neg\delta_i \mathrel{\vdash\mkern-7mu\sim} \delta_{i+1} \vee \cdots \vee \delta_n$$

The following result give an equivalent (and sometimes more convenient) description of Δ-reductive inference relations.

Lemma 7.8.3. *An inference relation is Δ-reductive if and only if it satisfies the following two conditions:*

1. *If $A^{\Delta} \mathrel{\vdash\mkern-7mu\sim} B$, then $A \mathrel{\vdash\mkern-7mu\sim} B$;*
2. *If $A \mathrel{\vdash\mkern-7mu\sim} B$, then $A \mathrel{\vdash\mkern-7mu\sim} (A \to B)_{\Delta}$.*

Proof. Assume first that an inference relation satisfies the above two conditions. Then $A^{\Delta} \mathrel{\vdash\mkern-7mu\sim} (A \to B)_{\Delta}$ implies $A^{\Delta} \mathrel{\vdash\mkern-7mu\sim} (A \to B)$ by Right Weakening, and hence $A \mathrel{\vdash\mkern-7mu\sim} A \to B$ by (1) above. But the latter is equivalent to $A \mathrel{\vdash\mkern-7mu\sim} B$, so we have a Δ-reduction from right to left. Assume now that $A \mathrel{\vdash\mkern-7mu\sim} B$ holds. Since A implies A^{Δ} (with respect to the internal logic $\mathrm{Th}_{\mathrel{\vdash\mkern-7mu\sim}}$), we have $A \wedge A^{\Delta} \mathrel{\vdash\mkern-7mu\sim} B$ (by left logical equivalence), and therefore $A^{\Delta} \mathrel{\vdash\mkern-7mu\sim} A \to B$. The latter implies $A^{\Delta} \mathrel{\vdash\mkern-7mu\sim} (A^{\Delta} \to (A \to B))_{\Delta}$ by the condition (2), and hence $A^{\Delta} \mathrel{\vdash\mkern-7mu\sim} (A \to B)_{\Delta}$ by Right Weakening. Therefore $\mathrel{\vdash\mkern-7mu\sim}$ satisfies Δ-reduction.

Assume now that our inference relation is Δ-reductive. Then $A^{\Delta} \mathrel{\vdash\mkern-7mu\sim} B$ implies $A^{\Delta} \mathrel{\vdash\mkern-7mu\sim} (A \to B)$ by Right Weakening, and hence Δ-reduction and idempotence of Δ-closure give us $A^{\Delta} \mathrel{\vdash\mkern-7mu\sim} (A^{\Delta} \to (A \to B))_{\Delta}$. As before, the conclusion of the above rule is equivalent to $(A \to B)_{\Delta}$, and hence we can use Δ-reduction once more to infer $A \mathrel{\vdash\mkern-7mu\sim} B$. Thus, condition (1) is satisfied.

To show (2), assume that $A \mathrel{\vdash\mkern-7mu\sim} B$ holds. Then $A^{\Delta} \mathrel{\vdash\mkern-7mu\sim} (A \to B)_{\Delta}$ by Δ-reduction. It turns out that $(A \to B)_{\Delta}$ logically implies $(A \to (A \to B)_{\Delta})_{\Delta}$; this follows from the fact that if δ is any default from Δ that implies $A \to B$, then δ implies $(A \to B)_{\Delta}$, and hence it implies $A \to (A \to B)_{\Delta}$. Consequently, $A^{\Delta} \mathrel{\vdash\mkern-7mu\sim} (A \to B)_{\Delta}$ implies $A^{\Delta} \mathrel{\vdash\mkern-7mu\sim} (A \to (A \to B)_{\Delta})_{\Delta}$ by Right Weakening. Applying Δ-reduction to the latter, we obtain $A \mathrel{\vdash\mkern-7mu\sim} (A \to B)_{\Delta}$. Therefore, (2) is satisfied. $\square$

Our next result shows that Δ-grounded epistemic states always produce Δ-reductive inference relations.

Lemma 7.8.4. *Any inference relation generated by a Δ-grounded epistemic states is Δ-reductive.*

Proof. Let $\mathbb{E}$ be a Δ-grounded epistemic states, $\vdash\!\!\!\sim$ the associated inference relation, and Th the classical subrelation of $\vdash\!\!\!\sim$. In order to prove the theorem, it sufficient to show the validity of the two conditions given in the preceding lemma.

(1). Assume that $A^\Delta \vdash\!\!\!\sim B$, but $A \not\!\vdash\!\!\!\sim B$. Then $\mathbb{E}$ must contain a preferred admissible state s consistent with A and such that $A \to B \notin l(s)$. By Lemma 7.8.2, an admissible state of $\mathbb{E}$ is consistent with A if and only if it is consistent with A^Δ. Therefore, s will also be a preferred state consistent with A^Δ. In addition, A implies A^Δ by the same lemma, and consequently $A^\Delta \to B \notin l(s)$. Thus, $A^\Delta \vdash\!\!\!\sim B$ does not hold, contrary to our assumptions.

(2). Assume that $A \vdash\!\!\!\sim B$, but $A \not\!\vdash\!\!\!\sim (A \to B)_\Delta$. Then there must exist a preferred state s that is consistent with A and $(A \to B)_\Delta \notin l(s)$. By Lemma 7.8.1, the latter condition holds if and only if $A \to B \notin l(s)$. But then $A \vdash\!\!\!\sim B$ is not valid in $\mathbb{E}$, contrary to our assumptions. $\qquad\square$

A finite set Δ will be called a *partition* with respect to a classical consequence relation Th if its elements are pairwise incompatible (with respect to Th) and $\bigvee \Delta \in \text{Th}(\emptyset)$. In this case it can be easily verified that the Δ-closure of any proposition A is equivalent to the disjunction of all defaults that are consistent with A, that is,

$$A^\Delta \text{ is equivalent to } \bigvee\{\delta \mid \delta \in \Delta \ \& \ \neg A \notin \text{Th}(\delta)\}$$

As a result, if Δ is a partition, conditionals of a Δ-reductive inference relation will all be reducible to conditionals of the form

$$\delta_1 \vee \cdots \vee \delta_i \vdash\!\!\!\sim \delta_{i+1} \vee \cdots \vee \delta_n$$

It turns out that, for partitions, the condition of Δ-reduction will be both necessary and sufficient for generation by a Δ-grounded epistemic state. Moreover, relevant epistemic states can be always chosen to be finite.

Theorem 7.8.1. *A preferential inference relation is Δ-reductive with respect to a partition Δ iff it is generated by a finite Δ-grounded epistemic state.*

Proof. Let $\vdash\!\!\!\sim$ be a Δ-reductive preferential inference relation with respect to a partition Δ, and $\mathbb{W}$ some its smooth possible worlds (KLM) model. We will use this model to construct a Δ-grounded epistemic state for $\vdash\!\!\!\sim$. Notice that, since Δ is a partition, each state s in $\mathbb{W}$ contains exactly one default from Δ; we will denote it by δ_s. Now we will replace the labelling function l of $\mathbb{W}$ with the following function: $l_\Delta(s) = \text{Th}_{\vdash\!\!\!\sim}(\delta_s)$, where $\text{Th}_{\vdash\!\!\!\sim}$ is the internal logic of $\vdash\!\!\!\sim$. Let us denote the resulting epistemic state by $\mathbb{E}$. Clearly, $\mathbb{E}$ will already be a Δ-grounded state. Moreover, we will show now that $\mathbb{E}$ also generates $\vdash\!\!\!\sim$.

We will say that a proposition A is Δ-*prime* if it is equivalent to a disjunction of some defaults from Δ. Notice that if A is Δ-prime, then, for any default $\delta \in \Delta$, either $A \in \text{Th}(\delta)$ or $\neg A \in \text{Th}(\delta)$. As a result, for any state

s, $A \in l(s)$ if and only if $A \in l_\Delta(s)$. It immediately follows that if A and B are Δ-prime, then $A \hspace{0.2em}\vdash\hspace{-0.9em}\sim\hspace{0.2em} B$ is valid in $\mathbb{W}$ if and only if it is valid in $\mathbb{E}$. Now, for arbitrary propositions A and B, $A \hspace{0.2em}\vdash\hspace{-0.9em}\sim\hspace{0.2em} B$ holds if and only if $A^\Delta \hspace{0.2em}\vdash\hspace{-0.9em}\sim\hspace{0.2em} (A \to B)_\Delta$. But A^Δ and $(A \to B)_\Delta$ are Δ-prime propositions, so the latter holds if and only if $A^\Delta \hspace{0.2em}\vdash\hspace{-0.9em}\sim\hspace{0.2em} (A \to B)_\Delta$ is valid in $\mathbb{E}$. Note now that $\mathbb{E}$ is a Δ-grounded state, so its generated inference relation satisfies Δ-reduction. Consequently, the conditional $A \hspace{0.2em}\vdash\hspace{-0.9em}\sim\hspace{0.2em} B$ belongs to $\hspace{0.2em}\vdash\hspace{-0.9em}\sim\hspace{0.2em}$ if and only if it is valid in $\mathbb{E}$.

Finally, we will transform $\mathbb{E}$ into a finite epistemic state. Note that, due to the smoothness of $\mathbb{W}$, the set of admissible states of $\mathbb{E}$ that support (equivalently, consistent with) some $\delta \in \Delta$ always has preferred elements. Accordingly, we will choose such preferred admissible states for each δ and remove the rest. Let us denote the resulting epistemic state by $\mathbb{E}_1$. Since the removed admissible states have not been normal, $\mathbb{E}_1$ will be normally similar to $\mathbb{E}$. Next, for any admissible state s from $\mathbb{E}_1$, we will consider the set $\hat{s}$ of all admissible states s_1 of $\mathbb{E}_1$ that are equal to s and such that $\Uparrow s = \Uparrow s_1$. Notice that, since $\mathbb{E}$ has only a finite number of admissible belief sets, the set of admissible states of $\mathbb{E}_1$ is partitioned by this into a finite number of sets of the form $\hat{s}$. Now we choose some such set $\hat{s}$ and identify all its elements into a single new admissible state $\tilde{s}$. The obtained epistemic state will be denoted by $\mathbb{E}_s$. Note that, since elements of $\hat{s}$ are incomparable with respect to preference, the resulting preference relation will also be a strict partial order. Moreover, we will show that $\mathbb{E}_s$ is similar to $\mathbb{E}_1$. Indeed, for any $t \notin \hat{s}$, we will take t itself as a counterpart in $\mathbb{E}_s$. If $t \prec r \neq \tilde{s}$ in $\mathbb{E}_s$, then clearly $t \prec r$ also in $\mathbb{E}_1$, while if $t \prec \tilde{s}$ in $\mathbb{E}_s$, then $t \prec s_1$ in $\mathbb{E}_1$, for some $s_1 \in \hat{s}$, as required by similarity. Finally, any $s_1 \in \hat{s}$ will be assigned $\tilde{s}$ as a counterpart in $\mathbb{E}_s$. Then $\tilde{s} \prec t$ in $\mathbb{E}_s$ only if $s_2 \prec t$, for some $s_2 \in \hat{s}$. But $\Uparrow s_2 = \Uparrow s_1$, so $s_1 \prec t_1$, for some t_1 equal to t. Consequently, $\Uparrow s_1$ dominates $\Uparrow \tilde{s}$. The proof for the second condition of similarity is perfectly similar. Thus, $\mathbb{E}_s$ is similar to $\mathbb{E}_1$.

Iterating the above reduction a finite number of times, we will obtain a required finite Δ-grounded epistemic state that still generates $\hspace{0.2em}\vdash\hspace{-0.9em}\sim\hspace{0.2em}$. This concludes the proof. $\qquad\qquad\qquad\qquad\qquad\qquad\qquad\qquad\qquad\qquad\quad$ $\square$

Δ-based inference

Now we will consider a more realistic setting in which a set of defaults Δ forms a base of an inference relation. Recall that base-generated epistemic states are epistemic states of the form $(\mathcal{P}(\Delta), l, \prec)$, where $\prec$ is a monotonic order on $\mathcal{P}(\Delta)$, while l assigns each $\Gamma \subseteq \Delta$ its closure with respect to some classical consequence relation Th. The syntactic characterization of Δ-grounded inference relations, given earlier, will help us in establishing the main result of this section, namely a syntactic description of inference relations corresponding to Δ-based epistemic states. The link is provided by the result given below.

Let Δ be a finite base, and Th a classical consequence relation. For any $\Gamma \subseteq \Delta$, we will denote by $\sigma(\Gamma)$ the conjunction of all propositions $\tilde{\delta}_i$, for

$\delta \in \Delta$, where $\tilde{\delta}_i$ is δ_i when $\delta_i \in \Gamma$, and $\neg \delta_i$ otherwise. As before, a subset $\Gamma \subseteq \Delta$ will be called *independent* if $\mathrm{Th}(\sigma(\Gamma))$ is consistent. We will denote by Δ^σ the set of all $\sigma(\Gamma)$ for independent subsets of Δ. As can be easily seen, Δ^σ is a partition. Moreover, it turns out that this partition can be used to generate the same inference relation.

Lemma 7.8.5. *For any Δ-based epistemic state there exists an inference-equivalent Δ^σ-grounded epistemic state.*

Proof. Let $\mathbb{E}$ be a Δ-based epistemic state, and Th its internal logic. We will construct a corresponding Δ^σ-grounded state $\mathbb{E}^\sigma$ as follows. First, we remove from $\mathbb{E}$ admissible states Γ that are not independent subsets of Δ with respect to Th. Second, for the remaining states we will define a new labelling function $\tilde{l}$ as follows: $\tilde{l}(\Gamma) = \mathrm{Th}(\sigma(\Gamma))$. As can be seen, the resulting epistemic state will be a Δ^σ-grounded. We will show now that $\mathbb{E}^\sigma$ generates the same preferential inference relation as $\mathbb{E}$.

To begin with, notice that the removal of admissible states corresponding to non-independent subsets of Δ does not change the generated inference relation, since the inferential reduction of a base-generated epistemic state involves only independent subsets of Δ (see above).

Let Γ be a preferred state in $\mathbb{E}$ that is consistent with A. Since $\mathbb{E}$ is semi-monotonic, Γ will be a maximal subset of Δ that is consistent with A, that is, $\neg \delta \in \mathrm{Th}(A, \Gamma)$, for any $\delta \notin \Gamma$. Therefore, $\mathrm{Th}(A, \Gamma) = \mathrm{Th}(A, \sigma(\Gamma))$. The latter equality means, in particular, that $\sigma(\Gamma)$ is consistent, and hence Γ will be retained in $\mathbb{E}^\sigma$. Moreover, Γ will also be a preferred state in $\mathbb{E}^\sigma$ that is consistent with A. So, any preferred state in $\mathbb{E}$ with respect to some proposition is also a preferred state in $\mathbb{E}^\sigma$ with respect to the same proposition.

Assume now that Γ is a preferred state in $\mathbb{E}^\sigma$ with respect to A. If it were the case that Γ is not a preferred state in $\mathbb{E}$ that is consistent in with A, then there would exist a preferred state Φ consistent with A such that $\Gamma \prec \Phi$. Our previous considerations would imply, however, that Φ is also an admissible state in $\mathbb{E}^\sigma$ that is consistent with A, contrary to the assumption that Γ is a preferred state. Consequently, for any proposition A, $\mathbb{E}$ and $\mathbb{E}^\sigma$ have the same preferred states consistent with A. Moreover, we have shown earlier that if Γ is such a state in $\mathbb{E}$, then $\mathrm{Th}(A, \Gamma) = Th(A, \sigma(\Gamma))$. The latter condition can now be rewritten as $\mathrm{Th}(A, l(\Gamma)) = \mathrm{Th}(A, \tilde{l}(\Gamma))$. In other words, for any proposition B, $A \to B \in l(\Gamma)$ if and only if $A \to B \in \tilde{l}(\Gamma)$. Therefore $A \hspace{1pt}\vert\hspace{-4pt}\sim B$ is valid in $\mathbb{E}$ if and only if it is valid in $\mathbb{E}^\sigma$. $\qquad\square$

Since Δ-based epistemic states are inference-equivalent to Δ^σ-grounded epistemic states, and the latter correspond to Δ^σ-reductive inference relations by Theorem 7.8.1, we acquire an opportunity to give a syntactic characterization of inference relations generated by Δ-based epistemic states. However, we must take into account the fact that the preference relation of a Δ-based epistemic state is monotonic on the subsets of Δ, and this property is transferred also to the associated Δ^σ-grounded epistemic state. Fortunately, this property can be captured by the following condition on the associated inference relation: for any independent subsets Γ, Φ of Δ such that $\Gamma \subset \Phi$,

Δ-monotonicity $\sigma(\Gamma) \vee \sigma(\Phi) \mathrel|\!\sim \sigma(\Phi)$.

As can be easily verified, the above condition is satisfied by the Δ^σ-grounded epistemic state constructed in the proof of the above lemma. Consequently, it should be satisfied by any inference relation generated by a Δ-based epistemic state. This suggests the following definition.

Definition 7.8.3. *An inference relation $\mathrel|\!\sim$ will be called Δ-based if it is Δ^σ-reductive and Δ-monotonic (with respect to $\mathrm{Th}_{\mathrel|\!\sim}$).*

Unfortunately, the above conditions are still insufficient for a complete description of inference relations generated by Δ-based epistemic states. This is because they are valid also for inference relations generated by arbitrary *sets* (disjoint unions) of Δ-based epistemic states. It will turn out, however, that this indeterminacy is precisely what we will need for describing defeasible inference in Chapter 8.

The following result shows that the above conditions provide a syntactic characterization of inference relations generated by sets of Δ-based epistemic states.

Theorem 7.8.2. *A preferential inference relation is Δ-based if and only if it is generated by a set of Δ-based epistemic states.*

Proof. If a preferential inference relation $\mathrel|\!\sim$ is determined by a set (= disjoint sum) of Δ-based epistemic states, then the preceding lemma shows that $\mathrel|\!\sim$ is determined also by a corresponding set of Δ^σ-grounded epistemic states. Clearly, the disjoint sum of the latter will also be Δ^σ-grounded, so $\mathrel|\!\sim$ will be Δ^σ-reductive. Also, each such component epistemic state will still be monotonic on independent subsets, that is, $\Gamma \subset \Phi$ will imply $\Gamma \prec \Phi$. This will immediately give us Δ-monotonicity of the associated inference relation. Consequently, $\mathrel|\!\sim$ will be Δ-based.

Assume now that a preferential inference relation $\mathrel|\!\sim$ is Δ-based. Since it is Δ^σ-reductive, it is determined by the finite Δ^σ-grounded epistemic state $\mathbb{E}$ constructed in the proof of Theorem 7.8.1. We will transform now the latter epistemic state into an inference-equivalent set of Δ-based epistemic states. To this end, we will first decompose $\mathbb{E}$ into a set $\mathfrak{E}$ of linear, standard and monotonic epistemic states. By the construction of this decomposition (described in Chapter 4), each $\mathbb{E}_i \in \mathfrak{E}$ is a normal reduction of some linear refinement of $\mathbb{E}$. Consequently, each $\mathbb{E}_i$ will be Δ^σ-grounded. Note also that each consistent theory $\mathrm{Th}(\sigma(\Gamma))$ will also be an admissible belief set in every $\mathbb{E}_i$; this is because different theories of the form $\mathrm{Th}(\sigma(\Gamma))$ are incomparable with respect to set inclusion, so any maximally preferred admissible state labelled with $\mathrm{Th}(\sigma(\Gamma))$ will also be normal, and hence will survive a normal reduction. As a result, each $\mathbb{E}_i$ is representable, in effect, as a set of all consistent theories $\text{Th}(\sigma(\Gamma))$ that is linearly ordered by preference. Moreover, this order will always be 'Δ-monotonic' in the sense that if $\Gamma \subset \Phi$, for two independent subsets of Δ, then $\text{Th}(\sigma(\Gamma)) \prec \text{Th}(\sigma(\Phi))$. Indeed, assuming otherwise, we would obtain $\text{Th}(\sigma(\Phi)) \prec \text{Th}(\sigma(\Gamma))$ by linearity, and hence $\sigma(\Gamma) \vee \sigma(\Phi) \hspace{0.1em}\vdash\hspace{-0.9em}\sim\hspace{0.4em} \sigma(\Gamma)$ would be valid in $\mathbb{E}_i$. By Δ-monotonicity we have, however, that $\sigma(\Gamma) \vee \sigma(\Phi) \hspace{0.1em}\vdash\hspace{-0.9em}\sim\hspace{0.4em} \sigma(\Phi)$ is valid in $\mathbb{E}$, so it will be valid also in $\mathbb{E}_i$ (recall that the latter is normally similar to some refinement of $\mathbb{E}$). Consequently, $\sigma(\Gamma) \vee \sigma(\Phi) \hspace{0.1em}\vdash\hspace{-0.9em}\sim\hspace{0.4em} \sigma(\Gamma) \wedge \sigma(\Phi)$, and therefore $\sigma(\Gamma) \vee \sigma(\Phi) \hspace{0.1em}\vdash\hspace{-0.9em}\sim\hspace{0.4em} \mathbf{f}$, since $\sigma(\Gamma)$ is incompatible with $\sigma(\Phi)$. But the latter conditional says, in effect, that neither $\text{Th}(\sigma(\Gamma))$, nor $\text{Th}(\sigma(\Phi))$ are admissible theories of $\mathbb{E}_i$ - a contradiction.

On a next step, we change the labelling function l_i of every $\mathbb{E}_i$ into a new labelling function l_i^0 as follows: If $l_i(s) = \text{Th}(\sigma(\Gamma))$, we define $l_i^0(s)$ to be equal to $\text{Th}(\Gamma)$. Let us denote the resulting epistemic states by $\mathbb{E}_i^0$. Such epistemic states can be seen already as consisting of independent subsets of Δ as their admissible states. Note that the proof of Lemma 7.8.5 can now be used to show that this transformation also does not change the generated inference relation.

As a final step, we extend each $\mathbb{E}_i^0$ by adding new admissible states Γ, for all non-independent subsets of Δ. Each such new admissible state Γ will also be labelled with $\text{Th}(\Gamma)$. In addition, the preference order of $\mathbb{E}_i^0$ will by extended by monotonicity with respect to Δ. The resulting epistemic states will be denoted by $\mathbb{E}_i^1$. It should be clear that each $\mathbb{E}_i^1$ will already be a Δ-based epistemic state. Moreover, since all the added admissible states are not independent in $\mathbb{E}_i^1$, the latter will be normally similar to $\mathbb{E}_i^0$. Consequently, the set of epistemic states $\{\mathbb{E}_i^1\}$ will generate the same inference relation as $\mathbb{E}$. This concludes the proof of the theorem.   □

The above result can be refined further if we notice that any Δ-based epistemic state is decomposable, in turn, into a set of linear Δ-based epistemic states. Consequently, we obtain

Corollary 7.8.1. *A preferential inference relation is Δ-based if and only if it is generated by a set of linear Δ-based epistemic states.*

Strong monotonicity

An inference relation $\hspace{0.1em}\vdash\hspace{-0.9em}\sim\hspace{0.4em}$ will be said to satisfy *strong Δ-monotonicity* if, for any two subsets Γ, Φ of Δ such that $\Gamma \subseteq \Phi$, and any proposition A such that $A \wedge \sigma(\Phi) \hspace{0.1em}\not\vdash\hspace{-0.9em}\sim\hspace{0.4em} \mathbf{f}$,

Strong Δ-monotonicity $A \wedge (\sigma(\Gamma) \vee \sigma(\Phi)) \hspace{0.1em}\vdash\hspace{-0.9em}\sim\hspace{0.4em} \sigma(\Phi)$

The condition $A \wedge \sigma(\Phi) \hspace{0.1em}\not\vdash\hspace{-0.9em}\sim\hspace{0.4em} \mathbf{f}$ above says that A is compatible with $\sigma(\Phi)$ with respect to the underlying classical consequence relation $\text{Th}_{\hspace{0.1em}\vdash\hspace{-0.55em}\sim\hspace{0.2em}}$. The above principle has actually been suggested in [TP95] as a way of 'correcting' the system Z of defeasible entailment (see Chapter 8).

The following lemma gives a semantic characterization of strong Δ-monotonicity for the finite case.

Lemma 7.8.6. *An inference relation $\vdash$ in a finite language satisfies strong Δ-monotonicity if and only if, for any KLM model $\mathbb{W}$ of $\vdash$ and any proposition A, s is a preferred state containing A only if $l(s) \cap \Delta$ is a maximal subset of Δ consistent with A (with respect to $\mathrm{Th}_{\vdash}$).*

Proof. Assume that there exists a KLM model $\mathbb{W}$ of $\vdash$, a proposition A, and a state s in $\mathbb{W}$ that do not satisfy the above condition. Let us denote by Γ the set $l(s) \cap \Delta$. Since Γ is not a maximal subset of Δ consistent with A, there must exist a subset Φ of Δ that is maximal consistent with A with respect to $\mathrm{Th}_{\vdash}$ and such that $\Gamma \subset \Phi$. Since Φ is consistent with A with respect to $\mathrm{Th}_{\vdash}$, $\mathbb{W}$ should contain a state t that support A and such that $l(t) \cap \Delta = \Phi$. Due to finiteness of the language, we can treat worlds (complete theories) as propositions. Let us denote by A_0 the proposition $A \wedge (l(s) \vee l(t))$. Then s should be a preferred state with respect to $A_0 \wedge (\sigma(\Gamma) \vee \sigma(\Phi))$. Consequently $A \wedge (\sigma(\Gamma) \vee \sigma(\Phi)) \not\vdash \sigma(\Phi)$, contrary to our assumption that $\vdash$ is strongly Δ-monotonic.

In the other direction, assume that there are Γ, Φ and A such that $\Gamma \subseteq \Phi \subseteq \Delta$, A is consistent with $\sigma(\Phi)$ with respect to $\mathrm{Th}_{\vdash}$, but $A \wedge (\sigma(\Gamma) \vee \sigma(\Phi)) \not\vdash \sigma(\Phi)$. Then there must exist a KLM model $\mathbb{W}$ and a state s in $\mathbb{W}$ such that s is a preferred state satisfying $A \wedge (\sigma(\Gamma) \vee \sigma(\Phi))$, but s does not validate $\sigma(\Phi)$. Then Γ coincides with $l(s) \cap \Delta$ and $\Gamma \subset \Phi$. We have, however, that A is consistent with $\sigma(\Phi)$ with respect to $\mathrm{Th}_{\vdash}$, and hence $\mathbb{W}$ must contain a state t validating A and such that $\Phi = l(t) \cap \Delta$. Consequently, $l(s) \cap \Delta$ is not a maximal subset of Δ consistent with A. This completes the proof. $\qquad\Box$

As can be anticipated on the basis of the above description, Δ-based inference relations should already satisfy strong Δ-monotonicity.

Lemma 7.8.7. *Any Δ-based inference relation is strongly Δ-monotonic.*

Proof. Assume that Γ, Φ are subsets of Δ, $\Gamma \subset \Phi$ and $\sigma(\Phi)$ is consistent with some proposition A. By Δ-monotonicity, we have $\sigma(\Gamma) \vee \sigma(\Phi) \vdash \sigma(\Phi)$. We will consider two cases.

(i) Assume that $\sigma(\Gamma)$ is also consistent with A. Then $\sigma(\Gamma) \vee \sigma(\Phi)$ coincides with the Δ^σ-interior of $A \wedge (\sigma(\Gamma) \vee \sigma(\Phi))$, and consequently $A \wedge (\sigma(\Gamma) \vee \sigma(\Phi)) \vdash \sigma(\Phi)$ by Δ^σ-reduction.

(ii) Assume that $\sigma(\Gamma)$ is inconsistent with A. Then $A \wedge (\sigma(\Gamma) \vee \sigma(\Phi))$ is equivalent to $A \wedge \sigma(\Phi)$, and hence we immediately obtain $A \wedge (\sigma(\Gamma) \vee \sigma(\Phi)) \vdash \sigma(\Phi)$. So, in both cases strong Δ-monotonicity holds. $\qquad\Box$

Thus, Δ-based inference relations can be alternatively characterized by Δ^σ-reduction and strong Δ-monotonicity. We will return to such inference relations in Chapter 8.

7.9 Injectivity and pure base-generation

A preferential inference relation will be called *injective* if it is generated by a standard (injective) KLM model in which different states are labelled with different worlds. In other words, if it is generated by a standard epistemic state in which all admissible belief sets are worlds.

Not all preferential inference relations, not even finite ones, are injective. An example of a finite non-injective inference relation has been given in the preceding section.

The class of injective inference relations is interesting for many reasons. First, because initial models of nonmonotonic inference (suggested by Shoham in [Sho88]) correspond to injective models. Also, we will see later that such models naturally correspond to common models of belief change. Finally, we will see that injective inference is intimately connected with base-generation, which allows to give it a very natural representation in the framework of epistemic states.

As we have shown in the preceding section, any preferential KLM model $\mathbb{W}$ can be transformed into a monotonic union-closed general epistemic state $\mathbb{E}_W$ by adding an inconsistent admissible state. Now, if $\mathbb{W}$ is an injective model, the corresponding epistemic state $\mathbb{E}_W$ will be standard. Consequently, we immediately obtain

Lemma 7.9.1. *Any injective inference relation is generated by some standard monotonic and union-closed epistemic state.*

Moreover, we will show now that the reverse claim is also true. More exactly, we will demonstrate that any preferential inference relation generated by a standard, maximizing and union-closed epistemic state will be injective.

Let $\mathbb{E}$ be a standard union-closed epistemic state. Then it can be easily shown that any world α containing at least one theory from $\mathbb{E}$ contains a greatest such theory.

Lemma 7.9.2. *Let $\mathbb{E}$ be a standard union-closed epistemic state, and α a world consistent with at least one theory from $\mathbb{E}$. Then there exists a theory $u \in \mathbb{E}$ consistent with α such that $v \subseteq u$, for any theory $v \in \mathbb{E}$ that is consistent with α.*

Proof. Follows immediately from the fact that the set of theories from $\mathbb{E}$ that are consistent with α is directed, and hence it has a supremum. $\square$

If $\mathbb{E}$ is a standard union-closed epistemic state, then, for any world α that includes some theory from $\mathbb{E}$, we will denote by u_α a unique maximal theory in $\mathbb{E}$ that is included in α. Let us consider now preferential KLM models generated by such epistemic states in accordance with Theorem 7.7.1. Since for any world there exists a unique maximal theory consistent with it, states of the corresponding preferential model are uniquely determined by their worlds. This means, in particular, that the relevant preferential models will be injective. The following construction gives a direct description of such injective models.

Let W_E be the set of all worlds that contain at least one theory from $\mathbb{E}$. We define a preference relation on this set as follows:

$$\alpha \prec_E \beta \quad \text{iff} \quad u_\alpha \prec u_\beta$$

Theorem 7.9.1. *If $\mathbb{E}$ is a standard union-closed and maximizing epistemic state, then $(W_E, \prec_E)$ is an injective preferential model that is inference-equivalent to $\mathbb{E}$.*

Proof. To begin with, we will check that the above definition gives us a smooth preferential model. Assume that α is a world containing A. Then u_α is consistent with A. Assume first that u_α itself is a preferred theory of $\mathbb{E}$ that is consistent with A. Then α will be a preferred world containing A. Indeed, assume that $\alpha \prec \beta$, for some world β. Then $u_\alpha \prec u_\beta \subseteq \beta$. But then $\neg A \in u_\beta$, and hence $\neg A \in \beta$. Assume now that u_α is not a preferred theory consistent with A. Then $u_\alpha \prec v$, for some preferred theory v consistent with A. Let β be a world containing v and A. Then v coincides with u_β. Indeed, otherwise we would have $v \subset u_\beta \subseteq \beta$, and hence v would not be a maximal theory consistent with A. Now, we have $\alpha \prec \beta$, and the same argument can be used to show that β is a preferred world containing A. Consequently, our definition determines a smooth order.

Assume first that $A \hspace{0.15em}\vdash\hspace{-0.8em}\sim\hspace{0.15em} B$ is valid in $\mathbb{E}$, but there exists a preferred A-world $\alpha \in W_E$ such that $\neg B \in \alpha$. Then $A \to B \notin u_\alpha$, and hence there must exist some preferred theory v in $\mathbb{E}$ that is consistent with A and such that $A \to B \in v$ and $u_\alpha \prec v$. Let β be a world containing v and including A. Then, as before, it can be shown that v coincides with u_β. Consequently, we have $\alpha \prec \beta$, contrary to our assumption that α is a preferred world containing A.

Assume now that $A \hspace{0.15em}\vdash\hspace{-0.8em}\sim\hspace{0.15em} B$ is not valid in $\mathbb{E}$, and let v be a preferred theory in $\mathbb{E}$ that is consistent with A and such that $A \to B \notin v$. Then there exists a world α containing v and such that $A \wedge \neg B \in \alpha$. We will show that α is a preferred A-world in W_E. Again, it can be shown that v coincides with u_α. Now, if it were the case that $\alpha \prec \beta$, for some A-world β, then we would have $v \prec u_\beta \subseteq \beta$, contrary to the assumption that v is a preferred theory in $\mathcal{E}$ that is consistent with A. Hence, α is a preferred A-world in W_E. But $\neg B \in \alpha$, and therefore $A \hspace{0.15em}\vdash\hspace{-0.8em}\sim\hspace{0.15em} B$ is not valid in the corresponding preferential model. This completes the proof. $\square$

As a first consequence of the above result, we obtain

Corollary 7.9.1. *A preferential inference relation is injective if and only if it is generated by a standard, union-closed and monotonic epistemic state.*

As has been shown in the preceding section, any preferential inference relation is generated by some standard, union-closed and weakly monotonic epistemic state. So, the only restriction needed to obtain injective inference relations in this setting amounts to strengthening weak monotonicity to monotonicity (or even to maximizing).

It was noticed by Poole and Makinson (see [Mak94]) that Poole's abductive system produces an injective preferential inference relation. This result can be obtained as a special case of the above construction. To begin with, we have the following consequence of the above theorem:

Corollary 7.9.2. *If $\mathcal{E}$ is a pure base-generated epistemic state, then $(W_{\mathcal{E}}, \prec_{\mathcal{E}})$ is an injective preferential model that generates the same preferential inference relation as $\mathcal{E}$.*

Proof. Immediate from the fact that a pure base-generated epistemic state is already monotonic and union-closed. □

If $\mathcal{E}$ is a pure union-closed epistemic state, then the corresponding preference order $\prec_{\mathcal{E}}$ on worlds corresponds to set inclusion among associated theories: $\alpha \prec_{\mathcal{E}} \beta$ holds iff $u_{\alpha} \subset u_{\beta}$. Moreover, if $\mathcal{E}$ is base-generated by a set Δ, then this preference order among worlds can be equivalently defined in terms of sets of defaults they contain:

$$\alpha \prec_{\mathcal{E}} \beta \quad \equiv \quad \alpha \cap \Delta \subset \beta \cap \Delta$$

Consequently, the resulting injective KLM model corresponding to $\mathcal{E}$ coincides with the model constructed in [Mak94].

Now we will describe the results about injective preferential inference relations obtained by Michael Freund in [Fre98][3]. These results will show that, in the finite case, an inference relation is injective if and only if it is produced by a pure base-generated epistemic state.

The following theorem can be seen as a special case of Theorem 7.7.3 above.

Theorem 7.9.2. *Let $(W, \prec)$ be a finite injective preferential model. Define $\mathcal{E}$ to be the set of theories corresponding to intersections of all $\prec$-closed sets of worlds. Then $\mathcal{E}$ is a union-closed pure epistemic state that generates the same preferential inference relation as $(W, \prec)$.*

Proof. To begin with, we will show that $\mathcal{E}$ is union-closed. Notice that if Γ and Δ are $\prec$-closed subsets of W, then $\Gamma \cap \Delta$ is also a $\prec$-closed subset of W. Consequently, it is sufficient to show that if u and v are, respectively, intersections of Γ and Δ, then $\mathrm{Cl}(u, v)$ is precisely the intersection of all worlds in $\Gamma \cap \Delta$.

If $\alpha \in \Gamma \cap \Delta$, then both u and v are clearly included in α. Hence $\mathrm{Cl}(u, v)$ is included in $\bigcap(\Gamma \cap \Delta)$.

Since W is a finite set of worlds, for any world α we can find a proposition A_{α} that distinguish it from all other worlds in W, that is, any world $\beta \in W$

---

[3] Similar results have been established in [Val94, Val97].

will contain A_α if and only if β coincides with α. Let $\{A_\alpha\}$ be an arbitrary, but fixed set of such propositions for all worlds in W. Also, for any subset Γ of W, we will denote by A_Γ the disjunction of all A_α, for $\alpha \in \Gamma$. As a special case, if $\Gamma = \emptyset$, we will put A_Γ to be equal to a contradictory proposition $\mathbf{f}$.

Assume now that a proposition A belongs to all worlds in $\Gamma \cap \Delta$. Then $A \vee A_{\Gamma \backslash \Delta}$ will belong to all worlds in Γ, and hence it will belong to their intersection u. Similarly, $A \vee \neg A_{\Gamma \backslash \Delta}$ will belong to all worlds in Δ, and hence it will belong to v. Consequently, $\mathrm{Cl}(u, v)$ will contain both $A \vee A_{\Gamma \backslash \Delta}$ and $A \vee \neg A_{\Gamma \backslash \Delta}$, and hence $A \in \mathrm{Cl}(u, v)$. This shows that $\mathrm{Cl}(u, v)$ coincides with the intersection of all worlds from $\Gamma \cap \Delta$, and hence it belongs to $\mathcal{E}$. Therefore, $\mathcal{E}$ is a union-closed set of theories.

Notice now that any $\prec$-closed set from W is representable as a union of sets of the form $\{\beta \mid \alpha \preceq \beta\}$, while the latter sets determine the set of theories $\mathcal{T}_W$ described before Theorem 7.7.3. Consequently, theories from $\mathcal{E}$ are precisely intersections of theories from $\mathcal{T}_W$ for our case, and hence $\mathcal{E}$ determines the same (semi-classical) consequence relation as $\mathcal{T}_W$. As a result, we can apply Theorem 7.7.3 to conclude that $\mathcal{E}$ determines the same inference relation as the initial injective model. $\square$

Example 7.9.1. (Continued). As we have seen, a finite preferential (non-injective) model from [KLM90], described in the preceding section, has an equivalent pure epistemic state consisting of four theories $\{\mathrm{Cl}(p \wedge \neg q), \mathrm{Cl}(\neg p \wedge \neg q), \mathrm{Cl}(p), \mathrm{Cl}(p \leftrightarrow q)\}$. This epistemic state is not union-closed: the union of $\mathrm{Cl}(p)$ and $\mathrm{Cl}(p \leftrightarrow q)$ would give us a theory $\mathrm{Th}(p \wedge q)$ which does not belong to the admissible states.

The above result establishes a correspondence between finite injective preferential models and pure union-closed epistemic states. Since any finitary and pure union-closed epistemic state is always base-generated, we obtain also

Corollary 7.9.3. *For any finite injective preferential model there exists a finitary base-generated pure epistemic state that produces the same preferential inference relation.*

Note that the above correspondence between injective inference relations and base-generated epistemic states is not one-to-one, since different such epistemic states may generate the same inference relation (and the same injective KLM model). We have, however, a one-to-one correspondence between finite injective inference relations and base-generated semi-classical consequence relations.

Corollary 7.9.4. *A finite preferential inference relation is injective if and only if its associated semi-classical consequence relation is base-generated.*

Proof. Follows from the fact that the consequence relation corresponding to the epistemic state $\mathcal{E}$ described in Theorem 7.9.2 is not only union-closed, but also semi-classical. $\square$

An interesting consequence of the above theorem arises when combined with Theorem 7.9.1. Since any finite epistemic state that is standard, base-generated and maximizing produces an equivalent finite injective model, and the latter is equivalent, in turn, to some pure base-generated epistemic state, we obtain that imposing maximizing preferences on theories of a base-generated epistemic state does not extend our expressive capabilities, since any such 'prioritized' state will be equivalent again to a certain pure base-generated state:

Corollary 7.9.5. *For any finite standard base-generated and maximizing epistemic state there exists an inference-equivalent pure base-generated epistemic state.*

The correspondence between injective models and base-generated consequence relations can be extended further. Thus, we will call *persistent* propositions that 'persist' relative to the preference order on worlds[4]:

If $\alpha \prec \beta$ and $A \in \alpha$, then $A \in \beta$.

The following results show that, at least in the finite case, persistent propositions are precisely default propositions as defined earlier (see Definition 7.4.2). Actually, this connection between persistent and default propositions has been pointed out in [Eng98].

The next lemma shows that persistent propositions are precisely basic propositions of the associated semi-classical consequence relation.

Lemma 7.9.3. *Let $\mathbb{W}$ be a finite injective preferential model and $\vdash_W$ its associated union-closed consequence relation. Then a proposition A is a default in $\mathbb{W}$ if and only if it is a basic proposition of $\vdash_W$.*

Proof. As has been established in Chapter 2, a proposition A is basic in a base-generated consequence relation $\vdash$ if and only if it is prime, that is, $Th_\vdash(A)$ is a theory of $\vdash$. By the construction of $\vdash_W$, this amounts to a claim that the set of worlds containing A is $\prec$-closed. $\square$

Finally, we can combine the above lemma with the characterization of default propositions with respect to an inference relation, given in Theorem 7.4.3, and obtain the following

Corollary 7.9.6. *If $\vdash$ is a finite injective inference relation, then persistent propositions are precisely default propositions with respect to $\vdash$.*

The above results establish a one-to-one correspondence between injective (Shoham) models and Poole's systems based on defaults. Speaking more generally, in the finite case we have that any strict partial order on worlds is representable as produced by some base (see [Fre98, Theorem 14]).

---

[4] [Fre98] has called such propositions *defaults*.

In general, not all injective inference relations are representable in terms of some base – a suitable counterexample can be found in [Fre98]. In addition, different bases can generate the same preferential inference relation. Still, it is interesting to note that in the finite case an injective inference relation uniquely determines its associated injective KLM model.

Lemma 7.9.4. *Two finite injective KLM models determine the same preferential inference relation only if they coincide.*

Proof. Let W_1 and W_2 be two finite injective KLM models that induce the same preferential inference relation $\vdash\!\sim$. We show first that these models contain the same worlds. Indeed, assume that a world α belong to model W_1, and let A_α be some distinguishing formula for α in W_1. Then it is easy to see that if $B \in \alpha$, then $A_\alpha \vdash\!\sim B$ is valid in W_1. Consequently, $\mathbb{C}(A_\alpha)$ should coincide with α. Note that A_α is consistent with respect to $\vdash\!\sim$, and hence W_2 should contain at least one world that includes A_α. Moreover, $\mathbb{C}(A_\alpha)$ should also be an intersection of all preferred worlds in W_2 that contain A_α, which is possible only if α belongs by itself to W_2.

Thus, W_1 and W_2 contain the same worlds. Consequently, for any α, A_α will be its distinguishing proposition in both models. In addition, for any two worlds of W_1 we have $\alpha \prec \beta$ if and only if $A_\alpha \vee A_\beta \vdash\!\sim A_\beta$. Therefore, the preference orders in both models coincide. Thus, W_1 coincides with W_2. □

The correspondence between injective models and base-generated states, established above, depends essentially on the assumption of finiteness. In general, not all injective models give rise to base-generated epistemic states. A further complication arises when the set of theories produced by an infinite base Δ is not compact. In this case the preferential inference relation determined by the corresponding epistemic state will be distinct, in general, from the inference relation produced by the associated consequence relation. The following lemma gives a description of the latter.

Lemma 7.9.5. *Let $\vdash$ be a consequence relation generated by a base Δ. Then $A \vdash\!\sim B$ holds with respect to $\vdash$ iff any finite subset of Δ that is consistent with A is included in a subset of Δ that is also consistent with A and implies $A \to B$.*

Proof. Follows from the fact that the above condition is equivalent to the admissibility of the rule $\dfrac{a, A \to B \vdash \neg A}{a \vdash \neg A}$ in $\vdash$. □

The above characterization immediately implies that if $A \vdash\!\sim B$ is valid in an epistemic state generated by Δ, it will be valid also with respect to the associated consequence relation. The following counterexample shows, however, that the reverse implication does not hold.

Example 7.9.2. Consider a base Δ consisting of atomic propositions p_i, for all $i \geq 0$, and all propositions of the form $q \wedge \neg p_i$, where q is an atomic proposition distinct from all p_i. Then the set of all atoms p_i is a maximal subset of the base that is consistent with p_0. Therefore $p_0 \hspace{0.1em}\vdash\hspace{-0.8em}\sim q$ is not valid in an epistemic state generated by Δ. However, any finite subset of Δ consistent with p_0 can be extended by adding some base proposition of the form $q \wedge \neg p_i$, where $i > 0$. Consequently, $p_0 \hspace{0.1em}\vdash\hspace{-0.8em}\sim q$ will be valid in the consequence relation generated by Δ.

The previous discussion shows that there are still many questions about injective inference relations that remain open in the infinite case. The next section will supply additional open questions about such inference relations.

7.9.1 Syntactic characterizations

Since injective inference relations constitute a proper sub-class of all preferential inference relations, they must have some properties that are valid only for them. It turns out, however, that the problem of syntactic characterization of injective inference relations does not admit a simple solution. To begin with, we will prove a negative result showing that injectivity cannot be characterized by additional rules of a usual kind imposed on preferential inference relations.

Recall that a *general rule* for an inference relation is a rule of the form $\Gamma \Vdash \Delta$, where Γ and Δ are finite sets of conditionals. All the rules for inference relations considered thus far (such as Reflexivity, And, or even Rational Monotony) have been rules of this form. Now, our initial question can be specified as a question whether there are additional general rules that could be used to characterize injective inference relations. Unfortunately, the answer to this question will be negative. This follows from the result given below.

Theorem 7.9.3. *A general rule is valid with respect to the class of all injective inference relations only if it is valid with respect to all preferential inference relations.*

Proof. Assume that the rule $\Gamma \Vdash \Delta$ is not valid for preferential inference relations. This means that there is a preferential inference relation $\hspace{0.1em}\vdash\hspace{-0.8em}\sim$ that includes Γ, but disjoint from Δ. Let $\mathbb{W}$ be a possible worlds (KLM) model of $\hspace{0.1em}\vdash\hspace{-0.8em}\sim$ (note that, due to finiteness of Γ and Δ, such a model can also be chosen to be finite). By Theorem 4.4.1 from Chapter 4, this model can be transformed into an equivalent standard monotonic epistemic state in some extended language. Moreover, adding an additional inconsistent admissible state we can, as before, transform the latter into a union-closed epistemic state that we will denote by $\mathbb{E}$. By Corollary 7.9.1, $\mathbb{E}$ generates an injective inference relation $\hspace{0.1em}\vdash\hspace{-0.8em}\sim_{\mathbb{E}}$ (in the extended language). Finally, notice that our transformations have not changed the validity of conditionals in the source language. Consequently, the rule $\Gamma \Vdash \Delta$ will not be valid also with respect to the class of injective inference relations. $\qquad\square$

The above result shows, in particular, that injectivity does not introduce new valid general rules for an inference relation. This does not mean, however, that injectivity cannot be characterized by means of some more complex conditions. This is precisely what we are going to do next.

Due to the fact that an inference relation is injective if and only if it is generated by a standard monotonic and union-closed epistemic state, we immediately obtain that an inference relation is injective if its associated semi-classical inference relation is union-closed. Consequently (see Lemma 2.5.6 from Chapter 2) we obtain the following sufficient condition of injectivity:

Lemma 7.9.6. *An inference relation is injective if its associated semi-classical consequence relation satisfies:*

($\wedge$-Covering) $Cn(A \wedge B) = Cl(Cn(A), Cn(B))$

Due to the fact that semi-classical consequence relations are directly definable in terms of preferential inference relations, the above condition of $\wedge$-Covering can be seen, in effect, as a condition on inference relations that guarantees injectivity. We will see below that this condition is equivalent to the sufficient condition of injectivity given in [Fre92] and other papers. Moreover, our earlier results have shown that in the finite case union-closure of semi-classical consequence relations is also a necessary condition of injectivity. So, in the finite case $\wedge$-Covering can be considered as a characteristic property of injective inference relations.

Actually, in the finite case, injectivity can be characterized by a much simpler and direct condition, given in the theorem below (see [KM91, Fre92]). The proof of the theorem uses also an important construction of a preference order on worlds that has its origin in studies on counterfactual conditionals. Since in the finite case worlds are reducible to propositional formulas, we can express the preference order among such worlds by stipulating

$$\alpha \prec \beta \text{ if and only if } \alpha \vee \beta \hspace{0.5pt}\mid\hspace{-3pt}\sim \beta.$$

It turns out that in the finite case the above defined relation satisfies all the required properties for an adequate model.

Theorem 7.9.4. *A preferential inference relation in a finite language is injective if and only if it satisfies*

($\vee$-Covering) $\mathcal{C}(A \vee B) \subseteq Cl(\mathcal{C}(A), \mathcal{C}(B))$

Proof. (1) In order to show the implication from left to right, we will demonstrate that $\wedge$-Covering for a semi-classical consequence relation implies $\vee$-Covering for the associated inference relation.

Assume that $A \vee B \hspace{0.5pt}\mid\hspace{-3pt}\sim C$ holds. Translated into the terminology of semi-classical consequence relations, this gives us $\neg(A \vee B) \vee \neg C \hspace{0.5pt}\mid\hspace{-3pt}\sim \neg(A \vee B)$. By

Left Equivalence, the latter is equivalent to $(\neg A \vee \neg C) \wedge (\neg B \vee \neg C \mathrel{\vdash\!\!\!\sim} \neg(A \vee B)$. So, we can apply $\wedge$-Closure and infer

$$\neg(A \vee B) \in \mathrm{Cl}(\mathrm{Cn}(\neg A \vee \neg C), \mathrm{Cn}(\neg B \vee \neg C))$$

The latter condition means that there exist propositions A' and B' such that $\neg A \vee \neg C \vdash A'$, $\neg B \vee \neg C \vdash B'$, and $A' \wedge B' \vDash \neg(A \vee B)$. Now let us denote by A_0 the following proposition: $A \wedge (A' \vee C)$. Similarly, we will denote by B_0 the proposition $B \wedge (B' \vee C)$. It turns out that $A \mathrel{\vdash\!\!\!\sim} A_0$ and $B \mathrel{\vdash\!\!\!\sim} B_0$. We will show only the first condition, the second one being quite similar.

Since $\neg A \vee \neg C \vdash A'$, we have $(\neg A \vee \neg C)(\neg A \vee \neg A') \vdash A' \wedge \neg A$, and hence by elementary transformations $\neg A \vee (\neg A' \wedge \neg C) \vdash \neg A$. The later condition is equivalent to $A \mathrel{\vdash\!\!\!\sim} A' \vee C$ for the corresponding preferential inference relation, and hence $A \mathrel{\vdash\!\!\!\sim} A \wedge (A' \vee C)$ by Antecedence. Thus, $A \mathrel{\vdash\!\!\!\sim} A_0$.

Finally, notice that, since $A' \wedge B' \vDash \neg(A \vee B)$, $A_0 \wedge B_0$ logically implies C. As a result, C belongs to $\mathrm{Cl}(\mathcal{C}(A), \mathcal{C}(B))$. This shows that $\vee$-Covering is valid for $\mathrel{\vdash\!\!\!\sim}$.

(2) Given a finite inference relation $\mathrel{\vdash\!\!\!\sim}$ satisfying $\vee$-Closure, we are going to construct for it a finite injective KLM-model. In what follows, for any world α (maximal deductively closed set) in the underlying finite language, we will denote by $\hat{\alpha}$ the conjunction of all logically distinct propositions belonging to it.

We will define the set W of worlds of the intended model as the set of all worlds α such that $\hat{\alpha} \mathrel{\vdash\!\!\!\sim} \mathbf{f}$ does not belong to the inference relation. Also, we will define the preference order on these worlds as follows:

$$\alpha \prec \beta \text{ if and only if } \alpha \neq \beta \text{ and } \hat{\alpha} \vee \hat{\beta} \mathrel{\vdash\!\!\!\sim} \hat{\beta}.$$

Notice first that the above relation is anti-symmetric. Indeed, if $\alpha \prec \beta$ and $\beta \prec \alpha$, then $\hat{\alpha} \vee \hat{\beta} \mathrel{\vdash\!\!\!\sim} \hat{\alpha} \wedge \hat{\beta}$, and hence $\hat{\alpha} \vee \hat{\beta} \mathrel{\vdash\!\!\!\sim} \mathbf{f}$. But in the latter case we would have $\hat{\alpha} \mathrel{\vdash\!\!\!\sim} \mathbf{f}$ and $\hat{\beta} \mathrel{\vdash\!\!\!\sim} \mathbf{f}$, contrary to our assumption about worlds from W. In addition, note that $\hat{\alpha} \vee \hat{\beta} \mathrel{\vdash\!\!\!\sim} \hat{\beta}$ is equivalent to $\neg \hat{\beta} \vdash \neg \hat{\alpha}$ for the associated semi-classical consequence relation. Consequently, the above preference relation is a strict partial order. Thus, our task has been reduced to showing that the resulting injective model is adequate for the source inference relation. Actually, we will prove a stronger claim, namely that a world α in W is a preferred world satisfying A if and only if α contains $\mathcal{C}(A)$.

Assume first that α contains $\mathcal{C}(A)$, though it is not a preferred world satisfying A. Then there must exist a world β in W that satisfies A and such that $\alpha \prec \beta$. Consequently, $\hat{\alpha} \vee \hat{\beta} \mathrel{\vdash\!\!\!\sim} \hat{\beta}$. Note that A belongs to both α and β, so $\hat{\alpha} \vee \hat{\beta}$ is logically equivalent to $A \wedge (\hat{\alpha} \vee \hat{\beta})$. As a result, $A \wedge (\hat{\alpha} \vee \hat{\beta}) \mathrel{\vdash\!\!\!\sim} \hat{\beta}$. Applying Deduction to the latter, we conclude $A \mathrel{\vdash\!\!\!\sim} \neg \hat{\alpha}$, which is impossible, since $\mathcal{C}(A) \subseteq \alpha$.

Assume now that α is a preferred world satisfying A, and let $\{\alpha_1, \ldots, \alpha_n\}$ be the set of all worlds from W satisfying A. Clearly, A is equivalent to $\bigvee(\hat{\alpha}_i)$ with respect to the internal logic of $\mathrel{\vdash\!\!\!\sim}$. In addition, for any α_i we have $\mathcal{C}(\hat{\alpha} \vee \hat{\alpha_i}) \subseteq \alpha$. Indeed, otherwise we would have $\hat{\alpha} \vee \hat{\alpha_i} \mathrel{\vnsim} \neg\hat{\alpha}$ and hence $\hat{\alpha} \vee \hat{\alpha_i} \mathrel{\vnsim} \hat{\alpha_i}$. Therefore $\alpha \prec \alpha_i$, contrary to our assumption that α is a preferred world satisfying A. Thus, $\mathcal{C}(\hat{\alpha} \vee \hat{\alpha_i}) \subseteq \alpha$. Now we can apply $\vee$-Covering to all such conditionals and obtain

$$\mathcal{C}(\hat{\alpha} \vee \bigvee(\hat{\alpha_i})) \subseteq \alpha,$$

or, in other words, $\mathcal{C}(A) \subseteq \alpha$. This concludes the proof. $\square$

This concludes our description of injective inference relations.

7.10 Weakly rational inference

The epistemic representation of preferential inference relations is sufficiently versatile to allow for interpreting various additional conditions imposed on preferential inference relations. In the rest of the chapter we will consider two particular kinds of preferential entailment obtained by imposing some meaningful conditions on epistemic states.

In this section we will show that inference relations generated by determinate epistemic states are precisely preferential inference relations satisfying the additional rule called Weak Rational Monotony in [GM94]:

Weak Rational Monotony   If $\mathrel{\vnsim} A \to B$ and $\mathrel{\not\vnsim} \neg A$, then $A \mathrel{\vnsim} B$.

Preferential inference relations satisfying Weak Rational Monotony will be called *weakly rational*. The following simple result shows that Weak Rational Monotony holds for determinate epistemic states.

Lemma 7.10.1. *If* $\mathbb{E}$ *is a determinate general epistemic state, then the associated inference relation is weakly rational.*

Proof. If $\mathrel{\vnsim} \neg A$ does not hold for an inference relation generated by $\mathbb{E}$, then the unique most preferred admissible state s of $\mathbb{E}$ is consistent with A. Consequently, s is a unique preferred state in $\mathbb{E}$ that is consistent with A. Now $\mathrel{\vnsim} A \to B$ implies that s supports $A \to B$, and hence $A \to B$ belongs to all preferred states of $\mathbb{E}$ that are consistent with A. Therefore, $A \mathrel{\vnsim} B$. $\square$

The following theorem will show that the correspondence between determinate epistemic states and weakly rational inference relations is bidirectional.

Theorem 7.10.1. *Any weakly rational inference relation is generated by some determinate consequence relation.*

Proof. Let $\vdash\!\sim$ be a weakly rational inference relation and $\vdash^s$ its associated semi-classical consequence relation. We will transform the latter into a determinate consequence relation as follows. Let us denote by K the belief set of $\vdash^s$; the latter will coincide also with the set $\{A \mid \mathbf{t} \vdash\!\sim A\}$. Now we will define the intended consequence relation $\vdash^K$ by restricting the set of theories of $\vdash^s$ to theories that are included in K. Syntactically, this can be made as follows (see Section 2.1.5 in Chapter 2):

$$A \vdash^K B \quad \text{iff} \quad A \notin K \text{ or } A \vdash^s B$$

The above consequence relation will already be determinate, with K as its greatest theory. We will show now that $\vdash\!\sim$ coincides with an inference relation generated by $\vdash^K$.

Assume that $A \vdash\!\sim B$ holds and $a, A \to B \vdash^K \neg A$. Then either $a \not\subseteq K$, or $A \to B \notin K$, or else $a, A \to B \vdash^s \neg A$. Note that $A \vdash\!\sim B$ implies $\vdash\!\sim A \to B$, and consequently $A \to B \in K$. Moreover, $a, A \to B \vdash^s \neg A$ implies $a \vdash^s \neg A$, since $A \vdash\!\sim B$ is valid in $\vdash^s$. Consequently we conclude that either $a \not\subseteq K$ or $a \vdash^s \neg A$, that is, $a \vdash^K \neg A$. Thus, $\vdash^K$ makes valid all rules of $\vdash\!\sim$.

Assume now that $A \vdash\!\sim B$ does not hold. We will consider two cases. Assume first that $\neg A \notin K$. Then $\not\vdash\!\sim \neg A$, and hence by Weak Rational Monotony $\not\vdash\!\sim A \to B$. Consequently $A \to B \notin K$. So in this case we have that the greatest theory of $\vdash^K$ (namely K) is consistent with A and does not contain $A \to B$. Therefore $A \vdash\!\sim B$ is not valid with respect to $\vdash^K$. So, let us that $\neg A \in K$. Then $\neg A \vee \neg B \in K$. In addition, $A \vdash\!\sim B$ implies that $\neg A \vee \neg B \not\vdash^s \neg A$. Let us denote $\neg A \vee \neg B$ by C. Then $C, A \to B \vdash^s \neg A$, and hence $C, A \to B \vdash^K \neg A$. But we also have $C \in K$ and $C \not\vdash^s \neg A$, so $C \not\vdash^K \neg A$. This shows that $A \vdash\!\sim B$ is nod valid in $\vdash^K$ in this case also. Therefore, $\vdash^K$ is a determinate consequence relation that generates $\vdash\!\sim$. $\square$

Determinate epistemic states and associated inference relations will play an important role in Part Three.

7.11 Linearity and rational inference

Rational inference relations (see [KLM90, LM92]) are obtained from preferential ones by adding the Rational Monotony rule:

Rational Monotony   If $A \vdash\!\sim C$ and $A \not\vdash\!\sim \neg B$, then $A \wedge B \vdash\!\sim C$.

As for the preferential inference above, we will establish first a correspondence between rational inference relations and their associated expectation relations.

Rational inference via expectations

Under the general correspondence between inference relations and expectation relations, rational inference relations turn out to correspond to modular entrenchment and plausibility relations, and to linear dependence relations. The simplest way to establish this correspondence consists in extending the ie-mapping between inference and simple entrenchment (see Chapter 6) to the rational case.

Theorem 7.11.1. *The ie-mapping determines a bijection between rational inference relations and simple modular entrenchment relations.*

Proof. We need to check only that Rational Monotony holds for an inference relation if and only if Modularity holds for the associated simple entrenchment relation.

Let $\vdash$ be a rational inference relation. Assume that $A < B$ and $A \not< C$ for the associated simple entrenchment relation. The first condition amounts to $\neg A \vee \neg B \vdash B$, which implies $\neg A \vee \neg B \vee \neg C \vdash B$ by basic inference. The second condition amounts to $\neg A \vee \neg C \not\vdash C$, which implies $\neg A \vee \neg B \vee \neg C \not\vdash B \wedge C$, again, by basic inference. Hence by Rational Monotony $\neg B \vee \neg C \vdash B$, which is equivalent to $C < B$. Therefore, $<$ satisfies Modularity.

Assume now that $<$ is a simple modular entrenchment relation, and we have $A \vdash C$ for the associated inference relation. This condition corresponds to $\neg A < A \rightarrow C$ for entrenchment, and hence by modularity either $\neg A < A \rightarrow \neg B$, or $\neg A \vee \neg B < A \rightarrow C$. In the first case we have $A \vdash \neg B$. In the second case we have $\neg A \vee \neg B < \neg A \vee \neg B \vee C$ by Right Weakening, which amounts to $A \wedge B \vdash C$. Thus, Rational Monotony holds for $\vdash$. This completes the proof.   □

As has been established in Chapter 5, the rs-mapping determines a bijection between simple and strict modular qualitative entrenchment, while the Converse Complement determines a bijection between the latter and linear dependence orders. These mappings can now be used to establish correspondences between rational inference, on the one hand, and strict modular qualitative entrenchment and linear dependence, on the other. More exactly, the correspondence between rational inference and strict modular qualitative entrenchment is determined by the is-mapping, defined in the preceding chapter as a composition of the ie-mapping and the rs-mapping between simple and strict entrenchment. We reproduce it below for convenience in a slightly modified, but equivalent, form.

(ISE) $A \vdash B \equiv \neg A < A \rightarrow B$ or $\neg A \not< \mathbf{t}$

(SEI) $A < B \equiv \neg (A \wedge B) \vdash B$ and $\neg A \not\vdash \mathbf{f}$

The above definitions are almost equivalent to the representation of inference relations in terms of expectation orderings, given in [GM94], with the only distinction that the authors used an auxiliary classical consequence relation Cn satisfying Consistency Preservation (see below). 'Pure' correspondences between rational inference and strict entrenchment relations that are equivalent to the above definitions were given in [Geo96].

Similarly, the composition of the is-mapping and Converse Complement (called the id*-mapping in the preceding chapter) will determine a correspondence between rational inference and linear dependence orders:

(ID*) $A \hspace{0.5mm}\vert\!\sim B \equiv A \to B \not< \neg A$ or $\mathbf{t} < \neg A$

(DI*) $A < B \equiv \neg(A \wedge B) \hspace{0.5mm}\vert\!\not\sim A$ or $\neg B \hspace{0.5mm}\vert\!\sim \mathbf{f}$

Just as for preferential inference relations, the above definitions will be used below for establishing completeness of rational inference with respect to linear epistemic states.

Rational inference in epistemic states

The following result shows that any epistemic state with a modular preference relation on admissible states produces a rational inference relation.

Lemma 7.11.1. *The skeptical inference relation induced by any modular epistemic state is rational.*

Proof. We need only to check Rational Monotony. Assume that $A \hspace{0.5mm}\vert\!\sim C$ is valid in a modular epistemic state $\mathbb{E}$, while $A \hspace{0.5mm}\vert\!\sim \neg B$ is not valid in it. The latter implies that there exists a preferred state s in $]\neg A[$ that does not support $A \to \neg B$, that is, s belongs to $]\neg(A \wedge B)[$. Consequently, s will also be a preferred state in $]\neg(A \wedge B)[$, since all 'better' states will already support $\neg A$. Due to modularity, all preferred states in $]\neg(A \wedge B)[$ will be belong to the same layer as s (since they are incomparable with s). Therefore, any preferred state in $]\neg(A \wedge B)[$ will also be a preferred state in $]\neg A[$, and hence it will support $A \to C$. As a result, any preferred state in $]\neg(A \wedge B)[$ will support also $(A \wedge B) \to C$, and hence $A \wedge B \hspace{0.5mm}\vert\!\sim C$ will be valid in $\mathbb{E}$.   □

Since any linear epistemic state is already modular, we conclude, in particular, that any pure linear epistemic state will generate a rational inference. Consequently, we immediately obtain the following

Corollary 7.11.1. *Any linear consequence relation generates a rational inference relation.*

As a preparation for the completeness result, the following lemma gives an alternative description of the inference relation generated by a linear consequence relation.

Lemma 7.11.2. *If $\vdash$ is a linear consequence relation, then $A \hspace{0.5mm}\vert\!\sim_\vdash B$ holds if and only if either $\vdash \neg A$ or $A \to B \not\vdash \neg A$.*

Proof. Assume first that $A \mathrel{|\!\sim_{\vdash}} B$ and $\nvdash \neg A$. Then there is a theory of $\vdash$ consistent with A. Let u be a maximal such theory. Then $A \to B \in u$ and $\neg A \notin u$, and consequently $A \to B \nvdash \neg A$. In the other direction, if $\vdash \neg A$, then there are no theories of $\vdash$ consistent with A, and hence $A \mathrel{|\!\sim} B$ is trivially satisfied. Assume now that $A \to B \nvdash \neg A$. This means that there is a theory u containing $A \to B$ but not $\neg A$. Notice that for linear consequence relations a maximal theory consistent with A is unique, if it exists. Let v be such a theory. Clearly, $u \subseteq v$ and consequently $A \to B \in v$. Therefore $A \mathrel{|\!\sim} B$ is valid in $\vdash$. $\square$

Notice now that the above characterization of $\mathrel{|\!\sim_{\vdash}}$ corresponds exactly to the definition of rational inference in terms of linear dependence (see the condition (ID*) above). As a result, we obtain

Theorem 7.11.2. *(Completeness) An inference relation is rational if and only if it is generated by a modular epistemic state.*

Proof. If an inference relation $\mathrel{|\!\sim}$ is rational, its associated dependence order is linear and hence corresponds to some linear consequence relation $\vdash$. Then the preceding lemma shows, in effect, that the pure epistemic state determined by the theories of $\vdash$ generates precisely $\mathrel{|\!\sim}$. $\square$

Note that semi-classical consequence relations used earlier for showing completeness for general preferential inference relations are not linear even for rational inference relations and consequently are not suitable for establishing the above correspondence. Hence the need for an alternative mapping.

The proof of the above completeness theorem shows also that any rational inference relation is generated by some pure linear epistemic state. In other words, pure linear epistemic states constitute a representative class of epistemic states with respect to rational inference.

Since any pure linear epistemic state is union-closed, we immediately obtain that any rational inference relation is injective. Moreover, the injective preferential KLM model generated by a pure epistemic state in accordance with Theorem 7.9.1 can easily be shown to be modular, or *ranked*. Therefore, we obtain the following strengthening of the well-known result from [LM92]:

Theorem 7.11.3. *Any rational inference relation is generated by an injective modular possible worlds model.*

A similar, though somewhat different construction of (nice) preferential models on the basis of expectation orderings was given in [GM94].

Rational extensions of preferential inference

As has been shown in Chapter 4, any epistemic state is decomposable into a set of linear epistemic states. Consequently, any skeptical (= preferential)

inference relation is determined by a set of linear epistemic states (see Theorem 4.6.2). Since any linear epistemic state determines a rational inference relation, we obtain the following

Theorem 7.11.4. *Any preferential inference relation is an intersection of the set of all rational inference relations that extend it.*

The above result has a number of important consequences concerning the relationship between preferential and rational inference. Thus, it implies, in particular, that rational derivability is reducible to preferential derivability.

Theorem 7.11.5. *([LM92]) A conditional $A \mathrel{|\!\sim} B$ is derivable from a set of conditionals Δ with respect to the rational inference only if it is derivable from the latter with respect to the preferential inference.*

Proof. If $A \mathrel{|\!\sim} B$ is not preferentially derivable from Δ, $A \mathrel{|\!\sim} B$ does not belong to the preferential closure of Δ, $\hat{\Delta}$. The latter is a preferential inference relation, and hence by the preceding theorem $A \mathrel{|\!\sim} B$ does not belong to at least one rational inference relation containing Δ. Consequently, $A \mathrel{|\!\sim} B$ is not derivable from Δ also with respect to the rules of the rational inference.   □

The above theorem says, in effect, that the rules of rational inference do not add new derivable conditionals as compared with preferential inference. The Rational Monotony rule is non-Horn, and hence it does not allow to derive new conditionals unconditionally; it only puts constraints on 'admissible' sets of conditionals. Accordingly, rational inference is a *conservative* extension of preferential inference that does not change the set of singular (Horn) rules. Consequently, rational inference is also a conservative extension of basic inference with respect to derivability among individual conditionals:

Corollary 7.11.2. *A conditional is derivable from another one with respect to the rational inference only if it is derivable from the latter already with respect to the basic inference.*

On the rationality of Rational Monotony. The system of rational inference has received its honorable name do to the conviction of its authors that it constitutes a rational standard of nonmonotonic inference. Our representation of skeptical nonmonotonic inference in terms of epistemic states implicitly suggests, however, that this role of a (skeptical) standard should be relegated to preferential inference in general. Our main argument in favor of this suggestion is based on the claim that we need the notion of an epistemic state in its full generality, rather than just linear states, in order to represent the main ingredients of nonmonotonic reasoning and belief change. Thus, the systems of defeasible and inheritance reasoning described in Chapter 8 will be preferential, but not rational. Similarly, the representations of belief change operations given in Part Three will naturally produce non-linear epistemic states.

Nevertheless, the above results indicate that the refusal to accept Rational Monotony is very much like the refusal to accept the logical rule of Excluded Middle on the basis of the claim that our knowledge is always partial, and hence leaves some propositions undecided. Notice that any preferential inference relation can be always consistently extended to a rational inference relation. This creates a permanent basis for a suspicion (or a temptation) that our current preferential inference system could perhaps be extended further with additional, possibly valuable, default information. Worse still, unlike the logical case mentioned above, our decisions cannot be immediately refuted by pointing out that they exclude some reasonable situations; in most cases there is no immediate penalty for accepting improper new defaults, especially if they are sanctioned by Rational Monotony. A true counterexample against Rational Monotony should apparently involve *variable preferences* among defaults, when we have two equally plausible alternative extensions for a situation in which $A \hspace{1pt}\vdash\hspace{-6pt}\sim C$ is accepted, one in which we accept $A \hspace{1pt}\vdash\hspace{-6pt}\sim \neg B$ and reject $A \wedge B \hspace{1pt}\vdash\hspace{-6pt}\sim C$, and another one where we accept $A \wedge B \hspace{1pt}\vdash\hspace{-6pt}\sim C$ but reject $A \hspace{1pt}\vdash\hspace{-6pt}\sim \neg B$. We are not aware of an uncontestable example of this kind (though a formal epistemic state for this situation can be easily constructed). Accordingly, we will restrain ourselves for the time being to a more pragmatic claim that we do not need Rational Monotony for doing nonmonotonic reasoning. In other words, even if it is rational to accept Rational Monotony, we nevertheless can also rationally reason without it.

Expectation-based inference. The notion of an *expectation inference* suggested in [GM94] is very similar to that of a rational inference, the only distinction being that it was formulated with respect to a pre-given classical consequence relation, that was required to satisfy, in addition, the rule of Consistency Preservation :

(Consistency Preservation) If $A \hspace{1pt}\vdash\hspace{-6pt}\sim \mathbf{f}$, then $A \vdash \mathbf{f}$.

As can be immediately seen, these conditions on the classical consequence relation Th amounts precisely to saying that the inference relation *preserves* Th in the sense defined in the preceding chapter (see Definition 6.5.3). In addition, we have that any preferential inference relation is already strongly regular. Consequently, we can apply Corollary 6.5.2 from the preceding chapter and conclude that expectation-based inference relations of Gärdenfors and Makinson are precisely rational inference relations with respect to their underlying classical sub-relations.

Theorem 7.11.6. $\hspace{1pt}\vdash\hspace{-6pt}\sim$ *is an expectation-based inference relation with respect to a classical consequence relation* Th *if and only if it is a rational inference relation, and* Th *coincides with* $\mathrm{Th}_{\hspace{1pt}\vdash\hspace{-6pt}\sim}$.

The above result demonstrates that expectation-based and rational inference are equivalent notions (and eliminates the need for an auxiliary classical consequence relation in the latter).

8. Prolegomena to a Theory of Defeasible Entailment

8.1 Nonmonotonic meta-reasoning

A most natural kind of default assumptions we use in commonsense reasoning are conditional in nature, such as "Birds fly" or "Adults are employed". Consequently, a theory of reasoning about such default conditionals should occupy a central place in the general theory of nonmonotonic reasoning.

The question whether a proposition B is derivable from an evidence A with respect to a given default base is reducible to the question whether the corresponding conditional $A \mathrel{|\!\sim} B$ is derivable from the base. In addition, a conditional default base is capable of representing not only our default beliefs, but also 'hard' facts that are taken as known. This means that practically all questions we could have about reasoning with default conditionals are reducible to the question what conditionals could be (defeasibly) derived from a current conditional default base. Consequently, the latter problem could be seen as the main task of a theory of default conditionals (cf. [LM92]).

A first step in constructing such a theory consists in the observation that default conditionals are not reducible to corresponding classical implications. Instead, their most plausible understanding is obtained by treating them as (skeptical) nonmonotonic inference rules in the framework of our epistemic states.

The fact that preferential inference relations give a sound and complete characterization for the semantic notion of skeptical nonmonotonic inference in epistemic states suggests that such inference relations can be considered as a *logical core* of nonmonotonic reasoning. In other words, it is reasonable to require that the rules valid for preferential inference relations should be taken for granted by the latter.

The above basic requirement does not imply, however, that nonmonotonic reasoning about default conditionals is reducible to preferential derivability. Preferential inference is severely sub-classical and does not allows us, for example, to infer "Red birds fly" from "Birds fly". As a matter of fact, this is precisely the reason why such inference relations are called nonmonotonic. Clearly, there are good reasons for not accepting such a derivation as a general rule for nonmonotonic *inference*; otherwise "Birds fly" would imply also that "Birds with broken wings fly" and even "Penguins fly". Still, this should not prevent us from accepting "Red birds fly" on the basis of "Birds fly" as a *reasonable default conclusion*, namely a conclusion made in the absence of information against it. Actually, by doing this, we would just follow the general strategy of nonmonotonic reasoning that involves making reasonable default assumptions on the basis of available information.

The above considerations suggest that the logical core of nonmonotonic inference, namely preferential inference relations, should be augmented with a mechanism of making default conclusions on the basis of available (default and factual) information. Note that this setting is slightly different from a general abductive framework in which we can choose, in principle, any hypothesis that would explain the evidence. In this particular case, the choice can be restricted to conditionals that are classically derivable from a given set of conditionals. Speaking generally, we would like to keep reasoning classically about default conditionals insofar as this does not conflict with the default base and given evidence.

The above kind of reasoning will clearly be *defeasible*, or, in other words, *meta-nonmonotonic* in the sense that addition of new conditionals (or other relevant information) could block some of the default conclusions made earlier. Recall in this respect that, though preferential inference is nonmonotonic with respect to strengthening the premises of conditionals, it is nevertheless (in fact, due to this) meta-monotonic: adding new conditionals does not change the validity of derivations made earlier.

There is a semantic side in the above (still rather rough) picture of defeasible entailment. Accepted default conditionals can be seen as constraints on our epistemic states in the sense that the latter should make them skeptically valid. Still, in most cases there is a huge number of epistemic states that satisfy a given set of conditionals, so we have both an opportunity and necessity to chose among them. Moreover, our guiding principle in this choice should be the same basic principle of nonmonotonic reasoning, namely that the intended, 'preferred' epistemic state(s) should be as normal as is permitted by the current constraints. By choosing such preferred states, we also adopt some further conditionals that will not be derivable from a given set of conditionals by preferential inference.

A complete description of the above notion of defeasible entailment will not be found in this book. Still, we will make two important steps toward a solution of this problem. First, we will narrow down the search area by suggesting a powerful general constraint on the intended epistemic states satisfying a given set of default conditionals. As we will see, already this constraint will successfully cope with the majority of simple 'benchmark' examples of defeasible entailment, suggested in the literature. As a second step, we will show that some important systems of defeasible entailment, such as Geffner's conditional entailment, are subsumed by our framework. Finally, we will give a complete characterization of inheritance reasoning as another special case of our construction. It will be shown, in particular, that in order to cope with the latter, we need to generalize the notion of priority among defaults to local (context-dependent) priority relations.

8.2 Desiderata for defeasible entailment

There is a large number of different systems of defeasible entailment in the literature; practically all prominent authors that have worked in the field of nonmonotonic reasoning have suggested at least one theory of this kind. A short history of studies in this field could be briefly summarized as follows. Initial formal systems of defeasible entailment, namely Pearl's system Z [Pea90] and Lehmann's rational closure [Leh89, LM92], have turned out to be equivalent[1]. This encouraging development has followed by a realization that both theories are still insufficient for representing defeasible entailment, since they do not allow to make certain intended conclusions. Hence, they have been refined in a number of ways, giving such systems as lexicographic inference [BCD+93, Leh95], and corresponding, quite similar, modifications of Pearl's system [GMP93, TP95]. Unfortunately, these refined systems have turned out to have an opposite problem, namely, together with some desirable properties, they invariably produce some unwanted conclusions that disagree with intuition.

All the above systems have been based on an (implicit or explicit) assumption that the intended notion of defeasible entailment should form a rational inference relation, that is, it should satisfy Rational Monotony. A more general approach in the framework of preferential inference has been suggested in [Gef92]. We will discuss this approach in what follows.

A radically different, more syntactic, approach to defeasible entailment has been pursued in the framework of inheritance nets (see, e.g., [HTT90], as well as an excellent overview in [Hor94]). Inheritance reasoning deals with a quite restricted class of conditionals that do not involve, in effect, compound logical formulas. Nevertheless, in this restricted domain it has achieved a remarkably close correspondence between what is derived and what is expected intuitively. In fact, since our intuitions about defeasible entailment are quite vague and often conflicted, inheritance reasoning has emerged as a quite important test bed for adjudicating proposed theories.

Despite the diversity, most of the above systems have a lot in common, and take as a starting point a few important principles, or desiderata, for defeasible reasoning. Our next task will consist in making such desiderata precise.

Direct inference and monotonic core

Until now, we have systematically overburdened our terminology and used $A \hspace{0.1em}\vdash\hspace{-0.55em}\sim\hspace{0.1em} B$ to denote both individual conditionals and the corresponding inference

---

[1] See also Rott's non-monotonic conditional logic for belief revision in [Rot91a].

relation. This abuse of notation will no longer be appropriate in our present context. Consequently, in what follows we will denote default conditionals by $A \Rightarrow B$; we will use also small Greek letters $\alpha, \beta, \ldots$ to refer to such default conditionals. In addition, for any such $\alpha = A \Rightarrow B$, we will denote by $\vec{\alpha}$ the corresponding classical implication $A \to B$, while $\mathcal{A}_\alpha$ and $\mathcal{C}_\alpha$ will denote, respectively, its antecedent (A) and its consequent (B). Similarly, for a set of default conditionals Δ, $\vec{\Delta}$ will denote the corresponding set of classical implications, while $\mathcal{A}_\Delta$ and $\mathcal{C}_\Delta$ will denote, respectively, the set of antecedents and the set of consequents of conditionals from Δ.

As has been said, the main task of a theory of defeasible entailment consists in determining what conditionals are defeasibly derivable from a given base of default conditionals $\mathfrak{B}$. It will be assumed throughout this chapter that the base $\mathfrak{B}$ is finite.

In what follows, the set of conditionals that are defeasibly derivable from $\mathfrak{B}$ will be denoted by $\vdash^{\mathfrak{B}}$. As a starting point in our exposition, we will suggest below our first general constraint on such sets.

As has been argued earlier, defeasible entailment should respect skeptical inference in the sense that the rules of the latter should be considered as valid rules of the former. This requirement, that we will call the principle of direct inference, can be formulated as follows.

Direct Inference   *The set of conditionals that are defeasibly entailed by $\mathfrak{B}$ should form a preferential inference relation that includes $\mathfrak{B}$.*

It should be clear that the above principle only sets up the stage and does not advance us, taken by itself, to the goal of defining a defeasible entailment. Indeed, if it were the only reasonable requirement on defeasible entailment, it would be only natural to restrict our attention to the least preferential inference relation satisfying the above condition, which would immediately reduce defeasible entailment to preferential derivability. Fortunately, there are also other plausible conditions that will move us beyond preferential derivability. Moreover, the principle of direct inference suggests actually an important way of choosing the intended inference relation. Namely, since any preferential inference relation is determined by some epistemic state, we obtain an opportunity to characterize the intended set of conditionals by choosing, or constructing, an appropriate epistemic state. Our main constraint on defeasible entailment will be formulated in these latter terms.

It is important to note that the above principle is intentionally weaker than the corresponding thesis advanced in [Leh89, LM92], since it does not require the resulting inference relation to be *rational* (cf. our discussion of Rational Monotony at the end of Chapter 7). In fact, due to this generality, practically all 'rich' systems of defeasible entailment will comply with the principle of direct inference.

The monotonic core. As before, $\hat{\mathfrak{B}}$ will denote the preferential closure of $\mathfrak{B}$, that is, a least preferential inference relation containing $\mathfrak{B}$. In addition,

Th$_\mathfrak{B}$ will denote the internal logic of $\hat{\mathfrak{B}}$. As we have seen in preceding chapters, Th$_\mathfrak{B}$ embodies what is considered as known with respect to the base $\mathfrak{B}$.

Defeasible entailment is based on making additional default assumptions, or beliefs, that are reasonable to accept with respect to a given default base. Accordingly, it is reasonable to require that the set of conditionals that are defeasibly derivable from $\mathfrak{B}$ should not change what is known to the agent. This intuition can be formulated as the following constraint on defeasible entailment:

Monotonic Core $\mathrel{\mid\!\sim}^\mathfrak{B}$ *should preserve* Th$_\mathfrak{B}$.

As has been shown in Chapter 6, a regular inference relation preserves a classical consequence relation Th if and only if the latter coincides with the internal monotonic logic of the former (see Corollary 6.5.2). Consequently, the above constraint reflects the requirement that defeasible entailment should have the same internal logic as the preferential closure of $\mathfrak{B}$. In other words, the above constraint fixes the monotonic part of defeasible entailment as coinciding with Th$_\mathfrak{B}$.

Recall now that any default base $\mathfrak{B}$ can be neatly split into two mutually independent components, namely its knowledge core $\mathfrak{B}_k$ and its belief core $\mathfrak{B}_b$. As has been shown in Chapter 7, the knowledge core is sufficient for determining the internal logic Th$_\mathfrak{B}$. Moreover, the preferential derivability from $\mathfrak{B}$ is reducible to preferential derivability from its belief core $\mathfrak{B}_b$ with respect to Th$_\mathfrak{B}$. Accordingly, the above constraint suggests that defeasible entailment from $\mathfrak{B}$ is also reducible to defeasible entailment from $\mathfrak{B}_b$ that respects Th$_\mathfrak{B}$. This means, in particular, that, once the underlying monotonic logic Th$_\mathfrak{B}$ is fixed, we can safely restrict our attention to the belief core of the default base.

Default-based entailment

The overwhelming majority of approaches to defeasible entailment in the literature are based on the idea that the intended model of such an entailment should be described, ultimately, in terms of the set of material implications corresponding to a given set of default conditionals. In other words, classical implications corresponding to default conditionals should serve as defaults in the nonmonotonic reasoning sanctioned by the default base $\mathfrak{B}$. We will also adopt this idea in our study. Moreover, we will make it precise by requiring that intended epistemic states should be base-generated by $\mathfrak{B}$.

For reasons that will become clear soon, we start with a simple-minded way of realizing the above requirement, namely, we will consider first the epistemic state that is generated by a pure base $\overrightarrow{\mathfrak{B}}$. It turns out that the skeptical inference relation generated by this epistemic state produces intuitively plausible results, but is in general too weak to give the intended notion of defeasible entailment. The following simple example illustrates the situations where it goes wrong.

Example 8.2.1. Let us take a default base $\mathfrak{B} = \{P \Rightarrow B, B \Rightarrow F, P \Rightarrow \neg F\}$ corresponding to the penguins-birds triangle, and consider an epistemic state $\mathbb{E}$ that is base-generated by the set of classical conditionals $\overrightarrow{\mathfrak{B}} = \{P \rightarrow B, B \rightarrow F, P \rightarrow \neg F\}$. This epistemic state makes valid, in particular, $B \hspace{1pt}\vert\!\sim\! F$ and even $B \hspace{1pt}\vert\!\sim\! \neg P$. However, $\mathbb{E}$ contains three maximal admissible states consistent with P, namely, $\Delta_1 = \{P \rightarrow B, P \rightarrow \neg F\}$, $\Delta_2 = \{P \rightarrow B, B \rightarrow F\}$ and $\Delta_3 = \{B \rightarrow F, P \rightarrow \neg F\}$. Consequently, it validates neither $P \hspace{1pt}\vert\!\sim\! \neg F$, nor $P \hspace{1pt}\vert\!\sim\! B$.

As can be seen, the pure base-generated state in the above example violates our earlier principle of direct inference, since the associated skeptical inference relation does not include $\mathfrak{B}$. Hence, pure bases of the form $\overrightarrow{\mathfrak{B}}$ are inappropriate for capturing the notion of defeasible entailment.

There exists, however, a natural remedy to this shortcoming consisting in imposing appropriate preferences on the subsets of defaults. Thus, in the above example making Δ_1 preferred to both Δ_2 and Δ_3 will give us already an epistemic state that satisfies direct inference with respect to $\mathfrak{B}$.

The above idea can be developed further to the claim that intended epistemic states for defeasible entailment should be some epistemic states that are base-generated by $\overrightarrow{\mathfrak{B}}$ in the sense defined earlier in this book. Namely, their admissible states should be formed by subsets of $\overrightarrow{\mathfrak{B}}$, and the preference order should be monotonic on the latter.

A further refinement of this suggestion stems from the observation that the set $\overrightarrow{\mathfrak{B}}$ obliterates the distinction between default conditionals of the form $A \Rightarrow B$ and knowledge conditionals $A \wedge \neg B \Rightarrow \mathbf{f}$ (since they correspond to logically equivalent material implications). Consequently, in order to obtain an adequate representation, we need to take into account the distinction between the knowledge core of a default base, and its belief core. More precisely, since the knowledge core determines what is known with respect to the default base, it should not participate in forming the (belief) base of the corresponding epistemic state; instead, it should determine the internal logic of the latter, namely $\mathrm{Th}_{\mathfrak{B}}$. Accordingly, the relevant epistemic states should be generated by the belief core $\mathfrak{B}_b$ *with respect to* $\mathrm{Th}_{\mathfrak{B}}$. In other words, their admissible states should be subsets Γ of $\mathfrak{B}_b$ that are labelled with $\mathrm{Th}_{\mathfrak{B}}(\overrightarrow{\Gamma})$.

As has been established in Chapter 7, Δ-based inference relations are precisely preferential inference relations that are generated by sets of Δ-based epistemic states. Accordingly, the above semantic requirement can now be reformulated as a following final constraint on defeasible entailment:

Base-generation $\vert\!\sim^{\mathfrak{B}}$ *should be a $\overrightarrow{\mathfrak{B}_b}$-based preferential inference relation that includes $\mathfrak{B}_b$ and preserves $\mathrm{Th}_{\mathfrak{B}}$.*

As can be seen, the above requirement includes already the two constraints described earlier, namely direct inference and monotonic core. This constraint is satisfied by many current systems of defeasible entailment, though not by all of them. Some further properties of this constraint will be helpful in assessing its impact on the intended theory of defeasible entailment.

Recall that Δ-based inference relations were defined as inference relations that satisfy Δ^σ-reduction and Δ-monotonicity. The role of Δ-monotonicity in this setting amounts precisely to the requirement that the preference relation should be monotonic on the subsets of Δ. This additional requirement turns out to be essential for an adequate representation of defeasible entailment. Actually, the condition of Δ-monotonicity has been suggested in [TP95] as a way of correcting Pearl's system Z.

The importance of the monotonicity principle is revealed by its correspondence with the subsumption principle described below.

Let us return to the epistemic state generated by a pure base $\overrightarrow{\mathfrak{B}}$. As we have seen, such an epistemic state ignores potential preferences among sets of defaults, and hence it is in general too weak for representing defeasible entailment based on $\mathfrak{B}$. Nevertheless, this epistemic state invariably produces *correct* (albeit weak) results vis-a-vis our intuitive understanding. Accordingly, it could be required that if a conditional is already valid with respect to this epistemic state, it should also be accepted in the resulting system of defeasible entailment.

Let $\vdash$ be an inference relation, $\mathbb{E}_\Delta$ an epistemic state that is purely base-generated by some base Δ with respect to the internal logic of $\vdash$, and $\vdash_\Delta$ the inference relation generated by $\mathbb{E}_\Delta$. Then we will say that $\vdash$ satisfies Δ-*subsumption* if $\vdash_\Delta$ is included in $\vdash$.

The following result shows that in the finite case Δ-subsumption is equivalent to strong Δ-monotonicity.

Theorem 8.2.1. *If Δ is finite, then a preferential inference relation satisfies Δ-subsumption if and only if it satisfies strong Δ-monotonicity.*

Proof. Assume that $\vdash$ satisfies Δ-subsumption, but there are subsets Γ, Φ of Δ and a proposition A such that $\Gamma \subset \Phi$, $A \wedge \sigma(\Phi) \not\vdash \mathbf{f}$, and $A \wedge (\sigma(\Gamma) \vee \sigma(\Phi)) \not\vdash \sigma(\Phi)$. By subsumption we have $A \wedge (\sigma(\Gamma) \vee \sigma(\Phi)) \not\vdash_\Delta \sigma(\Phi)$, which means that there exists a subset Ψ of Δ that is maximal consistent with $A \wedge (\sigma(\Gamma) \vee \sigma(\Phi))$ with respect to $\mathrm{Th}_\vdash$ and such that $A \wedge (\sigma(\Gamma) \vee \sigma(\Phi)) \wedge \Psi$ does not imply $\sigma(\Psi)$. The first condition holds if Ψ is a maximal set such that either $\Psi \subseteq \Gamma$ and A is consistent with Γ or else $\Psi \subseteq \Phi$, and A is consistent with Φ. Since $\Gamma \subseteq \Phi$, the latter can hold only if $\Psi = \Phi$. Substituting Φ for Ψ in the second condition, we obtain that $A \wedge (\sigma(\Gamma) \vee \sigma(\Phi)) \wedge \Phi$ does not imply $\sigma(\Phi)$, which is impossible, since, if Γ is a proper subset of Φ, then $A \wedge \sigma(\Gamma) \wedge \Phi$ is inconsistent. Consequently $\vdash$ should satisfy strong Δ-monotonicity.

Let us assume now that the inference relation $\vdash$ satisfies strong Δ-monotonicity, and suppose that $A \not\vdash B$. Then there must exist a KLM model

$\mathbb{W}$ of $\hspace{0.5pt}\vdash$ and a preferred A-state s in $\mathbb{W}$ that does not support B. By Lemma 7.8.6 from Chapter 7, $l(s) \cap \Delta$ is a maximal subset of Δ consistent with A, and it does not support $A \to B$. Consequently, $A \hspace{0.5pt}\nvdash_{\Delta} B$. Therefore, subsumption is satisfied. □

It is interesting to note that if the entire set $\overrightarrow{\mathfrak{B}}$ is consistent with a proposition A, then the subsumption principle already implies direct inference with respect to default conditionals of the form $A \Rightarrow B$ from $\mathfrak{B}$. Our earlier example shows, however, that in cases where we have a conflict, subsumption is not sufficient for direct inference.

Monotonicity is naturally satisfied by preference orders determined by prioritized bases (see Chapter 3); as we will see below, a restriction to the latter will give us Geffner's theory of conditional entailment. Note, however, that monotonic preference orders on the subsets of a base are much more general than orders generated by prioritization on defaults. Thus, we will see that monotonicity will hold also for local (context-dependent) priority relations. Moreover, there exist also a number of interesting monotonic preference relations that are not reducible to prioritization. In particular, it has been shown in [BDL+98] that the system of lexicographic entailment, suggested independently in [BCD+93] and [Leh95], and some other systems are describable in terms of such monotonic preference orders. Consequently, they are also subsumed by the above general constraint.

Let us consider now how our constraints deal with common examples and problems of defeasible entailment discussed in the literature.

To begin with, the restriction to epistemic states that are base-generated by the corresponding set of classical implications allows us in most cases to augment the antecedents of default conditionals with irrelevant assumptions. For example, a default conditional "Birds fly" will defeasibly imply "Red birds fly" in all contexts that do not contain any conflicting information about redness. Speaking generally, if $A \Rightarrow B$ belongs to the default base $\mathfrak{B}$, then $A \to B$ should belong to all preferred subsets $\overrightarrow{\Gamma}$ of $\overrightarrow{\mathfrak{B}}$ that are consistent with A (by direct inference). Consequently, if all such preferred subsets are consistent also with $A \land C$, then $A \land C \hspace{0.5pt}\vdash B$ will also hold in the intended epistemic state. This will clearly hold, for example, if C is a proposition that does not contain common propositional atoms with $\overrightarrow{\mathfrak{B}}$ and A.

In addition to the above property, the subsumption principle turns out to be essential in supporting defeasible entailment across exception classes.

Example 8.2.2. (*Inheritance across exceptions*) Let us consider a default base $\mathfrak{B} = \{P \Rightarrow B, P \Rightarrow \neg F, B \Rightarrow F, B \Rightarrow W\}$ saying, for instance, that penguins are birds that do not fly, while birds fly and have wings. The pure epistemic state that is base-generated by $\overrightarrow{\mathfrak{B}}$ validates $P \hspace{0.5pt}\vdash B \to W$. Consequently, the latter conditional should belong to $\hspace{0.5pt}\vdash^{\mathfrak{B}}$. Combined with $P \hspace{0.5pt}\vdash B$ (which is sanctioned by direct inference), this gives us $P \hspace{0.5pt}\vdash W$ by And and Right Weakening.

Consequently, we obtain that penguins normally have wings, despite being abnormal birds.

The above example shows also that our general constraint turn out to be discriminative. Thus, it excludes, in effect, Pearl's system Z and related systems of defeasible entailment that do not allow inheritance across exceptional classes. On the other hand, it is still quite weak, and consequently does not allow to make any problematic conclusions that plague many systems (such as Lex-entailment) that are based on some particular ways of constructing the relevant preference order.

The above general scheme of defeasible entailment is already sufficient for demonstrating that the latter is meta-nonmonotonic in the sense described earlier. Thus, the following example shows that defeasible entailment is not cumulative: if we add to a default base even conditionals that are defeasibly entailed by the latter, we may change the set of derivable conclusions.

Example 8.2.3. Let us consider a default base $\mathfrak{B} = \{A \Rightarrow B\}$ consisting of a single conditional. This base defeasibly derives $A \hspace{1pt}\vert\hspace{-3pt}\sim B \vee C$ (by preferential derivability), though it does not derive, in general, $A \wedge \neg B \hspace{1pt}\vert\hspace{-3pt}\sim C$. Still, subsumption gives us that the latter conditional is derivable from the base $\mathfrak{B}^+ = \{A \Rightarrow B, A \Rightarrow B \vee C\}$, obtained from $\mathfrak{B}$ by adding a derivable conditional.

Speaking generally, defeasible entailment is very sensitive to the syntactic description of the source default base. Thus, even though the base $\mathfrak{B}_1 = \{A \Rightarrow B, A \Rightarrow C\}$ is 'preferentially equivalent' to the base $\mathfrak{B}_2 = \{A \Rightarrow B \wedge C\}$, they will produce quite different defeasible conclusions. The reason is that the two conditionals are considered as two independent pieces of information in the first base, but form a single default in the second base. As a result, in the second case they stand or fall together. The following familiar example illustrates this.

Example 8.2.4. Consider a base $\mathfrak{B} = \{S \Rightarrow B, S \Rightarrow T\}$ saying, for instance, that Swedes are blond and Swedes are tall. Then $\mathfrak{B}$ defeasible entails $S \wedge \neg T \hspace{1pt}\vert\hspace{-3pt}\sim B$ saying that even non-tall Swedes are normally blond (by subsumption). However, a single default conditional $S \Rightarrow B \wedge T$ does not allow us to make this conclusion.

Though the above general constraint deals successfully with many simple examples of defeasible entailment, it is still insufficient for capturing some important forms of the latter. The following example can serve as a good illustration.

Example 8.2.5. (*Double preemption*) Let us consider a default base on Figure 8.1. The story behind this picture could be as follows (cf. [GV88]): John is a computer science professor at a junior college (q), and also a never-do-well, disinherited scion of a wealthy family (q_1). Now, computer science professors at junior colleges are normally poor (δ), though they normally have a Ph.D. in computer science (β), and people who have a Ph.D. in computer

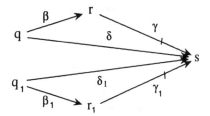

Fig. 8.1. Double preemption

science normally are not poor (γ). Also, never-do-well, disinherited scions of wealthy families are normally poor (δ_1), though scions of wealthy families normally are not poor (γ_1). Clearly, this default information should lead to an inevitable defeasible conclusion that John is poor, that is, $q \wedge q_1 \mathrel{\vrule height 1.1ex depth 0pt width 0pt}\joinrel\sim s$.

Let $\mathfrak{B}$ denote the set of all conditionals involved. Unfortunately, we can construct an epistemic state that satisfies our constraints, but still does not sanction this entailment. Namely, there is a monotonic preference order on the subsets of $\overrightarrow{\mathfrak{B}}$ that sanctions the validity of all conditionals from $\mathfrak{B}$, but still leaves the set $\{\beta, \gamma, \beta_1, \gamma_1\}$ as one of the preferred admissible states consistent with $q \wedge q_1$ (we leave here the details to the reader). As a result, the corresponding epistemic state will not validate $q \wedge q_1 \mathrel{\vrule height 1.1ex depth 0pt width 0pt}\joinrel\sim s$.

The above example shows clearly that we need some further constraints on the preference order of intended epistemic states that would sanction plausible conclusions in such cases. More precisely, it shows that such an order should be determined in terms of local preferences or priorities arising from conflicting sets of defaults. Note that the required conditional is valid for both inheritance inference and Geffner's system of conditional entailment (see below). The reason is that both these systems are based on some *systematic* ways of imposing preference relation on sets of defaults. It is precisely this feature that is missing in our construction. In fact, the whole problem of defeasible entailment is reducible on the suggested account to the solution of this latter problem, namely, to determining *principled ways of constructing a preference order on default sets*.

Unfortunately, the above problem has turned out to be far from being a non-trivial or univocal matter. In the following sections we will consider two most plausible solutions to this problem, namely conditional entailment and inheritance reasoning. These solutions can also be seen as two particular ways of implementing our general constraint on intended epistemic states.

8.3 Conditional entailment

In this section we will show that the system of conditional entailment suggested in [Gef92] can be seen as a particular realization of the above general constraint on defeasible entailment. More exactly, it amounts to restricting the class of intended epistemic states to states generated by *prioritized* default bases.

Practically all studies in defeasible entailment take as a starting point the following relation among default conditionals:

Definition 8.3.1. *Let $\mathfrak{B}$ be a default base. A conditional α will be said to dominate a set of conditionals Γ from $\mathfrak{B}$ if $\neg A_\alpha \in \mathrm{Th}_\mathfrak{B}(\overrightarrow{\Gamma}, \overrightarrow{\alpha})$.*

The above definition has actually been used in [Gef92], though the origins of this notion can be found already in Adams' book [Ada75]. A number of related notions have also been studied in the literature, such as α being exceptional with respect to Γ (in [LM92]), or Γ does not tolerate α (in [Pea90]). It constitutes also a generalization of the notion(s) of preemption used in inheritance reasoning (see below).

The importance of the above notion stems from the fact that intended epistemic states should consist of sets of the form $\overrightarrow{\Gamma}$ as their admissible states. In this context, sets of conditionals that are dominated by a given conditional are exactly the admissible states that block the application of this conditional. More precisely, if such a Γ is consistent with A_α, we have an admissible state that is consistent with A_α, though $\overrightarrow{\alpha}$ cannot be added to it without losing consistency with A_α. This is the source of potential violations of the principle of direct inference that we have discussed earlier: preferred sets of conditionals that are consistent with A_α should include $\overrightarrow{\alpha}$ (in order to make α skeptically valid), and hence they cannot contain sets that are dominated by α.

A suggestive reading of the above notion of dominance says that if α dominates Γ, it should have priority over at least some conditionals in Γ. This idea forms the basis of a theory of conditional entailment developed in [Gef92].

Let us assume that the belief core $\mathfrak{B}_b$ of a default base $\mathfrak{B}$ is ordered by some priority relation $\lhd$. This priority relation can be used to generate a preference relation $\prec_\lhd$ on the subsets of $\mathfrak{B}_b$ (by using the lexicographic rule – see Chapter 3). Then we can construct the associated prioritized base-generated epistemic state $(\mathcal{P}(\mathfrak{B}_b), l, \prec_\lhd)$ in which admissible states are subsets of $\mathfrak{B}_b$, and the labelling function assigns each such subset Γ a theory $\mathrm{Th}_\mathfrak{B}(\overrightarrow{\Gamma})$.

Note 8.3.1. The above description is a bit different from our earlier descriptions of base-generated epistemic states in that we use default conditionals themselves in forming admissible states, instead of taking their associated material implications. This allows us to make a clear distinction, for example, between conditionals $A \Rightarrow B$ and $\neg B \Rightarrow \neg A$ (that correspond to logically equivalent material implications). Recall in this respect that prioritized bases are quite sensitive to the syntactic descriptions, since they do not allow replacement of logical equivalents. Still, the above modification is not essential;

we could as well use $\overrightarrow{\mathfrak{B}}_b$ as our base, provided we take care that different default conditionals correspond to syntactically different classical implications.

Taken by itself, the restriction to prioritized bases does not give us satisfaction of direct inference. In order to comply with the latter, we need a certain constraint on priority orders. This constraint is provided by the following definition.

Definition 8.3.2. *([Gef92]) A priority order on the belief core of $\mathfrak{B}$ will be said to be* admissible *if it satisfies the following condition:*

Dominance   *If α dominates Γ, then $\alpha \lhd \beta$, for some $\beta \in \Gamma$.*

An epistemic state generated by a prioritized base $(\mathfrak{B}_b, \lhd)$ will be said to be *admissible* for the default base $\mathfrak{B}$ if $\lhd$ is an admissible priority order. The following result shows that such a priority order can always be constructed.

Lemma 8.3.1. *For any finite default base $\mathfrak{B}$ with a non-empty belief core there exists an admissible priority order.*

Proof. The proof is based on the well-known construction of a Z-ordering described, e.g., in [Pea90, LM92]. Notice first that if Γ is an arbitrary non-empty subset of $\mathfrak{B}_b$, then it contains at least one conditional that does not dominate Γ. Indeed, otherwise, for any $\alpha \in \Gamma$, we would have that $\overrightarrow{\Gamma}$ implies $\neg A_\alpha$ with respect to $\mathrm{Th}_{\mathfrak{B}}$. This would mean, however, that Γ is a clash with respect to $\mathrm{Th}_{\mathfrak{B}}$, and consequently Γ would be included into the knowledge core of $\mathfrak{B}$ (see Lemma 7.5.6 in Chapter 7).

Now we will construct a partition of $\mathfrak{B}_b$ as follows. First, we take the set Δ_0 of all conditionals from $\mathfrak{B}_b$ that are not dominated by $\mathfrak{B}_b$. Then we remove Δ_0 from the base, and if the set $\mathfrak{B}_b \setminus \Delta_0$ is not empty, we take the set Δ_1 of all conditionals from $\mathfrak{B}_b \setminus \Delta_0$ that are not dominated by the latter, and so on. Due to the above observation, on each stage we obtain a non-empty set Δ_i; moreover, this procedure will stop when, at some stage n, we will obtain a set Δ_n that is not dominated by any conditional from it.

As a result of the above procedure, we obtain a partition $(\Delta_0, \ldots, \Delta_n)$ of $\mathfrak{B}_b$ such that each $\alpha \in \Delta_i$ does not dominate $\bigcup_{j=i}^{n} \Delta_j$. This partition can also be seen as a modular priority order $\lhd_Z$ on $\mathfrak{B}_b$. Moreover, this priority order will be admissible with respect to $\mathfrak{B}$. Indeed, assume that α dominates Γ, and suppose that $\alpha \in \Delta_i$. Then, since α does not dominate $\bigcup_{j=i}^{n} \Delta_j$, it must be the case that $\Gamma \cap \Delta_m \neq \emptyset$, for some natural $m < i$. But if $\beta \in \Gamma \cap \Delta_m$, then $\alpha \lhd_Z \beta$, and hence Dominance holds for $\lhd_Z$. This completes the proof. $\square$

Note that, though the priority order described in the proof of the above lemma is modular, admissible priority orders need not be modular, in general. In fact, as was rightly noted already in [Gef92], the adherence to the above Z-ordering as the only 'right' priority order can be seen as the main source of problems with many current systems of defeasible entailment (including Pearl's system Z and the Lex-system, mentioned above).

The next result shows that admissible epistemic states in the above sense satisfy Direct Inference. The proof of this result can be found in [Gef92]. It will follow also from a more general result about local priorities that will be given later.

Theorem 8.3.1. *If $\mathbb{E}$ is an admissible epistemic state for a default base $\mathfrak{B}$, then conditionals from $\mathfrak{B}$ are skeptically valid in $\mathbb{E}$.*

The above result shows that admissible epistemic states will satisfy already all our earlier desiderata. Note, however, that in many cases there is no unique admissible priority order for a given default base (even if we take into account only minimal such orders – see below for an example). Consequently, an admissible epistemic state for a default base is not uniquely determined in general. In such cases we should take into account all such admissible states.

Definition 8.3.3. *A conditional will be said to be* conditionally entailed *by a default base $\mathfrak{B}$ if it is valid in all admissible epistemic states for $\mathfrak{B}$.*

The above definition coincides, in effect, with the semantic definition of conditional entailment, given in [Gef92][2].

The range of admissible epistemic states for a default base can be restricted in a number of ways. To begin with, since refinements of priority orders produce refinements of generated preference relations, we immediately obtain that conditional entailment is completely determined by admissible epistemic states corresponding to *minimal* admissible priority orders. On the other hand, we have shown in Chapter 4 that any prioritized base-generated state is similar to a set of epistemic states generated by linear refinements of the source priority order (see Theorem 4.2.2). Consequently, we can restrict our attention also to epistemic states corresponding to linear priority orders:

Theorem 8.3.2. *Conditional entailment is determined by the set of linear epistemic states generated by all admissible linear priority orders.*

The following example illustrates the use of admissible epistemic states in determining what is conditionally entailed by a default base.

Example 8.3.1. Let us return to the penguins-birds base

$$\mathfrak{B} = \{\alpha : P \Rightarrow B, \beta : B \Rightarrow F, \gamma : P \Rightarrow \neg F\}$$

This base has an empty knowledge core, and hence it coincides with its belief core. In addition, α and γ are dominated by $\mathfrak{B}$ (and this exhausts the domination relations in this case). As can be easily verified, there is a

---

[2] Provided we identify Geffner's notion of a background with that of the knowledge base of a default base.

unique minimal admissible priority order on $\mathfrak{B}$ that satisfies these conditions; according to it, both α and γ should be prior to β. This is also sufficient for making $\{\alpha, \gamma\}$ a unique preferred admissible state consistent with P. As a result, both $P \hspace{-0.5mm}\mid\hspace{-2mm}\sim B$ and $P \hspace{-0.5mm}\mid\hspace{-2mm}\sim \neg F$ will be valid in the associated epistemic state. In addition, the set $\mathfrak{B}$ itself is consistent with B, so $B \hspace{-0.5mm}\mid\hspace{-2mm}\sim F$ will also be valid. Thus, the resulting inference relation will satisfy Direct Inference.

Now let us modify the above default base as follows:

$$\mathfrak{B}^0 = \{\alpha_0 : P \wedge \neg B \Rightarrow \mathbf{f}, \beta : B \Rightarrow F, \gamma : P \Rightarrow \neg F\}.$$

The latter base provides an alternative description of the penguins-birds story; this time we assume that 'Penguins are birds' is a knowledge (strict) conditional that is formalized as $P \wedge \neg B \Rightarrow \mathbf{f}$. Clearly, the latter conditional will belong to the knowledge core of $\mathfrak{B}^0$, so its belief core $\mathfrak{B}^0_b$ will amount to $\{\beta, \gamma\}$. Note also that γ still dominates β in this case, *given the internal logic of* $\mathfrak{B}^0$. Consequently, there is a unique epistemic state that is generated by a prioritized base $\mathfrak{B}^0_b$; in this epistemic state $\{\gamma\}$ will be the only preferred admissible state consistent with P, and hence $P \hspace{-0.5mm}\mid\hspace{-2mm}\sim \neg F$ will be valid in the associated epistemic state. In addition, $P \wedge \neg B \hspace{-0.5mm}\mid\hspace{-2mm}\sim \mathbf{f}$ will be valid in this epistemic state due to the fact that its internal logic contains $P \to B$.

As can be seen from the above example, the knowledge core of a default base plays an essential role in determining an appropriate priority relation among defaults.

As we already noted earlier, Dominance does not determine, in general, a unique admissible priority order. The next example gives us an important illustration of this situation.

Example 8.3.2. The inheritance net on Figure 8.2 can be seen as yet another benchmark example that allows to differentiate theories of defeasible entailment.

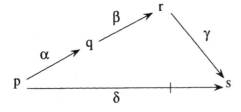

Fig. 8.2. Disjunctive priority

For this default base, both α and δ dominate the set of all defaults, and hence each should be prior to either β or γ. Since no further information is available, we obtain four minimal admissible priority orders that satisfy these constraints. So, the relevant defeasible entailments should be checked with respect to four admissible epistemic states. Note, in particular, that neither of these epistemic states validates $p \sim r$. Consequently, this conditional is not derivable, though it is sanctioned by inheritance reasoning for this net.

Conditional entailment has shown itself as a serious candidate on the role of a general theory of defeasible inference. In particular, the present author is unaware of any examples where the results produced by conditional entailment directly conflict with our intuition. The only essential reservation expressed against conditional entailment in the literature[3] is that it does not capture inheritance reasoning.

The relation between conditional entailment and inheritance reasoning has turned out to be quite complex and as much instructive for our study. To begin with, conditional entailment was designed to be a general theory of defeasible reasoning, while inheritance reasoning has intentionally imposed severe restrictions on the form of default conditionals it deals with. Still, inheritance nets are viewed as embodying much more information and priorities than it is assumed by conditional entailment, so in many cases they produce stronger results than the latter (witness the above example).

Taken by itself, this fact does not form an objection against conditional entailment, since it still leaves room for a possibility that inheritance reasoning is simply a special case of the latter (valid perhaps only for restricted domains). But unfortunately, the situation is not that simple.

Example 8.3.3. (*continued*) Let us return to the above example about disjunctive priorities in an attempt to 'improve' the relevant models in order to obtain the inference $p \sim r$ that holds for inheritance reasoning. A most natural, and practically the only, way to do this in the framework of prioritized bases consists in extending the relevant admissible priority orders by adding a new priority $\beta \lhd \gamma$. Then it is easy to verify that the required inference will be valid. Furthermore, we will see later that this additional priority is accepted also in inheritance reasoning. Unfortunately, it was noticed in [DS96] that this move creates an undesirable side effect in the framework of conditional entailment. Namely, as a by-product of this new priority, we obtain that δ should also be prior to γ for any admissible priority order. As a result, the conditional $p \wedge \neg q \wedge r \sim \neg s$ turns out to be derivable, since the set $\{\beta, \delta\}$ becomes a unique most preferred admissible state consistent with $p \wedge \neg q \wedge r$. However, the inheritance reasoning in this case gives two equally plausible extensions, namely $\{\beta, \gamma\}$ and $\{\beta, \delta\}$, and consequently neither s, nor $\neg s$ are inferred from this assumption. Note that $p \wedge \neg q \wedge r$ effectively excludes α from consideration, so the inheritance reasoning sensibly claims that in this situation (just as in Nixon's diamond) we have no grounds for preferring δ to γ.

The above example reveals a rather subtle conflict between the foundations of conditional entailment and that of inheritance reasoning. Namely, conditional entailment is based on imposing absolute, context-independent

---

[3] Except, of course, the qualms that it is too complex, that we dismiss outright as irrelevant for our discussion.

priorities among defaults, while inheritance reasoning determines such priorities in a context-dependent way, namely in presence of other defaults that provide a (preemption) link between the two. Thus, in the above example, δ will preempt γ according to inheritance reasoning only in presence of both α and β; when at least one of the latter is not accepted, no preferences can be established between γ and δ; in the latter case we have, instead, two equally plausible solutions, just as in the case of Nixon's diamond.

Though the above example still forms a somewhat hypothetical objection to conditional entailment, the next example shows already that, due to the above discrepancy, conditional entailment can sometimes produce stronger answers than that suggested by inheritance reasoning.

Example 8.3.4. Let us consider a net depicted on Figure 8.3.

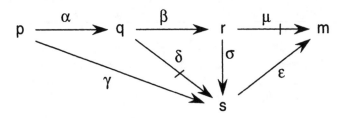

Fig. 8.3. Safety

For conditional entailment, this net determines a unique minimal admissible priority order; according to the latter, the set $\Gamma = \{\alpha, \beta, \gamma, \sigma, \mu\}$ is the only preferred set consistent with p, and hence $p \hspace{0.5mm}|\hspace{-1mm}\sim m$ is conditionally derivable. According to inheritance reasoning, however, σ is not a good basis for preferring μ over ε, and hence this net produces *two* extensions with respect to p, namely Γ and Γ_1 obtained from Γ by replacing μ with ε. As a result, neither m, nor $\neg m$ can be inferred from p according to inheritance reasoning.

In fact, the above example is intimately connected with the phenomenon of *reinstatement* discussed in [TTH91]. The following example illustrates the idea.

Example 8.3.5. Let us consider an example from [TTH91] that is depicted on Figure 8.4. In this figure the labels are self-explanatory, except that *J-ch* denotes a chicken with a jet-pack. As can be seen, this net is just a reduced net from the preceding example obtained by removing the arrows to m.

As has been argued in [TTH91], the flying ability of a chicken with a jet-pack should not be explained by its being a bird, though both *Bird* and *Fly* are defeasible consequences of *J-ch* according to the inheritance theory. Consequently, we should not accept the default conditional 'Birds fly' as a basis of further inferences in this context, despite the fact that it is 'reinstated' in

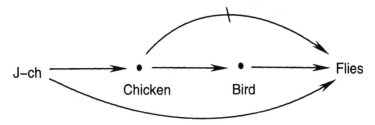

Fig. 8.4. Reinstatement

the sense that its conclusion is a consequence of *J-ch*. As can be seen, however, this is precisely what is done by conditional entailment in the previous example, since Dominance implies that μ should be invariably preferred to ε.

'Real-life' examples like the one given above are quite a shaky ground for forming a decisive objection against a particular theory of defeasible entailment. Furthermore, despite the above seemingly plausible arguments against reinstatement, the author was unable to find a clear example where it produces downright wrong conclusions. Still, one fact remains indisputable, namely that conditional entailment is incompatible with inheritance reasoning and hence cannot capture the latter.

As could be anticipated from the above discussion, in order to account for inheritance reasoning in our framework, we need to generalize the notion of priority among defaults to *conditional* priorities that depend on context. This is the subject of the next section.

8.4 Local priorities

We are going to describe now preference relations that are generated by conditional priorities among defaults.

A *conditional priority relation* on a set Δ is a three-place relation $\alpha \underset{\Gamma}{\lhd} \beta$ such that $\alpha, \beta \in \Delta$ and $\Gamma \subseteq \Delta$. It is interpreted as saying that α *is prior to β with respect to Γ*, or, in short, that α is Γ-*prior* to β. Accordingly, a conditional priority relation can also be seen as a set of ordinary priority relations $\{\underset{\Gamma}{\lhd} \mid \Gamma \subseteq \Delta\}$ on Δ that are indexed by the subsets of Δ. Moreover, we will say that the conditional priority relation is a *conditional priority order* if each $\underset{\Gamma}{\lhd}$ is a strict partial order. We will require, in addition, that such conditional priorities should be *local* in the following sense: for any default α, the set of defaults that are prior to α with respect to Γ should depend only on those elements of Γ that are themselves prior to α. This requirement is reflected in the following condition:

Locality If $\beta \underset{\Phi}{\lhd} \alpha$ and, for any γ such that $\gamma \underset{\Gamma}{\lhd} \alpha$, $\gamma \in \Gamma$ if and only if $\gamma \in \Phi$, then $\beta \underset{\Gamma}{\lhd} \alpha$.

Let us introduce some notation. For any default α, we will denote by $\downarrow_\Gamma \alpha$ the set of all defaults that are prior to α with respect to Γ. Then the following lemma gives a more convenient description of the locality condition.

Lemma 8.4.1. *A conditional priority order is local if and only if it satisfies the following condition:*

$$\text{If } \Gamma \cap \downarrow_\Gamma \alpha = \Phi \cap \downarrow_\Gamma \alpha, \text{ then } \downarrow_\Gamma \alpha = \downarrow_\Phi \alpha.$$

Proof. The implication from right to left is immediate, so we shall prove only that local conditional priority satisfies the above condition. Assume that $\Gamma \cap \downarrow_\Gamma \alpha = \Phi \cap \downarrow_\Gamma \alpha$, but $\downarrow_\Gamma \alpha \neq \downarrow_\Phi \alpha$. By locality, the latter can hold only if there exists β such that $\beta \underset{\Gamma}{\lhd} \alpha$ and $\beta \underset{\Phi}{\not\lhd} \alpha$. Locality implies now that there must exist $\gamma \underset{\Phi}{\lhd} \alpha$ such that γ belongs to the symmetric difference of Γ and Φ. But then by locality again we obtain $\gamma \underset{\Gamma}{\lhd} \alpha$, which contradicts our first assumption.   □

The following corollary can be obtained as an immediate consequence of the above result:

Corollary 8.4.1. *If a conditional priority is local, then*

$$\Gamma \cap \downarrow_\Gamma \alpha = \Phi \cap \downarrow_\Phi \alpha \text{ implies } \downarrow_\Gamma \alpha = \downarrow_\Phi \alpha.$$

Proof. From the fact that, for any Ψ, $\downarrow_\Psi \alpha = \downarrow_{\Psi \cap \downarrow_\Psi \alpha} \alpha$.   □

Though the above condition looks similar to locality, the following example shows that it is actually weaker than the latter.

Example 8.4.1. Let us consider a set of defaults $\Delta = \{\alpha, \beta\}$ with $\beta \underset{\{\beta\}}{\lhd} \alpha$ as the only conditional priority. It easy to check that this set validates the above condition, but is not local: we have $\beta \underset{\{\beta\}}{\lhd} \alpha$ and $\beta \underset{\{\alpha\}}{\not\lhd} \alpha$, though $\{\alpha\} \cap \downarrow_{\{\alpha\}} \alpha = \{\beta\} \cap \downarrow_{\{\alpha\}} \alpha = \emptyset$.

Now we will use conditional priorities to define a preference relation on sets of defaults in a way quite similar to the use of absolute priorities in Chapter 3. Namely, we will say that a set of defaults Φ is preferred to another set of defaults Γ if, for each default in $\Gamma \backslash \Phi$, there exists a Γ-prior default in $\Phi \backslash \Gamma$.

$$\Gamma \prec \Phi \equiv \Gamma \neq \Phi \ \& \ (\forall \alpha \in \Gamma \backslash \Phi)(\exists \beta \in \Phi \backslash \Gamma)(\beta \underset{\Gamma}{\lhd} \alpha)$$

The above preference relation provides an important generalization of the earlier construction based on absolute priorities, in that the very comparison among defaults with respect to priority is made now in a context-depended way, namely on the basis of sets of defaults involved. Note, however, that if conditional priority orders are actually independent of their contexts, that is, $\vartriangleleft$ coincides with $\vartriangleleft$, for any sets Γ and Φ, then the above construction Γ Φ is reducible, in effect, to the case of absolute priorities. Moreover, we are going to show now that the generalized preference relation has the same nice features as in the absolute case, namely it forms a monotonic strict partial order. But first we need to make some preparations.

We will say that a set of defaults is *well-founded* with respect to a set of conditional priority orders if it does not contain infinite descending chains with respect to some $\vartriangleleft$. Clearly, any finite set of defaults will be well-founded. Γ
The following lemma shows, in effect, that well-founded sets are smooth much in the same sense as it was defined earlier for general preference orders.

Lemma 8.4.2. *If Γ is well-founded and $\alpha \in \Gamma$, then, for any default set Φ, either $\Gamma \cap \downarrow_\Phi \alpha = \emptyset$, or there exists $\beta \in \Gamma$ such that $\beta \underset{\Phi}{\vartriangleleft} \alpha$ and $\Gamma \cap \downarrow_\Phi \beta = \emptyset$.*

Proof. If α itself is a minimal element of Γ with respect to $\underset{\Phi}{\vartriangleleft}$, then $\Gamma \cap \downarrow_\Phi \alpha = \emptyset$. Otherwise, since Γ is well-founded, it must contain a minimal element β below α (with respect to $\underset{\Phi}{\vartriangleleft}$). In this case, $\Gamma \cap \downarrow_\Phi \beta = \emptyset$. $\square$

The lemma below gives a convenient reformulation of the definition of the preference relation for well-founded sets.

Lemma 8.4.3. *If Γ and Φ are well-founded, then $\Gamma \prec \Phi$ iff $\Gamma \neq \Phi$ and $\Gamma \cap \downarrow_\Gamma \alpha \neq \Phi \cap \downarrow_\Gamma \alpha$, for any $\alpha \in \Gamma \backslash \Phi$.*

Proof. It is easy see that if $\Gamma \prec \Phi$, then the above condition is satisfied. In the other direction, assume that the above condition holds, and $\alpha \in \Gamma \backslash \Phi$. Notice that the symmetric difference $\Gamma \div \Phi$ is a well-founded set (since an infinite descending chain in $\Gamma \div \Phi$ would contain an infinite sub-chain included in either Γ or Φ). Consequently, $\Gamma \div \Phi$ should contain a minimal element β below α with respect to $\vartriangleleft$. Now, by the condition of the lemma, β cannot Γ belong to $\Gamma \setminus \Phi$. Therefore it belongs to $\Phi \setminus \Gamma$. Consequently, $\Gamma \prec \Phi$. This completes the proof. $\square$

The next lemma shows that, for any well-founded sets Γ, Φ, the preference relation $\Gamma \prec \Phi$ could as well be defined in terms of priorities with respect to their common part $\Gamma \cap \Phi$, or even with respect to Φ.

Lemma 8.4.4. *If Γ and Φ are well-founded, then $\Gamma \prec \Phi$ iff one of the following conditions is satisfied*

1. *$\Gamma \neq \Phi$ and for any $\alpha \in \Gamma \backslash \Phi$ there is $\beta \in \Phi \backslash \Gamma$ such that $\beta \underset{\Gamma \cap \Phi}{\vartriangleleft} \alpha$;*
2. *$\Gamma \neq \Phi$ and for any $\alpha \in \Gamma \backslash \Phi$ there is $\beta \in \Phi \backslash \Gamma$ such that $\beta \underset{\Phi}{\vartriangleleft} \alpha$.*

Proof. We will prove only the first equivalence, the second one being quite similar. Assume first that $\Gamma \neq \Phi$ and $\Gamma \not\prec \Phi$. By Lemma 8.4.3, this means that there exists $\alpha \in \Gamma \backslash \Phi$ such that $\Gamma \cap \downarrow_\Gamma \alpha = \Phi \cap \downarrow_\Gamma \alpha$. Clearly, $\Gamma \cap \downarrow_\Gamma \alpha = (\Gamma \cap \Phi) \cap \downarrow_\Gamma \alpha$, and hence by locality $\downarrow_\Gamma \alpha = \downarrow_{\Gamma \cap \Phi} \alpha$. Therefore $\Gamma \cap \downarrow_{\Gamma \cap \Phi} \alpha = \Phi \cap \downarrow_{\Gamma \cap \Phi} \alpha$, which implies that condition (1) above does not hold. Moving in the opposite direction, the later condition implies, in turn, $\Gamma \cap \downarrow_{\Gamma \cap \Phi} \alpha = (\Gamma \cap \Phi) \cap \downarrow_{\Gamma \cap \Phi} \alpha$, and hence $\downarrow_\Gamma \alpha = \downarrow_{\Gamma \cap \Phi} \alpha$ by locality. Therefore, $\Gamma \cap \downarrow_\Gamma \alpha = \Phi \cap \downarrow_\Gamma \alpha$, and consequently $\Gamma \not\prec \Phi$. This shows that condition (1) holds iff $\Gamma \prec \Phi$. $\square$

Finally, the following theorem shows that the above defined preference relation forms a strict partial order on well-founded sets.

Theorem 8.4.1. *The preference relation generated by a local conditional priority order is a monotonic strict partial order on well-founded sets of defaults.*

Proof. We need only to prove transitivity of the preference relation on well-founded sets. Let us assume that, for some well-founded sets, $\Gamma \prec \Psi$, $\Psi \prec \Phi$, but $\Gamma \not\prec \Phi$.

We assume first that $\Gamma \neq \Phi$. Then there must exist $\alpha \in \Gamma \backslash \Phi$ such that $\Gamma \cap \downarrow_\Gamma \alpha = \Phi \cap \downarrow_\Gamma \alpha$. We are going to show that in this case we will have also $\Gamma \cap \downarrow_\Gamma \alpha = \Psi \cap \downarrow_\Gamma \alpha$. Assume otherwise. Then there exists $\beta \in \Gamma \div \Psi$ such that $\beta \triangleleft_\Gamma \alpha$. Since Γ and Ψ are well-founded, $\Gamma \div \Psi$ is also well-founded. Consequently, the above β can be chosen in such a way that it will satisfy, in addition, $\Gamma \cap \downarrow_\Gamma \beta = \Psi \cap \downarrow_\Gamma \beta$. Moreover, since $\beta \triangleleft_\Gamma \alpha$, we have also $\Gamma \cap \downarrow_\Gamma \beta = \Phi \cap \downarrow_\Gamma \beta$. In other words, all three our sets coincide below β. By locality, this implies, in particular, $\downarrow_\Gamma \alpha = \downarrow_\Psi \alpha = \downarrow_\Phi \alpha$.

Since $\Gamma \prec \Psi$, β cannot belong to $\Gamma \backslash \Psi$. Consequently, $\beta \in \Psi \backslash \Gamma$. But $\Gamma \cap \downarrow_\Gamma \alpha = \Phi \cap \downarrow_\Gamma \alpha$, and hence $\beta \in \Psi \backslash \Phi$. We have, however, $\Psi \cap \downarrow_\Psi \beta = \Phi \cap \downarrow_\Psi \beta$, which contradicts our assumption that $\Psi \prec \Phi$. Thus, $\Gamma \cap \downarrow_\Gamma \alpha = \Psi \cap \downarrow_\Gamma \alpha$.

As a result, our three sets (and their corresponding priority orders) coincide below α. Assume now that $\alpha \in \Psi$. Since $\alpha \in \Gamma \backslash \Phi$, we have then $\alpha \in \Psi \backslash \Phi$, which contradicts $\Psi \prec \Phi$. So let us assume $\alpha \notin \Psi$. But then $\alpha \in \Gamma \backslash \Psi$, contrary to our assumption that $\Gamma \prec \Psi$.

Assume now that $\Gamma = \Phi$. Then our assumptions amount to $\Gamma \prec \Psi$ and $\Psi \prec \Gamma$. Then $\Gamma \neq \Psi$. Since $\Gamma \div \Psi$ is well-founded, let as assume that α is some $\triangleleft_\Gamma$-minimal element of $\Gamma \div \Psi$. Then $\Gamma \cap \downarrow_\Gamma \alpha = \Psi \cap \downarrow_\Gamma \alpha$. However, if $\alpha \in \Gamma \backslash \Psi$, this would contradict $\Gamma \prec \Psi$, while if $\alpha \in \Psi \backslash \Gamma$, it would contradict $\Psi \prec \Gamma$. Consequently, $\Gamma \neq \Phi$, contrary to our assumption that $\Gamma \not\prec \Phi$. This completes the proof. $\square$

The above theorem shows that non-local conditional priority orders are also capable of generating well-behaved preference relations. Such a priority order will be used below as a basis for representing inheritance reasoning in the framework of epistemic states.

8.4.1 Local dominance

As we have seen earlier, absolute priority orders on default conditionals that satisfy the condition of Dominance produce epistemic states that satisfy all our desiderata. It turns out that this result is extendable also to a certain broad class of conditional priority orders.

Given a conditional priority order $\underset{\Gamma}{\lhd}$, we will use $\uparrow_\Gamma \alpha$ to denote the set of defaults having a lower priority than α with respect to Γ, that is, $\{\beta \mid \alpha \underset{\Gamma}{\lhd} \beta\}$.

The locality condition for conditional priority states that a conditional priority of α to other defaults depends only on defaults that are themselves prior to α. This feature has turned out to be sufficient for establishing that the generated preference relation is a strict partial order. Still, this principle is naturally extendable to a stronger claim that all priority relations of a given default should be determined only by defaults prior to it. This intuition can be formalized as follows.

Definition 8.4.1. *A conditional priority order will be called* fully local *if it is local and satisfies*

U-Locality   If $\Gamma \cap \downarrow_\Gamma \alpha = \Phi \cap \downarrow_\Gamma \alpha$, then $\uparrow_\Gamma \alpha = \uparrow_\Phi \alpha$.

Taken together with locality, U-Locality says that all priority relations of α to other defaults in the context Γ are determined only by the elements of Γ that are also prior to α with respect to Γ. In fact, for local conditional priority orders, U-Locality is reducible to the following condition

$$\uparrow_\Gamma \alpha = \uparrow_{\Gamma \cap \downarrow_\Gamma \alpha} \alpha$$

Now we will say that a conditional priority order is *l-admissible* with respect to the default base $\mathfrak{B}$ if it is fully local and satisfies the following condition:

Local Dominance   If α dominates Γ, then $\alpha \underset{\Gamma}{\lhd} \beta$, for some $\beta \in \Gamma$.

As before, an epistemic state will be called l-admissible for a default base if it is generated by an l-admissible conditional priority order on its belief core. Then we have

Theorem 8.4.2. *If $\mathbb{E}$ is an l-admissible epistemic state for a default base $\mathfrak{B}$, then all conditionals from $\mathfrak{B}$ are skeptically valid in $\mathbb{E}$.*

Proof. Since the internal logic of $\mathbb{E}$ is $Th_\mathfrak{B}$, all conditionals from the knowledge core of $\mathfrak{B}$ will be (trivially) valid in $\mathbb{E}$. So, let us assume that $\alpha = A \Rightarrow B$ is a conditional belonging to $\mathfrak{B}_b$. Then we will show that, for any admissible state Γ that is consistent with A, but does not contain α, there exists an admissible state that is preferred to Γ and contains α. This will immediately give us that all preferred admissible states consistent with A will support $\vec{\alpha}$, and consequently α will be valid in $\mathbb{E}$.

Assume first that $\Gamma \cup \{\alpha\}$ is consistent with A. In this case we have that $\Gamma \prec \Gamma \cup \{\alpha\}$, and hence $\Gamma \cup \{\alpha\}$ is a required admissible state containing α. So, assume now that $\Gamma \cup \{\alpha\}$ is inconsistent with A. Then α dominates Γ, and hence $\alpha \underset{\Gamma}{\vartriangleleft} \beta$, for some $\beta \in \Gamma$. Let Γ^α denote the set of all defaults $\gamma \in \Gamma$ such that $\alpha \underset{\Gamma}{\ntriangleleft} \gamma$. Then clearly $\Gamma \prec \Gamma^\alpha \cup \alpha$ (since α is prior to the rest of defaults in Γ). Moreover, we will show that $\Gamma^\alpha \cup \alpha$ is consistent with A. Indeed, otherwise we would have that α dominates Γ^α, and hence α should be prior to some $\gamma \in \Gamma^\alpha$ with respect to Γ^α. Note, however, that $\Gamma \cap \downarrow_{\Gamma}\alpha = \Gamma^\alpha \cap \downarrow_{\Gamma}\alpha$. Consequently, by U-Locality α would be prior to γ with respect to Γ, contrary to our assumption that γ belongs to Γ^α. Thus, $\Gamma^\alpha \cup \alpha$ is consistent with A, and hence it forms a required admissible state that is preferred to Γ. This completes the proof.   □

As an immediate consequence of the above result, we obtain that l-admissible epistemic states will also satisfy all our desiderata for defeasible entailment. Note that ordinary (absolute) priority orders are trivially fully local. Consequently, the corresponding result for conditional entailment is obtainable as a special case of the above theorem.

In the next section, conditional priority orders will be shown to be adequate for representing inheritance hierarchies. Moreover, these orders will actually be fully local in the above sense. But unfortunately, they will not satisfy Local Dominance. The reason is that it might be a case that α dominates Γ, but Γ cannot support conditional priority of α to any of the defaults from Γ, because Γ is a 'bad' (preempted) default set by itself. This means that inheritance hierarchies produce conditional priority orders that satisfy some conditions more general than Local Dominance, though still sufficient for validating Direct Inference. Finding such conditions will amount also to finding a reasonably general solution to the problem of defeasible entailment.

8.5 Preferential inheritance

Inheritance hierarchies constitute a particular representation formalism for defeasible reasoning. They deal with default conditionals of a very simple kind, namely conditionals having propositional atoms as antecedents, and literals (atoms or their negations) as consequents. Chaining such conditionals into paths gives arguments supporting potential conclusions. However, different arguments may sometimes support contradictory conclusions, so we have to resolve such conflicts in order obtain consistent results. This is achieved by determining the relation of preemption between conflicting arguments (paths), according to which preempted arguments are discarded in favor of preempting ones.

Inheritance reasoning is primarily syntactic in nature, and so far it has been devoid of a semantic interpretation. Nevertheless, the results produced by such a reasoning stand remarkably close to what would be expected intuitively from defeasible reasoning in this restricted domain. This makes the task of finding a semantic representation for it an important matter; it could shed further light on the basic principles of defeasible reasoning in general.

In this section we will give a semantic representation for inheritance reasoning as yet another implementation of our general desiderata. More precisely, it will be shown that such a reasoning is representable in terms of certain conditional priority orders on default bases.

8.5.1 Inheritance argumentation frameworks

As a preparation, we will briefly describe the basic notions associated with an inheritance net: paths, arguments and credulous extensions. We will deviate, however, from the traditional exposition, and will base our description on the re-interpretation of inheritance hierarchies in terms of argumentation frameworks described in [DS96]. This representation involves, in particular, elimination of individual links and their replacement by the evidence set E. So, an *inheritance framework* will be defined as a pair $< \Delta, E >$, where E is a set (conjunction) of literals representing the evidence, while Δ is a set of default conditionals of the form $p \Rightarrow \tilde{q}$, where p is a propositional atom, while $\tilde{q}$ is a literal, that is, either q or $\neg q$. Such conditionals correspond to links of an inheritance net. Though the main construction of a credulous extension can be generalized to broader classes of conditionals (as is done, for example, in [DS96]), the original restrictions turn out to be essential for some of the key results in what follows.

In full accordance with general constraints commonly imposed on inheritance nets, we will assume below that Δ is a preferentially consistent set of conditionals, and hence its internal logic coincides with the classical entailment. This means, in particular, that Δ cannot contain two conditionals with the same antecedent and opposite consequents. In addition, we will assume also that the corresponding inheritance hierarchy is acyclic. Such inheritance hierarchies determine an absolute priority order $\trianglelefteq$ on their nodes and conditionals. This immediately distinguish inheritance reasoning from general defeasible entailment, since the relevant priority order is not determined by potential conflicts, but is based instead on the natural topology of the net. Thus, in the base $\{p \Rightarrow q, q \Rightarrow r\}$ the first conditional is considered as prior to the second one. The idea behind this priority order is that the structure of the net determines a *specificity relation* among propositions that should be respected in making plausible conclusions.

The above absolute priority order can be defined as follows. To begin with, for two propositional atoms, we define $p \lessdot q$ as holding if the default base contains a conditional of the form $p \Rightarrow \tilde{q}$. Then we define a weak priority order $\trianglelefteq$ on the set of propositional atoms as a reflexive and transitive closure of $\lessdot$.

An inheritance framework will be said to be *acyclic* if $\unlhd$ is an antisymmetric relation, that is, $p \unlhd q$ and $q \unlhd p$ hold only if p coincides with q.

It is important to observe that, due to the acyclicity condition, different conditionals from Δ cannot correspond to logically equivalent classical implications. Indeed, if $p_1 \Rightarrow \tilde{q}_1$ and $p_2 \Rightarrow \tilde{q}_2$ belong to an inheritance framework, and their corresponding material implications are logically equivalent, then one of these implications is obtainable as a contraposition of another, and this would immediately lead to violation of acyclicity. Consequently, conditionals from an acyclic inheritance framework can be safely identified with their associated classical implications. This identification will be implicitly used in what follows (e.g., in determining the logical consequences of a set of conditionals).

The above absolute priority ordering will also be extended to conditionals: $\alpha \unlhd \beta$ will denote the fact that $C_\alpha \unlhd C_\beta$. In addition, $\alpha \unlhd p$ will mean that $C_\alpha \unlhd p$. We will define also the corresponding strict priority order and equivalence as usual: $X \sim Y$ will mean $X \unlhd Y \wedge Y \unlhd X$, while $X \lhd Y$ will mean that $X \unlhd Y$ and not $Y \unlhd X$. We will occasionally use also the following 'lexicographic' order $\lhd^+$ on conditionals: $\alpha \lhd^+ \beta$ will mean that either $\alpha \lhd \beta$ or else $\alpha \sim \beta$ and $\mathcal{A}_\alpha \lhd \mathcal{A}_\beta$. Finally, we will use in what follows a derived priority order on *sets* of conditionals: $\Gamma \lhd \Phi$ will mean that, for any $\beta \in \Phi$, there exists $\alpha \in \Gamma$ such that $\alpha \lhd \beta$.

The following definition provides us with a notion of an argument in our present setting.

Definition 8.5.1. *A set of conditionals Γ is an E-argument with respect to an inheritance framework (Δ, E) if it is consistent with E, and $\Gamma, E \vDash \mathcal{A}_\Gamma$.*

If Γ is an E-argument, then its conditionals can be verified simultaneously, that is, $\Gamma \cup \mathcal{A}_\Gamma$ is a logically consistent set. Actually, the later set is consistent if and only if Γ is an E-argument, for some E (take $\mathcal{A}_\Gamma$ as an evidence). Moreover, it is easy to check that any set of conditionals that is consistent with E contains a greatest subset which is an E-argument.

Note that [DS96] (and most papers on inheritance) use a somewhat different notion of an argument which is based on treating conditionals as rules of inference rather than implications. This latter notion can be described as follows.

Let $\vdash_\Gamma$ denote a least supraclassical consequence relation containing rules $A \vdash B$, for all conditionals $A \Rightarrow B$ from Γ. Then Γ will be called a *strong E-argument* if $E \nvdash_\Gamma \mathbf{f}$ and $E \vdash_\Gamma \mathcal{A}_\Gamma$.

The following example shows that the two notions of an argument are different, in general.

Example 8.5.1. Let us consider the following set $\Gamma = \{p \Rightarrow q, q \Rightarrow p\}$ and take $p \vee q$ as an evidence E. Then Γ will be an E-argument according to our definition. Yet, it is easy to see that it is not a strong E-argument, since there is no way of proving the antecedents of the conditionals without reasoning by cases.

Still, the following result shows that for inheritance frameworks the two notions will coincide.

Lemma 8.5.1. *If E is a set of literals, then Γ is an E-argument if and only if it is a strong E-argument.*

Proof. Clearly, any strong E-argument will be an E-argument. Moving in the other direction, let us assume that Γ is an E-argument and denote by Γ^s the greatest strong E-argument contained in Γ. If $\Gamma^s = \Gamma$, then we are done. So let us assume that $\Gamma \setminus \Gamma^s \neq \emptyset$. As can be checked, this can happen only if $\Gamma^s, E \nvDash \mathcal{A}_\alpha$, for any $\alpha \in \Gamma \setminus \Gamma^s$. Moreover, since E is a set of literals, the latter holds if and only if $\mathcal{A}_\alpha$ appears neither in E, nor in Γ^s. Consequently, $E \cup \Gamma^s$ will be consistent with the set $\{\neg \mathcal{A}_\alpha \mid \alpha \in \Gamma \setminus \Gamma^s\}$. Since $\neg \mathcal{A}_\alpha$ implies $\overrightarrow{\alpha}$, we obtain that $\Gamma \cup E$ will also be consistent with this latter set, contrary to the assumption that Γ is an E-argument. $\qquad\square$

The above result establishes an equivalence between our notion of an argument and that given in [DS96]. Consequently, we can adapt the construction of extension given there to our needs. Notice in this respect that, for inheritance hierarchies, if Γ is a strong E-argument, then for any literal $\tilde{p}$, $\Gamma, E \vDash \tilde{p}$ if and only if Γ contains a ground path supporting $\tilde{p}$.

The next result describes an additional important property of arguments.

Lemma 8.5.2. *If Γ is a set of conditionals that is consistent with E, then, for any propositional atom p, $\Gamma, E \vDash p$ only if Γ contains an E-argument supporting p.*

Proof. Let Γ_E be the greatest E-argument in Γ, and suppose that $\Gamma, E \vDash p$, though $\Gamma_E, E \nvDash p$. Then $\Gamma_E, E \nvDash \mathcal{A}_\alpha$, for any $\alpha \in \Gamma \setminus \Gamma_E$. Since Γ_E is an E-argument, the latter holds if and only if $\mathcal{A}_\alpha$ does not belong to literals appearing in E or in Γ_E. Let us consider the set of propositions $a = \{\neg \mathcal{A}_\alpha \mid \alpha \in \Gamma \setminus \Gamma_E\}$. Then the above considerations imply that $\Gamma_E, E, a \vDash p$. But a contains only negated atoms, and hence $\Gamma_E, E \vDash p$ - contradiction. This concludes the proof. $\qquad\square$

The following example shows that the restriction of evidence E to conjunctions of literals is essential for the above result.

Example 8.5.2. Let us consider the following set $\Gamma = \{r \Rightarrow s, q \Rightarrow \neg s\}$, and take $(p \vee q) \wedge r$ as an evidence E. Then we obtain $\Gamma, E \vDash p$, though only $\{r \Rightarrow s\}$ constitutes an E-argument, and it does not support p.

We recall now some basic notions of the argumentation theory used in [DS96].

An *argumentation framework* is a pair (Δ, R), where Δ is a set of arguments, while R is an attack relation on Δ. A subset of arguments Γ attacks another subset Φ if $\alpha R \beta$, for some $\alpha \in \Gamma$ and $\beta \in \Phi$. A set Γ is *conflict-free* if it does not attack itself; it is *admissible* if it is conflict-free and (counter-)attacks any argument that attacks it. Finally, a set of arguments Γ is called a *stable extension* of an argumentation framework if it is conflict-free, but attacks any argument outside Γ. Clearly, any stable extension will also be admissible, though not vice versa.

The argumentation framework corresponding to an inheritance net was defined in [DS96] as a set of E-arguments with two kinds of attacks on them – conflict and preemption (specificity). Below we will give definitions of these notions that will be suitable for our purposes. The definition of conflict is quite simple.

Definition 8.5.2. *An E-argument Γ will be said to* conflict *with an E-argument Δ if their union $\Gamma \cup \Delta$ is not an argument.*

As can be seen, for inheritance hierarchies, Γ and Δ are in conflict only if they contain conditionals with opposite consequents.

The definition of a preemption attack is a bit more involved. We introduce first the following auxiliary notion.

Definition 8.5.3. *A conditional α will be said to* undermine *another conditional β with respect to a set of conditionals Γ if α and β have conflicting conclusions and $\mathcal{A}_\alpha, \Gamma \vDash \mathcal{A}_\beta$.*

The following lemma provides an important feature of this relation for inheritance frameworks.

Lemma 8.5.3. *If α undermines β wrt Γ, then there exists $\Gamma_0 \subseteq \Gamma$ such that $\gamma \lhd \mathcal{A}_\beta$, for any $\gamma \in \Gamma_0$, and α undermines β wrt Γ_0.*

Proof. Follows from the fact that $\Gamma, \mathcal{A}_\alpha \vDash \mathcal{A}_\beta$ only if Γ contains an $\mathcal{A}_\alpha$-argument supporting $\mathcal{A}_\beta$.   □

Note also that if α undermines β wrt Γ, then $\alpha \lhd^+ \beta$. Consequently, the relation of undermining is asymmetric.

The notion of undermining allows us now to define the main notion of preemption.

Definition 8.5.4. *An E-argument Γ will be said to* preempt *an E-argument Φ if there exist conditionals $\beta \in \Phi$ and $\alpha \in \Delta$ such that α undermines β wrt Γ.*

It can be shown that, for inheritance hierarchies, the above definition is equivalent to a (more complex) definition of an attack by specificity used in [DS96]. Without going into too much details, we note only that, in the above context, if Γ_0 is a minimal subset of Γ such that α undermines β wrt Γ_0, then the set $\Gamma_0 \cup \{\alpha, \beta\}$ forms a specificity relevant minimal conflict set (MCS) in the sense of [DS96]. In addition, α could undermine β wrt Γ only if $\mathcal{A}_\alpha$ is an antecedent of some conditional in Γ. But Γ is an E-argument, and consequently $\Gamma, E \vDash \mathcal{A}_\alpha$ – yet another condition required in [DS96] for an attack by specificity. As a result, the definition of the latter is reducible to the above notion of preemption.

Having at our disposal the above two kinds of an attack among arguments, namely conflict and preemption, we can define the notion of a stable extension of the associated argumentation framework. As was shown in [DS96], these stable extensions will correspond exactly to ground credulous extensions of the inheritance hierarchy. Moreover, the actual proof of this fact was based on the observation that ground credulous extensions exactly correspond to the set of all paths composed from conditionals appearing in corresponding arguments. This fact will allow us to formulate the relevant notion of an extension in terms of sets of conditionals, instead of sets of sets of conditionals (i.e., arguments), as in the original formulation.

A set of E-arguments $\mathfrak{G}$ will be called *regular*, if it coincides with a set of all E-arguments in $\bigcup \mathfrak{G}$. Then we have

Lemma 8.5.4. *Any stable extension is regular.*

Proof. Let us assume that $\mathfrak{G}$ is a stable extension with respect to E, and Γ is an E-argument included in $\bigcup \mathfrak{G}$, though it does not belong to $\mathfrak{G}$. By the definition of a stable extension, this can hold only if $\mathfrak{G}$ attacks Γ either by conflict or by preemption.

(i) Assume first that $\mathfrak{G}$ attacks Γ by conflict. Then there must exist $\alpha \in \Gamma$ that conflicts with some argument in $\mathfrak{G}$. But $\alpha \in \bigcup \mathfrak{G}$, so α belongs to some E-argument in $\mathfrak{G}$, and hence $\mathfrak{G}$ conflicts with itself - contradiction.

(ii) Assume now that $\mathfrak{G}$ attacks Γ by preemption, that is, there exists an E-argument $\Phi \in \mathfrak{G}$ such that α undermines some $\beta \in \Gamma$ wrt Φ. Again, β must belong to some argument from $\mathfrak{G}$, and hence $\mathfrak{G}$ will preempt itself, contrary to our assumptions. $\qquad\square$

Due to the above result, extensions are uniquely determined by the set of conditionals involved in its arguments. The following definition gives a direct description of such sets.

Definition 8.5.5. *A set of conditionals Γ will be called an E-extension if it is an E-argument that attacks any E-argument that is not included in Γ.*

The above rather brief description of inheritance hierarchies and their associated argumentation frameworks will be sufficient for our purposes.

8.5.2 Expanding extensions

In this section we will describe some logical properties of credulous extensions in inheritance hierarchies that will be used in what follows.

For the beginning, the result below shows that credulous extensions decide all conditionals that are 'accessible' with respect to them.

Lemma 8.5.5. *If Γ is an E-extension, and $\Gamma, E \vDash \mathcal{A}_\alpha$, for some $\alpha \in \Delta$, then either $\Gamma, E \vDash \alpha$ or $\Gamma, E \vDash \neg\alpha$.*

Proof. To begin with, if $\alpha \in \Gamma$, then clearly $\Gamma, E \vDash \alpha$. So, let us assume that $\alpha \notin \Gamma$ and that the claim holds for all β strictly below $\mathcal{A}_\alpha$ with respect to the priority order. Since $\mathcal{A}_\alpha$ is an atom, there must exist an E-argument supporting $\mathcal{A}_\alpha$ that is included in Γ. Consequently, since α does not belong to Γ, the latter must attack it. If Γ conflicts with α, then clearly $\Gamma, E \vDash \neg\alpha$. Otherwise it should preempt α. In this case there must exist a conditional β that contradicts α such that $\mathcal{A}_\beta \lhd \mathcal{A}_\alpha$ and $\Gamma, E \vDash \mathcal{A}_\beta$. According to our assumption, either $\Gamma, E \vDash \beta$ or $\Gamma, E \vDash \neg\beta$. But α and β have opposite conclusions, so we will have, respectively, that either $\Gamma, E \vDash \neg\alpha$ or $\Gamma, E \vDash \alpha$. $\square$

The following result will play an essential role in what follows.

Lemma 8.5.6. *If Γ_E is an E-extension, and Γ is a set of conditionals that is consistent with E and includes Γ_E, then for any propositional atom p, $\Gamma, E \vDash p$ only if $\Gamma_E, E \vDash p$.*

Proof. Assume that the claim is not true, and let Γ be a minimal set of conditionals that falsifies it with respect to some atom p. Then there must exist an E-argument $\Phi \subseteq \Gamma$ that supports p. Since Γ_E does not support p, Φ is not included in Γ_E. Let α be a minimal link in Φ (with respect to the priority order) that does not belong to Γ_E. Then $\Gamma, E \vDash \mathcal{A}_\alpha$, and by the preceding lemma either $\Gamma_E, E \vDash \alpha$ or $\Gamma_E, E \vDash \neg\alpha$. In the latter case we would have that Γ is not consistent with E, contrary to our assumption. So, $\Gamma_E, E \vDash \alpha$. But then $\Gamma \setminus \{\alpha\}, E \vDash p$. Due to minimality of Γ, we conclude that $\Gamma_E, E \vDash p$. Thus, the claim holds also for Γ - a contradiction. $\square$

As an immediate consequence of the above result, we obtain

Corollary 8.5.1. *If Γ_E is an E-extension, and Γ is consistent with E and includes Γ_E, then for any conditional α, $\Gamma, E \vDash \neg\alpha$ only if $\Gamma_E, E \vDash \neg\alpha$.*

Proof. Assume that $\Gamma, E \vDash \neg\alpha$. Then $\Gamma, E \vDash \mathcal{A}_\alpha$, and hence $\Gamma_E, E \vDash \mathcal{A}_\alpha$ by the previous lemma. By Lemma 8.5.5 either $\Gamma_E, E \vDash \alpha$ or $\Gamma_E, E \vDash \neg\alpha$. The first case is impossible, however, since otherwise Γ would not be consistent with E. Thus, $\Gamma_E, E \vDash \neg\alpha$. $\square$

Credulous extensions can be seen as providing particular ways of resolving inconsistencies involved in a set of inheritance claims. In other words, they make choices in all (minimal) conflicting sets of conditionals that lead to inconsistency. Hence, once the choices are made, adding 'irrelevant' conditionals does not create new contradictions. These considerations can be made more precise as follows.

Deciding sets

Let X be an arbitrary set of propositions. A subset Y of X will be called
E-*deciding*, for some proposition E, if it is consistent with E, and there
exists only one maximal subset of X that is consistent with E and includes
Y. Clearly, any maximal subset of X that is consistent with E will also be
E-deciding, but X may contain, in general, some smaller E-deciding sets. In
order to describe such sets, let us introduce the following notion:

Definition 8.5.6. *An* E-*expansion of a subset* Y *in* X *is a set*

$$[Y]_E = \{B \in X \mid Y \cup \{B\} \text{ is consistent with } E\}$$

To begin with, we have the following simple observation:

Lemma 8.5.7. *If* $[Y]_E$ *is consistent with* E, *then it is a greatest subset of*
X *that is consistent with* E *and includes* Y.

Proof. Follows from the fact that if $Y \subseteq Y_0$ and Y_0 is consistent with E, then
$Y \cup \{B\}$ is consistent with E, for any $B \in Y_0$.   □

Even if Y is consistent with E, the set $[Y]_E$ will not be, in general, jointly
consistent with E. It will be consistent, however, if Y is an E-deciding set.

Lemma 8.5.8. Y *is an* E-*deciding set in* X *iff both* Y *and* $[Y]_E$ *are consistent with* E.

Proof. If $[Y]_E$ is consistent with E, then it is easy to see that it is a unique
greatest set that is consistent with E and includes Y. In the other direction,
assume that Y is consistent with E, but $[Y]_E$ is inconsistent with E. Let b be
a minimal subset of $[Y]_E$ such that $Y \cup b$ is inconsistent with E. Since each
element of b, taken alone, can be added to Y without producing inconsistency
with E, b should contain at least two elements, say B and C. Now let us
consider the following two sets: $Y_1 = Y \cup (b \setminus \{B\})$ and $Y_2 = Y \cup (b \setminus \{C\})$.
Due to minimality of b, these sets are consistent with E. However, $Y_1 \cup Y_2$
is inconsistent with E, so these sets cannot belong to the same maximal set
consistent with E. Consequently, Y is included in at least two maximal sets
consistent with E, so it is not E-deciding. This completes the proof.   □

Returning to our discussion, the following result shows that E-extensions
are E-deciding sets with respect to the default base Δ.

Lemma 8.5.9. *Any* E-*extension is an* E-*deciding subset of* Δ.

Proof. Assume that the claim does not hold for an E-extension Γ, and let
Γ_0 be some minimal set of conditionals from $[\Gamma]_E$ that includes Γ and is
inconsistent with E. Let us take an arbitrary conditional α from $\Gamma_0 \setminus \Gamma$.
Then $\Gamma \setminus \{\alpha\}$ will already be consistent with E and, taken together with
E, will imply $\neg\alpha$. Therefore $\Gamma, E \models \neg\alpha$, contrary to the assumption that α
belongs to $[\Gamma]_E$.   □

The above result shows that if Γ is an E-extension, it generates a unique maximal subset of Δ that is consistent with E, namely its expansion. In other words, we have a one-to-one correspondence between E-extensions and certain maximal sets of conditionals that are consistent with E. This correspondence will allow us to raise inheritance reasoning to the level of defeasible entailment.

Internal extensions

In this section we will relativize the construction of extensions to particular sets of arguments.

Definition 8.5.7. *Let Γ be a set of conditionals. A subset Γ_0 of Γ will be called E-admissible in Γ if it is an E-argument that does not attack itself, but attacks any E-argument $\Phi \subseteq \Gamma$ such that Φ attacks Γ_0.*

The above definition says, in effect, that Γ_0 is an admissible set in the restricted argumentation framework consisting of E-arguments in Γ.

The following result shows that any set of conditionals consistent with the evidence contains a unique maximal admissible set.

Lemma 8.5.10. *If Γ is consistent with E, then it has a greatest E-admissible subset.*

Proof. It is sufficient to show that if Γ_1 and Γ_2 are admissible in Γ, then $\Gamma_1 \cup \Gamma_2$ is also admissible. To begin with, notice that since Γ is consistent with E, E-arguments in Γ cannot conflict with respect to consistency. Accordingly, the only attack possible in this case is preemption.

If Φ is an E-argument in Γ that preempts $\Gamma_1 \cup \Gamma_2$, then it should preempt either Γ_1 or Γ_2. Consequently, either Γ_1 or Γ_2 preempts Φ, and in either case $\Gamma_1 \cup \Gamma_2$ preempts Φ, as required.

Assume now that $\Gamma_1 \cup \Gamma_2$ preempts itself. Then $\Gamma_1 \cup \Gamma_2$ should preempt either Γ_1 or Γ_2, and hence Γ_1 or Γ_2 preempts $\Gamma_1 \cup \Gamma_2$. Consequently, either Γ_1 preempts Γ_2 or Γ_2 preempts Γ_1, and hence Γ_1 and Γ_2 preempt each other.

Let Φ_2 be a minimal E-argument in Γ_2 in the priority ordering $\lhd$ that is preempted by Γ_1. Then Γ_1 should contain an E-argument Φ_1 that preempts Φ_2 and such that $\Phi_1 \lhd \Phi_2$. Then Γ_2 should preempt Φ_1, and hence there exists an E-argument Ψ_2 in Γ_2 such that Ψ_2 preempts Φ_1 and $\Psi_2 \lhd \Phi_1$. But Γ_1 should preempt Ψ_2, contrary to our assumption about minimality of Φ_2. Hence $\Gamma_1 \cup \Gamma_2$ is conflict-free, and therefore it is E-admissible in Γ. $\square$

So, any set of conditionals Γ consistent with the evidence contains a greatest admissible set. Moreover, the following result shows that this set is actually an E-extension of the argumentation framework restricted to E-arguments from Γ.

Theorem 8.5.1. *Let Γ be a set of conditionals consistent with E, and Γ_E its greatest admissible subset. Then Γ_E is a stable extension in the set of E-arguments included in Γ.*

Proof. We need to show only that if Φ is an E-argument in Γ that is not included in Γ_E, then Γ_E preempts Φ. Assume otherwise, and let us choose an order-minimal such Φ. We are going to show that $\Gamma_E \cup \Phi$ is an admissible set in Γ.

Assume that Ψ is an E-argument in Γ that preempts $\Gamma_E \cup \Phi$. Then Ψ preempts either Γ_E or Φ. In the first case Γ_E preempts Ψ. In the second case there exists $\Psi_0 \subseteq \Psi$ that preempts Φ and such that $\Psi_0 \lhd \Phi$. Since Γ_E does not preempt Φ, Ψ_0 is not included in Γ_E. Our assumption about order-minimality of Φ implies then that Γ_E should preempt Ψ_0, and hence it preempts Φ.

Assume now that $\Gamma_E \cup \Phi$ preempts itself. If $\Gamma_E \cup \Phi$ preempts Γ_E, then the latter should preempt $\Gamma_E \cup \Phi$, which is impossible, since Γ_E preempts neither itself nor Φ. So, let us assume that $\Gamma_E \cup \Phi$ preempts Φ. In this case there must exist Ψ in $\Gamma_E \cup \Phi$ that preempts Φ and $\Psi \lhd \Phi$. Notice that Ψ cannot be included into Γ_E, so by our assumption about minimality of Φ, we have that Γ_E should preempt Ψ. Consequently, Γ_E preempts $\Gamma_E \cup \Phi$, which is impossible, since Γ_E preempts neither itself nor Φ. So, $\Gamma_E \cup \Phi$ is conflict-free.

Thus, $\Gamma_E \cup \Phi$ is an admissible set in Γ. But Γ_E is a maximal such set, so $\Phi \subseteq \Gamma_E$, contrary to our assumption. This completes the proof. $\qquad\square$

It should be clear that internal extensions as defined above are not, in general, extensions for the whole set of conditionals. It will be such, however, under certain additional conditions stated below.

Theorem 8.5.2. *If Γ is a maximal set of conditionals that is consistent with E, and Γ_E is its greatest admissible subset, then Γ_E is an E-extension if and only if, for any $\alpha \notin \Gamma$, $\Gamma_E, E \vDash \neg\alpha$.*

Proof. The direction from left to right follows from Corollary 8.5.1. For the opposite direction, it is sufficient to show that if the above condition is satisfied, then Γ_E attacks any E-argument Φ that is not included in Γ_E. Indeed, let α be a conditional in Φ that does not belong to Γ. Then $\Gamma_E, E \vDash \neg\alpha$, and hence Γ_E attacks Φ by consistency. $\qquad\square$

As a consequence of the above result, we will obtain that any set Γ consistent with E either does not include E-extensions at all, or else its greatest admissible set is (a unique) E-extension contained in it.

Corollary 8.5.2. *If Γ is consistent with E, then Γ contains an E-extension iff the latter coincides with the greatest admissible set of Γ.*

Proof. Let us assume that $\Gamma_0 \subseteq \Gamma$ is an E-extension. Then Γ_0 is clearly an admissible set in Γ, and hence it is included into its greatest admissible set Γ_E. Notice now that Γ_0 cannot attack arguments from Γ_E, and hence it should coincide with Γ_E. $\qquad\square$

Recall that any E-extension is expandable to a unique maximal set of conditionals that is consistent with E. The above results show also that there is a uniform way of discerning E-extensions from (appropriate) maximal consistent sets.

Quasi-extensions

All the notions described earlier have been defined as relative to a given evidence E. As a final step in our development, we will describe now an alternative notion of an extension that will already be independent of evidences.

Definition 8.5.8. *A set of conditionals Γ will be said to* preempt *a conditional α with respect to* another set Φ *if $\Gamma, \alpha \subseteq \Phi$, and there exists $\beta \notin \Phi$ such that β undermines α with respect to Γ.*

As can be seen, the above notion of preemption is already independent of the evidence. The following definition gives a notion of extension that is based on this notion of attack.

Definition 8.5.9. *A* quasi-extension *of a set of conditionals Φ is a subset of Φ that does not preempt itself wrt Φ, but preempts any conditional from $\Phi \setminus \Gamma$.*

Theorem 8.5.3. *Any set of conditionals in an inheritance framework contains a unique quasi-extension.*

Proof. To begin with, we will show that if Γ_1 and Γ_2 are admissible subsets with respect to a set of conditionals Φ, then $\Gamma_1 \cup \Gamma_2$ will also be admissible.

Assume first that $\Gamma_1 \cup \Gamma_2$ is not conflict-free. Due to locality of the above attack relation, this will hold only if $\Gamma_1 \cup \Gamma_2$ preempts either Γ_1 or Γ_2. We will consider only the first case, the second being quite similar. So, assume that $\Gamma_1 \cup \Gamma_2$ preempts Γ_1. Since Γ_1 is admissible, it should preempt, in turn, $\Gamma_1 \cup \Gamma_2$, and hence it should preempt Γ_2. Let β be a priority-minimal conditional in Γ_2 that is preempted by Γ_1. Then there must exist an argument $\pi \subseteq \Gamma_1$ that is strictly prior to β that preempts β. In this case Γ_2 should preempt π, and hence there exists $\rho \subseteq \Gamma_2$ strictly below β that attacks π. But Γ_1 is admissible, so it should preempt ρ, contrary to our assumption about minimality of β.

Assume now that some argument $\pi \subseteq \Phi$ preempts $\Gamma_1 \cup \Gamma_2$. Then it must preempt either Γ_1 or Γ_2. Consequently, either Γ_1 or Γ_2 should preempt π, and therefore $\Gamma_1 \cup \Gamma_2$ preempts π in both cases. Thus, $\Gamma_1 \cup \Gamma_2$ is an admissible set.

Since the union of any two admissible sets is admissible, there must exist a greatest admissible set in Φ. Let us denote it by Φ_0. We will show that Φ_0 is a quasi-extension.

Assume that Φ_0 is not a quasi-extension, and let α be a minimal conditional in $\Phi \setminus \Phi_0$ that is not attacked by Φ_0. Then we will show that $\Phi_0 \cup \{\alpha\}$ is admissible.

To begin with, suppose that some argument π preempts $\Phi_0 \cup \{\alpha\}$. Consider first the case when π preempts Φ_0. Since Φ_0 is admissible, it should preempt, in turn, π, and therefore $\Phi_0 \cup \{\alpha\}$ also preempts π, as required. Assume now that π preempts α. Then there must exist $\rho \subseteq \pi$ strictly below α that preempts α. Since Φ_0 does not preempt α, we infer that $\rho \not\subseteq \Phi_0$. Consequently, due to minimality of α, we conclude that Φ_0 preempts ρ, and therefore $\Phi_0 \cup \{\alpha\}$ preempts π also in this case.

Suppose now that $\Phi_0 \cup \{\alpha\}$ preempts itself. Assume first that $\Phi_0 \cup \{\alpha\}$ preempts Φ_0. In this case Φ_0 should preempt $\Phi_0 \cup \{\alpha\}$, and hence it would preempt α, contrary to our assumption. So, assume that $\Phi_0 \cup \{\alpha\}$ preempts α. But the latter is possible only if Φ_0 preempts α - contradiction.

Thus, we have shown that Φ_0 is a quasi-extension. Moreover, since any extension is also a maximal admissible set, it follows that Φ_0 is the only quasi-extension in Φ. This concludes the proof. $\square$

In what follows, we will denote by $S(\Gamma)$ the quasi-extension of Γ. In view of the above theorem, this notion is correctly defined.

Though quasi-extensions do not coincide, in general, with E-extensions, the following result shows that any credulous extension is included in the quasi-extension of its expansion.

Theorem 8.5.4. *If Γ is an E-extension, then $\Gamma \subseteq S([\Gamma]_E)$.*

Proof. It is sufficient to show that Γ is admissible in $[\Gamma]_E$. Clearly, Γ cannot preempt itself in $[\Gamma]_E$. Assume now that some $\pi \subseteq [\Gamma]_E$ preempts Γ and $\beta \notin [\Gamma]_E$ is a relevant conflicting link. Then π is not included in Γ. In addition, due to maximality of $[\Gamma]_E$, $E, [\Gamma]_E \vDash \neg\beta$, and hence $\Gamma, E \vDash \neg\beta$ by Corollary 8.5.1. Therefore there exists an E-argument ρ in Γ that supports $\mathcal{A}_\beta$. Consequently, $\pi \cup \rho$ contains an E-argument that preempts Γ, and hence Γ should attack $\pi \cup \rho$, which is possible only if it preempts π. Therefore, Γ is admissible in $[\Gamma]_E$, and hence is included in its quasi-extension. $\square$

Note that, in general, $S([\Gamma]_E)$ may contain many other conditionals beside Γ that are irrelevant (inaccessible) with respect to it.

As a final result in this section, we will prove a technical result showing that quasi-extensions can be coherently restricted to sets of conditionals that are prior to a given conditional. This result will be used in the next section.

As before, for any conditional α, we will denote by $\downarrow\alpha$ the set of conditionals that are prior to α with respect to the absolute priority order determined by the inheritance net.

Lemma 8.5.11. *For any Γ and α, $S(\Gamma \cap \downarrow\alpha) = S(\Gamma) \cap \downarrow\alpha$.*

Proof. For $S(\Gamma \cap \downarrow\alpha) \subseteq S(\Gamma) \cap \downarrow\alpha$, it is sufficient to show that $S(\Gamma \cap \downarrow\alpha)$ is admissible in Γ. Clearly, $S(\Gamma \cap \downarrow\alpha)$ is conflict-free also with respect to Γ. In addition, if $\Phi \subseteq \Gamma$ preempts $S(\Gamma \cap \downarrow\alpha)$ wrt Γ, then $\Phi \cap \downarrow\alpha$ will also preempt $S(\Gamma \cap \downarrow\alpha)$ wrt $\Gamma \cap \downarrow\alpha$ by the definition of preemption, and hence $S(\Gamma \cap \downarrow\alpha)$ will preempt Φ via some $\gamma \notin \Gamma \cap \downarrow\alpha$. Clearly, γ is prior to α, and hence $\gamma \notin \Gamma$. Consequently, $S(\Gamma \cap \downarrow\alpha)$ will preempt Φ wrt Γ, and therefore $S(\Gamma \cap \downarrow\alpha)$ is admissible in Γ.

In order to show the reverse inclusion, it is sufficient to demonstrate that $S(\Gamma) \cap \downarrow\alpha$ is admissible in $\Gamma \cap \downarrow\alpha)$. Assume that some $\Phi \subseteq \Gamma \cap \downarrow\alpha)$ preempts $S(\Gamma) \cap \downarrow\alpha$ wrt $\Gamma \cap \downarrow\alpha$. Then Φ will also preempt $S(\Gamma)$ wrt Γ, and hence $S(\Gamma)$ will preempt Φ wrt Γ. But since Φ is included in $\downarrow\alpha)$, we immediately obtain that already $S(\Gamma) \cap \downarrow\alpha$ will preempt Φ wrt $\Gamma \cap \downarrow\alpha)$. Hence, $S(\Gamma) \cap \downarrow\alpha$ is admissible in $\Gamma \cap \downarrow\alpha)$. This concludes the proof. $\square$

8.5.3 The representation

Now we have all the necessary components for representing inheritance reasoning in terms of epistemic states that are base-generated by the corresponding set of conditionals.

Let us define first the following auxiliary relation on conditionals:

$$\alpha \hookrightarrow_\Gamma \beta \ \equiv \ \alpha \neq \beta \ \& \ \alpha \sim \beta \ \& \ \mathcal{A}_\alpha, S(\Gamma) \vDash \mathcal{A}_\beta$$

The above relation holds when α and β has the same or opposite conclusions, and the quasi-extension of Γ contains a path from $\mathcal{A}_\alpha$ to $\mathcal{A}_\beta$. Informally speaking, the latter condition means that Γ contains a 'safe' support (path) for preferring α to β with respect to specificity.

Using the above notion, we define now the following conditional priority relation on Δ:

$$\alpha \underset{\Gamma}{\lessdot} \beta \ \equiv \ \alpha \lessdot \beta \ \text{or} \ \alpha \hookrightarrow_\Gamma \beta$$

As we will show, the above relation will be adequate for representing inheritance reasoning. But first, the next result shows that this is indeed a conditional priority in our sense.

Lemma 8.5.12. $\underset{\Gamma}{\lessdot}$ *is a local conditional priority order on* Δ.

Proof. Since $\alpha \underset{\Gamma}{\lessdot} \beta$ will hold only if $\alpha \lessdot^+ \beta$, this relation is clearly asymmetric. We will show that it is also transitive.

Assume that $\alpha \underset{\Gamma}{\lessdot} \beta$ and $\beta \underset{\Gamma}{\lessdot} \gamma$. If either $\alpha \lessdot \beta$, or $\beta \lessdot \gamma$, then clearly $\alpha \lessdot \gamma$. But if $\alpha \hookrightarrow_\Gamma \beta$ and $\beta \hookrightarrow_\Gamma \gamma$ then $\alpha \hookrightarrow_\Gamma \gamma$ by transitivity of classical entailment and acyclicity of the net. Hence $\underset{\Gamma}{\lessdot}$ is transitive.

Finally we show locality. Assume that $\Gamma \cap \downarrow_\Gamma \alpha = \Phi \cap \downarrow_\Gamma \alpha$. Then clearly $\Gamma \cap \downarrow\alpha = \Phi \cap \downarrow\alpha$. Consequently $S(\Gamma) \cap \downarrow\alpha = S(\Phi) \cap \downarrow\alpha$ by Lemma 8.5.11.

Therefore, for any β, $\beta \hookrightarrow_{\Gamma} \alpha$ is equivalent to $\beta \hookrightarrow_{\Phi} \alpha$, which is sufficient for showing that $\downarrow_{\Gamma}\alpha = \downarrow_{\Phi}\alpha$. Thus, $\underset{\Gamma}{\lhd}$ is a local conditional priority order. $\quad\square$

As has been established earlier, a local conditional priority order determines a monotonic preference order on sets of conditionals via the following definition:

$$\Gamma \prec \Phi \equiv \Gamma \neq \Delta \,\&\, (\forall \beta \in \Gamma \setminus \Phi)(\exists \alpha \in \Phi \setminus \Gamma)(\alpha \underset{\Gamma}{\lhd} \beta)$$

This preference order will be called an *inheritance preference relation* determined by an inheritance framework. The following example shows that this order already agrees with the results produced by inheritance reasoning.

Example 8.5.3. Let us return to the net depicted on Figure 8.3. In addition to $\Gamma = \{\alpha, \beta, \gamma, \sigma, \mu\}$, the inheritance preference order admits $\Gamma_1 = \{\alpha, \beta, \gamma, \sigma, \varepsilon\}$ as another preferred set with respect to p. This holds despite the fact that ε is undermined by a conflicting conditional μ. However, the basis of preemption, namely σ, is not safe, since it does not belong to the relevant quasi-extension. Consequently, it cannot be used for preempting ε. As a result, this net produces *two* preferred sets with respect to p, and consequently neither m, nor $\neg m$ can be derived from p.

Notice, however, that if we add δ to Γ, then σ will become safe, and hence this set can be 'improved' by replacing ε with μ. This reflects the fact that the set of all conditionals, except ε, is the only preferred set with respect to r, so $r \sim m$ holds.

As we are going to show, preferred admissible states with respect to the inheritance preference relation are precisely expansions of extensions. First, we will prove the following

Theorem 8.5.5. *If Γ is an E-extension, then $[\Gamma]_E$ is a preferred set consistent with E.*

Proof. Clearly, $[\Gamma]_E$ is consistent with E. Assume now that $[\Gamma]_E \prec \Delta$. If $[\Gamma]_E$ is a proper subset of Δ, then Δ will be inconsistent with E due to maximality of $[\Gamma]_E$. So let us assume that there exists some $\beta_0 \in [\Gamma]_E \setminus \Delta$. Then there must exist some $\alpha \in \Delta \setminus [\Gamma]_E$ that is prior to β_0 wrt $[\Gamma]_E$. Let us take a $\lhd$-minimal such α. Then $[\Gamma]_E$ will coincide with Δ strictly below α. We will show now that all conditionals from $S([\Gamma]_E)$ weakly below α belong to Δ. Indeed, assume that there exists $\gamma \in S([\Gamma]_E) \setminus \Delta$ is such that $\gamma \trianglelefteq \alpha$. Since γ belongs to $[\Gamma]_E \setminus \Delta$, there must exist $\beta \in \Delta \setminus [\Gamma]_E$ such that $\beta \underset{[\Gamma]_E}{\lhd} \gamma$. But this is impossible, since, if C_β coincides with C_γ, then β is consistent with $S([\Gamma]_E)$, and hence it should belong to $[\Gamma]_E$, while if γ and β have opposite conclusions, then $S([\Gamma]_E)$ would preempt itself.

Since $\alpha \notin [\Gamma]_E$, we have $[\Gamma]_E, E \vDash \neg\alpha$, and consequently $\Gamma, E \vDash \neg\alpha$ by Corollary 8.5.1. In addition, by Theorem 8.5.4 Γ is included into $S([\Gamma]_E)$. Consequently, all elements of Γ that are weakly below α are included in Δ.

Moreover, since Γ is an E-argument, we have that the subset of Γ weakly below α is sufficient for supporting $\neg\alpha$. As a result, the set of conditionals from Δ that are weakly below α clearly contain α, but support $\neg\alpha$ with respect to E. Consequently, Δ is inconsistent with E. This shows that $[\Gamma]_E$ is a preferred set of conditionals that is consistent with E. $\square$

In order to show that any preferred set consistent with the evidence is an expansion of some extension, we need to make some preparations.

For any set of conditionals Γ that is consistent with E, we will denote below by Γ_a the greatest E-argument included in Γ and by Γ_e the greatest E-admissible set in Γ. Clearly, $\Gamma_e \subseteq \Gamma_a$.

Lemma 8.5.13. *If Γ is a preferred admissible set consistent with E, then, for any literal $\tilde{p}$, $\Gamma_a, E \vDash \tilde{p}$ only if $\Gamma_e, E \vDash \tilde{p}$.*

Proof. Due to monotonicity, Γ is a maximal set of conditionals consistent with E.

Assume that the claim does not hold, and let p be an order-minimal atom that violates the above condition. We will show first that all conditionals in Γ_e strictly below p are included in $S(\Gamma)$.

Assume that β is an order-minimal conditional strictly below p that belongs to $\Gamma_e \setminus S(\Gamma)$. Then there exists $\gamma \notin \Gamma$ and some $\mathcal{A}_\gamma$-argument Φ included in $S(\Gamma)$ such that γ undermines β. Since γ does not belong to Γ, we have $\Gamma, E \vDash \neg\gamma$, and hence $\Gamma, E \vDash \mathcal{A}_\gamma$. But $\mathcal{A}_\gamma$ is an atom, and therefore $\Gamma_a, E \vDash \mathcal{A}_\gamma$. Moreover, $\mathcal{A}_\gamma$ is prior to p, and hence the condition of the lemma holds for it. Therefore $\Gamma_e, E \vDash \mathcal{A}_\gamma$, and hence Γ_e contains an E-argument Φ_0 below $\mathcal{A}_\gamma$ such that $\Phi_0, E \vDash \mathcal{A}_\gamma$. Consequently, $\Phi_0 \cup \Phi$ is an E-argument in Γ. This argument is not included in Γ_e, since it preempts β. Consequently, Γ_e should preempt $\Phi_0 \cup \Phi$, and hence Γ_e must contain an argument Ψ strictly below β that preempts $\Phi_0 \cup \Phi$. Due to order-minimality of β, however, Ψ, Φ and Φ_0 all belong to $S(\Gamma)$, which is impossible, since otherwise $S(\Gamma)$ would attack itself. Therefore all conditionals in Γ_e strictly below p are included in $S(\Gamma)$.

Let $\{\Phi_n\}$ be the set of all minimal E-arguments in Γ that support $\tilde{p}$, that is, $\Phi_n, E \vDash \tilde{p}$. Due to minimality, any Φ_n contains a unique conditional α_n having $\tilde{p}$ as its consequent. Since Γ_e does not support $\tilde{p}$, $\alpha_n \notin \Gamma_e$. On the other hand, Φ_n is an E-argument supporting $\mathcal{A}_{\alpha_n}$, so $\Gamma_a, E \vDash \mathcal{A}_{\alpha_n}$. Due to the order-minimality of p, we can conclude $\Gamma_e, E \vDash \mathcal{A}_{\alpha_n}$, and hence $\Gamma_e \cup \{\alpha_n\}$ is an E-argument. Consequently, Γ_e should attack it, which is possible only if there exists β_n such that β_n undermines α_n wrt Γ_e. Notice that β_n has $\neg\tilde{p}$ as its conclusion, and hence it does not belong to Γ. Moreover, since we have shown that all conditionals from Γ_e strictly below p are included in $S(\Gamma)$, we conclude that $\beta_n \hookrightarrow_\Gamma \alpha_n$. Now, for any Φ_n, we will choose one particular such β_n. Also, in the case when $\neg\tilde{p} = p$, we will denote by Γ_p the set of all conditionals from Γ that have p as its antecedent.

Let Ψ denote the set of conditionals obtained from Γ by adding all such β_n and removing all α_n, as well as all conditionals from Γ_p, if $\neg\tilde{p}$ is positive. It is easy to see that Ψ is preferred to Γ; indeed, for any removed conditional there exists some added conditional which is either strictly below it or preempts it. Since Γ is a preferred set consistent with E, Ψ should already be inconsistent with E. Let Γ^- denote the set $\Gamma \backslash (\{\alpha_n\} \cup \Gamma_p)$. Then $\{\beta_n\} \cup \Gamma^-$ is inconsistent with E. But each β_n has $\neg\tilde{p}$ as its conclusion, and hence $\neg\tilde{p}, \Gamma^-, E \vDash$, or, in other words, $\Gamma^-, E \vDash \tilde{p}$. But the latter is impossible, since conditionals from Γ^- do not contain p neither in its premises, nor in its conclusions. This completes the proof. $\qquad\square$

The above result will allow us to prove the following

Theorem 8.5.6. *If Γ is a preferred admissible set consistent with E, then its greatest E-admissible subset Γ_e is an E-extension.*

Proof. Due to Theorem 8.5.2, it is sufficient to show that, for any $\alpha \notin \Gamma$, $\Gamma_e, E \vDash \neg\alpha$. Since Γ is a maximal set consistent with E, the first condition implies $\Gamma, E \vDash \neg\alpha$. We will consider now two cases.

(i) If C_α is a negative literal, then $\neg\alpha$ is a set of positive literals, so $\Gamma_a, E \vDash \alpha$, and hence the required result follows immediately from the previous lemma.

(ii) Assume that C_α is a positive literal, say p. Let Γ_p denote the set of all conditionals in Γ having p as their antecedents. Consider a set of conditionals Φ obtained from Γ by adding α and removing Γ_p. Since Φ is clearly preferred to Γ, it is already inconsistent with E. Consequently, $\Gamma \backslash \Gamma_p, E \vDash \neg\alpha$. But $\Gamma \backslash \Gamma_p$ cannot contain 'backward arguments' supporting $\neg p$, so there must exist an E-argument in Γ supporting $\neg\alpha$, that is, $\Gamma_a, E \vDash \neg\alpha$. As before, the required result follows now from the preceding lemma. $\qquad\square$

Combining the above theorem with the results obtained earlier, we reach

Representation Theorem 8.1. *If $\prec$ is an inheritance preference relation on $\mathcal{P}(\Delta)$, then Γ is a preferred admissible state consistent with E iff Γ is an E-expansion of some E-extension.*

The above result gives a precise content to our claim that inheritance reasoning constitutes a particular form of defeasible entailment in the sense defined earlier. It establishes a one-to-one correspondence between credulous extensions of an inheritance hierarchy and preferred maximal sets of conditionals that are consistent with the evidence. As a result, it is easy to see that the corresponding defeasible entailment always subsumes inheritance reasoning:

Corollary 8.5.3. *If (Δ, E) is an inheritance framework, then a literal $\tilde{p}$ is derivable in it only if $E \hspace{0.1em}\vdash\hspace{-0.9em}\sim \tilde{p}$ is valid in the associated epistemic state.*

Note, however, that inheritance reasoning and corresponding defeasible entailment do not produce the same results. Defeasible entailment is more expressive than inheritance reasoning even in the restricted domain covered by the latter. The reason is that inheritance reasoning is forward-directed and does not capture backward (contrapositive) inference. Thus, already preferential inference derives that birds are normally not penguins (that is, $Bird \mathrel{|\!\sim} \neg Penguin$) in the penguins-birds example; such a result cannot be obtained by inheritance reasoning, since the conditionals derived by the latter always agree with the specificity order of the inheritance net. Nevertheless, the above results show not only that inheritance reasoning is subsumed by corresponding defeasible entailment; they demonstrate also that the inheritance reasoning captures the 'essence' of the corresponding defeasible reasoning. Since extensions are deciding sets of conditionals with respect to the evidence, once extensions are determined, the corresponding preferred sets of conditionals are obtainable as their (unique) expansions. In other words, the relevant defeasible entailment is uniquely determined, in effect, by the credulous extensions of the inheritance net.

As an additional consequence of the above correspondence, both systems produce the same *positive* conclusions.

Corollary 8.5.4. *If (Δ, E) is an inheritance framework, then a propositional atom p is derivable in it if and only if $E \mathrel{|\!\sim} p$ is valid in the associated epistemic state.*

Proof. Follows immediately from the fact that an expansion of an E-extension Γ supports a positive atom only if it is supported already by Γ (with respect to E). □

Thus, inheritance reasoning and corresponding defeasible entailment agree on their positive conclusions (on evidences that are conjunctions of literals). Consequently, defeasible entailment can also be seen as a conservative extension of inheritance reasoning obtained by expanding the latter with new negative backward conclusions.

This concludes our discussion of defeasible entailment. As the reader has seen, there is yet much to be done in order to obtain a fully fledged theory of this important concept.

9. Credulous Nonmonotonic Inference

Introduction

Skeptical inference relations described in Chapter 7 were designed to capture a skeptical approach to nonmonotonic reasoning, according to which if there is a number of equally preferred alternatives, we infer only what is common to all of them. However, works in nonmonotonic reasoning have suggested also an alternative approach, usually called *credulous* or *brave* reasoning, according to which each of the preferred alternatives is considered as an admissible solution to the nonmonotonic reasoning task. Actually, there are many important reasoning problems in AI and beyond, such as diagnosis, abduction and explanation, that are best seen as involving search for particular preferred solutions. This idea is implicit also in the notion of an extension in default logic [Rei80] and its generalizations, as well as in similar constructs in modal nonmonotonic logics.

There have been a few attempts in the literature to investigate the properties of credulous inference, mainly with negative conclusions that such an inference does not satisfy practically all 'respectable' rules (see, e.g., [Bra93, CLS95]). Thus, a distinctive feature of credulous reasoning is that it does not allow us to conjoin different conclusions derivable from the same premises (because they might be grounded on different preferred solutions). In other words, credulous inference renders invalid the rule And.

An especially illuminating discussion concerning the rule And and problems created by it in representing commonsense reasoning can be found in [Poo91]. The following example from this paper illustrates some of these problems.

Example 9.0.4. Assume that we accept the following conditionals taken from the famous 'penguins-birds' story: $B \mid\!\sim F$, $P \mid\!\sim B$ and $P \mid\!\sim \neg F$. Then the last two imply $P \wedge B \mid\!\sim \neg F$ by Cautious Monotony, and hence $B \mid\!\sim P \rightarrow \neg F$ by Deduction. Now we can apply And and Right Weakening to $B \mid\!\sim F$ and the latter conditional in order to conclude $B \mid\!\sim \neg P$. In other words, we have obtained that P is an exceptional condition for B. As is discussed in [Poo91], given an unrestricted use of And, this immediately produces a qualitative version of the lottery paradox in quite natural situations when B is logically equivalent to a disjunction of a set of propositions $\{P_1, P_2, \ldots, P_n\}$, each of which being exceptional for B in some respect or other.

As we have seen in Chapter 6, the rule And can be seen as a characteristic property of skeptical inference relations; in the framework of basic inference it implies the rest of the postulates for preferential entailment.

We suggest below both a formal characterization and semantic interpretation for a number of systems of non-skeptical nonmonotonic inference based on the notion of an epistemic state. This will give us a good opportunity to compare the two kinds of inference and study their relationship.

We will also establish a close connection between credulous inference relations and Tarski consequence relations. In fact, we will see that the main kinds of brave inference can also be described in these terms. Among other things, this will allow us to give a representation of credulous inference in the expectation-based framework suggested by Gärdenfors and Makinson in [GM94].

9.1 Credulous inference relations

As was defined in Chapter 3, a conditional $A \hspace{0.1em}\vert\!\sim B$ is *credulously valid* in an epistemic state $\mathbb{E}$ if either $\neg A$ is known in $\mathbb{E}$ or at least one preferred state consistent with A supports $A \to B$. In this section we are going to give a syntactic characterization of such credulous validity.

The following definition describes credulous inference relations as a certain extension of regular inference relations from Chapter 6.

Definition 9.1.1. *A regular inference relation will be called* credulous *if it satisfies Rational Monotony:*

Rational Monotony   *If $A \hspace{0.1em}\vert\!\sim B$ and $A \hspace{0.1em}\not\vert\!\sim \neg C$, then $A \land C \hspace{0.1em}\vert\!\sim B$.*

Credulous inference is clearly a weakening of a rational skeptical inference; the latter will be obtained if we add And to the postulates.

The next result shows that credulous inference relations are strongly regular.

Lemma 9.1.1. *Credulous inference satisfies Strong Regularity.*

Proof. Assume $A \hspace{0.1em}\vert\!\sim C$ and $B \hspace{0.1em}\vert\!\sim \mathbf{f}$, but $A \hspace{0.1em}\not\vert\!\sim \neg B \land C$. By Rational Monotony, we have $A \land (B \lor \neg C) \hspace{0.1em}\vert\!\sim C$, and hence $A \land (B \lor \neg C) \hspace{0.1em}\vert\!\sim B \land C$ by Antecedence. But $B \hspace{0.1em}\vert\!\sim \mathbf{f}$ implies $B \land C \hspace{0.1em}\vert\!\sim \mathbf{f}$ by the basic inference, so $A \land (B \lor \neg C) \hspace{0.1em}\vert\!\sim \mathbf{f}$ by Regularity. But the latter conditional implies $A \hspace{0.1em}\vert\!\sim \neg B \land C$ by Deduction, contrary to our assumptions. $\square$

The following lemma gives us an important property of credulous inference that will be used later. This is actually the same property as stated in

[LM92, Lemma 3.11] in the context of rational inference relations. It turns out, however, that the proof given there remains valid for credulous inference relations in general.

Lemma 9.1.2. *If $\neg(A \wedge C) \mathrel{|\!\sim} A$ and $\neg(B \wedge C) \mathrel{|\!\not\sim} B$, then $\neg(A \wedge B) \mathrel{|\!\sim} A$.*

Proof. If $\neg(A \wedge C) \mathrel{|\!\sim} A$, then $\neg(A \wedge B \wedge C) \mathrel{|\!\sim} A$ by (3) from Lemma 6.2.2. In addition, $\neg(B \wedge C) \mathrel{|\!\not\sim} B$ implies $\neg(A \wedge B \wedge C) \mathrel{|\!\not\sim} A \wedge B$ by (5) from the same lemma. Applying Rational Monotony to these two conditionals, we obtain $\neg(A \wedge B \wedge C) \wedge \neg(A \wedge B) \mathrel{|\!\sim} A$, which is equivalent to $\neg(A \wedge B) \mathrel{|\!\sim} A$. □

Rational Monotony is not a Horn rule. So it does not allow us to derive new conditionals directly from given ones; rather, it gives us alternative ways in which a given set of conditionals should be extended to comply with the rule. As we will see later, credulous inference does not give us new singular derivability rules as compared with strongly regular inference.

9.1.1 Credulous inference and expectation relations

Due to the general correspondence between basic inference relations and expectation relations, established in Chapter 6, credulous inference relations also correspond to a natural class of expectation relations. More exactly, it turns out that they are exact counterparts of dependence orders under the id*-mapping that we reproduce below for convenience.

(ID*) $A \mathrel{|\!\sim} B \;\equiv\; A \to B \not< \neg A$ or $\mathbf{t} < \neg A$

(DI*) $A < B \;\equiv\; \neg(A \wedge B) \mathrel{|\!\not\sim} A$ or $\neg B \mathrel{|\!\sim} \mathbf{f}$

As has been shown in Chapter 6, the above conditions determine a one-to-one correspondence between regular inference relations and regular dependence relations. The following theorem refines this result to a correspondence between credulous inference relations and dependence orders, that is, dependence relations that are already transitive.

Theorem 9.1.1. *1. If $\mathrel{|\!\sim}$ is a credulous inference relation, then (DI*) defines a dependence order that generates, in turn, $\mathrel{|\!\sim}$ via (ID*).*
2. If $<$ is a dependence order, then (ID) defines a credulous inference relation that produces, in turn, $<$ via (DI*).*

Proof. We need to check only that Rational Monotony corresponds to transitivity of dependence relations under the id*-mapping.

(i) Let $\mathrel{|\!\sim}$ be a credulous inference relation, and assume that the corresponding dependence relation is not transitive, that is, $A < B$ and $B < C$, but $A \not< C$. Translated into the conditions for the inference relation, this gives us $\neg(A \wedge B) \mathrel{|\!\not\sim} A$, $\neg(B \wedge C) \mathrel{|\!\not\sim} B$ and $\neg(A \wedge C) \mathrel{|\!\sim} A$. But the latter two conditions imply $\neg(A \wedge B) \mathrel{|\!\sim} A$ by Lemma 9.1.2 - a contradiction.

(ii) Assume that $<$ is a dependence order, $A \mathrel{\mid\!\!\!\sim\!\!\!\!\!\!\!\!\not\;\;} \neg B$ and $A \wedge B \mathrel{\mid\!\!\!\sim\!\!\!\!\!\!\!\!\not\;\;} C$ for the corresponding inference relation. The first condition implies $\neg(A \wedge B) < \neg A$ and $t \not< \neg A$, while the second condition gives $(A \wedge B) \to C < \neg(A \wedge B)$. Hence $(A \wedge B) \to C < \neg A$ by transitivity of $<$, and therefore $A \to C < \neg A$ by left monotonicity. Consequently, $A \mathrel{\mid\!\!\!\sim\!\!\!\!\!\!\!\!\not\;\;} C$ for the associated inference relation. This shows that Rational Monotony holds for $\mathrel{\mid\!\!\!\sim}$.   □

As has been shown in Chapter 5, dependence orders are equivalent to supraclassical consequence relations. And as for skeptical inference relations, this fact will allow us to prove a completeness of credulous inference relations with respect to credulous inference in epistemic states.

9.2 Semantic representations

To begin with, the following result shows that the semantic definition of credulous validity with respect to epistemic states determines a credulous inference relation.

Theorem 9.2.1. *The set of conditionals that are credulously valid in an epistemic state forms a credulous inference relation.*

Proof. Left Logical Equivalence, Right Weakening, Antecedence and Regularity are immediate.

Deduction. Let $A \wedge B \mathrel{\mid\!\!\!\sim} C$ be valid. Assume first that $\neg(A \wedge B)$ is known in $\mathbb{E}$. If $\neg A$ is not known, let s be a preferred admissible state consistent with A. Then s supports $\neg(A \wedge B)$, and hence it supports $A \to (B \to C)$. Thus, $A \mathrel{\mid\!\!\!\sim} B \to C$ is valid.

Assume now that $\neg(A \wedge B)$ is not known, and let t be a preferred state consistent with $A \wedge B$ that supports $(A \wedge B) \to C$. If t is also a preferred state in $]\neg A[$, then clearly $A \mathrel{\mid\!\!\!\sim} B \to C$ will be credulously valid. Otherwise there must exist a state s that is preferred in $]\neg A[$ and such that $t \prec s$. In this case $\neg(A \wedge B) \in l(s)$ (since t is preferred in $]\neg(A \wedge B)[$), and therefore $(A \to (B \to C)) \in l(s)$. So, in this case also $A \mathrel{\mid\!\!\!\sim} BtoC$ will be credulously valid.

Conjunctive Cautious Monotony. Let $A \mathrel{\mid\!\!\!\sim} B \wedge C$ be valid. If $\neg A$ is known, $\neg(A \wedge B)$ will also be known, and hence $A \wedge B \mathrel{\mid\!\!\!\sim} C$ will be valid. Assume, therefore, that $\neg A$ is not known, and let t be a preferred state in $]\neg A[$ that supports $A \to (B \wedge C)$. Then t will also belong to $]\neg(A \wedge B)[$ and hence it will also be preferred in $]\neg(A \wedge B)[$. In addition, $(A \wedge B) \to C \in l(t)$, and therefore $A \wedge B \mathrel{\mid\!\!\!\sim} C$ will be valid also in this case.

Rational Monotony. Assume that $A \mathrel{\mid\!\!\!\sim} B$ and $A \mathrel{\mid\!\!\!\sim\!\!\!\!\!\!\!\!\not\;\;} \neg C$ are valid. To begin with, the second condition implies that $\neg A$ is not known in $\mathbb{E}$. Accordingly, the first conditional implies that there exists some preferred state s in $]\neg A[$ that supports $A \to B$. Since $A \mathrel{\mid\!\!\!\sim} \neg C$ is not valid, $A \to \neg C \notin l(s)$, and hence s belongs to $]\neg(A \wedge C)[$. Therefore s should also be a preferred state in $]\neg(A \wedge C)[$ (since any more preferred state will already support $\neg A$). Also, $(A \wedge B) \to C \in l(s)$, and consequently $A \wedge B \mathrel{|\!\sim} C$ will be credulously valid. $\square$

Now we will show that credulous inference relations are actually complete with respect to this semantic representation. To this end we need only to collect some facts established earlier.

Let $\mathrel{|\!\sim}$ be a credulous inference relation, and $<$ its associated dependence order. The latter is equivalent to some supraclassical consequence relation $\vdash$. Accordingly, credulous inference relations are interdefinable with supraclassical consequence relations. Moreover, let us rewrite now the definition of credulous inference in terms of consequence relations:

$$A \mathrel{|\!\sim} B \ \equiv \ A \to B \nvdash \neg A \text{ or } \vdash \neg A$$

The above condition says, in effect, that $A \mathrel{|\!\sim} B$ holds iff either $\neg A$ belongs to all theories of $\vdash$, or there exists a theory of $\vdash$ that is consistent with A and contains $A \to B$. As can be seen, this means precisely that $A \mathrel{|\!\sim} B$ is credulously valid in the pure epistemic state consisting of theories of $\vdash$. Consequently, we immediately obtain

Representation Theorem 9.1. *An inference relation is credulous if and only if it coincides with the set of conditionals that are credulously valid in some epistemic state.*

Actually, the above considerations show also that pure epistemic states (and consequence relations) are sufficient for representing any credulous inference relation.

The above representation result can also be used to provide a semantic characterization for various extensions of credulous inference. In fact, the semantic characterization of rational inference relations, given in Chapter 7, can be viewed as a special case of the above construction. This is based on a simple, but important, observation that, *for linear epistemic states, credulous inference coincides with skeptical inference.* Accordingly, rational inference relations are both skeptical and credulous, and hence obliterate the distinction between skeptical and credulous inference.

In addition, it can be shown, for example, that credulous inference relations generated by determinate epistemic states are precisely characterized by the following weakening of the postulate And:

Weak And   If $t \mathrel{|\!\sim} A$ and $t \mathrel{|\!\sim} B$, then $t \mathrel{|\!\sim} A \wedge B$.

The coincidence of credulous and skeptical inference in the linear case will help us in establishing an important feature of credulous derivability.

Recall that a co-singular rule is valid for credulous inference relations if and only if it is valid for all such relations that are generated by linear epistemic states (see Theorem 4.7.2 in Chapter 4). Now, since each such relation is actually a rational inference relation, we immediately obtain

Theorem 9.2.2. *A co-singular rule is valid for credulous inference relations iff it is valid for rational inference relations.*

A good example of such a rule is Disjunctive Rationality studied in a number of works (see, e.g., [Fre92]):

(**Disjunctive Rationality**)   If $A \vee B \mathbin{\mid\!\sim} C$, then either $A \mathbin{\mid\!\sim} C$, or $B \mathbin{\mid\!\sim} C$.

The above rule is valid for rational inference, and it is co-singular. Consequently, it is valid also for credulous inference relations.

An immediate consequence of the above theorem is the fact that simple rules valid for credulous inference are precisely the rules valid for basic inference. This follows from the fact that simple rules of rational inference coincide with such rules for basic inference.

Corollary 9.2.1. *A simple rule is valid for credulous inference relations iff it is valid for basic inference.*

Though credulous inference is no less powerful than rational inference with respect to disjunctive co-singular rules, it turns to be quite weak in deriving particular conditionals. Thus, the following result shows, in effect, that credulous inference coincides in this respect with strongly regular basic inference.

Theorem 9.2.3. *A conditional $A \mathbin{\mid\!\sim} B$ is credulously derivable from the set of conditionals Γ only if it is derivable from the latter using the basic postulates and Strong Regularity.*

Proof. Assume that $A \mathbin{\mid\!\sim} B$ is not derivable from Γ with respect to strongly regular inference. Then we will construct an epistemic state $\mathbb{E}$ that credulously validates Γ, but not $A \mathbin{\mid\!\sim} B$.

As has been shown in Chapter 6 (see Theorem 6.5.2), regular derivability is reducible to the basic derivability with respect to the classical consequence relation Th_Γ that is determined by the monotonic core of Γ. Accordingly, Γ does not regularly entail $A \mathbin{\mid\!\sim} B$ if and only if no conditional $A_i \mathbin{\mid\!\sim} B_i$ from Γ regularly entails $A \mathbin{\mid\!\sim} B$ with respect to Th_Γ. The later means that $A \rightarrow B \notin \mathrm{Th}_\Gamma(\emptyset)$, and either $A \wedge B \notin \mathrm{Th}_\Gamma(A_i \wedge B_i)$, or $A \rightarrow B \notin \mathrm{Th}_\Gamma(A_i \rightarrow B_i)$.

Let Γ_0 be a subset of Γ containing all non-trivial conditionals $A_i \mathbin{\mid\!\sim} B_i$ that do not belong to the monotonic core of Γ (that is, $A_i \mathbin{\mid\!\sim} \mathbf{f}$ is not regularly derivable from Γ). For any such conditional $A_i \mathbin{\mid\!\sim} B_i$, we will add to $\mathbb{E}$ a new admissible state s_i and label it as follows: if $A \rightarrow B \notin \mathrm{Th}_\Gamma(A_i \rightarrow B_i)$, we put $l(s_i) = \mathrm{Th}_\Gamma(A_i \rightarrow B_i)$; otherwise it is easy to see that $A \notin \mathrm{Th}_\Gamma(A_i \wedge B_i)$, and we put $l(s_i) = \mathrm{Th}_\Gamma(A_i \wedge B_i \wedge \neg A)$. We will define $\mathbb{E}$ as the set of all such admissible belief states with an empty preference relation.

Clearly, each admissible state s_i is a preferred state in $\mathbb{E}$. Consequently, it is easy to see that each such state makes the corresponding conditional $A_i \mathbin{\mid\!\sim} B_i \in \Gamma_0$ credulously valid in $\mathbb{E}$. In addition, the rest of conditionals in

Γ will also be credulously valid in $\mathbb{E}$ due to the fact that each admissible belief set contains a monotonic core of Γ. Thus, all conditionals from Γ are credulously valid in $\mathbb{E}$. Note, however, that $A \mathrel{|\!\sim} B$ is not valid in $\mathbb{E}$, since each s_i either does not support $A \to B$, or else supports $\neg A$.

Since there exists an epistemic state that validates Γ, but falsifies $A \mathrel{|\!\sim} B$, the latter is not derivable from Γ also with respect to the credulous inference. This completes the proof. $\square$

The above results can be summarized roughly by saying that credulous inference is a combination of co-singular rules of rational inference and singular rules of regular inference. The latter fact might be seen as yet another justification for our claim (made in the Introduction) that there should be no hope to capture nonmonotonic reasoning by derivability in some ingenious 'nonmonotonic logic'. Some other ways of reaching this goal are discussed in Chapter 8, and also at the end of this chapter.

Expectation-based credulous inference

There exists a strong connection between the above representation of credulous inference in terms of dependence (consequence) relations, and representation of nonmonotonic inference relations based on expectation orders suggested in [GM94].

As one of the possible ways of understanding nonmonotonic inference, Gärdenfors and Makinson suggested the following formulation:

> A nonmonotonically entails B iff B follows logically from A together with "as many as possible" of the set of our expectations as are compatible with A.

As was rightly noted by the authors, this interpretation tends to suggest a multiplicity of possible sets of auxiliary premises. In other words, it admits a credulous reading:

> A nonmonotonically entails B iff B follows logically from A together with *some* consistent set of propositions that are "sufficiently well expected" in the light of A.

Recall now that a dependence order is actually a 'partial' generalization of an expectation order from [GM94]: it has all the properties of the latter except connectivity. Moreover, the above description of credulous inference in terms of dependence orders is equivalent to the 'standard' definition of expectation inference relations (see [GM94, Theorem 3.5]). Thus, our representation can be considered as a generalization of the corresponding interpretation for expectation inference given in [GM94]. Note also that, for the case of linear epistemic states, this interpretation will give a representation of skeptical rational inference relations that we described in Chapter 7.

9.2.1 Possible worlds semantics

It turns out that credulous inference relations also admit a possible worlds semantics. As for skeptical inference, this semantics can be obtained by transforming epistemic states into certain possible worlds models. This representation requires, however, the use of weak (reflexive) preference orders on worlds.

Let $\mathbb{W} = (W, l, \preccurlyeq)$ be a smooth possible world model such that $\preccurlyeq$ is a weak partial order on W. Such models will be called *reflexive* in what follows.

We define $s \sim t$ as $s \preccurlyeq t \wedge t \preccurlyeq s$; such admissible states will be called equally preferred.

Definition 9.2.1. *A credulously entails B in $\mathbb{W}$ if either $\neg A$ holds in all states of $\mathbb{W}$, or there exists a preferred state s supporting A such that, for any $t \sim s$, if t supports A, then t supports B. The set of conditionals that are credulously valid in $\mathbb{W}$ will be denoted by $\mathrel{\succcurlyeq}_{\mathbb{W}}$.*

The above definition says, in effect, that A credulously entails B in a possible worlds model if either A is false in all states of the model, or there exists a preferred state satisfying A such that all equally preferred states satisfying A will satisfy also B.

To begin with, the following lemma shows that the above definition determines a credulous inference relation.

Lemma 9.2.1. *For any reflexive possible worlds model $\mathbb{W}$, $\mathrel{\succcurlyeq}_{\mathbb{W}}$ is a credulous inference relation.*

Proof. Left Logical Equivalence, Right Weakening, Antecedence and Regularity are immediate.

Deduction. Let $A \wedge B \mathrel{\succ\!\!\mid} C$ be valid. Assume first that $\neg(A \wedge B)$ holds in all states of $\mathbb{W}$. If A holds in at least one state, let s be a preferred state supporting A. Then trivially any equally preferred state satisfying $A \wedge B$ will satisfy C (since there are no such states). Thus, $A \mathrel{\succ\!\!\mid} B{\to}C$ is valid in this case.

Assume now that $A \wedge B$ holds in at least one state, and let t be a preferred state satisfying $A \wedge B$ that 'realizes' $(A \wedge B) \mathrel{\succ\!\!\mid} C$, that is, all equally preferred states satisfying $A \wedge B$ will satisfy C. Notice that in this case any equally preferred state satisfying A will satisfy $B \to C$. Consequently, if t is also a preferred state satisfying A, then $A \mathrel{\succ\!\!\mid} B{\to}C$ is valid in this case. Otherwise there must exist a state s that is preferred among the states satisfying A and such that $t \prec s$. In this case $\neg(A \wedge B)$ will hold in s and all states s' equally preferred to s. Consequently, if such an s' satisfies A, it will satisfy also $\neg B$ and thereby $B{\to}C$. So, in this case also $A \mathrel{\succ\!\!\mid} BtoC$ will be credulously valid.

Conjunctive Cautious Monotony. Let $A \mathrel{\succ\!\!\mid} B \wedge C$ be valid. If A is false in all states of $\mathbb{W}$, then $A \wedge B$ will also be false in all states, and hence $A \wedge B \mathrel{\succ\!\!\mid} C$ will be credulously valid. Assume, therefore, that t is a preferred state satisfying

A such that all equally preferred states satisfying A satisfy also $B \wedge C$. In particular, t satisfies $A \wedge B$, and hence it will also be a preferred such state. In addition, all equally preferred states satisfying $A \wedge B$ will satisfy also C, and therefore $A \wedge B \mathrel{\vert\!\sim} C$ will be valid also in this case.

Rational Monotony. Assume that $A \mathrel{\vert\!\sim} B$ and $A \mathrel{\vert\!\not\sim} \neg C$ in $\mathbb{W}$. The second condition implies that A holds in at least one state of $\mathbb{W}$. Accordingly, the first conditional implies that there exists some preferred state s satisfying A such that B holds in all equally preferred states satisfying A. Since $A \mathrel{\vert\!\sim} \neg C$ is not valid, there must exist a state s_1 that is equally preferred to s and satisfies $A \wedge C$. Moreover, s_1 will be a preferred state satisfying $A \wedge C$, since any strictly more preferred state will satisfy $\neg A$. In addition, all states equally preferred to s_1 will also be equally preferred to s, and hence if such a state satisfies $A \wedge C$, it will satisfy also B. Consequently $A \wedge B \mathrel{\vert\!\sim} C$ will be credulously valid. $\qquad\qquad\qquad\qquad\qquad\qquad\qquad\qquad\qquad\qquad\qquad\qquad\square$

Now we are going to show that the above possible worlds models are adequate for representing credulous inference. To this end, we will transform any epistemic state into a reflexive possible worlds model generating the same credulous inference relation.

Given an epistemic state $\mathbb{E} = \langle S, l, \prec \rangle$, we define the corresponding reflexive possible worlds model $\mathbb{W}$ as follows. Let W be a set of all world-state pairs (α, s) such that $s \in S$ and $l(s) \subseteq \alpha$. Define a weak preference relation on W as follows:

$$(\alpha, s) \preccurlyeq (\beta, t) \text{ iff } s \preceq t.$$

As can be easily verified, $\preccurlyeq$ is a weak partial order. Note that $(\alpha, s) \sim (\beta, t)$ if and only $s = t$. In other words, states of $\mathbb{W}$ are equally preferred in this order if and only if they correspond to the same admissible state of $\mathbb{E}$. Finally, we define the corresponding labelling function l_0 on W in an obvious way: $l_0(\alpha, s) = \alpha$.

Theorem 9.2.4. *If $\mathbb{E}$ is an epistemic state, then $\mathbb{W}$ as defined above is a reflexive possible worlds model that determines the same credulous inference relation as $\mathbb{E}$.*

Proof. The smoothness of $\mathbb{W}$ immediately follows from the smoothness of $\mathbb{E}$. The limit case of known propositions is simple, so we will consider only the case when the credulous inference is non-trivial.

Assume first that $A \mathrel{\vert\!\sim} B$ is credulously valid in $\mathbb{E}$, and s is an admissible state in $\mathbb{E}$ that is preferred in $]\neg A[$ and supports $A \to B$. Since s is consistent with A, there must exist a world α including $l(s)$ that satisfies A. Let us consider the state (α, s) in $\mathbb{W}$. Clearly, (α, s) is a preferred state satisfying A. Moreover, all states that are equally preferred to s in $\mathbb{W}$ correspond to worlds that include $l(s)$, and hence they satisfy $A \to B$. This shows that $A \mathrel{\vert\!\sim} B$ is credulously valid in $\mathbb{W}$.

Assume now that $A \mathrel{\vdash\mkern-8mu\sim} B$ is credulously valid in $\mathbb{W}$, and (α, s) is a preferred state in $\mathbb{W}$ satisfying A such that all equally preferred states satisfy $A \rightarrow B$. The latter means that s supports $A \rightarrow B$ in $\mathbb{E}$. Moreover, s is a preferred admissible state in $\mathbb{E}$ that is consistent with A. Indeed, if we would have $s \prec t$, for some admissible state t consistent with A, then there must exist a world $\beta \supseteq l(t)$ that satisfies A. But then (β, t) would be a state in $\mathbb{W}$ that is strictly preferred to (α, s) and satisfies A, contrary to our assumption that (α, s) is a preferred such state. Thus, A credulously entail B in $\mathbb{E}$. This completes the proof. $\square$

Since any credulous inference relation is determined by some epistemic state, the above theorem gives a completeness of credulous inference with respect to reflexive possible worlds models.

Representation Theorem 9.2. *An inference relation is credulous if and only if it generated by some reflexive possible worlds model.*

9.3 Permissive inference

In this section we will describe another kind of non-skeptical inference which will turn out to be an exact dual of credulous inference.

Definition 9.3.1. *A basic inference relation will be called* permissive *if it satisfies the Cut rule:*

Cut   *If $A \mathrel{\vdash\mkern-8mu\sim} B$ and $A \wedge B \mathrel{\vdash\mkern-8mu\sim} C$, then $A \mathrel{\vdash\mkern-8mu\sim} C$.*

To begin with, the following result shows that any permissive inference relation satisfies Strong Regularity:

Lemma 9.3.1. *Any permissive inference relation is strongly regular.*

Proof. Assume $\neg B \mathrel{\vdash\mkern-8mu\sim} \mathbf{f}$ and $A \mathrel{\vdash\mkern-8mu\sim} C$. The first conditional gives us $\neg B \vee (A \wedge C) \mathrel{\vdash\mkern-8mu\sim} A \wedge B \wedge C$ by Confirmation, and hence $A \wedge C \mathrel{\vdash\mkern-8mu\sim} B \wedge C$ by Cautious Monotony. Applying Cut to the latter and to $A \mathrel{\vdash\mkern-8mu\sim} C$, we conclude $A \mathrel{\vdash\mkern-8mu\sim} B \wedge C$, as required. $\square$

Also, it has been shown in Chapter 6 that in the context of the basic postulates, Cut implies the rule Or:

(Or)   *If $A \mathrel{\vdash\mkern-8mu\sim} C$ and $B \mathrel{\vdash\mkern-8mu\sim} C$, then $A \vee B \mathrel{\vdash\mkern-8mu\sim} C$.*

The following result gives a more 'traditional' characterization of permissive inference relations:

Theorem 9.3.1. *Permissive inference relations are completely characterized by the postulates Reflexivity, Left Logical Equivalence, Right Weakening, Conjunctive Cautious Monotony, Cut and Or.*

Proof. We need only to show the derivability of Antecedence and Confirmation. To begin with, Cut and Reflexivity jointly imply Antecedence. Indeed, given $A \mathrel{|\!\sim} B$ we can use $A \wedge B \mathrel{|\!\sim} A \wedge B$ to conclude $A \mathrel{|\!\sim} A \wedge B$ by Cut. In addition, Confirmation is also derivable from the above postulates: If $A \mathrel{|\!\sim} B$, then $A \mathrel{|\!\sim} B \vee C$ by Right Weakening; also, $C \mathrel{|\!\sim} B \vee C$ by Reflexivity and Right Weakening. Applying Or, we obtain $A \vee C \mathrel{|\!\sim} B \vee C$. □

If we compare the above list of postulates with the characterization of preferential inference, given in Chapter 7, we can notice that the distinction of permissive inference from preferential one amounts simply to replacement of standard Cautious Monotony by Conjunctive Cautious Monotony. Nevertheless, we will see that permissive inference is not skeptical, since it does not satisfy And.

The following result shows that permissive and credulous inference relations are duals.

Theorem 9.3.2. $\mathrel{|\!\sim}$ *is a permissive inference relation iff* $\mathrel{|\!\sim}^{\circ}$ *is a credulous inference relation.*

Proof. We have to show, in effect, that Rational Monotony corresponds to Cut under the duality transformation.

$\mathrel{|\!\sim}^{\circ}$ satisfies Rational Monotony if and only if the source inference relation satisfies the following condition:

(*)   If $A \mathrel{|\!\sim} C$ and $A \wedge C \mathrel{|\!\sim} B$, then $A \mathrel{|\!\sim} B$ or $A \wedge C \mathrel{|\!\sim} \mathbf{f}$.

Moreover, if $A \wedge C \mathrel{|\!\sim} \mathbf{f}$ and $A \mathrel{|\!\sim} C$, then $A \mathrel{|\!\sim} C \wedge \neg(A \wedge C)$ by Regularity, and hence $A \mathrel{|\!\sim} \neg A$ by Right Weakening. The latter implies $A \mathrel{|\!\sim} \mathbf{f}$ and therefore $A \mathrel{|\!\sim} B$. Consequently, the second disjunct in the conclusion of (*) can be eliminated, and hence it amounts to

(**)   If $A \mathrel{|\!\sim} C$ and $A \wedge C \mathrel{|\!\sim} B$, then $A \mathrel{|\!\sim} B$.

which is nothing other than the Cut rule. In the same way it can be shown that $\mathrel{|\!\sim}^{\circ}$ satisfies Cut iff $\mathrel{|\!\sim}$ satisfies Rational Monotony. □

Using the above duality, we can obtain all the properties of permissive inference by 'dualizing' corresponding properties of credulous inference.

To begin with, the semantic interpretation of credulous inference immediately gives us the following semantic characterization of permissive inference in epistemic states:

Definition 9.3.2. *A conditional* $A \mathrel{|\!\sim} B$ *will be said to be* permissively valid *in an epistemic state* $\mathbb{E}$ *if any preferred state consistent with* A *is consistent also with* $A \wedge B$. *The set of all permissively valid conditionals in* $\mathbb{E}$ *will be denoted by* $\mathrel{|\!\sim}_{\mathbb{E}}^{p}$.

So, a permissive conditional says informally "A *is normally consistent with B*". Since the above semantic description corresponds precisely to the interpretation of the relation dual to credulous entailment, we immediately obtain

Lemma 9.3.2. *For any epistemic state* $\mathbb{E}$, $\vdash^{p}_{\mathbb{E}}$ *is a permissive inference relation.*

Moreover, the duality of credulous and permissive inference implies that the following mapping establishes a one-to-one correspondence between permissive inference relations and dependence orders.

(ID) $\qquad\qquad\qquad A \mathrel{\vdash} B \;\equiv\; \neg(A \wedge B) < \neg A$

(DI) $\qquad\qquad\qquad A < B \;\equiv\; \neg(A \wedge B) \mathrel{\vdash} \neg A$

The above pair of definitions is actually nothing other than the *id-mapping* introduced in Chapter 6, and used in Chapter 7 for a correspondence between skeptical inference relations and qualitative dependence orders (= semi-classical consequence relations). The following theorem states that the id-mapping provides also a bijection between permissive inference relations and dependence orders in general. The proof follows immediately by duality.

Theorem 9.3.3. *1. If* $\vdash$ *is a permissive inference relation, then (DI) defines a dependence order that generates, in turn,* $\vdash$ *via (ID).*
2. If $<$ *is a dependence order, then (ID) determines a permissive inference relation* $\vdash_{<}$, *and* $<$ *coincides with the dependence relation produced by* $\vdash_{<}$ *via (DI).*

Since dependence orders are interdefinable with consequence relations, we obtain that the above conditions determine also a one-to-one correspondence between permissive inference relations and supraclassical consequence relations. And just as for credulous inference, this correspondence allows us to show that the above semantic representation of permissive inference is adequate for representing all permissive inference relations.

Representation Theorem 9.3. *An inference relation is permissive if and only if it coincides with the set of conditionals that are permissively valid in some epistemic state.*

Finally, the possible worlds semantics for credulous inference gives us a semantic characterization of permissive inference in terms of reflexive possible worlds models:

Definition 9.3.3. *A permissively entails* B *in a reflexive possible worlds model* $\mathbb{W}$ *if, for any preferred state supporting* A *there exists an equally preferred state that supports* $A \wedge B$.

Notice that if the classes of equally preferred states are singletons, then the above definition will coincide with the definition of preferential entailment in KLM models. In the general case, however, this definition gives a semantic characterization of permissive inference.

Representation Theorem 9.4. *An inference relation is permissive if and only if it generated by some reflexive possible worlds model.*

X-logics

Siegel and Forget has suggested in [SF96] a new description of nonmonotonic inference relations that they called *X-logics*. For any set of propositions X, they define an inference relation $\vdash_X$ as follows:

$$A \vdash_X B \text{ iff } \text{Th}(A, B) \cap X \subseteq \text{Th}(A) \cap X$$

The authors have described a number of properties of this consequence relation and have shown, in particular, that it does not satisfy, in general, And and Cautious Monotony. At the end of the paper they have posed a question about a general characterization of such X-logics. A detailed study of such inference relations and their use for describing circumscriptions is given in [MR98]. The latter authors have established, in effect, that any X-logic is a permissive inference relation in our sense. Actually, the following result shows that, for finite languages, the two notions turn out to coincide.

Theorem 9.3.4. *Any X-logic is a permissive inference relation. Moreover, for any permissive inference relation $\vdash$ in a finite language there exists a set of propositions X such that $\vdash$ coincides with $\vdash_X$.*

Proof. The definition of $A \vdash_X B$ can be rewritten as follows:

For any $C \in X$, if $\neg C$ is consistent with A, then it is consistent with $A \wedge B$.

The above reformulation clearly shows that $\vdash_X$ is actually a permissive inference relation determined by a pure epistemic state consisting of the set of theories $\{\text{Th}(\neg C) \mid C \in X\}$. In addition, if $\vdash$ is a permissive inference relation in a finite language, and $\vdash$ is its associated supraclassical consequence relation, then any theory of $\vdash$ is representable as $\text{Th}(C)$, for some proposition C. Consequently, if Y is a set of such propositions corresponding to all (maximal) theories of $\vdash$, then $X = \{\neg C \mid C \in Y\}$ will determine an X-logic that will coincide with $\vdash$. $\qquad\square$

Since any preferential inference relation is permissive, the above result immediately implies that in the finite case any preferential inference relation will also coincide with some X-logic.

9.4 Safe credulous inference

As was defined in Chapter 6, an inference relation is *safe* if it satisfies the following rule:

Consistency   If $A \mathrel{|\!\sim} B$ and $A \mathrel{|\!\sim} \neg B$, then $A \mathrel{|\!\sim} \mathbf{f}$.

Unfortunately, many kinds of brave inference cannot be made safe without collapsing to scepticism. Thus, it turns out that a credulous inference relation will be safe only if it is already skeptical; this follows from the fact that Rational Monotony and Consistency imply And (see Theorem 6.7.1 in Chapter 6).

Lemma 9.4.1. *Any credulous and safe inference relation is rational.*

It can be shown that, for permissive inference relations, safety does not imply scepticism. However, permissive inference relations are not too natural candidates for representing brave inference, so we need to look elsewhere.

It was shown in Chapter 6 that there is a general way of constructing a safe counterpart for any regular inference relation. Namely, for any such inference relation $\mathrel{|\!\sim}$ we can define the corresponding safe inference relation $\mathrel{|\!\sim}^s$ by taking an intersection of $\mathrel{|\!\sim}$ with its dual:

$$A \mathrel{|\!\sim}^s B \;\equiv\; A \mathrel{|\!\sim} B \;\&\; A \mathrel{|\!\sim}^{\circ} B$$

Applying the above construction to credulous inference, we will obtain a natural safe inference relation that is still not skeptical.

Definition 9.4.1. *A conditional $A \mathrel{|\!\sim} B$ will be said to be safely valid in an epistemic state $\mathbb{E}$ if it is both credulously an permissively valid in $\mathbb{E}$.*

Unfolding the corresponding definitions of credulous and permissive validity, we obtain that $A \mathrel{|\!\sim} B$ is safely valid in $\mathbb{E}$ iff either $\neg A$ is known in $\mathbb{E}$, or there exists a preferred state consistent with A that supports $A \to B$, and no such preferred state supports $A \to \neg B$. In still other words, $A \mathrel{|\!\sim} B$ is safely valid in $\mathbb{E}$ iff either $\neg A$ is known in $\mathbb{E}$, or $A \mathrel{|\!\sim} B$ is credulously valid, while $A \mathrel{|\!\sim} \neg B$ is not credulously valid in $\mathbb{E}$.

An inference relation will be called *argumentative* (see [Cay95]) if it coincides with the set of safely valid conditionals determined by some epistemic state. Unfortunately, the problem of characterization for argumentative inference relations remains still open. We will give only a couple of facts that locate argumentative inference among other inference relations. To begin with, we clearly have

Lemma 9.4.2. *Any argumentative inference relation is regular and safe.*

Unfortunately, argumentative inference relations do not satisfy, in general any of the other rules discussed earlier in the book. On the other hand, it is strictly stronger than a combination of regularity and safety (Consistency). For example, it validates the following rule (that can be easily checked on the basis of the above semantic definition):

If $A \hspace{1pt}\vdash\hspace{-6pt}\sim\hspace{1pt} B$ and $A \land B \hspace{1pt}\vdash\hspace{-6pt}\sim\hspace{1pt} C$, then $A \land C \hspace{1pt}\vdash\hspace{-6pt}\sim\hspace{1pt} B$.

The above rule can be obtained as a consequence of Cut and Conjunctive Cautious Monotony. Consequently, it is valid also for permissive inference relations. However, Cut is not valid, in general, for argumentative inference. On the other hand, as can be anticipated, the above rule is not a consequence of Regularity and Consistency, so not all safe and regular inference relations are argumentative. This seems to confirm the suspicion that an adequate characterization of many brave inference relations cannot be achieved on the basis of rules and postulates designed for skeptical inference. Still, it can be shown that argumentative inference is weaker than rational one. In other words, the rules valid for argumentative inference should also be valid for rational inference relations. This immediately follows from the following simple observation:

Lemma 9.4.3. *Any rational inference relation is argumentative.*

Thus, rational inference relations constitute, in effect, an upper bound also for non-skeptical inference.

9.5 Some other kinds of brave inference

Kinds of non-skeptical nonmonotonic inference, described earlier, by no means exhaust plausible inference relations of this kind. In this section we will briefly sketch a couple of other opportunities.

An interesting kind of brave inference can be described as follows:

Definition 9.5.1. *A conditional $A \hspace{1pt}\vdash\hspace{-6pt}\sim\hspace{1pt} B$ will be said to be AP-valid in an epistemic state $\mathbb{E}$ if either $\neg A$ is known in $\mathbb{E}$ or there exists a belief state s consistent with A that supports $A \to B$, and no state consistent with A that is preferred to s supports $A \to \neg B$.*

The above description follows [Cay95] that is based, in turn, on [PL92]. It can acquire a natural reading when seen as representing preferences between arguments supporting, respectively, $A \to B$ and $A \to \neg B$. Namely, it says that there exists argument supporting B in the context of A that is not superseded by any argument to the opposite conclusion.

Below by an *AP-inference relation* we will mean any set of conditionals that are AP-valid with respect to some epistemic state. The following result shows that this is indeed an inference relation in our sense:

Lemma 9.5.1. *Any AP-inference relation is a regular inference relation.*

Proof. Left Logical Equivalence, Right Weakening, Antecedence and Strong Regularity are immediate.

Confirmation. Assume first that $\neg A$ is known in $\mathbb{E}$. Then if $\neg C$ is also known in $\mathbb{E}$, then $\neg(A \vee C)$ is known, and hence $A \vee C \hspace{1mm}\vdash\hspace{-3mm}\sim B \vee C$ will obviously hold. Otherwise there must exist some state s consistent with A. But s supports $A \vee C \to B \vee C$, since the latter is a logical consequence of $\neg A$, and the latter belongs to all states in $\mathbb{E}$. Hence $A \vee C \hspace{1mm}\vdash\hspace{-3mm}\sim B \vee C$ is valid also in this case.

Assume now that $\neg A$ is not known in $\mathbb{E}$. Then $A \hspace{1mm}\vdash\hspace{-3mm}\sim B$ implies that there exists a belief state s consistent with A that supports $A \to B$ and no state in $]\neg A[$ that is preferred to s supports $A \to \neg B$. Clearly, s is consistent with $A \vee C$. In addition, s supports $A \vee C \to B \vee C$ (since it supports $A \to B$). Finally, if $s \prec t$ and t is consistent with $A \vee C$, then t is consistent with either A or C. In the first case t should be consistent with $A \wedge B$, and hence in either case t is consistent with $(A \wedge B) \vee C$, which immediately implies that t does not support $A \vee C \to \neg(B \vee C)$. So, $A \vee C \hspace{1mm}\vdash\hspace{-3mm}\sim B \vee C$ will also be valid in this case.

Conjunctive Cautious Monotony. If $\neg A$ is known in $\mathbb{E}$, then $\neg(A \wedge B)$ is also known, and hence $A \wedge B \hspace{1mm}\vdash\hspace{-3mm}\sim C$ will trivially hold. Assume, therefore, that $\neg A$ is not known in $\mathbb{E}$. Then $A \hspace{1mm}\vdash\hspace{-3mm}\sim B \wedge C$ implies that there exists a belief state s consistent with A that supports $A \to (B \wedge C)$ and no state preferred to s and consistent with A supports $A \to \neg(B \wedge C)$. Now, s is obviously consistent with $A \wedge B$ and supports $(A \wedge B) \to C$. In addition, if $s \prec t$ and t is consistent with $A \wedge B$, then it is consistent with A, and therefore it does not support $A \to \neg(B \wedge C)$. But the latter is equivalent to $(A \wedge B) \to \neg C$, which is sufficient for the validity of $A \wedge B \hspace{1mm}\vdash\hspace{-3mm}\sim C$. $\qquad\square$

Since no constraints were imposed on the underlying epistemic states, some stronger inference systems can be obtained by imposing various conditions on the latter. For example, if $\prec$ were assumed to be modular and reflexive (that is, if its complement were a transitive and irreflexive relation), then the corresponding AP-inference would be safe. Note also that if we will require the relevant epistemic states are pure, or even persistent, then we will obtain, in effect, credulous validity. Hence, credulous inference is stronger than AP-inference:

Corollary 9.5.1. *Any credulous inference relation is an AP-inference relation.*

An additional interesting inference relation is produced by 'dualization' of AP-validity:

Definition 9.5.2. *A conditional $A \hspace{1mm}\vdash\hspace{-3mm}\sim B$ will be said to be AP°-valid in an epistemic state $\mathbb{E}$ if, for any state s consistent with A that supports $A \to \neg B$ there exists a state t consistent with A that is preferred to s and supports $A \to B$.*

As can be seen, the above defined validity is a precise dual of AP-validity, and hence it also determines a regular inference relation in accordance with our previous results.

9.6 Interrelations

In a certain sense, credulous reasoning provides a more fine-grained mechanism for inferring from incomplete and default assumptions. This can be seen already from the fact that knowing each of the preferred solutions is already sufficient for establishing what can be skeptically inferred (namely, what belongs to all of them). In particular, we will show below that credulous inference relations allow to restore their associated skeptical counterparts.

In this section we will invariably use $\vdash\!\!\!\sim$ to denote a skeptical (preferential) inference relation, while $\approx\!\!\!|$ will denote a credulous inference relation.

Clearly, any preferential inference relation determines an associated semi-classical consequence relation and thereby a corresponding credulous inference relation. In fact, the latter is definable directly as follows:

$$A \mathrel{\vcenter{\hbox{$\approx$}}}\!\!| B \ \text{ iff } \ A \not\!\!\mathrel{\vcenter{\hbox{$\approx$}}}| \neg B \text{ or } A \vdash\!\!\!\sim \mathbf{f}$$

Unfortunately, semi-classical consequence relations determine a rather special class of credulous inference relations that satisfy the following rule:

(Completeness)   If $A \mathrel{\vcenter{\hbox{$\approx$}}}\!\!| B \vee C$, then either $A \mathrel{\vcenter{\hbox{$\approx$}}}\!\!| B$ or $A \mathrel{\vcenter{\hbox{$\approx$}}}\!\!| C$.

In particular, we have that, for any A and B, either $A \mathrel{\vcenter{\hbox{$\approx$}}}\!\!| B$ or $A \mathrel{\vcenter{\hbox{$\approx$}}}\!\!| \neg B$. This feature implies the well-known property of Excluded Middle that characterizes Stalnaker's logic of counterfactuals.

A more natural and useful correspondence arises in the opposite direction. As we have established, supraclassical consequence relations in general are interdefinable with credulous inference relations. Consequently, any credulous inference determines an associated skeptical inference. Moreover, any preferential inference relation is definable in this way on the basis of some credulous inference relation. A direct description of such a preferential inference relation is given by the following condition:

$$A \vdash\!\!\!\sim B \ \text{ iff } \ C \to A \mathrel{\vcenter{\hbox{$\approx$}}}\!\!| C \text{ only if } C \to A \mathrel{\vcenter{\hbox{$\approx$}}}\!\!| C \wedge B, \text{ for any } C.$$

The above condition implies the following highly plausible property that connects skeptical and credulous inference:

Corollary 9.6.1. *If $\approx\!\!\!|$ is a credulous inference relation, and $\vdash\!\!\!\sim$ its associated skeptical inference relation, then, for any propositions A, B and C*

If $A \vdash\!\!\!\sim B$ and $A \mathrel{\vcenter{\hbox{$\approx$}}}\!\!| C$, then $A \mathrel{\vcenter{\hbox{$\approx$}}}\!\!| B \wedge C$.

The above condition says that skeptical consequences of some proposition can always be added to all its credulous consequences.

Unfortunately, the above rather natural condition is still insufficient for characterizing the skeptical inference associated with a given credulous one (hence the need in a more complex characterization, given earlier).

Example 9.6.1. Assume that $\mathbb{E}$ is a pure epistemic state determined by two theories, $u = \text{Th}(p)$ and $v = \text{Th}(q \to p, q \to r)$. As can be seen, both these theories are preferred among the states consistent with q. In addition, $\text{Th}(q, u) \subset \text{Th}(q, v) = \text{Th}(q, p, r)$. Consequently, for any proposition C, if $q \hspace{0.1em}\mid\!\approx\hspace{0.1em} C$, then $q \hspace{0.1em}\mid\!\approx\hspace{0.1em} C \wedge r$. However, $q \hspace{0.1em}\mid\!\sim\hspace{0.1em} r$ is not preferentially valid in $\mathbb{E}$, since u does not contain $q \to r$.

9.6.1 Credulous conditionals as default assumptions

In Chapter 8 we have described the notion of a defeasible entailment, a reasoning framework that is based on a general strategy of nonmonotonic reasoning consisting in making plausible assumptions that are compatible with a given default base. We have described in that chapter a semantic approach to defeasible entailment that amounted to choosing preferred epistemic states satisfying a given set of conditionals.

There exists, however, yet another, syntactic way to cope with defeasible entailment. It consists in adopting explicit default assumptions that would permit desirable inference steps, as well as prevent undesirable ones. Actually, such an explicit control on possible derivations has been suggested, in one form or another, in many studies of defeasible entailment (see, e.g., the assumption of independence, discussed in [Gef92]).

It turns out that default assumptions of the above kind cannot take, in general, the form of additional skeptical conditionals; rather, they should express our beliefs about relevance or irrelevance of particular propositions for a given default inference. For example, the conditional *Birds fly* defeasibly entails *Red bird fly* under a reasonable assumption that the color of birds is irrelevant to their flying ability. Our general experience suggests, however, that wounds could influence the ability of flying, even though we do not have sufficient grounds for inferring that *Wounded birds do not fly*. In other words, the appropriate assumption about relevance of wounds to flying cannot be expressed as a skeptical conditional. As we will see, however, such assumptions can often be expressed using appropriate credulous or permissive conditionals.

Using explicit assumptions in making defeasible derivations has a definite advantage over the semantic approach in that it allows us to keep most such derivations intact when we change the default base. On the semantic approach, the validity of defeasible derivations is determined in a global way by the whole default base. Consequently, changes made to the default base undermine, in general, all the conclusions made earlier.

The above ideas are a subject of an ongoing research, so we can only be brief here. Namely, we will give below two examples of the use of non-skeptical conditionals in supporting defeasible entailment.

Strengthening the Antecedent. The connection between brave inference relations and their associated skeptical ones allows to establish some interesting conditions permitting the strengthening of the antecedents of skeptical conditionals. Thus, we have the following simple observation:

Lemma 9.6.1. *If $\vdash$ and $\approx^\circ$ are, respectively, skeptical and permissive inference relation determined by some epistemic state, then*

$$\text{If } A \vdash B \text{ and } A \approx^\circ C, \text{ then } A \wedge C \vdash B.$$

The above condition is a kind of a 'mixed' Cautious Monotony rule that is valid for any skeptical inference relation. It says that if C is normally permitted for A, then it can be added to premises of any conditional of the form $A \vdash B$. For example, we can make an assumption $Birds \approx^\circ Red$ saying that redness is normally compatible with being a bird, and then $Bird \; fly$ would allow us to derive $Red \; birds \; fly$.

In this way, the above rule can be used for making defeasible derivations. This rule can be expressed also using the corresponding credulous conditional:

$$\text{If } A \vdash B \text{ and } A \not\approx \neg C, \text{ then } A \wedge C \vdash B.$$

The above condition gives a weaker variant of 'rational monotony' that hold for all skeptical inference relations. It allows to augment the antecedents of default conditionals with any proposition such that its negation is not credulously derivable. Actually, this condition captures much of the content of the full Rational Monotony rule, and explains thereby why the latter is seen as valid in many 'real' examples.

Credulous rules as defeaters. Credulous conditionals $A \approx B$ can be considered as *might*-conditionals saying that if A holds then it might be the case that B. Such conditionals are well-known in the literature on conditional logic at least since the time of David Lewis. They play also an important role in Nute's defeasible logic [Nut90] where they function primarily as *defeaters* that block applications of ordinary defeasible rules. This function can be justified via the following condition relating skeptical inference and its counterpart credulous inference:

$$\text{For any contingent } A, \text{ if } A \approx \neg B, \text{ then } A \not\vdash B.$$

The above condition says that if, given A, it might be the case that $\neg B$, then A should not skeptically entail B. Using our earlier example, we can accept as a default assumption *Wounded birds might not fly*, and this will block potential derivations of *Wounded birds fly* from *Birds fly*, without forcing us to accept a stronger claim *Wounded birds normally do not fly*.

Actually, instead of credulous inference in the above condition, we could as well use permissive inference. So, brave conditionals can function also as defeaters of ordinary skeptical rules.

10. Contraction Inference

In this chapter we will give a detailed description of contraction inference introduced in Chapter 3. As has been said, in the general correspondence between nonmonotonic inference and belief change, contraction inference corresponds to the basic operation of belief contraction. This augments the idea that belief change and nonmonotonic inference are "two sides of the same coin" and extends it to belief contractions.

This chapter deals mainly with technical issues and results concerning contraction inference relations. The discussion of their significance for the theory of belief change is postponed until Part Three. We will provide below an axiomatic characterization of contraction inference relations, and show its completeness with respect to epistemic states. We will also give a number of representation results for extensions of the contraction relation depending on various constraints imposed on epistemic states. These results will cover a broad range of possible belief contraction functions including traditional AGM contractions, as well as contractions that do not satisfy the recovery postulate.

10.1 Contraction inference relations

In this section we will give a syntactic description of contraction inference. Similarly to ordinary inference relations considered earlier, we will define a contraction inference relation as a certain set of contractionals of the form $A \mathbin{\sim\!\!\!\mid} B$ meaning "In the absence of A, normally B", or in short, "Unless A, B".

In what follows, we will denote by $-A$ the set of propositions that should be believed in the absence of A, that is,

$$-A = \{C \mid A \mathbin{\sim\!\!\!\mid} C\}$$

The above definition describes, in effect, the closure operator corresponding to contraction inference. In addition, sets of the form $-A$ will correspond to *contracted belief sets* in the theory of belief change.

10.1.1 Postulates of contraction inference

We will present below postulates that characterize general contraction relations. To begin with, we give the basic postulates.

Tautology $A \mathrel{\vrule height 1.6ex depth 0pt width 0.1ex\!\sim} t$

And   If $A \mathrel{\vrule height 1.6ex depth 0pt width 0.1ex\!\sim} B$ and $A \mathrel{\vrule height 1.6ex depth 0pt width 0.1ex\!\sim} C$, then $A \mathrel{\vrule height 1.6ex depth 0pt width 0.1ex\!\sim} B \wedge C$.

Right Weakening   If $B \vDash C$ and $A \mathrel{\vrule height 1.6ex depth 0pt width 0.1ex\!\sim} B$, then $A \mathrel{\vrule height 1.6ex depth 0pt width 0.1ex\!\sim} C$.

Extensionality   If $\vDash A \leftrightarrow C$ and $A \mathrel{\vrule height 1.6ex depth 0pt width 0.1ex\!\sim} B$, then $C \mathrel{\vrule height 1.6ex depth 0pt width 0.1ex\!\sim} B$.

The first three postulates amount to the requirement that the contracted belief set $-A$ should be deductively closed. Thus, they jointly correspond to the postulate of closure (K–1) in the AGM theory (see Chapter 12). Notice that, unlike ordinary nonmonotonic inference relations, studied earlier, we need the postulate of Tautology in order to secure that a contracted belief set is always nonempty. Given the supplementary postulates, however, Tautology is reducible to its very special case $t \mathrel{\vrule height 1.6ex depth 0pt width 0.1ex\!\sim} t$. The last postulate, Extensionality, says that logically equivalent propositions generate identical contractions. This postulate makes contraction a syntax-independent relation.

Now we present the supplementary postulates. As we will see below, their role consists, in effect, in determining a 'preferential' contraction that is based on a preference order among admissible states.

Partial Antitony   If $A \wedge B \mathrel{\vrule height 1.6ex depth 0pt width 0.1ex\!\sim} A$, then $A \wedge B \wedge C \mathrel{\vrule height 1.6ex depth 0pt width 0.1ex\!\sim} A$.

Cautious Antitony   If $A \wedge B \mathrel{\vrule height 1.6ex depth 0pt width 0.1ex\!\sim} A$ and $B \mathrel{\vrule height 1.6ex depth 0pt width 0.1ex\!\sim} C$, then $A \wedge B \mathrel{\vrule height 1.6ex depth 0pt width 0.1ex\!\sim} C$.

Distributivity   If $A \mathrel{\vrule height 1.6ex depth 0pt width 0.1ex\!\sim} C$ and $B \mathrel{\vrule height 1.6ex depth 0pt width 0.1ex\!\sim} C$, then $A \wedge B \mathrel{\vrule height 1.6ex depth 0pt width 0.1ex\!\sim} C$.

Cautious Monotony   If $A \wedge B \mathrel{\vrule height 1.6ex depth 0pt width 0.1ex\!\sim} A \wedge C$, then $B \mathrel{\vrule height 1.6ex depth 0pt width 0.1ex\!\sim} C$.

We will defer the discussion and justification of these postulates to Chapter 12. As we will see then, all the above postulates are already known from the literature on belief change. Moreover, in what follows we will show how other postulates for belief contractions can be satisfied by imposing additional constraints on epistemic states. Among other things, this will help us to reveal some constitutive principles underlying common approaches to belief change.

We will list now some of the derived features of our contraction relation that we will need in the sequel.

Lemma 10.1.1.   *1. If $A \mathrel{\vrule height 1.6ex depth 0pt width 0.1ex\!\sim} B$, then $-A = -(B \rightarrow A)$;*
  2. If $A \wedge B \mathrel{\vrule height 1.6ex depth 0pt width 0.1ex\!\sim} A \leftrightarrow B$, then $-A = -B$;
  3. If $A \mathrel{\vrule height 1.6ex depth 0pt width 0.1ex\!\sim} B$, then $A \wedge C \mathrel{\vrule height 1.6ex depth 0pt width 0.1ex\!\sim} A \vee B$;
  4. If $A \wedge B \mathrel{\vrule height 1.6ex depth 0pt width 0.1ex\!\sim} B$, then $A \mathrel{\vrule height 1.6ex depth 0pt width 0.1ex\!\sim} B$;

5. $A \wedge B \mathrel{\vdash\mkern-9mu\sim} B$ iff $A \wedge C \mathrel{\vdash\mkern-9mu\sim} B$, for any C;
6. If $A \mathrel{\vdash\mkern-9mu\sim} A$, then $B \mathrel{\vdash\mkern-9mu\sim} A$.
7. If $A \mathrel{\vdash\mkern-9mu\sim} A$, then $-A = -\mathbf{t}$;
8. If $A \wedge B \mathrel{\vdash\mkern-9mu\sim} B$, then $\mathbf{f} \mathrel{\vdash\mkern-9mu\sim} B$.
9. If $A \wedge B \mathrel{\vdash\mkern-9mu\sim} A{\to}B$ and $B \wedge C \mathrel{\vdash\mkern-9mu\sim} B{\to}C$, then $A \mathrel{\vdash\mkern-9mu\sim} B{\to}C$.

Proof. (1) and (2) directly follow from the combination of Cautious Antitony and Cautious Monotony. (3) follows from Right Weakening and Partial Antitony. (4) follows from Cautious Monotony. (5) follows from (4) and Partial Antitony. (6) is a consequence of Partial Antitony and Cautious Monotony. (7) is a special case of (2), while (8) is a consequence of Partial Antitony.

For (9). From $A \wedge B \mathrel{\vdash\mkern-9mu\sim} A{\to}B$ we infer $A \wedge B \wedge C \mathrel{\vdash\mkern-9mu\sim} A{\to}B$ by Partial Antitony. Similarly, $B \wedge C \mathrel{\vdash\mkern-9mu\sim} B{\to}C$ gives us $A \wedge B \wedge C \mathrel{\vdash\mkern-9mu\sim} B{\to}C$. Combining the two, we obtain

$$A \wedge B \wedge C \mathrel{\vdash\mkern-9mu\sim} (A{\to}B) \wedge (B{\to}C)$$

Applying now (4), we infer $A \mathrel{\vdash\mkern-9mu\sim} (A{\to}B) \wedge (B{\to}C)$, and consequently $A \mathrel{\vdash\mkern-9mu\sim} B{\to}C$.   □

Notice that, given Tautology and Right Weakening, the condition (2) in the above lemma implies (C4), (C6) and (C8). Consequently, our contraction relation can be compactly characterized by the following conditions on contracted belief sets:

(B1) $-A$ is a deductively closed theory;
(B2)   If $A \wedge B \mathrel{\vdash\mkern-9mu\sim} A \leftrightarrow B$, then $-A = -B$;
(B3)   If $A \wedge B \mathrel{\vdash\mkern-9mu\sim} A$, then $A \wedge B \wedge C \mathrel{\vdash\mkern-9mu\sim} A$;
(B4) $-A \cap -B \subseteq -(A \wedge B)$.

Now we are going to show that all our postulates for contraction relations are mutually independent.

Independence of Partial Antitony. Let u and v be two consistent theories such that $u \subset v$. For any $A \in v$, we put $-A = v$, while for any $A \notin u$, we define $-A$ to be equal to u. It is easy to check that this determines a contraction relation satisfying all the postulates except Partial Antitony. For the latter, notice that if we take an arbitrary A from $v \setminus u$ and $B \in v$, we will have $A \wedge B \mathrel{\vdash\mkern-9mu\sim} A$, but not $\mathbf{f} \mathrel{\vdash\mkern-9mu\sim} A$, contrary to Partial Antitony.

Independence of Cautious Antitony. Let u be a consistent theory. For any tautology A, we put $-A = \mathrm{Th}(\mathbf{f})$, while for any non-tautology we define $-A$ as equal to u. It is easy to check that this contraction relation satisfies all the postulates except Cautious Antitony.

Independence of Distributivity. The relevant counterexample that we have is a bit complicated. Consider a structure consisting of a base $\Delta = \{p \wedge (q \vee r), p \wedge r, q \wedge (p \vee r), q \wedge r, p \wedge q \wedge r\}$ and a selection function γ on the subsets of the base defined as follows:

• $\gamma(\Delta) = \{p \wedge q \wedge r\}$.

- $\gamma(\{p \wedge (q \vee r), p \wedge r\}) = \{p \wedge r\}; \quad \gamma(\{q \wedge (p \vee r), q \wedge r\}) = \{q \wedge r\}$
- γ is an identity on all other subsets Δ.

For any proposition A, we take $\Delta \perp A$ to be the set of all the subsets of Δ that do not imply A. Finally we define the contraction relation as follows

$$-A = \bigcap \{\mathrm{Cl}(\Gamma) \mid \Gamma \in \gamma(\Delta \perp A\}$$

It is easy to check that r belongs to both $-p$ and $-q$, though it does not belong to $-p \wedge q$. Hence the above structure violates Distributivity. It is also an easy but tedious exercise to check that the above finite model satisfies all the rest of our postulates.

Independence of Cautious Monotony. (Taken from [RP99]) For an arbitrary contraction relation $\sim\!\!\mid$, let us consider the following relation: $A \sim\!\!\mid^* B \equiv A \sim\!\!\mid B \,\&\, A \vDash B$. It is easily verified that $\sim\!\!\mid^*$ satisfies all the postulates except Cautious Monotony. For the latter, given $\mathbf{f} \sim\!\!\mid A$, we have $A \wedge \neg A \sim\!\!\mid^* A$, and hence Cautious Monotony would imply $\neg A \sim\!\!\mid^* A$, and therefore $\vDash A$. In other words, $-\mathbf{f}$ for $\sim\!\!\mid$ should contain only tautologies.

Belief and knowledge set of a contraction relation. Just as ordinary inference relations, every contraction relation also determines its own belief and knowledge sets. These sets will correspond, respectively, to belief and knowledge set of any epistemic state that generates it.

Contraction relations allow for a situation in which the contracted proposition is still retained in the contracted belief set. This is what is happening, for example, when we try to delete a logical tautology. This abnormal behavior points out that the proposition in question is considered as belonging to our knowledge rather than to our beliefs, and hence as impossible to retract. To make the discussion of such propositions more precise, let us introduce the following definition:

Definition 10.1.1. *A proposition A will be said to be* known *with respect to a contraction relation $\sim\!\!\mid$, if $A \sim\!\!\mid A$ holds; otherwise, it will be called* contingent. *The set of all propositions that are known with respect to $\sim\!\!\mid$ will be called the* knowledge set *of $\sim\!\!\mid$ and denoted by $\mathbf{K}_\sim$.*

According to the intended interpretation, $\mathbf{K}_\sim$ consists of propositions that are known in the associated epistemic state. As we will show in the next section, this set determines, in effect, the internal logic that governs the behavior of contractions.

Similarly, a proposition will be said to be believed with respect to a contraction relation if it normally holds in the absence of falsity.

Definition 10.1.2. *A proposition A will be said to be* believed *with respect to a contraction relation $\sim\!\!\mid$, if $\mathbf{f} \sim\!\!\mid A$ holds. The set of all such propositions will be called the* belief set *of $\sim\!\!\mid$ and denoted by $\mathbf{B}_\sim$.*

As can be seen, $\mathbf{B}_\sim$ coincides with $-\mathbf{f}$. Consequently, a belief set of a contraction relation is always deductively closed. On the intended interpretation, this set will correspond to the refined belief set of the associated epistemic state. As can be anticipated, it will play an important role in characterizing AGM contractions.

10.1.2 The internal logic of contractions and the success postulate

As we are going to show now, the knowledge set $\mathbf{K}_\sim$ of a contraction relation determines its underlying monotonic logic. Moreover, by fixing this underlying logic, we will make valid an important postulate of Success for contraction inference.

Below we will denote by $\mathrm{Th}_\sim$ the least classical consequence relation that includes $\mathbf{K}_\sim$.

To begin with, we will show that $\mathbf{K}_\sim$ is a deductively closed set.

Lemma 10.1.2. $\mathbf{K}_\sim$ *is a deductively closed set.*

Proof. To begin with, since $\mathbf{t} \sim \mathbf{t}$, every tautology belongs to $\mathbf{K}_\sim$. Now if $A, B \in \mathbf{K}_\sim$, then $A \sim A$ and $B \sim B$. Applying Partial Antitony to each, we obtain $A \wedge B \sim A$ and $A \wedge B \sim B$. Therefore by And, $A \wedge B \sim A \wedge B$, that is, $A \wedge B \in \mathbf{K}_\sim$. Finally, if $A \in \mathbf{K}_\sim$ and $A \vDash B$, then we have $A \sim A$ and $(A \wedge B) \leftrightarrow A$, and consequently $A \wedge B \sim A \wedge B$ by Right Weakening and Extensionality. Therefore, we have also $A \wedge B \sim A$. Applying Cautious Monotony to these two rules, we obtain $B \sim A \wedge B$, and hence $B \sim B$, that is $B \in \mathbf{K}_\sim$. This concludes the proof. $\square$

As a consequence of the above lemma, we immediately obtain the following characterization of $\mathrm{Th}_\sim$.

Corollary 10.1.1. $B \in \mathrm{Th}_\sim(A)$ *if and only if* $A \rightarrow B \sim A \rightarrow B$.

Proof. Since $\mathrm{Th}_\sim$ is a classical consequence relation, $B \in \mathrm{Th}_\sim(A)$ holds if and only if $A \rightarrow B \in \mathrm{Th}_\sim(\emptyset)$. Now, $\mathrm{Th}_\sim(\emptyset)$ is a least deductively closed set containing $\mathbf{K}_\sim$. But the latter set is deductively closed by itself, so $\mathbf{K}_\sim = \mathrm{Th}_\sim(\emptyset)$. Hence the result. $\square$

Similarly to inference relations, the following definition describes when a contraction relation respects and, respectively, preserves a classical consequence relation.

Definition 10.1.3. *1. A contraction relation $\sim$ will be said to* respect *a classical consequence relation* Th *if it satisfies*
   Closure $\mathrm{Th}(-A) = -A$.
   2. A contraction relation $\sim$ will be said to preserve Th *if it respects* Th *and satisfies, in addition,*

Success   If $A \notin \mathrm{Th}(\emptyset)$, then $A \not\sim A$.

The Closure postulate requires contracted belief sets to be closed theories in Th. The Success postulate says that if A is not a valid proposition with respect to Th, then it can be successfully contracted (accomplishing thereby the purpose of contraction). It plays the same role for contraction relations as the postulate of Consistency Preservation for nonmonotonic inference relations.

If a contraction relation respects Th, then it allows for replacement of Th-equivalent propositions not only in consequents, but also in antecedents of contractionals.

Lemma 10.1.3. *If a contraction relation $\sim$ respects* Th, *then it satisfies also*

Left Th-***Equivalence***   *If* $A \leftrightarrow B \in \mathrm{Th}(\emptyset)$, *then* $-A = -B$.

Proof. Assume that $A \leftrightarrow B \in \mathrm{Th}(\emptyset)$ and $A \sim C$. Then $A \wedge B \sim A \leftrightarrow B$ by Closure, and hence $A \wedge B \sim C$ by Cautious Antitony. By Left Logical Equivalence and Closure again,

$$B \wedge (A \leftrightarrow B) \sim C \wedge (A \leftrightarrow B).$$

Therefore, $B \sim C$ by Cautious Monotony. Thus, Left Th-Equivalence holds.
□

As we will see in Chapter 12, the above conditions exactly correspond to the AGM postulates for contraction that involve the underlying consequence relation.

The following result shows that $\mathrm{Th}_\sim$ provides an adequate description of the logic underlying a given contraction relation.

Theorem 10.1.1.   *1. Any contraction relation $\sim$ respects* $\mathrm{Th}_\sim$.
2. If a contraction relation $\sim$ preserves Th, *then the latter coincides with* $\mathrm{Th}_\sim$.

Proof. (1) In order to show the validity of Closure with respect to $\mathrm{Th}_\sim$, it is sufficient to demonstrate that if $A \sim B$ and $C \in \mathrm{Th}_\sim(B)$, then $A \sim C$. Since $\mathrm{Th}_\sim$ satisfies the deduction theorem, we have $B \rightarrow C \in \mathrm{Th}(\emptyset)$, and therefore $B \rightarrow C \sim B \rightarrow C$. But the latter implies $A \sim B \rightarrow C$ (see condition (6) from Lemma 10.1.1), and hence the result follows from the deductive closure of $-A$.

(2) Success gives us that if $A \in \mathrm{Th}_\sim(\emptyset)$, then $A \in \mathrm{Th}(\emptyset)$, while Closure implies that if $A \in \mathrm{Th}(\emptyset)$, then, in particular, $A \sim A$, and hence $A \in \mathrm{Th}_\sim(\emptyset)$. Thus, Th and $\mathrm{Th}_\sim$ have the same provable formulas, and this is sufficient for the coincidence of these two classical consequence relations.   □

As the above result shows, instead of the classical entailment, we could as well choose $\text{Th}_{\sim\!\!\mid}$ as our underlying logic. Moreover, in the latter case we would have that our contraction relation would satisfy the Success postulate. In other words, the effect of the latter amounts simply to 'fixing' the underlying logic of contraction.

10.1.3 Contraction and expectation relations

An informal characterization of entrenchment relations, suggested in Chapter 5, said that B is more entrenched than A if removal of $A \wedge B$ will normally retain B. This contraction-based criterion of epistemic entrenchment can now be made exact. Namely, it gives the following definition of entrenchment in terms of contraction relations:

$$\text{(EC)} \qquad\qquad A < B \;\equiv\; A \wedge B \sim\!\!\mid B$$

The following result shows that the above definition determines a simple qualitative entrenchment.

Theorem 10.1.2. *If $\sim\!\!\mid$ is a contraction relation, then $<$ as defined by (EC) is a simple qualitative entrenchment relation.*

Proof. We show first that $<$ is an expectation relation.

Right Weakening. Assume that $A \wedge B \sim\!\!\mid B$ and $B \vDash C$. Then $A \wedge B \wedge C \sim\!\!\mid B$ by Left Equivalence, which implies $A \wedge C \sim\!\!\mid B$ by (4) from Lemma 10.1.1, and hence $A \wedge C \sim\!\!\mid C$ by Right Weakening for $\sim\!\!\mid$. Thus, $A < C$, and consequently Right Weakening holds for $<$.

Left Strengthening. If $A \wedge B \sim\!\!\mid B$ and $C \vDash A$, then $C \wedge A \wedge B \sim\!\!\mid B$ by Partial Antitony, which is equivalent to $C \wedge B \sim\!\!\mid B$, and hence $C < B$ holds.

Now we will show that $<$ is a qualitative entrenchment relation. t-*reflexivity* and *Reduction* are immediate.

And. If $A \wedge B \sim\!\!\mid B$ and $A \wedge C \sim\!\!\mid C$, then $A \wedge B \wedge C \sim\!\!\mid B$ and $A \wedge B \wedge C \sim\!\!\mid C$ by Partial Antitony, and hence $A \wedge B \wedge C \sim\!\!\mid B \wedge C$ by And for contraction. Thus, $A < B \wedge C$, and therefore And holds for $<$. $\qquad\square$

The above proof uses actually a very small part of the rules valid for contraction relations. In fact, it shows that (EC) determines a simple qualitative entrenchment relation if $\sim\!\!\mid$ satisfies the basic postulates for contractions, Partial Antitony and the rule (4) from Lemma 10.1.1. Another aspect of this situation is that many quite different contraction relations can determine the same entrenchment relation. As we will see below, this will mean that they determine also the same inference relation.

Notice now that any simple qualitative entrenchment relation is also a contraction relation by itself; in other words, it satisfies all the above postulates for contraction. The following lemma shows that Left Strengthening is the only additional rule needed to characterize such contraction relations.

Lemma 10.1.4. *A contraction relation is a simple qualitative entrenchment relation if and only if it satisfies*

Left Strengthening   *If $A \mathbin{\vdash\mkern-7mu\mid} B$, then $A \wedge C \mathbin{\vdash\mkern-7mu\mid} B$.*

Proof. It is easy to check that all basic postulates for contraction relations are valid for simple qualitative entrenchment. In addition, Left Strengthening immediately implies all supplementary postulates for contraction, except Cautious Monotony, while the latter amounts to (2) from Lemma 5.2.1. Thus, any simple qualitative entrenchment relation is a contraction relation.

Assume now that $\mathbin{\vdash\mkern-7mu\mid}$ is a contraction relation satisfying Left Strengthening. Then it is clearly an expectation relation. In addition, it satisfies And, t-reflexivity (from Tautology), and Reduction (by (4) from Lemma 10.1.1). Therefore, it is a simple qualitative entrenchment relation.   □

An immediate consequence of the above lemma is that any simple qualitative entrenchment relation is determined by some contraction relation via (EC).

Corollary 10.1.2. *Any simple qualitative entrenchment relation is determined by some contraction relation via (EC).*

Proof. If $<$ is a simple qualitative entrenchment relation, it is also a contraction relation; moreover, it generates itself via (EC) due to the fact that, for entrenchment relations, $A < B$ is equivalent to $A \wedge B < B$.   □

Since qualitative entrenchment relations are interdefinable with qualitative dependence relations, the latter are also definable in terms of contractions as follows:

(DC) $$A < B \ \equiv \ A \wedge B \mathbin{\vdash\mkern-7mu\mid} A{\to}B$$

The following result is obtainable as an immediate consequence of Theorem 10.1.2 and the definition of dependence in terms of simple entrenchment, given in Chapter 5.

Lemma 10.1.5. *If $\mathbin{\vdash\mkern-7mu\mid}$ is a contraction relation, then (DC) determines a qualitative dependence relation.*

The above result will be used later in this chapter in the proof of the representation theorem.

Finally, we know also that qualitative entrenchment and dependence are interdefinable with preferential inference relations. This implies, in turn, that the latter are also definable in terms of contraction relations. This is the subject of the next section.

10.1.4 Contraction and preferential inference

As has been said in Chapter 3, skeptical inference $A \mathrel{|\!\sim} B$ with respect to an epistemic state is 'decomposable' into a contraction step consisting of restricting admissible states to states consistent with the antecedent A, and an expansion step consisting in adding A to propositions obtained on the contraction step. As a result, we have obtained the following correspondence between skeptical and contraction inference determined by an epistemic state:

(IC) $\qquad\qquad\qquad A \mathrel{|\!\sim} B \equiv \neg A \mathrel{\rightarrowtail} A \rightarrow B$

The above decomposition is actually an inferential counterpart of the famous Levi identity in belief change theory that will be discussed in Part Three. In this section we will explore syntactic aspects of this correspondence.

To begin with, the following result shows that any contraction relation determines a preferential inference relation in accordance with the above definition.

Theorem 10.1.3. *If $\mathrel{\rightarrowtail}$ is a contraction relation, then $\mathrel{|\!\sim}$ defined by (IC) is a preferential inference relation.*

Proof. Instead of a direct check of the postulates, we can notice that $\neg A \mathrel{\rightarrowtail} A {\rightarrow} B$ is equivalent to $A {\rightarrow} \neg B <_0 A {\rightarrow} B$ for the entrenchment relation $<_0$ determined by $\mathrel{\rightarrowtail}$, which is exactly the definition of the preferential inference relation corresponding to $<_0$. $\qquad\qquad\square$

Notice that, due to the fact that $-A$ is deductively closed, (IC) can be rewritten as follows:

$$A \mathrel{|\!\sim} B \text{ if and only if } A, -(\neg A) \vDash B$$

In other words, A preferentially entails B if B can be logically inferred from A together with a set of assumptions that 'survive' the deletion of $\neg A$.

Remark. The above description can also be considered as a generalization of the corresponding interpretation for expectation inference given in [GM94]. According to the latter, A nonmonotonically entails B if B follows from A together with all propositions that are "sufficiently well expected" in the light of A, where C is sufficiently well expected in view of A if $\neg A < C$ holds for the corresponding expectation relation. As we will see later, however, for modular expectation relations (considered by the authors) $\neg A < C$ is equivalent to $\neg A \mathrel{\rightarrowtail} C$. Thus, our representation provides, in effect, a smooth extension of the interpretation from [GM94] to preferential inference relations.

As for entrenchment relations earlier, it turns out that preferential inference relations are also equivalent to some (very special) contraction relations. Namely, a contraction relation will be called *complete* if it satisfies

Completeness $\quad A \mathrel{\rightarrowtail} \neg A$

Then the following result shows that complete contraction relations can be identified, in effect, with preferential inference relations.

Lemma 10.1.6. $\vdash$ *is a complete contraction relation if and only if the relation* $\vdash$ *defined as*

$$A \vdash B \equiv \neg A \vdash B$$

is a preferential inference relation.

Proof. If $\vdash$ is a complete contraction relation, then (IC) is reducible to $\neg A \vdash B$, so $\vdash$, as defined above, will be a preferential inference relation. In the other direction, if $\vdash$ is a preferential inference relation, then $A \vdash B$ defined as $\neg A \vdash B$ satisfies all the postulates of contraction inference as well as Completeness. Indeed, the basic postulates (C1)–(C4) are immediate, (C5) and (C8) follow by basic inference, while (C6) and (C7) are direct consequences of Cut and Or, respectively.   □

Since any contraction determines a preferential inference relation, it determines also an associated complete contraction relation via the following definition:

(CC) $A \vdash^i B \equiv A \vdash A \vee B$

As a consequence of the above lemma, we obtain a quite simple proof that any preferential inference relation is generated by some contraction relation.

Corollary 10.1.3. *Any preferential inference relation is generated via (IC) by some contraction relation.*

Proof. As can be seen, any preferential inference relation is (trivially) generated by the corresponding complete contraction relation.   □

Later we will obtain a more natural decomposition of preferential inference as a by-product of the semantic representation of contraction relations in terms of epistemic states.

10.1.5 Inference-equivalent contractions

Different contraction relations can generate the same inference relation. This naturally leads to the following notion of equivalence:

Definition 10.1.4. *Two contraction relations are* inference-equivalent *if they generate the same inference relation via (IC).*

As we will see in Part Three, this notion of equivalence coincides with the notion of revision equivalence introduced by Makinson in [Mak87].

As can be easily discerned from the condition (IC), contraction relations are inference-equivalent if and only if they coincide on contractionals $A \mathbin{\vert\!\sim} B$ for which A logically implies B. Such contraction relations have many common features. Most importantly, inference-equivalent contractions have the same belief sets (since the latter are determined by contractionals of the form $\mathbf{f} \mathbin{\vert\!\sim} A$) and same knowledge sets (determined by contractionals of the form $A \mathbin{\vert\!\sim} A$). Still, the equivalence classes determined by inference-equivalence are rather large and contain many quite different kinds of contractions. We will give below a rather simple description of the partition generated by the inference-equivalence on the set of all contraction relations.

For any contraction relation $\mathbin{\vert\!\sim}$, $\mathbin{\vert\!\sim}^e$ will denote the entrenchment relation generated by $\mathbin{\vert\!\sim}$ via (EC) (which is also a special contraction relation), while $\mathbin{\vert\!\sim}^i$ will denote the corresponding complete contraction relation produced by $\mathbin{\vert\!\sim}$ via (CC). As can be easily checked, $\mathbin{\vert\!\sim}$ is always included in $\mathbin{\vert\!\sim}^i$ and includes $\mathbin{\vert\!\sim}^e$. Moreover, both $\mathbin{\vert\!\sim}^i$ and $\mathbin{\vert\!\sim}^e$ are inference-equivalent to $\mathbin{\vert\!\sim}$.

Since preferential inference relations are interdefinable with both entrenchment relations and complete contraction relations, we immediately obtain that two entrenchment relations or, respectively, two complete contraction relations are inference-equivalent if and only if they coincide. Moreover, this implies also that inference-equivalence could be alternatively characterized in terms of coincidence of either generated entrenchment relations or complete contraction relations.

Lemma 10.1.7. *Contraction relations $\mathbin{\vert\!\sim}_1$ and $\mathbin{\vert\!\sim}_2$ are inference-equivalent if and only if one of the following conditions holds:*

1. $\mathbin{\vert\!\sim}_1^e = \mathbin{\vert\!\sim}_2^e$;
2. $\mathbin{\vert\!\sim}_1^i = \mathbin{\vert\!\sim}_2^i$.

Finally, the following result shows that the set of contraction relations that are inference-equivalent to a given contraction relation $\mathbin{\vert\!\sim}$ consists precisely of contraction relations that include $\mathbin{\vert\!\sim}^e$ and are included in $\mathbin{\vert\!\sim}^i$.

Theorem 10.1.4. *A contraction relation $\mathbin{\vert\!\sim}$ is inference-equivalent to $\mathbin{\vert\!\sim}_1$ if and only if*

$$\mathbin{\vert\!\sim}^e \subseteq \mathbin{\vert\!\sim}_1 \subseteq \mathbin{\vert\!\sim}^i.$$

Proof. The implication from left to right follows from the preceding lemma and the fact that $\mathbin{\vert\!\sim}^e \subseteq \mathbin{\vert\!\sim} \subseteq \mathbin{\vert\!\sim}^i$.

Assume that $A \vDash B$. Then it is easy to see that $A \mathbin{\vert\!\sim}^e B$ iff $A \mathbin{\vert\!\sim}^i B$ iff $A \mathbin{\vert\!\sim} B$. Consequently, if $\mathbin{\vert\!\sim}^e \subseteq \mathbin{\vert\!\sim}_1 \subseteq \mathbin{\vert\!\sim}^i$, then $\mathbin{\vert\!\sim}_1$ coincides with $\mathbin{\vert\!\sim}$ on contractionals $A \mathbin{\vert\!\sim} B$ for which $A \vDash B$. Consequently, the two contraction relations are inference-equivalent. $\square$

The above result shows, in particular, that $\rightvdash^e$ is a least contraction relation that is inference-equivalent to $\rightvdash$, while $\rightvdash^i$ is a greatest such relation.

10.1.6 Simple, conservative and cautious contractions

Known propositions of a contraction relation are propositions that the contraction relation is refusing to contract. But even if we know which propositions are known with respect to a contraction relation, this still does not determine what we should believe when we are required 'to do the impossible', that is, to delete such a proposition. The only constraint on such 'abnormal' belief sets is the condition (7) of Lemma 10.1.1 saying that the result of contracting a known proposition should be the same as that of contracting a tautology $\mathbf{t}$. Consequently, all such sets should coincide. Beyond that, the postulates of contraction inference do not say us what this abnormal belief set amounts to. This means also that our contraction relations are still under-determined in some sense. Though it is possible to give a semantic representation for all of them (see below), we will prefer in this study to consider more specialized classes of contraction relations, for which the above mentioned abnormal belief set is already fixed. Nevertheless, we have put the corresponding additional postulates separately from the rest in order to keep the notion of a contraction relation sufficiently general for potential representations beyond our immediate interests in this book.

A simplest possible way of fixing the result of impossible contractions is a 'classical' one, according to which if we are forced to disbelieve logical tautologies, we are allowed to believe anything. Consequently, the abnormal belief set will be an inconsistent theory in this case. This stipulation is akin to the classical logical principle that contradiction implies any proposition; it is preserved also by nonmonotonic inference formalisms. Most importantly, this stipulation is presupposed already by the semantic definition of contraction inference with respect to epistemic states, given in Chapter 3: when we are saying that $A \rightvdash B$ is valid in an epistemic state if B holds in all preferred belief states that do not satisfy A, this implies, in particular, that if A is known, then $A \rightvdash B$ will be (trivially) valid, for any B.

The above decision is reflected in the following definition.

Definition 10.1.5. *A contraction relation will be called* simple *if it satisfies*

Simple Failure   *If $A \rightvdash A$, then $A \rightvdash \mathbf{f}$.*

The above condition says that contracting a known proposition results in an inconsistent belief set. As we will show below, simple contraction relations provide a complete characterization of the contraction inference with respect to epistemic states. Notice, however, that *any* contraction relation can be transformed into a simple contraction relation by changing its behavior on known propositions. More exactly, for any contraction relation we can construct the following relation:

$$A \mathrel{\rlap{\hskip.1em/}\sim}^s B \;\equiv\; A \mathrel{\rlap{\hskip.1em/}\sim} B \text{ or } A \mathrel{\rlap{\hskip.1em/}\sim} A.$$

As can be easily seen, $\mathrel{\rlap{\hskip.1em/}\sim}^s$ will already be a simple contraction relation. though it will have the same known propositions and, moreover, will coincide with $\mathrel{\rlap{\hskip.1em/}\sim}$ on contingent propositions. In particular, $\mathrel{\rlap{\hskip.1em/}\sim}^s$ will also be inference-equivalent to $\mathrel{\rlap{\hskip.1em/}\sim}$. This shows, in effect, that the restriction to simple contractions is rather a matter of overall simplicity of the formalism and its interpretations, rather than a deep conceptual issue.

Though the above solution provides a really simple definition for 'impossible' contractions, it has an obvious drawback from the point of view of belief change in that it is careless about what we should do after the 'impossible' contraction is made (just as classical logic is careless about what we should do after deriving a contradiction). Common theories of belief change suggested a different solution for this case that was guided by the intention to preserve consistency of contracted belief sets. They adopted the principle that if we are required to do the impossible, we should do nothing. In particular, if A is known, then the contracted belief set $-A$ should coincide with the original belief set. This decision can be incorporated into our framework as follows.

Definition 10.1.6. *A contraction relation* $\mathrel{\rlap{\hskip.1em/}\sim}$ *will be called* conservative *if it satisfies the following postulate*

Failure   *If* $A \mathrel{\rlap{\hskip.1em/}\sim} A$*, then* $A \mathrel{\rlap{\hskip.1em/}\sim} B$ *iff* $\mathbf{f} \mathrel{\rlap{\hskip.1em/}\sim} B$.

The above postulate says, in effect, that if A is known, then $-A = -\mathbf{f}$. Thus, the effect of Failure consists in identifying the result of contracting a known proposition with the original belief set of a contraction relation. As can be seen, it is actually reducible to a simpler condition stating that contracting a tautology gives the belief set of a contraction relation:

$$-\mathbf{t} = -\mathbf{f}$$

As before, the difference between conservative and simple contractions pertains only to their behavior with respect to known propositions. Similarly to simple contractions, for any contraction relation we can construct a conservative contraction coinciding with the former on contingent propositions (which are common to both):

$$A \mathrel{\rlap{\hskip.1em/}\sim}^c B \;\equiv\; \begin{cases} A \mathrel{\rlap{\hskip.1em/}\sim} B & \text{if } A \mathrel{\rlap{\hskip.1em/}\not\sim} A, \\ \mathbf{f} \mathrel{\rlap{\hskip.1em/}\sim} B & \text{otherwise.} \end{cases}$$

Finally, we will briefly mention yet another decision that could be made in this case. A most cautious stipulation in our case consists in restricting the abnormal belief set to the set of known propositions. The following definition reflects this decision.

Definition 10.1.7. *A contraction relation will be called* cautious *if it satisfies*

Retreat   *If* t ⊣ A, *then* A ⊣ A.

As can be shown, Retreat amounts to the condition −t = **K**~. Thus, it amounts to removal of all our potential and actual beliefs and leave us only with what was known (firmly believed) beforehand. This is presumably not too wise a behavior, so it will not be used in our study. Still it is worth to mention for what follows that simple entrenchment relations, viewed as contraction relations, are cautious in this sense; t < A holds for them if and only if A < A.

The above three kinds of contraction relations apparently exhaust the range of interesting context-independent decisions that can be made about what we should believe when we are required to remove a known proposition.

10.2 Completeness

In this section we are going to show that simple contraction relations provide a complete description of contraction inference generated by epistemic states.

Recall that a contractional A ⊣ B is valid with respect to an epistemic state if B holds in all preferred states from]A[. The set of contractionals that are valid in 𝔼 will be denoted by ⊣$_𝔼$.

To begin with, we have the following soundness lemma.

Lemma 10.2.1. *If* 𝔼 *is an epistemic state, then* ⊣$_𝔼$ *is a simple contraction relation.*

Proof. The basic postulates (C1)–(C4) are immediate, so we will check only the supplementary ones.

Partial Antitony. Assume that A ∧ B ∧ C ⊣ A is not valid in 𝔼. Then there must exist a preferred state s in]A ∧ B ∧ C[such that A ∉ l(s). But then s is also preferred in]A ∧ B[, and hence A ∧ B ⊣ A is not valid in 𝔼.

Cautious Antitony and Cautious Monotony. Assume that A ∧ B ⊣ A is valid in 𝔼. Then both these postulates will immediately follow from the fact that in this case preferred states in]A ∧ B[will coincide with preferred states in]B[. Indeed, if s is preferred in]A ∧ B[, then it should satisfy A, and hence it cannot satisfy B. But then s will obviously be preferred in]B[. In the other direction, if s is a preferred state in]B[, then it belongs to]A ∧ B[. Assume that s is not preferred in]A ∧ B[. Then there must exist a more preferred state t that is preferred in]A ∧ B[. But then t should satisfy A and hence it cannot satisfy B, contrary to our assumption that s is a preferred state in]B[.

Distributivity. Assume that A ∧ B ⊣ C is not valid in 𝔼, that is, there exists a preferred state s in]A ∧ B[such that C ∉ l(s). Since s does not satisfy A ∧ B, either A or B does not hold in s. Assume that A does not hold in s. Then s will be preferred in]A[, and consequently A ⊣ C will not be valid in $\mathbb{E}$. Similarly, if B does not hold in s, the latter will be preferred in $]B[$, and consequently $B \vdash C$ will not be valid in $\mathbb{E}$. This concludes the proof.   □

Thus, any epistemic state generates a simple contraction relation. Moreover, we are going to prove now that any simple contraction relation is generated by some epistemic state.

We have shown earlier that preferential entailment corresponds to a special case of a contraction relation. Accordingly, the proof of the representation theorem, given below, will follow the general pattern of the ingenious proof given for preferential inference relations in [KLM90]. In order to highlight the similarity, we will use a terminology similar to that in [KLM90]. It should be kept in mind, however, that our definitions for the relevant notions will be very different from that given in [KLM90], and this will require, in turn, some drastic changes in the proof.

Recall first that the following definition

(DC) $A < B \equiv A \wedge B \vdash A \rightarrow B$

determines a qualitative dependence relation (see Lemma 10.1.5). We will use this relation now in order to define the notion of a normal theory for a proposition.

Definition 10.2.1. *A deductively closed theory u will be called* normal *for a contingent proposition A if $A \notin u$ and, for any B such that $A < B$, either $B \in u$ or $-B \subseteq u$.*

Notice that any normal theory for A should contain $-A$ (since $<$ is reflexive). The following lemma shows that for worlds (maximal deductively closed sets) this is already sufficient for normality.

Lemma 10.2.2. *A world α is normal for A iff it includes both $\neg A$ and $-A$.*

Proof. Assume that α includes both $\neg A$ and $-A$, and let $A < B$ and $B \vdash C$. By (3) from Lemma 10.1.1 we obtain $A \wedge B \vdash B \vee C$, and then applying Cautious Monotony to $A < B$ and $A \wedge B \vdash B \vee C$, we obtain $A \vdash B \vee C$. But $-A$ is included in α, and hence $B \vee C \in \alpha$. Since C was taken to be an arbitrary proposition from $-B$, this implies, in particular, that if $B \notin \alpha$, then $-B \subseteq \alpha$. This concludes the proof.   □

The following lemma constitutes the main step in the proof. Notice that the relevant result for preferential inference relations presents no difficulty and is proved in a few easy steps in [KLM90].

Lemma 10.2.3 (Basic Lemma). *If A is contingent, then $A \vdash B$ iff B belongs to all theories that are normal for A.*

Proof. The implication from left to right follows immediately from the definition of a normal theory. Assume that $A \not\mathrel{\mid\!\sim} B$. Two cases should be considered.

(a) $A \not\mathrel{\mid\!\sim} A \vee B$. Then, due to deductive closure of $-A$, there must exist a world α that includes $-A$ but not $A \vee B$. But then α is normal for A by Lemma 10.2.2 and $B \notin \alpha$.

(b) Assume now that $A \mathrel{\mid\!\sim} A \vee B$. Since $A \not\mathrel{\mid\!\sim} B$, there must exist a world β that includes $-A$ but not B. The assumption implies then that $A \in \beta$. Let us denote by u the following set of propositions:

$$\{\neg A\} \cup -A \cup \{C \mid A < C \ \& \ -C \not\subseteq \beta\}$$

We will prove first that u is logically consistent. Indeed, otherwise there must exist propositions C_i, D_i, for $1 \le i \le n$, such that, for all i, (i) $A < C_i$, (ii) $C_i \mathrel{\mid\!\sim} D_i$, (iii) $D_i \notin \beta$, and (iv) $-A, C_1, \ldots, C_n \vDash A$. Let C denote the conjunction of all C_i, and D denote the disjunction of all D_i. Then (i) implies $A < C$; (ii) implies $C_i \mathrel{\mid\!\sim} D$, for all i, and hence $C \mathrel{\mid\!\sim} D$ by Distributivity; (iii) implies $D \notin \beta$, and (iv) gives $-A \vDash C{\to}A$ and hence $A \mathrel{\mid\!\sim} C{\to}A$ (since $-A$ is deductively closed). Since A is equivalent to $(C \vee A) \wedge (C{\to}A)$, we can apply Partial Antitony and conclude $A \wedge C \mathrel{\mid\!\sim} C{\to}A$. Combining this with $A < C$, we finally obtain $A{\wedge}C \mathrel{\mid\!\sim} A \leftrightarrow C$. But then by (2) from Lemma 10.1.1 we have $-A = -C$, and therefore $A \mathrel{\mid\!\sim} D$. But $-A$ is included in β, which contradicts the assumption that $D \notin \beta$. Thus, u should be logically consistent.

Now we take α to be an arbitrary world including u and consider a theory $v = \alpha \cap \beta$. Clearly, $-A \subseteq v$ and neither A nor B belong to v. Hence, to prove our lemma, we need only to show that v is a normal theory for A. Assume that $A < C$ and $C \notin v$. By Cautious Monotony, we have $A \mathrel{\mid\!\sim} A{\to}C$, and hence $A{\to}C \in \beta$. But $A \in \beta$, and therefore $C \in \beta$. Since v is an intersection of α and β, C does not belong to α. By Lemma 10.2.2, α is normal for A, and consequently $-C \subseteq \alpha$. Moreover, u is included in α, and hence $C \notin u$. But then the definition of u gives us $-C \subseteq \beta$, and consequently $-C$ is included in v. This concludes the proof.   □

It is important for what follows to notice that the set of normal theories needed for the validity of the Basic Lemma can be restricted in various ways. In fact, the above proof shows that

normal theories for A can be chosen to be either worlds or intersections of pairs of worlds $\alpha \cap \beta$ such that $\neg A \in \alpha$ and $A \in \beta$.

Now we define a canonical epistemic state for a given contraction relation. The following definition coincides, in effect, with the corresponding definition in [KLM90][1].

- Admissible belief states are pairs (u, A), where A is contingent, and u is a normal theory for A.

---

[1] The only change we make is that we reverse the direction of the preference relation, since we are seeking to maximize preference, not to minimize it.

- $(v, B) \prec (u, A) \equiv A < B$ and $B \in u$.

The results that follow are exact counterparts of the corresponding auxiliary results proved in [KLM90]. The proofs, however, are different.

Lemma 10.2.4. *If $A < B$, u is a normal theory for A and $B \notin u$, then u is normal for B.*

Proof. The result follows directly from the definition of normality and transitivity of $<$. □

Lemma 10.2.5. *If $A < B$, $B < C$, u is a normal theory for A and $B \in u$, then $C \in u$.*

Proof. By (9) from Lemma 10.1.1, $A < B$ and $B < C$ imply $A \multimap B \rightarrow C$. Since u is normal for A, $-A \subseteq u$, and hence $B \rightarrow C$ belongs to u. Then the result follows from the fact that u is deductively closed and $B \in u$. □

Lemma 10.2.6. $\prec$ *is a strict partial order on states.*

Proof. Irreflexivity immediately follows from the definition of $\prec$. Assume now that $(v, B) \prec (u, A)$ and $(w, C) \prec (v, B)$. Then we have $A < C$ (by transitivity of $<$). In addition, since $B \in u$, Lemma 10.2.5 gives us that $C \in u$, and hence $(w, C) \prec (u, A)$. □

The following lemma is an analogue of Lemma 5.14 from [KLM90].

Lemma 10.2.7. (u, B) *is a preferred state in* $]A[$ *iff* $A \notin u$ *and* $B < A$.

Proof. Assume that (u, B) is preferred in $]A[$, but $B < A$ does not hold. Then there must exist a world α that includes $-A \wedge B$ and $B \wedge \neg A$. By Lemma 10.2.2, α is normal for $A \wedge B$. Since $A \wedge B < B$ always holds, we would have $(\alpha, A \wedge B) \succ (u, B)$, which contradicts the assumption that (u, B) is preferred in $]A[$.

Assume now that $A \notin u$, $B < A$, but (u, B) is not preferred in $]A[$, that is, there exists a state $(u, B) \prec (v, C)$ such that $A \notin v$. Then we have $C < B$, $B \in v$ and v is normal for C – a contradiction with Lemma 10.2.5. □

Now we can show that the canonical epistemic state satisfies the smoothness condition.

Lemma 10.2.8. *For any A, $]A[$ is smooth.*

Proof. Assume that (u, B) is a state such that $A \notin u$. If $B < A$, then (u, B) will be preferred in $]A[$ (by the previous lemma). Now if $B < A$ does not hold, the construction in the proof of the previous lemma gives us a state $(u, B) \prec (\alpha, A \wedge B)$ such that $A \notin \alpha$. It is easy to see that $(\alpha, A \wedge B)$ is a required state that is preferred in $]A[$. □

Thus, we have shown that the canonical epistemic state is indeed a smooth epistemic state in our sense. The following result demonstrates that this state provides an adequate model for our contraction relation.

Lemma 10.2.9. *If $\mathbb{E}$ is the canonical epistemic state of $\sim\!|$, then $A \sim\!|_{\mathbb{E}} B$ iff $A \sim\!| B$.*

Proof. The claim is obvious if A is a known proposition. So, assume that A is contingent. By the definition of $\prec$, if u is a normal theory for A, then (u, A) will always be preferred in $]A[$. Consequently, if $A \sim\!|_{\mathbb{E}} B$ holds, B will belong to all theories that are normal for A. Hence we have $A \sim\!| B$ by the Basic Lemma. In the other direction, if (u, C) is a preferred state in $]A[$, then u is normal for C and $C < A$ by Lemma 10.2.7. But then Lemma 10.2.4 implies that u is normal for A, and therefore $-A \subseteq u$. Consequently, any state preferred in $]A[$ should contain $-A$. This concludes the proof.   □

It is easy to see that the above lemma provides us with all we have needed in order to prove the following

Representation Theorem 10.1. *$\sim\!|$ is a simple contraction relation iff there exists an epistemic state $\mathbb{E}$ such that $\sim\!|$ coincides with $\sim\!|_{\mathbb{E}}$.*

Proof. If $\sim\!|$ is a simple contraction relation, then the preceding lemma implies that the canonical epistemic state for $\sim\!|$ generates exactly $\sim\!|$. The other direction follows from Lemma 10.2.1.   □

Thus, simple contraction relations provide a complete description of contraction validity with respect to epistemic states. This theorem (and especially its proof) will also be used for obtaining most of our subsequent representation results.

The representation of contraction relations in terms of epistemic states allows to see clearly the distinctions as well as similarities between contraction and preferential inference relations. Recall that preferential models from [KLM90] can be identified with epistemic states in which admissible belief states are labelled by worlds. Such 'complete' admissible states do not support A if and only if they support $\neg A$. In other words, for such epistemic states a contractional $A \sim\!| B$ will be obviously equivalent to the preferential conditional $\neg A \mathrel{|\!\sim} B$. This gives a semantic face to the correspondence between preferential inference relations and complete contraction relations, described earlier. At the same time, this shows clearly why general epistemic states are essential for an adequate representation of general, non-complete, contraction relations.

10.2.1 Representation of conservative, cautious and general contractions

The representation theorem proved in the preceding section will allow us to give representation of particular classes of contraction relations in the framework of epistemic states. To begin with, we will show in this section that the representation of conservative, cautious and even general contraction relations can be obtained simply by modifying the definition of contraction inference with respect to epistemic states.

Conservative contractions. As we have seen earlier, conservative contraction relations are contraction relations for which the contraction of known propositions results in the original belief set. A semantic counterpart of such contractions can be obtained using the notion of conservative contraction inference described in the following definition.

Definition 10.2.2. *A contractional* $A \sim\!\mid B$ *will be said to be* conservatively valid *with respect to an epistemic state* $\mathbb{E}$ *if either* A *is known and* B *is believed in* $\mathbb{E}$, *or* B *holds in all preferred admissible states in* $]A[$.

As can be seen, the above definition of conservative validity is obtained from the original definition of contraction inference by changing the behavior of contractionals on known propositions. As a result, we obtain that it determines conservative contraction relations.

Lemma 10.2.10. *The set of contractionals that are conservatively valid with respect to an epistemic state forms a conservative contraction relation.*

Proof. It is easy to check that conservative validity still preserves all the postulates for general contraction relations. In addition, $A \sim\!\mid A$ is conservatively valid in an epistemic state $\mathbb{E}$ if and only if A is known in $\mathbb{E}$. Accordingly, in this case $-A$ will coincide with the belief set of $\mathbb{E}$, and hence the postulate of Failure will hold also. $\square$

Moreover, the following theorem shows that conservative validity with respect to epistemic states provides a complete semantic description of conservative contraction relations.

Representation Theorem 10.2. *A contraction relation* $\sim\!\mid$ *is conservative if and only if it coincides with the set of contractionals that are conservatively valid in some epistemic state.*

Proof. The direction from right to left follows from the preceding lemma. In order to prove that any conservative contraction relation $\sim\!\mid$ is generated by some epistemic state, we can use the canonical epistemic state $\mathbb{E}_{\sim\!\mid}$ constructed in the proof of the main representation theorem. Since $\mathbb{E}_{\sim\!\mid}$ was constructed, in effect, on the basis of contingent propositions of a contraction relation, Lemma 10.2.9 above can be reformulated now as saying that, for contingent A, $A \sim\!\mid B$ holds if and only if B belongs to all preferred states in $]A[$. So we need only to consider the case of known propositions.

If A is known, that is $A \sim\!\mid A$, then $C \sim\!\mid A$, for any C (by (6) from Lemma 10.1.1), and hence A belongs to all states of $\mathbb{E}_{\sim\!\mid}$. Consequently, $A \sim\!\mid B$ is conservatively valid in $\mathbb{E}_{\sim\!\mid}$ if and only if B belongs to all preferred states of $\mathbb{E}_{\sim|}$ or, in other words, when $\mathbf{f} \mathrel{\vphantom{|}\smash{\sim}\mkern-5mu|} B$ is conservatively valid in $\mathbb{E}_{\sim|}$ (since $\mathbf{f}$ is a contingent proposition). On the other hand, the Failure postulate implies that $A \mathrel{\vphantom{|}\smash{\sim}\mkern-5mu|} B$ holds iff $\mathbf{f} \mathrel{\vphantom{|}\smash{\sim}\mkern-5mu|} B$, which is equivalent to (conservative) validity of $\mathbf{f} \mathrel{\vphantom{|}\smash{\sim}\mkern-5mu|} B$ in $\mathbb{E}_{\sim|}$. This completes the proof.   □

Cautious contractions. Similarly, the following definition of cautious validity will provide a representation for cautious contraction relations in epistemic states.

Definition 10.2.3. *A contractional $A \mathrel{\vphantom{|}\smash{\sim}\mkern-5mu|} B$ will be said to be* cautiously valid *with respect to an epistemic state $\mathbb{E}$ if either both A and B are known in $\mathbb{E}$, or A is contingent and B holds in all preferred admissible states from $]A[$.*

The following theorem shows that cautious validity with respect to epistemic states provides a complete semantic description of cautious contraction relations. The proof is quite similar to the previous one, and hence we omit it.

Representation Theorem 10.3. *A contraction relation is cautious if and only if it coincides with the set of contractionals that are cautiously valid with respect to some epistemic state.*

Representation of general contractions.. Actually, the canonical epistemic state used in the proof of the main representation theorem above allows to give a representation for all contraction relations (not necessary simple ones) in terms of pairs $(\mathbb{E}, \mathfrak{a})$, where $\mathbb{E}$ is an epistemic state, and $\mathfrak{a}$ is what can be called an *abnormal belief set*, which is just some deductively closed theory.

Definition 10.2.4. *A contractional $A \mathrel{\vphantom{|}\smash{\sim}\mkern-5mu|} B$ will be said to be* valid *with respect to a pair $(\mathbb{E}, \mathfrak{a})$ if either A is known in $\mathbb{E}$ and $B \in \mathfrak{a}$, or A is contingent in $\mathbb{E}$, and B holds in all preferred states from $]A[$ in $\mathbb{E}$.*

As can be checked, the above definition of validity still satisfies all the postulates for general contraction relations. Thus, we have

Lemma 10.2.11. *The set of contractionals that are valid with respect to a pair $(\mathbb{E}, \mathfrak{a})$ is a contraction relation.*

Moreover, the following theorem shows that any contraction relation is representable in this way.

Representation Theorem 10.4. *Any contraction relation coincides with the set of contractionals that are valid with respect to some pair $(\mathbb{E}, \mathfrak{a})$.*

Proof. Let $\mathrel{\vphantom{|}\smash{\sim}\mkern-5mu|}$ be an arbitrary contraction relation, and $\mathrel{\vphantom{|}\smash{\sim}\mkern-5mu|}^{s}$ the corresponding simple contraction relation, defined as follows (see above)

$$A \mathrel{\vphantom{|}\smash{\sim}\mkern-5mu|}^{s} B \equiv A \mathrel{\vphantom{|}\smash{\sim}\mkern-5mu|} B \text{ or } A \mathrel{\vphantom{|}\smash{\sim}\mkern-5mu|} A$$

Due to the main representation theorem, this latter contraction relation is representable by some epistemic state, say $\mathbb{E}$. Now, let as denote by $\mathfrak{a}$ the set $-\mathfrak{t}$. Then (using (7) from Lemma 10.1.1) it is easy to check that the source contraction relation can be 'restored' from $\curlywedge^s$ and $\mathfrak{a}$ as follows:

$A \curlywedge B$ iff either $A \not\curlywedge^s A$ and $A \curlywedge^s B$ or $A \curlywedge^s A$ and $B \in \mathfrak{a}$

Let as consider now the pair $(\mathbb{E}, \mathfrak{a})$. Then the above description can be easily shown to be equivalent to the condition of validity of $A \curlywedge B$ with respect to $(\mathbb{E}, \mathfrak{a})$. Consequently, $\curlywedge$ coincides with the set of contractionals that are valid in $(\mathbb{E}, \mathfrak{a})$. □

10.2.2 A refined representation

A careful reading of the proof given for the Representation Theorem allows us to single out a certain restricted class of epistemic states that will be still adequate for representing all contraction relations. The corresponding results will show, in particular, that there exists a number of constraints and conditions that can be safely imposed on the notion of an epistemic state while preserving the class of generated contraction relations.

Recall that a deductively closed theory is *saturatable* with respect to A if adding $\neg A$ transforms it into a world (cf. Definition 2.3.1 in Chapter 2). Let us introduce now the following definition:

Definition 10.2.5. *An epistemic state $\mathbb{E}$ will be called* saturatable *if, for any state s that is preferred in* $]A[$, $l(s)$ *is an A-saturatable theory.*

The following result shows that the above condition can be safely imposed on epistemic states without changing the class of contraction relations that are generated by them.

Corollary 10.2.1. *Any contraction relation is generated by some weakly monotonic and saturatable epistemic state.*

Proof. If $(u, A) \prec (v, B)$ holds in the canonical epistemic state for $\curlywedge$, then, by the definition of the preference relation, $A \notin u$ and $A \in v$, and hence $v \not\subseteq u$. Thus, the canonical epistemic state is already weakly monotonic. Moreover, we have said already that the set of normal theories for A can be restricted to either worlds or intersections of pairs of worlds $\alpha \cap \beta$ such that $\neg A \in \alpha$ and $A \in \beta$. As can be seen, each such theory will be A-saturated, and this immediately implies that the 'reduced' canonical epistemic state generated by such theories will be saturatable. □

As we will see in Part Three, the above representation constitutes actually a formal justification for some of the suggestions made by Isaac Levi in [Lev91].

10.2.3 Possible worlds semantics

In this section we will give a representation of contraction inference in terms of reflexive possible worlds models that were used in Chapter 9 for describing credulous and permissive inference relations.

Recall that a reflexive possible worlds model is a structure of the form $\mathbb{W} = (W, l, \preccurlyeq)$ such that $\preccurlyeq$ is a weak partial order on W. A contraction inference with respect to such models is definable as follows:

Definition 10.2.6. *B is a* contraction consequence *of A in $\mathbb{W}$ if either A holds in all states of $\mathbb{W}$, or there exists a preferred state s supporting $\neg A$ such that all equally preferred states support B. The set of contractionals that are valid in $\mathbb{W}$ in this sense will be denoted by $\mathbin{\vert\!\sim}_{\mathbb{W}}$.*

The following lemma shows that the above definition determines a simple contraction inference relation.

Lemma 10.2.12. *For any reflexive possible worlds model $\mathbb{W}$, $\mathbin{\vert\!\sim}_{\mathbb{W}}$ is a simple contraction inference relation.*

Proof. The basic postulates for contraction are immediate, so we will check only the supplementary ones.

Partial Antitony. If $A \wedge B \wedge C \mathbin{\vert\!\sim} A$ is not valid in $\mathbb{W}$, then there must exist a preferred state s supporting $\neg(A \wedge B \wedge C)$ such that $\neg A$ belongs to some equally preferred state t. But then t will be a preferred state containing $\neg(A \wedge B)$, and hence $A \wedge B \mathbin{\vert\!\sim} A$ will not be valid in $\mathbb{W}$.

Cautious Antitony and Cautious Monotony. It is sufficient to show that if $A \wedge B \mathbin{\vert\!\sim} A$ is valid in $\mathbb{W}$, then preferred admissible states containing $\neg(A \wedge B)$ coincide with preferred admissible states containing $\neg B$.

Assume first that s is a preferred state containing $\neg(A \wedge B)$. Then A should hold in this state (since $A \wedge B \mathbin{\vert\!\sim} A$), and consequently $\neg B \in l(s)$. As a result, s is also a preferred state containing $\neg B$. Assume now that s is a preferred state containing $\neg B$, and suppose that it is not a preferred state containing $\neg(A \wedge B)$. Then there must exist a preferred state t containing $\neg(A \wedge B)$ such that $s \prec t$. Again, A should belong to t, and hence $\neg B \in l(t)$, contrary to our assumption that s is a preferred state containing $\neg B$.

Distributivity. Assume that $A \mathbin{\vert\!\sim} C$ and $B \mathbin{\vert\!\sim} C$ are valid in $\mathbb{W}$, and let s be a preferred state containing $\neg(A \wedge B)$. Then either $\neg A$, or $\neg B$ should belong to s. In the first case s will be a preferred state containing $\neg A$, and hence C will belong to all equally preferred states. In the second case s will be a preferred state containing $\neg B$, and hence in this case also C will belong to all equally preferred states. Therefore $A \wedge B \mathbin{\vert\!\sim} C$ will be valid in $\mathbb{W}$. $\square$

Now we will show that reflexive possible worlds models are also adequate for contraction inference. As before, this will be done by transforming any epistemic state into a reflexive possible worlds model generating the same contraction inference relation.

We recall that the corresponding reflexive possible worlds model for an epistemic state is defined as follows: W is a set of all world-state pairs (α, s) such that $s \in S$ and $l(s) \subseteq \alpha$, while the preference relation on W is given by

$$(\alpha, s) \preccurlyeq (\beta, t) \text{ iff } s \preceq t.$$

Then we can show the following

Theorem 10.2.1. *If* $\mathbb{E}$ *is an epistemic state, then its corresponding reflexive possible worlds model determines the same simple contraction inference relation as* $\mathbb{E}$.

Proof. Assume first that $A \mathbin{\rightthreetimes} B$ is not valid in $\mathbb{E}$, and s is an admissible state in $\mathbb{E}$ that is preferred in $]A[$ and does not support B. Then there must exist worlds α, β including $l(s)$ such that $\neg A \in \alpha$ and $\neg B \in \beta$. Let us consider the states (α, s) and (β, s) in W. Clearly, these states are equally preferred in W. Moreover, (α, s) is a preferred state satisfying $\neg A$, since all better states in W will be obtained from admissible states of $\mathbb{E}$ that are preferred to s. Consequently $A \mathbin{\rightthreetimes} B$ is not valid in W.

Assume now that $A \mathbin{\rightthreetimes} B$ is not valid in W. Then there must exists worlds α, β and an admissible state s in $\mathbb{E}$ such that (α, s) is a preferred state in W satisfying $\neg A$, and $\neg B$ holds in (β, s). The latter means that s does not support B in $\mathbb{E}$. Moreover, s is a preferred admissible state in $]A[$ with respect to $\mathbb{E}$. Indeed, if we would have $s \prec t$, for some admissible state $t \in]A[$, then there must exist a world $\gamma \supseteq l(t)$ that contains $\neg A$. But then (γ, t) would be a state in W that is strictly preferred to (α, s) and satisfies $\neg A$, contrary to our assumption that (α, s) is a preferred such state. Thus, $A \mathbin{\rightthreetimes} B$ is not valid also in $\mathbb{E}$. This completes the proof. $\square$

Since any contraction inference relation is determined by some epistemic state, the above theorem gives a completeness of contraction inference with respect to reflexive possible worlds models.

Representation Theorem 10.5. $\mathbin{\rightthreetimes}$ *is a contraction inference relation iff it generated by some reflexive possible worlds model.*

10.3 Contraction inference in standard and pure epistemic states

The representation theorem was formulated in terms of general epistemic states. This naturally poses the question whether this class can be restricted to standard, or even to pure epistemic states, since, as we have seen in Chapter 7, skeptical inference relations are representable using only pure epistemic states. It turns out, however, that contraction inference is much more sensitive to the structure of the underlying epistemic states than skeptical inference. Thus, each of these restrictions reduces also the class of generated contraction relations.

Standard contraction relations. Contraction relations determined by standard epistemic states will themselves be called *standard* in what follows. There exists a clear analogy between standard contraction relations and injective preferential inference relations discussed in Chapter 7.

We begin with an example showing that not all contraction relations are representable by standard epistemic states. It uses, in effect, the same model from [KLM90] that we used in Chapter 7 for demonstrating that not all preferential inference relations are definable by injective models.

Example 10.3.1. Let us consider a general epistemic state $\mathbb{E}_0$ in a finite language determined by four states $\{s_1, s_2, s_3, s_4\}$ such that $s_3 \prec s_1$, $s_4 \prec s_2$, and the labelling function defined as follows: $l(s_1) = \mathrm{Cl}(p \wedge \neg q)$, $l(s_2) = \mathrm{Cl}(\neg p \wedge \neg q)$, and $l(s_3) = l(s_4) = \mathrm{Cl}(p \wedge q)$. Assume that there exists a standard epistemic state $\mathbb{E}$ *in the same language* that determines the same contraction relation as $\mathbb{E}_0$.

To begin with, we have that $q{\to}p$ is known in $\mathbb{E}_0$, and this reduces the set of potential belief sets of $\mathbb{E}$ to six theories, namely, $\mathrm{Cl}(p \wedge q)$, $\mathrm{Cl}(p \wedge \neg q)$, $\mathrm{Cl}(\neg p \wedge \neg q)$, $\mathrm{Cl}(p)$, $\mathrm{Cl}(\neg q)$ and $\mathrm{Cl}(p \leftrightarrow q)$. Moreover, since $\neg p \vee \neg q \mathrel{\substack{\sim\\\mid}} p \wedge q$, $p{\to}q \mathrel{\substack{\sim\\\mid}} p \wedge \neg q$ and $p \vee q \mathrel{\substack{\sim\\\mid}} \neg p \wedge \neg q$ are valid in $\mathbb{E}_0$, the first three theories must belong to $\mathbb{E}$ (since they cannot be obtained as intersections of other theories). In addition, $\neg p \vee \neg q \mathrel{\substack{\sim\\\mid}} p \wedge q$ implies also that even if $\mathrm{Cl}(p)$ and $\mathrm{Cl}(p \leftrightarrow q)$ belong to $\mathbb{E}$, they must be subordinated to $\mathrm{Cl}(p \wedge q)$. Similarly, the other two contractionals can be used to show that $\mathrm{Cl}(p)$ and $\mathrm{Cl}(\neg q)$ should be subordinated to $\mathrm{Cl}(p \wedge \neg q)$ and, finally, $\mathrm{Cl}(p \leftrightarrow q)$ and $\mathrm{Cl}(\neg q)$ should be subordinated to $\mathrm{Cl}(\neg p \wedge \neg q)$. In short, $\mathbb{E}$ should also be a monotonic epistemic state.

Now, $\mathbf{f} \mathrel{\substack{\sim\\\mid}} \neg q$ is valid in $\mathbb{E}_0$, which is possible in $\mathbb{E}$ only if $\mathrm{Cl}(p \wedge q)$ is subordinated to either $\mathrm{Cl}(p \wedge \neg q)$ or $\mathrm{Cl}(\neg p \wedge \neg q)$. Assume first that it is subordinated to $\mathrm{Cl}(p \wedge \neg q)$. Then we would have that $\neg p \wedge \neg q \mathrel{\substack{\sim\\\mid}} \neg q$ is valid in $\mathbb{E}$, though it is not valid in $\mathbb{E}_0$. Similarly, if $\mathrm{Cl}(p \wedge q)$ were subordinated to $\mathrm{Cl}(\neg p \wedge \neg q)$, we would have that $p \wedge \neg q \mathrel{\substack{\sim\\\mid}} \neg p \wedge \neg q$ is valid in $\mathbb{E}$, though it is not valid in $\mathbb{E}_0$. This shows that a standard state $\mathbb{E}$ simply does not exist.

As has been said in Chapter 3, a most plausible way of understanding non-standard epistemic states consists in the assumption that such states involve information that is not expressible in the current language. Moreover, we have seen in Chapter 4 that any general epistemic state can be viewed as a language-restricted part of some standard and monotonic epistemic state. Accordingly, any contraction relation determined by a general epistemic state is also always representable as a language restriction of some contraction relation determined by a standard monotonic epistemic state in some extended language, though it may well happen that it is not representable by any standard epistemic state in the same language. An important technical consequence of the above result, obtained in Chapter 4, is that restricting the set of epistemic states to standard monotonic ones will not give us new valid inference rules for contraction relations.

Thus, standardness and monotonicity, though reduce the class of generated contraction relations, do not introduce new valid general rules for them. The problem of characterizing standard contraction relations (by some more complex conditions) appears to be an important (and still unresolved) problem in our framework. As we will see later, however, some 'rich' contraction relations are representable by standard epistemic states in the same language.

Pure and persistent contraction relations. A contraction relation will be called *pure* if it is generated by a pure epistemic state. Pure contractions have been introduced in [Boc99b, Boc00c] as part of a foundationalist approach to belief change. And though the approach itself has turned out to by flawed, pure contractions have retained their importance for the theory of nonmonotonic reasoning and belief change described in this book.

To begin with, since pure epistemic states are describable by Scott consequence relations, they are definable also in the framework of the latter. Thus, we will say that a pure contraction relation $\sim\!\mid$ is *determined by a consequence relation* $\vdash$ if it is determined by the pure epistemic state consisting of theories of $\vdash$. The following lemma gives a syntactic description of such contraction relations.

Lemma 10.3.1. *If $\sim\!\mid$ is contraction relation determined by a consequence relation $\vdash$, then $A \sim\!\mid B$ holds if and only if $\vdash$ validates the following rule, for any set a:*

$$\frac{a, B \vdash A}{a \vdash A}$$

Proof. It is easily verified that the above rule holds if and only if all maximal theories of $\vdash$ that do not contain A include B.   □

Now, since any preferential inference relation is generated by some consequence relation, we immediately obtain

Lemma 10.3.2. *Any contraction relation is inference-equivalent to some pure contraction.*

Proof. Let $\sim\!\mid$ be an arbitrary contraction relation, and $\mid\!\sim$ its associated preferential inference relation. As has been shown in Chapter 7, any such inference relation is generated by some consequence relation $\vdash$. It can be easily seen that the contraction relation determined by $\vdash$ gives rise to the same inference relation, and hence is inference-equivalent to $\sim\!\mid$.   □

Thus, as far as inference relations are concerned, pure contraction relations turn out to be as expressive as contraction relations in general.

Unfortunately, a complete characterization for pure contractions in terms of relevant postulates remains an open problem, though we will present later such an axiomatization for the linear case. Below we will point out some distinctive features of such a characterization in the general case.

To begin with, it has been established in Chapter 4 that pure epistemic states are representable as language-restricted persistent epistemic states. Consequently, pure contractions satisfy the same general rules as contractions generated by persistent epistemic states. It remains to be seen whether these two classes of epistemic states determine the same set of contraction relations.

Second, pure and persistent contractions constitute a proper subset of general contraction relation, since they satisfy the following characteristic postulate:

Persistence   If $A \mathbin{\sim\!\!\!\mid} B$ and $A \wedge B \mathbin{\sim\!\!\!\mid} C$, then $A \mathbin{\sim\!\!\!\mid} C$.

The above postulate constitutes a strengthening of Cautious Monotony that is not valid for general contractions. In fact, there are some reasonable grounds for conjecturing that adding this postulate will give a required complete characterization for (at least) persistent contraction relations. Anyway, we will see later that this postulate is incompatible with the postulates for AGM contractions on pain of trivialization. In other words, pure and persistent contractions constitute a true alternative to the AGM approach.

10.4 Determination and vacuity

Using epistemic states as our semantic representation, we acquire an opportunity to determine the meaning of additional postulates for contraction suggested in the literature on belief change. This is what we are going to do in the following sections.

As we already mentioned, common representations of belief change give rise to determinate epistemic states. Such epistemic states validate the following well-known postulate for contractions.

Vacuity   If $\mathbf{f} \mathbin{\not\sim\!\!\!\mid} A$, then $A \mathbin{\sim\!\!\!\mid} B$ if and only if $\mathbf{f} \mathbin{\sim\!\!\!\mid} B$.

The above postulate can be rewritten in the form

If $A \notin \mathbf{B}_{\sim}$, then $- A = \mathbf{B}_{\sim}$

and hence it corresponds to the vacuity postulate for AGM contractions (see Chapter 12).

Definition 10.4.1. *A contraction relation will be called* determinate *if it satisfies Vacuity.*

Vacuity requires, in effect, that the corresponding epistemic state $\mathbb{E}$ should be determinate, that is, it must contain a consistent admissible belief state k preferred to all other admissible states in $\mathbb{E}$. Clearly, the state k will determine the belief set of the epistemic state. The following theorem shows that simple determinate contractions provide a complete description of contraction inference in determinate epistemic states[2].

---

[2] The proof given below is much simpler than a direct proof given in [Boc00a].

Representation Theorem 10.6. *A simple contraction relation $\sim\mid$ is determinate if and only if there exists a determinate epistemic state $\mathbb{E}$ such that $\sim\mid$ coincides with $\sim\mid_{\mathbb{E}}$.*

Proof. It is easy to check that determinate epistemic states validate Vacuity. So, we will show only that any simple determinate contraction relation is generated by some determinate epistemic state.

Let $\sim\mid$ be a simple determinate contraction relation, and $\mathbb{E}$ some (not necessarily determinate) epistemic state that generates $\sim\mid$. We will transform $\mathbb{E}$ into a determinate epistemic state as follows. Let S_b be the set of all admissible states s from $\mathbb{E}$ that support the belief set of $\sim\mid$, that is, $\mathbf{B}_\sim \subseteq l(s)$. We will identify all such admissible states into a new admissible state k while preserving all their preference relations with states outside S. In other words, if $t \notin S_b$, then $t \prec k$ will hold if and only if $t \prec s$, for some $s \in S_b$. Finally, we will label k with the belief set $\mathbf{B}_\sim$ of $\sim\mid$.

We will denote the resulting epistemic state by $\mathbb{E}_0$. As can be seen, $\mathbb{E}_0$ will already be a determinate epistemic state. Moreover, we will show that it also represents $\sim\mid$.

Assume first that $A \not\sim\mid B$. Then there must exist an admissible state s in $\mathbb{E}$ which is preferred in $]A[$ and $B \notin l(s)$. Assume first that $s \in S_b$, that is $\mathbf{B}_\sim \subseteq l(s)$. Then both A and B do not belong to $\mathbf{B}_\sim$. Consequently, $A \notin l(k)$, and hence k will be a (unique) preferred state in $]A[$ with respect to $\mathbb{E}_0$. Moreover, we have $B \notin l(k)$, and therefore the contractional $A \sim\mid B$ is not valid in $\mathbb{E}_0$, as required. So, assume now that $s \notin S_b$. If s is also a preferred state in $]A[$ with respect to $\mathbb{E}_0$, then $A \sim\mid B$ is not valid also in $\mathbb{E}_0$. So, assume that s is not a preferred state in $]A[$ with respect to $\mathbb{E}_0$. Then there must exist an admissible state t in $\mathbb{E}_0$ such that $s \prec t$ and $A \notin l(s)$. Since s is preferred in $]A[$ with respect to $\mathbb{E}$, this can happen only if t coincides with k. In this case $A \notin \mathbf{B}_\sim$, and therefore k will be a preferred state in $]A[$ with respect to $\mathbb{E}_0$. In addition, given that $A \not\sim\mid B$, we infer $B \notin \mathbf{B}_\sim$ by Vacuity, and hence $B \notin l(k)$. Consequently, $A \sim\mid B$ is not valid in $\mathbb{E}_0$ in this case also.

Assume now that $A \not\sim\mid_{\mathbb{E}_0} B$. Then there must exist an admissible state s in $\mathbb{E}_0$ which is preferred in $]A[$ and $B \notin l(s)$. Assume first that $s = k$. Then both A and B do not belong to $\mathbf{B}_\sim$, and hence $A \not\sim\mid B$ by Vacuity. So, assume now that $s \neq k$. Then $A \in \mathbf{B}_\sim$, since $s \prec k$ in $\mathbb{E}_0$. Consequently, all states in S_b support A. But then s is a preferred state in $]A[$ also with respect to $\mathbb{E}$, and therefore $A \sim\mid B$ is not valid in $\mathbb{E}$. This concludes the proof, since $\mathbb{E}$ is adequate for $\sim\mid$. $\square$

Notice that if $\mathbb{E}$ is a determinate epistemic state generating a given contraction relation $\sim\mid$, then the set of contractionals that are conservatively valid in $\mathbb{E}$ will generate the conservative contraction relation corresponding to $\sim\mid$. As can be seen, this latter contraction relation will also be determinate. Consequently, we immediately obtain

Corollary 10.4.1. *Any conservative determinate contraction coincides with the set of contractionals that are conservatively valid in some determinate epistemic state.*

The above fact will be used in the next section.

10.5 Rational contractions

Here we will describe contraction relations determined by modular (ranked) epistemic states. Such contractions join company with a number of other contraction functions, suggested in the literature, that satisfy all the AGM postulates except recovery (see Chapter 12). As we will see, the framework of epistemic states allows to single out a number of interesting classes of rational contractions that are indistinguishable in the AGM framework. We will show also that such contraction relations are always representable by standard monotonic epistemic states.

We will begin with the general notion of a rational contraction relation.

Definition 10.5.1. *A contraction relation will be called* rational *if it satisfies the following two postulates:*

Rational Monotony   *If $A \wedge B \not\sim A$ and $A \wedge B \sim C$, then $A \sim C$.*
Priority   *If $A \sim B$ and $B \not\sim A$, then $A \wedge B \sim B$.*

Rational Monotony corresponds to the last postulate (K–8) in the AGM theory of belief contractions. As to Priority, it seems to be new. Notice that its conclusion states that B is more entrenched than A for the associated entrenchment relation. Accordingly, Priority says, in effect, that B is more entrenched than A if deletion of A retains B, while deletion of B does not retain A.

As we will see later, Priority is a consequence of Rational Monotony in presence of the recovery postulate. Still, the following example shows that, in general, this postulate is independent of the rests of the postulates for contractions.

Example 10.5.1. Let us consider a standard and determinate epistemic state consisting of four theories $u_1 = \text{Th}(p \wedge q)$, $u_2 = \text{Th}(q)$, $u_3 = \text{Th}(p)$, $u_4 = \text{Th}(p \vee q)$ that are ordered as follows: $u_1 \succ u_2, u_3$ and $u_3 \succ u_4$. We will show that this epistemic state validates Rational Monotony. Notice first that, for any formula A, $p \vee q$ is included in $-A$. Hence Rational Monotony will be trivially satisfied in the case when $-A \wedge B = \text{Th}(p \vee q)$. Now, $-A \wedge B$ will be distinct from $\text{Th}(p \vee q)$ only in two cases:

(i) $A \wedge B \notin \text{Th}(p \wedge q) = \mathbf{B}_\sim$, in which case $-A \wedge B = \mathbf{B}_\sim$. But then $A \wedge B \not\sim A$ implies $A \notin \mathbf{B}_\sim$, and hence $-A$ is also equal to $\mathbf{B}_\sim$. Hence, Rational Monotony holds.

(ii) $A \wedge B \in u_2$ and $A \wedge B \notin u_3$. Then $-A \wedge B = \mathrm{Th}(p)$ and $A \in u_2$. Now, $A \wedge B \not\vdash\!\!\!\mid A$ implies $A \notin \mathrm{Th}(p)$, and hence $-A$ is also equal to $\mathrm{Th}(p)$. Thus, Rational Monotony is satisfied in this case also.

Finally, let us take $A = q$, $B = p$. Then it is easy to see that $A \vdash\!\!\!\mid B$ (since $-A = \mathrm{Th}(p)$), $B \not\vdash\!\!\!\mid A$ (since $-B = \mathrm{Th}(p \vee q)$) and $A \wedge B \not\vdash\!\!\!\mid B$ (since $-A \wedge B = \mathrm{Th}(p \vee q)$. Therefore, Priority is violated.

Rational contractions have already a quite organized structure. Thus, the following result shows that contraction of conjunction of propositions can be described in terms of contracted sets of conjuncts.

Lemma 10.5.1. *If $\vdash\!\!\!\mid$ is a rational contraction relation, then $-(A \wedge B)$ is equal either to $-A$ or to $-B$, or to $-A \cap -B$.*

Proof. If $A \wedge B \vdash\!\!\!\mid A$, then $-(A \wedge B) = -B$ by Cautious Antitony and Cautious Monotony. Similarly, $A \wedge B \vdash\!\!\!\mid B$ implies $-(A \wedge B) = -A$. Assume now that $A \wedge B \not\vdash\!\!\!\mid A$ and $A \wedge B \not\vdash\!\!\!\mid B$. Then $-(A \wedge B) \subseteq -A \cap -B$ by Rational Monotony, and hence $-(A \wedge B) = -A \cap -B$ by Distributivity. $\qquad \Box$

Perhaps the most important property of rational contraction relations is that they generate rational inference relations.

Lemma 10.5.2. *If $\vdash\!\!\!\mid$ is a rational contraction relation, then its corresponding inference relation is also rational.*

Proof. Assume that $A \vdash\!\!\sim B$ and $A \not\vdash\!\!\sim \neg C$ for the associated inference relation, that is, $\neg A \vdash\!\!\!\mid A \rightarrow B$ and $\neg A \not\vdash\!\!\!\mid A \rightarrow \neg C$. Then Rational Monotony for $\vdash\!\!\!\mid$ gives $\neg A \vee \neg C \vdash\!\!\!\mid A \rightarrow B$, and hence $\neg(A \wedge C) \vdash\!\!\!\mid (A \wedge C) \rightarrow B$ by Right Weakening. But the latter amounts to $A \wedge C \vdash\!\!\sim B$ for the associated inference relation, and therefore $\vdash\!\!\sim$ satisfies Rational Monotony. $\qquad \Box$

As we have seen in Chapter 7, rational inference relations are determined by linear epistemic states, but the actual completeness proof required a different definition of the associated consequence relation. This alternative definition will also be required in the present case. We will reproduce it below for convenience.

(DI*) $\qquad\qquad A < B \equiv \neg(A \wedge B) \vdash\!\!\sim A$ or $\neg B \vdash\!\!\sim \mathbf{f}$

As has been shown in Chapter 7, if $\vdash\!\!\sim$ is a rational inference relation, then the above definition determines a linear consequence relation. Rewriting it in terms of contraction relations, we obtain

(DC) $\qquad\qquad A < B \equiv A \wedge B \not\vdash\!\!\!\mid A$ or $B \vdash\!\!\!\mid B$

Combining our previous results, we conclude with

Lemma 10.5.3. *If $\vdash\!\!\!\mid$ is a rational contraction, then the condition (DC) defines a linear consequence relation.*

We will use this fact in the following completeness proof. As a preparation, we will prove first some additional properties of rational contractions.

Lemma 10.5.4. *If $\sim\!\mid$ is a simple rational contraction, $A < B$ and $B \sim\!\mid C$, then*

1. *either $A \vee B \sim\!\mid C$, or $A \sim\!\mid A \vee B$;*
2. *either $A \vee C \sim\!\mid B$, or $A \sim\!\mid A \vee C$;*
3. *if $A \sim\!\mid C \to A$, then $A \sim\!\mid B$;*
4. *if $A \sim\!\mid B \to A$, then $A \sim\!\mid C$.*

Proof. The above conditions are immediate if B is a known proposition. So, we will restrict the following proofs to the case when B is contingent.

(1) If $A \wedge B \not\sim\!\mid A$ and $A \not\sim\!\mid A \vee B$, then we have $A \wedge B \not\sim\!\mid A \vee B$ by Rational Monotony, and hence $B \not\sim\!\mid A \vee B$ by Partial Antitony. Combining the latter with $B \sim\!\mid C$, we can use Rational Monotony once more to infer $A \vee B \sim\!\mid C$.

(2) If $A \not\sim\!\mid A \vee C$, then $A \vee C < A$, and hence we have $A \vee C < B$ by transitivity of $<$. But $B \sim\!\mid C$ implies $B \sim\!\mid A \vee C$, and hence Priority gives $A \vee C \sim\!\mid B$.

(3) Notice first that $A < B$ (that is, $A \wedge B \not\sim\!\mid A$) implies that A is contingent. Now, applying (2) to the first two assumptions of (3), we infer that either $A \vee C \sim\!\mid B$, or $A \sim\!\mid A \vee C$. In the second case, however, the third assumption, $A \sim\!\mid C \to A$, would give us $A \sim\!\mid A$, contrary to contingency of A. Hence $A \vee C \sim\!\mid B$. Combining the latter with $A \sim\!\mid C \to A$, we finally infer $A \sim\!\mid B$ by applying Cautious Antitony.

In a similar way, it can be shown that (4) follows from (1). We leave the proof to the reader.   □

For a set of propositions B_i, where $1 \leq i \leq n$, we will denote below by $\bigwedge B$ ($\bigvee B$) the conjunction (respectively, disjunction) of all B_i. Now we have the following technical result:

Auxiliary Lemma. *Let B_i, C_i, D_j, E_j, where $1 \leq i \leq n$, $1 \leq j \leq m$, and A be propositions such that, for all i, j, $A < B_i$, $A < D_j$, $B_i \sim\!\mid C_i$, $D_j \sim\!\mid E_j$ and $A \sim\!\mid (\bigwedge B \wedge \bigwedge E) \to A$. Then $A \sim\!\mid \bigvee C \vee \bigvee D$.*

Proof. We are going to prove the claim by induction on the sum $n + m$. For the basis of induction, assume that $A < B$, $A < D$, $B \sim\!\mid C$, $D \sim\!\mid E$ and $A \sim\!\mid (B \wedge E) \to A$. We have to prove $A \sim\!\mid C \vee D$. Now, the previous lemma gives us that either $A \vee B \sim\!\mid C$ or $A \sim\!\mid A \vee B$, and either $A \vee E \sim\!\mid D$ or $A \sim\!\mid A \vee E$. A number of cases should be considered.

(1) Assume first that $A \sim\!\mid A \vee B$. Then $A \sim\!\mid (B \wedge E) \to A$ implies $A \sim\!\mid E \to A$, and hence by (3) of Lemma 10.5.4, we have $A \sim\!\mid D$. But the latter implies $A \sim\!\mid C \vee D$, and we are done.

Similarly it can be shown that $A \sim\!\mid A \vee E$ implies $A \sim\!\mid C$ and hence, again, $A \sim\!\mid C \vee D$.

(2) Assume now that both $A \vee B \mid\sim C$ and $A \vee E \mid\sim D$ hold. Then $A \vee B \mid\sim C \vee D$ and $A \vee E \mid\sim C \vee D$, and hence Distributivity implies $A \vee (B \wedge E) \mid\sim C \vee D$. Now notice that A is equivalent to $(A \vee (B \wedge E)) \wedge ((B \wedge E) \to A)$, and hence we can use $A \mid\sim (B \wedge E) \to A$ to infer $A \mid\sim C \vee D$ by Cautious Antitony. This completes the proof of the inductive basis.

Assume now that the premises of the assertion hold for some m and n and the assertion itself holds for all m' and n' such that $m' + n' < m + n$.

Let us assume first $A \mid\sim A \vee B_l$, for some l. Then, combined with $A \mid\sim (\bigwedge B \wedge \bigwedge E) \to A$, this would give us $A \mid\sim (B_\wedge^l \wedge \bigwedge E) \to A$, where $B_\wedge^l$ is a conjunction of all B_i, except B_l. Now we can apply the inductive hypothesis and infer $A \mid\sim C_\vee^l \vee \bigvee D$, where $C_\vee^l$ is a disjunction of all C_i, except C_l. But now the required conclusion follows by And. Similarly it can be shown that any assertion $A \mid\sim A \vee E_l$ leads to the same required conclusion.

Since we have covered 'one half' of the possibilities implied by (1) and (2) of Lemma 10.5.4, we can assume now that, for all i and j, $A \vee B_i \mid\sim C_i$ and $A \vee E_j \mid\sim D_j$. Then we have $A \vee B_i \mid\sim \bigvee C \vee \bigvee D$ and $A \vee E_j \mid\sim \bigvee C \vee \bigvee D$, and hence Distributivity will imply $A \vee (\bigwedge B \wedge \bigwedge E) \mid\sim \bigvee C \vee \bigvee D$. Finally, as in the base case, we can use the latter condition and $A \mid\sim (\bigwedge B \wedge \bigwedge E) \to A$ to infer the required conclusion by applying Cautious Antitony. This completes the proof. $\qquad\square$

Now we are going to construct the canonical epistemic state for a given rational contraction relation.

Definition 10.5.2. *A theory u will be said to* decide *a proposition A if, for any B such that $A < B$, either $B \in u$ or $-B \subseteq u$. A theory u will be called* r-normal *for a contingent proposition A if u decides A and $A \notin u$.*

In what follows we will use the following two properties of deciding:

Lemma 10.5.5.   *1. If u decides A, and $A < B$, then u decides B;*
  2. If u decides A and B, then it decides $A \wedge B$.

Proof. (1) follows immediately from transitivity of $<$, while (2) is a consequence of the fact that, for linear consequence relations, $A \wedge B < C$ holds only if either $A < C$ or $B < C$ (see Lemma 2.3.10 in Chapter 2). $\qquad\square$

Again, any r-normal theory for A should contain $-A$. The following lemma shows that for worlds this is also a sufficient condition.

Lemma 10.5.6. *Any world including $-A$ decides A.*

Proof. Assume that α is a world that includes $-A$, and let $A < B$. If B is known, then $B \in -A$, and hence $B \in \alpha$. So assume that B is contingent, $A \wedge B \not\vdash A$ and $B \mid\sim C$. Then by (3) from Lemma 10.1.1 we obtain $A \wedge B \mid\sim B \vee C$, and hence applying Rational Monotony, we obtain $A \mid\sim B \vee C$. But $-A$ is included in α, and hence $B \vee C \in \alpha$. Since C was taken to be an arbitrary proposition from $-B$, this implies that if $B \notin \alpha$, then $-B \subseteq \alpha$. This concludes the proof. $\qquad\square$

Lemma 10.5.7 (Basic Lemma 2). *If A is contingent, then $A \nmid B$ iff B belongs to all theories that are r-normal for A.*

Proof. Since $A < A$, for any r-normal theory u we have $-A \subseteq u$ (because $A \notin u$). This gives the direction from left to right.

Assume that $A \nmid B$. Two cases should be considered.

(a) $A \nmid A \vee B$. In this case there must exist a world α that includes $-A$ but not $A \vee B$. But then α is r-normal for A by the preceding lemma and $B \notin \alpha$.

(b) Assume now that $A \nmid A \vee B$. Since $A \nmid B$, there must exist a world β that includes $-A$ but not B. The assumption implies then that $A \in \beta$. Let us denote by u the following set of propositions:

$$\{\neg A\} \cup -A \cup \{C \mid A < C \ \& \ -C \nsubseteq \beta\} \cup \{-C \mid A < C \ \& \ C \notin \beta\}$$

We will prove first that u is consistent. Indeed, otherwise there must exist propositions C_i, D_i, for $1 \le i \le n$, and E_j, F_j, for $1 \le j \le m$, such that, for all i, j, (i) $A < C_i$ and $A < E_j$, (ii) $C_i \nmid D_i$ and $E_j \nmid F_j$, (iii) $D_i, E_j \notin \beta$, and

(iv) $$-A, C_1, \ldots, C_n, F_1, \ldots, F_m \vDash A$$

Let D and E denote, respectively, disjunction of all D_i and disjunction of all E_j. Then we can use Auxiliary Lemma and conditions (i), (ii) and (iv) to conclude that $A \nmid D \vee E$. But $-A$ is included in β, and hence $D \vee E \in \beta$, contrary to (iii).

Now, since u is consistent, we take α to be an arbitrary world including u, and consider the theory $v = \alpha \cap \beta$. Clearly, $-A \subseteq v$ and neither A nor B belong to v. Hence, to prove our lemma, we need only to show that v decides A. Assume that $A < C$ and $C \notin v$, that is, either $C \notin \alpha$ or $C \notin \beta$. We consider only the first case, the second being completely analogous.

If $C \notin \alpha$, then $-C$ is included in α by Lemma 10.5.6. Moreover, u is included in α, and hence $C \notin u$. But then the definition of u gives us $-C \subseteq \beta$, and consequently $-C$ is included in v. This concludes the proof. $\square$

Note that, as in the proof of the first Basic Lemma, the above proof shows that

r-normal theories for A can be chosen to be either worlds or intersections of pairs of worlds $\alpha \cap \beta$ such that $\neg A \in \alpha$ and $A \in \beta$.

Now we define a canonical *standard* epistemic state for a given contraction relation as follows:

- The set of admissible belief sets is the union of all r-normal theories for contingent propositions of the language.
- $v \prec u \equiv A \in u$, for any proposition A decided by v.

Lemma 10.5.8. $\prec$ *is a modular partial order on admissible states.*

Proof. If u is an r-normal theory for A, then $u \prec u$ would imply $A \in u$. Hence $\prec$ is irreflexive. To show transitivity, assume that $w \prec v \prec u$, but $w \not\prec u$. Then there exists A such that w decides A and $A \notin u$. Consequently v does not decide A, and hence there exists B such that $A < B$ and $B \notin v$. But w decides A and hence it should decide B (due to transitivity of $<$). However, $w \prec v$, and hence B should belong to v - a contradiction.

In order to show modularity of $\prec$, assume that for some admissible states u, v, w we have $u \not\prec w$ and $w \not\prec v$. We need to show that in this case $u \not\prec v$. Now, the first condition implies that u decides some proposition A such that $A \notin w$. Similarly, the second condition means that w decides some B such that $B \notin v$. Suppose that $A \not< B$. Then $B < A$ due to linearity of $<$, and hence w should decide $A \wedge B$ (see Lemma 10.5.5). We have, however, that $A \wedge B \notin w$, and therefore $-(A \wedge B) \subseteq w$. But $A \not< B$ implies $A \wedge B \dashv A$, and hence we obtain $A \in w$, which contradicts our assumptions. Thus, $A < B$. But in this case we have that u decides $A \wedge B$, though $A \wedge B \notin v$. Consequently, $u \not\prec v$, which concludes the proof. □

Lemma 10.5.9. *A theory u is preferred in $]A[$ iff it is r-normal for A.*

Proof. If u is r-normal for A and $u \prec v$, then $A \in v$ by the definition of $\prec$. This gives the direction from right to left.

Let u be a preferred state in $]A[$. We consider the following set of propositions:

$$v = \{\neg A\} \cup -A \cup \{B \mid u \text{ decides } B\}$$

Assume first that v is consistent, and let α be a world containing v. Then α is r-normal for A (by Lemma 10.5.6) and, moreover, $u \prec \alpha$ by the construction of v, contrary to the assumption that u is a preferred state in $]A[$. Thus, v is inconsistent. This implies, in turn, that there exist propositions B_i, $1 \leq i \leq n$, such that u decides all B_i and $-A, B_1, \ldots, B_n \vDash A$. Let B denote the conjunction of all B_i. Then we have that u decides B and $A \dashv B {\rightarrow} A$. The latter implies $A \wedge B \dashv B {\rightarrow} A$ by Partial Antitony, and hence $A \wedge B \not\dashv B$ (since otherwise A will not be contingent), that is, $B < A$. But then u should decide A, and hence u is r-normal for A. □

The construction in the above proof gives us another necessary property of a model.

Lemma 10.5.10. $\prec$ *is a smooth order.*

Proof. Let u be an admissible belief set from $]A[$. If v in the proof of the preceding lemma is inconsistent, then it was shown that u is preferred in $]A[$. Otherwise it was shown there that there exists a world α that is r-normal for A and such that $u \prec \alpha$. This concludes the proof. □

Now we have all that is necessary for

Representation Theorem 10.7. $\mathrel{\vdash\mkern-10mu\dashv}$ *is a simple rational contraction if and only if there exists a standard modular epistemic state* $\mathbb{E}$ *such that* $\mathrel{\vdash\mkern-10mu\dashv}_{\mathbb{E}}$ *coincides with* $\mathrel{\vdash\mkern-10mu\dashv}$.

Proof. The direction from right to left is shown by checking the validity of the rules for rational contraction in any modular epistemic state. The opposite direction follows from the construction of the canonical model, Lemma 10.5.9 and Basic Lemma. □

Refined representation. As we have mentioned after the Basic Lemma, r-normal theories can also be restricted to worlds or intersections of pairs of worlds. Therefore, in the rational case we also have

Corollary 10.5.1. *Any rational contraction relation is generated by some weakly monotonic, saturatable, modular and standard epistemic state.*

As we will see in Part Three, the above result makes a rational contraction a faithful formalization of Levi's notion of contractions suggested in [Lev91].

Our final result in this section shows that standard monotonic epistemic states are sufficient for representing rational contractions.

Theorem 10.5.1. $\mathrel{\vdash\mkern-10mu\dashv}$ *is a rational contraction if and only if it is generated by some standard, monotonic and modular epistemic state.*

Proof. Notice first that the intersection of any set of r-normal theories for some proposition A that is linearly ordered with respect to inclusion is also an r-normal theory for A. Consequently, any r-normal theory for A contains a minimal such theory. Actually, such minimal theories are sufficient for determining the contracted belief set $-A$.

Let $\mathbb{E}_0$ be the canonical epistemic state for $\mathrel{\vdash\mkern-10mu\dashv}$ constructed in the proof of the Representation theorem. We will construct a new epistemic state $\mathbb{E}$ by removing from $\mathbb{E}_0$ any theory that is not a *minimal* r-normal theory for at least one proposition. Clearly, $\mathbb{E}$ will determine the same contraction relation as $\mathbb{E}_0$. It remains to show that $\mathbb{E}$ satisfies monotonicity. Assume that $u \subset v$ for two theories from $\mathbb{E}$ and v is a minimal r-normal theory for A. If u and v were belong to the same layer in $\mathbb{E}$, then, since $A \notin u$, we would have that u would also be preferred in $]A[$, and hence would be an r-normal theory for A, contrary to minimality of v. Hence, u and v should be comparable with respect to $\prec$, that is, either $u \prec v$ or $v \prec u$. But $\mathbb{E}$ is weakly monotonic, and hence $u \prec v$ is the only possibility. This concludes the proof. □

Thus, we have shown that rational contraction relations provide a complete description of contraction inference with respect to modular epistemic states. For rational inference relations such a result gave already the whole picture, since further restriction of modular epistemic state even to pure linear ones does not lead to restricting the class of generated inference relations. Contraction relations, however, are more sensitive to the structure of epistemic states. In the following sections we will describe two important subclasses of rational contraction relations that are generated, respectively, by linear and pure linear epistemic states.

10.5.1 Linear contractions

Recall that an epistemic state is *linear*, if the preference relation is a linear (total) order on admissible states, that is, for any two distinct states s and t, either $s \prec t$ or $t \prec s$. It turns out that such epistemic states determine a restricted class of rational contraction relations described in the following definition.

Definition 10.5.3. *A contraction relation will be called* linear *if it satisfies Rational Monotony and*

Rational Antitony   *If $A \wedge B \nmid A$ and $A \mid\!\sim C$, then $A \wedge B \mid\!\sim C$.*

As can be easily seen, Priority is a consequence of Rational Antitony. Therefore, any linear contraction relation will already be rational.

If we rewrite both Rational Monotony and Rational Antitony in terms of contracted belief sets, we will obtain the following condition:

Linearity   If $A \wedge B \nmid A$, then $-(A \wedge B) = -A$.

A further interesting property of linear contractions is obtainable when we notice that Cautious Antitony and Cautious Monotony jointly amount to

If $A \wedge B \mid\!\sim A$, then $-(A \wedge B) = -B$.

Consequently, linear contractions satisfy the following *Decomposition property* (see [AGM85]):

$$-(A \wedge B) = -A \quad \text{or} \quad -(A \wedge B) = -B$$

For reasons that will become clear soon, in the case of linear contraction relations, we will be especially interested in their associated entrenchment relations. Since any rational contraction generates a rational inference relation, its associated simple entrenchment relation $A < B \equiv A \wedge B \mid\!\sim B$ will be qualitative and modular. Consequently, it will form a strict modular order on contingent propositions of $\mid\!\sim$.

The following result shows that, for linear contraction relations, the associated entrenchment relations will be 'almost linear'.

Lemma 10.5.11. *If $<$ is an entrenchment relation generated by a linear contraction relation $\mid\!\sim$, then, for any A and B,*

$$\text{either } -A = -B \text{ or } A < B \text{ or } B < A.$$

Proof. If $A \not< B$ and $B \not< A$, then Linearity implies, respectively, $-(A \wedge B) = -B$ and $-(A \wedge B) = -A$. Consequently, $-A = -B$. □

As can be easily verified, Rational Antitony is valid in all linear epistemic states. To prove the corresponding representation theorem, for any linear contraction relation we will construct a canonical *standard* epistemic state as follows:

1. Admissible belief sets are theories of the form $-A$, where A is contingent;
2. $-B \prec -A$ iff $A < B$ (where $<$ is the corresponding entrenchment relation).

To begin with, we need to check that above definition of the preference relation is correct, that is, it does not depend on the choice of propositions representing admissible belief sets. To this end, we need to check the following two properties of the associated entrenchment relation:

1. If $A < B$ and $-B = -C$, then $A < C$;
2. If $A < B$ and $-A = -C$, then $C < B$.

We show only the first property, the second one being perfectly similar. Since $B \not\prec B$, we have $C \not\prec B$ and consequently $B \wedge C \not\prec B$, that is, $C \not< B$. Now $A < C$ follows from $A < B$ due to modularity of $<$.

Let us denote the above constructed epistemic state by $\mathbb{E}$. Then we have

Lemma 10.5.12. $\mathbb{E}$ *is a standard, linear and monotonic epistemic state.*

Proof. Recall that $A <$ is a strict partial order. In addition, it is linear due to Lemma 10.5.11. To show monotonicity, assume that $-A \subset -B$, but $-A \not\prec -B$. Then $-B \prec -A$ by linearity, and hence $A \wedge B \prec B$. The latter implies $A \prec B$, that is, B belongs to $-A$. But then B should belong to $-B$, contrary to the assumption that B is contingent. □

The following lemma gives us, in effect, all that is needed for the representation theorem.

Lemma 10.5.13. *If A is contingent, then $-A$ is the only preferred theory in $]A[$.*

Proof. Due to linearity of the preference order, it is sufficient to show that $-A$ is a preferred theory in $]A[$. Assume that $-A \prec -B$. Then $A \wedge B \prec A$, and consequently $B \prec A$, that is, A belongs to $-B$. □

As a consequence of the above lemma we immediately obtain that $\prec$ is a smooth order on our admissible theories.

Corollary 10.5.2. $\prec$ *is a smooth preference relation.*

Proof. If A does not belong to $-B$, then $B \not\prec A$, and hence $A \wedge B \not\prec A$. Consequently, $-A \not\prec -B$, and therefore by linearity either $-A = -B$ or $-B \prec -A$. This concludes the proof, since $-A$ is a preferred theory in $]A[$. □

Finally, we can state the following

Representation Theorem 10.8. $\prec$ *is a linear contraction relation if and only if there exists a standard linear monotonic epistemic state S that generates $\prec$.*

Proof. If $\mathbb{E}$ is the canonical epistemic state for a linear contraction relation $\prec$, then $A \prec B$ iff B belongs to the unique preferred state in $]A[$ (namely $-A$). Consequently, $\mathbb{E}$ generates $\prec$. □

As has been shown in Chapter 4, any epistemic state is decomposable into a set of standard linear and monotonic epistemic states. As a result, linear contraction relations do not validate any new singular (Horn) derivation rules as compared with general contraction relations.

10.5.2 Severe contractions

A further constraint that can be imposed on linear epistemic states consists in considering only pure linear epistemic states. The resulting contraction relations will be both linear and pure. Such contraction relations will correspond to belief contraction functions suggested by Rott and Levi (see below).

Definition 10.5.4. *A contraction relation will be said to be* severe *if it satisfies Rational Monotony and*

Entrenchment   *If $A \not\prec A$ and $A \prec B$, then $A \wedge B \prec B$.*

Notice that $A \wedge B \prec B$ always implies $A \prec B$. Consequently, the above Entrenchment postulate says, in effect, that the contraction relation coincides with its associated entrenchment relation on contingent propositions. Note, in particular, that $A \wedge B \prec B$ implies $A \wedge C \prec B$, for any C. Consequently, severe contractions satisfy the following restricted version of Strengthening the Antecedent[3]:

CSA   If $A \not\prec A$ and $A \prec B$, then $A \wedge C \prec B$.

Now we will show that any severe contraction relation will be linear.

Lemma 10.5.14. *Any severe contraction relation is linear.*

Proof. We need only to show the validity of Rational Antitony. Assume that $A \wedge B \not\prec A$ and $A \prec C$. The first condition implies $A \not\prec A$ (see (6) from Lemma 10.1.1), and hence A is contingent. Consequently $A \prec C$ implies $A \wedge C \prec C$, and therefore $A \wedge B \prec C$, as required. □

---

[3] This postulate was used in [RP99].

As we will show below, severe contraction relations are precisely contraction relations determined by linear pure epistemic states. In anticipation for this, the following result shows that simple severe contractions are exactly linear contractions satisfying the Persistence postulate (see Section 10.3 above). It shows also that such contractions can be characterized by a single requirement of being *modular relations*:

Modularity   If $A \sim\!\!\!\!/\ B$, then either $A \sim\!\!\!\!/\ C$, or $C \sim\!\!\!\!/\ B$.

Rewritten in terms of contracted belief sets, Modularity amounts to the following postulate (cf. [RP99]):

SW   If $A \not\sim\!\!\!\!/\ C$, then $-A \subseteq -C$.

Lemma 10.5.15. *A simple contraction relation is severe if and only if it satisfies one of the following conditions:*

1. *it is linear and satisfies the Persistence postulate;*
2. *it satisfies Modularity.*

Proof. We will show first that any simple severe contraction is modular. Assume first that A is contingent and $A \sim\!\!\!\!/\ B$. Then $A \wedge B \sim\!\!\!\!/\ B$ by Entrenchment. Consequently, due to modularity of the corresponding entrenchment relation, either $A \wedge C \sim\!\!\!\!/\ C$ or $B \wedge C \sim\!\!\!\!/\ B$, and therefore either $A \sim\!\!\!\!/\ C$ or $C \sim\!\!\!\!/\ B$, as required. In addition, if A is not contingent, then $A \sim\!\!\!\!/\ C$ holds for any C. Thus, Modularity holds in each case.

Now we will show that Modularity implies Linearity and Persistence.

Linearity. Notice first that Rational Monotony is a special case of Modularity. To show the validity of Rational Antitony, assume that $A \wedge B \not\sim\!\!\!\!/\ A$. If $A \not\sim\!\!\!\!/\ A \wedge B$, then Modularity gives $-A \subseteq -(A \wedge B)$, as required. Otherwise $A \sim\!\!\!\!/\ A$, and hence $A \wedge B \sim\!\!\!\!/\ A$, contrary to our assumption.

Persistence. Assume $A \sim\!\!\!\!/\ B$. If $A \wedge B \not\sim\!\!\!\!/\ A$, then $-(A \wedge B) \subseteq -A$ by Modularity, as required. So, assume $A \wedge B \sim\!\!\!\!/\ A$. Now, $A \sim\!\!\!\!/\ B$ implies that either $A \sim\!\!\!\!/\ (A \wedge B)$ or $A \wedge B \sim\!\!\!\!/\ B$. In the first case $A \sim\!\!\!\!/\ A$, and hence $-(A \wedge B) \subseteq -A$ (since $\sim\!\!\!\!/$ is simple). In the second case we have $A \wedge B \sim\!\!\!\!/\ A \wedge B$ by And, and hence $A \sim\!\!\!\!/\ A$ in this case also. Thus, Persistence holds.

In order to complete the circle, we will show finally that Linearity and Persistence jointly imply Entrenchment. Assume that $A \not\sim\!\!\!\!/\ A$ and $A \sim\!\!\!\!/\ B$. Suppose that $A \wedge B \sim\!\!\!\!/\ A$. But then Persistence implies $A \sim\!\!\!\!/\ A$, contrary to our assumption. Consequently, $A \wedge B \not\sim\!\!\!\!/\ A$, and hence $-A = -(A \wedge B)$ by Linearity. But we have $A \sim\!\!\!\!/\ B$, so $A \wedge B \sim\!\!\!\!/\ B$, as required. This completes the proof.   □

Now we are going to show that severe contractions provide a complete description of contraction relations determined by pure linear epistemic states.

Theorem 10.5.2. *A simple contraction is severe if and only if it is generated by some pure linear epistemic state.*

Proof. Any contraction relation generated by a pure linear epistemic state is obviously both pure and linear. Consequently, it is a severe contraction. In the other direction, given a simple severe contraction relation, we define the following consequence relation:

(LSC) $A \vdash B \equiv B \not\sim A$ or $B \sim B$

We will show that this is a linear consequence relation.

Dominance. If $A \vDash B$ and $B \sim A$, then $B \sim B$ by Right Weakening. Thus, Dominance holds.

Antecedence. If $A \vdash B$ then either $B \not\sim A$ or $B \sim B$. In the first case we have $A \land B \not\sim A$, and hence $A \vdash A \land B$. In the second case we can assume also that $A \land B \sim A$. Then $B \sim B$ implies $A \land B \sim B$ by Partial Antitony, and hence $A \land B \sim A \land B$ by And. But the latter implies $A \vdash A \land B$ in this case also.

Transitivity. Assume that $A \vdash B$ and $B \vdash C$. If $C \sim C$, then $A \vdash C$, as required. Also, if $B \sim B$, then $C \sim B$ (see (6) in Lemma 10.1.1). What remains is the case when $B \not\sim A$ and $C \not\sim B$. But then $C \not\sim A$ by Modularity, and hence $A \vdash C$.

Thus, $\vdash$ is indeed a consequence relation.

Linearity. If $A \not\sim B$, then $B \vdash A$, and if $B \not\sim A$, then $A \vdash B$. So, assume that $A \sim B$ and $B \sim A$. If $A \land B \sim A$, then $A \sim A$ by Persistence, and hence $A \vdash B$. Similarly, if $A \land B \sim B$, then $B \vdash A$. Now if $A \land B \not\sim A$ and $A \land B \not\sim B$, then Linearity gives, respectively, $-(A \land B) = -A$ and $-(A \land B) = -A$, and therefore $-A = -B$. But then we have both $A \sim A$ and $B \sim B$, and consequently $A \vdash B$ and $B \vdash A$. So, in all cases either $A \vdash B$ or $B \vdash A$.

Thus, $\vdash$ is a linear consequence relation. Moreover, we will show that it generates $\sim$. Indeed, it is easy to see that a contractional $A \sim B$ is valid with respect to a linear consequence relation $\vdash$ if and only if either $\vdash A$ or $B \nvdash A$. In our case, this will hold iff either $A \sim A$ or $A \sim B$. But $\sim$ is a simple contraction relation, so the later condition is equivalent to $A \sim B$. This completes the proof.   □

The above proof is based on the fact that a severe contraction defines a consequence relation generating it. Actually, the proof shows also that the two are interdefinable. Namely, the following two simple conditions provide a mutual definability of simple severe contractions and linear consequence relations that generate them.

(LSC) $A \vdash B \equiv B \not\sim A$ or $B \sim B$
(SLC) $A \sim B \equiv B \nvdash A$ or $\vdash A$

Thus, severe contractions can be adjoined to the list of interdefinable concepts containing linear consequence relations, modular qualitative entrenchment and rational inference relations.

10.6 Withdrawals

A common feature of current theories of belief contraction is that contracted belief sets are always subsets of the original belief set. In other words, they satisfy the AGM postulate of inclusion. Such contractions are clearly not simple in our sense; instead, they are commonly supposed to be conservative. In addition, they are supposed also to satisfy Vacuity. This covers, in effect, all basic AGM postulates for contractions, except Recovery. Following Makinson, such contractions are often called withdrawals. Accordingly, we will introduce the following definition.

Definition 10.6.1. *A contraction relation will be said to be a* withdrawal *if it is conservative, determinate and satisfies*

Inclusion   If $A \mathbin{\rlap{\sim}{\dashv}} B$, then $\mathbf{f} \mathbin{\rlap{\sim}{\dashv}} B$.

As can be seen, Inclusion can be rewritten as $-A \subseteq \mathbf{B}_\sim$; it corresponds to the AGM postulate of inclusion.

Though withdrawals constitute a sub-class of all determinate contractions, they do not reduce the class of generated inference relations. To see this, notice that for any determinate contraction relation, we can construct a corresponding withdrawal simply by restricting the contracted belief sets:

$$A \mathbin{\rlap{\sim}{\dashv}}^w B \;\equiv\; A \mathbin{\rlap{\sim}{\dashv}} B \text{ and } \mathbf{f} \mathbin{\rlap{\sim}{\dashv}} B$$

As can be easily checked, if $\mathbin{\rlap{\sim}{\dashv}}$ is a determinate contraction, then $\mathbin{\rlap{\sim}{\dashv}}^w$ is a withdrawal. Moreover, the two contraction relations are actually inference-equivalent; this follows from the fact that if $A \vDash B$, then $A \mathbin{\rlap{\sim}{\dashv}} B$ implies $\mathbf{f} \mathbin{\rlap{\sim}{\dashv}} B$ by Partial Antitony. As a result, we obtain

Lemma 10.6.1. *For any determinate contraction relation there exists an inference-equivalent withdrawal.*

In what follows, we will call $\mathbin{\rlap{\sim}{\dashv}}^w$ the **B**-*restriction* of $\mathbin{\rlap{\sim}{\dashv}}$. Thus, the above results can be described shortly as saying that the **B**-restriction of any determinate contraction relation is a withdrawal that is inference-equivalent to it.

A semantic representation of withdrawals can be given in the framework of **B**-determinate epistemic states defined as follows.

Definition 10.6.2. *A determinate epistemic state* $\mathbb{E}$ *with a belief set* **B** *will be called* **B**-*determinate, if* $l(s) \subseteq \mathbf{B}$, *for any admissible state s of* $\mathbb{E}$.

The class of **B**-determinate epistemic states is quite broad; for example, any determinate monotonic epistemic state will be **B**-determinate. The following example shows, however, that Inclusion, taken by itself, does not imply determination (Vacuity).

Example 10.6.1. Let us consider a standard epistemic state $\mathbb{E}$ consisting of three theories $w \subset u \subset v$ and the preference relation $w \prec v$. Consequently u and v are preferred theories of $\mathbb{E}$, and hence u is a belief set of $\mathbb{E}$.

Assume that B is some proposition that belongs to u, but not to w, while A belongs only to v. Then B is believed in $\mathbb{E}$, A is not believed in $\mathbb{E}$ (since u is also a preferred state), and $A \mathbin{\rightharpoonup} B$ is not valid in $\mathbb{E}$ (since w is also a preferred theory in $]A[$). Consequently, Vacuity is violated. Still, it is easy to check that Inclusion holds; this follows from the fact that, for any proposition C, $]C[$ contains v only if it contains also u.

It can be easily verified that any **B**-determinate epistemic state makes valid all postulates for withdrawals. Moreover, we are going to show now that withdrawals provide a complete description of conservative contraction inference with respect to such epistemic states.

Representation Theorem 10.9. *A contraction relation $\mathbin{\rightharpoonup}$ is a withdrawal if and only if it coincides with the set of contractionals that are conservatively valid in some **B**-determinate epistemic state.*

Proof. Let $\mathbin{\rightharpoonup}$ be a withdrawal, $\mathbb{E}$ a determinate epistemic state that generates $\mathbin{\rightharpoonup}$, and k a maximally preferred admissible state in $\mathbb{E}$. Clearly, $l(k) = \mathbf{B}_{\sim}$.

This time we will transform $\mathbb{E}$ into a **B**-determinate epistemic state by restricting the labelling function l of $\mathbb{E}$ as follows: $l_0(s) = l(s) \cap l(k)$. We will denote the resulting **B**-determinate epistemic state by $\mathbb{E}_0$. As we will show now, $\mathbb{E}_0$ will also represent $\mathbin{\rightharpoonup}$. Since we consider conservative validity, we can restrict our attention to contingent propositions.

Assume first that A is contingent and $A \mathbin{\not\rightharpoonup} B$. Then there must exist an admissible state s in $\mathbb{E}$ which is preferred in $]A[$ and $B \notin l(s)$. Assume now that $A \notin l(k)$. Then k will be a unique preferred state in $]A[$ with respect to $\mathbb{E}_0$. In addition, $A \notin \mathbb{E}_{\sim}$ and $A \mathbin{\not\rightharpoonup} B$ give $B \notin \mathbb{E}_{\sim}$ by Vacuity. Consequently, $A \mathbin{\rightharpoonup} B$ is not valid in $\mathbb{E}_0$. So, let us assume now that $A \in l(k)$. in this case s will also be preferred state in $]A[$ with respect to $\mathbb{E}_0$. Indeed, otherwise we would have $s \prec t$, for some t such that $A \notin l_0(t)$. But then $A \notin l(t)$ (since $A \notin l(k)$), which contradicts the assumption that s is preferred in $]A[$ with respect to $\mathbb{E}$. Thus, s is a preferred state in $]A[$ with respect to $\mathbb{E}_0$. In addition, we have $B \notin l_0(s)$. Therefore $A \mathbin{\rightharpoonup} B$ is not valid in $\mathbb{E}_0$.

Assume now that A is contingent and $A \mathbin{\rightharpoonup} B$ is not valid in $\mathbb{E}_0$. Then there must exist an admissible state s in $\mathbb{E}_0$ which is preferred in $]A[$ and $B \notin l_0(s)$. If $s = k$, then we have $B \notin \mathbf{B}_{\sim}$, and hence $A \mathbin{\not\rightharpoonup} B$ by Inclusion. So assume $s \neq k$. Then it must be that $A \in l(k)$, and hence $A \notin l(s)$. Moreover, s will then be a preferred state in $]A[$ also with respect to $\mathbb{E}$. Let us consider two cases. If $B \notin l(k)$, then $\mathbf{f} \mathbin{\not\rightharpoonup} B$, and hence $A \mathbin{\not\rightharpoonup} B$ by Inclusion. So assume that $B \in l(k)$. Then $B \notin l(s)$, and consequently $A \mathbin{\rightharpoonup} B$ is nor valid in $\mathbb{E}$. But $\mathbb{E}$ generates exactly $\mathbin{\rightharpoonup}$, and therefore $A \mathbin{\not\rightharpoonup} B$. This concludes the proof. $\square$

It is interesting to note that the transformation described in the above proof preserves saturatedness of admissible belief sets. This follows from the fact that if u is an A-saturatable theory, and $A \in \mathbf{B}$, then $u \cap \mathbf{B}$ will also be an A-saturatable theory. Therefore, withdrawals also posses a refined representation we have given for other main kinds of contractions.

Corollary 10.6.1. *Any withdrawal is generated by some epistemic state that is saturatable and* **B**-*determinate.*

The above observation can be seen as a relational refinement of a nice general representation result, established in [HO95], according to which any withdrawal function in the sense of Makinson is representable as a partial meet contraction on saturatable theories.

10.6.1 Rational, linear and severe withdrawals

A withdrawal will be called *rational, (linear, severe)* if it is also a rational (respectively, linear or severe) contraction relation. Such withdrawals can be obtained as **B**-restrictions of corresponding simple rational contraction relations. Moreover, an obvious adaptation of the basic representation result for withdrawals will give us immediately representations of rational and linear withdrawals in terms of modular and, respectively, linear **B**-restricted epistemic states that are also both standard and monotonic. We leave details to the reader. For severe withdrawals (which is the main subject of [RP99]) we even do not have to modify anything. This is due to the following

Lemma 10.6.2. *Severe withdrawals coincide with conservative severe contractions.*

Proof. Since severe contractions are already determinate, we need to show only that conservativity (Failure) is already sufficient for the validity of Inclusion. If $A \mathbin{\rlap{\,/}\sim} A$, then $-A \subseteq -\mathbf{f}$ by Failure. So, assume that A is contingent, and $A \mathbin{\rlap{\,/}\sim} B$. Then $A \wedge B \mathbin{\rlap{\,/}\sim} B$ by Entrenchment, and consequently $\mathbf{f} \mathbin{\rlap{\,/}\sim} B$ by Partial Antitony. Therefore $-A \subseteq -\mathbf{f}$ also in this case, and hence Inclusion holds. $\square$

Notice now that pure linear epistemic states are already **B**-determinate. Consequently, we immediately obtain

Corollary 10.6.2. *A contraction relation is a severe withdrawal if and only if it coincides with the set of contractionals that are conservatively valid in some pure linear epistemic state.*

10.7 Recovering contraction relations

Finally, we consider the postulate of recovery that constitutes one of the main rationality postulates in the AGM theory of belief change. In our setting, it amounts to the following condition:

Recovery   If $\mathbf{f} \mathbin{\rightharpoondown} B$, then $A \mathbin{\rightharpoondown} A{\rightarrow}B$.

A contraction relation will be called a *recovering contraction*, if it is a withdrawal and satisfies Recovery. Notice that Inclusion and Recovery already imply Failure, so recovering contractions could be alternatively characterized as contraction relations that satisfy Vacuity, Inclusion and Recovery. In other words, they satisfy, in effect, all the basic postulates of the AGM theory.

Recovery and Inclusion jointly amount to the following equivalence:

Gärdenfors Identity $A \mathbin{\rightharpoondown} B$ if and only if $A \mathbin{\rightharpoondown} A{\vee}B$ and $\mathbf{f} \mathbin{\rightharpoondown} B$.

As can be seen, $A \mathbin{\rightharpoondown} A{\vee}B$ coincides with $\neg A \mathrel{\vert\!\sim} B$ for the preferential inference relation generated by $\mathbin{\rightharpoondown}$. Thus, any recovering contraction is determined, in turn, by the generated inference relation. In fact, the above equivalence constitutes an inferential counterpart of the Gärdenfors (or Harper) Identity in the theory of belief change.

Another look at the above identity reveals that $A \mathbin{\rightharpoondown} A \vee B$ defines a complete contraction relation corresponding to $\mathbin{\rightharpoondown}$. This gives us the following

Lemma 10.7.1. *Recovering contractions are precisely* **B**-*restrictions of complete contraction relations.*

We have seen already that the **B**-restriction of a contraction relation gives an inference-equivalent contraction relation. Consequently, we obtain the following result that can be attributed, in effect, to Makinson (see [Mak87]).

Corollary 10.7.1. *Any determinate contraction is inference-equivalent to some recovering contraction.*

Proof. For any contraction relation $\mathbin{\rightharpoondown}$, we can define the following relation:

$$A \mathbin{\rightharpoondown}^{*} B \;\equiv\; A \mathbin{\rightharpoondown} A \vee B \text{ and } \mathbf{f} \mathbin{\rightharpoondown} B$$

It can be easily checked that this is a contraction relation that already satisfies Inclusion and Recovery, and that it is inference-equivalent to $\mathbin{\rightharpoondown}$. $\square$

Finally, recall that two complete contraction relations are inference-equivalent only if they coincide. Consequently, the above lemma implies also that each equivalence class of contraction relations with respect to this equivalence can contain no more than one recovering contraction:

Corollary 10.7.2. *Two recovering contractions are inference-equivalent only if they coincide.*

Now we will turn to a semantic representation of recovering contractions. Let **B** be a consistent deductively closed theory. As usual in the literature on belief change, we will denote by **B**$\perp$ the set of theories consisting of **B** itself and all its maximal proper subtheories.

Definition 10.7.1. *A determinate epistemic state* $\mathbb{E}$ *with a belief set* **B** *will be called an* epistemic AGM-state *if all its admissible belief sets belong to* **B**⊥.

Epistemic AGM-states realize the idea that the only admissible options for choice in contracting a belief set are its maximal deductively closed subsets. As we will see in Chapter 11, such epistemic states constitute actually a generalization of the AGM models of belief change. They are equivalent also to monotonic **B**-homogeneous epistemic states (see Chapter 3).

As can be seen, an epistemic AGM-state is also **B**-determinate, since any admissible belief set is included in the belief set. In addition, it is easy to check that the conservative contraction relation generated by such an epistemic state already satisfies Recovery. Accordingly, any epistemic AGM-state generates a recovering contraction. We are going to show also that such epistemic states provide an adequate representation for the latter. The proof of the following representation theorem is based, in effect, on the *Grove connection*, according to which **B**⊥ is precisely the set of theories of the form **B** ∩ α, where α is a world (see [Gro88]).

Representation Theorem 10.10. ⊣ *is a recovering contraction if and only if it coincides with the set of contractionals that are conservatively valid in some epistemic AGM state.*

Proof. Let ⊣ be a recovering contraction relation with a belief set **B**, ⊢ its generated preferential inference relation, and $\mathbb{W}$ some possible worlds (KLM) model of ⊢. We will transform $\mathbb{W}$ into an epistemic AGM-state in two steps. First, we change the labelling function of $\mathbb{W}$ as follows: for any state $s \in \mathbb{W}$, we define $l^0(s)$ as equal to $l(s) \cap \mathbf{B}$. Notice that all maximally preferred states will be labelled now with **B**. So, as a second step, we amalgamate all such preferred states into a single state, say k, and put $l^0(k) = \mathbf{B}$.

Let us denote the resulting epistemic state by $\mathbb{E}$. Due to the Grove connection, $l^0(s)$ belongs to **B**⊥, for any admissible state s. Accordingly, $\mathbb{E}$ is an AGM-state. Moreover, we are going to show that $\mathbb{E}$ also generates ⊣. To this end, we will make use of the Gärdenfors Identity; in other words, we will show that the contractional $A \dashv B$ is conservatively valid in $\mathbb{E}$ if and only if $B \in \mathbf{B}$ and $\neg A \hspace{0.3em}\vdash\hspace{-0.9em}\sim\hspace{0.3em} B$ belongs to the above preferential inference relation.

Assume first that the contractional $A \dashv B$ is not conservatively valid in $\mathbb{E}$, but $B \in \mathbf{B}$. The latter condition implies that A is contingent and, moreover, $A \in \mathbf{B}$ (since otherwise we would have that $A \dashv B$ is valid in $\mathbb{E}$). Consequently, $\mathbb{E}$ must contain an admissible state s which is preferred in $]A[$ and such that $B \notin l^0(s)$. Since $A, B \in \mathbf{B}$, we have also $A, B \notin l(s)$. In addition, s will also be a preferred state in $\mathbb{W}$ that contains $\neg A$. Indeed, otherwise we would have that there exists an admissible state t in $\mathbb{W}$ such that $s \prec t$ and $\neg A \in l(t)$. But then $A \notin l^0(t)$, contrary to the assumption that s is preferred in $]A[$ with respect to $\mathbb{E}$. Consequently, $\neg A \hspace{0.3em}\not\vdash\hspace{-0.9em}\sim\hspace{0.3em} B$, and therefore $A \dashv B$ does not belong to the source contraction relation.

Assume now that the contractional $A \sim\!\!\mid B$ is conservatively valid in $\mathbb{E}$. Then $B \in \mathbf{B}$, since any admissible belief set in $\mathbb{E}$ is included in $\mathbf{B}$. Assume that $\neg A \not\!\!\sim B$. Then $\mathbb{W}$ must contain a preferred state s containing $\neg A$ for which $B \notin l(s)$. But then $A \notin l^0(s)$. Moreover, s will be a preferred state in $]A[$ with respect to $\mathbb{E}$. Indeed, assume that $s \prec t$, for some state t such that $A \notin l^0(t)$. Then $A \notin \mathbf{B}$, since otherwise we would have $\neg A \in l(t)$, contrary to our assumption that s is a preferred state in $\mathbb{W}$ containing $\neg A$. Consequently, $A \sim\!\!\mid B$ by Vacuity, and therefore $\neg A \!\sim B$, and hence $A \sim\!\!\mid B$ by Gärdenfors Identity. This concludes the proof.   □

Thus, any recovering contraction is determined by some epistemic AGM-state. It is important to note, however, that the above representation result refers to arbitrary AGM states, not only to standard ones. This additional freedom as compared with the standard AGM setting turns out to be essential, which can be anticipated on the basis of a tight correspondence (namely, inter-definability) between recovering contractions and preferential inference relations. Thus, the following example shows that even in the finite case there are recovering contractions that are not representable by standard AGM models.

Example 10.7.1. [Rot93] Let us consider a contraction relation determined by the (non-standard) epistemic AGM state having five admissible belief states with the following labels: $l(s_1) = \mathrm{Cl}(p \wedge q)$, $l(s_2) = \mathrm{Cl}(p)$, $l(s_3) = \mathrm{Cl}(q)$ and $l(s_4) = l(s_5) = \mathrm{Cl}(p \leftrightarrow q)$, ordered as follows $s_4 \prec s_2 \prec s_1$, $s_5 \prec s_3 \prec s_1$. Restricted to the finite language $\{p, q\}$ this contraction relation is fully characterized by the following list of contracted belief sets:

$$-\mathbf{t} = \mathrm{Cl}(p \wedge q) \qquad -(p \wedge q) = \mathrm{Cl}(p \vee q)$$
$$-(\neg p \vee q) = \mathrm{Cl}(p) \qquad -p = \mathrm{Cl}(\neg p \vee q)$$
$$-(p \vee \neg q) = \mathrm{Cl}(q) \qquad -q = \mathrm{Cl}(p \vee \neg q)$$
$$-(p \vee q) = \mathrm{Cl}(p \leftrightarrow q) \qquad -(p \leftrightarrow q) = \mathrm{Cl}(p \vee q)$$

and $A \sim\!\!\mid p \wedge q$ for any other proposition of the language. This contraction has been used in [Rot93] as an example of a recovering contraction that does not satisfy R-Covering; consequently, it is not representable by a standard AGM-state (see below).

Remark. We should warn the reader that the question whether a recovering contraction is representable by a standard AGM-state, though obviously related, is distinct from the question whether it is standard, that is, representable by a standard epistemic state in general. Thus, the contraction relation from the above example is actually representable by a standard (non-determinate) epistemic state having six theories ordered as follows:

$$\mathrm{Cl}(\neg p \wedge \neg q) \prec \mathrm{Cl}(p \wedge \neg q) \prec \mathrm{Cl}(p \wedge q)$$
$$\mathrm{Cl}(p \leftrightarrow q) \prec \mathrm{Cl}(q) \prec \mathrm{Cl}(p \wedge q)$$
$$\mathrm{Cl}(p) \prec \mathrm{Cl}(p \wedge q)$$

As can be seen from the construction given in the proof of the above theorem, standard AGM-states correspond to injective KLM models. Let us say that a recovering contraction relation is *AGM-standard* if it is generated by a standard epistemic AGM-state. Then we immediately obtain the following

Corollary 10.7.3. *A recovering contraction relation is AGM-standard if and only if its associated inference relation is injective.*

As has been shown in Chapter 7, in the finite case an inference relation is injective if and only if it satisfies $\vee$-Covering (see Theorem 7.9.4). This condition can be immediately translated into the following condition for contraction relations:

(C-Covering) $$-(A \wedge B) \subseteq \mathrm{Cl}(A, -A, B, -B)$$

Then we obtain

Corollary 10.7.4. *In the finite case a recovering contraction is AGM-standard if and only if it satisfies C-Covering.*

Just as for inference relations, little is known so far about characterization of standard recovering contractions in the infinite case. Further properties and characterizations of such contractions can be found in [Rot93]. Rott has shown, in particular, that in the finite case the above condition could actually be simplified to the following constraint:

(R-Covering) $$-(A \wedge B) \subseteq \mathrm{Cl}(-A, -B)$$

10.7.1 Rational recovering contractions

A recovering contraction relation will be called *rational* if it satisfies Rational Monotony. Such contraction relations will correspond already to AGM contractions satisfying the full list of its rationality postulates.

It turns out that, for recovering contractions, Rational Monotony already implies Priority. Consequently, we have

Lemma 10.7.2. *Any rational recovering contraction is a rational contraction relation.*

Proof. Let $\mathrel{\vrule height 1.6ex depth 0pt width 0.1ex\kern-0.1ex\sim}$ be a rational recovering contraction, $A \mathrel{\vrule height 1.6ex depth 0pt width 0.1ex\kern-0.1ex\sim} B$ and $A \wedge B \not\mathrel{\vrule height 1.6ex depth 0pt width 0.1ex\kern-0.1ex\sim} B$. In order to demonstrate that Priority is valid, we need to show that $B \mathrel{\vrule height 1.6ex depth 0pt width 0.1ex\kern-0.1ex\sim} A$. Note first that B is believed in $\mathrel{\vrule height 1.6ex depth 0pt width 0.1ex\kern-0.1ex\sim}$ (by Inclusion). But then A is also believed in $\mathrel{\vrule height 1.6ex depth 0pt width 0.1ex\kern-0.1ex\sim}$. Indeed, otherwise we would have that $A \wedge B$ is not believed, and hence $A \wedge B \mathrel{\vrule height 1.6ex depth 0pt width 0.1ex\kern-0.1ex\sim} B$ by Vacuity, contrary to our assumptions.

If A is believed, then $B \mathrel{\vrule height 1.6ex depth 0pt width 0.1ex\kern-0.1ex\sim} B{\rightarrow}A$ by Recovery. In addition, $A \mathrel{\vrule height 1.6ex depth 0pt width 0.1ex\kern-0.1ex\sim} A \vee B$, and hence $A \wedge B \mathrel{\vrule height 1.6ex depth 0pt width 0.1ex\kern-0.1ex\sim} A \vee B$ by Partial Antitony. Applying now Rational Monotony, we obtain $B \mathrel{\vrule height 1.6ex depth 0pt width 0.1ex\kern-0.1ex\sim} A \vee B$. Combined with $B \mathrel{\vrule height 1.6ex depth 0pt width 0.1ex\kern-0.1ex\sim} B{\rightarrow}A$, this gives us $B \mathrel{\vrule height 1.6ex depth 0pt width 0.1ex\kern-0.1ex\sim} A$, as required. $\square$

Thus, rational recovering contractions is a species of rational contractions.

Extending our previous results, we can immediately give a semantic representation of rational recovering contractions in terms of *rational AGM-states*:

Definition 10.7.2. *An epistemic state will be called a* rational AGM-state *if it is a standard epistemic AGM-state in which the preference order is modular.*

Rational AGM-states are essentially equivalent to the transitively relational models used in [AGM85] for representing AGM contractions. Accordingly, the following result is just a reformulation of the corresponding result established in [AGM85] in terms of contraction relations.

Theorem 10.7.1. *A contraction relation is a rational recovering contraction if and only if it coincides with the set of contractionals that are conservatively valid in some rational AGM-state.*

Proof. If ∼| is a rational recovering contraction, its generated preferential inference relation is rational, and hence it has a standard (injective) modular KLM model W. Then it can be easily checked that the transformation of this model into an epistemic AGM-state described in the proof of the representation theorem for general recovering contractions will give us a rational AGM-state.   □

This completes our description of contraction relations. We will return to them in Chapter 12 that will discuss contractions of epistemic states.

Part III

Belief Change

11. Belief Change and Its Problems

11.1 The problem of belief change

We have seen in Part Two that epistemic states provide a powerful and versatile representation for nonmonotonic reasoning. In this part we are going to show that epistemic states also constitute a very useful tool for representing and studying belief change. To begin with, we will briefly describe in this chapter the main approaches to representing belief change, as well as common problems arising with these representations. Then we will indicate how these problems can be resolved by taking epistemic states as an alternative background for belief change processes. We will also sketch new opportunities and directions of research about belief change arising in the suggested framework.

The problem of how to revise our theories and beliefs in response to new information has long been an important self-contained area of research in philosophical and logical literature. It has received a new, more practical motivation, however, with the realization that this aspect of our intellectual activity has immediate relevance for Artificial Intelligence, and is tightly connected with nonmonotonic reasoning. As a result, belief revision is commonly considered now as an integral part of the artificial intelligence research. We refer the reader to [GR95] for a comprehensive survey of current approaches in this area and their applications.

Two main approaches to representing belief change have been suggested in the literature. The first is a so-called AGM theory of belief change [AGM85, Gär88], a starting point in the formal study of the problem. It suggested a systematic approach to the problem both in terms of general rationality postulates that a belief change should satisfy, and in developing semantic representations that conform to these postulates.

The AGM theory was intended to give a representation for a process of revising *belief states* considered simply as deductively closed sets of propositions. According to this theory, a revision of a belief state with a new, possibly incompatible proposition is considered as a two-step process: on the first step, the belief state is *contracted* as little as possible in order to make it consistent with the new data, while on the second step the contracted belief set is *expanded* by adding the new proposition and taking the logical closure of the result. It has turned out, however, that a straightforward, naive realization of this procedure immediately runs into difficulties. A reduction of a beliefs state in order to restore consistency with the new data usually does not give a unique result; in most cases we obtain a number of maximal subsets that are compatible with the proposition being added. Furthermore, neither each maximal subset taken alone (*maxichoice* contraction), nor their common part (*full meet* contraction) can serve as reasonable solutions; the first solution is inappropriate because it contains in general too many propositions, whereas the second one contains far fewer than is expected (see [AM82, AGM85]).

As a way out of the above problem, the AGM theory suggested adding a preference mechanism allowing the choice among admissible maximal subtheories of the belief set. In [AGM85] this was achieved using a suitable *selection function* on the maximal subsets of the source belief set; the contracted belief set was then identified with the intersection of all selected maximal theories (*partial meet* contraction). The authors also focused on an important special case of the suggested construction in which the selection function is *relational*, that is, based on a preference order among the maximal subtheories. A complete description of the corresponding relational belief change operations, however, has turned out to be a difficult task. The reasons for this difficulty will become clear in what follows.

Gärdenfors has also proposed the use of epistemic entrenchment relations (see Chapter 5) as an alternative preference mechanism for choosing appropriate solutions. According to [Gär90], the belief set coupled with the associated relation of epistemic entrenchment constitutes the second level of representing epistemic states in the AGM theory. It has been shown that both constructions lead to the same results for 'rich' contraction and revision operations satisfying all the AGM postulates.

A major alternative solution to the problem of belief revision was based on the supposition that our corpus of beliefs is usually generated by some set of *basic* propositions (see, e.g., [Fuh91, Han91, Neb89]). This base approach embodied an important aspect of our beliefs that did not find its proper place in the AGM theory, namely that some of our beliefs are purely derivative and arise as logical consequences of other beliefs we have. From this point of view, it is natural to require that such derived beliefs should be withdrawn when we remove beliefs that served as their justification. Accordingly, contraction and expansion of belief sets are determined on this approach by contraction and expansion of their underlying bases. This drastically reduces the set of alternatives and avoids, in particular, trivialization of both maxichoice and full meet revision. Still, the resulting belief set on most of these accounts is also determined by imposing preference relations on such alternatives; the latter are purported to resolve residual choice problems that are not decided by bases alone.

Iterative change and categorial matching

As can be seen from the above short descriptions, both the AGM and base approach to belief change have agreed that the set of beliefs alone is insufficient for grounding a reasonable belief revision process; some more structure need to be discerned from our epistemic states in order to guide our decisions about what to retain and what to retract in the process of revising our beliefs. This understanding has created, however, problems of its own.

It is natural to suppose that belief change is an iterative process; we constantly obtain new data that require, from time to time, new revisions of our current beliefs. In order to perform such changes, we should have at each point not only the current belief set, but also the current preference mechanism that will determine the next revised belief set. Unfortunately, the source AGM theory does not account for this situation. Though the revised belief set is determined by the initial belief set and its associated selection function or an epistemic entrenchment order, the corresponding constructions do not (and have no means to) determine the preference structure associated with the resulting belief set. This is the source of the well-known shortcoming of the AGM theory, namely its inability to deal with iterated belief change.

Remark. Life would be much simpler if we could suppose that the above mentioned preference mechanism is representable as a background factor specifiable once and for all, independently of changes in beliefs. In fact, a number of earlier studies in the literature have been based, implicitly or explicitly, on such a supposition[1]. However, as has been argued by many authors, such an "epistemic determinism" is not a realistic supposition; the same belief set should be assigned sometimes different selection functions or entrenchment orderings, depending on its past history or other circumstantial factors. Thus, Lehmann has shown in [Leh95] that the supposition that belief revision operations can be defined as functions on belief sets alone may lead to trivialization given some plausible assumptions about iterated revisions.

A most natural solution to this problem of iterated changes consists in taking belief change as an operation on more complex epistemic states that incorporate not only the belief set, but also the associated preference mechanism. The resulting framework will satisfy then the *principle of categorial matching*, stated in [GR95], according to which the representation of the epistemic state after a change should be of the same kind as that before the change. For example, the AGM framework can be modified to provide a representation for 'real' changes that revise not only belief sets, but also

---

[1] For example, [Gär88, pp. 87–88] came very close to this supposition in claiming that the relation of epistemic entrenchment can be established independently of what happens to the belief set in contractions and revisions. Though Gärdenfors did not exclude changes to the entrenchment relation, he compared such changes with scientific revolutions and paradigm shifts. However, in a later paper [Gär90], he argued already that previous belief states can determine the current entrenchment order.

their associated entrenchment orderings. The idea that revision should be performed on epistemic entrenchment relations rather than on belief sets was expressed first in [Rot91b]. Actually, a number of different 'entrenchment revision' models of this kind have been proposed since then – see, e.g., [Bou96, Leh95, Nay94, Wil94]. As we will see, such models can be considered as instances of the general approach to belief change described below.

Let us turn now to the alternative base approach. If belief states are viewed as generated by bases alone (without the preference order), then it is easy to see that this representation conforms to the principle of categorial matching: belief change operations are defined then as operations on belief bases, rather than on belief sets (notice that belief sets are uniquely determined as logical closures of their bases, so the base representation subsumes belief sets). The situation will be different, however, if we will impose a preference (or selection) mechanism on the bases. Then we will be in the same situation as with the AGM approach, namely we have to determine also how belief change operations influence the associated preferences. And (contrary to the claim made in [Han92]) it seems that also in this context it is impossible to see the relevant selection mechanism as an invariant, background factor determined by the bases themselves.

Some of the relevant problems arising with the base approach are best illustrated by the following example (adapted from [Han92]).

Example 11.1.1. Let p and q denote, respectively, propositions "There is a university in Niamey", and "Niamey is a town in Nigeria". In the first situation a student sees a book titled *The University at Niamey*, and a fellow student says to her that Niamey is a town in Nigeria. In the second situation (not appearing in [Han92]) the title of the book is simply *Niamey*, and two equally good and reliable friends of the student say, respectively, that Niamey is a Nigerian town, and that Niamey has a university. Now, in both cases our student should subsequently retract her acquired belief that Niamey is a university town in Nigeria.

It is reasonable to assume that in the first case the student should retain her belief that p, due to a presumably high reliability of printed publications. Hansson's recipe suggests that in this case we have a selection mechanism that retains p when contracting $p \land q$ from the base $\{p, q\}^2$. It is much less clear, however, what the student should believe in the second case, since the relevant situation is perfectly symmetrical with respect to p and q, so no preferences could be established between them. Still, it is natural to require that the student should still believe that $p \lor q$.

The second situation in the above example is especially important; in fact, it can be seen as a benchmark problem for any theory of belief change. The situation can be described in general terms as a contraction of $A \land B$

---

² Note in passing that the same result can be achieved without introducing any preferences; instead, we could assume that the belief state is generated by the base $\{p, p \land q\}$.

from the (belief set generated by the) base $\{A, B\}$ in the case when A and B are equally preferred propositions. As has been noted in [GR95], this small example constitutes a mayor stumbling block for the base approach to belief change. Actually, we will see that none of the approaches suggested in the literature handles adequately this example. We will return to this problem later.

The above simple example reveals, however, yet another important problem arising in assuming that belief change operations should also change the underlying preference mechanism. Namely, we have seen that the resulting epistemic state obtained by incorporating two propositions depends essentially on the priority relation between the latter. Where such priorities came from? More exactly, whether we can assume that such priorities are created by the very operation of incorporating a new proposition into a current epistemic state? This supposition seems to be inevitable if we want to define a belief change *operation* producing a unique resulting state in response to a given informational input. But this means also that the new proposition alone is insufficient for determining the resulting epistemic state, since the result of the corresponding operation should also determine the place of this proposition in the new, revised preference structure.

The above considerations will have far reaching consequences for our study, since they undermine, in effect, a traditional view of the expansion operation in the framework of epistemic states. If epistemic states involve more than just belief sets, the corresponding operation(s) on such states should receive as an input not only the new proposition, but also an information sufficient for establishing where precisely it should be placed in the resulting preference structure. As we will see, this can be achieved if the relevant expansion operation will be defined as a *merge* of a given epistemic state with another epistemic state representing the required information.

Informational economy and minimality of change

The problem we are going to describe now is related to the problems described earlier, and concerns the principles of informational economy and minimality of change that lie at the heart of practically all approaches to belief change. The principle of informational economy says that information is valuable, and hence removal of information in contractions should be as small as possible (given the aim of restoring consistency). The related, though more general, principle of minimality of change requires that any kind of change made to belief or epistemic states should produce a minimal change to the source state that would achieve the purposes of the change.

An interesting puzzle arises with the implementation of the above principles in the AGM framework. A straightforward application of the principle of informational economy points out to (preferred) maximal subtheories of the belief set as the most appropriate options for choice. The suggested partial meet construction, however, takes the intersection of such theories as the final solution. As was rightly noted by Levi in [Lev91], such a solution violates the very principle of informational economy it was based on, since the intersection of maximal subtheories is already not maximal by itself, and hence is far from being optimal in the sense of preserving as much information as possible.

There is more to the above argument than an intellectual puzzle. True, facing a number of equally acceptable alternatives, it is reasonable to believe only what is common to all of them. However, if all we will remember after the change is what is common to all these alternatives, we put ourselves into a risk of losing important information *for subsequent changes.* Thus, it may well happen that subsequent data will show that some of these alternatives were wrong, and hence they should not be taken into account. In such a case remembering the source options would definitely help in producing a more adequate and informed solution.

The above problem acquires an especially vivid form in the base approach. Let us return to the situation when we have to contract $A \wedge B$ from the belief set generated by the base $\{A, B\}$ containing two equally preferred propositions. At the first step, we retreat to the two sub-bases $\{A\}$ and $\{B\}$ of the original base that do not imply $A \wedge B$. But since both these sub-bases are equally preferred, we have to form their intersection which happens to be empty! In other words, we have lost all the information contained in the initial base, so all subsequent changes should start from a scratch.

It seems reasonable to expect that, on any approach, the contracted belief set in the above situation should contain $A \vee B$, since each of the acceptable alternatives support this belief. In fact, this result is naturally sanctioned by the AGM theory. Furthermore, it seems also reasonable to require that if subsequent evidence rules out A, for example, we should believe that B. In other words, contracting first $A \wedge B$ and then A from the initial belief state should make us believe in B. Note that the AGM theory already cannot produce this result. The reason is that the first contraction gives the logical closure of $A \vee B$ as the contracted belief set, and hence the subsequent contraction of A will not have any effect on the corresponding belief state. This can serve as a good illustration of our claim that reducing our options to the intersection of preferred alternatives may lead to a loss of information for subsequent changes. Unfortunately, the majority of existing approaches to belief change do not produce this result. Notice that the loss of the above kind is not 'seen' so far as we are seeking only to find belief sets produced by one-step changes; it is revealed, however, in subsequent changes. It should also be clear that imposing preferences on the available alternatives cannot give a comprehensive solution to the problem, unless the alternatives are always totally ordered with respect to preference, and this is hard to achieve in most situations.

As we see it, the source of the above problem is that the above approaches to belief change force us to choose in situations we have no grounds for choice. And our suggested solution here amounts to retaining all the preferred alternatives as parts of the new epistemic state. In other words, we insist that all these alternatives should remain vivid in the representation of the resulting state rather than transformed into a single 'combined' solution. Otherwise we may lose important information. This does not prevent us from determining each time a unique current set of beliefs; but we should remember more than that.

11.2 Epistemic states as a framework of belief change

As will be shown below, epistemic states in the sense used in this book can be seen as a common generalization of both approaches to belief change sketched above. Accordingly, the theory of belief change in the framework of epistemic states that will be developed in subsequent chapters is intended to provide foundations for a general theory of belief change.

We begin with the assumption that belief change operations on belief sets should be seen as by-products of corresponding operations on the underlying epistemic states that explicitly include in some form or other the above mentioned preference mechanisms and/or generating bases. As a result, our representation will satisfy the principle of categorial matching, and consequently will freely admit iterative changes.

Our second major assumption concerning the representation of belief change will amount to the well-known claim that "a rational choice should be a relational choice" (see [Rot93] for a similar position). In other words, in accordance with our earlier decision made for nonmonotonic inference, and unlike the basic AGM approach and some of the studies in base-generated change, we will not consider in this book arbitrary selection functions. Instead, we will assume from the very beginning that a proper selection mechanism should be based on the underlying preference relation among admissible alternatives. In this case the common structure of the AGM and base representations will amount to a standard epistemic state consisting of (some) subtheories of the belief set, ordered by a preference relation.

11.2.1 AGM states and base-generated states

We will establish now a formal correspondence between our notion of an epistemic state and the two major representations of belief change. These correspondences will provide us with a first guidance for subsequent general constructions.

AGM states. In the relational case, the AGM framework consists of three components: an underlying classical consequence relation Th, a belief set **B**, which is a theory with respect to Th, and a preference relation on the maximal sub-theories of **B** (with respect to Th). As usual, for any proposition A, we will denote by **B**$\perp A$ the set of all maximal subsets of **B** that do not imply A with respect to Th. Note that each element of **B**$\perp A$ is a theory in Th. In addition, we will denote by **B**$\perp$ the union of all sets of the form **B**$\perp A$, where A is not an axiom of Th (that is, $A \notin$ Th($\emptyset$)). As can be easily shown, **B**$\perp$ consists of **B** itself and all its maximal proper subtheories with respect to Th.

The above AGM structure can be represented directly as a standard and determinate epistemic state (**B**$\perp$, $\prec$), where $\prec$ is a monotonic preference relation on **B**$\perp$. Then, for any proposition A that is inconsistent with the belief set **B**, it is easy to check that $]A[$ will coincide with **B**$\perp A$, and hence preferred theories in $]A[$ will be exactly selected maximal subsets of **B** that do not imply A according to AGM. If A is consistent with **B**, $]A[$ will coincide with the whole set **B**$\perp$. However, due to monotonicity of the preference relation $\prec$, **B** will be a unique preferred theory in $]A[$ in this case. This corresponds exactly to the behavior of relational selection functions in the AGM theory.

Epistemic states of the above form will be called *standard AGM-states* in what follows. The following observation shows that such epistemic states are equivalent (in the exact sense defined in Chapter 4) to monotonic **B**-homogeneous epistemic states.

Proposition 11.2.1. *Any standard AGM-state is equivalent to some standard monotonic **B**-homogeneous epistemic state and vice versa.*

Proof. Given a belief set **B**, we will denote by **B**$\downarrow$ the set of all subtheories of **B** with respect to Th. Then, if (**B**$\perp$, $\prec$) is a standard AGM-state, we add to it all theories from **B**$\downarrow$ and define the new preference relation as follows: if R is a union of the source preference order $\prec$ and the relation of set inclusion $\subseteq$ on **B**$\downarrow$, then the new preference relation will be defined as a transitive closure of R. As can be seen, the resulting epistemic state will be **B**-homogeneous and monotonic. Note also that the source preference relation $\prec$ coincides with the restriction of the new relation to **B**$\perp$. Moreover, due to the monotonicity of the new preference relation, preferred alternatives of the new epistemic state will always coincide with preferred theories of **B**$\perp$, so the two epistemic states will determine the same choice function. Thus, any standard AGM-state is extendable to an equivalent monotonic **B**-homogeneous epistemic.

Moving in the other direction, it is sufficient to observe that any monotonic **B**-homogeneous epistemic state is equivalent to its restriction to theories from **B**$\perp$; the latter is nothing other than an epistemic AGM-state.   □

In view of the above bidirectional correspondence, standard monotonic **B**-homogeneous epistemic states will also be considered as representatives of the AGM framework.

Epistemic AGM-states have a number of distinctive features that have played already an important role in our study of nonmonotonic reasoning. Thus, all such states are determinate, since the belief set **B** is also the most preferred theory in such states. In fact, they satisfy an even stronger property of *union-closure* (see Chapter 3): if u and v are admissible belief states, then $\text{Th}(u \cup v)$ is also an admissible belief state. The latter property turns out to be a common feature of both the AGM and base representations.

Base-generated states. Let **B** be a belief set generated by some base Δ with respect to a certain underlying classical consequence relation Th (that is, $\mathbf{B} = \text{Th}(\Delta)$). We will denote by $\mathcal{B}$ the set of theories determined by the subsets of the base:

$$\mathcal{B} = \{\text{Th}(\Delta_0) \mid \Delta_0 \subseteq \Delta\}$$

As we have shown in Chapter 4, the set of theories $\mathcal{B}$ provides a 'descriptively equivalent' representation for the base Δ. Consequently, base-generated belief states can be identified with another special class of epistemic states in our sense, namely with pure epistemic states of the form $\mathcal{B}$. A characteristic feature of such epistemic states is union-closure. As a result, all such epistemic states will also be determinate.

As we mentioned, however, the majority of current approaches in the base-generation camp eventually impose some kind of preference structure on the subsets of the base. This kind of structures can be captured by using standard epistemic states of the form $(\mathcal{B}, \prec)$, where $\prec$ is some preference relation on $\mathcal{B}$. Moreover, in most cases this preference relation is defined in such a way that it also satisfies the monotonicity property, though it is restricted now to the theories from $\mathcal{B}$. Thus, compared with epistemic AGM-states, the role of bases amounts to restricting the set of subtheories of the belief set that are considered as admissible belief sets; in other words, bases are used to constrain the set of alternatives that are admitted as options for a choice.

11.2.2 Determination, union-closure, monotonicity, and standardness

Summing up the above descriptions, we can conclude that the two major paradigms of belief change representation give raise to epistemic states that are standard, monotonic and union-closed (and hence determinate). Without diminishing the importance of such epistemic states, we will show in what follows, however, that in order to obtain a truly general and versatile theory of belief change, all these additional constraints on epistemic states should be rejected or relaxed.

Determination and union-closure. Recall that determinate epistemic states are epistemic states that contain a unique most preferred admissible belief state. The belief set of such an epistemic state coincides with the set of propositions supported by this preferred belief state. On the other hand, non-determinate epistemic states allow for a number of maximally preferred belief states; the belief set of such an epistemic state is determined as an intersection of the latter. This possibility has not been exploited so far in the literature on belief change, with [FUKV86] as a notable exception[3].

We have seen in the preceding chapters that non-determinate epistemic states suggest a more realistic representation of quite common epistemic situations that involve conflicting default assumptions. This suggests that determination should not be taken as a 'rationality constraint' on epistemic states. Moreover, as could be anticipated from our earlier discussion in this chapter, we see adherence to determination as the source of potential loss of information in iterative changes. Facing a set of equally preferred alternatives, the AGM procedure produces a unique new belief state which is the common part of these alternatives. Consequently, on all accounts that would agree with the original AGM representation, any further change will be confined to the new belief set and its subsets. In other words, any information concerning the source alternatives will be forgotten, and hence it will not be used even when subsequent data will reject some of these alternatives.

While for the AGM representation the influence of determination is not immediate, it has a direct impact on the base approach. Just as the AGM theory, given a set of equally preferred sub-bases, a theory of base change produces a new resulting base containing the elements that are common to these sub-bases. As shows the example of contracting $A \wedge B$ from the base $\{A, B\}$, however, the loss of information on this step may be immediate and painful.

Note that, for the base approach, determination (as well as union-closure) is not an independent property, but a by-product of the very representation in terms of bases; as our reconstruction shows, any consistent base corresponds to a determinate epistemic state in which the most preferred belief state is generated by the whole base. Moreover, the above procedure of forming intersections of preferred sub-bases is almost inevitable on the base approach, since we need to obtain a unique resulting base; otherwise we would face violation of the principle of categorial matching.

The above considerations imply that rejection of determination in this case cannot be made without rejecting the base representation itself as a general framework for representing belief change. In other words, even though many 'well-organized' epistemic states may be base-generated, belief change operations can transform such epistemic states into states that are not representable already by using bases. Furthermore, determination is actually a consequence of a stronger property of union-closure, a property that is common to epistemic AGM-states and base-generated states. Accordingly,

---

[3] A related idea of epistemic states consisting of several belief sets was expressed by in [Sta84] (and discussed in [Gär88]), though he considered such epistemic states as abnormal in some sense.

rejection of determination leads also to abandoning of union-closure as a constraint on epistemic states.

Monotonicity. Monotonicity of the preference relation can be seen as another characteristic feature of the current approaches to belief change. Basically, it stems from the principle of informational economy: belief sets preserving more information should be preferred to sets containing less. Note, however, that the principle of informational economy sanctions monotonicity of the preference relation only under an assumption that any proposition from a belief state contributes to its informational content. This assumption has been challenged by Isaac Levi in [Lev91]. He argued that not all additions of propositions produce a growth of information; only *valuable* information is relevant for establishing preferences between admissible alternatives. Consequently, monotonicity should not be accepted. Still, this understanding sanctions the property of *weak monotonicity* (see Chapter 3), according to which smaller belief sets should not be preferred to larger ones.

It has been shown in the preceding chapters that the class of monotonic epistemic states is sufficient for representing both skeptical and credulous inference. Still, we have also seen that the representation of contraction relations can be given only in the framework of epistemic states that are not monotonic in general, though they can be made weakly monotonic. In view of the correspondence between contraction relations and belief contraction functions that will be established in what follows, only weak monotonicity will be considered as a generally acceptable constraint on epistemic states.

Standardness. The preceding study has already shown the importance of general (non-standard) epistemic states for a perspicuous representation of nonmonotonic reasoning. As we will see, a similar generalization is required for an adequate representation of belief change operations. Actually, the restriction to standard epistemic states will be shown to be responsible for the difficulties in giving a characterization of relational belief change operations in the AGM framework.

As we have seen in Chapter 4, general epistemic states arise naturally in conjoining (taking sums of) a number of standard epistemic states. In addition, any general epistemic state could be seen as arising from a standard epistemic state by restricting available (or accepted) linguistic means. Accordingly, belief change operations on general epistemic states can also be seen as language-restricted descriptions of some quite regular changes in standard epistemic states, though defined with respect to extended languages.

11.2.3 Coherence versus foundations

The destiny of derived beliefs in belief change, and the role of justification in belief acceptance lie at the heart of the dispute between coherentist and foundational approaches to belief and knowledge. It should be noted, however, that the understanding of both coherentism and foundationalism when applied to the problem of belief change is somewhat different from the traditional, epistemological understanding of these notions (see, e.g., [Sos80, Har86]), and is far from being equivocal. We will suggest below a certain understanding of these doctrines in the theory of belief change, which is based on the above representation of the AGM and base approach in epistemic states. Whatever the relation of this understanding to the traditional opposition of coherence and foundations, we will see that our classification will provide us with an important viewpoint for analyzing different approaches to belief change.

A coherentist approach is based on the assumption that justifications and, in general, pedigree of one's beliefs should not matter for their acceptance or rejection. What matters, instead, is an overall coherence of sets of potential beliefs. Consequently, the only guiding principles for choosing the right set of beliefs on this view are consistency and preference relations among alternative sets of beliefs that reflect the level or degree of their coherence. In particular, *no set of beliefs should be excluded as a potential option for choice*, though it can be excluded as a solution to the choice task, if it happens to be a less coherent option than others. This latter claim, called the *homogeneity principle* in what follows, can be seen as a guiding principle behind the AGM theory. The principle is also forcefully advocated by Isaac Levi [Lev91, Lev97] in his alternative theory of belief change. Accordingly, we will consider the homogeneity principle as the characteristic property of the coherentist approach. This will agree with the traditional understanding that the AGM theory constitutes one of the main coherentist models (see, e.g., [Gär90]), though it permits also other coherentist modelling, provided it complies with the homogeneity principle.

The foundational approach to belief change explicitly accounts for the fact that some of our beliefs are derivative and depend on other, more basic, beliefs for their justification. On this view, our epistemic states involve some dependence, or justificational structure that constrain the set of admissible options for choice to 'well-formed' ones that accord with this structure. As a result, foundational approach leads to rejection of the above-mentioned homogeneity principle. Note that the preference relation among the alternatives is not essential on this view; a 'pure' foundationalist approach could be expressed by the claim that the dependence structure among beliefs (that is determined, for instance, by a set of basic beliefs) should be seen as the only principle guiding our choice decisions in belief change. Due to the principle of informational economy, the preference relation is reduced in this case simply to the relation of set inclusion among admissible options, and hence is wholly determined by the underlying dependence structure. On this account, the representation of belief states as determined by their bases constitutes a paradigmatic example of foundational modelling (cf., [Val97]).

Now let us see how the above conceptions are interpreted in the framework of epistemic states. The two components of a standard epistemic state

$\mathbb{E} = (\mathcal{E}, \prec)$ can be seen as reflecting two basic kinds of relations holding among propositions. The first component, $\mathcal{E}$, represents a foundational structure by the very fact that it restricts the set of admissible alternatives. As we have seen, this restriction can be alternatively described in terms of dependence consequence relations holding among propositions. On the other hand, the preference relation $\prec$ reflects a coherentist selection structure that allows us to choose among the available alternatives. Note that this structure of an epistemic state embodies a priority of dependence constraints with respect to preferential ones: preference relations hold only among the alternatives that are already admissible from the point of view of the underlying dependence relationships. Now, eliminating (more exactly, reducing to a necessary minimum) each of the two components, we obtain, respectively, the representations of the foundational and coherentist approaches in the framework of epistemic states.

Coherentism and homogeneous epistemic states. As we said, the homogeneity principle can be seen as a characteristic feature of the coherentist approach. The notion of a homogeneous epistemic state, defined in Chapter 3, provides a realization of this principle in the framework of epistemic states.

Recall that an epistemic state is homogeneous if the set of its admissible belief sets coincides with the set of all deductively closed theories that include the knowledge set. Current coherentist theories assume, however, a restricted version of the homogeneity principle, according to which only subsets of the belief set should be taken as options for choice. This version corresponds to the notion of a **B**-homogeneous state, in which the set of admissible belief sets is the set of all theories that include the knowledge set and are included in the belief set of the epistemic state. Such epistemic states presuppose, in effect, that no dependence relations hold among believed propositions, except for logical ones, and hence any deductively closed subset of the belief set is admissible. Consequently, the structure of such a state is determined solely by a preference relation on all subtheories of the belief set. Notice that the AGM paradigm belongs to this class, but involves an additional property that the preference relation should be monotonic.

As was argued in [Gär90], the AGM theory augmented with an entrenchment ordering is capable to reflect justifications (reasons) for our beliefs, so it is able, in principle, to capture belief changes sanctioned by the foundational approach. As a further confirmation of this thesis, we will see in the next chapter that homogeneous epistemic states are adequate for representing all belief contraction functions generated by epistemic states. This expressivity will essentially depend, however, on the assumption that the preference relation in such homogeneous states is not in general monotonic. Moreover, we will see also that pure epistemic states generate in this sense only a restricted class of (pure) belief contractions, and hence are incapable to directly capture the whole range of reasonable belief contractions. Thus, the coherentist approach will prove to be superior to the foundational one on this score.

Still, there is a general problem with the coherentist approach that undermines somewhat the significance of the above mentioned results, and reduces the whole approach, for the time being, to the level of a purely theoretical opportunity.

The problem with the coherentist approach appears first as a practical (computational) problem. A prerequisite for a successful implementation of a coherentist representation consists in determining an adequate preference relation on *all* subsets of the belief set. In most cases such a task poses an unbearable burden on our capabilities, especially in the absence of clear principles on the basis which we could determine such preferences. If we know, however, that the belief set is base-generated, or even has a more general dependence structure, as described earlier, we can drastically reduce the set of alternatives for choice, and in this way would obtain a much more feasible (and computable) representation. As was aptly remarked by Hansson in [Han92], the base of a belief set can relieve the preference mechanism of the majority of its functions.

The same problem reappears in a more severe form in an attempt to implement the coherentist framework to representing iterated belief changes. In order to represent such changes preserving at the same time the principle of categorial matching, we must know how to change the preference relation on all theories of the language. Once more, in the absence of clear principles for forming such preference relations, it is difficult to give a principled general recipe how to do this. Furthermore, we will see below that the actual contraction operation suggested by the AGM theory leads to an inevitable loss of information in iterative changes. This leaves us without a clear understanding whether and how an adequate representation of iterated changes could be achieved in the coherentist framework.

Foundationalism and pure epistemic states. Pure epistemic states trivialize the preferential component of the notion of an epistemic state by reducing it to the relation of set inclusion among admissible theories. So, a pure epistemic state is identified, in effect, with a set of theories. We have seen also that such epistemic states can be described in terms of *dependence relations dependence relations* holding between propositions. Accordingly, pure epistemic states apparently suggest themselves as a most natural framework for representing a foundationalist approach to belief change. Actually, they have been used for this purpose in [Boc99b, Boc00c].

On the one hand, the above representation can be viewed as reflecting a rigid foundationalist position according to which dependence relations among propositions is the only essential factor in determining our epistemic states and changes made to it. On the other hand, this version of foundationalism is very moderate, since the net of dependencies is not assumed in general to have a well-founded structure starting with universally acceptable self-justified 'basic' propositions. In this way it avoids much of the criticism raised against the traditional foundationalist approach. In fact, all it assumes is that there is some dependence relation between propositions that should determine the result of changes made to epistemic states.

Unfortunately, the approach described in the above mentioned papers has turned out to be flawed both technically and conceptually. Namely, it turns out that pure epistemic states do not give an adequate representation of expansions. As we will see, a nearest counterpart of pure epistemic states that will be still adequate for representing the main belief change operations amounts to the class of persistent epistemic states. This undermines a strong foundationalist claim that the structure of an epistemic state should be completely determined by the dependence (justification) relations; persistent epistemic state allow for preference relations that are not reducible to set inclusion. Furthermore, even simplest operations on epistemic states turn out to produce epistemic states that are not even standard. All this raises a suspicion that a fruitful theory of belief change cannot be constructed on a pure ideological basis of either coherentism or foundationalism.

To end our (inconclusive) discussion of coherentism and foundationalism, it is interesting to note that both these approaches can be fully realized in the restricted case of linear epistemic states. For this latter case, the AGM theory, on the one hand, and the foundational approach described in [Boc99b, Boc00c], on the other, provide, respectively, a purely coherentist and purely foundational representations of belief change.

11.2.4 Changing epistemic states

In accordance with the general approach to belief change, sketched above, our primary objects of interest will be operations that change epistemic states in response to new information. Two kinds of such changes immediately suggest themselves as most fundamental. The first consists in removing information from epistemic states, while the second one results in adding information to epistemic states. As can be anticipated, these main kinds of change in epistemic states will be intimately connected with the corresponding pair of fundamental operations on belief sets, namely contractions and expansions. The shift in the level of representation will imply, however, some drastic changes in the character of the corresponding operations. In particular, our classification of operations on epistemic states will not correspond exactly to the distinction between contractions and expansions of belief sets. We will see, for example, that contractions of epistemic states may sometimes lead to a growth of their associated belief sets. In addition, quite different operations on epistemic states may result in the same change of belief sets. Actually, these discrepancies could be seen as a further confirmation of the claim that belief sets alone do not give a full representation of the information embodied in epistemic states.

The belief set of an epistemic state was defined in Chapter 3 as the set of propositions supported by all preferred admissible belief states. Consequently, belief sets are uniquely determined by epistemic states, and hence change operations on epistemic states will determine also corresponding operations on belief sets. The description of such generated belief change functions, and their comparison with existing characterizations will be an important part of our study in what follows.

It is important to observe that the two major representations of belief change, namely the AGM theory and the theory of base change, fully agree with the above mentioned definition of belief. As a result, both these theories will be reconstructed in our framework by defining appropriate operations on the associated epistemic states.

Belief change versus nonmonotonic reasoning. By taking epistemic states as a common background for both nonmonotonic reasoning and belief change, we lay down a firm basis for the claim that both these theories are intimately related. Moreover, it will be shown that both skeptical and contraction inference relations directly correspond to two important belief change operations, namely revisions and contractions. Still, a general comparison between these two theories reveals also significant differences. To begin with, nonmonotonic reasoning captures only a flat, non-iterative aspect of belief change, whereas one of the main tasks of the latter consists in describing an iteration of belief change operations. Moreover, many of the operations on epistemic states, discussed in this part of the book, have no counterparts in the theory of nonmonotonic reasoning. In additional discrepancy between the use of epistemic states in nonmonotonic reasoning and belief change arises upon realizing that nonmonotonic reasoning usually do not involve real changes in epistemic states; all it requires is a *suppositional change* (see [Lev97]), in which the input proposition (the evidence) is temporarily assumed as true. Changing the evidence does not necessarily lead to changing epistemic states, since the latter contain a general default information that is applicable in many factual circumstances. Actually, this kind of representation has already been suggested, for example, in [Bre91a]. Clearly, supposing that a proposition is true (for the purposes of argumentation, or as holding in a given situation) is different from "actually coming to believe the proposition in earnest", using Levi's phrase. Accordingly, though a nonmonotonic inference is representable via revisions of an epistemic state, it does not require such revisions in order to produce answers to our queries.

11.3 Sums and contractions

The first basic kind of changes in epistemic states amounts to removing information from the latter. It turns out that there are two essentially different, in fact opposite, ways of achieving this in the framework of epistemic states. The first, more familiar way consists in deleting admissible belief states containing the proposition being removed. This gives us the notion of a contraction of epistemic states. This operation will be studied in details in Chapter 12.

The second, less direct way consists in extending epistemic states by adding new admissible belief states. A further refinement of this idea leads to accepting the operation of taking sums as a full-fledged belief change operation on epistemic states.

11.3.1 Sums of epistemic states

The operation of taking a disjoint sum of epistemic states has already been introduced in Chapter 4 in defining decomposition of epistemic states. From the point of view of belief change, this operation amounts to combining a number of epistemic states as (aggregated) options for choice.

Nobody wants to lose beliefs one has, unless compelled to do so. This seems to be the reason why, despite its naturalness, the above operation of taking sums of epistemic states does not correspond to anything in the existing literature. The sum of epistemic states combines admissible belief states rather than beliefs supported by them; in other words, it accumulates options for choice (serious possibilities). As a result, the belief set of a sum of epistemic states is in general smaller than belief sets of its component states. Furthermore, in most regular cases, the belief set of the sum is just an intersection of the component belief sets. In this sense, the operation of taking sums is a form of a belief contraction operation. On the other hand, it is similar to the operations of merge and expansion (see below) in that it does not remove admissible states, but only adds new ones.

The above operation arises naturally in the context of a theoretical research when a theory is generalized in order to subsume a number of alternative approaches to the same problem. It has also a natural meaning in the context of expert systems, when a number of experts suggest different opinions on the same subject. Notice that such opinions cannot be combined, in general, by conjunction; this is especially evident when the opinions are incompatible with each other. But even in the consistent case, when one expert says that the share can only rise, but no more than on one point, while the second one claims that it can only fall, up to ten points, then it would be unwise to assume that the share will preserve its value, since this is the only possibility allowed by both experts. Instead, a reasonably cautious (skeptical) evaluation of these opinions would lead to a plausible belief in the disjunction of these opinions, namely that the range of changes of the share will be confined to the interval (-10,+1) around the current value. In many cases, even this, presumably weak, yet valuable, information could serve as a basis of a reasonable behavior on the stock market.

A further justification for the necessity of this operation in the framework of epistemic states will be given in Chapter 14, where the sum operation will be shown to be essential for constructing the main classes of epistemic states.

11.3.2 Contraction

A partial compensation for raising the complexity of representation for belief change consists in the fact that it allows us to give a quite simple and natural definition of a contraction operation.

Admissible belief states of an epistemic state constitute all potential alternatives that are considered as 'serious possibilities' by the agent. In accordance with this, the contraction of a proposition A from an epistemic state $\mathbb{E}$ will be defined as an operation that consists simply in removal of all admissible belief states from $\mathbb{E}$ that support A. We will denote the resulting epistemic state by $\mathbb{E} - A$.

The above contraction operation on epistemic states will be studied in details in the next chapter. As we will see, it has quite regular properties, most important of which being commutativity: a sequence of contractions can be performed in any order yielding the same resulting epistemic state.

In order to assess the similarities and differences between the above contraction operation on epistemic states and common accounts of belief contraction, it is instructive to consider the behavior of this operation on epistemic AGM-states and base-generated states.

Contracting AGM and base-generated states. If the AGM framework is represented by what we have termed AGM states, then, for any proposition A, the belief set of $\mathbb{E} - A$ will be precisely the contracted belief set according to the AGM definition. In this respect, the AGM belief contraction functions are subsumed by our general construction. Still, there is an important difference between the two frameworks, since what we obtain in our construction is not only the new belief set, but also a new epistemic state. Consequently, our contraction operation can be iterated, which is impossible in the original AGM framework. Note also that the new epistemic state runs against the basic assumption of the AGM approach, since in most cases it will not already be determinate.

A more complex situation arises when comparing our contraction operation with base contractions. According to the general construction given in [Han93b], the first step in performing a base contraction of A consists in finding preferred (selected) subsets of the base that do not imply A. So far, this fits well with our reconstruction, since the latter subsets exactly correspond to preferred admissible theories of the associated contracted epistemic state. Then our definition says, in effect, that the contracted belief set should be equal to the intersection of all these preferred theories. Unfortunately, such a solution cannot be considered as a principled solution from the point of view of the base paradigm, since according to the latter we need to construct a unique contracted base; only this latter will determine the resulting belief set. Accordingly, [Han93b] defines first the contracted base as the intersection of all preferred subsets of the base ('partial meet base contraction'), and then the contracted belief set is defined as the set of all propositions that are implied by the new base.

Returning once more to the example of contracting $A \wedge B$ from the base $\{A, B\}$, the base contraction gives in this case the empty base, while our contraction results in a quite reasonable new belief set $\text{Th}(A \vee B)$, as well as a new epistemic state $\{\text{Th}(A), \text{Th}(B)\}$ consisting of two theories. This latter epistemic state, however, is not base-generated (since it is not union-closed).

Remark. An apparent solution to the above problem (explored by Hansson in [Han93a]) consists in allowing disjunctions of base propositions as legitimate elements of the base. Then in the above example we could take $\{A \vee B\}$ as representing the contracted base, and this would give us the desired new belief set. Actually, this partial departure from the base ideology would make the base representation quite similar to the AGM framework. Unfortunately, it would retain also the main shortcoming of the latter that we have mentioned earlier in this chapter. Notice that a subsequent deletion of A from this new base does not produce any effect, since A is already not believed in it. On our account, however, if we take the initial base $\{A, B\}$ and delete both $A \wedge B$ and A from it, then B will be believed in the resulting epistemic state. Speaking more generally, in this case also taking intersections of the preferred alternatives would lead to a loss of information, with the only distinction that, just as in the AGM approach, this loss will not be seen so far as we are seeking to find belief sets produced by one-step changes. It will revealed, however, in subsequent changes.

Contraction of flocks. As we have seen, contraction of base-generated epistemic states often produces epistemic states that are not base-generated. It turns out, however, that contraction of pure bases is representable using flocks of bases (see Chapter 3). Namely, we will see that a contraction of A from a base Δ could be modeled by a flock $\{\Delta_i\}$, where each Δ_i is a maximal subset of Δ that does not imply A. Speaking more generally, flocks will emerge as a nearest counterpart of bases that will already be closed with respect to the contraction operations. Moreover, the latter will correspond to the operation of deletion on flocks suggested in [FUKV86]. Still, the differences in our understanding of flocks (described in Chapter 3) will result in a different (and simpler) behavior of the contraction operation, as illustrated by the following example from [FUKV86].

Example 11.3.1. Let $\mathcal{E}$ be a pure epistemic state generated by the base $\{A, B, A \leftrightarrow B\}$, and suppose we contract it with respect to the set $\{A, B\}$. Then the resulting epistemic state on both our account and flock theory will amount to a single theory $\text{Cl}(A \leftrightarrow B)$. In our approach, this will also be the result of changing $\mathcal{E}$ by a sequence of contractions $\langle -A; -B \rangle$. The construction of deletion in [FUKV86], however, gives for this latter case a flock $\{\emptyset, \{A \leftrightarrow B\}\}$, which is treated, in effect, as identical with its least element $\{\emptyset\}$, while in our construction it is reducible to $\{\{A \leftrightarrow B\}\}$. As a result, multiple deletions are not equivalent to sequences of singular deletions in [FUKV86].

Meet contraction. Though we opt for a different understanding of contractions in this book, there is no technical difficulty in defining a contraction operation on epistemic states that will be in accord with both the AGM and base contractions. In fact, the following contraction operation on standard epistemic states gives the required behavior:

Definition 11.3.1. *A meet contraction of a standard epistemic state* $\mathbb{E}$ *with respect to a proposition* A *is a restriction of* $\mathbb{E}$ *to the set of admissible belief sets that are included in all preferred theories from* $]A[$.

As can be seen, the above contraction operation respects categorial matching, since it transforms epistemic states into epistemic states. In addition, it can be easily checked that it preserves already union-closure and base-generation, on the one hand, and **B**-homogeneity, on the other. Moreover, if we apply it to a monotonic **B**-homogeneous state corresponding to the AGM framework with a belief set **B**, we will obtain a monotonic **B**-homogeneous state corresponding to the contracted belief set in the sense of AGM. Similarly, being applied to a base-generated state, the meet contraction will produce exactly the epistemic state corresponding to the contracted base in the sense of Hansson. Thus, meet contraction operation seems to capture faithfully the common idea behind AGM and base contractions.

The reader could also notice the similarity between the above meet contraction operation and the notion of a careful inference sketched in Section 3.6.5 of Chapter 3. In fact, these notions have also much in common in terms of their (computational) advantages and (expressive) shortcomings. It is important to note, in particular, that our contraction and meet contraction will coincide on epistemic states in which the preference relation is a linear (total) order on admissible belief sets. This setting corresponds also to the AGM representations satisfying all AGM rationality postulates.

Belief contractions and contraction inference. If $\mathbb{E}$ is an epistemic state with a belief set $\mathbf{B}_{\mathbb{E}}$, then the belief set of a contracted epistemic state $\mathbb{E} - A$ (that is, $\mathbf{B}_{\mathbb{E}-A}$), can also be viewed as a contraction of the source belief set $\mathbf{B}_{\mathbb{E}}$ with respect to A. In order to highlight this understanding, we will denote this contracted belief set by $\mathbf{B}_{\mathbb{E}} - A$. Moreover, if $\mathbb{E}$ is fixed and known from the context, we will drop the subscript $\mathbb{E}$ and write simply **B** for the initial belief set and $\mathbf{B} - A$ for the contracted belief set. The latter notation will already be quite similar to the one adopted in the literature[4].

Since $\mathbf{B}_{\mathbb{E}} - A$ is a belief set of the contracted epistemic state, it is an intersection of all preferred admissible belief sets from $\mathbb{E}$ that do not contain A. Therefore, B belongs to $\mathbf{B}_{\mathbb{E}} - A$ if and only if the contractional $A \dashv B$ is valid in $\mathbb{E}$ (see Chapter 10). Accordingly, contractions of belief sets on the above understanding can also be described in terms of associated contraction inference relations. This correspondence adds another face to the thesis of

---

[4] Except that we use **B** instead of **K**, since we insist that we are talking about belief rather than knowledge.

Gärdenfors and Makinson that belief change and nonmonotonic inference are two sides of the same coin.

The above correspondence will be intensively used in what follows. It will allow us, in particular, to transfer the representation results obtained in Chapter 10 into corresponding representation results for belief contractions.

11.4 Merge and expansion

The second major kind of epistemic change consists in incorporating new information into an epistemic state. As we have said, however, this kind of change cannot be modeled via a simple addition of a new proposition to an epistemic state, since the resulting epistemic state should also reflect the corresponding change in the preference structure. In fact, the very picture of naked input propositions appearing out of the blue becomes patently insufficient for describing realistic processes of adding information to epistemic states. It turns out that there is a lot of ways in which new information can be incorporated into epistemic states, not all of them producing an immediate gain in associated belief sets. Accordingly, this kind of change will be modeled as a special case of a general *merge* operation on epistemic states.

A merge operation on epistemic states will be defined as a species of a well-known general notion of a product of mathematical structures. Unlike the sum operation, discussed earlier, the merge of epistemic states combines the beliefs determined by these states, so the belief set of the resulting epistemic state will ordinarily include the component belief sets. Moreover, implementing the results obtained in [ARS95], we define two binary merge operations, *pure merge* and *prioritized merge*, that will be sufficient for representing a large variety of merge operations satisfying Arrow's conditions. These two merge operations will correspond to two principal ways of combining informational sources, namely when the two epistemic states are equally reliable, and when one has a priority over the other.

These two merge operations will be used, in turn, for defining two basic *expansion* operations that will correspond to two main senses in which a proposition can be added to an epistemic state. Namely, an expansion of an epistemic state $\mathbb{E}$ with a proposition A will be defined as a merge of $\mathbb{E}$ with a primitive epistemic state $\mathbb{E}^A$ that is normally base-generated by the base $\{A\}$. This construction will determine a unique expanded epistemic state for each of the two basic merge operations. The primitive epistemic state $\mathbb{E}^A$ consists of just two theories, namely $Cl(A)$ and $Cl(\mathbf{t})$, and it can be seen as expressing a 'pure' belief in A, so the relevant expansion will represent the result of incorporating this belief into $\mathbb{E}$. As will be shown, the change in belief sets determined by such expansion operations will invariably coincide with the corresponding AGM expansions; nevertheless, different expansion operations will produce different epistemic states, and this will influence our beliefs in subsequent changes.

Finally, we describe in Chapter 13 a couple of alternative expansion operations, most important of which being a *knowledge expansion* that amounts to incorporating the new proposition into the knowledge set of an epistemic state.

11.5 Derived changes

The main belief change operations, described above, can be combined in various ways and produce some more complex changes. In addition, by changing epistemic states, we change also not only their belief sets, but also the generated inference relations, as well as their associated expectation relations. In the last chapter of the book we will discuss some of the issues arising in taking this broader perspective on epistemic change.

Consolidation and revision. One of the main concerns of the traditional theory of belief change consists in preserving consistency of belief sets in performing belief change operations. This concern is clearly justifiable in the framework of belief states, since an inconsistent belief state constitutes on this account a dead end for any epistemic process; no meaningful information could be discerned from inconsistent theories. However, this concern is less significant in the framework of epistemic states, since the latter carry much more information than just belief sets, so, even if an epistemic state has an inconsistent belief set, it is still capable of producing a consistent response on many queries. In particular, it usually produces a nontrivial *refined* belief set (see Chapter 3).

Using our present terminology, the refined belief set of an epistemic state $\mathbb{E}$ is nothing other than the belief set of an epistemic state $\mathbb{E} - \mathbf{f}$ obtained by contracting $\mathbb{E}$ with respect to falsity. Hansson has called such an operation a *consolidation*. As we will see, this operation produces desired results in many circumstances that create inconsistent belief sets.

A more drastic transformation of epistemic states that secure consistency of belief sets has been suggested by Isaac Levi and adopted by the AGM theory. It consists in defining a *revision* of an epistemic state with respect to A as a two-step procedure consisting of contracting $\neg A$ followed by an expansion with respect to A.

Revisions of epistemic states will always produce consistent belief sets that include the new proposition. Moreover, the corresponding belief revision function generated by revisions of a given epistemic state coincides, in effect, with the skeptical inference relation determined by this epistemic state. This fact constitutes the basis of the already mentioned claim that belief revision and nonmonotonic inference are two sides of the same coin.

The above correspondence will be used for proving a number of representation results for belief revision functions determined by epistemic states. It will be shown, in particular, that epistemic states provide a natural extension of the above correspondence between belief revision and nonmonotonic inference to preferential inference relations.

Inference and entrenchment change. Changes made to epistemic states lead also to changes in their associated inference relations. In fact, changes of belief sets can be seen as a special case of this broader change, since (refined) belief sets are definable as sets of the form $\{A \mid \mathbf{t} \vdash A\}$, for the preferential inference relation $\vdash$ generated by an epistemic state. Note also that inference relations are interdefinable with all the different kinds of expectation relations (see Chapter 6). Consequently, an inference change can be described, for instance, as an entrenchment change, and vice versa.

We will describe in Chapter 14 a number of different kinds of inference change determined by expansions and revisions of epistemic states. It will be shown, in particular, that inference changes produced by expansions of epistemic states satisfy all the postulates for such a change, suggested in [DP97]. It will also be shown that some natural and already known operations of this kind are describable directly as operations on inference relations, without any reference to underlying epistemic states.

Constructibility and natural classes of epistemic states. The theory of belief change in the framework of epistemic states, sketched above, deals mainly with the question what kinds of changes made to epistemic states constitute 'rational' changes in response to various informational inputs. Yet another perspective on this subject suggests, however, that such a theory can be viewed also as a *constructive theory of epistemic states* that describes the ways of building epistemic states satisfying given requirements. This perspective naturally raises the question of expressive capabilities of our belief change operations in constructing epistemic states.

As will be shown in Chapter 14, sum, merge and contraction turn out to be jointly sufficient for constructing any finitary epistemic state. In fact, sums, contractions and prioritized expansions are sufficient for this purposes. Moreover, it will be shown that the operation of taking sums is essential for this representation capability.

By restricting the set of allowable operations on epistemic states, we will obtain some natural sub-classes of epistemic states. It turns out, for example, that the two basic merge operations are sufficient for constructing any base-generated epistemic state. Also, removing prioritized merge from the set of allowable operations will reduce the range of constructible epistemic states to persistent ones. Finally, by restricting our tools to contractions and prioritized merge operations, we will obtain precisely the class of linear epistemic states. These results provide a primary description of the representation opportunities created by various 'ideological' constraints that might be imposed on the belief change operations. Such constraints are naturally arising, for instance, in pursuing a purely foundational or, alternatively, coherentist approach to belief change.

12. Contractions of Epistemic States

12.1 Definition and properties

As we argued in the preceding chapter, belief change operations should be defined primarily as operations on epistemic states; though any epistemic state has an associated belief set, changes to the latter will be determined by changes made to the underlying epistemic state. In this chapter we will describe this process for the case of contractions.

Contraction is one of the two complementary primitive operations, or steps, in the process belief change. Its role consists in removing information from epistemic states. The contraction operation cannot be reduced, however, to removal of a single proposition; in most cases the latter is supported by other beliefs we have, so its removal cannot be achieved without removing its supports, etc. Accordingly, the most radical way to achieve this consists in removing all admissible belief states that support the information being contracted.

The following definition describes a contraction of a set of propositions from an epistemic state.

Definition 12.1.1. *A* contraction *of an epistemic state $\mathbb{E}$ with respect to a set of propositions w is an epistemic state, denoted by $\mathbb{E} - w$, obtained by restricting the set of admissible states to belief states that support no proposition from w.*

Thus, a contraction of a set w from an epistemic state $\mathbb{E}$ is obtained by removing admissible belief states that support at least one proposition from w (and restricting the preference relation to the reduced set of admissible states). A *singular* (or ordinary) contraction is a contraction by a singleton set $\{A\}$, otherwise it will be called a *multiple contraction* (see [Fuh96]).

Recall that a proposition is *disbelieved* in an epistemic state $\mathbb{E}$ if it is supported by no admissible state from $\mathbb{E}$. Then a contraction of a set of propositions w can also be seen as a minimal reduction of an epistemic state that makes us disbelieve every proposition from w. It should be kept in mind, however, that disbelief is a stronger notion than simple absence of belief (and it is incomparable with the belief in the negation of the proposition). Accordingly, a change resulting in disbelief in A is much more radical, in general, than what would be required in order to just remove the belief in A. Furthermore, the contraction of A can result in a non-trivial change of an epistemic state even if A is not believed in it (but is not disbelieved either).

It turns out that the notion of disbelief can be defined, in turn, in terms of contractions. Namely, a proposition A is disbelieved in an epistemic state $\mathbb{E}$ if and only if the contraction of A from $\mathbb{E}$ does not change the epistemic state, that is, $\mathbb{E} - A = \mathbb{E}$. This fact will play an important role in what follows.

As can be easily verified, the set of admissible states $]x[$ in a contracted epistemic state $\mathbb{E} - w$ coincides with the set $]x \cup w[$ in $\mathbb{E}$. As a result, s is a preferred admissible state in $]x[$ with respect to $\mathbb{E} - w$ if and only if it is a preferred admissible state in $]x \cup w[$ with respect to $\mathbb{E}$. To begin with, this shows that contractions preserve m-smoothness of epistemic states. In addition, we immediately obtain the following characterization of the selection function corresponding to the contracted epistemic state:

Lemma 12.1.1. *For any set x, $f_{\mathbb{E}-w}(x) = f_{\mathbb{E}}(w \cup x)$.*

Thus, the selection function of the contracted epistemic state is uniquely determined by the selection function of the source epistemic state. As a result, we immediately obtain that contractions preserve the relation of equivalence among epistemic states.

Corollary 12.1.1. *If $\mathbb{E}_1 \approx \mathbb{E}_2$, then $\mathbb{E}_1 - w \approx \mathbb{E}_2 - w$.*

Clearly, a multiple contraction with a set of propositions cannot be replaced by a singular contraction with respect to their conjunction. Still, the following simple observation shows that any set of contracted propositions can be replaced by a basically equivalent set (see Chapter 4 for a definition).

Theorem 12.1.1. *If w_1 is basically equivalent to w_2, then $\mathbb{E} - w_1 \approx \mathbb{E} - w_2$.*

Proof. Follows from the fact that if w_1 is basically equivalent to w_2, then $]w_1[$ coincides with $]w_2[$ for any epistemic state. □

To simplify the notation, we will denote by $\mathbb{E} - u; v$ the epistemic state obtained by contracting $\mathbb{E}$ first with respect to u and then with respect to v, that is, the state $(\mathbb{E} - u) - v$. Also, we will use $\mathbb{E} - A$ as a shorthand for $\mathbb{E} - \{A\}$.

The following lemma gives two basic properties of contractions on general epistemic states. The proof presents no difficulties, and will be left to the reader. As we will see in what follows, these properties provide, in effect, a complete characterization of our contraction operation.

Lemma 12.1.2. *1.* $\mathbb{E} - v; u = \mathbb{E} - (u \cup v)$;
2. If $\mathbb{E} - B; A = \mathbb{E} - B$, then $\mathbb{E} - A \wedge B = \mathbb{E} - A$.

The first condition above states that a successive contraction of v and then u amounts to contracting $u \cup v$; this immediately implies that contraction operations *commute*:

$$\mathbb{E} - u; v \; = \; \mathbb{E} - (u \cup v) \; = \; \mathbb{E} - v; u$$

As a result, iterated contractions can be performed in any order, and any finite multiple contraction can be achieved through a sequence of corresponding singular contractions. Note that commutativity can be viewed as one of the distinguishing properties of our contraction operation; as we have seen in the preceding chapter, both for (a suitably extended) AGM approach and for the base theory, the order of performing contractions can influence the resulting belief set.

The second condition above says that if contracting B already makes us disbelieve A in the resulting epistemic state, then contracting the conjunction $A \wedge B$ from the source epistemic state amounts to contracting A. Formally speaking, this property is valid for AGM contractions satisfying all the rationality postulates of the AGM theory (see below), though it is not valid for relational AGM contractions in general. It is not valid also for the base approach.

Contraction turns out to be a very tolerant operation in the sense that it preserves many structural properties of epistemic states. Thus, a contraction of a monotonic, standard, or persistent epistemic state is again a monotonic, standard, or, respectively, persistent epistemic state. Consequently, contractions of pure epistemic states produce pure epistemic states. In addition, contractions preserve linearity of epistemic states; this fact will be important for representing the AGM theory in our framework.

12.1.1 Contractions of bases and flocks

Unfortunately, contractions do not preserve two important features of epistemic states, namely union-closure and determination. This means, in particular, that base-generated epistemic states are insufficient for representing belief changes. Still, contractions preserve persistence, and it has been shown in Chapter 4 that persistent epistemic states are representable by flocks of bases. Accordingly, flock-generated epistemic states will emerge as a smallest class of epistemic states that is closed under belief change operations.

The following definition provides a direct description of contraction for flocks that will correspond to contraction of associated epistemic states. It is actually equivalent to the definition of deletions for flocks given in [FUKV86].

Definition 12.1.2. *A contraction of a flock* $\mathcal{F} = \{\Delta_i\}$ *with respect to* w *(notation* $\mathcal{F} - w$*) is a flock consisting of all maximal subsets of each* Δ_i *that do not imply any proposition from* w.

If we represent a base Δ by a singular flock $\{\Delta\}$, then the contraction of the latter with respect to w will be a flock consisting of all maximal subsets of Δ that do not imply propositions from w. In other words, contractions of bases transform the latter into genuine flocks. For example, the contraction of the base $\{p, q\}$ with respect to $p \wedge q$ gives a flock $\{\{p\}, \{q\}\}$ consisting of two one-element bases. As can be verified, the belief set of the epistemic state generated by the latter flock is $\mathrm{Cl}(p \vee q)$, which exactly reflects our intuitions about this situation.

The following result confirms that the above operation on flocks corresponds to contraction of associated epistemic states.

Lemma 12.1.3. *If $\mathbb{E}_{\mathcal{F}}$ is an epistemic state generated by a flock $\mathcal{F}$, then, for any set w, $\mathbb{E}_{\mathcal{F}} - w = \mathbb{E}_{(\mathcal{F}-w)}$.*

Proof. Follows immediately from the fact that $(\mathcal{F} - w)_{\downarrow}$ is precisely the set of admissible states of $\mathbb{E}_{\mathcal{F}}$ that do not support propositions from w. $\square$

It should be pointed out, however, that despite the similarity of the above definition of contraction with that given in [FUKV86], the resulting contraction operation will behave differently in our framework. The reason is that, since only maximal elements of a flock are essential for its informational content, the definition could be replaced with the following condition:

A contraction of a flock $\mathcal{F} = \{\Delta_i\}$ with respect to w is a flock consisting of all *maximal* sets among subsets of Δ_i that do not imply propositions from w.

In other words, the contracted flock can be obtained by taking all maximal sets of propositions that do not imply w and are included in at least one base from the source flock, instead of taking all maximal such subsets in each base belonging to the flock. Clearly, the original definition permit inclusion of sets that are not absolutely maximal, but only with respect to some base from the source flock. The following example illustrates this.

Example 12.1.1. Let us return to the flock $\mathcal{F} = \{\{p\}, \{q\}\}$ obtained by contracting the base $\{p, q\}$ with $p \wedge q$. The contraction of the latter with respect to p, that is, $\mathcal{F} - p$, is a flock $\{\emptyset, \{q\}\}$, which is identical with $\{\{q\}\}$. Accordingly, the resulting epistemic state will be base-generated by $\{q\}$, and hence q will be believed in it. This behavior seems also to agree with our intuitions, since eliminating p as an option will leave us with a single solution, namely q. In the representation of [FUKV86], however, $\{\emptyset, \{q\}\}$ is not reducible to $\{\{q\}\}$. Consequently, nothing will be believed in the resulting epistemic state. Furthermore, this also makes the corresponding operation of deletion in [FUKV86] non-commutative: deletion of p and then $p \wedge q$ from the original base $\{p, q\}$ will give a different flock, namely $\{\{q\}\}$.

12.1.2 Abstract contraction systems

We will give now an abstract description of the contraction operation in terms of a set of postulates that characterizes its dynamic behavior. This description will not even presume what an epistemic state is. Our construction will remind the reader Gärdenfors' dynamic representation of classical logic, given in [Gär88], where propositions are identified with functions on epistemic states.

An abstract *contraction system* is a pair $\langle \mathfrak{E}, \sim \rangle$, where $\mathfrak{E}$ is a set of objects called (abstract) *epistemic states*, while $\sim$ is a mapping from the set of propositions to the set of unary (contraction) functions on $\mathfrak{E}$. For any proposition A and an epistemic state $\mathbb{E} \in \mathfrak{E}$, we will denote by $\mathbb{E} \sim A$ the result of applying the associated function to $\mathbb{E}$; the epistemic state $\mathbb{E} \sim A$ will be said to be obtained by *contracting* $\mathbb{E}$ with respect to A. As before, we will use also the notation $\mathbb{E} \sim A; B$ as a shorthand for $(\mathbb{E} \sim A) \sim B$.

A proposition A will be said to be *disbelieved* in an epistemic state $\mathbb{E}$, if $\mathbb{E} \sim A = \mathbb{E}$.

Any contraction systems will be supposed to satisfy the following postulates:

Equivalence   If $\vDash A \leftrightarrow B$, then $\mathbb{E} \sim A = \mathbb{E} \sim B$.

Idempotence $\mathbb{E} \sim A; A = \mathbb{E} \sim A$

Commutativity $\mathbb{E} \sim A; B = \mathbb{E} \sim B; A$

Inversion   If $\mathbb{E} \sim B; A = \mathbb{E} \sim B$, then $\mathbb{E} \sim A \wedge B = \mathbb{E} \sim A$.

The first postulate says that contraction does not depend on the syntactic form of the contracted proposition, but only on its logical content. The second postulate states that contraction with respect to the same proposition is an idempotent operation — the second application of the same contraction does not produce any effect. Taking into account our earlier definition, it says also that contracting A results in disbelieving A. The third postulate, Commutativity, says that contractions can be performed in any order with the same result. As can be seen, the first three postulates are not specific for contraction functions (they are valid, for example, for the above mentioned Gärdenfors's belief models). So the only non-trivial contraction postulate is Inversion. It states in this setting the property of contractions described in Lemma 12.1.2. Namely, it says that if A is disbelieved after contracting B, then contractions of A and $A \wedge B$ produce the same epistemic state.

Taken together with other properties of contraction, Inversion determines, in effect, that the set of contraction operations forms a lattice in which contraction of $\{A, B\}$ and of $A \wedge B$ play, respectively, the roles of meet and join with respect to singular contractions of A and B.

As we have seen, all the above postulates hold for contraction operations on general epistemic states. Moreover, we will show later that these postulates provide, in effect, a complete description of the behavior of contractions on epistemic states. Namely, we will demonstrate in the next section that any abstract contraction system can be realized as a set of pure epistemic states in such a way that contraction functions of the contraction system will exactly correspond to contractions of these epistemic states.

12.2 Contractions of pure epistemic states

Contractions of pure epistemic states play an important role in our theory. The main reasons is that the behavior of contractions on general epistemic states can be analyzed to a large extend through their behavior on pure epistemic states.

Notice that the contraction operation on general epistemic states does not depend on the preference relation on admissible belief states; the removal of the latter is determined only by the belief set supported by an admissible state, not by its position in the preference structure. This means, in particular, that the behavior of contractions on general epistemic states is wholly determined by their behavior on the associated pure epistemic states formed by admissible belief sets. More exactly, if $\mathcal{E}$ is a pure epistemic state corresponding to a general epistemic state $\mathbb{E}$, then $\mathbb{E} - w$ is obtainable by restricting the set admissible belief states of $\mathbb{E}$ to states supporting $\mathcal{E} - w$. Accordingly, the effect of a sequence of successive contractions applied to a general epistemic state can also be determined by computing the result of this sequence on the associated pure epistemic state.

Pure epistemic states have a very simple structure; they are just sets of theories. As a result, the contraction operation on such epistemic states admits a quite simple characterization. Thus, the following lemma shows that both sequences of contractions and contractions of conjunctions are determined as set theoretical combinations of contractions with respect to their components.

Lemma 12.2.1. *If $\mathcal{E}$ is a pure epistemic state, then*

1. $\mathcal{E} - v; u = \mathcal{E} - u \cap \mathcal{E} - v;$
2. $\mathcal{E} - A \wedge B = \mathcal{E} - A \cup \mathcal{E} - B.$

The first equation of the above lemma says, in effect, that any multiple contraction is determined as an intersection of epistemic states determined by corresponding singular contractions. The second equation says that any singular contraction is determined, ultimately, by contractions with respect to disjunctive clauses containing only propositional literals.

A further insight into the nature of belief contractions, as well as a powerful tool for their syntactic description, will be obtained in the next section where we will consider their reformulation in terms of contraction operations on consequence relations.

12.2.1 Contractions of consequence relations

As has been established in Chapter 2, pure epistemic states can be described syntactically using Scott consequence relations. Due to this correspondence, belief change operations on pure epistemic states are representable also as operations on consequence relations. Such a reformulation will provide us with a useful tool for studying such changes.

To begin with, the following definition describes an operation on consequence relations that will correspond to the contraction operation on associated pure epistemic states.

Definition 12.2.1. *A contraction of a Scott consequence relation $\Vdash$ with respect to a set of propositions w, denoted by $\Vdash_{-w}$, is a least consequence relation including $\Vdash$ and sequents $A \Vdash$, for all $A \in w$.*

The following lemma provides a direct description of the contracted consequence relation.

Lemma 12.2.2. *For any finite sets a and b,*

$$a \Vdash_{-w} b \quad \text{iff} \quad a \Vdash b, w.$$

Proof. It is easy to check that a consequence relation $\Vdash^*$ defined as follows:

$$a \Vdash^* b \equiv a \Vdash b, w$$

is a supraclassical Scott consequence relation containing $\Vdash$. Moreover, $C \Vdash^*$, for any $C \in w$. Since $\Vdash_{-w}$ is a least such consequence relation, we immediately obtain that $\Vdash \subseteq \Vdash^*$.

If $a \Vdash b, w$, then $a \Vdash_{-w} b, w$, and hence $a \Vdash_{-w} b, c$, for some finite $c \subseteq w$. But $C \Vdash_{-w}$, for any $C \in c$. Hence, applying Cut, we obtain $a \Vdash_{-w} b$. Thus, $\Vdash_{-w}$ coincides with $\Vdash^*$.   □

Now we will demonstrate that contraction of a consequence relation corresponds to contraction of the associated pure epistemic state.

Theorem 12.2.1. *If a consequence relation $\Vdash$ is generated by a pure epistemic state $\mathcal{E}$, then $\Vdash_{-w}$ is generated by the epistemic state $\mathcal{E} - w$.*

Proof. Notice first that $C \Vdash_{\mathcal{E}-w}$ holds for any $C \in w$. Hence $\Vdash_{-w}$ is included in $\Vdash_{\mathcal{E}-w}$. In addition, if $a \nVdash_{-w} b$, then $a \nVdash b, w$, and hence there is a theory u from $\mathcal{E}$ that includes a and disjoint from both b and w. Consequently, u belongs to $\mathcal{E}-w$, and therefore $a \nVdash_{\mathcal{E}-w} b$. Thus, $\Vdash_{-w}$ coincides with $\Vdash_{\mathcal{E}-w}$.   □

The above theorem establishes a tight correspondence between contractions of pure epistemic states and contractions of consequence relations. As a first important consequence, this theorem implies that contractions preserve finiteness and groundedness of consequence relations. Thus, if a consequence relation is generated by a set of propositions Δ, then its contraction with respect to a set w is generated by the set of propositions Δ_w consisting of all propositions from Δ that imply no proposition from w.

The following lemma follows immediately from the fact that disbelief with respect to epistemic states is definable in terms of contractions.

Lemma 12.2.3. *If $\Vdash$ is a consequence relation, then $A \Vdash$ holds if and only if $\Vdash_{-A}$ coincides with $\Vdash$.*

As for general epistemic states, we will denote by $\Vdash_{\langle -A_1;...;A_n \rangle}$ the result of applying to $\Vdash$ a sequence of contractions of A_i in that order. Then the next lemma is actually a consequence of the fact that a sequence of contractions of an epistemic state always amounts to a multiple contraction. It is obtainable also directly as an immediate corollary of Lemma 12.2.2.

Lemma 12.2.4. $\Vdash_{\langle -A;B \rangle} = \Vdash_{-\{A,B\}}$.

The above result reaffirms in the new setting that contractions commute, and that any finite multiple contraction can be achieved through a sequence of corresponding singular contractions.

As for contractions of general epistemic states, the properties of contractions of consequence relations, described below, constitute their basic structural features. To begin with, the following lemma shows that contractions of $A \wedge B$ and $\{A, B\}$ can be considered, respectively, as 'joins' and 'meets' of singular contractions with respect to A and B.

Lemma 12.2.5.   *1.* $\Vdash_{-(A \wedge B)} = \Vdash_{-A} \cap \Vdash_{-B}$;
  2. $\Vdash_{-\{A,B\}}$ *is a least consequence relation containing both $\Vdash_{-A}$ and $\Vdash_{-B}$.*

Proof. (i) Immediate from the fact that $a \Vdash b, A \wedge B$ holds in a supraclassical consequence relation if and only if $a \Vdash b, A$ and $a \Vdash b, B$.

(ii) Clearly, $\Vdash_{-\{A,B\}}$ includes both $\Vdash_{-A}$ and $\Vdash_{-B}$. In addition, if $\Vdash^*$ is any consequence relation that includes the latter two, it includes also $\Vdash$ and contains both $A \Vdash^*$ and $B \Vdash^*$. But then $\Vdash_{-\{A,B\}}$ is included in $\Vdash^*$, since it is defined as a least consequence relation satisfying these conditions. $\square$

The following result provides another 'lattice' property of contractions, namely Inversion.

Lemma 12.2.6. *If A is disbelieved in $\Vdash_{-B}$, then $\Vdash_{-(A \wedge B)}$ coincides with $\Vdash_{-A}$.*

Proof. $A \Vdash_{-B}$ holds iff $A \Vdash B$. The latter implies $A \Vdash A \wedge B$, and hence $A \wedge B$ is provably equivalent to A in $\Vdash$. But then $a \Vdash b, A \wedge B$ holds iff $a \Vdash b, A$. This concludes the proof. $\square$

Finally, the next result shows that Scott consequence relations are uniquely determined by their behavior in contractions. An informal consequence of this fact is that pure epistemic states constitute a minimum of complexity required from our epistemic states in order to give an adequate representation of contraction operations.

Lemma 12.2.7. *For any supraclassical consequence relation, $a \Vdash b$ holds if and only if contractions of $\Vdash$ with respect to b and $b \cup \{\bigwedge a\}$ coincide.*

Proof. For any sets c, d, $c \Vdash_{-(b \cup \{\bigwedge a\})} d$ holds if and only if $c \Vdash d, b, \bigwedge a$. Similarly, $c \Vdash_{-b} d$ amounts to $c \Vdash d, b$. Now, if $a \Vdash b$, these two sequents are equivalent, and this gives the direction from left to right. In addition, if $\Vdash_{-(b \cup \{\bigwedge a\})}$ coincides with $\Vdash_{-b}$, then, in particular, $a \Vdash_{-(b \cup \{\bigwedge a\})}$ should imply $a \Vdash_{-b}$. But the former sequent belongs to $\Vdash_{-(b \cup \{\bigwedge a\})}$, and hence $a \Vdash_{-b}$ holds, which is reducible to $a \Vdash b$. □

The above equivalence can be formulated as saying that $a \Vdash b$ holds if and only if b can be disbelieved only if $\bigwedge a$ is also disbelieved. We will use this fact in the next section.

It turns out that above result can be strengthened further to a claim that pure epistemic states are uniquely determined already by belief 'outputs' resulting from contractions. Accordingly, the differences between pure epistemic states will be always disclosed in producing different beliefs under some contractions.

Two consequence relations will be called *contraction-equivalent* if they produce identical belief sets under any contraction. Then the following result shows, in effect, that any epistemic state is uniquely determined by such contracted belief sets.

Theorem 12.2.2. *Two consequence relations are contraction-equivalent only if they coincide.*

Proof. Let $\Vdash^1$ and $\Vdash^2$ be two contraction-equivalent consequence relations. If they are distinct, they must have distinct theories. Assume that u is a theory of $\Vdash^1$, but not of $\Vdash^2$. We contract both these consequence relations with a set $\bar{u}$ of all propositions that do not belong to u. Clearly, u is still a theory and, moreover, a greatest theory of $\Vdash^1_{-\bar{u}}$, and hence it coincides with its belief set. Assume that u is also a belief set of $\Vdash^2_{-\bar{u}}$. Since any belief set is an intersection of maximal theories, and $\Vdash^2_{-\bar{u}}$ does not have theories above u, the latter should be a theory of $\Vdash^2_{-\bar{u}}$, which is impossible, since u is not a theory of $\Vdash^2$. □

As our last observation, we will describe the impact of contractions on basic propositions of a consequence relation.

Clearly, contractions cannot preserve all the original basic propositions. Yet, the following result shows that a basic proposition of a consequence relation will remain to be a basic proposition of a contracted consequence relation if and only if it is still believed in the latter.

Theorem 12.2.3. *A basic proposition B of a consequence relation $\Vdash$ will also be basic in $\Vdash_{-w}$ if and only if $B \in \mathbf{B}_{\Vdash} - w$.*

Proof. We will prove first the following auxiliary result:

Auxiliary Lemma. *If B is a basic proposition of $\Vdash$, then it will also be a basic proposition of $\Vdash_{-w}$ iff $B \to A \Vdash w$, for each $A \in w$.*

Proof. Assume that B is a basic proposition of $\Vdash_{-w}$. $B, B \to A \Vdash A$ is a valid sequent of $\Vdash$, and hence also $B, B \to A \Vdash w$, for each $A \in w$. The latter sequents are equivalent to $B, B \to A \Vdash_{-w}$. Since B is a basic proposition of $\Vdash_{-w}$, we conclude that $B \to A \Vdash_{-w}$, that is, $B \to A \Vdash w$.

In the other direction, if $a, B \Vdash_{-w} b$, then $a, B \Vdash w, b$, and hence $a, B \Vdash c, b$, for some finite $c \subseteq w$. Since B is a basic proposition of $\Vdash$, we obtain $a \Vdash B \to c, B \to b$. But $B \to A \Vdash A$, for any $A \in c$, and consequently we have $a \Vdash c, B \to b$ and therefore $a \Vdash w, B \to b$. But the latter sequent is equivalent to $a \Vdash_{-w} B \to b$, and hence B is a basic proposition of $\Vdash_{-w}$. □

Now if B is basic in $\Vdash_{-w}$, it is clearly believed in $\Vdash_{-w}$. Assume that B is believed in $\Vdash_{-w}$ As in the proof of the auxiliary lemma, we have $B, B \to A \Vdash_{-w}$, for any $A \in w$. By Lemma 3.2.1 from Chapter 2 we conclude $B \to A \Vdash_{-w}$, and now the result follows from the auxiliary lemma. □

12.2.2 Contraction dynamics

As we have mentioned already, contraction operations on general epistemic states do not depend on the preference relation among admissible states; whatever the preference order, a contraction of a set of propositions w will remove the same admissible states. This suggests, in particular, that the dynamic behavior of contractions can be modeled already on the level of pure epistemic states. And indeed, we will demonstrate now that any abstract contraction system can be mapped into a set of pure epistemic states in such a way that contraction functions of the abstract contraction system will exactly correspond to contractions of these epistemic states.

Let $\mathfrak{E}$ be an abstract contraction system. Due to commutativity, for any finite set of propositions a, we can safely denote by $\mathbb{E} \sim a$ the result of contracting $\mathbb{E}$ with respect to all propositions in a in some order. We will also abuse somewhat our notation and write $\mathbb{E} \sim a; A$ instead of $\mathbb{E} \sim a \cup \{A\}$.

To begin with, we will assign any abstract epistemic state $\mathbb{E}$ from $\mathfrak{E}$ a Scott consequence relation $\Vdash^{\mathbb{E}}$ defined as follows:

$$a \Vdash^{\mathbb{E}} b \text{ iff } \mathbb{E} \sim b \cup \{\wedge a\} = \mathbb{E} \sim b.$$

The above definition says that $a \Vdash b$ holds if and only if b can be disbelieved only if $\wedge a$ is also disbelieved (cf. Lemma 12.2.7 above). The following lemma shows that this is a supraclassical consequence relation:

Lemma 12.2.8. *For any abstract epistemic state $\mathbb{E} \in \mathfrak{E}$, $\Vdash^E$ is a supraclassical Scott consequence relation.*

Proof. Supraclassicality. Assume that $A \vDash B$. We have $\mathbb{E} \sim B; B; A = \mathbb{E} \sim B; A$ by Idempotence, and hence $\mathbb{E} \sim B; A \wedge B = \mathbb{E} \sim B; B$ by Inversion. But $A \wedge B$ is logically equivalent to A, and hence $\mathbb{E} \sim B; A = \mathbb{E} \sim B$ by Equivalence and Idempotence. The latter is equivalent to $A \Vdash^E B$, and we are done.

Monotonicity. To show Monotonicity, it is sufficient to demonstrate that an arbitrary proposition can be always added to the premises and conclusions of a valid sequent. Now, $\mathbb{E} \sim b; \wedge a = \mathbb{E} \sim b$ implies $\mathbb{E} \sim b; A; \wedge a = \mathbb{E} \sim b; A$ by commutativity, and hence any proposition can be added to the conclusions. In addition, if $\mathbb{E} \sim B = \mathbb{E}$, then $\mathbb{E} \sim B; A = \mathbb{E} \sim A$, and hence by Inversion $\mathbb{E} \sim A \wedge B = \mathbb{E} \sim B$, that is, $\mathbb{E} \sim A \wedge B = \mathbb{E}$. Consequently, any proposition can also be always added to the premises of a valid sequent.

Cut. If $\mathbb{E} \sim B; A = \mathbb{E} \sim B$ and $\mathbb{E} \sim A \wedge B = \mathbb{E}$, then $\mathbb{E} \sim A \wedge B = \mathbb{E} \sim A$ by Inversion from the first equality, and hence $\mathbb{E} \sim A = \mathbb{E}$. This shows the validity of the Cut rule. □

Now, for any $\mathbb{E} \in \mathfrak{E}$, we will denote by $\mathcal{E}_\mathbb{E}$ the pure epistemic state determined by the theories of $\Vdash^E$. Then the following result shows that contraction functions on $\mathbb{E}$ exactly correspond to contraction operations on the corresponding pure epistemic states.

Theorem 12.2.4. *For any proposition A, $\mathcal{E}_{\mathbb{E} \sim A} = \mathcal{E}_\mathbb{E} - A$.*

Proof. Due to the correspondence between pure epistemic states and Scott consequence relations, contractions of pure epistemic states can be described in terms of contractions of Scott consequence relations. In particular, if $\Vdash$ is a Scott consequence relation corresponding to a pure epistemic state $\mathcal{E}$, then $\mathcal{E} - A$ will exactly correspond to the consequence relation $\Vdash_{-A}$ defined as follows (see Lemma 12.2.2 above):

$$a \Vdash_{-A} b \quad \text{iff} \quad a \Vdash b, A.$$

Now, $a \Vdash^{\mathbb{E} \sim A} b$ amounts to $\mathbb{E} \sim b; A; \wedge a = \mathbb{E} \sim b; A$. By commutativity, the latter is equivalent to $\mathbb{E} \sim b; A; \wedge a = \mathbb{E} \sim b; A$, which is translatable as $a \Vdash^E b, A$. Due to the above mentioned result, the latter is equivalent to $a \Vdash^E_{-A} b$. This concludes the proof. □

The above result formally justifies our claim that the dynamic behavior of epistemic states in contractions can be analyzed on the level of pure epistemic states. This still does not say, however, that the postulates of contraction dynamics, given earlier, provide a *complete* description of the contraction operation on epistemic states. The reason is that our mapping is not injective: different abstract epistemic states may correspond to the same consequence relation. Nevertheless, the above mapping can be used to show that the postulates for abstract contractions give a faithful description for assertions of the form $\mathbb{E} \sim a = \mathbb{E} \sim b$ that are derivable with respect to epistemic states.

By a *contraction rule* we will mean below a rule of the form

$$\text{If } A_1, \ldots, A_m, \text{ then either } A_{m+1}, \text{ or } \ldots \text{ or } A_n;$$

where each A_i is an assertion of the form $\mathbb{E} \sim a_i = \mathbb{E} \sim b_i$, for some finite sets of propositions a_i, b_i.

The following result shows, in effect, that abstract contraction systems provide a complete characterization for rules of this kind.

Theorem 12.2.5. *A contraction rule is valid for contractions of epistemic states if and only if it is valid for abstract contraction systems.*

Proof. Clearly, if a contraction rule is valid for all abstract contraction systems, it will be valid also for contractions of epistemic states. In order to prove the claim in the other direction, notice first that the consequence relation $\Vdash^{\mathbb{E}}$ associated with an abstract epistemic state $\mathbb{E}$ is uniquely determined by all assertions of the form $\mathbb{E} \sim a; A = \mathbb{E} \sim a$ that hold in a given abstract system. We will show now that such assertions determine, in turn, all assertions of the form $\mathbb{E} \sim a = \mathbb{E} \sim b$ that hold in this contraction system.

Assume that $\mathbb{G} \sim a = \mathbb{G} \sim b$, for some abstract epistemic state $\mathbb{G}$ and finite sets a, b. By idempotence, this condition implies the following two:

$$\mathbb{G} \sim a; b = \mathbb{G} \sim b \text{ and } \mathbb{G} \sim a; b = \mathbb{G} \sim a$$

Note also that $\mathbb{G} \sim a = \mathbb{G} \sim b$ is in turn a consequence of the above two conditions. Furthermore, an assertion of the form

$$(*) \qquad\qquad\qquad \mathbb{G} \sim a; b = \mathbb{G} \sim a$$

is equivalent to the set of assertions $\mathbb{E} \sim a; B = \mathbb{E} \sim a$, for all $B \in b$. Indeed, if $B \in b$, then $\mathbb{E} \sim a; B = \mathbb{G} \sim a; b; B$ by (*), and hence $\mathbb{E} \sim a; B = \mathbb{G} \sim a; b$ by idempotence. Consequently, $\mathbb{E} \sim a; B = \mathbb{E} \sim a$, for all $B \in b$. The other direction follows immediately by commutativity and idempotence.

Thus, all assertions of the form $\mathbb{E} \sim a = \mathbb{E} \sim b$ that hold in an abstract contraction system are determined, ultimately, by its subset consisting of assertions of the form $\mathbb{E} \sim a; A = \mathbb{E} \sim a$, while the latter sets stand in one-to-one correspondence with consequence relations determined by abstract epistemic states. Consequently, if a contraction rule is invalid in a contraction system for some abstract epistemic state $\mathbb{E}$, it will not be valid also with respect to the pure epistemic state $\mathcal{E}_{\mathbb{E}}$, since the latter is determined by the consequence relation associated with $\mathbb{E}$. $\qquad\square$

The above result means that a contraction rule is valid for contractions of (pure) epistemic states if and only if it is a logical consequence of the postulates for contraction systems. It is an interesting question to what extent the restriction to contraction rules in this result could be relaxed when applied to general epistemic states. Note, however, that the postulates of abstract contraction systems still do not provide a complete characterization for contractions of pure epistemic states. In order to obtain such a characterization, we need a kind of Leibnitz principle of identity of indistinguishables. Namely, we need an additional postulate saying that different epistemic states cannot have identical behavior in contractions. The following postulate reflects this idea.

Identity   If $\mathbb{E}$ and $\mathbb{F}$ are two abstract epistemic states such that, for any finite sets of propositions a, b, $\mathbb{E} \sim a = \mathbb{E} \sim b$ if and only if $\mathbb{F} \sim a = \mathbb{F} \sim b$, then $\mathbb{E} = \mathbb{F}$.

The above condition states in precise terms that abstract epistemic states $\mathbb{E}$ and $\mathbb{F}$ have identical behavior in contractions. The Identity postulate requires that this can happen only if these epistemic states coincide. Note that consequence relations (and hence *compact* pure epistemic states) satisfy the above postulate – see Lemma 12.2.7.

An abstract contraction system will be called *pure* if it satisfies Identity. Then the following result shows that, for pure abstract contraction systems, the mapping to pure epistemic states is injective.

Lemma 12.2.9. *If $\mathbb{E}$ and $\mathbb{F}$ are epistemic states of a pure contraction system, then $\mathbb{E} = \mathbb{F}$ if and only if $\mathcal{E}_{\mathbb{E}} = \mathcal{E}_{\mathbb{F}}$.*

Proof. It follows from the definition of the mapping that $\mathcal{E}_{\mathbb{E}} = \mathcal{E}_{\mathbb{F}}$ holds if and only if $\mathbb{E}$ and $\mathbb{F}$ generate the same consequence relation, while the latter will hold iff, for any proposition A and set a we have

$$\mathbb{E} \sim a; A = \mathbb{E} \sim a \text{ if and only if } \mathbb{F} \sim a; A = \mathbb{F} \sim a$$

In the proof of the preceding theorem it has been established, in effect, that the above condition is sufficient for fulfilling the condition of the Identity postulate, and hence $\mathbb{E} = \mathbb{F}$. This completes the proof.   □

The above result implies, in particular, that pure abstract contraction systems provide a complete description of contraction in consequence relations and compact pure epistemic states.

12.2.3 Conditional contractions

The contraction operation involves an unconditional removal of admissible states that support the propositions being contracted. It seems reasonable, however, to constrain sometimes such removals by allowing certain such admissible states to be exempted from deletion. This is reflected in the following definition of a conditional contraction operation.

Definition 12.2.2. *A conditional contraction of a general epistemic state* $\mathbb{E}$ *with respect to a set of propositions* w *modulo* u *is an epistemic state, denoted by* $\mathbb{E} - (w|u)$, *obtained by restricting the set of admissible states to belief states that either support no proposition from* w, *or support some proposition from* u.

The above contraction operation amounts to deletion of admissible states that contain at least one proposition from w, *unless* they contain some proposition from u. Just as for original contraction operations, if w is finite, then $\mathbb{E} - (w|u)$ can be obtained by a sequence of singular conditional contractions of the form $-(A|u)$, for every $A \in w$. Accordingly, we will restrict ourselves below to singular conditional contractions.

The following definition provides a quite simple description of singular conditional contractions in the framework of consequence relations.

Definition 12.2.3. *A conditional contraction of a Scott consequence relation* $\Vdash$ *with respect to* A *modulo* u *(notation* $\Vdash_{-(A|u)}$*), is a least consequence relation including* $\Vdash$ *and the sequent* $A \Vdash u$.

Thus, a conditional contraction of a consequence relation amounts to adding a new sequent to it. As a result, conditional contractions provide a simple criterion for presence of rules in a consequence relation:

Lemma 12.2.10. *If* $\Vdash$ *is a supraclassical Scott consequence relation, then* $a \Vdash b$ *holds if and only if* $\Vdash_{-(\bigwedge a|b)}$ *coincides with* $\Vdash$.

Note that the contraction of the form $-(\mathbf{t}|A)$ results in adding $\Vdash A$ to the consequence relation; in other words, it amounts to adding A to the underlying logic (see Chapter 13). In fact, conditional contraction is in a sense a *functionally complete* contraction operation: any finite Scott consequence relation is determined by a finite set of sequents, so it can be obtained now by an appropriate sequence of conditional contractions starting from the classical entailment.

It remains to be seen whether conditional contractions could be useful in representing common belief changes.

12.3 Belief contraction functions

Contractions of epistemic states generate corresponding contraction operations on their belief sets. In this section we will give a formal characterization of such belief contraction functions in terms of 'rationality postulates' they satisfy.

If $\mathbb{E}$ is an epistemic state, then the contracted belief set $\mathbf{B}_\mathbb{E} - A$ is an intersection of all preferred admissible belief sets that do not contain A.

Consequently, any belief contraction function can be alternatively described in terms of the associated contraction inference relation defined as follows:

$$A \dashv_{\mathbb{E}} B \; \equiv \; B \in \mathbf{B}_{\mathbb{E}} - A$$

Indeed, given the above contraction relation, we can define, in turn, the associated contraction function:

$$\mathbf{B}_{\mathbb{E}} - A \; = \; \{B \mid A \dashv_{\mathbb{E}} B\}$$

So, the two notions turn out to be interdefinable. As has been said, this correspondence provides an extension of the thesis suggested by Gärdenfors and Makinson that belief change and nonmonotonic inference are two sides of the same coin.

The above correspondence will allow us to transfer the representation results obtained in Chapter 10 into corresponding representation results for belief contractions.

12.3.1 Postulates

Now we are going to present the postulates that characterize belief contraction functions generated by contractions of epistemic states. By a *preferential belief contraction function* we will mean any function on belief sets satisfying the following conditions:

$(B1)$	$\mathbf{B} - A$ is a deductively closed set	(closure)
$(B2)$	If $\vDash A \leftrightarrow B$, then $\mathbf{B} - A = \mathbf{B} - B$	(extensionality)
$(B3)$	If $A \in \mathbf{B} - A \wedge B$, then $A \in \mathbf{B} - A \wedge B \wedge C$	(partial antitony)
$(B4)$	$\mathbf{B} - A \bigcap \mathbf{B} - B \subseteq \mathbf{B} - A \wedge B$	(distributivity)
$(B5)$	If $A \in \mathbf{B} - A \wedge B$, then $\mathbf{B} - A \wedge B = \mathbf{B} - B$	(cumulativity)

The above postulates are actually direct translations of the corresponding postulates for contraction inference, given in Chapter 10. Thus, the first three postulates of contraction inference are jointly equivalent to (B–1); left equivalence corresponds to (B–2), the above postulates of partial antitony and distributivity are translations of the corresponding postulates for contraction inference, while cumulativity (B–5) is equivalent to a combination of Cautious Antitony and Cautious Monotony. As was said in Chapter 10, (B–2) and (B–5) can be combined into a single postulate

If $A \leftrightarrow B \in \mathbf{B} - A \wedge B$, then $\mathbf{B} - A = \mathbf{B} - B$.

It turns out that all the above postulates correspond to well-known postulates that have already been suggested in the belief change literature. For a comparison, we present first the AGM postulates for contraction.

(K–1) $\text{Th}(K \div A) = K \div A$ (closure)

(K–2) $K \div A \subseteq K$ (inclusion)

(K–3) If $A \notin K$, then $K \div A = K$ (vacuity)

(K–4) If $A \notin \text{Th}(\emptyset)$, then $A \notin K \div A$ (success)

(K–5) If $\text{Th}(A) = \text{Th}(B)$, then $K \div A = K \div B$ (extensionality)

(K–6) $K \subseteq \text{Th}((K \div A) \cup \{A\})$ (recovery)

(K–7) $(K \div A) \cap (K \div B) \subseteq K \div (A \wedge B)$ (conjunction1)

(K–8) If $A \notin K \div (A \wedge B)$, then $K \div (A \wedge B) \subseteq K \div A$ (conjunction2)

It turns out that only three of the above postulates are valid for belief contraction functions on general epistemic states, namely closure (K–1), extensionality (K–5) and conjunction1 (K–7); they correspond, respectively, to our postulates (B–1), (B–2) and (B–4). However, the rest of our postulates are also known from the literature. Thus, partial antitony (E–4) can be found already in the initial AGM study [AGM85], where it was shown to be equivalent to (K–7), though with an essential use of the recovery postulate (K–6) which is absent from our list. Partial antitony was also used in [Han93a] under the name 'conjunctive trisection'. Finally, cumulativity (B–5) corresponds to a combination of the two 'AGM-like' postulates introduced by Hans Rott in [Rot92b]:

(K–7c)   If $A \in K \div (A \wedge B)$, then $K \div B \subseteq K \div (A \wedge B)$

(K–8c)   If $A \in K \div (A \wedge B)$, then $K \div (A \wedge B) \subseteq K \div B$

These postulates were extensively used in [Rot93] for describing contraction functions definable by relational AGM frames (see below).

As can be seen, our postulates preserve much of the 'rationality' behind AGM contractions. In what follows we will see also that the rest of the AGM postulates can be satisfied by imposing additional constraints on epistemic states. Among other things, this will help us to reveal some constitutive principles underlying the AGM approach.

12.3.2 Failure and success

In Chapter 10 we have shown that belief contractions functions uniquely determine the sets of propositions that are, respectively, believed and known in any epistemic state that generate them. The following definitions provide a description of such sets in the terminology of belief contraction functions.

Definition 12.3.1. *A proposition A will be said to be* known *with respect to a contraction function, if $A \in \mathbf{B} - A$; otherwise, it will be called* contingent. *The set of known propositions will be called the* knowledge set of the contraction *function and denoted by* $\mathbf{K}_-$.

According to the intended interpretation, $\mathbf{K}_-$ consists of propositions that are known in the associated epistemic state (and hence they cannot be deleted by contractions)[1]. As has been shown in Chapter 10, $\mathbf{K}_-$ is a deductively closed set that determines the internal logic governing the behavior of contractions. Below we will reformulate these results in the terminology of belief contraction functions.

Now we will turn to the belief set associated with a belief contraction function.

Definition 12.3.2. *A proposition A will be said to be* believed *with respect to a contraction function, if $A \in \mathbf{B} - \mathbf{f}$. The set $\mathbf{B} - \mathbf{f}$ will be called the* belief set of *the contraction function.*

Thus, the belief set of a contraction function is a set of propositions that are believed in the absence of falsity. This set will play an important role in our representation of AGM contractions.

Remark. Note that our postulates for preferential belief contractions deal exclusively with contracted belief sets, and hence say nothing about their relations to the source belief set $\mathbf{B}$. The AGM postulate of vacuity (K–3) implies, however, that if $\mathbf{B}$ is consistent, it will coincide with $\mathbf{B} - \mathbf{f}$. Unfortunately, this identity, and the vacuity postulate itself, are not valid for general belief contraction functions on our interpretation. It will hold, however, for epistemic states that have no inconsistent admissible states, as well as for determinate epistemic states (see below).

Failure. As we have seen in Chapter 10, general contraction relations do not determine the result of contracting known propositions, apart from the fact that all such contracted belief sets should coincide with the contraction of truth, that is, with $\mathbf{B} - \mathbf{t}$ (see equation (7) in Lemma 10.1.1). The definition of the contraction operation on epistemic states, given at the beginning of this chapter, says, however, that if A is known in an epistemic state $\mathbb{E}$, then $\mathbb{E} - A$ will be an empty epistemic state. Any proposition whatsoever will be (trivially) believed in such an epistemic state, so $\mathbf{B}_{\mathbb{E}} - A$ will coincide with the inconsistent belief set $\mathrm{Cl}(\mathbf{f})$. Corresponding contraction relations were called simple in Chapter 10. Accordingly, we will introduce the following definition:

Definition 12.3.3. *A preferential belief contraction function will be called* simple *if it satisfies*

$$\text{If } A \in \mathbf{B} - A, \text{ then } \mathbf{B} - A = \mathrm{Cl}(\mathbf{f}) \qquad \text{(simple failure)}$$

The above condition says that contracting a known proposition results in an inconsistent belief set. Actually, the above postulate is reducible to the following special case dealing with contraction of tautologies:

$$\mathbf{B} - \mathbf{t} = \mathrm{Cl}(\mathbf{f})$$

---

[1] The knowledge set has been called the *taboo set* in [Rot96].

Simple belief contraction functions will be shown to provide a complete characterization of belief changes generated by contractions of epistemic states. Notice, however, that *any* preferential belief contraction function can be transformed into a simple one by changing its behavior on known propositions. More exactly, for any contraction function we can construct the following belief function (cf. Chapter 10):

$$\mathbf{B} -_s A = \begin{cases} \mathbf{B} - A & \text{if } A \notin \mathbf{K}_-, \\ \text{Cl}(\mathbf{f}) & \text{otherwise.} \end{cases}$$

The above condition determines a simple belief contraction function that coincides with the original function on contingent propositions. As we already mentioned, this observation shows, in effect, that the restriction to simple contractions is rather a matter of overall simplicity of the formalism and its interpretations, rather than a deep conceptual issue.

Both the AGM theory and base approach adopt, however, a different stipulation according to which if we are required to contract a proposition which is valid (known) with respect to the underlying classical consequence relation Th, the source belief state should remain intact. Corresponding contraction relations were called *conservative* in Chapter 10; they were characterized by an additional postulate that we can rewrite now as follows:

If $A \in \mathbf{B} - A$, then $\mathbf{B} - A = \mathbf{B} - \mathbf{f}$ (conservative failure)

The above postulate corresponds to the *postulate of failure* introduced in [FH94]. The postulate identifies the result of contracting a known proposition with the belief set of the contraction function. Thus, it embodies, in effect, the above mentioned 'opportunistic' stipulation that contractions of known propositions do not change belief sets. Preferential belief contraction functions satisfying conservative failure will also be called *conservative* in what follows. As before, the above postulate is actually reducible to its special case stating that contracting a tautology results in a belief set of the contraction function:

$\mathbf{B} - \mathbf{t} = \mathbf{B} - \mathbf{f}$

As for simple contractions, any preferential belief contraction function can be 'normalized' to a conservative contraction function via the following definition:

$$\mathbf{B} -_c A = \begin{cases} \mathbf{B} - A & \text{if } A \notin \mathbf{K}_-, \\ \mathbf{B} - \mathbf{f} & \text{otherwise.} \end{cases}$$

The above equation determines a conservative contraction which coincides with the source contraction function on contingent propositions. Accordingly, it will retain most of the regular properties of the latter.

A direct semantic representation for conservative belief contraction functions requires, however, a modification of the contraction operation on epistemic states in order to make it conservative.

Definition 12.3.4. *A* conservative contraction *of a general epistemic state* $\mathbb{E}$ *with respect to a proposition* A *is an epistemic state that coincides with* $\mathbb{E} - A$ *if* A *is contingent in* $\mathbb{E}$, *and with* $\mathbb{E}$ *if* A *is known in* $\mathbb{E}$.

Conservative contraction operation directly implements the principle that if we are required to contract a known proposition, we refuse to make any change to the source epistemic state. As can be immediately seen, this modified contraction operation already validates the above postulate of conservative failure. Moreover, we will see later that it gives an adequate representation for all conservative belief contraction functions. Note, however, that conservative contraction operations do not satisfy the postulates of contraction dynamics given earlier in this chapter. More exactly, they violate Inversion: if A is known, while B is contingent, then contracting B and then A amounts to contracting B (though A is not disbelieved). Moreover, contracting $A \wedge B$ in this case amounts to contracting B, which is clearly different from contracting A, as required by Inversion. As a result, conservative contractions have a more complex (and less natural) dynamic behavior than our 'official' contractions. Still, conservative contractions stand closer to the common models of belief contraction, and this makes them a useful notion for studying such models.

In what follows, we are intending to remain impartial about the above two possible behaviors of belief contraction functions on known propositions. Fortunately, the characterizations of different kinds of belief contractions, given in the next section, permit us to do this, since in most cases the two variants, simple or conservative, are obtainable just by adding the relevant failure postulate to the basic description. Accordingly, when we will say that some class of belief contraction functions is generated by contractions of certain epistemic states, this will mean that simple belief contraction functions in this class are produced by our 'official' contraction operation, while conservative belief contraction functions from this class are generated by conservative contractions of these epistemic states. This will allow us to avoid doubling of our representation results in order to give a separate description for simple and conservative contractions.

Success. If we compare our formalization of belief contractions with that of the AGM theory, we can notice that the underlying logic presupposed by the latter is not restricted to the classical entailment, but is represented by some Tarski consequence relation Th. Actually, following the lead of [AGM85], the logic presupposed in practically all current studies of belief change is taken to be an arbitrary classical Tarski consequence relation, that is, a consequence relation satisfying compactness, supraclassicality and the deduction theorem (see Chapter 2). It turns out, however, that this underlying logic of a contraction function can be 'reconstructed' on the basis of our postulates, and this will show, in particular, how the relevant AGM postulates can be satisfied in our framework.

Any classical consequence relation can be seen as a classical entailment augmented with some auxiliary non-logical axioms. And it turns out that the underlying logic of any belief contraction function is uniquely determined by taking the knowledge set $\mathbf{K}_-$ as the set of such non-logical axioms. Below we will denote by Th^- the least classical consequence relation that includes $\mathbf{K}_-$. Then the following results are obtainable by a direct reformulation of the corresponding results for contraction relations, established in Chapter 10. Due to this, we can afford to omit the corresponding proofs.

When we consider the role the underlying logic plays in the AGM theory of contractions, we find three AGM postulates that depend on this consequence relation; translated into our present terminology, they read as follows:

(K–1) $\mathrm{Th}(\mathbf{B}-A) = \mathbf{B}-A$ (Th-closure)

(K–4) If $A \notin \mathrm{Th}(\emptyset)$, then $A \notin \mathbf{B}-A$ (success)

(K–5) If $\mathrm{Th}(A) = \mathrm{Th}(B)$, then $\mathbf{B}-A = \mathbf{B}-B$ (Th-extensionality)

Repeating the terminology from Chapter 10, we will say that a contraction function *respects* a consequence relation Th, if it satisfies Th-closure. As has been shown there, if a contraction function respects Th, it will satisfy also Th-extensionality. Similarly, we will say that a contraction function *preserves* a consequence relation Th, if it respects it and satisfies, in addition, the success postulate. In other words, a contraction function preserves Th, if it satisfies the above three postulates. Then the following theorem shows that Th^- provides an adequate description of the logic underlying a given contraction function; it is a straightforward reformulation of Theorem 10.1.1 from Chapter 10.

Theorem 12.3.1.   *1. Any contraction function respects* Th^-.

2. If a contraction function preserves a classical consequence relation Th, *then the latter coincides with* Th^-.

The above result shows, in effect, that the introduction of an auxiliary background consequence relation Th does not extend our expressive capabilities in representing belief contraction functions: the above three AGM postulates provide only a definitional extension of the source formalism in which the underlying logic Th is definable as the consequence relation generated by the knowledge set of the contraction function. In other words, all these postulates (including the postulate of success!) are just consequences of a single rational assumption that Th^- constitutes the 'right' underlying logic for belief contractions.

12.4 Kinds of belief contractions

In this section we will establish the completeness of our postulates for belief contraction functions with respect to their intended interpretation in terms of epistemic states, as well as the role of additional postulates for belief contractions that have been suggested in the literature. In order to do this, we will make use of the correspondence between belief contraction functions and contraction inference relations; this will allow us to translate the representation results of Chapter 10 into corresponding results for belief contraction functions.

Recall that if a contraction inference relation is generated by some epistemic state $\mathbb{E}$, then contractions of this epistemic state produce exactly the simple belief contraction function corresponding to this contraction relation. In addition, conservative belief contraction functions are generated in this sense by conservative contractions of epistemic states. As a result, all the representation results for contraction relations, established in Chapter 10, can be immediately transformed into the corresponding representation results for belief contraction functions. This is precisely what we are going to do in this section.

To begin with, since general epistemic states have been shown to be adequate for the representation of general contraction relations (see Representation Theorems 10.1 and 10.2 in Chapter 10), we immediately obtain

Representation Theorem 12.1. *Preferential belief contraction functions are precisely belief functions generated by contractions of epistemic states.*

In view of the above theorem, the postulates for preferential belief contractions, coupled with the postulate of simple or conservative failure, respectively, give a complete characterization of belief contraction functions generated by simple and conservative contractions of epistemic states.

Below we will provide representations for additional postulates of belief contractions suggested by the AGM theory and beyond. These postulates will be shown to correspond to certain meaningful constraints on underlying epistemic states.

12.4.1 Determinate contractions

As we have seen in the preceding chapter, common representations of the contraction operation on belief sets give rise to determinate epistemic states. For the AGM theory, this assumption is actually a consequence of its basic assumption that epistemic states should be identified with belief sets. The assumption turns out to be valid, however, also for the rival base approach, due to the fact that base-generation implies determination.

It turns out that determinate epistemic states validate the AGM postulate of vacuity:

If $A \notin \mathbf{B} - \mathbf{f}$, then $\mathbf{B} - A = \mathbf{B} - \mathbf{f}$ (vacuity)

As in Chapter 10, a belief contraction function will be called *determinate* if it satisfies the above vacuity postulate. As has been shown there, determinate contraction relations (both simple and conservative) provide a complete description of contraction relations on determinate epistemic states (see Representation Theorem 10.6 and Corollary 10.4.1). Consequently, we have also

Representation Theorem 12.2. *Determinate belief contraction functions are exactly belief functions generated by contractions of determinate epistemic states.*

Finally, note that if an epistemic state is determinate, and its belief set $\mathbf{B}$ is consistent, then it will coincide with $\mathbf{B} - \mathbf{f}$. Consequently, the above vacuity postulate can be safely rewritten also in its original AGM form involving the source belief set, namely

$$\text{If } A \notin \mathbf{B}, \text{ then } \mathbf{B} - A = \mathbf{B} \qquad\qquad (vacuity_0)$$

The above postulate implies, in particular, that if $\mathbf{B}$ is consistent (that is, $\mathbf{f} \notin \mathbf{B}$), then it coincides with $\mathbf{B} - \mathbf{f}$. As a result, it is reducible, in effect, to the previous postulate of vacuity.

12.4.2 Withdrawals

In addition to determination (= vacuity), the main models of belief contraction sanction yet another common property, namely that contracted belief sets are always subsets of the original belief set. In other words, they satisfy the AGM postulate of inclusion (K–2). Such belief contraction functions will satisfy already all the basic AGM postulates for contractions, except the postulate of recovery. Following [Mak87], they are commonly called withdrawals. Notice that withdrawals cannot in general be simple belief contractions, since the contraction of a known proposition should also be a subset of the belief set. Accordingly, the following definition is formulated only with respect to conservative contractions.

Definition 12.4.1. *A conservative and determinate contraction function will be said to be a* withdrawal *if it satisfies*

$$\mathbf{B} - A \subseteq \mathbf{B} - \mathbf{f} \qquad\qquad (inclusion)$$

As we have seen in Chapter 10, withdrawal functions can be obtained in a systematic way from determinate contractions in general by forming their **B**-*restrictions*:

$$\mathbf{B} -^w A = \mathbf{B} - A \bigcap \mathbf{B} - \mathbf{f}$$

A semantic representation of withdrawals has been given in Chapter 10 in terms of $\mathbf{B}$-determinate epistemic states, that is, determinate epistemic states in which all admissible belief sets are included in the belief set of the epistemic state (see Representation Theorem 10.9). This representation result can now be formulated as follows:

Representation Theorem 12.3. *A belief contraction function is a withdrawal if and only if it is generated by conservative contractions of some* **B***-determinate epistemic state.*

We have argued in the preceding chapter that determination should not be considered as a rationality constraint on our epistemic states. But if an epistemic state is not determinate, it may include a number of preferred belief states, and then contraction of some of these possibilities may actually result in a *growth* of what is believed. Consequently, such epistemic states provide a natural and 'rational' way of violating both inclusion and vacuity postulates.

Example 12.4.1. Let us consider a pure epistemic state $\mathcal{E}$ consisting of the following theories: $\{\mathrm{Cl}(p \to q), \mathrm{Cl}(p \vee q), \mathrm{Cl}(p), \mathrm{Cl}(q)\}$. This epistemic state is not determinate and, as is easy to see, its belief set coincides with $\mathrm{Cl}(p \vee q)$. Contracting p from this epistemic state, however, will give us a new and greater belief set $\mathrm{Cl}(q)$. Thus, both inclusion and vacuity fail in this case.

12.4.3 Recovering contractions

The famous and much disputed AGM postulate of recovery (K–6) amounts in our present setting to the following condition:

$$\mathbf{B} - \mathbf{f} \subseteq \mathrm{Cl}(A, \mathbf{B} - A) \qquad\qquad \text{(recovery)}$$

A belief contraction function will be called a *recovering contraction*, if it is a withdrawal and satisfies the above recovery postulate. Note that if Th is an arbitrary classical consequence relation, then the above postulate immediately implies the more familiar AGM postulate of recovery with respect to Th:

$$\mathbf{B} - \mathbf{f} \subseteq \mathrm{Th}(A, \mathbf{B} - A) \qquad\qquad \text{(Th-recovery)}$$

Moreover, the postulates of inclusion and recovery jointly imply the postulate of conservative failure. Consequently, recovering contractions could be alternatively characterized as contraction relations that satisfy vacuity, inclusion and recovery. In other words, they will already be AGM contractions, since they will satisfy all the basic postulates for AGM contraction functions[2]. The following definition gives an 'AGM-like' description of such contraction functions.

Definition 12.4.2. *A belief contraction function will be called a* preferential AGM contraction *if it satisfies the basic AGM postulates and supplementary postulates (K–7) and Rott's (K–8c).*

As was shown in [AGM85], in the presence of recovery the partial antitony postulate (B–3) becomes equivalent to the AGM postulate (K–7), which is

---

[2] Taking into account our treatment of the Success postulate.

equivalent, in turn, to our distributivity postulate (B–4). Recall also that the cumulativity postulate (B–5) is equivalent to a conjunction of two Rott's postulates (K–7c) and (K–8c). Now, given recovery, (K–7c) is also a consequence of (K–7) (see [Rot92b]). So, all our postulates will turn out to be consequences of the above AGM postulates characterizing preferential AGM contractions. Hence, we immediately obtain

Lemma 12.4.1. *Recovering contractions coincide with preferential AGM contractions.*

In Chapter 10 we have shown that *epistemic AGM-states* provide an adequate representation for recovering contractions. This result can be used now to obtain the following representation result for preferential AGM contractions.

Representation Theorem 12.4. *A belief contraction function is a recovering (= preferential AGM) contraction if and only if it is generated by conservative contractions of some epistemic AGM state.*

Recall that the above representation refers to general AGM states, not only to standard ones. As we have seen already in Chapter 10, this generalization of the standard AGM models is essential for an adequate representation of preferential AGM contractions; even in the finite case there are preferential AGM contraction functions that are not representable by standard AGM states. This explains also the difficulty of giving an adequate characterization for belief contractions generated by standard AGM states. Further details on this problem can be found in Chapter 10.

It has often been claimed that recovery is a characteristic property of the coherentist approach to belief change. And indeed, recovery can be seen as a consequence of the homogeneity principle discussed in the preceding chapter; combined with monotonicity of the preference relation, it implies that only maximal sub-theories of the belief set should be considered as options for choice, and this immediately leads to recovery. Note, however, that monotonicity of the preference relation is also an essential ingredient of this result. In fact, if we drop this monotonicity requirement, we can obtain a purely coherentist interpretation for the whole class of preferential contraction functions.

12.4.4 Pure belief contractions

Belief contraction functions generated by contractions of pure epistemic states will be called *pure* belief contractions. As we mentioned in Chapter 10, an axiomatic characterization of such belief contractions is still missing. It is known, however, that all such contractions satisfy the following characteristic postulate:

If $B \in \mathbf{B}{-}A$, then $\mathbf{B}{-}(A \wedge B) \subseteq \mathbf{B}{-}A$ (persistence)

The above postulate is valid actually for all persistent epistemic states. In fact, the above postulate is expressible as some general rule for contractionals, and it has been shown in Chapter 4 that pure and persistent epistemic states are indistinguishable in terms of such general rules.

Just as contraction operations on pure epistemic states, pure belief contraction functions can also be analyzed in the framework of consequence relations. To begin with, the following important result shows that Tarski consequence relations are sufficient for representing pure belief contractions. It is an immediate consequence of Lemma 4.5.1.

Theorem 12.4.1. *If $\vdash$ is a Tarski subrelation of a Scott consequence relation $\Vdash$, then $\Vdash$ and $\vdash$ determine the same belief contraction function.*

As a result, the class of pure belief contraction functions coincides with the class of belief contraction functions generated by (supraclassical) Tarski consequence relations. Consequently, so far as we are interested only in belief functions resulting from one-step changes, we can restrict our attention to simpler and more familiar Tarski consequence relations.

The following theorem describes pure belief contractions directly in terms of the underlying consequence relation. It is an immediate consequence of Lemma 12.2.2 above and Lemma 3.2.1.

Theorem 12.4.2. $B \in \mathbf{B}_{\vdash} - A$ *if and only if, for any set a, if $a, B \vdash A$, then $a \vdash A$.*

Thus, B belongs to $\mathbf{B}_{\vdash} - A$ if the rule

$$\frac{a, B \vdash A}{a \vdash A}$$

is *admissible* with respect to $\vdash$. This condition can also be formulated as saying that B is *independent of A* in the sense that any admissible set of beliefs that does not depend on A can be always extended to an admissible set that includes B but still does not depend on A. And due to this independence, belief in B 'survives' the deletion of A. Note also that, since the relevant Tarski consequence relation is supraclassical, the condition of the above theorem can be reformulated in terms of qualitative dependence relations as follows:

$B \in \mathbf{B} - A$ if and only if $B \wedge C < A$ implies $C < A$, for any C.

The above condition gives a direct definition of pure belief contractions in terms of dependence relations.

Pure belief contractions embody an alternative understanding of contraction change as compared with AGM contractions. Thus, there are contraction functions that are perfectly reasonable from the point of view of the AGM theory, though they are not pure contractions. The following example shows that the difference can also be explained by appeal to the difference between (coherentist) entrenchment versus (foundational) dependence relations.

Example 12.4.2. Consider belief contractions from a belief set $\mathbf{B} = \mathrm{Cl}(p \wedge q)$, where p and q are contingent atomic propositions. According to the AGM theory, if q is more entrenched than p, then contracting $p \wedge q$ should retain q and remove p. This is perfectly compatible with retaining p when we are required to contract q anyway; the entrenchment relation determines only our choices in cases of conflict, so it does not require to delete less entrenched propositions when we remove more entrenched ones, unless this is required to restore consistency. Accordingly, we can have both $q \in \mathbf{B} - (p \wedge q)$ and $p \in \mathbf{B} - q$. This situation is impossible, however, for pure contractions: the above two conditions imply $q \in \mathbf{B} - q$ by persistence, which is possible only if q is a known proposition. Note also that if p depends on q (that is, $p \vdash q$), then pure contraction of $p \wedge q$ could retain q, but contraction of q would also delete p.

Pure belief contractions are different from the AGM contractions also in terms of their properties. Thus, the following example demonstrates that even quite simple pure epistemic states invalidate most of the AGM postulates.

Example 12.4.3. Let us return to the epistemic state consisting of the following theories: $\{\mathrm{Cl}(p \rightarrow q), \mathrm{Cl}(p \vee q), \mathrm{Cl}(p), \mathrm{Cl}(q)\}$. As we have seen earlier, this non-determinate epistemic state violates both inclusion (K–2) and vacuity (K–3). In addition, contracting q gives $\mathrm{Cl}(\emptyset)$ as a belief set, and hence recovery (K–6) also fails. Finally $q \notin \mathbf{B} - (p \wedge q)$, but $\mathbf{B} - (p \wedge q) = \mathrm{Cl}(p \vee q) \not\subseteq \mathbf{B} - q = \mathrm{Cl}(\emptyset)$. Therefore, (K–8) fails as well.

The situation improves, however, if we consider contractions of determinate epistemic states. Then the corresponding pure belief contractions will satisfy also the AGM postulate of vacuity (K–3). Moreover, if we will consider only conservative contractions, they will satisfy also the postulate of inclusion (K–2), since all contracted belief sets will be subsets of the initial belief set. Accordingly, in this case they will be withdrawal functions satisfying all the AGM postulates except recovery (K–6) and the last postulate (K–8).

As a matter of fact, in the determinate case pure contractions can be seen as a straightforward generalization of *full meet contractions* in the AGM theory.

If $\vdash$ is a supraclassical Tarski consequence relation with a belief set $\mathbf{B}$, then, for any proposition A, $\mathbf{B} - A$ is an intersection of all maximal theories of $\vdash$ that do not contain A. If $\vdash$ is determinate, then each such maximal theory is a subset of $\mathbf{B}$. Accordingly, the resulting framework in this case can be viewed as a generalization of the AGM paradigm obtained by replacing its underlying classical consequence relation Th by a *supra-classical* one. The possibility of such a generalization of the basic AGM setting was envisaged, for example, by David Makinson in [Mak87]. Note that pure contraction corresponds in this sense to the full meet contraction in the AGM theory. However, due to the fact that the underlying consequence relation is only supraclassical, the full meet contraction does not lead to trivialization as in the AGM setting.

The above analogy between pure belief contractions and full meet contractions reveals, however, not only the similarity, but also an essential difference between pure contractions and partial meet contractions of the AGM theory. Pure contractions embody essential features of full meet contractions (reflected in the above persistence postulate) which have been the source of trivialization in the AGM setting. As a result, the postulate of persistence cannot even be added to the basic AGM postulates, on pain of collapsing to full meet contractions:

Theorem 12.4.3. *A contraction function satisfies the basic AGM postulates and the persistence postulate if and only if it is a full meet contraction.*

Proof. As was shown in [AGM85], full meet AGM contractions are characterized by the basic AGM postulates and the following *Monotony property*:

(M)   If $B \in \mathbf{B}$, then $\mathbf{B} - (A \wedge B) \subseteq \mathbf{B} - A$

Now, if $B \in \mathbf{B}$, then $A \to B \in \mathbf{B} - A$ by recovery, and hence $\mathbf{B} - A \wedge B \subseteq \mathbf{B} - A$ by persistence. Consequently, a contraction function satisfying the above postulates satisfies also Monotony, and hence is a full meet contraction. □

Thus, pure contractions are also AGM contractions only in the trivial case of full meet contractions. Consequently, pure contractions stem form an alternative understanding of belief contractions that is not subsumed by the AGM theory.

Belief contractions in base-generated states. Pure base-generated epistemic states have many interesting features that do not hold for a general case. Thus, we will show now that any such state is uniquely determined by its associated belief contraction function. As a result, it is possible in principle to give an abstract characterization of 'base-generated' contractions in terms of the properties of the associated belief contraction functions. However, as can be seen from Hansson's results in [Han93b, Han93a], no characterization of this kind is going to be simple. So, we will state here only the basic facts.

Our first result shows that the Tarski subrelation of a base-generated Scott consequence relation is uniquely determined by its associated belief contraction function.

Theorem 12.4.4. *If $\Vdash$ is a base-generated consequence relation, then $A \Vdash C$ holds iff, for any proposition B, $A \in \mathbf{B}_{\Vdash} - B$ implies $C \in \mathbf{B}_{\Vdash} - B$.*

Proof. The direction from left to right is immediate. Assume that $A \nVdash C$. Then there must exist a base proposition B_0 such that $A \in \mathrm{Th}_{\Vdash}(B_0)$ and $C \notin \mathrm{Th}_{\Vdash}(B_0)$. Let us denote by B a proposition $B_0 \to C$. Then B_0 belongs to $\mathbf{B} - B$ (see Lemma 12.4.2), and hence A also belongs to $\mathbf{B} - B$. In addition, $C \notin \mathbf{B} - B$. Indeed, otherwise B would belong to $\mathbf{B} - B$, and hence we would have $\Vdash B_0 \to C$, which contradicts the assumption that $C \notin \mathrm{Th}_{\Vdash}(B_0)$. Thus, the implication from right to left also holds. □

The above theorem shows that the Tarski subrelation of a base-generated Scott consequence relation is determined by contracted belief sets. In fact, the above property can be seen as a 'logical source' of Hansson's symmetry postulate in [Han93b]. An additional consequence of the above result that plays an important role in Hansson's characterization is that in the finite case any theory of a base-generated consequence relation has the form $\mathbf{B} - A$, for some A (this follows immediately from compactness of finite sets of theories).

Finally, it turns out that basic propositions of any consequence relation can also be 'restored' from the associated belief contraction function. The following result shows that if arbitrary contractions of propositions of the form $B \to C$ preserve the belief in B, then B is a basic proposition.

Lemma 12.4.2. *B is a basic proposition of $\Vdash$ iff, for any set c, B is believed in $\Vdash_{-(B \to c)}$.*

Proof. Notice first that $a, B \Vdash c$ is always equivalent to $a, B \Vdash B \to c$. Consequently, B is a basic proposition if and only if $a, B \Vdash B \to c$ always implies $a \Vdash B \to c$. Now the result follows from Lemma 12.2.2. $\qquad\square$

The above results demonstrate that, for base-generated states, the associated belief contraction functions are already sufficient for recovering their structure. This property, however, is highly specific for base-generated states and is not extendable even to finite grounded epistemic states.

12.4.5 Rational contractions

So far we have discussed the basic AGM postulates and their interpretation in our framework. The last two AGM postulates, (K–7) and (K–8), were called supplementary postulates in the AGM approach, since they are not valid for general partial meet contractions. We have seen, however, that the postulate (K–7) is valid for relational (preferential) AGM contractions; it corresponds to our postulate of distributivity (B–4). In this section we will show that the last AGM postulate (K–8) corresponds to restriction of epistemic states to states in which the preference order is modular (ranked).

As can be easily checked, contraction functions determined by modular epistemic states satisfy already the last AGM postulate (K–8). Still, the class of belief contraction functions determined by such epistemic states is much larger than the class of AGM contractions, since it includes also contractions that do not satisfy the recovery postulate. It includes, for example, contraction functions called Levi contractions in [HO95] (see below). Moreover, modular epistemic states allow for some fine-grained distinctions inside this class, many of them corresponding to belief contraction functions already suggested in the literature.

A belief contraction function will be called *rational* if it satisfies the following two postulates:

If $A \notin \mathbf{B}-A \wedge B$, then $\mathbf{B}-A \wedge B \subseteq \mathbf{B}-A$ (rational monotony)

If $B \in \mathbf{B}-A$ and $A \notin \mathbf{B}-B$, then $B \in \mathbf{B}-A \wedge B$ (priority)

Rational monotony is nothing other than the last AGM postulate (K-8). Notice that it already implies the vacuity postulate. The priority postulate has been discussed in Chapter 10. We have shown, in particular, that for recovering contractions, it is a consequence of rational monotony.

As we have seen in Chapter 10, rational contractions satisfy the following *weak decomposition property*:

$$\mathbf{B} - (A \wedge B) \text{ is equal to } \mathbf{B} - A \text{ or } \mathbf{B} - B, \text{ or } \mathbf{B} - A \bigcap \mathbf{B} - B.$$

As before, our results for contraction relations in Chapter 10 imply that rational contractions provide a complete description of belief contraction functions generated by modular epistemic states. Thus, we can formulate the following

Representation Theorem 12.5. *A belief contraction function is rational if and only if it is generated by a modular epistemic state.*

An epistemic state will be called *rational* if it is modular, standard and monotonic. We have shown in Chapter 10 that such epistemic states are sufficient for representing all rational contractions (both simple and conservative ones). Consequently, we have also

Representation Theorem 12.6. *Any rational contraction function is generated by a rational epistemic state.*

Thus, rational belief contractions have a pleasant property that they can be always represented by standard monotonic epistemic states in the same language.

Levi contractions and rational withdrawals. A formalization of some of the ideas of Isaac Levi on contractions has been suggested in [HO95]. According to this formalization, a *value-based Levi contraction* is representable, in effect, as a contraction operation on the set of saturatable subsets of the belief set that are ordered by a modular (ranked) preference relation. The authors have shown that such contractions satisfy already the two supplementary postulates for AGM contractions, but they have left open the problem of their complete characterization. It has been established in Chapter 10, however, that any rational contraction is representable by a standard saturatable epistemic state with a modular preference order. We have shown, in addition, that **B**-restrictions of saturatable epistemic states produce again saturatable epistemic states. Accordingly, we can state the following result that provides, in effect, a formalization for Levi contractions.

Theorem 12.4.5. *Value-based Levi contractions coincide with rational withdrawals.*

In the AGM framework, the full set of eight postulates for contractions provides, in a sense, a final step in the development of a general theory. Rational contractions allows, however, for a number of further concretizations beside AGM contractions, each leading to an interesting class of belief contraction functions. Thus, two important subclasses of rational contraction functions, described below, are generated, respectively, by linear and pure linear epistemic states.

Linear contractions

A belief contraction function will be called *linear* if it satisfies rational monotony and

If $A \notin \mathbf{B} - A \wedge B$, then $\mathbf{B} - A \subseteq \mathbf{B} - A \wedge B$ (rational antitony)

Since the priority postulate is a consequence of rational antitony, any linear contraction relation will already be rational. Rational monotony and rational antitony can be combined into the following single condition:

If $A \notin \mathbf{B} - A \wedge B$, then $\mathbf{B} - A = \mathbf{B} - A \wedge B$ (linearity)

The above condition has been called *hyperregularity* in [Han93b]. As we have shown in Chapter 10, this property implies, in turn, the following *strong decomposition property* (see [AGM85]):

$$\mathbf{B} - (A \wedge B) = \mathbf{B} - A \ \text{ or } \mathbf{B} - (A \wedge B) = \mathbf{B} - B$$

Recall that an epistemic state is *linear*, if the preference relation is a linear (total) order on admissible states. As we have seen in Chapter 10, such epistemic states provide a semantic representation for linear contractions. Accordingly, we have

Representation Theorem 12.7. *A belief contraction function is linear if and only if it is generated by a linear standard and monotonic epistemic state.*

Severe contractions

A further constraint that can be imposed on linear epistemic states consists in considering only pure epistemic states. In other words, we can consider pure epistemic states in which the set of theories is linearly ordered by inclusion. The resulting contraction relations will be both linear and pure. Their conservative versions will correspond to belief contraction functions suggested by Rott and Levi.

Definition 12.4.3. *A belief contraction function will be said to be* severe *if it satisfies rational monotony and the following postulate from [RP99]:*

If $A \notin \mathbf{B} - A$, then $\mathbf{B} - A \subseteq \mathbf{B} - A \wedge C$ (severe antitony)

All severe contractions will already be linear. The following result from Chapter 10 gives a couple of alternative characterizations for severe contractions:

Lemma 12.4.3. *A contraction relation is severe if and only if it satisfies one of the following conditions:*

1. *It is linear and satisfies the persistence postulate;*
2. *It satisfies the following postulate (see [RP99]):*

$$\text{If } B \notin \mathbf{B} - A, \text{ then } \mathbf{B} - A \subseteq \mathbf{B} - B \qquad \text{(modularity)}$$

In view of the representation result stated below, the first characterization above shows that the persistence postulate in this setting is sufficient for the restriction to pure epistemic states.

Now the following result shows that severe contractions provide a complete description of contraction relations determined by pure linear epistemic states. It is an immediate consequence of the corresponding result for severe contraction relations proved in Chapter 10.

Theorem 12.4.6. *A belief contraction function is severe if and only if it is generated by some pure linear epistemic state.*

Severe withdrawals. It turns out that conservative belief contractions generated by linear pure epistemic states coincide with *severe withdrawals* suggested recently by Rott and Pagnucco [RP99]. A similar notion, called *mild contraction* has been introduced by Levi in [Lev97].

The following representation result can be established syntactically by showing the equivalence between the postulates for severe withdrawals from [RP99] and postulates for conservative severe contractions. It can also be easily discerned from the relevant representation results, proved in [RP99], that establish a correspondence between severe withdrawals and epistemic entrenchment relations (see their Observation 19).

Theorem 12.4.7. *A contraction function is a severe withdrawal if and only if it is generated by conservative contractions of a linear pure epistemic state.*

It is interesting to note that, though [RP99] and [Lev97] gave quite different descriptions for this kind of contraction, in both cases the authors have given a broadly coherentist justification for this notion. Our results show, however, that a purely foundational approach can suggest here a viable and natural alternative to coherentism.

Linearity is a severe constraint on epistemic states. For example, severe withdrawals satisfy the following *expulsiveness* property (see [RP99]): if A and B are arbitrary contingent propositions, then either $A \notin \mathbf{B} - B$ or $B \notin \mathbf{B} - A$. So, in the linear case any two sentences may affect one another in contractions. We agree here with Rott and Pagnucco that this is an undesirable property. However, as can be easily checked, this property is not germane to pure contractions in general, so we can simply turn expulsiveness into an argument against taking linearity as a rationality constraint on epistemic states.

Rational recovering contractions

If we add recovery to the postulates of rational contractions, we obtain precisely contraction functions satisfying all the AGM postulates. In fact, combining our results on recovering and rational contractions, we could immediately rediscover the representation of AGM contractions, given in [AGM85].

Recall that by a *rational AGM-state* we mean a standard epistemic AGM-state in which the preference order is modular. Such epistemic states are essentially equivalent to the transitively relational models from [AGM85]. Consequently, the following result is just a reformulation of the corresponding result established in the AGM theory.

Representation Theorem 12.8. *A belief contraction function is a rational recovering contraction if and only if it is generated by conservative contractions of some rational AGM-state.*

12.5 Refined representations

The construction of a canonical epistemic state for a given contraction relation, described in Chapter 10, allows to single out a number of special classes of epistemic states that will be still adequate for representing all contraction functions. The results stated below will show that there exists a number of interesting conditions that can be safely imposed on the notion of an epistemic state in this sense.

Weak monotony and saturatedness. Isaac Levi has suggested in [Lev91] that the AGM framework for representing belief change should be extended; instead of the set of all maximal subsets of a belief set, that constitutes the primary set of alternatives for choice in the AGM approach, we should consider a broader class of *saturatable theories* that satisfy the condition that adding $\neg A$ transform them into worlds. As we already mentioned in Chapter 3, Levi argued also that the monotonicity property of the AGM framework should be replaced by the principle of weak monotonicity.

In confirmation of Levi's claims, the following result shows that the above conditions can be safely imposed on epistemic states without changing the class of generated belief contraction functions. It is a reformulation of the corresponding result for contraction relations proved in Chapter 10.

Corollary 12.5.1. *Any belief contraction function is generated by some weakly monotonic and saturatable epistemic state.*

The coherentist paradigm. As has been established in Chapter 4, homogeneous epistemic states are sufficient for representing any belief contraction function. This makes the coherentist approach a viable option for representing one-step belief changes.

As a special case of this result, the following theorem shows that **B**-homogeneous epistemic states are sufficient for representing any determinate belief contraction.

Representation Theorem 12.9. *Any determinate contraction function is generated by some **B**-homogeneous epistemic state.*

Proof. We will transform the canonical determinate epistemic state $\mathbb{E}_0$ for a given determinate contraction function into a **B**-homogeneous state. Let $\mathcal{U}$ be the set of all deductively closed theories u that are not admissible belief sets of $\mathbb{E}_0$ and such that $\mathbf{K}_- \subseteq u \subseteq \mathbf{B}_-$. We will consider all such u as new admissible belief states and extend the preference order as follows. A theory will be called **B**-maximal if it is representable as $\alpha \cap \mathbf{B}_-$, for some world α. Similarly, an admissible state s will be called **B**-maximal if $l(s)$ is **B**-maximal. Now if $u \in \mathcal{U}$ is not **B**-maximal, we will subordinate u to all **B**-maximal theories and states that include u. If u is already **B**-maximal, we will subordinate it to all **B**-maximal states s from $\mathbb{E}_0$. In this way we will obtain a new state $\mathbb{E}$ that will already be **B**-homogeneous. We will show that $\mathbb{E}$ and $\mathbb{E}_0$ generate the same belief contraction function. If $s \in \mathbb{E}$ is an 'old' state, then it is easy to see that it has the same more preferred states in $\mathbb{E}$ as it had in $\mathbb{E}_0$. Consequently, for any A, such a state will be maximal in $]A[$ with respect to $\mathbb{E}$ iff it was maximal in $\mathbb{E}_0$. Moreover, we will show that no new state $u \in \mathcal{U}$ can be maximal in $]A[$. Indeed, if u is such a new state and $A \notin u$, then there must exist a world α including u such that $\neg A \in \alpha$. Then $v = \alpha \cap \mathbf{B}_-$ is a **B**-maximal theory including u and $A \notin v$. Now if v does not coincide with u, then $u \prec v$ in the new order, and hence u is not maximal in $]A[$. Otherwise $u = v$, and hence u is **B**-maximal. Since $\mathbf{K}_-$ is included in u, A does not belong to $\mathbf{K}_-$ and hence it is contingent. Consequently there must exist a world β that is normal for A. But then $s = (\beta \cap \mathbf{B}_-, A)$ should be an admissible state of $\mathbb{E}_0$, and $u \prec s$. Thus, in this case also u cannot be maximal in $]A[$.

Thus, we have shown, in effect, that a state s is maximal in $]A[$ with respect to $\mathbb{E}$ iff s is a state of $\mathbb{E}_0$ and is also maximal in $]A[$ with respect to $\mathbb{E}_0$. Consequently, both epistemic states should generate the same contraction function. $\square$

The above results can be seen, in a sense, as a formal justification of Levi's approach to belief change. Note that we cannot impose strong monotonicity in this setting, since this would immediately imply the validity of the recovery postulate. Thus, the generality of our coherentist representation essentially depends on non-acceptance of the strong monotonicity principle.

As we have shown, the coherentist paradigm provides a powerful representation framework allowing us to capture all belief contraction functions in our sense. In particular, it allows in principle to represent pure belief contractions that we have considered as paradigmatic for a purely foundationalist approach. Speaking more generally, an appropriately chosen preference relation can incorporate all the relevant information embodied in the dependence structure of an epistemic state. This can be seen as a generalization of the claim made by Gärdenfors [Gär90] that a suitable entrenchment relation can incorporate the functions served by bases. Note also that the pure foundationalist approach turns out to be inferior in this respect, since the class of contraction functions representable by pure epistemic states is restricted to pure contractions.

All this facts notwithstanding, the above picture should not be construed as demonstrating the 'final victory' of coherentism. As we discussed in the preceding chapter, there are some general problems with the coherentist approach, both practical and theoretical, that undermine the overall impact of the above results.

13. Merge and Expansion

Whereas the general purpose of the contraction operation amounts to removing information (that is no longer believed), the operation of expansion consists in adding information to epistemic states. In the AGM theory this is achieved through a straightforward addition of the new proposition to the belief set, while in the base approach the new proposition is added directly to the base.

The framework of epistemic states drastically changes, however, the form and content of expansion operations. This stems already from the fact that adding a proposition to an epistemic state is no longer reducible to adding it to the belief set; it should also determine the place of the newly added proposition in the structure of the expanded epistemic state. This will establish the degree of firmness with which we should believe the new proposition, as well as its dependence and justification relations with other beliefs. In many cases the differences between various kinds of expansion operations will not even result in different 'expanded' belief sets. The auxiliary information will determine, however, the behavior of the resulting expanded epistemic state in subsequent changes.

As a way of modelling this additional information required for the expansion operation, we suggest treating the latter as a special case of merging the source epistemic state with another epistemic state that will represent the added information. Accordingly, we will describe first the general notion of a merge (product) of epistemic states, and introduce two basic merge operations that will be sufficient for representing any 'rational' merge of a set of epistemic states. Then an expansion operation $\mathbb{E} + A$ will be defined roughly as a merge of $\mathbb{E}$ with a rudimentary epistemic state $\mathbb{E}_A$ expressing a belief that A. We will study the properties of these expansion operations and show, in particular, that the belief change sanctioned by such expansions of epistemic states coincides with the belief expansion in the traditional AGM sense. In addition, we will consider a number of alternative expansion operations that correspond to existing proposals.

13.1 Merging epistemic states

Merge is yet another procedure of combining a number of epistemic states into a single epistemic state. In contrast to disjoint sum, however, by merging epistemic states we seek to combine information that is supported by the source epistemic states.

It turns out that this notion of merging can be captured using another well-known algebraic construction, namely the *product* of epistemic states. For reasons that will be made clear later, we can restrict our attention to merge of two epistemic states. The following definition gives a generic description of this notion. This means that it still does not define an operation of merging; rather, it stipulates some general constraints such an operation should satisfy in order to count as a merge of two epistemic states.

Definition 13.1.1. *An epistemic state* $\mathbb{E} = (S, l, \prec)$ *is a* merge *of two epistemic states* $\mathbb{E}_1 = (S_1, l_1, \prec_1)$ *and* $\mathbb{E}_2 = (S_2, l_2, \prec_2)$ *if it satisfies the following conditions:*

- $S = S_1 \times S_2$;
- *For any* $s = (s_1, s_2) \in S$, $l(s) = \text{Cl}(l_1(s_1) \cup l_2(s_2))$;
- *The preference relation* $\prec$ *is a strict partial order on* S *that satisfies the following two conditions:*
  (i) $(s_1, s_2) \prec (t_1, s_2)$ *if and only if* $s_1 \prec_1 t_1$;
  (ii) $(s_1, s_2) \prec (s_1, t_2)$ *if and only if* $s_2 \prec_2 t_2$.

Thus, a merge of two epistemic states $\mathbb{E}_1$ and $\mathbb{E}_2$ is an epistemic state in which the admissible states are all combinations of admissible states from $\mathbb{E}_1$ and $\mathbb{E}_2$, the labelling function assigns each such pair the deductive closure of their corresponding labels, while the preference relation agrees with the 'component' preferences *ceteris paribus*, that is, all else being equal.

The two conditions on the combined preference relation in the above definition are rather weak, since they determine only the order among pairs in which one of the components is fixed. Still, they jointly imply the following general constraint:

$$\text{If } s_1 \preceq_1 t_1 \text{ and } s_2 \preceq_2 t_2, \text{ then } (s_1, s_2) \preceq (t_1, t_2).$$

In general, however, the reverse implication does not hold; additional preferences may be determined, for example, by the relative priority of the defaults constituting one of the component epistemic states with respect to the defaults belonging to the other epistemic state (see below).

We present now a couple of results that are intended to demonstrate that the chosen generalization captures some key intuitions behind the notion of merging.

To begin with, it is natural to assume that a merge of two (prioritized) bases should produce a union of these bases. The following results confirm this intuition. As a general preparation, we will show that merging preserves basic propositions and union-closure.

Lemma 13.1.1. *If $\mathbb{E}$ is a merge of $\mathbb{E}_1$ and $\mathbb{E}_2$, then basic propositions of $\mathbb{E}_1$ and $\mathbb{E}_2$ are basic propositions of $\mathbb{E}$.*

Proof. Assume that A is a basic proposition of $\mathbb{E}_1$, and let (s,t) be an admissible state in $\mathbb{E}$ such that $A \notin l((s,t))$. Then clearly $A \notin l_1(s)$, and hence there must exist an admissible state s_1 in $\mathbb{E}_1$ such that $s \prec_1 s_1$ and $l_1(s_1) = \text{Cl}(A, l_1(s))$. But then we have $(s,t) \prec (s_1,t)$ and $l((s_1,t)) = \text{Cl}(l_1(s_1), l_2(t)) = \text{Cl}(A, l((s,t)))$. Consequently, A is a basic proposition in $\mathbb{E}$. $\qquad\square$

As we have said in Chapter 3, union-closure can be seen as a characteristic property of base-generated epistemic states. Our next result shows that merging preserves also this property.

Lemma 13.1.2. *A merge of two union-closed epistemic states is also union-closed.*

Proof. If $\mathbb{E}$ is a union-closed epistemic state, then, for any two admissible states s,t from $\mathbb{E}$ there exists an admissible state r such that $s,t \preceq r$ and $l(r) = \text{Cl}(l(s), l(t))$. We will call the latter admissible state a *covering* of s and t.

Assume now that $\mathbb{E}$ is a merge of two union-closed epistemic states $\mathbb{E}_1$ and $\mathbb{E}_2$, and let (s_1, s_2), (t_1, t_2) be two admissible states in $\mathbb{E}$. Consider an admissible state (r_1, r_2), where r_i are respective coverings of s_i and t_i in $\mathbb{E}_i$ (where $i = 1, 2$). Clearly, $(s_1, s_2), (t_1, t_2) \preceq (r_1, r_2)$. Moreover, it is easy to check that $l((r_1, r_2)) = \text{Cl}(l((s_1, s_2)) \cup l((t_1, t_2)))$. Thus, (r_1, r_2) is a covering of (s_1, s_2) and (t_1, t_2). Therefore, $\mathbb{E}$ is also union-closed. $\qquad\square$

Finally, the result below shows that the above defined notion of merging agrees with an intuitive understanding of merging for prioritized bases.

Given two prioritized bases $(\Delta_1, \lhd_1)$ and $(\Delta_2, \lhd_2)$ such that Δ_1 and Δ_2 are disjoint sets, we will consider a 'combined' base $(\Delta_1 \cup \Delta_2, \lhd)$ such that $\lhd$ is a conservative extension of $\lhd_1$ and $\lhd_2$ (in other words, $\lhd$ coincides with $\lhd_1$ on Δ_1, and with $\lhd_2$ on Δ_2).

The result below shows that the above combination of prioritized bases corresponds to merging of epistemic states that are normally base-generated by these bases (see Chapter 3 for the definition of normal base-generation).

Theorem 13.1.1. *An epistemic state that is normally base-generated by $(\Delta_1 \cup \Delta_2, \lhd)$ is isomorphic to a merge of epistemic states that are normally base-generated, respectively, by $(\Delta_1, \lhd_1)$ and $(\Delta_2, \lhd_2)$.*

Proof. Let $\mathbb{E}$ be the epistemic state that is normally generated by $(\Delta_1 \cup \Delta_2, \lhd)$, and $\prec_\lhd$ its preference relation. $\mathbb{E}$ contains admissible states of the form $\Gamma_1 \cup \Gamma_2$, where $\Gamma_1 \subseteq \Delta_1$ and $\Gamma_2 \subseteq \Delta_2$. Let i be a function mapping each such admissible state to a pair (Γ_1, Γ_2). Due to the assumption that Δ_1

and Δ_2 are disjoint, the mapping will be one-to-one[1]. Now we will define a preference relation $\prec$ on such pairs in accordance with the ordering on their counterparts:

$$(\Gamma_1, \Gamma_2) \prec (\Phi_1, \Phi_2) \text{ iff } \Gamma_1 \cup \Gamma_2 \prec_\lhd \Phi_1 \cup \Phi_2$$

Finally, we will label such pairs as follows: $l((\Gamma_1, \Gamma_2)) = \text{Cl}(\Gamma_1 \cup \Gamma_2)$.

The resulting epistemic state, that we will denote by $\mathbb{E}_+$, will be a merge of the epistemic states generated, respectively, by $(\Delta_1, \lhd_1)$ and $(\Delta_2, \lhd_2)$. Indeed, by the lexicographic rule, if Γ is disjoint from both Φ and Ψ, then $\Gamma \cup \Phi \prec \Gamma \cup \Psi$ holds if and only if $\Phi \prec \Psi$. This immediately gives us the two conditions on the merged preference relation. Moreover, it is easy to check that the above identification of admissible states $\Gamma_1 \cup \Gamma_2$ with pairs (Γ_1, Γ_2) actually establishes an isomorphism between $\mathbb{E}_+$ and $\mathbb{E}$. This completes the proof. $\qquad\square$

It is important to observe that the condition of disjointness for the bases Δ_1 and Δ_2 was essential for the above result. Note, however, that this requirement is a purely syntactic constraint that can be easily met by replacing some of the propositions in Δ_1 or in Δ_2 with logically equivalent, though syntactically different propositions. This 'trick' will be extensively used in what follows.

The above result also shows clearly that our generic definition does not determine an operation of merging. This is because any conservative extension of the two original priority orders determines some merge of the two base-generated epistemic states. As the following example shows, we may have, in particular, that two admissible states of the merge are related by preference, though their components are not related in the source epistemic states.

Example 13.1.1. Given two pure bases $\{A_1, B_1\}$ and $\{A_2, B_2\}$ (that is, bases with empty priority relations), let us consider a prioritized base $(\{A_1, B_1, A_2, B_2\}, \lhd)$ such that $A_1 \lhd B_2$ and $A_2 \lhd B_1$. Clearly, $\lhd$ is a conservative extension of the (empty) priority relations corresponding to the component bases. It is easy to see, however, that $\{A_1, A_2\} \prec_\lhd \{B_1, B_2\}$ holds in the epistemic state generated by the latter base.

Merging operations

The diversity of possible ways of merging epistemic states makes the task of defining plausible merging *operations* a nontrivial matter. However, the way of solving this problem will become obvious once we notice that this task is a special case of the problem of combining preference relations that we have discussed in Chapter 3.

Generalizing the notion of merging for two epistemic states, described above, a merge of a finite set of epistemic states $\{\mathbb{E}_i = (\mathcal{S}_i, l_i, \prec_i)\}$, where

---

[1] The assumption of *normal* base-generation is essential here.

$1 \leq i \leq n$, can be taken to be an epistemic state $\mathbb{E} = (\mathcal{S}, l, \prec)$, where $\mathcal{S} = \prod \mathcal{S}_i$, l assigns each n-tuple $(s_1, \ldots, s_n)$ from $\mathcal{S}$ a theory $\mathrm{Cl}(\bigcup l_i(s_i))$, while $\prec$ is a certain (yet to be defined) preference relation on $\mathcal{S}$. Thus, the merge operation will be completely specified once we define the resulting 'merged' preference relation. Notice now that each component preference relation $\prec_i$ determines a corresponding preference relation on $\prod \mathcal{S}_i$:

$$(s_1, \ldots, s_n) \prec_i' (t_1, \ldots, t_n) \equiv s_i \prec_i t_i$$

Moreover, the resulting preference relation can be naturally required to satisfy Arrow's conditions with respect to these component preferences. Then the basic result of [ARS95] (described in Chapter 3) will imply that any merge operator of this kind will be definable by some priority graph on the component preferences.

As a matter of fact, the conditions stated in our earlier generic definition of merge are consequences of the unanimity postulate, which constitutes one of the main Arrow's conditions. Still, the generic definition does not fully reflect even the unanimity condition, and hence it allows, in particular, merging in which the resulting preference depends on the relative priority of defaults occurring in different epistemic states. The unanimity postulate implies, however, that if two elements are comparable with respect to the resulting preference, then they should be comparable with respect to at least one argument preference. In our case, this amounts to the following additional condition:

If $(s_1, s_2) \prec (t_1, t_2)$, then either $s_1 \prec t_1$, or $s_2 \prec t_2$.

The above Example 13.1.1 shows, in effect, that there are merges that does not satisfy this condition, so it is independent from the conditions stated in the generic definition.

[ARS95] contains yet another important result, namely that any priority-based operator for combining preferences is constructible, in effect, by composing two basic binary operators of this kind. The following definition provides a description of these basic operations for the case of merging.

Definition 13.1.2. *1. A* pure merge *of epistemic states* $\mathbb{E}_1 = (\mathcal{S}_1, l_1, \prec_1)$ *and* $\mathbb{E}_2 = (\mathcal{S}_2, l_2, \prec_2)$ *is a merge of* $\mathbb{E}_1$ *and* $\mathbb{E}_2$ *in which the preference relation is defined as follows*
$(s_1, s_2) \preceq (t_1, t_2)$ *iff* $s_1 \preceq_1 t_1$ *and* $s_2 \preceq_2 t_2$.
The pure merge of $\mathbb{E}_1$ *and* $\mathbb{E}_2$ *will be denoted by* $\mathbb{E}_1 \times \mathbb{E}_2$.
2. A prioritized merge *of* $\mathbb{E}_1$ *with* $\mathbb{E}_2$ *(notation* $\mathbb{E}_1 \ltimes \mathbb{E}_2$) *is a merge of* $\mathbb{E}_1$ *and* $\mathbb{E}_2$ *in which the preference relation is defined as*
$(s_1, s_2) \prec (t_1, t_2)$ *iff either* $s_2 \prec_2 t_2$, *or* $s_2 = t_2$ *and* $s_1 \prec_1 t_1$.

In the following sections we will give a detailed description of these operations. Also, it will be shown in the next chapter that the above two operations are sufficient for constructing any prioritized base.

13.1.1 Pure merge

A pure merge is a merge operation that treats the two component epistemic states as two equally reliable sources. In other words, neither epistemic state is considered as having a higher priority than the other. Consequently, the resulting preference relation amounts to a full agreement between the component preferences. As a result, it is easy to see that pure merge is a commutative operation, unlike the prioritized merge that will be considered later. It can also be verified that pure merge is an associative operation, that is,

$(\mathbb{E}_1 \times \mathbb{E}_2) \times \mathbb{E}_3$ is isomorphic to $\mathbb{E}_1 \times (\mathbb{E}_2 \times \mathbb{E}_3)$

Though the resulting preference was defined above via weak preference, the corresponding strict preference is easily definable as follows:

$(s_1, s_2) \prec (t_1, t_2)$ iff either $s_1 \prec_1 t_1$ and $s_2 \preceq_2 t_2$, or $s_1 \preceq_1 t_1$ and $s_2 \prec_2 t_2$.

Alternatively, a pure merge can be defined by the requirement that the resulting preference relation is a *least* strict partial order satisfying the conditions in the generic definition of merging. Each of these characterizations fully determine the resulting preference relation, so a pure merge turns out to be an operation on epistemic states.

Being applied to base-generated epistemic states, the operation of pure merging corresponds to a straightforward union of two prioritized bases:

Lemma 13.1.3. *If $\mathbb{E}_1$ and $\mathbb{E}_2$ are epistemic states that are normally generated, respectively, by prioritized bases $(\Delta_1, \lhd_1)$ and $(\Delta_2, \lhd_2)$ such that $\Delta_1 \cap \Delta_2 = \emptyset$, then $\mathbb{E}_1 \times \mathbb{E}_2$ is isomorphic to an epistemic state normally generated by $(\Delta_1 \cup \Delta_2, \lhd_1 \cup \lhd_2)$.*

Proof. Given the isomorphism described in Theorem 13.1.1, we need only to show that the corresponding merge $\mathbb{E}_+$ is pure. But this follows from the fact that, since propositions from Δ_1 are nor related by priority to propositions from Δ_2, $\Gamma_1 \cup \Gamma_2 \preceq_\lhd \Phi_1 \cup \Phi_2$ in $\mathbb{E}$ if and only if $\Gamma_1 \preceq_1 \Phi_1$ and $\Gamma_2 \preceq_2 \Phi_2$, by the definition of the preference relation. $\square$

Thus, pure merge does not introduce new priorities in addition to those holding in the component bases. In particular, a pure merge of two pure bases amounts to a simple union of these bases.

Important note. Pure merge is an operation defined for any pair of epistemic states. In particular, it is defined even if the relevant epistemic states are generated by bases that are not disjoint. In this case the result of merging can also be modeled on the level of bases, provided we replace first the relevant common basic propositions by their logical equivalents in a way that secure disjointness. Similar observation will hold also for the prioritized merge that we will consider below.

As a final result in this section, we will show that pure merge allows for replacement of (normally) similar epistemic states. Due to commutativity of the pure merging, it is sufficient to prove the claim for one of the components.

Theorem 13.1.2. *If $\mathbb{E}_1$ is (normally) similar to $\mathbb{E}$, then $\mathbb{E}_1 \times \mathbb{E}_2$ is (normally) similar to $\mathbb{E} \times \mathbb{E}_2$.*

Proof. We will prove first the preservation of normal similarity.

Assume that (s_1, s_2) is a normal admissible state in $\mathbb{E}_1 \times \mathbb{E}_2$. Then both s_1 and s_2 are normal admissible states in their respective epistemic states. Indeed, assume, for example, that $s_1 \prec t_1$ in $\mathbb{E}_1$, for some t_1 such that $l(t_1) \subseteq l(s_1)$. Then clearly $(s_1, s_2) \prec (t_1, s_2)$ in $\mathbb{E}_1 \times \mathbb{E}_2$, and, moreover, $l((t_1, s_2)) = \mathrm{Cl}(l(t_1), l(s_2)) \subseteq l((s_1, s_2))$, contrary to normality of (s_1, s_2).

Now, since $\mathbb{E}_1$ is normally similar to $\mathbb{E}$, there must exist an admissible state s in $\mathbb{E}$ such that $s \stackrel{\circ}{=} s_1$ and $\Uparrow s_1 \ll \Uparrow s$. Let us consider an admissible state (s, s_2) in $\mathbb{E} \times \mathbb{E}_2$. Clearly, $(s_1, s_2) \stackrel{\circ}{=} (s, s_2)$. Consequently, in order to complete the proof, it is sufficient to show that $\Uparrow(s_1, s_2) \ll \Uparrow(s, s_2)$.

Assume that $(s, s_2) \prec (t, t_2)$ in $\mathbb{E} \times \mathbb{E}_2$. Then $s \preceq t$ in $\mathbb{E}$ and $s_2 \preceq t_2$ in $\mathbb{E}_2$. Assume first that $s \prec t$. Since $\Uparrow s_1 \ll \Uparrow s$, there must exist t_1 in $\mathbb{E}_1$ such that $s_1 \prec t_1$ and $l(t_1) \subseteq l(t)$. Consequently, $(s_1, s_2) \prec (t_1, t_2)$ in $\mathbb{E}_1 \times \mathbb{E}_2$. Moreover, $l((t_1, t_2)) \subseteq l((t, t_2))$, as required. Assume now that $s = t$. Then $s_2 \prec t_2$ in $\mathbb{E}_2$, and hence $(s_1, s_2) \prec (s_1, t_2)$ in $\mathbb{E}_1 \times \mathbb{E}_2$. In addition, (s, t_2) and (s_1, t_2) are equal admissible states. This shows that $\Uparrow(s_1, s_2) \ll \Uparrow(s, s_2)$.

The above proof has demonstrated that pure merge preserves normal similarity. Actually, the proof for preservation of similarity can be easily discerned from the above proof by simply eliminating all references to normality. $\square$

It remains an open question whether pure merge preserves equivalence of epistemic states. Note, however, that, due to the correspondence between equivalence and normal similarity, established in Chapter 4, a potential counterexample should be rather complex. The same question remains open also for prioritized merges described below. It will be shown later, however, that both these merge operations preserve equivalence in the special case of expansions.

Yet another open question concerns smoothness of the epistemic states resulting from the two merge operations. Again, smoothness will be shown to be preserved, however, for the special case of expansion operations.

Merging flocks. To begin with, the following simple result shows that pure merge preserves persistence of epistemic states.

Lemma 13.1.4. *A pure merge of two persistent epistemic states is also a persistent epistemic state.*

Proof. If $(s_1, s_2) \prec (t_1, t_2)$ in a pure merge of two persistent epistemic states $\mathbb{E}_1$ and $\mathbb{E}_2$, then $s_1 \preceq t_1$ and $s_2 \preceq t_2$. Consequently, $l_1(s_1) \subseteq l_1(t_1)$ and $l_2(s_2) \subseteq l_2(t_2)$ by persistence, and hence $\mathrm{Cl}(l_1(s_1) \cup l_2(s_2)) \subseteq \mathrm{Cl}(l_1(t_1) \cup$

$l_2(t_2)$). Thus, $l((s_1, s_2)) \subseteq l((t_1, t_2))$, and therefore $\mathbb{E}_1 \times \mathbb{E}_2$ is a persistent epistemic state. $\square$

As we have established in Chapter 4, persistent epistemic states are representable by flocks. Consequently, a pure merge gives rise to a certain operation on flocks. This operation can be described as follows:

Let us consider two flocks $\mathcal{F}_1$ and $\mathcal{F}_2$ that have no propositions in common. Then a *merge* of $\mathcal{F}_1$ and $\mathcal{F}_2$ will be a flock

$$\mathcal{F}_1 \times \mathcal{F}_2 = \{\Delta_i \cup \Delta_j \mid \Delta_i \in \mathcal{F}_1, \Delta_j \in \mathcal{F}_2\}$$

Thus, the merge of two disjoint flocks is obtained by a pairwise combination of bases belonging to each flock. Note, however, that, as before, the assumption of disjointness turns out to be essential for establishing the correspondence between merge of flocks and pure merge of associated epistemic states. But as we said earlier, this constraint can be easily satisfied by replacing 'offending' propositions with their logical equivalents. A suitable example will be given later in this chapter when we will consider expansions of flocks that are based on the above notion of merge.

The following result shows that merge of flocks corresponds to a pure merge of associated epistemic states.

Theorem 13.1.3. *If $\mathbb{E}_\mathcal{F}$ and $\mathbb{E}_\mathcal{G}$ are epistemic states that are normally generated, respectively, by disjoint flocks $\mathcal{F}$ and $\mathcal{G}$, then $\mathbb{E}_\mathcal{F} \times \mathbb{E}_\mathcal{G}$ is isomorphic to an epistemic state that is normally generated by the flock $\mathcal{F} \times \mathcal{G}$.*

Proof. Let $\mathbb{E}_{\mathcal{F} \times \mathcal{G}}$ denote the epistemic state that is normally generated by the flock $\mathcal{F} \times \mathcal{G}$. This epistemic state contains admissible states of the form $\Gamma \cup \Phi$, where $\Gamma \in \mathcal{F}_\downarrow$ and $\Phi \in \mathcal{G}_\downarrow$, while admissible states of $\mathbb{E}_\mathcal{F} \times \mathbb{E}_\mathcal{G}$ are pairs (Γ, Φ). However, due to the disjointness assumption, we can establish an obvious one-to-one correspondence between these two sets of admissible states. Clearly, counterpart admissible states under this correspondence have the same label, namely $\mathrm{Cl}(\Gamma \cup \Phi)$. Moreover, it is easy to verify that this correspondence preserves the preference relation, namely

$$(\Gamma, \Phi) \prec (\Gamma', \Phi') \text{ in } \mathbb{E}_\mathcal{F} \times \mathbb{E}_\mathcal{G} \text{ iff } \Gamma \cup \Phi \subset \Gamma' \cup \Phi' \text{ in } \mathbb{E}_{\mathcal{F} \times \mathcal{G}}$$

This shows that the above correspondence is actually an isomorphism between $\mathbb{E}_\mathcal{F} \times \mathbb{E}_\mathcal{G}$ and $\mathbb{E}_{\mathcal{F} \times \mathcal{G}}$. $\square$

13.1.2 Prioritized merge

A prioritized merge of an epistemic state $\mathbb{E}_1$ with an epistemic state $\mathbb{E}_2$ is obtained as a merge in which the state $\mathbb{E}_2$ is assigned a higher priority than $\mathbb{E}_1$. Accordingly, the resulting preference relation is defined as a lexicographic order in which we compare first the admissible states from $\mathbb{E}_2$, and only if they are equal, compare the corresponding admissible states of $\mathbb{E}_1$. This order assigns a greater importance to the admissible states of $\mathbb{E}_2$, so an admissible state (s_1, s_2) will be preferred to any admissible state (t_1, t_2) for which $t_2 \prec s_2$, irrespective of the preferences between s_1 and t_1. Clearly, $\mathbb{E}_1 \ltimes \mathbb{E}_2$ will not be a commutative operation. It can be easily verified, however, that prioritized merge is an associative operation, that is,

$(\mathbb{E}_1 \ltimes \mathbb{E}_2) \ltimes \mathbb{E}_3$ is isomorphic to $\mathbb{E}_1 \ltimes (\mathbb{E}_2 \ltimes \mathbb{E}_3)$

Let us consider now the behavior of prioritized merge on base-generated epistemic states. Given two disjoint prioritized bases $(\Delta_1, \lhd_1)$ and $(\Delta_2, \lhd_2)$, we will construct a combined base $(\Delta_1 \cup \Delta_2, \vec{\lhd})$ such that $\vec{\lhd}$ is defined as follows:

$A \vec{\lhd} B \equiv$ either $(A, B \in \Delta_1 \wedge A \lhd_1 B)$, or $(A, B \in \Delta_2 \wedge A \lhd_2 B)$, or $(A \in \Delta_2 \wedge B \in \Delta_1)$.

Thus, $\vec{\lhd}$ is obtained by combining the source priority relations and making any propositions from Δ_2 prior to all propositions in Δ_1. The following result shows that the resulting prioritized base gives an adequate representation of the prioritized merge of the epistemic states that are normally generated by the source bases.

Lemma 13.1.5. *If $\mathbb{E}_1$ and $\mathbb{E}_2$ are epistemic states that are normally generated, respectively, by prioritized bases $(\Delta_1, \lhd_1)$ and $(\Delta_2, \lhd_2)$ such that $\Delta_1 \cap \Delta_2 = \emptyset$, then $\mathbb{E}_1 \ltimes \mathbb{E}_2$ is isomorphic to an epistemic state that is normally generated by $(\Delta_1 \cup \Delta_2, \vec{\lhd})$.*

Proof. Using once more the isomorphism described in the proof of Theorem 13.1.1, we need only to show that the corresponding merge $\mathbb{E}_+$ is a prioritized merge. Since all propositions from Δ_2 are prior to propositions from Δ_1, $\Gamma_1 \cup \Gamma_2 \preceq_{\vec{\lhd}} \Phi_1 \cup \Phi_2$ in $\mathbb{E}$ if and only if either $\Gamma_2 \prec_2 \Phi_2$ (in which case for any proposition from $\Gamma_1 \backslash \Phi_1$ there is a prior proposition in $\Phi_2 \backslash \Gamma_2$), or else $\Gamma_2 = \Phi_2$ and $\Gamma_1 \prec \Phi_1$. $\square$

Now we will show that prioritized merge also preserves normal similarity. Coupled with similar results for contraction and pure merge, proved earlier, this will demonstrate, in effect, that normal similarity of epistemic states is preserved by all basic belief change operations.

Theorem 13.1.4. *If $\mathbb{E}_1$ and $\mathbb{E}_2$ are normally similar, respectively, to $\mathbb{E}_1'$ and $\mathbb{E}_2'$, then $\mathbb{E}_1 \ltimes \mathbb{E}_2$ is normally similar to $\mathbb{E}_1' \ltimes \mathbb{E}_2'$.*

Proof. It is sufficient to show the claim separately for the two component epistemic states. Moreover, since the proofs are completely analogous, we will prove only that if $\mathbb{E}_1$ is normally similar to $\mathbb{E}$, then $\mathbb{E}_1 \ltimes \mathbb{E}_2$ is normally similar to $\mathbb{E} \ltimes \mathbb{E}_2$.

Let (s_1, s_2) be a normal admissible state in $\mathbb{E}_1 \times \mathbb{E}_2$. Then both s_1 and s_2 are normal admissible states in their respective epistemic states (see the corresponding proof for pure merge). Consequently, there must exist an admissible state s in $\mathbb{E}$ such that $s \overset{\circ}{=} s_1$ and $\Uparrow s_1 \ll \Uparrow s$. Let us consider an admissible state (s, s_2) in $\mathbb{E} \times \mathbb{E}_2$. Clearly, $(s_1, s_2) \overset{\circ}{=} (s, s_2)$. Consequently, it is sufficient to show that $\Uparrow(s_1, s_2) \ll \Uparrow(s, s_2)$.

Assume that $(s, s_2) \prec (t, t_2)$ in $\mathbb{E} \times \mathbb{E}_2$. Suppose first that $s_2 \prec t_2$. Note that by Lemma 4.3.3, $\mathbb{E}$ contains a normal admissible state t' such that $t \preceq t'$ and $l(t') \subseteq l(t)$. Consequently, there exists an admissible state t_1 in $\mathbb{E}_1$ that is equal to t'. Since $s_2 \prec t_2$, we have that $(s_1, s_2) \prec (t_1, t_2)$ in $\mathbb{E}_1 \times \mathbb{E}_2$. In addition, $l((t_1, t_2)) \subseteq l((t, t_2))$, as required. Suppose now that $s_2 = t_2$, and hence $s \prec t$. Since $\Uparrow s_1 \ll \Uparrow s$, there must exist t_1 in $\mathbb{E}_1$ such that $s_1 \prec t_1$ and $l(t_1) \subseteq l(t)$. Consequently, $(s_1, s_2) \prec (t_1, t_2)$ in $\mathbb{E}_1 \times \mathbb{E}_2$, and $l((t_1, t_2)) \subseteq l((t, t_2))$. This shows that $\Uparrow(s_1, s_2) \ll \Uparrow(s, s_2)$. A similar proof can be given for the second condition of normal similarity. Consequently, $\mathbb{E}_1 \ltimes \mathbb{E}_2$ is normally similar to $\mathbb{E} \ltimes \mathbb{E}_2$. $\qquad \Box$

For what follows, it is important to observe that prioritized merge preserves linearity of epistemic states. This follows immediately from the definition of the combined preference relation.

Lemma 13.1.6. *If $\mathbb{E}_1$ and $\mathbb{E}_2$ are linear epistemic states, then $\mathbb{E}_1 \ltimes \mathbb{E}_2$ will also be linear.*

As we will see in the next chapter, in the linear case the operation of prioritized merge will correspond to the entrenchment revision operation suggested in [Nay94].

13.2 Basic expansions

In a somewhat roundabout way, we have nevertheless reached the point where we can give a definition of expansion in the framework of epistemic states.

Generally speaking, while contractions remove admissible belief states, expansions of epistemic states with a new proposition should involve creating new admissible belief states, namely belief states that support the proposition being added. A simplest and most natural way to achieve this, which is actually suggested by the AGM theory, consists in adding the new proposition to existing admissible belief sets and taking the logical closure of the result. There are two main choices, however, that are open for us in doing this in the framework of epistemic states. First, we can create in each case a new admissible state side by side with the old one or, alternatively, label an existing admissible state with a new, expanded belief set. For reasons that will become clear, the latter operation will be called a *knowledge expansion* in what follows. Second, we can add the new proposition to all admissible belief states, or only to some of them (e.g., to preferred ones). This distinction is reflected below in the difference between *basic* and *flat* expansions.

In addition to the above options, expansions of epistemic states have also another, no less important task, namely determining the place of the newly added admissible states in the preference structure; this will reflect the priority of the new proposition with respect to the information represented by the epistemic state. Accordingly, the new proposition is not sufficient, by itself, for determining the resulting expansion, unless we know (or stipulate) in advance its priority relations to admissible states of the source epistemic state. Actually, this idea has already been exploited in the literature; for linear (ranked) epistemic states, it takes the form of adding a proposition supplied with its rank (see, e.g., [Bre91a, Wil94]). It turns out, however, that we have an opportunity to describe the process of expansion in a purely qualitative and context-independent way.

The framework of epistemic states suggests that a strongest way of adding a new *belief* consists in making it a basic proposition of the new epistemic state. This is captured by the notion of a basic expansion described in this section.

Basic expansions introduce new propositions into an epistemic framework in such a way that they are treated as freely combined with other potential beliefs. As we will see, if an epistemic state is base-generated, such an expansion amounts to an addition of a proposition to the base. This understanding of expansions is presupposed in practically all foundational approaches to belief change. In addition, the expansion operation should determine the place of the newly added proposition in the dependence (or priority) structure. This is achieved by defining the preferences between newly added admissible belief states and old ones.

The following definition provides a *generic* description of basic expansions on epistemic states that is based on a generic notion of merging.

For any proposition A, we will denote by $\mathbb{E}^A$ an epistemic state that is normally generated by a singular base $\{A\}$. This epistemic state consists of just two theories, $\mathrm{Cl}(\mathbf{t})$ and $\mathrm{Cl}(A)$, and it gives a most 'pure' expression of the belief in A. Now the main idea behind the definition below is that an expansion of an epistemic state with respect to A amounts to merging it with $\mathbb{E}^A$.

Definition 13.2.1. *A basic expansion of an epistemic state $\mathbb{E}$ with respect to a proposition A is a merge of $\mathbb{E}$ and the epistemic state $\mathbb{E}^A$.*

Unfolding the above definition, we obtain that each admissible state s from $\mathbb{E}$ is transformed into two admissible states, namely $(s, \{A\})$ and $(s, \emptyset)$. Note that the latter admissible state have the same label as s. Moreover, the constraints on the combined preference relation imply that such admissible states are ordered in the expanded epistemic state exactly as their counterparts in $\mathbb{E}$. Consequently, the expanded epistemic state can actually be seen as an 'expansion' of the source epistemic state with new admissible states. Using this identification, we can give the following direct generic definition of basic expansions; as can be easily verified, it is equivalent to the source one.

Definition 13.2.2. *A basic expansion of an epistemic state* $\mathbb{E} = (\mathcal{S}, l, \prec$
*) with respect to a proposition A is an epistemic state $\mathbb{E}_+ = (\mathcal{S}_+, l_+, \prec_+)$
satisfying the following conditions:*

- *$\mathcal{S}_+ = \mathcal{S} \cup \mathcal{S}^A$, where $\mathcal{S}^A = \{s_A \mid s \in \mathcal{S}\}$ is a set of new admissible belief
  states;*
- *The labelling function l_+ coincides with l on admissible states from $\mathcal{S}$, while
  for any $s_A \in \mathcal{S}^A$, $l_+(s_A) = \mathrm{Cl}(A, l(s))$;*
- *The preference relation $\prec_+$ coincides with $\prec$ on $\mathcal{S}$ and satisfies the following two conditions, for any $s, t \in \mathcal{S}$:*
  1. $s \prec_+ s_A$;
  2. $s_A \prec_+ t_A$ if and only if $s \prec t$.

As we said, the aim of a basic expansion consists in adding a proposition
to an epistemic state as a basic proposition. To begin with, the following
result shows that basic expansion preserves basic propositions; it is immediate
consequence of our earlier results on merging.

Lemma 13.2.1. *If $\mathbb{E}_+$ is a basic expansion of $\mathbb{E}$ with respect to A, then A
itself, and any basic proposition of $\mathbb{E}$ are basic propositions of $\mathbb{E}_+$.*

An interesting question that might arise at this point is what will happen
if we will expand an epistemic state with a proposition that is already basic
in it. As we have said, however, an expansion operation not only adds new
propositions, it also establishes their place in the priority structure. For example, it may raise the priority of a given basic proposition in an epistemic
state. In this case, basic expansion may produce a non-trivial change even
when we add a proposition that is already basic. Examples of such changes
will be given below.

As an application of the general result proved in the preceding section,
we have that basic expansions of base generated states correspond to adding
the new proposition to the base. Namely, given a prioritized base $(\Delta, \lhd)$ and
a new proposition $A \notin \Delta$, we will consider an extended base $(\Delta \cup \{A\}, \lhd_+)$
such that $\lhd$ coincides with the restriction of $\lhd_+$ to Δ. Then we have:

Lemma 13.2.2. *If $\mathbb{E}$ is an epistemic state that is normally generated by
$(\Delta, \lhd)$, then the epistemic state normally generated by $(\Delta \cup \{A\}, \lhd_+)$ is isomorphic to a basic expansion of $\mathbb{E}$ with respect to A.*

13.2.1 Belief expansions

As any other kind of change in epistemic states, expansions generate corresponding changes in belief sets of epistemic states. As we will show now, basic
expansions generate in this sense precisely AGM belief expansion functions.

Recall that ordinary AGM expansions of belief sets are defined directly
via the equation

$$\mathbf{K} + A = \mathrm{Th}(\mathbf{K} \cup \{A\}),$$

where Th is the background classical consequence relation (see [Gär88]). Notice, however, that the latter consequence relation does not play an essential role in this definition, since it can be easily shown that if $\mathbf{K}$ is a theory of Th, then $\mathrm{Th}(\mathbf{K} \cup \{A\})$ will coincide with $\mathrm{Cl}(\mathbf{K} \cup \{A\})$.

The following lemma shows that basic expansions generate the same change in belief sets as corresponding AGM expansions:

Lemma 13.2.3. *If $\mathbb{E}_+$ is a basic expansion of $\mathbb{E}$ with respect to A, then its belief set coincides with $\mathrm{Cl}(\mathbf{B}_\mathbb{E} \cup \{A\})$.*

Proof. In order to prove the claim, it is sufficient to show that maximally preferred admissible states of $\mathbb{E}_+$ are precisely admissible states of the form s_A, where s is a maximally preferred admissible state in $\mathbb{E}$. We show first that each such state is preferred in $\mathbb{E}_+$. Indeed, if $s_A \prec t_A$, then $s \prec t$, which is impossible. Similarly, if $s_A \prec t$, then $s_A \prec t_A$, and we return to the first case. In the other direction, any old state t is subordinated to the new state t_A, so only new admissible states could be preferred. In addition, if $s \prec t$ implies $s_A \prec t_A$, so any preferred admissible state s_A should be such that s is a maximally preferred admissible state in $\mathbb{E}$.

As a result, the belief set of $\mathbb{E}_+$, which is an intersection of all theories corresponding to preferred admissible states, can be obtained by adding A to the intersection of all theories corresponding to preferred admissible states of $\mathbb{E}$, while the latter intersection is precisely the belief set of $\mathbb{E}$. Hence the result. $\qquad\square$

Thus, belief expansions generated by basic expansions of epistemic states behave just as AGM expansions: the underlying epistemic state plays no role in determining the resulting expanded belief set, since the latter can be obtained by a direct addition of new propositions to the source belief set.

The following example shows, however, that the above result cannot be generalized to arbitrary merges.

Example 13.2.1. Let $\mathbb{E}_1$ and $\mathbb{E}_2$ be pure epistemic states such that $\mathbb{E}_1$ contains all theories of the form $\mathrm{Cl}(p_i \to q)$, while $\mathbb{E}_2$ contains a single theory u which is a deductive closure of all p_i. The belief set of $\mathbb{E}_1$ is an intersection of all theories of the latter, so it contains only logical tautologies. However, the belief set of $\mathbb{E}_1 \times \mathbb{E}_2$ is $\mathrm{Cl}(\{q\} \cup u)$, which is distinct from $\mathrm{Cl}(u \cup \mathbf{B}_{\mathbb{E}_1})$.

It should also be kept in mind that identical expansions of belief sets can be produced by expansions of different epistemic states, and even by different basic expansions of the same epistemic state. These differences will be revealed in subsequent contractions and revisions of the expanded belief set.

Example 13.2.2. Expansions of an epistemic state with $A \wedge B$ will always produce the same expanded belief set as a sequence of expansions with respect to A and B, but only the latter sequence of expansions makes both A and B basic propositions. Consequently, subsequent contraction of $A \wedge B$ will delete all new admissible states introduced after expanding with $A \wedge B$. In the second case, however, the subsequent contraction of $A \wedge B$ will usually retain theories of the form $\mathrm{Cl}(u, A)$ and $\mathrm{Cl}(u, B)$ introduced on the preceding step. In the principal case this would retain $A \vee B$ in the resulting belief set.

13.2.2 Pure expansion

Just as with merge operations, there are two basic expansion *operations* on epistemic states that conform to the generic definition. For these operations, the resulting expanded epistemic state will already be uniquely determined, since they will be based on context-independent conditions establishing the priority of the newly added proposition.

A pure basic expansion is a change resulting from adding the new proposition as an independent piece of information, that is, as a proposition that is not related to others with respect to priority. As could be anticipated, such an expansion is definable as a special case of pure merge.

Definition 13.2.3. *A pure basic expansion of* $\mathbb{E}$ *with respect to* A *(denoted by* $\mathbb{E} + A$*) is a pure merge of* $\mathbb{E}$ *with* $\mathbb{E}^A$.

Alternatively, a pure basic expansion can be defined by the requirement that the new preference relation is a *least* strict partial order satisfying the conditions in the explicit generic definition of a basic expansion. Being applied to base-generated epistemic states, the operation of a pure expansion corresponds to the straightforward extension of a prioritized base $(\Delta, \lhd)$ to the prioritized base $(\Delta \cup \{A\}, \lhd)$ which keeps the source priority relation intact. In other words, in the extended base A is not related by priority to any proposition from Δ. In the special case when there is no priority relation, a pure basic expansion amounts simply to an addition of A to the base.

Corollary 13.2.1. *If* $\mathbb{E}$ *is normally generated by* $(\Delta, \lhd)$, *and* $A \notin \Delta$, *then* $\mathbb{E} + A$ *is isomorphic to an epistemic state normally generated by* $(\Delta \cup \{A\}, \lhd)$.

Recall that the condition that A does not belong to Δ is essential for the adequacy of the above claim. As we have said, however, this condition can be easily satisfied, for example by replacing A by its logical equivalent that does not appear in Δ. Let us consider the following example that illustrates the behavior of pure basic expansions in a rather special, but instructive, case.

Example 13.2.3. A prioritized default base $\Delta = \{A_1, B_1\}$ consists of two logically independent propositions such that $B_1 \lhd A_1$. This prioritized base generates a corresponding epistemic state $\mathbb{E}$, which is actually a standard epistemic state having four theories that are linearly ordered by preference:

$$\mathrm{Cl}(\emptyset) \prec \mathrm{Cl}(A_1) \prec \mathrm{Cl}(B_1) \prec \mathrm{Cl}(A_1 \wedge B_1)$$

A pure basic expansion $\mathbb{E} \overset{\sim}{+} A$ of this epistemic state with respect to a proposition A that is distinct, but logically equivalent, to A_1 results in an epistemic state that contains eight admissible belief states; clearly, it will be non-standard. But since it will be union-closed, by eliminating non-normal admissible states we can reduce it to a standard epistemic state, which in our case is describable as follows:

$$\mathrm{Cl}(\emptyset) \prec \mathrm{Cl}(A_1) \prec \mathrm{Cl}(A_1 \wedge B_1) \qquad \mathrm{Cl}(\emptyset) \prec \mathrm{Cl}(B_1) \prec \mathrm{Cl}(A_1 \wedge B_1)$$

As can be easily verified, the above epistemic state coincides with an epistemic state generated by a pure base Δ with an empty priority relation. This is because the expansion improved the priority status of A_1 from the lowest priority to a neutral one. Note in this respect that if we would have an opposite prioritization on Δ, that is, $A_1 \lhd B_1$, then the same expansion would not change, in effect, the source epistemic state. In other words, $\mathbb{E} + A$ would be equivalent to $\mathbb{E}$.

The above example shows, in particular, that pure basic expansions can produce a non-trivial change in an epistemic state even if the added proposition is already basic in the latter. Note also that, though the source epistemic state in the above example was linear, the expanded epistemic state will not be linear. So, pure expansions do not preserve linearity of epistemic states (unlike the prioritized expansion described below).

Since pure merge is a commutative and associative operation, pure expansions will also be commutative. Actually, if $\mathbb{E}^A$ and $\mathbb{E}^B$ are epistemic states generated, respectively, by distinct bases $\{A\}$ and $\{B\}$, then their pure merge $\mathbb{E}^A \times \mathbb{E}^B$ is isomorphic to an epistemic state $\mathbb{E}^{\{A,B\}}$ normally generated by the base $\{A, B\}$. Consequently, we immediately obtain

$$(\mathbb{E} + A) + B = (\mathbb{E} + B) + A = \mathbb{E} \times \mathbb{E}^{\{A,B\}}$$

Clearly, the above equalities are extendable to arbitrary sequences of pure expansions.

As before, for a set of propositions w, we will denote by $A \to w$ the set of all implications $A \to B$ such that $B \in w$. Note that, for an admissible state s, $s \in]A \to w[$ means then that $\mathrm{Cl}(A, l(s))$ is disjoint from w.

The following technical lemma gives an explicit description of preferred admissible states in $\mathbb{E} + A$ in terms of preferred admissible states of $\mathbb{E}$. The proof presents no difficulty, and we leave it to the reader.

Lemma 13.2.4. *If $\mathbb{E} + A$ is a pure expansion of $\mathbb{E}$, then*

- *s_A is a preferred admissible state in $]w[$ wrt $\mathbb{E} + A$ iff s is a preferred admissible state in $]A \to w[$ wrt $\mathbb{E}$;*
- *s is a preferred admissible state in $]w[$ wrt $\mathbb{E} + A$ iff it is a preferred admissible state in $]w[$ wrt $\mathbb{E}$, and $s \notin]A \to w[$.*

As an immediate consequence of the above lemma, we have the following characterization of the selection function of $\mathbb{E} + A$ in terms of the selection function of $\mathbb{E}$.

Corollary 13.2.2. *If f and f_A are selection functions corresponding, respectively, to $\mathbb{E}$ and $\mathbb{E} + A$, then, $u \in f_A(w)$ iff either $u = \mathrm{Cl}(A, v)$, for some $v \in f(A{\to}w)$, or $u \in f(w)$ and $\mathrm{Cl}(A, u) \cap w \neq \emptyset$.*

The most important fact about the above description is that the selection function of $\mathbb{E} + A$ is completely determined by the selection function of $\mathbb{E}$. Consequently, pure basic expansion preserves the relation of equivalence among epistemic states.

Corollary 13.2.3. *If $\mathbb{E}_1 \approx \mathbb{E}_2$, then $\mathbb{E}_1 + A \approx \mathbb{E}_2 + A$.*

It is important to observe in this respect that pure expansions do not preserve belief equivalence. The following example shows this.

Example 13.2.4. Let us return to Example 4.5.2 we have considered in Chapter 4. The example involved two belief equivalent standard epistemic states, namely $\mathbb{E}_1$ consisting of two theories $\mathrm{Cl}(p)$ and $\mathrm{Cl}(p \wedge q)$ with an empty preference relation, and $\mathbb{E}_2$ consisting of a single theory $\mathrm{Cl}(p)$. Now, let us expand both these epistemic states with r. Then the belief set of $\mathbb{E}_1 + r - (q \wedge r)$ will be $\mathrm{Cl}(p \wedge (q \vee r))$, while the belief set of $\mathbb{E}_2 + r - (q \wedge r)$ will be $\mathrm{Cl}(p \wedge r)$. This shows that $\mathbb{E}_1 + r$ is not belief equivalent to $\mathbb{E}_2 + r$.

The above example shows, in effect, that belief equivalence could not be taken as a general equivalence notion for epistemic states.

Another consequence of Lemma 13.2.4 is that pure basic expansions preserve smoothness of epistemic states.

Lemma 13.2.5. *If $\mathbb{E}$ is an m-smooth epistemic state, then $\mathbb{E} + A$ is m-smooth.*

Proof. Assume first that $s \in]w[$ in $\mathbb{E} + A$. Then $s \in]w[$ in $\mathbb{E}$, and hence there must exist a preferred admissible state t in $]w[$ such that $s \preceq t$. Now if $t \notin]A{\to}w[$, then t is clearly a preferred admissible state in $]w[$ wrt $\mathbb{E} + A$. Otherwise, t_A will be such a preferred state by Lemma 13.2.4.

Assume now that $s_A \in]w[$ in $\mathbb{E} + A$. Then $s \in]A{\to}w[$ in $\mathbb{E}$, and hence there must exist a preferred admissible state t in $]A{\to}w[$ such that $s \preceq t$. Clearly, $s_A \preceq t_A$, and t_A will be a preferred admissible state in $]w[$ by Lemma 13.2.4. Therefore, $\mathbb{E} + A$ is a smooth epistemic state. $\square$

Expansions of flocks. As we have seen earlier, pure merge generates a corresponding merge operation on flocks. Consequently, pure expansion corresponds in this sense to a certain expansion operation on flocks. This operation is described in the following definition.

Definition 13.2.4. *A basic expansion of a flock $\mathcal{F} = \{\Delta_i \mid i \in I\}$ with respect to a proposition A that does not belong to $\mathcal{F}$ is a flock $\mathcal{F} + A = \{\Delta_i \cup \{A\} \mid i \in I\}$.*

Thus, an expansion of a flock is obtained simply by adding the new proposition to each base from the flock. Our earlier results immediately imply that this operation exactly corresponds to a pure expansion of the associated epistemic state with A:

Theorem 13.2.1. *If $\mathbb{E}_{\mathcal{F}}$ is an epistemic state normally generated by the flock $\mathcal{F}$, and A does not belong to $\mathcal{F}$, then $\mathbb{E}_{\mathcal{F}} + A$ is isomorphic to the epistemic state normally generated by the flock $\mathcal{F} + A$.*

The above operation is quite similar in spirit to the operation of insertion into flocks used in [FUKV86], though the latter was intended to preserve consistency of the component bases, so they defined, in effect, the corresponding revision operation based on contraction and expansion in our sense (see the next chapter). Note, however, that our flock expansion is defined only when the added proposition does not appear in the flock. This constraint turns out to be essential for an intuitively satisfactory representation of expansions on flocks. The following example illustrates this.

Example 13.2.5. Let us return to the flock $\mathcal{F} = \{\{p\}, \{q\}\}$, where p and q denote, respectively, propositions "There is a university in Niamey", and "Niamey is a town in Nigeria". Recall that this flock is obtainable by contracting $p \wedge q$ from the base $\{p, q\}$. In other words, it reflects an informational situation in which we have reasons to believe in each of these propositions, but cannot believe in both.

Now let us expand the epistemic state $\mathbb{E}_{\mathcal{F}}$ with p. In accordance with the said above, this expansion can be modeled by expanding $\mathcal{F}$ with some proposition p' that is logically equivalent to p. In other words, the epistemic state generated by the flock $\mathcal{F} + p' = \{\{p', p\}, \{p', q\}\}$ will be equivalent to the expansion of $\mathbb{E}_{\mathcal{F}}$ with p. This flock sanctions belief in p in full accordance with our intuitions. Actually, it can be shown that the latter flock is reducible to a flock $\{\{p\}, \{p', q\}\}$ in the sense that the latter flock will produce an equivalent epistemic state, or even to a flock $\{\{p'\}, \{p, q\}\}$. However, p' cannot be replaced with p in all these flocks: the flock $\{\{p\}, \{p, q\}\}$ is already reducible to a single base $\{\{p, q\}\}$ in which both p and q are believed, contrary to our intuitions about the relevant situation: receiving a new support for believing that there is a university in Niamey should not force us to believe also that Niamey is a town in Nigeria. This also shows most vividly that a straightforward addition of p to each base in the flock $\{\{p\}, \{q\}\}$ does not produce intuitively satisfactory results.

An additional interesting aspect of the above representation is that, though we fully believe in p in the flock $\{\{p\}, \{p', q\}\}$, the option q has not been forgotten; if we will contract now p from the latter flock, we will obtain the flock $\{\{q\}\}$ which supports belief in q. A little reflection shows that this is exactly what would be reasonable to believe in this situation.

Remark. Unfortunately (especially for the author), the above example can also serve as a counterexample for the approach to expansions suggested in

[Boc99b, Boc00c]. Namely, the expansion operation on pure epistemic states defined in these papers also sanctioned an unjustified belief in $p \wedge q$ when p is added to the epistemic state corresponding to the flock $\{\{p\}, \{q\}\}$. It also has other shortcomings that we will discuss later. As we see it now, an adequate theory of belief change is not representable in the framework of pure epistemic states.

13.2.3 Prioritized expansion

The operation of a prioritized basic expansion is obtained as a result of assigning the added proposition a highest priority. It is representable via a prioritized merge of an epistemic state with the epistemic state normally generated by a base $\{A\}$.

Definition 13.2.5. A prioritized basic expansion *of an epistemic state* $\mathbb{E}$ *with respect to A (notation $\mathbb{E} \overrightarrow{+} A$) is an epistemic state* $\mathbb{E} \ltimes \mathbb{E}^A$.

By definition of the prioritized merge, the resulting preference relation makes any new admissible state s_A preferred to any old admissible state from $\mathbb{E}$.

Given a prioritized base $(\Delta, \lhd)$ and a proposition $A \notin \Delta$, a prioritized expansion with respect to A produces a prioritized base $(\Delta \cup \{A\}, \overrightarrow{\lhd})$ such that $\overrightarrow{\lhd}$ is obtained from $\lhd$ by adding priorities of the form $A \lhd D$, for every $D \in \Delta$:

Lemma 13.2.6. *If* $\mathbb{E}$ *is an epistemic state normally generated by* $(\Delta, \lhd)$*, and* $A \notin \Delta$*, then* $\mathbb{E} \overrightarrow{+} A$ *is isomorphic to an epistemic state normally generated by* $(\Delta \cup \{A\}, \overrightarrow{\lhd})$.

Let us return to the example we have considered in the preceding section.

Example 13.2.6. Let $\Delta = \{A_1, B_1\}$ be a prioritized default base consisting of two logically independent propositions such that $B_1 \lhd A_1$. As we have said, the corresponding base-generated epistemic state $\mathbb{E}$ is equivalent to a standard epistemic state having four theories that are linearly ordered by preference:

$$\mathrm{Cl}(\emptyset) \prec \mathrm{Cl}(A_1) \prec \mathrm{Cl}(B_1) \prec \mathrm{Cl}(A_1 \wedge B_1)$$

Let us consider now a prioritized expansion of $\mathbb{E}$ with respect to a proposition A that is logically equivalent to A_1. Then the resulting expanded epistemic state will be reducible to a standard epistemic state having the same admissible belief sets, though ordered as follows:

$$\mathrm{Cl}(\emptyset) \prec \mathrm{Cl}(B_1) \prec \mathrm{Cl}(A_1) \prec \mathrm{Cl}(A_1 \wedge B_1)$$

Thus, the prioritized expansion of $\mathbb{E}$ with respect to A resulted in reversing preferences between theories $\mathrm{Cl}(A_1)$ and $\mathrm{Cl}(B_1)$. Furthermore, it is easy to check that the latter epistemic state is generated by the same base Δ, though with an opposite priority between its elements, that is, by putting $A_1 \lhd B_1$. This shows that the net effect of adding A to the source prioritized base consists in raising the priority of A_1.

The above example shows that also for prioritized expansions adding a proposition that is already basic can lead to a non-trivial change corresponding to changing the priority relations of the proposition with other propositions from the base.

It can be easily seen that prioritized expansions do not commute: expanding with A and then with B makes B prior to A, while the reverse sequence of prioritized expansions would make A prior to B.

The following lemma describes preferred admissible states of an expanded epistemic state in terms of preferred admissible states of the source epistemic state. As for pure expansions above, this characterization will turns out to be useful in proving some important properties of prioritized expansions.

Lemma 13.2.7. *Let* $\mathbb{E}\overrightarrow{+}A$ *be a prioritized expansion of* $\mathbb{E}$. *Then*

- s_A *is a preferred admissible state in* $]w[$ *wrt* $\mathbb{E}\overrightarrow{+}A$ *iff* s *is a preferred admissible state in* $]A{\rightarrow}w[$ *wrt* $\mathbb{E}$;
- s *is a preferred admissible state in* $]w[$ *wrt* $\mathbb{E}\overrightarrow{+}A$ *iff it is a preferred admissible state in* $]w[$ *wrt* $\mathbb{E}$, *and* $]A{\rightarrow}w[= \emptyset$.

As an immediate consequence of the above lemma, we have the following characterization of the selection function of $\mathbb{E}\overrightarrow{+}A$ in terms of the selection function of $\mathbb{E}$.

Corollary 13.2.4. $u \in f_{\mathbb{E}\overrightarrow{+}A}(w)$ *iff either* $u = \mathrm{Cl}(A,v)$, *for some* $v \in f_{\mathbb{E}}(A{\rightarrow}w)$, *or* $u \in f(w)$ *and* $f_{\mathbb{E}}(A{\rightarrow}w) = \emptyset$.

The above description shows that the selection function of $\mathbb{E}\overrightarrow{+}A$ is completely determined by the selection function of $\mathbb{E}$. Consequently, prioritized expansions preserve the relation of equivalence among epistemic states.

Corollary 13.2.5. *If* $\mathbb{E}_1 \approx \mathbb{E}_2$, *then* $\mathbb{E}_1 \overrightarrow{+} A \approx \mathbb{E}_2 \overrightarrow{+} A$.

Another consequence of Lemma 13.2.7 is that prioritized expansions preserve smoothness of epistemic states. The proof is similar to the corresponding proof for pure basic expansions, so we leave it as an exercise to the reader.

Lemma 13.2.8. *If* $\mathbb{E}$ *is an* m-*smooth epistemic state, then* $\mathbb{E}\overrightarrow{+}A$ *is* m-*smooth.*

13.3 Knowledge expansion

In the following sections we will briefly consider a number of other expansion operations that are definable in the framework of epistemic states. Knowledge expansions, described in this section, constitute perhaps the most important kind among them.

By a knowledge expansion we will mean an operation on epistemic states that amounts to *replacement* of admissible belief sets by their expansions. Thus, the main difference between knowledge expansions and basic expansions described earlier is that knowledge expansions 'forget' the original admissible belief states and replace them with new ones. This distinction allows to account for some subtle differences between various revision operations suggested in the literature.

Let us denote by $\mathbb{E}_A$ an epistemic state that is base-generated by $\{A\}$. This epistemic state contains a single theory $\mathrm{Cl}(A)$, and hence it naturally represents an information that A is known. Now, a *knowledge expansion* of $\mathbb{E}$ with A is definable as a merge of $\mathbb{E}$ with $\mathbb{E}_A$. Note that any merge operation produces the same result in this case; the resulting epistemic state can be described directly as follows.

Definition 13.3.1. *A* knowledge expansion *of a state* $\mathbb{E} = (\mathcal{S}, l, \prec)$ *with respect to* A *is an epistemic state* $\mathbb{E} \oplus A = (\mathcal{S}, l^A, \prec)$ *such that, for any* $s \in \mathcal{S}$, $l^A(s) = \mathrm{Cl}(l(s), A)$.

By the above definition, a knowledge expansion of an epistemic state is obtained by replacing all original admissible belief sets with their expansions that already include the new proposition. The name knowledge expansion is justified by the fact that this change amounts, in effect, to incorporating the new proposition into the knowledge set of an epistemic state. In other words, it amounts to changing the internal logic of an epistemic state. Apparently, it gives a faithful representation of the proposal made [FH97, FH99], according to which addition of new factual observations should be considered as an addition to the knowledge of the agent rather to her beliefs.

There exists a significant similarity between basic expansions and knowledge expansions. Note that any expansion of an epistemic state conforming to the generic definition of a basic expansion uniquely determines the preference order among new admissible states. And it can be easily seen that knowledge expansion coincides with basic expansion when restricted to the new admissible states.

Despite the above similarity, there is an essential difference between the two kinds of expansions: basic expansions incorporate new propositions as new beliefs, while knowledge expansions treat them as new knowledge. Thus, knowledge expansion is *irreversible*: if A is added to the knowledge set of an epistemic state, then neither contractions, nor expansions of this state could remove it from there. This means, in particular, that all subsequent expansions and additions have to be consistent with such an addition. In other words, inconsistent sequences of knowledge expansions should be excluded (cf. [FH99]).

There is also another, global effect of using knowledge expansions. Notice that contraction reduces, in general, the number of admissible belief states in an epistemic state, while knowledge expansion retains the number of admissible states intact. Consequently, if we would restrict our belief change operations only to contractions and knowledge expansions, this would lead to an inevitable 'degradation' of any epistemic state in a sufficiently long series of belief changes to rudimentary epistemic states consisting, at best, of a single admissible belief state. In such epistemic states belief and knowledge would coincide. Note that this observation does not depend on whether expansions extend knowledge or not. Rather, it refers to the forgetful character of knowledge expansions that eliminate old admissible states while adding new ones.

The following lemma describes the selection function of $\mathbb{E} \oplus A$ in terms of the selection function for $\mathbb{E}$. The proof is immediate.

Lemma 13.3.1. $u \in f_{\mathbb{E} \oplus A}(w)$ *iff* $u = \mathrm{Cl}(v \cup \{A\})$, *for some* $v \in f_{\mathbb{E}}(A \rightarrow w)$.

Again, since the new selection function is uniquely determined by the source one, we have that knowledge expansions preserve equivalence of epistemic states.

Corollary 13.3.1. *If* $\mathbb{E}_1 \approx \mathbb{E}_2$, *then* $\mathbb{E}_1 \oplus A \approx \mathbb{E}_2 \oplus A$.

Knowledge expansions have a quite simple dynamic behavior. Actually, most of their dynamic properties are obtainable as a consequence of the following dynamic postulate:

Conjunction $\mathbb{E} \oplus A \oplus B = \mathbb{E} \oplus A \wedge B$.

The above postulate can be considered as a characteristic property of knowledge expansions. It implies, in particular, that knowledge expansions commute, that is, $\mathbb{E} \oplus A \oplus B = \mathbb{E} \oplus B \oplus A$. Also, it shows that multiple expansions are reducible to singular ones, namely to expansions with conjunction of corresponding propositions.

13.4 Flat expansions

Flat expansion, described in this section, is actually a generalization of the system suggested by Boutilier in [Bou96]. It produces smaller changes in the underlying epistemic state as compared with basic expansions, though in appropriate circumstances it will also achieve the aim of adding the new proposition to the resulting belief set. In the general case, however, the belief change produced by such expansion operations will correspond to belief revision (see the next chapter). These operations could serve as an illustration that possible ways of expanding epistemic states are not restricted, in principle, to basic expansions and merge operations.

To begin with, note that only admissible states consistent with the added proposition A are relevant for producing *consistent* output in response to expansion with respect to A. Moreover, it is natural to assume that only preferred admissible states among them should participate in forming such an output. Clearly, we can achieve consistency by contracting $\neg A$ from the epistemic state before (or after) performing the expansion with respect to A. Actually, this will give us the notion of *revision* of epistemic states that we will discuss in the next Chapter. It turns out, however, that revisions are by no means the only way of preserving consistency in the framework of epistemic states. For example, the same resulting belief set will be obtained if we will expand only preferred admissible states consistent with A, but will make these expanded admissible states preferred to all old admissible states. This operation, that we will call flat expansion, is described in the following definition.

Definition 13.4.1. *A flat expansion of epistemic state* $\mathbb{E} = (\mathcal{S}, l, \prec)$ *with respect to A is an epistemic state* $\mathbb{E} \hat{+} A = (\mathcal{S}_A, l_A, \prec_A)$ *such that:*

- $\mathcal{S}_A = \mathcal{S} \cup \mathcal{S}^A$, *where* $\mathcal{S}^A = \{s_A \mid s \text{ is preferred in }]\neg A[\}$ *is a new set of admissible belief states;*
- *The labelling function l_A coincides with l on $\mathcal{S}$, while for any $s_A \in \mathcal{S}^A$, $l_A(s_A) = \mathrm{Cl}(A, l(s))$;*
- *The preference relation $\prec_A$ is a least extension of $\prec$ that satisfies the condition $t \prec_A s_A$, for any $t \in \mathcal{S}$ and $s_A \in \mathcal{S}^A$.*

Thus, a flat expansion of an epistemic state with A is obtained by expanding its preferred admissible states consistent with A, and making any new, expanded admissible state preferred to any old admissible state. Actually, this operation has the same design as the prioritized expansion described earlier, except that it produces a smaller change in epistemic states.

[Bou96] has suggested a 'natural' revision operation on epistemic entrenchment relations intended to produce a minimal transformation of the latter that would give a required revision of associated belief sets. In the context of associated Grove's possible worlds models, this operation amounted to 'elevating' all preferred possible worlds satisfying the added proposition to the status of maximally preferred worlds (so they will determine the new belief set), while the ordering for the rest of the worlds was retained intact. As can be easily verified, this operation corresponds to a flat expansion of the associated epistemic state (more exactly, it is similar to the latter). Accordingly, Boutilier's operation can be seen as a special (i.e. modular) case of flat expansion.

To begin with, we have the following characterization of the selection function of $\mathbb{E} \hat{+} A$ in terms of the selection function of $\mathbb{E}$.

Lemma 13.4.1. $u \in f_{\mathbb{E}+A}(w)$ *iff either* $u \in f_{\mathbb{E}}(w)$ *and* $\mathrm{Cl}(v, A) \cap w \neq \emptyset$, *for any* $v \in f_{\mathbb{E}}(\neg A)$, *or else* $u \cap w \neq \emptyset$, *and there exists* $v \in f_{\mathbb{E}}(\neg A)$ *such that* $u = \mathrm{Cl}(A, v)$.

Proof. The above description follows from the following two conditions that can be easily verified.

(a) A new admissible state s_A is a preferred state in $]x[$ with respect to $\mathbb{E}\hat{+}A$ iff s is a preferred state consistent with A with respect to $\mathbb{E}$, and $l_A(s_A) \cap x = \emptyset$;

(b) An old admissible state s is a preferred state in $]x[$ with respect to $\mathbb{E}\hat{+}A$ iff s is a preferred state $]x[$ with respect to $\mathbb{E}$, and no new admissible state belongs to $]x[$. $\qquad\square$

The above description shows that the selection function of $\mathbb{E} + A$ is completely determined by the selection function of $\mathbb{E}$. Consequently, flat expansions preserve the relation of equivalence among epistemic states.

Corollary 13.4.1. *If* $\mathbb{E}_1 \approx \mathbb{E}_2$, *then* $\mathbb{E}_1 \hat{+} A \approx \mathbb{E}_2 \hat{+} A$.

Unlike the basic expansions, flat expansions do not preserve union-closure, so flat expansions of base-generated epistemic states are not representable in terms of transformations of bases. Flat expansions also do not commute. However, just as basic prioritized expansions, they preserve linearity of epistemic states. Actually, we will see that in the latter case flat expansions will correspond to Boutilier's natural revisions of epistemic entrenchment.

Finally, notice that, though flat expansions are expansions of epistemic states in the sense that they add new admissible states, changes of belief sets, generated by such expansions will not correspond to AGM expansions. Rather, they will correspond to belief revisions in the AGM sense (see the next chapter).

Flat L-expansions. Flat L-expansion is a variant of a flat expansion in which the new admissible states replace the old ones (similarly to knowledge expansions).

Definition 13.4.2. *Let* $\mathbb{E} = \langle S, l, \prec \rangle$ *be an epistemic state, and* S^A *the set of preferred admissible states in* $]\neg A[$. *Then a flat L-expansion of* $\mathbb{E}$ *with respect to* A *is an epistemic state* $\mathbb{E}\hat{\oplus} A = \langle S, l_A, \prec \rangle$ *such that* $l_A(s) = l(s)$, *for any* $s \in S \setminus S^A$, *and* $l_A(s) = \mathrm{Cl}(l(s), A)$, *for any* $s \in S^A$.

In most cases, flat L-expansion does not change the knowledge set of an epistemic state, so it behaves differently from knowledge expansion in this respect. An important property of flat L-expansions is that they preserve linearity of epistemic states. Actually, we will see in the next chapter that in the latter case revision operations based on this notion of expansion correspond to belief revision operations suggested by Lehmann in [Leh95].

Note that flat L-expansions share with knowledge expansions the property of preserving the set of admissible belief states. As we have said earlier, this leads to an inevitable degradation of belief change systems based solely on contractions and flat L-expansions. Actually, this feature can be taken to be responsible for a similar degradation behavior of the corresponding belief revision operation discussed in [Leh95]. Furthermore, flat L-expansions fall out of our general approach in yet another respect, namely, they do not preserve equivalence of epistemic states.

Example 13.4.1. Let us consider the following two epistemic states. A state $\mathbb{E}_1$ contains three admissible states such that $l(s) = l(t) = \mathrm{Cl}(C)$, $l(r) = \mathrm{Cl}(B)$, and $t \prec r$. The second epistemic state $\mathbb{E}_2$ is obtained from $\mathbb{E}_1$ by removing the admissible state t; as can be seen, its preference relation will be empty.

It can be easily checked that $\mathbb{E}_1$ and $\mathbb{E}_2$ are equivalent epistemic states (moreover, they are similar — see the corresponding definitions in Chapter 4). Now, let us perform a flat L-expansion of both these states with a proposition A that is consistent with both B and C. Then the labels of the admissible states s and r will be expanded with A. Since $t \not\prec s$ in $\mathbb{E}_1 \hat{\oplus} A$, both s and t will be preferred admissible states in $]B[$ with respect to $\mathbb{E}_1 \hat{\oplus} A$, and hence we would have $f_{\mathbb{E}_1 \hat{\oplus} A}(B) = \{\mathrm{Cl}(C), \mathrm{Cl}(A \wedge C)\}$. It can be easily seen, however, that $f_{\mathbb{E}_2 \hat{\oplus} A}(B) = \{\mathrm{Cl}(A \wedge C)\}$, so the resulting epistemic states $\mathbb{E}_1 \hat{\oplus} A$ and $\mathbb{E}_2 \hat{\oplus} A$ will not be equivalent.

This ends our rather cursory overview of the alternative notions of expansion that are definable in the framework of epistemic states. As the reader could notice, we have not attempted to adjudicate between different options. Rather, our aim was to give a general picture of the opportunities open to us in modelling addition of information to epistemic states. A further insight into these options will be obtained in the next chapter, where these kinds of expansion will be put to use as part of more complex epistemic changes.

14. Compound and Derived Changes

In this last chapter we will study some compound operations that are definable in our framework, the most important among them being the revision operation. Also, we will briefly discuss changes in inference and entrenchment relations that are generated by expansions and revisions of epistemic states. Finally, we will single out sets of epistemic states that form 'natural classes' with respect to the main operations discussed in the previous chapters.

14.1 Consolidation and revision

Expansions may sometimes produce inconsistent admissible belief sets, or even expanded epistemic states with an inconsistent set of beliefs. Unlike the AGM setting, however, the framework of epistemic states is much more tolerant to such outcomes. For example, such epistemic states still produce non-trivial inference relations; in particular, they give consistent responses to factual inputs. Moreover, it turns out that inconsistent admissible states are irrelevant for determining such responses.

A most obvious way of dealing with inconsistent admissible states consists simply in eliminating them. This is the essence of Hansson's consolidation operation that amounts to contracting falsity $\mathbf{f}$ from an epistemic state. Note that, since the selection function associated with an epistemic state cannot choose inconsistent admissible belief sets, we immediately obtain that *any epistemic state $\mathbb{E}$ is equivalent to its consolidation $\mathbb{E} - \mathbf{f}$*. Consequently, inconsistent admissible states can be eliminated from epistemic states without changing their functional behavior. In particular, the refined belief set, that is, the belief set of $\mathbb{E} - \mathbf{f}$, constitutes an arguably reasonable answer to the question of what we should believe in epistemic states containing inconsistent admissible states.

Since inconsistency may arise only in expansions or merge, we can keep our epistemic states consistent by performing consolidation after each such operation. Note, however, that if an epistemic state is expanded with A and then consolidated, then A will not always be believed in the resulting epistemic state. As a simplest example, take an epistemic state $\mathbb{E}_{\neg A}$ that is generated by the base $\{\neg A\}$. A pure expansion of $\mathbb{E}_{\neg A}$ with A and subsequent consolidation will result in an epistemic state generated by a flock $\{\{A\}, \{\neg A\}\}$; neither A, nor $\neg A$ is believed in this epistemic state.

A more radical way of preserving consistency has been suggested, in effect, by the AGM theory. It consists in performing contraction of $\neg A$ before an expansion with respect to A. The rationale behind this operation consists in ensuring that A will be believed in the resulting epistemic state. This is achieved by invalidating all conflicting potential beliefs supported by an epistemic state.

A well-known principle, called *Levi identity* in [Gär88], identifies a *revision* of a belief set with respect to a proposition A with a sequence of changes consisting of contracting $\neg A$ and subsequent expansion with A. Generalizing this principle to epistemic states and basic expansions, we introduce the following generic definition.

Definition 14.1.1. *A basic revision of an epistemic state $\mathbb{E}$ with respect to A is a basic expansion of an epistemic state $\mathbb{E} - \neg A$ with respect to A.*

The above definition gives a *generic* definition of basic revisions, since it is based on the generic definition of basic expansions given in the preceding chapter. Still, just as all basic expansions have a lot in common, basic revisions will also have a number of important properties that will be common to all of them.

To begin with, the contraction of $\neg A$ eliminates all admissible states that are incompatible with A. Consequently the revised epistemic state will contain only consistent admissible states. In addition, all basic expansions with respect to A determine the same resulting belief set, namely $\text{Cl}(\mathbf{B}, A)$. As a result, all basic revisions with respect to A will also determine the same revised belief set. If we denote this revised belief set by $\mathbf{B} * A$ (where $\mathbf{B}$ is the belief set of the source epistemic state), we will immediately obtain the following equality:

$$\mathbf{B} * A = \text{Cl}(A, \mathbf{B} - \neg A)$$

The above equality is nothing other than the *Levi identity for belief sets*. Thus, the revisions of epistemic states preserve this basic feature of the AGM theory.

Recall that a contraction with respect to $\neg A$ always commutes with a basic expansion with respect to A. So, for a revision with respect to A, the order of performing its underlying contraction and expansion does not matter; in each case we will obtain the same revised epistemic state. As can be expected, however, revisions do not commute: the sequence of revisions $\langle *A, *\neg A \rangle$ produces a belief in $\neg A$ and hence does not coincide with $\langle *\neg A, *A \rangle$ that leads to a belief in A.

The so-called *Gärdenfors (or Harper) identity* (see [Gär88]) states that contraction of a belief set $\mathbf{B}$ with respect to A is precisely the common part of $\mathbf{B}$ and its revision with respect to $\neg A$, that is,

$$\mathbf{B} - A \; = \; (\mathbf{B} * \neg A) \cap \mathbf{B}$$

This identity does not hold for our belief operations. To see this, it is sufficient to note that it implies recovery for contractions that is not valid in our framework. Still, the following result shows that the corresponding 'generalized' Gärdenfors identity holds for epistemic states:

Lemma 14.1.1. *If $\mathcal{E} * \neg A$ is a basic revision of an epistemic state $\mathbb{E}$ with respect to $\neg A$, then $\mathcal{E} - A$ is a restriction of $\mathcal{E} * \neg A$ to admissible states from $\mathbb{E}$.*

In other words, the contracted epistemic state contains exactly the admissible belief states that are common to both the source epistemic state and its revision with respect to $\neg A$. The proof presents no difficulty, and we leave it to the reader.

Consolidation produces in most cases a different epistemic state from the corresponding revision. Still, in many cases this operation generates the same resulting belief set as the revision. Suitable examples will be given below. For prioritized expansions, for example, consolidating $\mathbb{E} + A$ will give the same belief set as the revision of $\mathbb{E}$. As we will see below, this operation corresponds actually to Nayak's model of entrenchment change.

14.2 Belief revision and nonmonotonic inference

As with operations on epistemic states, studied earlier, revisions of epistemic states generate a certain change in their belief sets. As before, the belief change function produced by revisions of an epistemic state will be called a *belief revision function* associated with the epistemic state. In this section we give a detailed description of such belief revision functions. As a first step, we will establish an intimate connection between the latter and skeptical inference.

Notice that the very definition of revision is quite similar to the procedure of evaluating conditionals, described in Chapter 3. Indeed, a conditional $A \sim B$ is valid in an epistemic state $\mathbb{E}$ if and only if each preferred admissible belief set in $\mathbb{E}$ that is consistent with A, taken together with A itself, implies B. Now, preferred admissible belief states in $\mathbb{E}$ that are consistent with A are precisely preferred admissible states of the contracted epistemic state $\mathbb{E} - \neg A$. In addition, their expansions with A produce preferred admissible states of the resulting revised epistemic state. Consequently, if $\neg A$ is not disbelieved in $\mathbb{E}$, a conditional $A \sim B$ will be valid in $\mathbb{E}$ if and only if B is believed in the epistemic state revised with A.

Theorem 14.2.1. *If $*$ is a belief revision function associated with an epistemic state $\mathbb{E}$, then $B \in \mathbf{B} * A$ if and only if $A \sim B$ is valid in $\mathbb{E}$, for any contingent A.*

The above result gives a succinct expression to the claim made first by Gärdenfors and Makinson in [MG91], that belief revision and nonmonotonic inference are actually 'two sides of the same coin'. Due to the above correspondence, belief revision functions generated by epistemic states can also be seen as a natural generalization of AGM revisions; in particular, they extend the scope of the correspondence between belief revision and nonmonotonic inference from rational inference relations to a broader class of preferential ones. Accordingly, belief revision functions generated by basic revisions of epistemic states will be called below *preferential belief revision functions*.

Remark. The expansion operation on pure epistemic states, introduced in [Boc99b, Boc00c], does not produce AGM expansions of associated belief sets. Consequently, it violates Levi's identity for belief sets. The author has overlooked, however, that this leads also to violation of the above correspondence between preferential inference and revision operations based on this notion of expansion. In particular, Theorem 5.1 stated in [Boc00c] has turned out to be wrong in its 'easy' direction, namely, such revisions do not always produce preferential inference (though any preferential inference relation still can be modeled via such a revision). Actually, this was the main reason for abandoning the whole foundationalist approach described in the above papers. As we already mentioned, we do not believe now that a general theory of belief change can be confined to pure epistemic states. Still, it is worth mentioning that the approach remains adequate for linear epistemic states.

It is important to note that revision of epistemic states is by no means the only way of producing preferential belief revision. Actually, we will describe now a number of alternative ways of doing this.

To begin with, the following result shows that preferential belief revision can be modeled by consolidating prioritized expansions.

Theorem 14.2.2. *If $*$ is a belief revision function associated with $\mathbb{E}$, then, for any contingent A, $\mathbf{B} * A$ coincides with the refined belief set of $\mathbb{E} + A$.*

Proof. If A is compatible with at least one admissible state of $\mathbb{E}$ (that is, $\neg A$ is not a known proposition in $\mathbb{E}$), then preferred consistent admissible states of $\mathbb{E} + A$ are precisely new admissible states of the form s_A such that s is a preferred admissible state in $\mathbb{E}$ that is consistent with A. Hence the result. $\qquad\square$

The above result shows, in affect, that any preferential belief revision function can be obtained by combining prioritized expansion with consolidation.

Our second result shows that flat expansions, discussed in the preceding chapter, produce preferential belief revision functions directly, without further ado. The result is immediate due to the fact that preferred admissible belief sets of $\mathbb{E} \hat{+} A$ are precisely theories of the form $\mathrm{Cl}(A, l(s))$, where s ranges over preferred admissible states of $\mathbb{E}$ that are consistent with A.

Theorem 14.2.3. *If* * *is a belief revision function associated with* $\mathbb{E}$, *then, for any contingent* A, $\mathbf{B} * A$ *coincides with the belief set of* $\mathbb{E} \hat{+} A$.

Finally, the following result shows that preferential belief revision is obtainable also by consolidating knowledge expansions.

Theorem 14.2.4. *If* * *is a belief revision function associated with* $\mathbb{E}$, *then, for any contingent* A, $\mathbf{B} * A$ *coincides with the refined belief set of* $\mathbb{E} \oplus A$.

The above observations show, in effect, that belief revision does not determine, by itself, the kind of the underlying process producing it.

14.2.1 Completeness results

Using the above correspondence between belief revision and nonmonotonic inference, we can immediately give an axiomatic description of belief revision functions in terms of their 'rationality postulates' of an AGM-kind. To this end we can simply translate the postulates for preferential inference into the corresponding conditions for belief revision. To simplify the discussion, however, we will consider in what follows only the case of a consistent belief set $\mathbf{B}$.

$(K * 1)$ $\text{Th}(\mathbf{B} * A) = \mathbf{B} * A$		(closure)
$(K * 2)$ $A \in \mathbf{B} * A$		(success)
$(K * 3)$ $\mathbf{B} * A \subseteq \text{Th}(\mathbf{B}, A)$		(expansion1)
$(K * 4c)$ If $A \in \mathbf{B}$, then $\mathbf{B} \subseteq \mathbf{B} * A$		(expansion0)
$(K * 5)$ If $\mathbf{B} * A = \mathbf{B}_{\perp}$, then $\neg A \in \text{Th}(\emptyset)$		(cons. preservation)
$(K * 6)$ If $\text{Th}(A) = \text{Th}(B)$, then $\mathbf{B} * A = \mathbf{B} * B$		(extensionality)
$(K * 7)$ $\mathbf{B} * A \wedge B \subseteq \text{Th}(\mathbf{B} * A, B)$		(conjunction)
$(K * 8c)$ If $B \in \mathbf{K} * A$, then $\mathbf{K} * A \subseteq \mathbf{K} * (A \wedge B)$		(cautious monotony)

Preserving the AGM tradition, the above postulates are formulated with respect to some auxiliary classical consequence relation Th. It has been shown in Chapter 6, however, that if an inference relation satisfies Consistency Preservation with respect to Th (which is exactly what the postulate (K*5) says), then the latter consequence relation coincides with the internal logic of the inference relation (see Corollary 6.5.2). Consequently, the above postulates amount, in effect, to the postulates of preferential inference.

The above postulates almost coincide with the corresponding characterization of AGM belief revision functions (see [Gär88]), except that the postulates (K*4c) and (K*8c) replace the original, stronger AGM postulates (K*4) and (K*8), given below.

$(K * 4)$ If $\neg A \notin \mathbf{B}$, then $\mathbf{B} + A \subseteq \mathbf{B} * A$		(expansion2)
$(K * 8)$ If $\neg B \notin \mathbf{B} * A$, then $(\mathbf{B} * A) + B \subseteq \mathbf{B} * (A \wedge B)$		(rat. monotony)

Violation of the above postulates in our setting stems already from the fact that we admit epistemic states that are not determinate. Still, we will show below that these postulates can be satisfied using appropriate restrictions on the class of generating epistemic states.

Preferential belief revision functions represent a very natural and regular kind of belief revisions. Unfortunately, just as for preferential AGM contractions, such revision functions cannot be characterized in terms of AGM models, since the latter correspond to injective models for inference relations; as we have seen in Chapter 7, such models are insufficient for representing all preferential inference relations.

Remark. We have seen in Chapter 7 that a complete characterization of injective inference relations can be given at least in the finite case by imposing a condition of ∨-covering (see Theorem 7.9.4). In fact, the corresponding characterization of belief revision functions generated by relational AGM models has been given in [KM91]; it is obtainable by adding the following postulate[1]:

$$(K * I) \ \mathbf{B} * (A \vee B) \subseteq \mathrm{Th}(\mathbf{B} * A, \mathbf{B} * B) \qquad \text{(covering)}$$

The next result shows that adding postulate (K*4) amounts to restricting generating epistemic states to determinate ones.

Theorem 14.2.5. *A belief revision function satisfies the AGM postulates (K*1)–(K*7) and (K*8c) iff it is generated by some determinate epistemic state.*

Proof. It can be easily verified that the postulate (K*4) corresponds to the rule Weak Rational Monotony for inference relations, and hence belief revision functions satisfying the above postulates will correspond exactly to weakly rational inference relations. As has been shown in Chapter 7, these are precisely the inference relations that are generated by determinate epistemic states. □

Finally, the last AGM postulate, (K*8), corresponds to the rule of Rational Monotony for inference relations. Consequently, in order to satisfy all AGM postulates for revision, we need to restrict the class of generating epistemic states to modular ones (see Theorem 7.11.2 in Chapter 7).

Theorem 14.2.6. *A belief revision function satisfies all the AGM postulates iff it is determined by some modular epistemic state.*

The above theorem provides, in effect, a canonical reformulation in the framework of epistemic states for the main result of the AGM theory of belief revision.

---

[1] This postulate corresponds to the postulate (R8) in [KM91].

14.3 Inference and entrenchment change

Changes made to epistemic states produce not only changes in corresponding belief sets, they change also inference relations associated with these epistemic states. By our earlier observations, this amounts to change in the revision functions associated with epistemic states. Recall also that inference relations are interdefinable with epistemic entrenchment and related notions (see Chapter 6). Consequently, inference change can also be studied in terms of changes in epistemic entrenchment, and vice versa.

Though epistemic states are not reducible, in general, to their associated entrenchment orders, this holds, however, for special kinds of epistemic states, e.g., for pure epistemic states. It will hold, in particular, for linear pure epistemic states and their associated linear consequence relations. Recall that the latter can be seen as an alternative description of standard epistemic entrenchment relations of Gärdenfors and Makinson. Accordingly, viewed 'from within' the AGM paradigm, changes of linear pure epistemic states amount to changes of linear epistemic entrenchment relations. In fact, practically all models of entrenchment change, described in the literature, belong to this latter class. The idea that revision should be performed on epistemic entrenchment relations rather than on belief sets was first expressed by Rott in [Rot91b]. Changes of this kind have received recently a considerable attention in the literature (see, e.g., [Bou96, DP97, Leh95, Nay94]). As we will see below, many such changes can be captured by choosing suitable operations on epistemic states.

14.3.1 Inference change generated by expansions

It turns out that the most natural initial setting for studying changes in inference relations consists in considering such changes that are produced by expansions of epistemic states.

If $\vdash$ is a preferential inference relation generated by an epistemic state $\mathbb{E}$, then we will denote by $\vdash_{+A}$ an inference relation generated by an expansion of $\mathbb{E}$ with respect to A. Thus, $\vdash_{+A}$ can be seen as a result of incorporating the belief in A into $\vdash$. Accordingly, $\vdash_{+A}$ will also be called an *expansion* of $\vdash$ with respect to A. We will also use the terms basic, knowledge and flat expansions in denoting inference changes produced by these kinds of expansions of epistemic states.

Clearly, such an expansion cannot amount, in general, to a certain extension of the source inference relation; some old conditionals should be abandoned in order to incorporate the new belief. Still, it turns out that such a change has a quite regular character that can be described in terms of natural 'rationality postulates'.

The following theorem describes the main properties of changes in inference relations generated by basic expansions of epistemic states. Though we do not claim completeness here, these properties seems to capture the essence of the change involved.

Theorem 14.3.1. *If* $\vdash_{+A}$ *is a basic expansion of* $\vdash$, *then*

(I1) *If* $B \vdash C$ *and* $A \wedge B \vdash C$, *then* $B \vdash_{+A} C$;
(I2) *If* $B \vdash_{+A} C$, *then* $B \vdash A \rightarrow C$;
(I3) *If* $B \vdash_{+A} (\neg A \wedge C)$, *then* $B \vdash C$.

Proof. Let us denote by $\mathbb{E}$ the epistemic state produced $\vdash$, while $\mathbb{E}_+$ will denote the basic expansion of $\mathbb{E}$ that produced $\vdash_{+A}$.

(I1) Assume that $B \vdash C$, but $B \not\vdash_{+A} C$. The latter condition means that there exists a preferred admissible state in $\mathbb{E}_+$ that is consistent with B and does not support $B \rightarrow C$. Due the fact that $B \vdash C$, this admissible state cannot be an old admissible state, so it is a new admissible state, say s_A. Since $A \in l(s_A)$, we obtain that s_A is compatible with $A \wedge B$. Let us consider now the corresponding source admissible state s. Clearly, s is also consistent with $A \wedge B$ and does not support $(A \wedge B) \rightarrow C$, since otherwise s_A would support $B \rightarrow C$. In addition, s is actually preferred among admissible states of $\mathbb{E}$ that are consistent with $A \wedge B$. Indeed, if $s \prec t$, for some t consistent with $A \wedge B$, we would obtain that t_A is consistent with B and $s_A \prec_A t_A$, by the properties of the expanded preference relation. But this contradicts the assumption that s_A is a preferred such state. Now, since t is a preferred admissible state consistent with $A \wedge B$, and it does not support $(A \wedge B) \rightarrow C$, we conclude that $A \wedge B \not\vdash C$. Consequently, (I1) holds.

(I2) If $B \not\vdash A \rightarrow C$, then there is an admissible state s in $\mathbb{E}$ that is preferred in $]\neg B[$ and does not support $B \rightarrow (A \rightarrow C)$. Clearly, s is consistent with $A \wedge B$, so the corresponding new admissible state s_A in $\mathbb{E}_+$ will be consistent with B and will not support $B \rightarrow C$. Moreover, s_A will be a preferred state in $\mathbb{E}_+$ that is consistent with B. Indeed, if $s_A \prec_A t$ in $\mathbb{E}_+$, then $s \prec t$ in $\mathbb{E}$, and hence t supports $\neg B$. Similarly, if $s_A \prec_A t_A$, then again $s \prec t$, and hence t and t_A support $\neg B$. Now, since s_A is preferred in $]\neg B[$ and does not support $B \rightarrow C$, we have $B \not\vdash_{+A} C$. Thus, (I2) holds.

(I3) It is sufficient to show that if $B \not\vdash C$ and $B \vdash_{+A} C$, then $B \not\vdash_{+A} \neg A$. Now, $B \not\vdash C$ implies that there exists an admissible state s in $\mathbb{E}$ that is preferred in $]\neg B[$ and does not support $B \rightarrow C$. But s is not a preferred such state also in $\mathbb{E}_+$, since otherwise $B \vdash_{+A} C$ would imply that it supports $B \rightarrow C$. Consequently, there is a new admissible state t_A that is preferred among admissible states consistent with B and such that $s \prec_A t_A$. But t_A supports A, so it cannot support $B \rightarrow \neg A$. Thus, $B \not\vdash_{+A} \neg A$. This shows that (I3) holds. $\qquad\square$

The above postulates are sufficient for showing that the expansion-based inference change satisfies, in particular, the counterparts of all the four postulates for iterated revision suggested in [DP97]:

Lemma 14.3.1. *If* $\vdash_{+A}$ *is a basic expansion of* $\vdash$, *then*

(C1) $A \wedge B \vdash_{+A} C$ *iff* $A \wedge B \vdash C$;
(C2) If $A \wedge B \vdash \mathbf{f}$, then $B \vdash_{+A} C$ iff $B \vdash C$;
(C3) If $B \vdash A$, then $B \vdash_{+A} A$;
(C4) If $B \vdash_{+A} \neg A$, then $B \vdash \neg A$.

Proof. For (C1). The implication from right to left follows from (I1), while the opposite implication follows from (I2) (by substituting $A \wedge B$ for B in both cases).

For (C2). The implication from right to left follows from (I1). For the opposite direction, note that $A \wedge B \vdash \mathbf{f}$ implies $A \wedge B \vdash_{+A} \mathbf{f}$ by (C1), while the latter implies $B \vdash_{+A} \neg A$ by the properties of preferential inference. Consequently, the result follows by (I3).

Finally, (C3) follows from (I1) (substituting A for C), while (C4) follows from either (I2) or (I3) (substituting $\neg A$ for C). □

Despite the fact that inference changes generated by expansions satisfy all the above postulates, the relation between such changes and the system described in [DP97] is somewhat complicated. This is because the latter was intended to be based on *revisions* of epistemic states. Accordingly, the resulting belief set was required to be a revision of the initial belief set. Still, we will see that the established similarity is not accidental. For the time being, however, we will present a somewhat unexpected result that inference change based on revisions instead of expansions fails to satisfy the postulate (C2) above.

Example 14.3.1. Let us consider a pure epistemic state $\mathbb{E}$ that is normally generated by a singular base $\{\neg A \wedge D\}$. If a proposition C is consistent with $\neg A \wedge D$, then clearly $\neg A \wedge C \vdash D$ is valid in $\mathbb{E}$. Now let us perform a basic revision of $\mathbb{E}$ with respect to A. Since the contraction of $\neg A$ removes the only non-trivial admissible state $\mathrm{Cl}(\neg A \wedge D)$ in $\mathbb{E}$, the resulting revised epistemic state will be uniquely determined and will amount to the epistemic state generated simply by the base $\{A\}$. Clearly, $\neg A \wedge C \vdash D$ will not be valid in the latter, though A is inconsistent with $\neg A \wedge D$. Hence, (C2) is violated.

As has been shown earlier, the invalidated part of (C2) is actually a consequence of (I1). Thus, the above example can also serve as a counterexample to (I1).

The above result seems to disqualify (C2) and (I1) as general postulates for revisions of epistemic states. Still, we will see below that some natural operations on epistemic states will produce revised belief sets while satisfying all the above postulates.

If an expansion operation preserves inferential equivalence, then the expanded inference relation will be uniquely determined by the source inference relation and the added proposition. This is not always the case, however. Thus, the following example shows that pure expansions do not satisfy this property.

Example 14.3.2. Let us consider once more Example 13.2.4 we have discussed in the preceding chapter. In this example we had two belief equivalent epistemic states $\mathbb{E}_1$ and $\mathbb{E}_2$ such that their pure expansions with respect to r produced non-equivalent epistemic states. Moreover, it can be easily checked that $\mathbb{E}_1 + r$ and $\mathbb{E}_2 + r$ are even not inference-equivalent, since $\neg(q \wedge r) \hspace{0.5mm}\vdash\hspace{-2.5mm}\sim\hspace{0.5mm} r$ is valid in $\mathbb{E}_2 + r$, but is not valid in $\mathbb{E}_1 + r$.

The above example shows that pure expansions of an inference relation can produce different results depending on the underlying epistemic state.

It turns out, however, that prioritized basic expansion, as well as both flat and knowledge expansions preserve inferential equivalence. Consequently, the corresponding expansions of inference relations for these cases can be described directly as certain operations on inference relations. These operations are discussed in more details in the following sections.

14.3.2 Prioritized inference change

Inference change produced by prioritized expansions of epistemic states turns out to admit an especially simple and explicit characterization. Namely, the following result shows that the expanded inference relation in this case is definable directly in terms of the source inference relation.

Theorem 14.3.2. $\vdash\hspace{-2.5mm}\sim_{+A}$ *is a prioritized expansion of* $\vdash\hspace{-2.5mm}\sim$ *iff, for any* B, C,

$$B \vdash\hspace{-2.5mm}\sim_{+A} C \quad iff \quad \begin{cases} A \wedge B \vdash\hspace{-2.5mm}\sim C & when\ A \wedge B \hspace{0.5mm}\vdash\hspace{-2.5mm}\sim\hspace{-2mm}/\hspace{1mm} \mathbf{f}, \\ B \vdash\hspace{-2.5mm}\sim C & otherwise. \end{cases}$$

Proof. Let $\mathbb{E}$ and $\mathbb{E} + A$ be epistemic states generating, respectively, $\vdash\hspace{-2.5mm}\sim$ and $\vdash\hspace{-2.5mm}\sim_{+A}$. As can be seen from the above description, two cases should be considered.

(a) Assume first that $A \wedge B \hspace{0.5mm}\vdash\hspace{-2.5mm}\sim\hspace{-2mm}/\hspace{1mm} \mathbf{f}$. The latter condition implies that there is an admissible state of $\mathbb{E}$ that is consistent with $A \wedge B$, and hence there are new admissible states in $\mathbb{E} + A$ that are consistent with B. Since new admissible states in $\mathbb{E} + A$ are preferred to all source admissible states from $\mathbb{E}$, $B \hspace{0.5mm}\vdash\hspace{-2.5mm}\sim\hspace{-2mm}/\hspace{1mm}_{+A} C$ holds in this case if and only if there exists a new admissible state s_A in $\mathbb{E} + A$ that is preferred in $]\neg B[$ and does not support $B \rightarrow C$. Now, the latter holds if and only if s is a preferred admissible state among admissible states of $\mathbb{E}$ that are consistent with $A \wedge B$, and s does not support $A \rightarrow (B \rightarrow C)$. As can be seen, this amounts to saying that $A \wedge B \vdash\hspace{-2.5mm}\sim C$ is not valid in $\mathbb{E}$.

(b) Assume now that $A \wedge B \vdash\hspace{-2.5mm}\sim \mathbf{f}$. Then there are no new admissible states in $\mathbb{E} + A$ that are consistent with B. Consequently, $\mathbb{E}$ and $\mathbb{E} + A$ have the same preferred admissible states that are consistent with B, and hence $B \vdash\hspace{-2.5mm}\sim C$ holds in $\mathbb{E}$ if and only if it holds in $\mathbb{E} + A$. This completes the proof. $\square$

The above characterization of prioritized inference expansion can be given the following somewhat shorter formulation:

$B \mathbin{\vert\!\sim}_{+A} C$ iff $A \wedge B \mathbin{\vert\!\sim} C$, and either $A \wedge B \mathbin{\not\!\!\vert\!\sim} \mathbf{f}$, or $B \mathbin{\vert\!\sim} C$.

An interesting fact about prioritized expansions of inference relations is that the resulting inference relation satisfies the condition that if $B \mathbin{\vert\!\sim}_{+A} C$, then $A \wedge B \mathbin{\vert\!\sim}_{+A} C$. In other words, prioritized expansion of an inference relation with respect to A always makes A a *default proposition* of the expanded inference relation (see Chapter 7 for the definition of this notion). Note, however, that this property does not hold for all basic expansions of inference relations.

Since the expanded inference relation in our case is uniquely determined by the source inference relation, we immediately obtain that prioritized expansion preserves inferential equivalence. This means also that the corresponding inference change can be studied independently of its realization in terms of epistemic states.

Recall now that inference relations are interdefinable with entrenchment relations and semi-classical consequence relations. As for inference relations, we will say that an entrenchment or a consequence relation is a (prioritized) expansion of another entrenchment or a consequence relation, if it is produced by a (prioritized) expansion of the underlying epistemic state.

The following result gives a description of the change in consequence (dependence) relations corresponding to prioritized expansions. The proof follows immediately by applying an id-mapping between inference relations and semi-classical consequence relations (see Chapter 7).

Lemma 14.3.2. *If $\vdash_{+A}$ is a prioritized expansion of a semi-classical consequence relation $\vdash$, then*

$$B \vdash_{+A} C \quad \textit{iff} \quad A{\to}B \vdash A{\to}C \textit{ and either } \nvdash A{\to}B, \textit{ or } \vdash B{\to}C.$$

Recall that any consequence relation can be considered as a syntactic representation of a pure epistemic state consisting of its theories. It is interesting to observe in this respect that the above transformation of consequence relations corresponds to the following transformation of the associated sets of theories: any theory u of $\vdash$ is replaced with two theories, namely $\mathrm{Cl}(A, u)$ and $u \cap \mathrm{Th}_{\vdash}(A)$, where $\mathrm{Th}_{\vdash}$ is a classical sub-relation of $\vdash$. Actually, this transformation is intimately connected with the procedure of purifying epistemic states we have used in Chapter 7.

Similarly, the prioritized expansion of inference relations is representable also via a certain change of epistemic entrenchment relations. The corresponding change for simple entrenchment relations is describable as follows:

$$B <_{+A} C \quad \textit{iff} \quad A{\to}B < A{\to}C \textit{ and either } A{\to}B \not< A{\to}B, \textit{ or } B < C.$$

Recall that prioritized expansion preserves modularity and linearity of epistemic states. Prioritized expansions and prioritized merge correspond in this case to the revision of epistemic entrenchment relations suggested by Nayak in [Nay94]. Now, preservation of modularity implies that prioritized expansions of rational inference relations produce again rational inference relations. Moreover, since rational inference relations are interdefinable with linear consequence (alias entrenchment) relations via an id*-mapping, prioritized expansions of linear consequence relations produce linear 'expanded' consequence relations. Actually, the following somewhat surprising result shows that, despite the differences in the corresponding mappings, the relevant expansion operation on linear consequence relations coincides with the corresponding operation on semi-classical consequence relations:

Lemma 14.3.3. *If $\vdash_{+A}$ is a prioritized expansion of a linear consequence relation $\vdash$, then*

$$B \vdash_{+A} C \text{ iff } A{\to}B \vdash A{\to}C \text{ and either } \nvdash A{\to}B, \text{ or } \vdash B{\to}C.$$

Proof. Assume that $B \vdash_{+A} C$. By id*-mapping, this holds iff either $\neg(B \wedge C) \hspace{1pt}\not\!\sim_{+A} B$, or $\neg C \hspace{1pt}\sim_{+A} \mathbf{f}$. Unfolding these conditions, we obtain

$$A \wedge \neg(B \wedge C) \hspace{1pt}\not\!\sim B \vee [A \wedge \neg(B \wedge C) \hspace{1pt}\sim \mathbf{f} \& \neg(B \wedge C) \hspace{1pt}\not\!\sim B] \vee \neg C \hspace{1pt}\sim \mathbf{f}$$

Now we apply the reverse id*-mapping and obtain

$$[A{\to}B \vdash A{\to}C \& \nvdash A{\to}(B \wedge C)] \vee [\nvdash A{\to}(B \wedge C) \& B \vdash C \& \nvdash B] \vee \vdash C$$

which can be simplified to the required condition

$$A{\to}B \vdash A{\to}C \& (\nvdash A{\to}B \vee B \vdash C)$$

$\square$

Thus, prioritized expansions of epistemic states generate a uniform expansion operation on consequence relations.

Finally, we recall that consolidation of a prioritized expansion produces a revision of the associated belief set. Moreover, any epistemic state is equivalent to its consolidation. This means, in particular, that the two produce the same inference relations. Consequently, prioritized inference change can also be seen as a kind of revision of inference relations. In this sense, it turns out to be a special, constructive case of the system from [DP97].

14.3.3 Flat inference change

It turns out that flat expansions also posses the property that the expanded inference relation is wholly determined by the source inference relation.

Theorem 14.3.3. $\hspace{1pt}\sim_{\dot{+}A}$ *is a flat expansion of $\hspace{1pt}\sim$ if and only if, for any B, C,*

$$B \hspace{1pt}\sim_{\dot{+}A} C \text{ iff } \begin{cases} A \hspace{1pt}\sim B \to C & \text{when } A \hspace{1pt}\not\!\sim \neg B, \\ B \hspace{1pt}\sim C & \text{otherwise.} \end{cases}$$

Proof. Let $\mathbb{E}$ and $\mathbb{E}\hat{+}A$ be epistemic states generating, respectively, $\vdash$ and $\vdash_{\hat{+}A}$, and $\mathcal{S}^A$ is a set of preferred admissible states consistent with A in $\mathbb{E}$. Two cases should be considered.

(a) Assume first that $A \not\vdash \neg B$. Then some $s \in \mathcal{S}^A$ is consistent with $A \wedge B$, and hence there are new admissible states in $\mathbb{E}\hat{+}A$ that are consistent with B. Since new admissible states in $\mathbb{E}\hat{+}A$ are preferred to all source admissible states from $\mathbb{E}$, $B \not\vdash_{\hat{+}A} C$ holds in this case if and only if there exists a new admissible state s_A in $\mathbb{E}\hat{+}A$ that does not support $B \to C$. Now, the latter holds if and only if $s \in \mathcal{S}^A$ does not support $A \to (B \to C)$. As can be seen, this amounts to saying that $A \vdash B \to C$ is not valid in $\mathbb{E}$.

(b) Assume now that $A \vdash \neg B$. Then there are no new admissible states in $\mathbb{E}\hat{+}A$ that are consistent with B. Consequently, $\mathbb{E}$ and $\mathbb{E}\hat{+}A$ have the same preferred admissible states that are consistent with B, and hence $B \vdash C$ holds in $\mathbb{E}$ if and only if it holds in $\mathbb{E}\hat{+}A$. This completes the proof. $\square$

The above characterization of a flat inference expansion can be given the following more compact description:

$B \vdash_{\hat{+}A} C$ iff $A \vdash B \to C$, and either $A \not\vdash \neg B$, or $B \vdash C$.

Notice also that flat expansion produces actually a revision of the source belief set. Accordingly, just as prioritized expansions, flat expansions of inference relations could also be seen in this sense as a kind of revision. Note, however, that flat expansion is not a basic expansion, so it does not have to comply with the postulates (I1)–(I3) we have given earlier. Actually, flat expansions violate, in general, (I2). However, it turns out that this postulate is satisfied for rational inference relations.

Recall that flat expansions also preserve modularity of epistemic states, so flat expansions of rational inference relations produce again rational inference relations. Moreover, in the rational case, the characterization of the expanded inference relation can be modified as follows (due to Rational Monotony):

$$B \vdash_{\hat{+}A} C \quad \text{iff} \quad \begin{cases} A \wedge B \vdash C & \text{when } A \not\vdash \neg B, \\ B \vdash C & \text{otherwise.} \end{cases}$$

The above characterization can actually be found in [Bou96]. Notice that in the rational case the only difference between prioritized and flat expansions of inference relations amounts to the difference in the condition that 'switches' between $B \vdash C$ and $A \wedge B \vdash C$.

Since inference relations are interdefinable with entrenchment relations, flat expansions of epistemic states correspond also to certain operations on entrenchment relations. The corresponding flat expansion of simple entrenchment orders can be described as follows.

$B <_{\hat{+}A} C$ iff $\neg A < A \to C$ and either $\neg A \not< A \to B$, or $B < C$.

Lehmann's revisions. If we would use flat L-expansions instead of basic expansions in our the definition of a revision operation, we will obtain a revision operation that preserves linearity and determines the same revised belief set. We will call the corresponding revision operation on inference relations an *L-revision*, due to its connection with the revision operation described in [Leh95].

Unfortunately, an L-revision of inference relations does not admit an elementary syntactic description of the kind given above for prioritized and flat expansions. Still, its semantic description is fairly simple. And it can be used to show that this kind of revision exactly corresponds to a revision operation suggested by Lehmann in [Leh95].

It is interesting to observe that the two preceding kinds of inference change have been based on expansions rather than revisions. So, only Lehmann's model is actually constructible as a certain revision of epistemic states.

14.3.4 Knowledge-based inference change

Inference change due to knowledge expansions has an especially simple characterization. The proof is quite similar to other proofs of this kind, given earlier, so we omit it.

Theorem 14.3.4. $\vdash_{\oplus A}$ *is a knowledge expansion of* $\vdash$ *if and only if*

$$B \vdash_{\oplus A} C \quad \text{iff } A \to B \vdash A \to C$$

The following result shows that $\vdash_{\oplus A}$ is actually a minimal transformation of $\vdash$ securing that A is a new knowledge.

Lemma 14.3.4. $\vdash_{\oplus A}$ *coincides with a least extension* $\vdash'$ *of* $\vdash$ *in which* A *is known (that is,* $\neg A \vdash' \mathbf{f}$ *).*

Proof. Since $B \vdash C$ implies $A \to B \vdash A \to C$, $\vdash$ is included into $\vdash_{\oplus A}$. In addition, $\neg A \vdash_{\oplus A} \mathbf{f}$, and hence A is known in $\vdash_{\oplus A}$.

Assume that $\vdash'$ is an extension of $\vdash$ such that $\neg A \vdash' \mathbf{f}$, and $B \vdash_{\oplus A} C$. Then $A \to B \vdash A \to C$, and consequently $A \to B \vdash' A \to C$. By Regularity, we have also $A \to B \vdash' A \land (A \to C)$, and hence by Cautious Monotony $A \land B \vdash' C$. The latter implies $B \vdash' A \to C$ by Deduction, and hence $B \vdash' A \land (A \to C)$ by Regularity. Therefore, $B \vdash' C$, and consequently $\vdash_{\oplus A}$ is included into $\vdash'$. This completes the proof. $\square$

As before, knowledge expansions of inference relations can be modeled in terms of entrenchment changes. The knowledge expansion of simple epistemic entrenchment relations is definable just as for inference relations:

$$B <_{\oplus A} C \quad \text{iff } A \to B < A \to C$$

It is interesting to note that such an entrenchment change corresponds actually to Rott's abandoned proposal in [Rot91b]. Rott has rejected this proposal due to the (right) observation that such a change is not reversible, so it cannot serve as a representation of changes in beliefs.

14.4 Constructibility and natural classes

In this final section we will consider some global questions concerning the emerging general theory of belief change. Namely, we will consider expressivity of our belief change operations in the range of all epistemic states.

The theory of belief change can also be viewed as a constructive theory of epistemic states purported to provide us with means of creating and modifying epistemic states. We have seen that the suggested operations on epistemic states allows to construct quite complex epistemic states. Now we will turn to a more systematic analysis of these expressive capabilities.

Three fundamental operations on epistemic states have been considered in this book, namely sum, merge (product) and contraction. An important question arises now as to what is the range of epistemic states that can be constructed using these operations. In order to answer this question, we must stipulate first which epistemic states could be considered as primitive, 'initial' ones.

Our preceding discussion (see especially Chapter 13) suggests that there are two kinds of epistemic states that can be considered as primitive. The first comprises epistemic states $\mathbb{E}^A$ that are normally generated by singular bases $\{A\}$. An epistemic state $\mathbb{E}^A$ consists, in effect, in two theories, namely $Cl(\mathbf{t})$ (that is, the set of tautologies) and $Cl(A)$ such that the second theory (the belief set) is preferred to the first. Such epistemic states can be seen as expressing an explicit belief in A.

The second kind consists of unitary knowledge states $\mathbb{E}_A$ that contain a single theory $Cl(A)$; such epistemic states are expressing the knowledge that A. Note that belief and knowledge coincide in such epistemic states. In other words, such states do not involve genuine beliefs that are distinct from knowledge[2].

For obvious reasons, we will restrict our attention in what follows to finite operations on epistemic states. Accordingly, an epistemic state will be called *constructible* if it can be obtained from the above primitive epistemic states by applying singular contractions and binary operations of taking sum and merging.

Due to the finiteness restriction on the basic operations, it should be clear that any constructible epistemic state will be finitary. Moreover, our main result in this section will show that any finitary epistemic state is equivalent

---

[2] Compare this with Gärdenfors' identification of knowledge with full belief in [Gär88].

to some constructible epistemic state. As a preparation, we will consider first the case of linear epistemic states. It turns out that such epistemic states are constructible using only contractions and prioritized expansions.

Theorem 14.4.1. *Any linear finitary epistemic state is equivalent to an epistemic state that is constructible using contractions and prioritized expansions.*

Proof. Recall that any linear epistemic state is equivalent to a linear state that is standard and monotonic. Consequently, it is sufficient to show the claim for the latter class of epistemic states.

Let $\mathbb{E}$ be a finitary linear standard epistemic state. Due to finiteness, its internal logic Th is representable as a classical entailment augmented with a singe axiom, say A. Then we will represent such an epistemic state by a sequence $(\mathbf{t}, A_1, \ldots, A_n)$, where $\mathrm{Th}(A_i)$ and $\mathrm{Th}(\mathbf{t})$ are admissible belief sets of $\mathbb{E}$, and $\mathrm{Th}(A_i) \prec \mathrm{Th}(A_j)$ if and only if $i < j$. The epistemic state is standard if and only if the set $\{A_i\}$ does not contain Th-equivalent propositions or tautologies. It is monotonic if and only if $A_i \vDash A_j$ holds only if $j < i$.

We will prove the claim by induction on the number of admissible belief sets. To begin with, notice that an epistemic state corresponding to the sequence $(\mathbf{t})$ coincides with a primitive knowledge state of the form $\mathbb{E}^A$, where A is a proposition determining its internal logic.

Assume now that an epistemic state $\mathbb{E}$ is representable by a sequence $(\mathbf{t}, A_1, \ldots, A_{n-1}, A_n)$. By the inductive assumption, the epistemic state $\mathbb{E}_0$ corresponding to the sequence $(\mathbf{t}, A_1, \ldots, A_{n-1})$ is constructible. Now we will construct $\mathbb{E}$ as follows.

As a first step, we expand $\mathbb{E}_0$ with A_n by prioritized expansion. As can be verified, the expanded epistemic state $\mathbb{E}_0 + A_n$ will be representable by a sequence

$$(\mathbf{t}, A_1, \ldots, A_{n-1}, A_n, A_1 \wedge A_n, \ldots, A_{n-1} \wedge A_n)$$

Now we contact $\mathbb{E}_0 + A_n$ with respect to all conjunctions $A_i \wedge A_n$ from the above sequence that are not equivalent to A_n. As we are going to show, no proposition A_i is removed by such contractions.

Suppose first that a contraction of $A_i \wedge A_n$ removes some A_j, where $j < n$. This can happen only if $A_i \wedge A_n \in \mathrm{Th}(A_j)$, and hence $A_n \in \mathrm{Th}(A_j)$. By monotonicity, the latter condition implies, however, $\mathrm{Th}(A_n) \prec \mathrm{Th}(A_j)$, contrary to our assumptions about $\mathbb{E}$. Also, a contraction of $A_i \wedge A_n$ cannot remove A_n, since, by the same argument, this could happen only if A_n is equivalent to $A_i \wedge A_n$.

Let us denote by $\mathbb{E}_1$ the epistemic state obtained as a result of all such contractions. Due to above considerations, $\mathbb{E}_1$ contains only $\mathrm{Th}(A_i)$ as admissible belief sets. Still, it may be distinct from $\mathbb{E}$, since it may be non-standard and contains multiple copies of $\mathrm{Th}(A_n)$. This means, however, that the normal reduction of $\mathbb{E}_1$ will coincide with $\mathbb{E}$. This completes the proof. $\square$

As has been established earlier, any epistemic state is equivalent to a disjoint sum of its linear refinements. Now, since any finitary linear epistemic state is constructible, we immediately obtain

Theorem 14.4.2. *Any finitary epistemic state is equivalent to a constructible epistemic state.*

The above result shows that our system of belief change provides, in effect, a constructive theory of epistemic states. The importance of this fact cannot be overestimated. According to it, for example, any intended inference behavior that is expressible in terms of epistemic states is obtainable by a suitable composition of primitive epistemic states.

14.4.1 Natural kinds of epistemic states

By restricting or modifying the set of allowable operations on epistemic states, we obtain some interesting classes of epistemic states. In this section we will consider a number of such classes that are constructible without the sum operation.

To begin with, we will show that removing the sum operation, we restrict essentially the set of generated epistemic states. To this end, we will present a rather simple epistemic state that is not constructible without taking sums.

Let us consider a standard finitary epistemic state $\mathbb{E}_s$ consisting of three theories $\mathrm{Cl}(\mathbf{t})$, $\mathrm{Cl}(p)$ and $\mathrm{Cl}(p \wedge q)$ such that both $\mathrm{Cl}(p)$ and $\mathrm{Cl}(p \wedge q)$ are preferred to $\mathrm{Cl}(\mathbf{t})$. As can be seen, $\mathbb{E}$ is persistent; in fact, it is representable by a flock $\{\{p\}, \{p \wedge q\}\}$.

Lemma 14.4.1. $\mathbb{E}_s$ *is not equivalent to any epistemic state constructible using contractions and merging only.*

Proof. The proof of this fact is rather involved and tedious, so we will provide only an extended outline, leaving some small details to the reader.

Suppose that there exists an epistemic state $\mathbb{E}$ that is constructible in the above sense and is equivalent to $\mathbb{E}_s$. Notice first that the internal logic of $\mathbb{E}_s$ coincides with the classical entailment, so the construction of $\mathbb{E}$ can involve only primitive belief states of the form $\mathbb{E}_A$. Assume that $\mathbb{E}_{A_i}$, for $1 \leq i \leq n$, are all the primitive epistemic states used in the construction of $\mathbb{E}$. For each $\mathbb{E}_{A_i}$, we will denote by s_i^+ and s_i^0 the admissible states corresponding, respectively, to $\mathrm{Cl}(A_i)$ and $\mathrm{Cl}(\mathbf{t})$. Then any admissible state of $\mathbb{E}$ can be 'parsed' into a binary tree with admissible states of $\mathbb{E}_{A_i}$ as its leaves. All such trees have the same structure and differ only in which of the two admissible states of each $\mathbb{E}_i$, s_i^+ or s_i^0, is placed as a leaf. We will represent such admissible states simply as lists $(s_1^*, \ldots, s_n^*)$, keeping in mind, however, that the actual sequence of merge operations determines how such lists are 'parsed'.

Due to possible contraction operations intertwined with merging, not all possible lists of the above kind will represent admissible states of $\mathbb{E}$. There is, however, an important regularity in the set of such lists that 'survived' all contractions. Namely, it can be easily verified that if $s = (s_1^*, \ldots, s_n^*)$ is an admissible state of $\mathbb{E}$, then the replacement of any s_i^+ in s with s_i^0 will give again an admissible state of $\mathbb{E}$.

Now we will show that if s is an admissible state of $\mathbb{E}$ and s_i^+ appears in s, then $A_i \vDash p$. Assume that this does not hold, and let s' be a list obtained from s by replacing each s_j^+, for $i \neq j$, with s_j^0. By our earlier observation, s' will also be an admissible state of $\mathbb{E}$, and it will be labelled with $\mathrm{Cl}(A_i)$. Consequently, the contraction of $\mathbb{E}$ with respect to p will retain s'. Let t be an admissible state of $\mathbb{E}$ that has a minimal nontrivial label that is included in $\mathrm{Cl}(A_i)$. Since $A_i \nvDash p$, t will also belong to $\mathbb{E} - p$. Moreover, since all other admissible belief sets in $\mathbb{E} - p$ are not included in $l(t)$, all of them can be eliminated by appropriate contractions that still retain t. Consequently, if w is the corresponding set of contracted propositions, then $\mathbb{E} - p; w$ will contain $l(t)$ as its only nontrivial admissible belief set, and hence $l(t)$ will coincide with the belief set of the latter epistemic state. Note, however, that $\mathbb{E}_s - p; w$ contains only $\mathrm{Cl}(t)$ as its admissible theory, which contradicts our supposition that $\mathbb{E}$ is equivalent to $\mathbb{E}_s$.

Let f_s be a selection function of $\mathbb{E}_s$. Then $f_s(\mathbf{f}) = \{\mathrm{Cl}(p), \mathrm{Cl}(p \wedge q)\}$, and consequently $\mathbb{E}$ should contain at least two maximally preferred admissible states s and t that are labelled, respectively, with $\mathrm{Cl}(p)$ and $\mathrm{Cl}(p \wedge q)$. Note that, for any s_i^+ appearing in s, A_i should be a consequence of p, and hence A_i and p will be equivalent. In other words, all s_i^* appearing in s will be labelled with either $\mathrm{Cl}(t)$, or $\mathrm{Cl}(p)$.

Given the above two admissible states s and t, we will construct their cover r by taking, for each i, s_i^+ when it appears in either s or t, and s_i^0 otherwise. It turns out that r is also an admissible state of $\mathbb{E}$. This can be shown by induction on the construction of r. To this end, we will consider all well-formed sub-states $s^k = (s_{k_1}^*, \ldots, s^* k_m)$ that were constructed 'on the way' of constructing admissible states of $\mathbb{E}$. If such a sub-state is a part of some admissible state of $\mathbb{E}$, we will say that such a sub-state is *admissible* with respect to $\mathbb{E}$.

Note first that some s_i^* belongs to r only if it belongs to either s or t, and hence the initial sub-state (s_i^*) of r will be admissible with respect to $\mathbb{E}$. This gives us the basis of induction. Let us assume then that, for some sub-states r_1 and r_2 of r, the pair $r_0 = (r_1, r_2)$ is also a sub-state of r. By the inductive assumption, we can assume that both r_1 and r_2 are admissible with respect to $\mathbb{E}$. Suppose that r_0 is not admissible. This could happen only if a contraction has been performed on subsequent stages of the construction removing some proposition A such that $A \in l(r_0)$. Now, r_0 is also a cover of the corresponding sub-states s_0 and t_0 of s and t, respectively. Since s_0 is admissible with respect to $\mathbb{E}$, r_0 should be distinct from s_0, so r_0 must contain at least one s_i^+ from t. Recall that in this case A_i implies p. But then t_0 will have the same label as r_0; indeed, r_0 is obtainable from t_0 by possible replacement of some s_j^0 with s_j^+, when the latter appears in s_0. We have noted earlier, however, that the label of any such s_j^+ is $\mathrm{Cl}(p)$, so it is subsumed by the label $\mathrm{Cl}(A_i)$ of s_i^+. As a result, t_0 will also be eliminated by the contraction with respect to A, contrary to the fact that it is admissible with respect to $\mathbb{E}$. This shows that r_0 is admissible. Consequently, we can conclude by induction that r is an admissible state of $\mathbb{E}$.

By the construction of r and the generic definition of merge, we obtain that r is preferred to both s and t in $\mathbb{E}$. But this contradicts our assumption that s and t are maximally preferred admissible states of $\mathbb{E}$. The obtained contradiction shows that the relevant constructible epistemic state $\mathbb{E}$ does not exist. This completes the proof.   □

The above result shows that we lose expressivity if we do not use sums in constructing epistemic states. Still, the class of epistemic states that are constructible without taking sums is quite large, and it contains many 'well-behaved' epistemic states. We have seen already that linear epistemic states are included in this class. In addition, the following important result shows that any epistemic state generated by some finite prioritized base is constructible by using the two basic merge operations, namely pure and prioritized merge. This result is actually an adaptation in our context of the general result proved in [ARS95], namely that any priority-based preference is constructible using two binary operators for combining preference relations.

Theorem 14.4.3. *Any finite base-generated epistemic state is equivalent to an epistemic state constructible using the two basic merge operations.*

Proof. As has been established in Lemma 4.1.3, any prioritized base is similar to a tree-ordered base. Consequently, it is sufficient to prove the claim only for the bases of the latter kind.

Let $(\Delta, \lhd)$ be a tree-ordered base. We construct the epistemic state corresponding to this base in a top-down way as follows: on each stage we perform one of the two decompositions of a current base $\Gamma \subseteq \Delta$, and construct the corresponding epistemic state $\mathbb{E}_\Gamma$ by merging the epistemic states associated with its components. The two ways of decomposition are as follows:

- If Γ consists of disjoint components $\Gamma_1, \ldots, \Gamma_n$, we set $\mathbb{E}_\Gamma$ to be a pure merge of all $\mathbb{E}_{\Gamma_i}$;
- else, Γ is a connected tree, and hence it has a unique most prior element, say A. Then, if $\Gamma = \{A\}$, we set $\mathbb{E}_\Gamma = \mathbb{E}^A$; otherwise it is set as a prioritized merge $\mathbb{E}_A \ltimes \mathbb{E}_{\Gamma \setminus \{A\}}$.

As can be easily verified, if we start with Δ, the above procedure will result in constructing an epistemic state similar to the epistemic state generated by $(\Delta, \lhd)$.   □

Pure change

Our suggested theory of belief change has led us far away from the traditional distinction between coherentism and foundationalism (see Chapter 11). Still, some reflection of this opposition can be found in the distinction between pure and prioritized change, described below.

By removing prioritized merge from the set of allowable operations, we restrict ourselves to operations on epistemic states that do not create priorities among defaults. Accordingly, this kind of epistemic change could be called a *pure change*.

Recall that pure merge allows to combine simple (non-prioritized) bases into a new base. Consequently, any epistemic state that is generated by a finite pure base is constructible using pure basic expansion as the only operation. However, contractions do not preserve base-generation, so the class of epistemic states constructible using contraction and pure merge is significantly larger than the class of pure base-generated states.

In order to establish an 'upper bound' on the class of epistemic states that are constructible in this case, note that contractions, sums and pure merges preserve persistence of epistemic states. Moreover, primitive epistemic states are actually pure, and hence they are also persistent. Consequently, the relevant belief change operations allow to construct only persistent epistemic states. Moreover, we will take a risk and advance the following

Conjecture. *Any finitary persistent epistemic state is constructible using sums, contractions and pure expansions.*

It has been established earlier that finitary persistent epistemic states are representable by flocks. Moreover, we have also seen that contractions, sums and pure merging give rise to the corresponding operations on flocks. Accordingly, the theory of flock change emerges as an important alternative representation of pure change. Note in passing that the epistemic state $\mathbb{E}_s$, used earlier for showing that not all epistemic states are constructible without sums, corresponds actually to the flock $\{\{p\}, \{p \wedge q\}\}$. Consequently, the operation of taking sums turns out to be essential for constructibility of flocks.

We have seen already that there are flock-generated epistemic states that are not equivalent to any standard epistemic state. The following example shows that there are constructible flocks such that their associated epistemic states are essentially non-standard.

Example 14.4.1. Let us consider an epistemic state generated by a flock

$$\mathcal{F} = \{\{p, p_1, p \leftrightarrow q\}, \{q, q_1, p \leftrightarrow q\}\}.$$

It can be verified that this flock can be constructed from the base $\{p, p_1, q, q_1\}$ by applying first contraction with respect to $(p \vee p_1) \wedge (q \vee q_1)$, and then expanding the result with $p \leftrightarrow q$. Consequently, this flock is constructible.

The corresponding epistemic state $\mathbb{E}_{\mathcal{F}}$ contains two admissible belief states that are labelled with the theory $u = \text{Cl}(p \wedge q)$, so it is not standard. We will denote by $f_{\mathcal{F}}$ the selection function associated with $\mathbb{E}_{\mathcal{F}}$. Assume now that there exists a standard epistemic state $\mathbb{E}$ that is equivalent to $\mathbb{E}_{\mathcal{F}}$. Note first that $f_{\mathcal{F}}(p_1 \vee q_1) = \{u\}$ and $f_{\mathcal{F}}(\mathbf{f}) = \{u_1, u_2\}$, where $u_1 = \text{Cl}(p, p_1, q)$ and $u_2 = \text{Cl}(p, q, q_1)$. Consequently, all these theories should belong to admissible belief sets of $\mathbb{E}$. Moreover, the second condition shows that u is not a preferred admissible state in $\mathbb{E}$, so it should be subordinated to either u_1, or u_2. Assume that $u \prec u_1$. But this is incompatible with the fact that $f_{\mathcal{F}}(q_1) = \{u, u_1\}$. Similarly $u \prec u_2$ is incompatible with the fact that $f_{\mathcal{F}}(p_1) = \{u, u_2\}$. The obtained contradiction shows that there is no standard epistemic state that is equivalent to $\mathbb{E}_{\mathcal{F}}$.

As we have seen in Chapter 12, persistent epistemic states generate a restricted class of contraction functions, so the restriction to pure change involves also a restriction on the class of belief contraction functions. Still, this does not lead to a restriction on the class of representable belief revision functions. Indeed, we have seen that all preferential inference relations are representable in the framework of pure epistemic states. This fact can also be used for showing that any belief revision function is representable via a revision of some persistent epistemic state.

Prioritized change

If we take prioritized merge and contraction as the only belief change operations, we produce precisely the class of linear finitary epistemic states. Indeed, both these operations preserve linearity, and the primitive epistemic states are also linear. Consequently, any epistemic state that is constructible in this way will be linear. In addition, it has been established earlier that contractions and prioritized expansions are sufficient for constructing any finitary linear epistemic state.

Linear epistemic states and their equivalents occupy a large part of the literature on nonmonotonic reasoning and belief change. Some studies are even based on an implicit or explicit presupposition that 'rational' inference relations and belief change functions should be rational in the technical sense sanctioned by the KLM and AGM theories (see, e.g., [LM92]). Under this presupposition, contraction and prioritized expansion can be seen as a fully expressive set of belief change operations.

Our study, however, has been thoroughly non-rational in this respect. Though we have seen that linear epistemic states are important also for analyzing general epistemic states, we believe that linearity constraint imposes an unbearable burden on our representation capabilities, since it requires us, in effect, to establish a linear priority order on defaults. This is especially evident in the above representation in terms of prioritized expansions: any sequence of prioritized expansions produces not only a default base, but also a linear prioritization on it. As has been noticed by many, this could be a problem if we are dealing with mutually independent defaults. Borrowing an example from [DP97], if we acquire first a belief that something seen is red, and then that it is a bird, then we will persist in believing that it is bird even when required to retract the belief that it is a red bird. This is because the second expansion assigned a higher priority to the belief that it is a bird as compared with being red. Clearly, such a reasoning behavior is not especially rational.

References

[ACS92] H. L. Arlo-Costa and S. J. Shapiro, *Maps between nonmonotonic and conditional logics*, Proceedings of KR'92, Morgan Kaufmann, 1992, pp. 553–564.

[Ada75] E. W. Adams, *The Logic of Conditionals*, Reidel, Dordrecht, 1975.

[AGM85] C. Alchourrón, P. Gärdenfors, and D. Makinson, *On the logic of theory change: Partial meet contraction and revision functions*, J. of Symbolic Logic **50** (1985), 510–530.

[AM82] C. Alchourrón and D. Makinson, *On the logic of theory change: contraction functions and their associated revision functions*, Theoria **48** (1982), 14–37.

[ARS95] H. Andreka, M. D. Ryan, and P.-Y. Schobbens, *Operators and laws for combining preference relations*, Information Systems: Correctness and Reusability (Selected Papers) (R. J. Wieringa and R. B. Feenstra, eds.), World Scientific Publ. Co., 1995.

[BCD+93] S. Benferhat, C. Cayrol, D. Dubois, J. Lang, and H. Prade, *Inconsistency management and prioritized syntax-based entailment*, Proceedings of IJCAI'93 (Chambery, France) (R. Bajcsy, ed.), Morgan Kaufmann, 1993, pp. 640–645.

[BDKT97] A. Bondarenko, P. M. Dung, R. A. Kowalski, and F. Toni, *An abstract, argumentation-theoretic framework for default reasoning*, Artificial Intelligence **93** (1997), 63–101.

[BDL+98] S. Benferhat, D. Dubois, J. Lang, H. Prade, A. Saffiotti, and P. Smets, *A general approach for inconsistency handling and merging information in prioritized knowledge bases*, Proceedings Sixth Int. Conference on Principles of Knowledge Representation and Reasoning, KR'98 (San Francisco, CA) (A. G. Cohn, L. Schubert, and S. C. Shapiro, eds.), Morgan Kaufmann, 1998, pp. 466–477.

[BDP97] S. Benferhat, D. Dubois, and H. Prade, *Nonmonotonic reasoning, conditional objects and possibility theory*, Artificial Intelligence **92** (1997), 259–276.

[Ben84] J. Van Benthem, *Foundations of conditional logic*, J. of Philosophical Logic **13** (1984), 303–349.

[Ben86] J. Van Benthem, *Essays in Logical Semantics*, D. Reidel, 1986.

[Ben88] J. Van Benthem, *A Manual of Intensional Logic*, second ed., CSLI, Stanford, 1988.

[Boc92] A. Bochman, *Mereological Semantics*, Ph.D. thesis, Tel-Aviv University, 1992.

[Boc96] A. Bochman, *Biconsequence relations for nonmonotonic reasoning*, Principles of Knowledge Representation and Reasoning. Proc. Fifth Int. Conference, KR'96 (L. C. Aiello, J. Doyle, and S. C. Shapiro, eds.), Morgan Kaufmann, 1996, pp. 482–492.

[Boc99a] A. Bochman, *Credulous nonmonotonic inference*, Proceedings IJCAI'99 (Stockholm) (T. Dean, ed.), Morgan Kaufmann, 1999, pp. 30–35.

[Boc99b] A. Bochman, *A foundational theory of belief and belief change*, Artificial Intelligence **108** (1999), 309–352.

[Boc00a] A. Bochman, *Belief conraction as nonmonotonic inference.*, Journal of Symbolic Logic **65** (2000), 605–626.

[Boc00b] A. Bochman, *Contraction of epistemic states: A general theory*, Frontiers of Belief Revision (H. Rott and M.-A. Williams, eds.), Kluwer, 2001, (to appear).

[Boc00c] A. Bochman, *A foundationalist view of the AGM theory of belief change*, Artificial Intelligence **116** (2000), 237–263.

[Bou96] C. Boutilier, *Iterated revision and minimal change of conditional beliefs*, J. of Philosophical Logic **25** (1996), 263–305.

[Bra93] S. Brass, *On the semantics of supernormal defaults*, Proceedings IJCAI-93, 1993, pp. 578–583.

[Bre91a] G. Brewka, *Belief revision in a framework for default reasoning*, The Logic of Theory Change (A. Fuhrmann and M. Morreau, eds.), Springer-Verlag, 1991, Lecture Notes in AI 465, pp. 206–222.

[Bre91b] G. Brewka, *Nonmonotonic Reasoning: Logical Foundations of Commonsense*, Cambridge Tracts in Theoretical Computer Science, Cambridge UP, 1991.

[Bro90] F. M. Brown, *Boolean Reasoning*, Kluwer, 1990.

[Cay95] C. Cayrol, *From non-monotonic syntax-based entailment to preference-based argumentation*, Symbolic and Qualitative Approaches to Reasoning and Uncertainty, ECSQARU'95 (Fribourg, Switzerland) (C. Froidevaux and J. Kohlas, eds.), Springer-Verlag, Lecture Notes in AI, 946, pp. 99–106.

[CLS95] C. Cayrol and M.-C. Lagasquie-Shiex, *Non-monotonic syntax-based entailment: A classification of consequence relations*, Symbolic and Qualitative Approaches to Reasoning and Uncertainty, ECSQARU'95 (Fribourg, Switzerland) (C. Froidevaux and J. Kohlas, eds.), Springer-Verlag, Lecture Notes in AI, 946, pp. 107–114.

[DP91] D. Dubois and H. Prade, *Epistemic entrenchment and possibilistic logic*, Artificial Intelligence **50** (1991), 223–239.

[DP97] A. Darwiche and J. Pearl, *On the logic of iterated belief revision*, Artificial Intelligence **89** (1997), 1–29.

[DS96] P. M. Dung and T. C. Son, *An argumentation-theoretic approach to reasoning with specificity*, Proc. Fifth Int. Conference on Principles of Knowledge Representation and Reasoning, KR'96, (L. C. Aiello, J. Doyle, and S. C. Shapiro, eds.), Morgan Kaufmann, 1996, pp. 506–517.

[DW91] J. Doyle and M. P. Wellman, *Impediments to universal preference-based default theories*, Artificial Intelligence **49** (1991), 97–128.

[Eng98] J. Engelfriet, *Monotonicity and persistence in preferential logics*, J. of Artificial Intelligence Research **8** (1998), 1–21.

[FH94] A. Fuhrmann and S. O. Hansson, *A survey of multiple contractions*, J. of Logic, Language and Information **3** (1994), 39–76.

[FH97] N. Friedman and J. Y. Halpern, *Modeling belief in dynamic systems, part I: Foundations*, Artificial Intelligence **95** (1997), 257–316.

[FH98] N. Friedman and J. Y. Halpern, *Plausibility measures and default reasoning*, J. of ACM, to appear.

[FH99] N. Friedman and J. Y. Halpern, *Modelling belief in dynamic systems. part II: Revision and update*, J. of Artificial Intelligence Research **10** (1999), 117–167.

[Fla98] P. A. Flach, *Comparing consequence relations*, Proc. Sixth Int. Conf. On Principles of Knowledge Representation and Reasoning (KR'98) (A. G. Cohn, L. Shubert, and S. C. Shapiro, eds.), Morgan Kaufmann, 1998, pp. 180–189.

[Fre92] M. Freund, *Injective models and disjunctive relations*, J. of Logic and Computation **3** (1992), 231–247.

[Fre98] M. Freund, *Preferential reasoning in the perspective of Poole default logic*, Artificial Intelligence **98** (1998), 209–235.

[Fuh91] A. Fuhrmann, *Theory contraction through base contraction*, J. of Philosophical Logic **20** (1991), 175–203.

[Fuh96] A. Fuhrmann, *An Essay on Contraction*, Studies in Logic, Language and Information, The University of Chicago Press, 1996.

[FUKV86] R. Fagin, J. D. Ullman, G. M. Kuper, and M. Y. Vardi, *Updating logical databases*, Advances in Computing Research, vol. 3, 1986, pp. 1–18.

[Gab76] D. M. Gabbay, *Investigations in Modal and Tense Logics*, D. Reidel, 1976.

[Gab81] D. M. Gabbay, *Semantical Investigations in Heyting's Intuitionistic Logic*, D. Reidel, 1981.

[Gab85] D. M. Gabbay, *Theoretical foundations for non-monotonic reasoning in expert systems*, Logics and Models of Concurrent Systems (Berlin) (K. R. Apt, ed.), NATO ASI Series F, vol. 13, 439–457, Springer-Verlag, 1985.

[Gär88] P. Gärdenfors, *Knowledge in Flux: Modeling the Dynamics of Epistemic States*, Bradford Books, MIT Press, 1988.

[Gär90] P. Gärdenfors, *The dynamics of belief systems: Foundations vs. coherence theories*, Revue Internationale de Philosophie **44** (1990), 24–46.

[Gef92] H. Geffner, *Default Reasoning. Causal and Conditional Theories*, MIT Press, 1992.

[Geo96] K. Georgatos, *Ordering-based representations of rational inference*, Logics in Artificial Intelligence (JELIA '96) (Berlin) (José Júlio Alferes, Luís Moniz Pereira, and Ewa Orlowska, eds.), Lecture Notes in AI 1126, Springer-Verlag, 1996, pp. 176–191.

[Geo99] K. Georgatos, *To preference via entrenchment*, Annals of pure and applied logic **96** (1999), 141–155.

[GM88] P. Gärdenfors and D. Makinson, *Revisions of knowledge systems using epistemic entrenchment*, Proc. Second Conference on Theoretical Aspects of Reasoning about Knowledge (M. Vardi, ed.), Morgan Kaufmann, Los Altos, CA, 1988, pp. 83–95.

[GM94] P. Gärdenfors and D. Makinson, *Nonmonotonic inference based on expectations*, Artificial Intelligence **65** (1994), 197–245.

[GMP93] M. Goldszmidt, P. Morris, and J. Pearl, *A maximum entropy approach to nonmonotonic reasoning*, IEEE Transactions on Pattern Analysis and Machine Intelligence **15** (1993), 220–232.

[GR95] P. Gärdenfors and H. Rott, *Belief revision*, Handbook of Logic in Artificial Intelligence and Logic Programming. Vol. 4 (D. M. Gabbay et al., ed.), Clarendon Press, 1995, pp. 35–132.

[Gro88] A. Grove, *Two modelings for theory change*, J. of Philosophical Logic **17** (1988), 157–170.

[Gro91] B. N. Grosof, *Generalising prioritization*, Proc. Second International Conference on Principles of Knowledge Representation and Reasoning, KR'91 (J. Allen, R. Fikes, and E. Sandewall, eds.), Morgan Kaufmann, 1991, pp. 289–300.

[GV88] P. Geerts and D. Vermeir, *Defeasible logics*, Handbook of Defeasible Reasoning and Uncertainty Management Systems, Vol. 2: Reasoning with Actual and Potential Contradictions (D. M. Gabbay and P. Smets, eds.), Kluwer, 1988, pp. 175–210.

[Han91] S. O. Hansson, *Belief contraction without recovery*, Studia Logica **50** (1991), 251–260.

[Han92] S. O. Hansson, *In defense of base contraction*, Synthese **91** (1992), 239–245.

[Han93a] S. O. Hansson, *Changes of disjunctively closed bases*, J. of Logic, Language and Information **2** (1993), 255–284.

[Han93b] S. O. Hansson, *Theory contraction and base contraction unified*, J. of Symbolic Logic **58** (1993), 602–625.

[Han99] S. O. Hansson, *A Textbook of Belief Dynamics*, Kluwer, 1999.

[Har86] G. Harman, *Change in View*, Bradford Books, MIT Press, 1986.

[Hem88] C. G. Hempel, *Provisoes: A problem concerning the inferential function of scientific theories*, Erkenntnis **28** (1988), 147–164.

[HO95] S. O. Hansson and E. J. Olsson, *Levi contractions and AGM contractions: a comparison*, Notre Dame J. of Formal Logic **36** (1995), 103–119.

[Hor94] J. F. Horty, *Some direct theories of nonmonotonic inheritance*, Handbook of Logic in Artificial Intelligence and Logic Programming **3**: Nonmonotonic Reasoning and Uncertain Reasoning (D. M. Gabbay, C. J. Hogger, and J. A. Robinson, eds.), Oxford University Press, Oxford, 1994.

[HTT90] J. F. Horty, R. H. Thomason, and D. S. Touretzky, *A sceptical theory of inheritance in nonmonotonic semantic networks*, Artificial Intelligence **42** (1990), 311–348.

[KLM90] S. Kraus, D. Lehmann, and M. Magidor, *Nonmonotonic reasoning, preferential models and cumulative logics*, Artificial Intelligence **44** (1990), 167–207.

[KM91] H. Katsuno and A. O. Mendelzon, *Propositional knowledge base revision and minimal change*, Artificial Intelligence **52** (1991), 263–294.

[Kra81] A. Kratzer, *Partition and revision: The semantics of counterfactuals*, J. of Philosophical Logic **10** (1981), 201–216.

[Leh89] D. Lehmann, *What does a conditional knowledge base entail?*, Proc. 2nd Int. Conf. On Priniciples of Knowledge Representation and Reasoning, KR'89 (R. Brachman and H. J. Levesque, eds.), Morgan Kaufmann, 1989, pp. 212–222.

[Leh95] D. Lehmann, *Belief revision, revised*, Proceedings IJCAI'95, Morgan Kaufmann, 1995, pp. 1534–1540.

[Leh98] D. Lehmann, *Nonmonotonic logics and semantics*, Tech. Report TR-98-6, Institute of Computer Science, Hebrew University, May 1998.

[Lev91] I. Levi, *The Fixation of Belief and Its Undoing*, Cambridge University Press, 1991.

[Lev97] I. Levi, *Contraction and Informational Value*, Columbia University, fifth version, August 1997.

[Lew73] D. Lewis, *Counterfactuals*, Basil Blackwell, Oxford, 1973.

[Lew81] D. Lewis, *Ordering semantics and premise semantics for counterfactuals*, Journal of Philosophical Logic **10** (1981), 217–234.

[LM92] D. Lehmann and M. Magidor, *What does a conditional knowledge base entail?*, Artificial Intelligence **55** (1992), 1–60.

[LR91] S. Lindström and W. Rabinowicz, *Epistemic entrenchment with incomparatibilities and relational belief revision*, The Logic of Theory Change (A. Fuhrmann and M. Morreau, eds.), Springer-Verlag, 1991, Lecture Notes in AI 465, pp. 93–126.

[Mak87] D. Makinson, *On the status of the postulate of recovery in the logic of theory change*, J. of Philosophical Logic **16** (1987), 383–394.

[Mak89] D. Makinson, *General theory of cumulative inference*, Nonmonotonic Reasoning (M. Reinfrank, ed.), Springer-Verlag, 1989, Lecture Notes in AI 346, pp. 1–18.

[Mak94] D. Makinson, *General patterns in nonmonotonic reasoning*, Handbook of Logic in Artificial Intelligence and Logic Programming, Vol. 3, Nonmonotonic and Uncertain Reasoning (D. M. Gabbay et al., eds.), vol. 2, Oxford University Press, Oxford, 1994, pp. 35–110.

[McC80] J. McCarthy, *Circumscription – a form of non-monotonic reasoning*, Artificial Intelligence **13** (1980), 27–39.

[MG91] D. Makinson and P. Gärdenfors, *Relations between the logic of theory change and nonmonotonic logic*, The Logic of Theory Change (A. Fuhrmann and M. Morreau, eds.), Springer-Verlag, 1991, Lecture Notes in AI, 465, pp. 185–205.

[MR98] Y. Moinard and R. Rolland, *Circumscriptions from what they cannot do (preliminary report)*, Working papers of Common Sense'98 (University of London), 1998, pp. 20–41.

[MS91] D. Makinson and K. Schlechta, *Floating conclusions and zombie paths: Two deep difficulties in the "directly sceptical" approach to defeasible inheritance nets*, Artificial Intelligence **48** (1991), 199–209.

[MS93] Y. Moses and Y. Shoham, *Belief as defeasible knowledge*, Artificial Intelligence **64** (1993), 298–321.

[MT93] W. Marek and M. Truszczyński, *Nonmonotonic Logic. Context-dependent Reasoning*, Springer-Verlag, 1993.

[Nay94] A. C. Nayak, *Iterated belief change based on epistemic entrenchment*, Erkenntnis **41** (1994), 353–390.

[Neb89] B. Nebel, *A knowledge level analysis of belief revision*, Proc. First Int. Conference on Principles of Knowledge Representation and Reasoning (R. J. Brachman et al., eds.), Morgan Kauffman, 1989, pp. 301–311.

[Neb92] B. Nebel, *Syntax-based approaches to belief revision*, Belief Revision (P. Gärdenfors, ed.), Cambridge University Press, 1992, pp. 52–88.

[Nut90] D. Nute, *Defeasible logic and the frame problem*, Knowledge Representation and Defeasible Reasoning (R. Loui H. Kyburg and G. Carlson, eds.), Kluwer, Boston MA, 1990, pp. 3–24.

[Pea90] J. Pearl, *System Z: A natural ordering of defaults with tractable applications to default reasoning*, Proceedings of the Third Conference on Theoretical Aspects of Reasoning About Knowledge (TARK'90), Morgan Kaufmann, 1990, pp. 121–135.

[PL92] G. Pinkas and R. P. Loui, *Reasoning from inconsistency: A taxonomy of principles for resolving conflict*, Proceedings of the Third Conference on Principles of Knowledge Representation and Reasoning, KR'92 (Cambridge, Mass.), Morgan Kaufmann, 1992, pp. 709–719.

[Poo88] D. Poole, *A logical framework for default reasoning*, Artificial Intelligence **36** (1988), 27–47.

[Poo91] D. Poole, *The effect of knowledge on belief: conditioning, specificity and the lottery paradox in default reasoning*, Artificial Intelligence **49** (1991), 281–307.

[Ram78] F. P. Ramsey, *Foundations*, Routledge & Kegan Paul, London, 1978.

[Rei80] R. Reiter, *A logic for default reasoning*, Artificial Intelligence **13** (1980), 81–132.

[Rot91a] H. Rott, *A non-monotonic conditional logic for belief revision*, The Logic of Theory Change (A. Fuhrmann and M. Morreau, eds.), Springer-Verlag, 1991, Lecture Notes in CS 465, pp. 135–181.

[Rot91b] H. Rott, *Two methods of constructing contractions and revisions of knowledge systems*, J. of Philosophical Logic **20** (1991), 149–173.

[Rot92a] H. Rott, *Modellings for belief change: Prioritization and entrenchment*, Theoria **58** (1992), 21–57.

[Rot92b] H. Rott, *Preferential belief change using generalized epistemic entrenchment*, J. of Logic, Language and Information **1** (1992), 45–78.

[Rot93] H. Rott, *Belief contraction in the context of the general theory of rational choice*, J. of Symbolic Logic **58** (1993), 1426–1450.

[Rot94] H. Rott, *Coherent choice and epistemic entrenchment (preliminary report)*, Proceedings ISMIS'94 (Z. W. Raz and M. Zemankova, eds.), Springer-Verlag, 1994, Lecture Notes in AI 869, pp. 284–295.

[Rot95] H. Rott, *"Just because": Taking belief bases seriously*, Logic for a Change. Essays Dedicated to Sten Lindström on the Occasion of his 50th Birthday (S. O. Hansson, W. Rabinowicz, and K. Segerberg, eds.), 1995, Version of October 30, 1998, pp. 106–124.

[Rot96] H. Rott, *Makig Up One's Mind: Foundations, Coherence, Nonmonotonicity*, Habilitationsschrift, Universität Konstanz, 1996.

[RP99] H. Rott and M. Pagnucco, *Severe withdrawal (and recovery)*, Journal of Philosophical Logic **28** (1999), 501–547.

[Sch93] K. Schlechta, *Directly sceptical inheritance cannot capture the intersection of extensions*, J. of Logic and Computartion **3** (1993), 455–467.

[Sch97] K. Schlechta, *Nonmonotonic Logics: Basic Concepts, Results, and Techniques*, Lecture Notes in AI 1187, Springer-Verlag, 1997.

[Sco74] D. Scott, *Completeness and axiomatizability in many-valued logic*, Proc. Symp. In Pure Math., No. 25, 1974, pp. 431–435.

[Seg82] K. Segerberg, *Classical Propositional Operators*, Clarendon Press, 1982.

[SF96] P. Siegel and L. Forget, *A representation theorem for preferential logics*, Principles of Knowledge Representation and Reasoning. Proc. Fifth Int. Conference, KR'96 (L. C. Aiello, J. Doyle, and S. C. Shapiro, eds.), Morgan Kaufmann, 1996, pp. 453–460.

[Sho88] Y. Shoham, *Reasoning about Change*, Cambridge University Press, 1988.

[Sos80] E. Sosa, *The raft and the pyramid: Coherence versus foundations in the theory of knowledge*, Midwest Studies in Philosophy **5** (1980), 3–25.

[SS78] D. J. Shoesmith and T. J. Smiley, *Multiple-conclusion Logic*, Cambridge University Press, 1978.

[Sta84] R. Stalnaker, *Inquiry*, MIT Press, Cambridge, Mass., 1984.

[TP95] S.-W. Tan and J. Pearl, *Specificity and inheritance in default reasoning*, Proceedings IJCAI-95, 1995, pp. 1480–1486.

[TTH91] D. S. Touretzky, R. H. Thomason, and J. F. Horty, *A skeptic's menagerie: Conflicors, preemptors, reinstaters, and zombies in nonmonotnic inheritance*, Proceedings of IJCAI-91, 1991, pp. 478–483.

[Val94] A. Del Val, *On the relation between the coherence and foundations theories of belief revision*, Proceedings AAAI-94, 1994, pp. 909–914.

[Val97] A. Del Val, *Non-monotonic reasoning and belief revision: Syntactic, semantic, foundational, and coherence approaches*, Journal of Applied Non-Classical Logics **7** (1997), 213–240.

[Vel76] F. Veltman, *Prejudices, presuppositions and the theory of conditionals*, Amsterdam Papers on Formal Grammar (J. Groenendijk and M. Stokhof, eds.), vol. 1, Centrale Interfaculteit, Universiteit van Amsterdam, 1976, pp. 248–281.

[Wil94] M.-A. Williams, *Transmutations of knowledge systems*, Principles of Knowledge Representation and Reasoning (KR'94) (J. Doyle, E. Sandewall, and P. Torasso, eds.), Morgan Kaufmann, 1994, pp. 619–629.

Index

Springer Series
Artificial Intelligence

N. J. Nilsson: Principles of Artificial Intelligence. XV, 476 pages, 139 figs., 1982

J. H. Siekmann, G. Wrightson (Eds.): Automation of Reasoning 2. Classical Papers on Computational Logic 1967–1970. XXII, 638 pages, 1983

R. S. Michalski, J. G. Carbonell, T. M. Mitchell (Eds.): Machine Learning. An Artificial Intelligence Approach. XI, 572 pages, 1984

J. W. Lloyd: Foundations of Logic Programming. Second, extended edition. XII, 212 pages, 198

N. Cercone, G. McCalla (Eds.): The Knowledge Frontier. Essays in the Representation of Knowledge. XXXV, 512 pages, 93 figs., 1987

G. Rayna: REDUCE. Software for Algebraic Computation. IX, 329 pages, 1987

L. Kanal, V. Kumar (Eds.): Search in Artificial Intelligence. X, 482 pages, 67 figs., 1988

H. Abramson, V. Dahl: Logic Grammars. XIV, 234 pages, 40 figs., 1989

P. Besnard: An Introduction to Default Logic. XI, 201 pages, 1989

A. Kobsa, W. Wahlster (Eds.): User Models in Dialog Systems. XI, 471 pages, 113 figs., 1989

Y. Peng, J. A. Reggia: Abductive Inference Models for Diagnostic Problem-Solving. XII, 284 pages, 25 figs., 1990

A. Bundy (Ed.): Catalogue of Artificial Intelligence Techniques. Fourth revised edition. XVI, 141 pages, 1997 (first three editions published in the series)

R. Kruse, E. Schwecke, J. Heinsohn: Uncertainty and Vagueness in Knowledge Based Systems. Numerical Methods. XI, 491 pages, 59 figs., 1991

Z. Michalewicz: Genetic Algorithms + Data Structures = Evolution Programs. Third, revised and extended edition. XX, 387 pages, 68 figs., 1996 (first edition published in the series)

V. W. Marek, M. Truszczyński: Nonmonotonic Logic. Context-Dependent Reasoning. XIII, 417 pages, 14 figs., 1993

V. S. Subrahmanian, S. Jajodia (Eds.): Multimedia Database Systems. XVI, 323 pages, 104 figs., 1996

Q. Yang: Intelligent Planning. XXII, 252 pages, 76 figs., 1997

J. Debenham: Knowledge Engineering. Unifying Knowledge Base and Database Design. XIV, 465 pages, 288 figs., 1998

H. J. Levesque, F. Pirri (Eds.): Logical Foundations for Cognitive Agents. Contributions in Honor of Ray Reiter. XII, 405 pages, 32 figs., 1999

K. R. Apt, V. W. Marek, M. Truszczynski, D. S. Warren (Eds.): The Logic Programming Paradigm. A 25-Year Perspective. XVI, 456 pages, 57 figs., 1999

W. Wahlster (Ed.): Verbmobil: Foundations of Speech-toSpeech Translation. XII, 677 pages. 224 figs., 2000

A. Bochman: A Logical Theory of Nonmonotonic Inference and Belief Change. XII, 434 pages, 2001